CHASE COUNTY, KANSAS

PrairyErth

(a deep map)

By William Least Heat-Moon

Blue Highways:
A Journey into America

PrairyErth (a deep map)

William
Least Heat-Moon

PrairyErth

(a deep map)

A PETER DAVISON BOOK

Houghton Mifflin Company

BOSTON · 1991

For information about permission to reproduce selections
from this book, write to Permissions, Houghton Mifflin
Company, 2 Park Street, Boston, Massachusetts 02108.

Library of Congress Cataloging-in-Publication Data
Heat-Moon, William Least.
PrairyErth : (a deep map) / William Least Heat-Moon ; [maps and
Kansas petroglyphs drawn by author].
p.   cm.
"A Peter Davison Book."
ISBN 0-395-48602-5
1. Chase County (Kan.) — Description and travel.   2. Chase County
(Kan.) — History, Local.   3. Heat-Moon, William Least — Journeys
— Kansas — Chase County.   I. Title.
F687.C35H44   1991   91-23250
917.81'59 — dc20   CIP

Printed in the United States of America

HAD 10 9 8 7 6 5 4 3 2 1

Book design by Robert Overholtzer

Maps and Kansas petroglyphs drawn by the author.

This book is printed on acid-free paper.

PrairyErth speaks in many voices. The author thanks
the numerous writers, alive and dead, whose descriptions
of Chase County and Kansas and the American prairie,
indeed the globe itself, have informed and advised
him — and contributed to the scope and substance of
the Commonplace Books.

Acknowledgments for the use of lengthy quotations
from previously published works are given on page 624.

FOR LKT:
TO THE PRAIRIE
IN A
DREAMTIME LILAC BUSH

Contents

Crossings
From the Commonplace Book   3
On Roniger Hill   10

I. Saffordville
From the Commonplace Book   21
In the Quadrangle   27
Upon the First Terrace   31
Under Old Nell's Skirt   40
Along the Ghost Highway   46
On the Town: Cottonwood Falls   49

II. Gladstone
From the Commonplace Book   59
In the Quadrangle   66
Between Pommel and Cantle   71
About the Red Buffalo   76
Atop the Mound   81
On the Town: Courthouse   85

III. Thrall-Northwest
From the Commonplace Book   93
In the Quadrangle   100
Of Recharging the System   106
Down in the Hollow   113
By Way of Spelling Kansas   118
On the Town: The Emma Chase   123

IV. Fox Creek

From the Commonplace Book   133
In the Quadrangle   142
After the Sixteen-Sixty-Six Beast   147
Above the Crystalline Basement   156
Outside the Z Bar   162
On the Town: Gabriel's Inventory   167

V. Bazaar

From the Commonplace Book   175
In the Quadrangle   181
In Ecstasy   187
Beneath a Thirty-Six-Square Grid   194
Within Her Pages   202
On the Town: A Night at Darla's   207

VI. Matfield Green

From the Commonplace Book   215
In the Quadrangle   222
En las Casitas   230
Ex Radice   237
Via the Short Line to China   244
On the Town: Versus Harry B. (I)   253

VII. *Hymer*

From the Commonplace Book   259
In the Quadrangle   265
Underneath the Overburden   272
With the Grain of the Grid   279
Around Half Past   288
On the Town: Versus Harry B. (II)   295

VIII. *Elmdale*

From the Commonplace Book   303
In the Quadrangle   309
Up Dead-End Dirt Roads   317
In Kit Form: The Cottonwood Chapter   326
Across Osage Hill   334
On the Town: Versus Harry B. (III)   346

IX. *Homestead*

From the Commonplace Book   353
In the Quadrangle   363
Beyond the Teeth of the Dragon   371
Amidst the Drummers Desirous   381
Regarding Fokker Niner-Niner-Easy   386
On the Town: The Life and Opinions of Sam Wood (I)   400

X. Elk

From the Commonplace Book   415
In the Quadrangle   421
Among the *Hic Jacets*   430
Out of the Totem Hawk Lexicon   439
At the Diamond of the Plain   446
On the Town: The Life and Opinions of Sam Wood (II)   465

XI. Cedar Point

From the Commonplace Book   477
In the Quadrangle   484
To Consult the Genius of the Place in All   493
Concerning the Glitter Weaver   505
According to the *Leader*   513
On the Town: The Life and Opinions of Sam Wood (III)   531

XII. Wonsevu

From the Commonplace Book   539
In the Quadrangle   547
Toward a Kaw Hornbook   561
Beside Coming Morning   583
Below the Turf   592
Until Black Hole XTK Yields Its Light   597

Circlings

From the Commonplace Book   603
Over the Kaw Track   608

In Thanks   623

Crossings

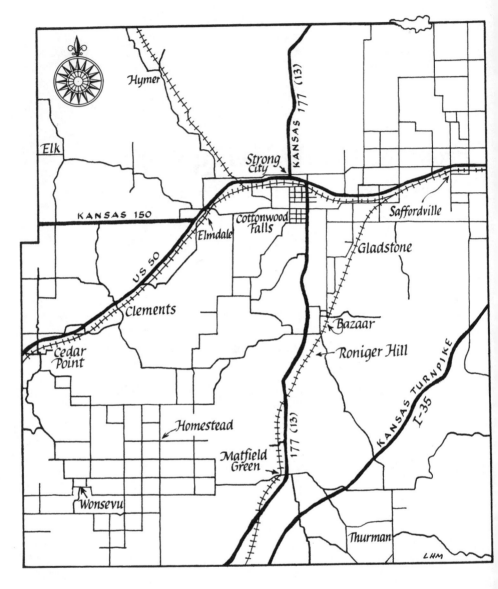

CHASE COUNTY, KANSAS
SCALE: ³⁄₁₆ inch = 1 mile

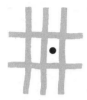

From the Commonplace Book: Crossings

WHAT TO TAKE: *Let your trunk, if you have to buy one, be of moderate size and of the strongest make. Test it by throwing it from the top of a three-storied house; if you pick it up uninjured, it will do to go to Kansas. Not otherwise.*

> — James Redpath and Richard Hinton,
> *Hand-Book to Kansas Territory* (1859)

The stranger [to Kansas], if he listened to the voice of experience, would not start upon his pilgrimage at any season of the year without an overcoat, a fan, a lightning rod, and an umbrella.

> — John James Ingalls,
> "In Praise of Blue Grass" (1875)

It was probably necessary that we develop an American name system, for many of our native soils are unique and should bear their own identities. In a stroke of scientific shorthand, the soils of our central grasslands are sometimes called simply "prairyerths."

> — John Madson,
> *Where the Sky Began* (1982)

I would like to tell you how to get there so that you may see all this for yourself. But first a warning: you may already have come across a set of detailed instructions, a map with every bush and stone clearly marked, the meandering courses of dry rivers and other geographical features noted, with dotted lines put down to represent the very faintest of trails. Perhaps there were also warnings printed in tiny red letters along the margin, about the lack of water, the strength of the wind and the swiftness of the rattlesnakes. Your confidence in these finely etched maps is understandable, for at first glance they seem excellent, the best a man is capable of; but your confidence is misplaced. Throw them out. They are the wrong sort of map. They are too thin. They are not the sort of map that can be followed by a man who knows what he is doing. The coyote, even the crow, would regard them with suspicion.

> — Barry Lopez,
> *Desert Notes* (1976)

Maps are a way of organizing wonder.

> — Peter Steinhart,
> "Names on a Map" (1986)

Once in his life a man ought to concentrate his mind upon the remembered earth, I believe. He ought to give himself up to a particular landscape in his experience, to look at it from as many angles as he can, to wonder about it, to dwell upon it. He ought to imagine that he touches it with his hands at every season and listens to the sounds that are made upon it. He ought to imagine the creatures there and all the faintest motions of the wind. He ought to recollect the glare of noon and all the colors of the dawn and dusk.

> — N. Scott Momaday,
> *The Way to Rainy Mountain* (1969)

Our present "leaders" — the people of wealth and power — do not know what it means to take a place seriously: to think it worthy, for its own sake, of love and study and careful work. They cannot take any place seriously because they must be ready at any moment, by the terms of power and wealth in the modern world, to destroy any place.

> — Wendell Berry,
> "Out of Your Car, Off Your Horse"
> (1991)

All nature is so full, that that district produces the greatest variety which is the most examined.

> — Gilbert White,
> *The Natural History and Antiquities
> of Selborne* (1768)

You expect to wait. You expect night to come. Morning. Winter to set in. But you expect sometime [the land] will loosen in pieces to be examined.
— Barry Lopez,
Desert Notes (1976)

I like to think of landscape not as a fixed place but as a path that is unwinding before my eyes, under my feet.

To see and know a place is a contemplative act. It means emptying our minds and letting what is there, in all its multiplicity and endless variety, come in.
— Gretel Ehrlich,
"Landscape," introduction to *Legacy of Light* (1987)

Eternal prairie and grass, with occasional groups of trees. [Captain John] Frémont prefers this to every other landscape. To me it is as if someone would prefer a book with blank pages to a good story.
— Charles Preuss,
Exploring with Frémont (1842)

Tourists through Kansas would call this place dull enough, but then so much of the interest of a place depends on its traditions. For a passing traveler in search of pleasure, it certainly possesses few attractions. But a [correspondent], in pursuit of useful knowledge for the reading public, observes things differently.
— Henry Stanley,
My Early Travels and Adventures in America (1867)

No one, I discover, begins to know the real geographic, democratic, indissoluble American Union in the present, or suspect it in the future, until he explores these Central States, and dwells awhile on their prairies or amid their busy towns.
— Walt Whitman,
Specimen Days (1879)

The prairie, in all its expressions, is a massive, subtle place, with a long history of contradiction and misunderstanding. But it is worth the effort at comprehension. It is, after all, at the center of our national identity.
— Wayne Fields,
"Lost Horizon" (1988)

I have resented that prairie was not an Indian word. It should have been, and sounds as if it might have been. The one thing the Indian came nearer owning than any other, was prairie.

America's unique province is her prairie, [yet] how slightingly American authors have behaved toward the prairie.

— William A. Quayle,
The Prairie and the Sea (1905)

So far as we know, no modern poet has written of the Flint Hills, which is surprising since they are perfectly attuned to his lyre. In their physical characteristics they reflect want and despair. A line of low-flung hills stretching from the Osage Nation on the south to the Kaw River on the north, they present a pinched and frowning face to those who gaze on them. Their verbiage is scant. Jagged rocks rise everywhere to their surface. The Flint Hills never laugh. In the early spring when the sparse grass first turns to green upon them, they smile saltily and sardonically. But, as spring turns to summer, they grow sullen again and hopeless. Death is no stranger to them. For there nature struggles always to survive.

— Jay E. House,
Philadelphia Public Ledger (1931)

Some persons have failed to see anything beautiful in this region, and the hills have been called "barren" and "depressing." Perhaps the Flint Hills are more pleasing when they are at least in part understood.

— J. M. Jewett,
*Second Geologic Field Conference in
the Flint Hills Guidebook* (1958)

The statistics of the census tables are more eloquent than the tropes and phrases of the rhetorician. The story of Kansas needs no reinforcement from the imagination.

Kansas is the navel of the nation.

— John James Ingalls,
"Kansas: 1541–1891" (1892)

Take it by any standard you please, Kansas is not in it.

— William Allen White,
"What's the Matter with Kansas?"
(1896)

When anything is going to happen in this country, it happens first in Kansas.

— William Allen White,
Editorial, *Emporia Gazette* (1922)

Kansas is no mere geographical expression, but a "state of mind," a religion, and a philosophy in one.

The Kansas spirit is the American spirit double-distilled. It is a new-grafted product of American individualism, American idealism, American intolerance. Kansas is America in microcosm: as America conceives itself in respect to Europe, so Kansas conceives itself in respect to America.

— Carl Becker,
"Kansas" (1910)

Before Kansas could legally acquire title to public land the federal government had to clear the way. The Indian title had to be extinguished and public surveys carried out preliminary to the opening of a land office. A surveyor general for Kansas and Nebraska was appointed in August, 1854, and three months later surveying began. . . . No mapping has ever so profoundly affected the physical appearance of land as did the township surveying method. Those who have flown over Kansas can appreciate its results. Visibly the land is divided into endlessly repeated squares, reflecting the pattern of survey and sale. Road building and farming generally follow the pattern marked out by the General Land Office.

— Robert W. Baughman,
Kansas in Maps (1961)

County lines do make separate kinds of community life, each a little different from the other.

— William Allen White,
Chase County Historical Sketches
(1940)

It is the nature of the soil to be highly complex and variable, to conform very inexactly to human conclusions and rules. It is itself easily damaged by the imposition of alien patterns. Out of the random grammar and lexicon of possibilities — geological, topographical, climatological, biological — the soil of any one place makes its own peculiar and inevitable sense.

It is impossible to contemplate the life of the soil for very long without seeing it as analogous to the life of the spirit.

— Wendell Berry,
The Unsettling of America (1977)

Words are the daughters of earth, and things are the sons of heaven.

> — Samuel Johnson (paraphrasing Samuel
> Madden),
> *A Dictionary of the English
> Language* (1755)

In anthropology now, the term "thick description" refers to a dense accumulation of ordinary information about a culture, as opposed to abstract or theoretical analysis. It means observing the details of life until they begin to coagulate or cohere into an interpretation. . . . I'd like to see thick description make a comeback. Apart from sheer sensuous pleasure, it gives you the comforting feeling that you're not altogether adrift, that at least you have an actual context to enter into and real things to grapple with. The protectors of the environment are a powerful group in the United States. Perhaps they should extend their concern to the country of the imagination.

> — Anatole Broyard,
> *New York Times Book Review* (1985)

The European writing I know rarely recognizes a power in the land that corresponds to a power of being, while one of the things that distinguishes American literature, especially in the West, is that you expect to see the land turn up in a powerful or a mysterious or an affecting way.

> — Barry Lopez,
> "An Interview," in *Western American
> Literature* (1986)

The indivisible is not to be put into compartments.

Every fact is a logarithm; one added term ramifies it until it is thoroughly transformed. In the general aspect of things, the great lines of creation take shape and arrange themselves into groups; beneath lies the unfathomable.

Which of our methods of measuring could we apply to this eddying mass that is the universe? In the presence of the profundities our sole ability is to dream. Our conception, quickly winded, cannot follow creation, that vast breath.

> — Victor Hugo,
> *The Toilers of the Sea* (1866)

Our religion is the traditions of our ancestors — the visions of our sachems and the dreams of our old men, given them in the solemn hours of night by the Great Spirit — and it is written in the hearts of our people.

> — Chief Seattle,
> "Address to Governor Isaac Stevens"
> (1855)

The Dreaming is the founding story, the great drama of the creative era, in which the landscape took its present form and the people, animals, plants, and elements of the known world were created. But the Dreaming is also the inner or spiritual dimension of the present. Things contain their own histories. There is no contrast of the natural and the spiritual, and there is no geography without history and meaning. The land is already a narrative — an artefact of intellect — before people represent it.

In the Dreaming, heroic characters travelled about the land, doing the ordinary good and evil things people do today, and also performing extraordinary feats of creation and destruction, cooperation and conflict. These characters, the Ancestral Beings, who are also called the Dreamings, have their visible manifestations now in the form of animals, plants, elements, places, and people.

> — Peter Sutton,
> Exhibition brochure for "Dreamings:
> The Art of Aboriginal Australia"
> (1988)

Geography blended with time equals destiny.

> — Joseph Brodsky,
> "Strophes" (1978)

The moment comes: we intersect a history, a long existence, offering it our fresh discovery as regeneration.

> — Shirley Hazzard,
> "Points of Departure" (1983)

New earths, new themes expect us.

> — Henry David Thoreau,
> The Journal (1857)

On Roniger Hill

Sundown: I am standing on Roniger Hill, and I am trying to see myself as if atop a giant map of the United States. If you draw two lines from the metropolitan corners of America, one from New York City southwest to San Diego and another from Miami northwest to Seattle, the intersection would fall a few miles from my position. I am on a flat-topped ridge 155 miles southeast of the geographic center of the contiguous states, 130 miles from the geodetic datum (the point from which all North American mapping originates), and about three miles from the precise middle of Chase County, Kansas. Were you to fold in half a three-foot-long map of the forty-eight states north to south then east to west, the creases would cross within an inch of where I stand, and you would see that Roniger Hill is nearly at the heart of the nation; but I think that is only incidental to my reason for being here. In truth, I don't much understand why I *am* here, but, whatever the answer, it's strong enough to pull me five hours by interstates from home, eight hours if I follow a route of good café food through the Missouri hills.

For years, outsiders have considered this prairie place barren, desolate, monotonous, a land of more nothing than almost any other place you might name, but I know I'm not here to explore vacuousness at the heart of America. I'm only in search of what *is* here, here in the middle of the Flint Hills of Kansas. I'm in quest of the land and what informs it, and I'm here because of shadows in me, loomings about threats to America that are alive here too, but things I hope will show more clearly in the spareness of this county.

The Flint Hills: if you drive from the Atlantic Ocean to the Pacific by the most central yet least traveled national route, you set off on U.S. 50 from Ocean City, Maryland, pass before the Capitol, ride down Constitution Avenue, past the Declaration of Independence in the National Archives, past the Washington Monument and the Truman Balcony of the White House and the Zero Milestone it looks out upon, past the Lincoln Memorial, and then head into the countryside where the places are Hayfield, Virginia; Coolville, Ohio; Loogootee, Indiana; Flora, Illinois; Useful, Missouri; Dodge City, Kansas; the Royal Gorge of Colorado; Deseret, Utah; Eureka, Nevada; Placerville, California. You'll run out of route 50 only on the Embarcadero along San Francisco Bay, and behind will lie your course over four time zones, over the Alleghenies, along the northern edge of the broken Ozark Plateau, across the Rockies, over the Sierra Nevadas. At times you will have followed the routes of the Overland-Butterfield Stage, the Pony Express, the Oregon, Santa Fe, and California trails, and the Lincoln Highway; along the entire three thousand miles between Washington and San Francisco, you'll have seen only four other cities: Cincinnati, St. Louis, Kansas City, Sacramento. You will have closely paralleled the old "Main Street of America," highway 40, a road that has taken most of the cities and congestion and four-lane life, and, for half the trip, you will also have roughly paralleled route 66, the so-called Mother Road of the thirties. People write books about 40 and 66, but I know of nobody writing or singing about 50 (considering what fame can do, travelers of this transcontinental highway can be thankful Bobby Troup drove route 66). Yet, for at least the last couple of generations, the westering center of American population has followed 50, at times edging precisely along it like an aerialist on his wire. For the unhurried, this little-known highway is the best national road across the middle of the United States.

When an English woman, inspired by Isabella Bird's travels in nineteenth-century America, asked me last year how she might see the full dimension of the country, I said to drive highway 50 from ocean to ocean. If she begins in the East, I know the very mile where she will exclaim from behind her windshield that she has at last arrived in the American West. That spot is in Kansas in the Flint Hills in Chase County: if highway 50 is a belt across the midriff of America, then the Flint Hills make a buckle cinching East to West. From where I stand above what's left of the village of Bazaar, I can nearly see that stretch of road where the West begins. The traditional hundredth meridian be damned; at this latitude the West starts here, obviously, definitively. What's more, Chase County, Kansas, is the most easterly piece of the American Far West.

For twelve hundred miles, ever since driving smack through the morning shadow of the Washington Monument, my English traveler will pass from woodland to woodland — central Virginia looks much like central Missouri — but, several miles across the Kansas line, she'll begin to see fewer trees, see them thinning out and clustering in draws and valleys until she notices from the first rise of highway 50 in Chase County that, but for the wooded vales, the trees have nearly disappeared altogether. To encounter treelessness of such distance has often moved eastern travelers — and sometimes natives — more to discomfiture than rapture. Of the prairie, Willa Cather wrote in *My Ántonia: Between that earth and that sky I felt erased, blotted out.* The protection and sureties of the vertical woodland, walled like a home and enclosed like a refuge, are gone, and now the land, although more filled with cellulose than ever, is a world of air, space, apparent emptiness, near nothingness, where once the first travelers could walk for twelve hours and believe they had taken only a dozen steps. On a clear day of summer along this section of highway 50, the world changes in a few miles from green to blue, from shadows to nearly unbroken sunlight, from intermittent breezes to a wind blowing steadily as if out of the lungs of the universe.

The Flint Hills are the last remaining grand expanse of tallgrass prairie in America. On a geologic map, their shape something like a stone spear point, they cover most of the two-hundred-mile longitude of Kansas from Nebraska to Oklahoma, a stony upland twenty to eighty miles wide. At their western edge, the mixed-grass prairie begins and spreads a hundred or so miles to the shortgrass country of the high plains. On the eastern side, settlement and agriculture have all but obliterated the whilom tallgrass prairie so that it is hardly visible to anyone who would not seek it out on hands and knees; although the six million acres of the Flint Hills — also called the Bluestem Hills — were once a mere four percent of the American long-grass prairie, they are now nearly all of it. The grasses can grow to ten feet, high enough that red men once stood atop their horses to see twenty yards ahead; that wasn't common, but it occurred, and, even today in moist vales protected from development and cattle, I've found big bluestem and sloughgrass, the grandest of the tallgrasses, eight feet high. In season, these and their relatives make the Flint Hills an immense pasturage nutritionally richer than the Bluegrass country of Kentucky. During the warm season, a big steer will gain two pounds a day, and the 120,000 beeves in the uplands will put on twenty-two million pounds.

Although the height of the Hills here is not remarkable, never rising more than three hundred feet from base to crest, their length and breadth would make them noteworthy even in places outside the somewhat level horizon of eastern Kansas, but, were they forested, my English traveler would hardly know she was crossing them. Because they belong to the open world of grasses, they dominate if not the sky then surely the horizon with their symmetrical and flattened tops, their trapezoidal slopes, and (at dawn and sunset) their shadows that can stretch unbrokenly and most visibly for a prairie mile.

These hills are largely limestones and shales distilled from the Permian seas that covered most of middle America off and on for fifty million years in the days when — had human beings and cities been around — a man could have paddled from Pittsburgh to Denver. Those seas were of such size that their sediments buried a mountain range with an eastern front once the equivalent to the New Mexico Rockies. Beneath Chase County, the great Nemaha Ridge, sometimes called the Kansas Mountains, lies about three thousand feet down, but its presence below the Flint Hills is coincidental: these tilted uplands are largely the result of erosion and not, like the Ridge or the Rockies, of upthrust. Still, today, the ancient Nemahas, as if gods buried alive, move their stone shoulders below and rattle the county atop its three fault zones, and, in time, the Flint Hills could split open and part like a biblical sea and the Nemahas may come again into the sun to throw the grassed slopes aside like so much surf.

Let this book page, appropriate as it is in shape and proportion, be Chase County. Lay your right hand across the page from right edge to left; tuck middle finger under palm and splay your other fingers wide so that your thumb points down, your little finger nearly upward: you have a configuration of the county watercourses, a manual topography of the place. Everything here has been and continues to be shaped by those four drainages: the South Fork of the Cottonwood River (thumb), the Cottonwood (index finger), Middle Creek (ring), Diamond Creek (little finger). Many more streams and brooks are here, but these four control the country, and where they have gone and are going and what they have done and are doing mark out where and what men have gone and done.

I am standing on Roniger Hill: I am facing west, dusk creeping up my back to absorb my thirty-foot shadow, the sun now a flattened crescent so dull I can look directly into it. The month is November, and, behind me, a nearly full moon will soon rise, and I am standing on this hill. I've been to this place before. Up here in the thirties Frank and George Roniger built three stone markers to honor Indian remains they unearthed atop the ridge. The Roniger brothers were bachelors, farmers, and collectors of stone artifacts from their fields lying below, and they believed this hill sacred to the people living around it in the time when Europeans were building cathedrals and sending children off to take holy cities from desert tribes. To me, this ridge is singular and, at night, almost unearthly, and I come here, in a friend's words, as *a two-bit mystic,* but I believe I've found my way onto the top by some old compass in the blood.

I've already said that what's left of Bazaar, Kansas, lies below. Lights in houses are coming on, but I can't make out the Ronigers' old brick home, and that's good because it's the nearest one, and when I come here I want Anglo civilization and its disruptions of the prairie contours far enough away so they soften and simplify into mere silhouettes. When the darkness is complete — before the moon blanches the valley — house lights will appear as campfires, and the hills can again assume their ancient aspect. Only the ponderous throb and roll of the Atchison, Topeka and Santa Fe Railroad, approaching now as it does about every half hour, breaks the illusion, an illusion that helps me see things here, to imagine how things have been. I've come into the county from that dreaming, and from it, finally, all my questions proceed, and, if things run true, I believe they will return to it.

I am standing on Roniger Hill to test the shape of what I'm going to write about this prairie place. For thirty months, maybe more, I've come and gone here and have found stories to tell, but, until last week, I had not discovered the way to tell them. My searches and researches, like my days, grew more randomly than otherwise, and every form I tried contorted them, and each time I began to press things into cohesion, I edged not so much toward fiction as toward distortion, when what I wanted was accuracy; even when I got a detail down accurately, I couldn't hook it to the next without concocting theories. It was connections that deviled me. I was hunting a fact or image and not a thesis to hold my details together, and so I arrived at this question: should I just gather up items like creek pebbles into a bag and then let them tumble into their own pattern? Did I really want the reality of randomness? Answer: only if it would yield a landscape with figures, one that would unroll like a Chinese scroll painting or a bison-skin drawing where both beginnings and ends of an event are at once present in the conflated time of the American Indian. The least I hoped for was a topographic map of words that would open inch by inch to show its long miles.

Early, I aimed to write about a most spare landscape, seemingly poor for a reporter to poke into, one appearing thin and minimal in history and texture, a stark region recent American life had mostly gone past, a still point, a fastness an ascetic seeking a penitential corner might discover. Chase County fit. Then, a week ago, at home in the second-story room where I write, I laid over the floor the twenty-five U.S. Geological Survey maps that cover Chase County to the measure of an inch and a half to the mile, maps so detailed that barns and houses and windmills appear. On the carpet, the county was about seven feet by six, and I had to walk from the north border to read the scale at the south end. As I traipsed around this paper land, a shape came to me: while thirteen of the maps contain only narrow strips of Chase, the central twelve hold almost all of it, and their outlines form a kind of grid such as an archaeologist lays over ground he will excavate. Wasn't I a kind of digger of shards? Maybe a grid was the answer: arbitrary quadrangles that have nothing inherently to do with the land, little to do with history, and not much to do with my details. After all, since the National Survey of 1785, seventy percent of America lies under such a grid, a system of coordinates that has allowed wildness to be subdued. Would coordinates lead to connections? Were they themselves the only links we can truly understand? Could they lead into the dark loomings that draw me here?

Now: I am standing on Roniger Hill to test the grid. I'm not waiting for revelation, only watching to see whether my notions will crumble like these old, eroding slopes. Standing here, thinking of grids and what's under them, their depths and their light and darkness, I'm watching, and in an hour or so I'll lie down and sleep on this hill and let it and its old shadows work on me, let the dark have at my own shadows and assail my sleep. If my configuration is still alive by morning, then I'll go down off this ridge, and, one more time, begin walking over Chase County, Kansas, grid by topographic grid, digging, sifting, sorting, assembling shards, and my arbitrary course will be that of a Japanese reading a book: up to down, right to left.

So.

Sunrise: sometime last night just before I went into my sleeping bag, the south wind — the one that so blows here the Kansa Indians may have taken their name from it, South Wind People — eased to a brief stillness almost unnatural. (I once asked a countian when this Kansas wind would stop. He said, *Never.*) It seemed to sit on the land, on Roniger Hill, on me, pushing me down into a burden of sleep, leaning heavily as if to impress me into the prairie earth, and then, I don't know when, it rose once more and fetched up chilled bird calls from the south valley, dumped them over me as if from a pitcher of drawn well-water, poured them down, and I got up and rolled my bag, not hurrying before the lightning and murk of clouds coming on, hurrying only a little in the sparse raindrops. Then, as often happens in the Flint Hills, the morning shifted, rearranged itself, all the while getting cooler and clearer, and I went off up-county with a tool kit not of shovels and trowels but of imaginary lines and questions and loomings and the archaeologist's perpetual unease that time is running out before the obliteration hits. And that's how I started off my fourth term in Chase County, Kansas.

Again: let the book page represent this county in east-central Kansas. Divide it horizontally into thirds and split those vertically into quarters so you see twelve sections of a grid that looks like a muntin-bar window of a dozen lights. These are their names north to south, east to west: Saffordville, Gladstone, Thrall-Northwest, Fox Creek, Bazaar, Matfield Green, Hymer, Elmdale, Homestead, Elk, Cedar Point, Wonsevu.

To them attach this old Indian story: The white man asked, *Where is your nation?* The red man said, *My nation is the grass and rocks and the four-leggeds and the six-leggeds and the belly wrigglers and swimmers and the winds and all things that grow and don't grow.* The white man asked, *How big is it?* The other said, *My nation is where I am and my people where they are and the grandfathers and their grandfathers and all the grandmothers and all the stories told, and it is all the songs, and it is our dancing.* The white man asked, *But how many people are there?* The red man said, *That I do not know.*

The population of Chase County is 3,013 at the last counting (about what it was in 1873 when its remarkable courthouse was built), and that's four persons to the square mile, roughly as many as in a Brooklyn apartment. Chase is thirty miles long north to south, twenty-six miles east to west on the south border and a mile shorter on the north. Five hundred twenty-six miles of county road run Chase, 403 of them gravel, seventy-six broken asphalt, forty-six dirt, and one concrete; except for lanes twisting down creek hollows, these roads follow the cardinal compass points along section lines. Three state and federal highways traverse it: Kansas 177 splits it longitudinally, U.S. 50 crosses near its middle before breaking off into a forty-five-degree angle, and Interstate 35 (the Kansas Turnpike) takes a similar angle to link Kansas City, a hundred miles northeast, with Wichita, thirty-five miles southwest. Chase countians use these cities, but more commonly they drive to Emporia, twenty-five miles east of county center.

Of a dozen settlements, three or four still can be called villages and two are towns — Cottonwood Falls, the county seat, and Strong City. Only in these, once linked by a horse trolley, can you buy gasoline *and* groceries. When citizens want a new car or the latest novel or a pair of spectacles, they must drive to Emporia in Lyon County. Chase no longer has a resident physician, dentist, or a pharmacist, but it does have six lawyers, six insurance and thirteen real estate agents. There is one high school, one middle school, two grammar schools, and sixty teachers; within seventy miles of its borders are a couple of dozen colleges and universities. Chase has eleven sites on the National Register of Historic Places (more per citizen than any other Kansas county), a single newspaper (the weekly *Leader-News*), one public library, sixty-six volunteer firemen, six filling stations, one sheriff and two deputies, one barber, and one traffic light (flashing). Also: a nine-hole golf course (sand "greens," players in coveralls, hazards of curious cattle pressed to the barbed-wire fences), an annual rodeo, an airfield (grass), a gun club (Friday night shoots), a movie house (piano still down front), a nursing home. And so on. Before the last world war there was more of almost everything except abandoned farmhouses and collapsing windmills.

You may see the county from one of the many transcontinental flights that pass right over it, or you may view it from an Amtrak window (no stops in the county), or you can get fired down the long, smoking bore of the turnpike that shoots across it. You may also see it from its graveled roads, dirt lanes, pasture tracks, or vestiges of historic trails, or from its couple of hundred miles of canoe-navigable waters, and you can travel it by leg and butt — that is, by walking and reading. There's another means too: call it dreaming, where the less conscious mind can mouse about.

People passing through from other counties have sometimes found it a good spot to get thumped. A man from Marion, immediately west of here (now residing safely in Colorado), told me: *We used to call it Chasem County. The story there was chase 'em, catch 'em, kick 'em.* I add only that people in Cottonwood Falls will comment on the number of federal marshals shot down in Marion. But one thing is surely here: Chase County, Kansas, looks much the way visitors want rural western America to look. A college student, a Pennsylvanian working on a ranch near Matfield Green, said to me: *I can't believe this county. I can't believe it's still like this. I mean, it's so Americana.*

I

Saffordville

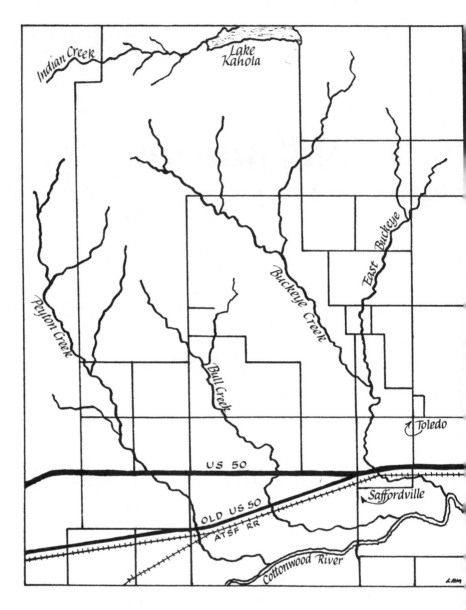

SAFFORDVILLE QUADRANGLE

From the Commonplace Book: Saffordville

I must describe it. Its physical characteristics are somehow close to the heart of the matter.

> — Mark Helprin,
> "Mar Nueva" (1988)

There is no describing [the prairies]. They are like the ocean in more than one particular but in none more than this: the utter impossibility of producing any just impression of them by description. They inspire feelings so unique, so distinct from anything else, so powerful, yet vague and indefinite, as to defy description, while they invite the attempt.

> — John C. Van Tramp,
> *Prairie and Rocky Mountain
> Adventures* (1860)

Creeds and carrots, catechisms and cabbages, tenets and turnips, religion and rutabagas, governments and grasses all depend upon the dewpoint and the thermal range. Give the philosopher a handful of soil, the mean annual temperature and rainfall, and his analysis would enable him to predict with absolute certainty the characteristics of the nation.

> — John James Ingalls,
> "In Praise of Blue Grass" (1875)

The first experience of the plains, like the first sail with a "cap" full of wind, is apt to be sickening. This once overcome, the nerves stiffen, the senses expand, and man begins to realize the magnificence of being.

— Richard Irving Dodge,
The Plains of the Great West (1877)

As to scenery (giving my own thought and feeling), while I know the standard claim is that Yosemite, Niagara Falls, the Upper Yellowstone, and the like afford the greatest natural shows, I am not so sure but the prairies and plains, while less stunning at first sight, last longer, fill the esthetic sense fuller, precede all the rest, and make North America's characteristic landscape. Even [the prairie's] simplest statistics are sublime.

— Walt Whitman,
Specimen Days (1879)

Prairies let us out. . . . They aid to grow a roomy life.

— William A. Quayle,
The Prairie and the Sea (1905)

The children of the American Revolution hesitated forty years at the western edges of the forest because they didn't trust the grasslands.

— Sellers Archer and Clarence Bunch,
The American Grass Book (1953)

Let no one think he may as well keep away from these regions, or pass through at night. There is no part of Kansas where the visitor who would know America can afford to be careless of his surroundings.

— John T. Faris,
Seeing the Middle West (1923)

For more than a generation, [pioneer] Americans viewed this [prairie] expanse, greater in size than the vast wooded regions they had just crossed, as some huge ocean separating east from west, itself no place at all.

[The prairie] immensity, its apparent visual redundancy, makes pointless a rush to somewhere else and creates an overwhelming suspicion that there is nowhere else.

— Wayne Fields,
"Lost Horizon" (1988)

An alert race cannot develop in a forest — a forested country can never be the center of radiation for [pro-dawn] man. Nor can the higher type

*of man develop in a lowland river-bottom country with plentiful food
and luxuriant vegetation. It is on the plateau and relatively level
uplands that life is most exciting and response to stimulus most beneficial.*

> — Henry Fairfield Osborn,
>   "The Plateau Habitat of Pro-Dawn
>   Man" (1928)

The Kiowas reckoned their stature by the distance they could see.

> — N. Scott Momaday,
>   *The Way to Rainy Mountain* (1969)

*Kansas is not a community of which it can be said, "happy is the
people without annals."*

> — Carl Becker,
>   "Kansas" (1910)

*In all the world there is no more peaceful, prosperous scene than in the
"bottomlands" of the thousands and thousands of Kansas creeks. . . .
Here are the still waters, here are the green pastures. Here, the fairest
of the world's habitations.*

> — William Allen White,
>   *Emporia Gazette* (1925)

*I've wondered sometimes if geography might not have been among the
chief determinants of our Kansas mind.*

> — Kenneth S. Davis,
>   "What's the Matter with Kansas?"
>   (1954)

*There are few regions in the United States that are more important
and less known than this bluestem-pasture region of Kansas.*

> — James C. Malin,
>   "An Introduction to the History of
>   the Bluestem-Pasture Region of
>   Kansas" (1942)

*There is no need to personify a river: it is much too literally alive in its
own way, and like air and earth themselves is a creature more powerful, more basic, than any living thing the earth has borne. It is one of*

*those few, huge, casual and aloof creatures by the mercy of whose
existence our own existence was made possible.*
> — James Agee,
> *Let Us Now Praise Famous Men* (1939)

*Kansas brags on its thunder and lightning, and the boast is well
founded.*
> — Horace Greeley,
> *An Overland Journey* (1859)

No Kansan likes to do anything easy.
> — Paul Wellman,
> *The Bowl of Brass* (1944)

*We who live in Kansas know well that its climate is superior to any
other in the world, and that it enables one, more readily than any
other, to dispense with the use of ale.*
> — Carl Becker,
> "Kansas" (1910)

*With the exception of the high character of its people, the greatest
asset of Kansas is its climate. Yet, there seems to have been an unfortunate tendency from the first settlement to exaggerate spectacular
and unfavorable features.*
> — S. D. Flora,
> "The Climate of Kansas" (1918)

*[Kansas is] a state like nothing so much as some scriptural kingdom —
a land of floods, droughts, cyclones, and enormous crops, of prophets
and plagues.*
> — Julian Street,
> *Abroad at Home* (1926)

*The special quality of fine prairie weather isn't necessarily one of
intrinsic merit, but of contrast with what has gone just before.*
> — John Madson,
> *Where the Sky Began* (1982)

*The Tibetans ... revere the wind and sky. Blue and white are the
celestial colors of the B'on sky god, who is seen as an embodiment of
space and light, and creatures of the upper air become B'on symbols —*

the griffon, the mythical garuda, and the dragon. For Buddhist Tibetans, prayer flags and windbells confide spiritual longings to the winds.

— Peter Matthiessen,
The Snow Leopard (1978)

Wind is a plant's only chance to make music.

Cook Islanders had names for thirty-two different winds.

The Jews, Arabs, Romans, Greeks, and Aztecs all took their word for spirit from the word for wind.

In the 1880's, an American at Point Barrow, Alaska, watched Eskimo women chase the wind from their houses with clubs and knives, while the men waited around a fire that had been built to draw the wind. When the men decided the wind had come to the fire, they shot it with rifles and poured a cauldron of water on the fire. As the dying wind tried to rise in steam from the smouldering embers, they crushed it with a heavy stone.

Of all the phenomena of nature, wind is probably the least understood and the least controlled.

— Peter Steinhart,
"Tracks of the Wind" (1988)

A single, severe thunderstorm supercell can hold more energy than a hydrogen bomb.

— John G. Fuller,
Tornado Watch #211 (1987)

A few very fortunate people have gone aloft in tornadoes and survived. During [a] tornado in Wichita Falls, a man was blown out of his exploding house. Like Dorothy, he glimpsed others in the funnel. A house trailer rotated near him, and in the window he could see the terrified face of one of his neighbors. (She did not survive.) Flying ahead of him was a mattress. If I could reach that, he thought, I'd just go to sleep. He then lost consciousness and woke on the ground, wrapped in barbed wire. Flying splinters had made a pincushion of his body.

— William Hauptman,
"On the Dryline" (1984)

From what angle does the mysterious ordainer see causes and effects? Is there any sense in the elements, those intermediaries between him and us?

— Victor Hugo,
The Toilers of the Sea (1866)

"Things have a life of their own," the gypsy proclaimed with a harsh accent. "It's simply a matter of waking up their souls."

> — Gabriel García Márquez,
> *One Hundred Years of Solitude* (1967)

Each hamlet or village or town should be a place, its own place. This is not a matter of fake historicism or artsy-craftsy architecture. It is a matter of respect for things existing, subtle patterns of place woven from vistas and street widths and the siting and color and scale of stores, houses, and trees. . . . If the countryside is to prosper, it must be different from city or suburb. . . . That difference is in part the simple business of containing our towns and giving them boundaries.

> — Robert B. Riley,
> "New Mexico Villages in a
> Future Landscape" (1969)

Gain! Gain! Gain! Gain! Gain! is the beginning, the middle and the end, the alpha and omega of the founders of American towns.

> — Morris Birkbeck,
> *Notes on a Journey in America* (1818)

We always need theres, spots which happily aren't like ours, to validate heres. Mostly theres are inert supports, silent witnesses to the quality of here.

> — Robert B. Heilman,
> "We're Here" (1987)

Chase County has 2,839 people. There is one blind person, one insane person, and 745 voters.

> — News item,
> *Chase County News* (1873)

Maybe you never heard of Cottonwood Falls, but the philosopher who said that the whole universe was reflected in a drop of dew may have had that particular town in mind.

> — King Features news item,
> "Here's America's Progress at a
> Glance" (1936)

In the Quadrangle:
Saffordville

In 1952, when I first crossed Chase County, I was twelve years old and riding in the front seat as navigator while my father drove our Pontiac Chieftain with its splendid hood ornament, an Indian's head whose chromium nose we followed for half a decade over much of America. In the last weeks, I've probed my memory to find even one detail of that initial passage into the western prairies. What did I see, feel? Nothing now except our route returns. My guess is that I found the grasslands little more than miles to be got over — after all, that's the way Americans crossed Kansas. Still do.

In 1965, when I came out of the navy, I drove across the prairie again on a visit to California, and the grasslands looked different to me, so alive and varied, and now I believe that two years of watching the Atlantic Ocean changed the way I viewed landscape, especially levelish, rolling things. I also began to see the prairies as native ground, the land my hometown sat just out of sight of, and I began to like them not because they demand your attention like mountains and coasts but because they almost defy absorbed attention. At first, to be *here*, to be here *now*, was hard for me to do on the prairie. I liked the clarity of line in a place that seemed to require me to bring something to it and to open to it actively: see far, see little. I learned a prairie secret: take the numbing distance in small doses and gorge on the little details that beckon. Like its moisture, the prairie doesn't give up anything easily, unless it's horizon and sky. Search out its variation, its colors, its subtleties. It's not that I had to learn to think flat — the prairies rarely are — but I had to begin thinking open and lean, seeing without set points of obvious focus, noticing first the horizon and then drawing my vision back toward middle distance where so little appears to exist. I came to understand that the prairies are nothing but grass as the sea is nothing but water, that most prairie life is *within* the place: under the stems, below the turf, beneath the stones. The prairie is not a topography that shows its all but rather a vastly exposed place of concealment, like the geodes so abundant in the county, where the splendid lies within the plain cover. At last I realized I was not a man of the sea or coasts or mountains but a fellow of the grasslands. Once I understood that, I began to find all sorts of reasons why, and here comes one:

I am driving west of Emporia, Kansas, on highway 50 where it takes up the course of the two-mile-wide and shallow valley of the east-running Cottonwood River, and I've just entered the prairie hills through a trough of a wooded bottom on this route that runs some way into the uplands before it rises out of the floodplain to reveal the open spread of grasses. The change is sudden, stark, surprising. If I kept heading west, I would ride among the grasses — tall, middle, short — until I crossed the prairie and the plains (the words are not synonyms) and climbed into the foothills of the Rockies. By following route 50 into Chase County, up out of the shadowed woodlands, out of the soybean and sorghum bottoms and into the miles of something too big, too wild to be called a meadow, I am recapitulating human history, retracing in an hour the sixty-five-million-year course of our evolution from some small, bottom-dwelling mammal that began to crawl trees and evolve and then climb down and move into the East African savannahs. It was tall grass that made man stand up: to be on all fours, to crouch in a six-foot-high world of thick cellulose, is to be blind and vulnerable. People may prefer the obvious beauty of mountains and seacoasts, but we are bipedal because of savannah; we are human because of tallgrass. When I walk the prairie, I like to take along the notion that, while something primal in me may long for the haven of the forest, its apprenticeship in the trees, it also recognizes this grand openness as the kind of place where it became itself.

Now: I am in the grasses, my arms upraised: spine and legs straight, everything upright like the bluestem, and I can walk a thousand miles over this prairie, but I can't climb a tree worth a damn.

On highway 50, two miles west of the eastern Chase County line exactly (man-made things are often exact distances here because they grow up along section-line junctures), a gravel road crosses the highway; I am walking it southward, toward where it passes over old route 50 and then over the old Santa Fe tracks, then over the new tracks, and then drops steeply down the high grade to the oldest route 50 and runs a mile to the Cottonwood River. Between tracks and river stand four houses, a brick school, and, off in a grove, a wooden depot used as a storage shed, and the sign still says, although fading, SAFFORDVILLE.

Saffordville: population five, the youngest fifty-five, the oldest eighty-two. The village, briefly called Kenyon (I haven't discovered why), takes its name from a Kansas judge who advocated passage of the Homestead Act of 1862. I am in the grass and scrub where the town once was, and I climb concrete steps leading to nothing, shuffle down native-stone sidewalk slabs going nowhere, and ahead is the concrete cooler of a grocery and, behind it, the block shell of an auto garage. In 1940, two hundred people lived here. No town in the county has increased its population since World War II, and what I am about to say is true of other villages nearby, the twin towns of Cottonwood and Strong excepted; as a form of shorthand, let me call this dying the Saffordville Syndrome: in the thirties, the town had a doctor, three stores, two schools, one hotel, a blacksmith shop, lumberyard, grain elevator, implement dealer, creamery, café, barber and butcher shops, bank, garage, a church, and five "lodges" (Masons, Woodmen, Eastern Star, Royal Neighbors, Ladies' Aid). These happened: farmers needed fewer hands to get a good crop from the rich bottoms, and bigger implements required more land to make them pay; automobiles and paved roads opened the commerce of Emporia (so properly named); county schools consolidated.

That much is general American history. Saffordville added a detail that, in one Kansan's words, *capped the climax*. Town speculators trying to make a killing by inventing towns and then selling lots laid out Saffordville not just between Buckeye and Bull creeks, but also on the first terrace of the Cottonwood River so that heavy rains rush the village from three sides, and, on the south, a bluff forces the Cottonwood in flood northward toward Saffordville where the railroad grade dams it. The effect is something like building a town at the bottom of a funnel; even after the citizens cut away a loop in the river, it didn't drain fast enough during flood. In the 1940s, an old raconteur wrote:

The Indians used to warn settlers who settled near the river. They said they had seen the water from bluff to bluff. The settlers did not pay any attention to the Indian warnings, and in 1904, there came a flood and the Cottonwood River overflowed its banks and flooded Everything. Two weeks later it overflowed again, which was the last flood for nineteen years. Again in 1923, there came another flood. It was the last one until 1926. In 1929 there were two floods — one in June and the other in November. From 1923 to 1929, the river overflowed eight times.

And then, as if to prove these were not mere and rare chances of nature, in 1951 the Cottonwood flooded four times, the last the worst in white man's memory. Less than a hundred feet wide here, this river, which had caught fire from an oil-well spill a generation earlier and two generations before that had gone dry (countians tell of walking the twelve miles to Emporia on the riverbed and of helplessly standing by their empty wells and watching their houses burn to the ground that summer), this same river gathered the waters of its tributaries running full of July rains, and went overnight from five feet deep to thirty feet, and took off once again across the valley, just as it was to do in 1965, 1973, 1985. Had there been an economic reason for Saffordville to continue, these repetitions of muddy water would have been serious drawbacks, but, without reasons beyond the inertia of initial settlement, the Cottonwood, like a wronged red man, finally drove out the town. A fellow told me, *That river ate our dinner once too often.* The residents packed up possessions, picked up their houses and church and even some of the stone-slab sidewalks, and moved a mile north to the higher ground of faceless Toledo, a mere cluster of buildings that happen to stand in some proximity. Since the big flood of 1951, only two families have stayed on in Saffordville, and, a couple of decades ago, another moved in. To my knowledge, no one around here thinks them crazy.

Upon the First Terrace

Now, this is Tom Bridge: *Most of the dust storms in southeastern Colorado blew in from the north. I was a boy — seven, eight, nine — in the early thirties, Dust Bowl days. For a long distance we could see them coming, the dusters. We looked north and there was a curtain of brown dust, sometimes black. The storm came on like a cliff. The sun shone right into the irregularities in that wall, and it was like looking into a canyon. There was a period of quiet: the air got still as the dust came on. It was hundreds of feet high. And then the high-velocity winds that were riding over the top of the storm roared in. It turned so dark I could hardly see the end of my arm. We watched from the house, and we felt the grit between our teeth, and pressure changes pulled dust into the house and into everything — linens, trunks, hatboxes. Lids weren't any use, so my mother hung wet towels over the windows, and when we went out, she had us wrap wet cloths over our mouths and noses. The dust was silt — fine quartz sand pulled up off the alluvial fan east of the Rockies.*

I am at the dinner table in the Bridges' house, a solid, one-and-a-half-story, red-brick, red-tile-roofed place built in 1921 in Saffordville. Although it's not a big home, even today it stands out in the county. For twenty-two years, Tom Bridge, tall and angular, has taught geology at Emporia State University, but he grew up on the Colorado grasslands at the foot of the Front Range.

After a duster, we'd go out and hunt arrowheads: the wind had carried off the lighter topsoil and the flint points lay shining on the hardpan. I had cigar boxes of them "dug up" by the wind. We lived near a leg of the Santa Fe Trail, where the ruts were compacted so hard that the wind would blow away the soil around them, and following a storm we'd find ruts raised like railroad tracks. We never had to open a gate after a duster: the fences would catch the tumbleweed and make a windbreak, and the drifts covered the barbed wire. We rode our horses right over the fences.

In 1966, he got lost and drove into Saffordville and asked the old banker's son for directions to a piece of land Tom was considering buying. The son said he might sell him his house, and later he did, and all along Bridge knew that the house sat in the floodplain of the Cottonwood River. Anybody who grows up inhaling dry bits of the Rocky Mountains might do the same. He moved in with his wife, Syble, and their four children, and it's quite possible that they will be the last citizens in Saffordville. From 1966 to 1973 they averaged a flood a year, but the water never got higher than the basement. Tom didn't complain about the flooding but he did about Syble's overstocking canned goods because they seemed a needless burden. In 1985 the river began to swell, and the Bridges began raising furniture, but they were soon out of bricks and concrete blocks, and they started setting cans of corn, tomato soup, and V-8 juice under the furniture legs. Of the three inhabited houses remaining in Saffordville, the Bridges' is the farthest from the river but on the lowest ground, and it isn't feasible to raise the brick house as their neighbors the Staedtlers did their big, two-story frame place. So, while the radio crackled out flood updates, the Bridges put down cans of chili, and pork and beans, their sole defense against the river and not much more effective than wet towels against dusters.

As goes the Cottonwood River, so goes Chase County: through the quarter-billion-year-old limestone hills, the typically slow waters have cut a sixty-mile dogleg trough, northeast, east. Before the recent building of several impoundments, all the storm runoff in the county, but for two small portions in the south, as well as much of the drainage of Marion County, rolled past Saffordville. While nearly every village in Chase sits in the valley of the Cottonwood or one of its tributaries, only Saffordville on the east, sooner or later, gets the runoff from seventeen hundred square miles, an immense drainage for such a small channel. Without the Cottonwood watershed there would never have been much settlement in

Chase or agriculture other than upland grazing, and the railroad and highway 50 would not likely have passed this way, since transport crosses the hills through the gaps cut by the Cottonwood and South Fork. The valleys hold the towns and the cultivation, but only fourteen percent of the county is bottomland, and it is the rain that falls on the other eighty-six percent, the uplands, that creates floods. Like Kane, the ancient Hawaiian shark-god, the Cottonwood gives life and destruction with equal nonchalance.

Now the river is rising:

the uplands in saturation, they can no longer hold the rain, and they slough it down the slopes to the creeks, where a few days earlier quiet waters flowed blue-gray, the color of moonstone, but now they climb banks and rip off ledges with mad turnings of earthen roil, and where they join larger streams they meet walls of water and back up until the whole county, its veinings of waterways become a massive thrombus, starts to overflow, and the word goes out by radio, by neighbors in pickups: *River's on the rise!* And all the time it's raining, raining so long that the *Emporia Gazette* has time to print front-page jokes about it. *If you've been saving for a rainy day, brother, this is it.* Raining, and the Cottonwood, now thirty feet deep, tops out and starts across the bottoms and begins losing its hundred serpentines as it straightens itself to fit the more linear contours of the valley, and the word goes out, *Take high ground!* and people wonder, *Am I high enough?* and now only parallel lines of cottonwoods and sycamores and willows mark the usual river course, and a man stands on a bridge and remembers how last week his rowboat hardly moved in the slow river when he fished east of the old milldam, and now the silent river has voice, loud, and one fellow says to his son, *It's that sound I don't like,* and farmers start their combines and tractors (and one machine won't fire up) and move them to higher ground: *How high is high enough?* and, *Is there time to get the cattle out?* and everywhere along the South Fork and the Cottonwood the usual argument: *I'm not leaving. This is where I live. This is mine.* And the old, benign river turns malevolent, and a farmer shouts at his wife, *It's sweeping us away!* and she won't listen because women here are always the last to leave, and out back the corn and milo are slipping under, green to brown, and she shouts, *I'm going upstairs!* and he shouts too, *No you're not!* And she: *It's not taking my house while I stand up on the bluff, not this river!* And he: *It ain't no river now!* It's a thing moving as if it knows what made this valley and knows its million-year right of tenancy, and it's going to tear out the fences and flush the squatters and their privies away and scrub the valley of the septic intrusion and let them go down with their hogs and stories of Noah:

the river has risen.

This is Syble Bridge, small and trim. She says to me: *The problem isn't the water really: it's the mud that stays behind. The water drains out but the mud settles.* And Tom says, and he is thinking of Dust Bowl days too: *We get that same layer, that same type of dust or mud precipitated out of water.* I'm laughing and I say, all your life you keep getting soil in your house from one agency or another. You're an earth scientist and earth keeps coming in to live with you. It must make you glad you're not an entomologist. Or a mortician.

I ask, where did you see the water first, and she says: *In '85 I opened the basement door, and it was coming up the stairs at me. It was rising faster than we'd seen it do before. I'd already gotten my home-canned goods from down below, and then they went under up here: sweet pickles and dills. Afterward, we were afraid to eat them, but we ate the stuff in tin cans. Two dozen jars of pickles, still pretty and green, went to the dump along with some furniture and mattresses and rugs: three flatbed truckloads. You understand, in '85 we never left the house. That's the way it is for us here — our neighbors don't leave either. We have one room upstairs, and Tom and I go up to it, but we come down in our rubber boots and sit in the water to eat at the table. The man who built this house, Bill ImMasche, the banker, did the same thing: went upstairs and waited it out. During a flood, Stanley North would come up to the back of the house in a rowboat to bring Bill his paper and mail and milk every day. In '51 they took the screen off the upstairs window to pass things in. Before he pulled away, Stanley said, "You want this screen back on?" "No," says Bill. "Leave it off. I'll swat flies. It'll give me something to do." The floods never bothered him, but people say that his wife's severe heart trouble came from worrying over this house flooding. He watched his pennies, but she shook him loose to build this place.*

The Bridges have lived here twenty-two years, and I ask why they don't at least build a levee around the house, a four-foot berm should do it, and Tom says, *When we get time.* I ask whether living here makes them watch the sky, and he says, *We've had floods when we've had no rain on our place. We have to listen to the radio, go down to the bridge to check on the river, especially at night when we can't see it coming over the fields.*

Syble says, *When the forecast is for flood, Tom starts moving vehicles to higher ground, and I mow the lawn so the grass clippings will wash away. If the forecast was for flooding tomorrow, I'd head right now for the canned goods, especially juice cans, the forty-six-ounce size. Two years ago it was ten inches in this room, but in '51 it was five feet, and that's what damaged the house. When we bought it, we had to put everything inside back together. We decorated with the idea that things would probably get wet.* Now Syble is setting the table to serve a roast and mashed potatoes and broccoli, and she says, *In high water it gets quiet. About all we hear is the water slopping outside.*

Tom: *This house is a riverboat that won't float. I'll look out a window and see carp jumping on the lawn. Frogs in the basement. Cordwood floating off the porch.*

And Syble: *I looked out the window in '85 and saw the workbench float out the garage. An eddy carried it away. It wasn't a regular workbench: it was an old grand piano that had been gutted, but it had fancy carved legs. We kept tools and nails sitting on. We watched it float out, go past the house, moving right along. It stopped over east in Edith's field, tools still on top of it.*

Tom: *I had three Honda motorcycles in the garage. They went beneath. There isn't time to get everything, so we go for the books first, then things in the basement. I turn off the electricity if water's coming upstairs. Syble got shocked the last time. You'll feel the electric current in the water, a kind of vibrating: it can kill you. We take oil lamps to the second floor. The toilet stops working, the bathtub backs up with foul stuff. There's no question a flood's inconvenient.*

Syble: *You don't live in a floodplain and get excited about water. Now, a tornado gets us excited. Tom calls us collectors who need a flood every so often to clear things out anyway. When the water drops, we get the brooms and hose and squirt it and keep the water riled up, make it take the mud back out. If you let the mud dry, it's like concrete. We pump out the basement.*

The Bridges have no flood insurance, and Tom tells me he sold their canoe, and Syble says, *I wouldn't want out in a flood in a canoe or anything else.* They don't have a CB to make up for losing the telephone when the buried lines short out. I ask Tom if he will see water in this house again, and he says, *That's a real possibility, but I don't worry about it. Our lives aren't threatened. Our possessions, yes.*

The meal is over, and we are talking about geology, and someone has said that the Kansas pioneers' great fear was drought. I say, since erosion is the primary geologic force in Kansas, isn't it appropriate for a geologist to live amidst the cycle of flood, erosion, and deposition, and Tom says, *Twenty-two years here now and I really understand sedimentary layering, what made these hills.*

II

Edith McGregor lives across the road — that's all it can be called now, although it once was Hunt Street — from the Bridges, and she also knows that sedimentary layering is the real enemy. Her home is a large, two-story frame house, immaculately white, the kind you find along old, tree-lined, front-porch streets in America, and she isn't much slowed by her eighty-two years, she of the young hands. Her husband died a few years ago, yet she's a jolly woman, a former schoolteacher as are all five people who live in Saffordville, and, like the others, she owns no boat and would have to be unconscious before she would take to the flood in anything other than the second floor of her house. She has a master's degree in psychology. I am seated at her kitchen table in front of the window where, six months ago, she watched the tornado come down on Toledo, a mile north, and she says, *I didn't go to the basement. I wasn't turning my back on that thing,* and she sets down thick slices of her wheat bread and pushes the butter toward me; she has already explained how she gets fresh Chase County wheat from the small grain elevator by the Santa Fe tracks and how she grinds it to add to her store flour. It's ten in the morning, and she's wiping off a jar of home-canned pears.

Dean and I came here in 1947, and we saw floods about every year, but the water never got out of the yard until '51. It came up early on Wednesday morning, and it rolled across those west bean fields like a wall, it seems. We didn't have much time before it started up the porch steps and under the front door and then through the windows. They're low like old windows are. This is the highest house here: built in 1913 for seven thousand dollars and paid for with one crop of alfalfa seed. My husband was head wire-

chief in Emporia, in telegraph communications for the Santa Fe, and whenever it looked like high water, he'd take out for town so he wouldn't get cut off. That Wednesday he got the horse to higher ground and went on to work. I was here with my daughter and son, both still in school. First we crated up the chickens and took them up to the sun porch on the second floor, and that was our mistake: it took too much time to run down three dozen fryers. We got the dining table up on boxes and the piano up on something — got it up a foot or so — we thought that was enough, and she smiles at her naiveté and says, *They tell that the Indians believed a big flood would come every hundred years, but our people who build on high ground have their wells go dry in the summer: we located down in here to have water. My well's been polluted by floods, but it's never gone dry.*

There's a story of the woman who in the drought of 1929 prayed hard for rain, even asking that the river overflow and water their dying corn, and it began raining, and the Cottonwood rose and washed out their whole crop, and I ask, *did you pray?* and she says, *I suppose we did. My son got scared when the water started rising in the house, but he got over it. The first floor is four feet above the yard: I measured the water in this kitchen, and it came to the top of the table, thirty-three inches. We took canned goods upstairs: I remember a lot of hominy and mackerel. Haven't eaten hominy since.*

Edith sets preserves and a glass of cold water on the table, and she says, *When the river's coming on, I always fill the bathtub so we can wash up and flush the toilet. Somebody will bring us drinking water. In '51, a boat was at the house by noon to pick us up, but when the water's six feet deep with a current like we get here, I don't go outside.* She says that as if speaking of spring showers. *That boat wasn't big enough. I can't swim. Besides, I had no reason to get out. I like to stay and take care of things. I guess I'm an old river rat.*

She slows as she recalls the details, and she says, *We stayed and watched the river rise: the chicken coop washed away, and that was it for us raising chickens. The soybean crop went, but the wheat we'd already harvested. Then, the second day my son got restless, and he went up on the roof with the dog and his twenty-two and shot at trash floating by. An airplane flew over and saw him and passed word that the McGregors were signaling for help. I wasn't scared, really wasn't. My husband couldn't get away from*

*all the stopped trains in Emporia: every stranded passenger wanted
to send a message. He didn't come home until Monday. But every
night he drove up to the south bluff to see if the oil lamp was
burning in the window — that was our signal that we were all
right. On Friday I started stirring the water with a broom so the
mud would go out with it. I went round and round the rooms, and
finally, when the water was out of the house, I went to the porch
time and again and brought in buckets of water to throw on the
floors. You don't wait until you need a shovel. These pine floors
held up, but all the veneer furniture and the doors and the piano
just fell apart.*

She's watching to see whether I find all this eccentric, and she
says, *I walked out of the house Sunday, but my son put a bundle of
clean clothes over his head and waded out Saturday evening —
went to town for a good meal. When I came out, first thing I did
was get a drink of cold water and a big slice of fruit pie someone
brought — peach it was. Then strangers started coming out to stare
and pick through our fields and houses. They carried off more than
the river did.* For the first time she shows irritation.

She says, *I remember that before the water started rising, animals did strange things. Groundhogs, skunks, snakes all moving:
they weren't waiting for the water. A mother skunk got trapped in
the barn with her two little ones, and my son lifted the babies up
on a feed box, and then the mother climbed up but never raised her
tail. She seemed to understand. A neighbor, the French war bride,
stopped her pickup on the highway and opened the door to see if a
big old hog was all right. He climbed up in the seat and sat down
beside her, she said, "just like he knowed me."*

Now Edith is looking out the window where she could once count
eight houses along Hunt Street. She says this seriously: *If people
don't know any better than to live down here, they'll have to suffer
the consequences, but I never knew anyone to die in our floods.*

III

In the early summer of 1951, Frances Staedtler's husband's parents
jacked up their big house, added three feet to the foundation, and
set the house back down on it. Six days later the Cottonwood was
at the door, and then in the kitchen, the living room, and the family
went upstairs. Frances spoke to me for a while about the floods, her

story paralleling the others', and, when she began talking about her mother-in-law taking the ironing board to the second floor in case she needed a raft, Frances had to stop, and she struggled to say, *I'm afraid I can't go on. It's too much remembering how we all were in those days, when we were strong enough to fight it. We were together.*

These people of Saffordville, the whole population, all five of them, as they talk their way back into the big floods, grow animated, and sorrows and smiles come and go so quickly about their faces that I almost don't see them, and their eyes are widened and keen. They are not boastful, but they relish, not having beaten the river, but having held their own with it and not yielding to it other than by climbing a flight of stairs, and the whole time they realize the battle is a little foolish — just the way they want it. They recognize but do not say how the river whets a fine edge on their lives, and I never heard any of them speak love for the river, or hate. These are not people locked in the floodplain by poverty; they are held here by recollections of what the river has given them: hours of a family bound tightly like shocks of wheat, of moments when all their senses were almost one with the land, of times when they earned the right to be tenants on the first terrace of the Cottonwood River. One afternoon, Edith McGregor said to me: *Not everybody gets the chance to live like this.*

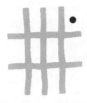

Under Old Nell's Skirt

I know a man, a Maya in the Yucatán, who can call up wind: he whistles a clear, haunting, thirteen-note melody set in the Native American pentatonic scale. He whistles, the wind moves, and for some moments the heat of the tropical forest eases. It's a talent there to appreciate. But does he summon the wind, or does he know just the right time to whistle before the wind moves? He says, in effect, that he is on speaking terms with the wind, and by that he means it is a phenomenon, yes, but also a presence, and it has a name, Ik, and it is Ik that brings the seasonal rain to Yucatán. You may call such a notion pantheism or primitivism or mere personification: he wouldn't care, because for him, for the Maya, for all of tribal America, the wind, the life bringer, is something to heed, to esteem: Ik.

In Kansas I've not heard any names for the nearly constant winds, the oldest of things here. When the Kansa Indians were pushed out of the state, they carried with them the last perception of wind as anything other than a faceless force, usually for destruction, the power behind terrible prairie wildfires, the clout in blizzards and droughts, and, most of all, in tornadoes that will take up everything, even fenceposts. But people here know wind well, they often speak of it, yet, despite the several names in other places for local American winds, in this state, whose very name may mean "wind-people," it has no identity but a direction, no epithet but a curse. A local preacher told me: *Giving names to nature is un-*

christian. I said that it might help people connect with things and who knows where that might lead, and he said, *To idolatry.* Yet the fact remains: these countians are more activated by weather than religion.

Almost everything I see in this place sooner or later brings me back to the grasses; after all, this is the prairie, a topography that so surprised Anglo culture when it began arriving that it found for this grand-beyond no suitable word in its immense vocabulary, and it resorted to the French of illiterate trappers: prairie. Except in accounts of novice travelers, these grasslands have never been meadows, heaths, moors, downs, wolds. A woman in Boston once said to me, *Prairie is such a lovely word — and for so grim a place.*

More than all other things here, the grasses are the offspring of the wind, the power that helps evaporation equal precipitation to the detriment of trees, the power that breaks off leaves and branches, shakes crowns and rigid trunks to tear roots and disrupt transpiration, respiration, nutrient assimilation. But grasses before the wind bend and straighten and bend and keep their vital parts underground, and, come into season, they release their germ, spikelets, and seeds to the wind, the invisible sea that in this place must carry the code, the directions from the unfaced god, carry the imprint of rootlet and rhizome, blade and sheath, culm and rachis: the wind, the penisless god going and coming everywhere, the intercourse of the grasses, the sprayer of seed across the opened sex risen and waiting for the pattern set loose on the winds today of no name; and so the grasses pull the energy from the wind, the offspring of sunlight, to transmute soil into more grasses that ungulates eat into flesh that men turn into pot roasts and woolen socks.

Now: I am walking a ridge in the southern end of Saffordville quadrangle, and below me in the creek bottom are oaks of several kinds, cottonwood, hackberry, walnut, hickory, sycamore. Slippery elms, once providing a throat emulcent, try to climb the hills by finding rock crevices to shield their seed, and, if one sprouts, it will grow straight for a time, only to lose its inborn shape to the prevailing southerlies so that the windward sides of elms seem eaten off but the lee sides spread north like tresses unloosed in March. If a seedling succeeds on a ridge top, it will spread low as if to squat under the shears of windrush, and everywhere the elm trunks lean to the polestar and make the county appear as if its southern end had been lifted and tilted before the land could dry and set. A windmill must stand straight and turn into the wind to harvest

water, but the slippery elm turns away to keep the wind from its
wet pulp.

And there is another face to this thing from which life proceeds.
Yesterday I walked down a ridge to get out of the November wind
while I ate a sandwich, and I came upon a house foundation on a
slope bereft of anything but grasses and knee-high plants. It was
absolutely exposed, an oddity here, since most of the homes sit in
the shelter of wooded vales. This one faced east — or it would have,
had it still been there — and the only relief from the prevailing
winds that the builder had sought was to set the back of the house
to them. There was the foundation, some broken boards, a few
rusting things, and, thirty feet away, a storm cellar, its door torn off,
and that was all except for a rock road of two ruts. The cave, as
people here call tornado cellars, was of rough-cut native stone with
an arched roof, wooden shelves, and a packed-earth floor with
Mason jar fragments glinting blue in the sunlight; one had been so
broken that twin pieces at my feet said:

The shards seemed to be lost voices locked in silica and calling still.

These cellars once kept cool home-canned food (and rat snakes),
and, when a tornado struck like a fang from some cloud-beast, they
kept families that mocked their own timorousness by calling them
'fraidy holes, and it did take nerve to go into the dim recesses with
their spidered corners and dark, reptilian coils. I stepped down
inside and sat on a stone fallen from the wall and ate safely in the
doorway, but, even with the sun shafts, there was something dismal
and haunted in the shadowed dust of dry rot here and dank of wet
rot there. Things lay silent inside, the air quite stilled, and I felt
something, I don't know what: something waiting. ·

Was there a connection between this cave and that house absent
but for its foundation? The site, sloping southwest, seemed placed
to catch a cyclone in a county in the heart of the notorious Tornado
Alley of the Middle West, a belt that can average 250 tornadoes a
year, more than anywhere else in the world. A hundred and sixty
miles from here, Codell, Kansas, got thumped by a tornado every
twentieth of May for three successive years, and five months ago a
twister "touched down," mashed down really, a mile north of Saffordville at the small conglomeration of houses and trailers called

Toledo, and the newspaper caption for a photograph of that crook'd finger of a funnel cloud was HOLY TOLEDO! Years earlier a cyclone wrecked a Friends meetinghouse there, but this time it skipped over the Methodists' church and went for their houses. In Chase County I've found a nonchalance about natural forces born of fatalism: *If it's gonna get me, it'll get me.* In Cottonwood Falls, on a block where a house once sat, the old cave remains, collapsing, yet around it are six house trailers. Riding out a tornado in a mobile home is like stepping into combine blades: trailers can become airborne chambers full of flying knives of aluminum and glass. No: if there is a dread in the county, it is not of dark skies but of the opposite, of clear skies, days and days of clear skies, of a drought nobody escapes, not even the shopkeepers. That any one person will suffer losses from a tornado, however deadly, goes much against the odds, and many residents reach high school before they first see a twister; yet, nobody who lives his full span in the county dies without a tornado story.

Tornado: a Spanish past participle meaning turned, from a verb meaning to turn, alter, transform, repeat, *and* to restore. Meteorologists speak of the reasons why the Midlands of the United States suffer so many tornadoes: a range of high mountains west of a great expanse of sun-heated plains at a much lower altitude, where dry and cold northern air can meet warm and moist southern air from a large body of water to combine with a circulation pattern mixing things up: that is to say, the jet stream from Arctic Canada crosses the Rockies to meet a front from the Gulf of Mexico over the Great Plains in the center of which sits Kansas, where, since 1950, people have sighted seventeen hundred tornadoes. It is a place of such potential celestial violence that the meteorologists at the National Severe Storms Forecast Center in Kansas City, Missouri, are sometimes called the Keepers of the Gates of Hell. Countians who have smelled the fulminous, cyclonic sky up close, who have felt the ground shake and heard the earth itself roar and have taken to a storm cellar that soon filled with a loathsome greenish air, find the image apt. The Keepers of the Gates of Hell have, in recent years, become adept at forecasting tornadoes, and they might even be able to suggest cures for them if only they could study them up close. Years ago a fellow proposed sending scientists into the eye of a tornado in an army tank until he considered the problem of transporting the machine to a funnel that usually lasts only minutes, and someone else suggested flying into a cyclone, whereupon a weather-research pilot said, yes, it was feasible if the aviator would first practice by flying into mountains.

Climatologists speak of thunderstorms pregnant with tornadoes, storm-breeding clouds more than twice the height of Mount Everest; they speak of funicular envelopes and anvil clouds with pendant mammati and of thermal instability of winds in cyclonic vorticity, of rotatory columns of air torquing at velocities up to three hundred miles an hour (although no anemometer in the direct path of a storm has survived), funnels that can move over the ground at the speed of a strolling man or at the rate of a barrel-assing semi on the turnpike; they say the width of the destruction can be the distance between home plate and deep center field and its length the hundred miles between New York City and Philadelphia. A tornado, although more violent than a much longer lasting hurricane, has a life measured in minutes, and weathercasters watch it snuff out as it was born: unnamed.

I know here a grandfather, a man as bald as if a cyclonic wind had taken his scalp — something witnesses claim has happened elsewhere — who calls twisters Old Nell, and he threatens to set crying children outside the back door for her to carry off. People who have seen Old Nell close, up under her skirt, talk about her colors: pastel-pink, black, blue, gray, and a survivor said this: *All at once a big hole opened in the sky with a mass of cherry-red, a yellow tinge in the center,* and another said: *a funnel with beautiful electric-blue light,* and a third person: *It was glowing like it was illuminated from the inside.* The witnesses speak of shapes: a formless black mass, a cone, cylinder, tube, ribbon, pendant, thrashing hose, dangling lariat, writhing snake, elephant trunk. They tell of ponds being vacuumed dry, eyes of geese sucked out, chickens clean-plucked from beak to bum, water pulled straight up out of toilet bowls, a woman's clothes torn off her, a wife killed after being jerked through a car window, a child carried two miles and set down with only scratches, a Cottonwood Falls mother (fearful of wind) cured of chronic headaches when a twister passed harmlessly within a few feet of her house, and, just south of Chase, a woman blown out of her living room window and dropped unhurt sixty feet away and falling unbroken beside her a phonograph record of "Stormy Weather."

London Harness, an eighty-five-year-old man who lives just six miles north of the county line, told me: *I knew a family years ago that was crossing open country here in a horse and wagon. A bad storm come on fast, and the man run to a dug well and said, "I'm going down in here — you do the best you can!" The wife hollered and screamed and run to a ditch and laid down with their two little kids. That funnel dropped right in on them. After the storm passed over, she and the kids went to the well to say, "Come on up, Pappy," but there weren't no water down there, and he weren't down there. If you're in that path, no need of running.*

Yesterday: in the sun the broken words on the Mason jar glinted and, against the foundation, the wind whacked dry grasses and seed pods, *tap-tap-tap, rasp-rasp,* and a yellow light lay over the November slope, and Ma and son: did they one afternoon come out of the cave to see what I see, an unhoused foundation, some twisted fence wire, and a sky turning golden in all innocence?

Along the Ghost Highway

Unless you count possums, skunks, raccoons, and deer, there's no coming and going on this road, a quarter-mile-long strip of concrete, twenty feet wide, running nearly atop an east-west section line, and so concealed two miles east of Saffordville that many countians don't know it still exists. I am walking it, and I believe it to be the last exposed piece of the original concrete, however broken, of what was once U.S. 50 South in or touching Chase. These fractures, a crazed pattern of cracks and crevices crammed with plants, give it the look of the slabbed Appian Way. On each of its long sides, the Santa Fe trackbeds seal it in, and two raised section-line roads close its ends to give it the appearance of an empty moat; these closures have largely kept this strip from being torn out. The railroad grades slide right down to what was once the highway shoulder, and, a hundred feet south, the Cottonwood River, just below where Buckeye Creek joins, begins turning a nicely cut **W** in the valley as it meanders toward junction with the Neosho River. Three hundred feet north and several feet higher and sitting atop the second road lies the newest highway 50, twenty-four feet wide; this one has yet to be flooded. Three highways, three trackbeds, and one river have made for much passage, much fluxion of one kind and another: flatboats, the El Capitan and Super Chief, flivvers and roadsters and runabouts, Chevy coupes, Marmon sedans, Hudson Terraplanes, pickups, long-haul transports heading to California and Chicago. The concrete, in the right angle of light, shows four parallel depressions, wheel tracks, worn by all that traffic, and I'm dreaming it, dreaming lives going east and west, conversations at a mile a minute, people riding and listening in the dark to "The Great Gildersleeve" and "Inner Sanctum," to home runs and field goals, vehicles full of expectation, boredom, anger, laughter, dread, drowsiness, passenger-side sleep, back-seat sex, drunkenness, and whatever they said about coming into the prairie for the first time.

Today the new highway takes the passage, and, in so doing, takes its toll: six thousand cars and trucks rip over it each day, and their occasional meetings have given this stretch in the vale of the river the name Death Valley. Because the highway is straight as an axle, because its hills are long and gentle with good sight-lines, because this appears a most undangerous place, and because people still stack up here and die, one politician called it a Bermuda Triangle. Two years ago the county led the state in traffic deaths, and most of them happened on this open stretch of new U.S. 50 that runs the east valley. A man said to me: *Pile up the bodies killed in the last thirteen months on that nine miles between the Chase line and Strong City, and it would look like we'd just had a bounty hunt. Hell, we don't even have that many coyotes here anymore.*

But I am speaking of the old highway, this ghost of a road, the one under my boots, this one quiet for thirty years and starting to disappear under sediment and scrub: it reveals better than any other place nearby the power of prairie, its continuous insistence, its opportunism, its capacity to lie unheeded and let human intrusion pass and only then to begin to creep back from what seemed nonexistence, to germinate and grow and build a bed of litter that needs only a loose spark to clear away the new and competing trees and really open things again for the grasses, for the native essence of the region.

Along this fossil highway, even though it lies in the bottomlands that have always belonged mostly to the trees, I am walking in the time of the birth of the tallgrass prairie, that epoch when turfy perennials — bluestems and gramas, panicums and ryes — began covering the American interior as the old sea, now turned to a limestone anchor, once did. Down in here, the rock is the worn concrete, yet, as hard as it is, the cement road is nevertheless a fissured seedbed, a string of a glade full of brand-new prairie, an extinct highway giving birth to grassland.

Now: I've walked half this remnant, and I've found big bluestem and little bluestem, silvery bluestem, cord grass, wild rye, sunflower, bundle flower, catclaw sensitive briar, and also plants of the woodlands, including a clump of garden iris from I don't know where. But this strip is not a relict Pleistocene prairie because there probably never was much grass in this low spot in the bottoms: a vestigial highway, yes, but a new prairie. The native forbs and grasses have come in on the wind and maybe on the floods, and now they have roots under the pavement, and soon the prairie plants will need fire to clear away the shading and moisture-sucking trees, and until then the infant prairie can do little more than begin.

Prairie birth: in an earlier time, men believed the grasslands came as a consequence of infertile ground, or an absence of coarse soil material, or from glaciation, from bison trampling, lightning fires, Indian fires, from persistent wind, drought, temperature extremes. But Chase County has good soil of various composition, the ice sheets did not reach here, and the temperature range and rainfall differ only a little from the woodlands of Missouri. The other "reasons" — fire, wind, grazing — contribute less to the birth of prairie than to its maintenance. No: the source of the prairie is its midcontinental position, far from tempering seas, where it lies under an eolian cleavage zone that mixes westerlies, wrung dry by the Rocky Mountains, with humid air from the Gulf: here, inches of evaporation and precipitation are nearly equal, and here, above my head, the rain-shadow of the Rockies meets in commensurate strength the humid Gulf fronts so that this land can grow ten-foot grasses and ninety-foot sycamores, and which one prevails depends mostly on one thing: fire. In the last half-century, the balance has careened toward trees because white men have suppressed the keeper of the grasses. To the prairie, the voice of the Great Mysterious speaks in three tongues: water, wind, flame. This glade beginning in the abandoned highway has heard the first two, and now this slender quarter mile of incipient prairie could use a tossed cigarette from a Santa Fe trackman so that the highway can flourish as never before.

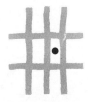

On the Town:
Cottonwood Falls

The name sounds like something from a 1939 *Saturday Evening Post* story or a name on a depot in a Norman Rockwell illustration: Cottonwood Falls. Cottonwood Falls, Chase County, Kansas. Last year a New Yorker asked me: *Is the cottonwood a real tree?* A real tree, yes, but its white, fluffy seeds have only a poetic relation to cotton. As for the river, it's real too, but the falls these days have to be dreamed, buried as they are under a small milldam; before the gristmill, Cottonwood *Rapids* would have been more accurate, or *Ford*, or *Crossing*, or *Shallows*. The dam, at the foot of the wide main street, makes a nice pool and a pleasant falling of water that you can hear, if the wind is from the north and the town quiet, along Broadway, the commercial street of red brick that runs from the falls due south three blocks to a slight rise where stands the red-roofed (the color of blood), Second Empire–style, 1873 courthouse, the oldest edifice in the state still serving the ends of county justice. It — like the milldam and the three biggest commercial buildings and a half-dozen houses — is built of local cut rock, a thing so important that the only drama ever written about the county is titled *Native Stone.*

In my last three years visiting here as an inspector of the ordinary, the courthouse clock has told two times: one-thirty and four-forty. There is something to be said for aging only three hours and ten minutes in thirty-six months. Until I climbed up in the courthouse cupola last week and saw the stilled works of the timepiece,

COTTONWOOD FALLS, KANSAS

Drawn by D. D. Morse, 1878

I'd thought that workmen merely painted a different hour on a false clock face whenever they spruced up the building. The other three sides of the cupola were also apparently designed to carry clocks, but instead each bears a painted black star, as if to remind people of time in its longer dimension.

A clock that lightning strikes every few months is bound to run slow, and the big bell under it hasn't been used for years, except last week when I gave it a good whack and managed to bring three merchants and one lawyer out onto Broadway to see if the cupola was on fire again. For writers hunting symbols of this and that, the courthouse clock serves well, suggesting as it does the herky-jerky passage of time here. A few days ago, at the crossing of Broadway and Friend Street, I stood with an 1878 bird's-eye-view engraving of the town in my hands and compared it to what I saw, and it was plain that history in Cottonwood proceeds at about the rate of an hour a year.

From its founding in 1856 through the following generation, changes were radical, but the old print shows a postbellum village quite recognizable today, although the gristmill is gone but for a piece of foundation and part of the turbine that appears at low water. McWilliams Creek, which once split open Broadway, has disappeared in a long, stone-arched conduit; the iron bridge is also gone, but the second and third ones still stand. Because the nineteenth century shows up so plainly, more than one reporter passing through has described the town as sleepy, and perhaps also this sense of drowsing comes from time stretched out, from a clock that moves even slower than the official state reptile, the ornate box turtle, which the county is properly full of.

A century ago there were 550 people in the Falls, as it was popularly known then (residents have progressed to calling it Cottonwood), and a half-century later there were 880; the town added one person every couple of years until this last decade when it lost seven percent of its people. Citizens and visitors alike take pleasure in a place that remains recognizable not just from generation to generation but from century to century, and, in this way, it is like a good English village. But I wouldn't claim, except in my more cynical moments, that the main progress since the last world war has been the disappearance of merchants, even if it is evident that there used to be at least two of many kinds of businesses and now there's only one of a few and none of most. Cottonwood Falls is probably not dying, but without the courthouse that issue would be moot: of the thirty enterprises along Broadway, the lone commercial street, half are federal, state, or county offices.

In my time here, I've seldom heard anyone speak of the town and in the same sentence use the word "energy" positively. After all, it's a rare county seat that can't keep at least one eatery open, but the Emma Chase Café has just closed, reopened, and closed again, and the only place on Broadway now for a cup of coffee is at the Senior Citizens' Center. One Saturday night a couple of years ago, the Emma put on a Mexican Nite Special: a hungry countian in pressed overalls and shined shoes came in, sat down at the next table, read the blackboard menu, said for more than his wife to hear, *This goddamn place*, and got up and left.

While Broadway has generally shifted from shopkeepers to workers in bureaucracies, Judy and Ken Mackey have tried to help revive commercial life by opening in the old jewelry store an art gallery, a nice little shop of the kind you'll find in Taos, New Mexico, and someone else told me he might buy the decrepit Cottonwood Falls Hotel a block south and renovate the two-story brick building (it later sold for forty dollars) and, maybe, make it a bed-and-breakfast for tourists who cruise the Flint Hills and drive through town to photograph the courthouse, an event happening so often that Whitt Laughridge, whose realty business faces Broadway, wants to paint an X in the middle of the street to show photographers the nearest spot where the whole building will fit into a point-and-shoot camera frame. (I digress here to speak of Whitt, because you will meet him again: although the pronunciation of his last name belies the spelling and his nature, say the "Laugh-" as "lock." From the eyebrows up to his burnished pate, he looks like a small and jolly Buddhist monk, and from the brows down to the thrust jaw he's Gilbert Stuart's George Washington.)

I've heard a few citizens say about the Mackeys' gallery, *What's it good for?* but that doesn't mean that negativism, conservatism, and unimaginativeness are any more prevalent here than elsewhere in village America (although the title of a 1957 *Saturday Evening Post* article on the county was "They Don't Need Progress"). In fact, the Exchange National Bank enlarged its old, native-stone place in a pleasing — if not historic — way, the county historical society moved into and preserved the best cut-rock building, after the courthouse, in town, and on highway 177 a plastic-roofed convenience store recently opened, the first franchise here. In a display of civic vigor unseen in half a century, Cottonwood not long ago linked with Strong City and joined the Kansas Main Street Program to revitalize the twin towns and the county.

One of the fortunate things for Cottonwood Falls, something that has aided its inadvertent preservation, is that the disfiguring enterprises of our time — drive-thrus, motels, truck stops, mobile-home sales lots — have descended upon Strong City, two miles north on highway 50, and the absence of strip-development in the Falls leaves it with a rare thing today — neatly circumscribed limits. Visitors know when they have arrived in Cottonwood and when they have left it, and they can clearly distinguish town from country: should residents want, they could wall the village at its perimeter streets and not leave out more than a dozen houses. On the west, just beyond Spring Street, the prairie grows right up to the backyards and stops clean, and, if I lived here, my sunset porch would have prairie, prairie, prairie to the horizon.

A Kansas City reporter once called Cottonwood Falls *a dusty jewel,* but it has more fundamental substance, more usefulness than that. Rather, it's a chiseled block of native stone, burnt by the sun, otherwise plain, practical, humble, and ordinary except for the tarrying past that each year makes Cottonwood stand out a little more from other Flint Hills towns either dying or embracing some prostitute of progress that eats away their history as syphilis does a nose.

At one time, it looked as if the Falls might see a significant improvement in its economy: in the late 1970s some people thought the town would soon stand just ten miles from the edge of the first national park in Kansas, the only federal one anywhere devoted entirely to the tall prairie. Several groups, all of them out-of-county, wanted to buy sixty thousand acres in southeastern Chase and adjoining counties to establish the Tallgrass Prairie Park, and there was logic to the idea: absentee landlords owned much of the proposed area, rangeland had declined in value, the population density was quite low, and, preeminently, Chase County holds the largest and least corrupted stand of tallgrass left in America. Many citizens realized that much pasture (they rarely call it prairie) was being overgrazed and suffering the consequences: erosion, loss of species, lowered productivity. What's more, the residents admire the beauty of the land in a way not always common among people so closely linked with agriculture. But most of them disliked the park proposal. Indeed, it would have changed some lives and maybe not for the better in every instance, but the plan did not merit certain stories that got concocted: *Farmhouses robbed by niggers from Chicago. Watermelon rind all over the streets. Daughters assaulted by New Yorkers. Buildings burned by drug dealers.* For a while it was difficult to tell whether a countian was speaking of an American tourist or a Mongolian horse soldier.

A couple of groups organized meetings, leaned on legislators, printed bumper-sticker threats, and finally drove the park proponents toward a site ninety miles south in Oklahoma, a state as much associated with the tallgrass prairie as Georgia is with the Appalachian Mountains. It seemed to me then, were I to line up all three thousand countians along Broadway and ask every environmentalist to step forward, even the closet ones, I could take them all into the Emma Chase and buy them a Mexican Nite Special on a single twenty-dollar bill. Of the several reasons for killing off the prairie park, this sentence I heard a few days ago in the Wagon Wheel Café in Strong City is the fundamental one: *I don't say that the prairie park was all that bad an idea — I just say I don't want some government telling me what to do.* Those words, better than any others I know, situate Chase County in the American West.

Cottonwood Falls sits only seven miles northeast of county center, about a mile south of the Santa Fe line and U.S. 50. The main north-south road of both the county and the Flint Hills, Kansas 177, forms the eastern boundary of the town, so that a traveler must turn off to get into Cottonwood, and many residents like living in a place that an outsider can hardly help passing by, cannot readily enter even by accident. Although its length is only a mile and its width half that, it began as two towns, and the evidence of its dual birth lies today along historically and ironically named Union Street, once the divider between the hamlets: the north-south streets don't align, so a driver must jog left or right at Union, a reminder of how poorly during the first days of the Falls the nation itself conjoined.

Of the fifteen longitudinal streets, ten have the names of trees and none of a prairie grass or native forb or legume. These names are fossil history of attitudes that town promoters employed to attract settlers from the eastern woodlands, people who had experienced little to prepare them for this big grassland, even the pioneers from the smaller and wetter prairies of Illinois and Indiana. The homesteaders brought with them a notion corroborated by their Christianity that this hugely open spread was a kind of failed forest that needed only the hand of civilized man to redeem it from its appalling waste, and they reversed here their usual practice of axing wilderness: they planted trees to remove it. Rather than learning what the prairie could provide and then changing their ways to harmonize with a land new to them, the settlers began trying to remake it into the East. Early photographs of the Falls reveal it wonderfully nude, but a snapshot I took from a light plane last month shows it a woody knot in the grasses.

The first waves of settlement passed over the Flint Hills for destinations much farther west, but, as those lands filled, people began looking again at the eastern portion of what an 1823 map based on Stephen Long's exploration four years earlier called the Great American Desert. They discovered not aridity and sand but something closer to the earlier meaning of the word: deserted — at least empty of white farmers. The land was not at all barren, and, when the immigrants of Cottonwood Falls and Council Grove and a hundred other Hills places saw their apple trees bloom and their corn and oats grow, all that remained was to get clear title and evict the inhabitants of the last ten thousand years. Anglo society accomplished that deed in only ten years by odious methods governments and churches condoned, by an ethic that taints every Pioneer Mother statue put up by the Daughters of the American Revolution.

The nineteenth-century dumping ground, a kind of huge ghetto that Kansas had become for eastern tribes forced in with the native Kansa and Osage, had to be emptied so that Indian Territory (I.T.) could become Kansas Territory (K.T.), could become Kanzas (Kan.), could become Kansas (KS). And so, a decade after its founding, the Falls and its county were free of tribal Americans except for occasional wanderers from the new Indian Territory, a place the next wave of Anglo usurpers, the Boomers and Sooners of Oklahoma, would soon take. Today there is not even a half-blood Indian living in the county, although the aboriginal presence was once so great that anybody who will walk the plowed bottoms can still find stone points. The Roniger Museum behind the courthouse has thousands of them, a collection once coveted by the Smithsonian Institution.

A few weeks ago I sat in the last row of the Chase County High School auditorium, and before me was an assembly of blond heads with last names from Kent and Antrim and Bavaria by way of New York, Indiana, Illinois, Missouri, and I remembered what a New Jersey visitor once said to me: *The people here look so American.*

II

Gladstone

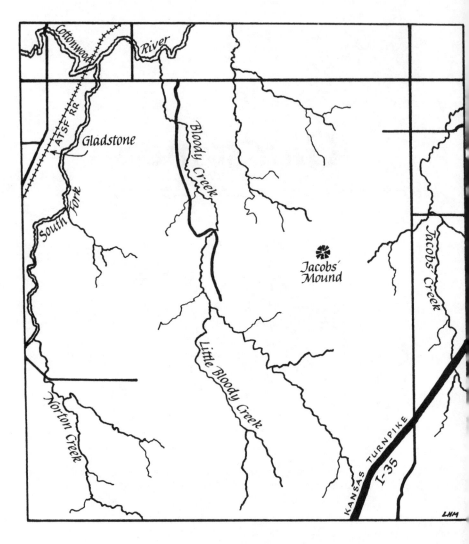

GLADSTONE QUADRANGLE

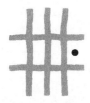

From the Commonplace Book: Gladstone

The true state of every nation is the state of common life.

> — Samuel Johnson,
> *A Journey to the Western Islands of Scotland* (1775)

Nowhere in America, probably, is the contrast between the Northern and the Southern man exhibited in so marked a manner as in Kansas. He who would see the difference between comfort and discomfort, between neatness and disorder, cleanliness and filth, between farming the land and letting the land farm itself, between trade and stagnation, stirring activity and reigning sloth, between a wide-spread intelligence and an almost universal ignorance, between general progress and an incapacity for all improvement or advancement, has commonly only to cross the border-line which separates a free from a slave State. But he who would see these broad contrasts in a single view, the evidences of well-directed enterprise and intelligent energy mixed up with the ugly features of backgoing and barbarity, should seek out Kansas and make its strange varieties of inhabitants his study.

> — T. H. Gladstone,
> *The Englishman in Kansas* (1857)

June 15th, 1856: Others have written of a vitality in the atmosphere of Kansas that is truly wonderful, "it breathes new life around, and vigor and buoyancy is felt coming back to old limbs." My health has not been so good for years as since I have been in the Territory; my headaches have lost the greater share of their severity, and I feel equal for any task. I never was so thin in flesh, and never felt such agility.

November 29th, 1856: Often father Colt would say when we urged him to leave Kansas with us, "I had as lief lay my bones in Kansas as in any other place"; and so it has come to pass. But to think of a death in Kansas, in that wild though beautiful country — to be laid away in a rough box, in a grave marked only while the mound looks newly made, away from all kindred and friends who would drop on it a tear or plant on it a flower, seems to me horrible in the extreme.

> — Miriam Davis Colt,
> *Went to Kansas, Being a Thrilling
> Account of an Ill-Fated Expedition to
> That Fairy Land and Its Sad Results*
> (1862)

Pioneer life was usually duller and safer than it is generally imagined.

The Wilderness was no "heritage" to folk who had to cope with it; it became one only when it no longer had to be lived in.

> — David Lowenthal,
> "Not Every Prospect Pleases" (1962)

Nature is uncommonly helpful to the settler here.

> — Ernst von Hesse-Wartegg,
> "Across Kansas by Train" (1877)

Until 1895 the whole history of the state was a series of disasters, and always something new, extreme, bizarre, until the name Kansas became a byword, a synonym for the impossible and the ridiculous, inviting laughter, furnishing occasion for jest and hilarity. "In God we trusted, in Kansas we busted."

> — Carl Becker,
> "Kansas" (1910)

As in all other things, the myth of the Great American Desert is an asset of no mean proportion to the Kansas man. All of which serves to establish, in a way, the boast that what is a calamity for other countries is often a valuable asset for Kansas.

> — William Connelley,
> *History of Kansas* (1928)

Water runs off these rolling prairies so rapidly that a stream which a three-year-old child might ford at night will be running water enough to float a steamboat before morning.

> — Horace Greeley,
> *An Overland Journey* (1859)

March the 3rd, 1857
Dear Brother and Sister we received your letter March the Second with much pleasure and glad to here from you all and much to here that you had sole out to come to Kansas for I think it is the best thing you can do the sooner you come out the beter it will be for you We are all well at present and we hope these few lines may find you injoying the same blessing I will go and se farther Jacobs and take your letter along and he can se and know your Request of him I thot it best to rite to you so you would get the Waybill in good time I now want to inform you that when you come to the perraryes that you had beter take a little wood along in yor fead troft or else you mite miss your coffee some night because that when I came out I had to burn cobs or get no coffee also when you get to Kansas City if your woman neads any thing Hannah says that is the time to get it whatever it may be you can get things closer but not so cheap before you get through the state of Mosoury get some fead for your horses if you have any and if you have cattle you won't nead any grane for you will finde plenty of grass of the best kinds bring ropes and drive little stakes and tie some of your horses and let the Rest go and they wont nead much hay Hannah wants you to bring roses sprouts lalock sprouts curns sprouts tansy and roots and a little whiskey to keep the roots alive for Jackson peach seeds aple seed and all kinds of garden seeds that you suppos to be neadful because they are scarce out here they are nothing like sweet potatoes here If you can bring a few Irish potatoes or good ones some [of] a good kind We have had toler colde winter but it has not been long about two months and then the winter was over. . . . Now I will clos these few lines so no more at present but remains effectionet friends until Deth
    Jackson Holmes
    Hannah [Jacobs] Holmes

> — *Chase County Historical Sketches*
> (1948)

Much of the population in many American small towns would be either marginal or unemployable in any city. In their hometowns, such people usually have the advantages of roots, family, some kind of standing within a group, and often have their own homes.

> — Albert Solnit,
> "What's the Use of Small Towns?"
> (1966)

Urban-oriented students of small central places are afflicted by a kind of metropolitan myopia, which makes them act as though they think that rural residents somehow are just not quite as smart and clever as city people.

> — John Fraser Hart,
> *The Look of the Land* (1975)

The earth is a fire planet, and Homo sapiens, *a fire creature. The earth has fire because it has life.*

> — Stephen J. Pyne,
> "The Summer We Let Wild Fire
> Loose" (1989)

Haveing nothing else to do, I set fire to the Prairies.

> — Francis Chardon,
> *Fort Clark Journal* (1839)

The Indians now set fire to the prairies and woods all around us, and the chance of good sport daily diminished. These malicious neighbours were determined to drive us from the district; they evidently watched our every motion; and whenever we entered a wood or grove to hunt, they were sure to set the dry grass on fire. Half a mile to the windward they pursued this plan so effectually, as not only to spoil our hunting, but on two occasions to oblige me to provide hastily for my personal safety: on the first of these, they set fire to a wood where I was passing, and compelled me to cross a creek for fear of being overtaken by the flames; on the second, having watched me as I crossed a large dry prairie, beyond which was some timber that I wished to try for deer, they set fire to the grass in two or three places to the windward; and as it was blowing fresh at the time, I saw that I should not have time to escape by flight; so I resorted to the simple expedient, in which lies the only chance of safety on such occasions: I set the prairie on fire where I myself was walking, and then placed myself in the middle of the black barren space which I thus created, and which covered many acres before the advancing flames reached its border; when they did so they naturally expired for want of fuel, but they continued their leaping, smoking, and crackling way on each side of me. It was altogether a disagreeable sensation, and I was half choked with hot dust and smoke.

— Charles Augustus Murray,
Travels in North America (1839)

Over the elevated lands and prairie bluffs, where the grass is thin and short, the fire slowly creeps with a feeble flame, which one can easily step over; where the wild animals often rest in their lairs until the flames almost burn their noses, when they will reluctantly rise, and leap over it, and trot off amongst the cinders, where the fire has passed and left the ground black as jet. These scenes become indescribably beautiful, when their flames are seen at many miles distance, creeping over the sides and tops of the bluffs, appearing to be sparkling and brilliant chains of liquid fire (the hills being lost to view), hanging suspended in graceful festoons from the skies.

But there is yet another character of burning prairies. . . . There are many meadows on the Missouri, the Platte, the Arkansas, of many miles in breadth, which are perfectly level, with a waving grass, so high, that we are obliged to stand erect in our stirrups, in order to look over its waving tops as we are riding through it. The fire in these, before a [strong] wind, travels at an immense and frightful rate, and often destroys, on their fleetest horses, parties of Indians, who are so unlucky as to be overtaken by it; not that it travels as fast as a horse at full speed, but that the high grass is filled with wild pea-vines, and other impediments, which render it necessary for the rider to guide his horse in the zig-zag paths of the deers and buffaloes, retarding his progress, until he is overtaken by the dense column of smoke that is swept before the fire — alarming the horse, which stops and stands terrified and immutable, till the burning grass which is wafted in the wind, falls about him, kindling up in a moment a thousand new fires, which are instantly wrapped in the swelling flood of smoke that is moving on like a black thunder-cloud, rolling on the earth, with its lightning's glare, and its thunder rumbling as it goes.

— George Catlin,
*Letters and Notes on the Manners,
Customs, and Conditions of the North
American Indians* (1841)

We stood in the dark on the platform of our Pullman, fearfully and in awe, marveling at the gruesome yet sublime spectacle: flames as far as the eye can see in every direction, nothing but flames leaping twenty feet and higher, filling the sky with black clouds, a sea of flames racing toward us and threatening to swallow us and all travelers, as the Red Sea swallowed Pharaoh's armies. But such a threat looms only when grass is very dry and exceptionally tall. Otherwise, fire is merely a long line about six feet wide, easily jumped to safety. Fire therefore seldom frightens settlers; their lives and possessions are usually safe. The most dangerous of these blazes rage in novels.

> — Ernst von Hesse-Wartegg,
> "Across Kansas by Train" (1877)

When a tiny flame is discovered in Kansas, or other states where the wind blows a hurricane so much of the time, there is not a moment to lose. . . . The resort of a frontiersman, if the flames are too much for him to overcome, is to take refuge with his family, cattle, horses, etc. in the garden, where the growing vegetables make an effectual protection.

> — Elizabeth (Mrs. George) Custer,
> *Tenting on the Plains* (1887)

Perhaps one day prairie burning will be one of the great ritual occasions of the Midwest, a sort of festival of Dionysus, the god of the inexhaustible life — an occasion for drama, music, poetry, and storytelling.

> — Frederick Turner,
> "A Field Guide to the Synthetic
> Landscape" (1988)

Phenomena intersect; to see but one is to see nothing.

> — Victor Hugo,
> *The Toiler of the Sea* (1866)

I saw that a little height on the prairie was enough to look like much more — every detail as to height becoming intensely significant, breadth all falling short.

> — Frank Lloyd Wright,
> *An Autobiography* (1943)

Stone was a noble material, not just because it was used for noble purposes, noble buildings. It was noble because it had been extracted from the depths of the earth and was timeless.

We have all but entirely broken away from the Renaissance concept of an architecture standing for permanence and political power, an architecture of stone celebrating an unchangeable political and religious order. The notion of building a symbol for posterity — much less a symbol for the ages — is no longer, except in the case of a few commemorative monuments, taken seriously.

In hard times (which eventually come to every community no matter what its size or wealth) what makes survival possible and desirable is not its archeological identity but its ability to continue, and it continues because some structures, some institutions and facilities provide continuity. These are the landmarks, [and they] stand for continuity, community identity, for links with the past and the future. In the contemporary American community these roles are what counteract our mobility and fragmentation and forgetfulness of history.

— J. B. Jackson,
"Stone and Its Substitutes" (1984)

Whatever the character of the thinking, just so was the character of the building.

— Henry Van Brunt,
Original source unknown

You may have believed that the land itself is what matters, that men may come and go, and their names be unimportant — that one may sow an acre where another reaps, and the change be nothing, since it is the same acre, and the wheat or corn is wheat or corn, whoever the plowman or the reaper. Farmers, so far as history knows, are stripped of their personal idiosyncracies; in all that makes them essential to the nation, they are alike. You may have believed this — but the activity in these [county clerks'] rooms proves that it is man's relation to the land, whether he be its owner or its slave, that is important to him and to the society he has created here in the shadow of the courthouse.

— Helen Hooven Santmyer,
Ohio Town (1963)

In the Quadrangle: Gladstone

Now, three miles south of Saffordville: I'm walking in the Gladstone quadrangle, some seventy square miles of grassland, draws,
and hollows devoid of roadways but for those at its perimeter and
the Bloody Creek Road, which follows the wooded stream to a dead
end in the heart of the rectangle (even before the first settlers here
saw their children finish school, seven men had been murdered on
Bloody Creek). The South Fork bounds the western side of the
quadrangle, and Jacobs' Creek nicks the northeastern corner, and
along this fluvial notching, and in a smaller strip farther south on
the Verdigris River, lie the most ancient things of substance in
Chase County — 260-million-year-old shales and limestones, strata
formed when the seven continents lay as one.

The Gladstone area today is nearly all rangeland, a place where I
sometimes must stop my car on the rock roads to let pass approaching Hereford and Angus and crossbreeds moved by mounted pasturemen, the animals pressing against the car, their flanks rubbing
doors and fenders clean, gently rocking me inside as they bellow at
who knows what. Nearly all things in the quadrangle lie within
sight of the most distinctive natural feature in the county, Jacobs'
Mound; even though it is several feet lower than knobs a few miles
south, its abrupt rise from a rolling plain and its isolation and
symmetry have made it the best landmark around. The first settlers
and wagon freighters sighted on it as a coastal pilot would a sea
stack, but no one other than a cowboy or hunter has navigated by it

for years, and the travelers on Interstate 35, that open-air tunnel from Lake Superior to the Rio Grande, ignore it, if they even see it, preferring to rely on green signs and concrete strips.

I'm walking along Jacobs' Creek — clear water and mellow riffles over a stone-broken bed that bends every twenty yards like a small and maddened viper and cuts a course under redbud, burr oak, walnut, hickory. It is quiet and alluring today, a New England brook, but like other things here, its nature is most mutable; it has several faces, and it can turn a new one on you suddenly. Gabriel Jacobs, born in Pennsylvania, came to the Hills in 1856 from Indiana. His biographer, with only slight exaggeration, wrote in the *Chase County Historical Sketches: As far as is known, no white man had ever set foot on this rock- and grass-bound place before the Jacobs family settled here.* Gabriel, drawn west by his son, was an old man when he arrived, but he lived long enough to build a log house in the rich land by the creek, and he fielded a couple of good harvests before the great "drouth" (the local pronunciation) of 1859 and 1860, when the Cottonwood River ran dry, did him in. He was a Dunkard preacher, and the creek vale became a settlement of followers named for their full-immersion baptisms but better known for their practice of mutual foot washing. The Dunkers eventually lost the county to the less damp but more practical Methodists. An old resident wrote: *They just preached themselves out. We could not stand it. Some of their sermons were three hours long.* The Methodists here also watched disappear the Soul Sleepers, a sect believing that the spirit was a mortal substance slumbering within the body, like a woodchuck in winter, until the noise of the resurrection would awaken it. The log schoolhouse and its stone and frame successors that these sects shared with the Baptists and Presbyterians have fallen or been scavenged for later barns, while the old chimneys and foundations lie hidden in rock fences. The Jacobs' Creek community, known today as Grandview, shows itself only in a county-line cemetery and a few incidents in the *Historical Sketches,* where a later resident of Gabriel's cabin tells of the partition between rooms that her mother brightened up with pages of the *Emporia News: from that wall young Josephine Makemson learned to read.*

And, in the *Sketches,* Helen Austin writes this about an 1885 cloudburst: *By ten o'clock it was raining hard. The sound filled our little house. Water poured off the roof and ran over the yard like oil. By eleven o'clock the muddy water from the creek was spread-*

ing over the fields. It made a roaring noise as it ate away the furrows. Ben Jacobs, Gabriel's grandson, living along the creek near the ford, got his brother, Will, and loaded his wife and two children into the mule wagon and started fast for higher ground across the creek, usually no wider than a half-dozen tall men lying head to toe. At the crossing Ben looked up the creek and saw what he'd never seen before, a wall of violent, muddy water, *waves rolling over and over,* higher than the ears of his mules. The uproar hit the wagon and capsized it and flushed the little family toward the Cottonwood River. Ben caught hold of a limb, and Will snatched up the boy and held him above the brown swirl and suck until he could climb into a tree, but the creek pulled Mattie and her baby on north. By three o'clock the sky blew clear, the stream fell back to size, and Ben went down along the creek and climbed the slick banks to hunt his wife and child. Just before dusk, in a field he found a small, lumpen shape, and under a coverlet of soft mud lay his daughter, her nose and eyes stoppered with earth. She was drowned. Hoping for a miracle, he kept searching for Mattie. Three days later, on the bottom of the creek carrying his family name, he found her, the flesh already defiled, her torn and beslimed dress snagged on a sunken limb. From then on, they say, *Ben was here and there,* mostly living away from the county. His end was the reverse of what he'd found along his stream: in 1901, he died in a prairie fire.

And it was on Jacobs' Creek where Josephine Makemson, four years after she learned her letters from a papered wall, received something rare in the hard land: a new dress, white and trimmed in lace, *to wear to Sunday school and church and to other happy places.* She was nine, and in the next few months she watched die her cousin of diphtheria, her eldest brother from blood poisoning after he cut himself recovering his hatchet from the creek, and an uncle from a spinal injury. When she was seventy-five, Josephine wrote: *The little white dress after being worn to three funerals no longer was a joy to me. It was just a sad little dress, and I could not be happy in it again.*

It was north of where the creek makes its east turn out of the county, close to where I'm walking, that the wife of Gabriel's grandson often allowed their six-month-old boy to go in the arms of an admiring Kansa woman across the Cottonwood to the Indian camp where she would care for him half the day. One afternoon Mrs. Jacobs learned that her son would not be returning until the Indians received in exchange a particularly fine rooster. It was purely business.

The creek-bottom community, even in its isolation, was a stop on the underground railroad. One escaped slave, Charlie, last name unknown, arrived and made a reputation as *a wizard of the fiddle,* and he played so exuberantly for all the dances around that a free black man warned him, *They'll get you sure if you don't stay at home. You better keep quiet beins you got no free papers if you don't want to go back to slavery.* One day Moses Jacobs, Gabriel's son, brought word that a Missouri slave owner named, of all things, Freeman, was on the creek and hunting Charlie. The fiddleman hid in that old frontier-prairie refuge, a cornfield, and a woman delayed Freeman and asked him whether he wasn't ashamed to be *chasing a poor colored boy,* and the Missourian admitted, yes, but couldn't help himself. That night, the Haworths, a white family, rigged Charlie up in a dress, shawl, and veiled sunbonnet, and Moses Jacobs took him by buggy to the next fugitive station, and that was the last they heard from the wizard of the fiddle.

Once in a while I hear Kansans congratulate themselves on the part the state played in ending American slavery, and it's true that Bleeding Kansas earned its epithet over that issue, and it's also fact that a century later one of the most important pieces of litigation in the civil rights movement began sixty miles northeast of here: *Brown v. Board of Education of Topeka.* But the full truth is more convoluted. Countians, at the time Gabriel Jacobs' sons were helping escaped slaves, voted against a statewide amendment to extend suffrage to blacks — in Chase it lost by three votes and women's suffrage by seven — and both amendments lost across the state. At that time, the county Republicans, supporters of Lincoln, passed several resolutions; this is one:

> We urge upon Congress the propriety of purchasing Sonora [Mexico] or some other suitable Territory for the purpose of settling the negroes of this country with a view to the entire separation of the races.

Sam Wood, who named the county, an abolitionist of whom I'll tell you more, believed in this idea: wishing to see a people free is not the same thing as wanting to see them equal.

When Charlie disappeared in Mrs. Haworth's dress and sunbonnet, when Kansas was bleeding and the house dividing, there arrived in Lawrence, seventy-five miles northeast, Thomas Gladstone, an English journalist and a kinsman of Queen Victoria's four-time prime minister, Sir William. Thomas reached Lawrence in 1856, the day after the first sack of the town by pro-slavery ruffians (a euphemism) and the day before John Brown and his sons retaliated by slashing to death five men on Pottawatomie Creek, the two signal events in the Border War. Young Gladstone traveled the northeast corner of the state for several weeks and then returned east to write his powerful reports that were quickly published as a book called *The Englishman in Kansas, or, Squatter Life and Border Warfare*. One historian claimed that Gladstone's pen helped make Kansas free. I can't say nobody in Chase County has ever read the book — if a copy exists here today — but I do say I've not found anyone who's heard of it, and I've found nobody who knows that Gladstone, Kansas, once a collection of a few homes and a school seven miles from Jacobs' Creek, was probably named for Thomas.

The settlement never had a post office or any official recognition beyond the sign that the Santa Fe Railroad put up by the stockpens, and today it's nothing more than two widely separated houses along perpendicular roads that join at the tracks, where the old marker still says GLADSTONE, a place the trainmen call Happy Rock. Now the history of the quadrangle is hardly more than pentimento, little more than the earthen circles near where Jacobs' Creek meets the Cottonwood — the circles that seasonally reappear when the new grass comes up to reveal where the Kansa camped — and the old stories of the hollow and its creek that seemed to take people one way or another (a stream that gave life and exacted it) have not much more presence than the fairy rings that crop up overnight on the lawns of the countians.

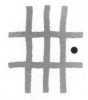

Between Pommel and Cantle

This is Slim, and he isn't, his circumference nearly his height, five feet four inches. Now that all the ranch hands from the first half of the century are gone, Slim Pinkston is the most famous cowboy in the county. It's Saturday morning and sunny, cold, November. Slim has parted and oiled his hair flat in the style of another time, and he just opened the door to me and the prairie wind that pushes me into the room but doesn't disturb his hair, and still he gives the wind a round of cussing and shuts the door to the dim little frame house where he has lived as a bachelor for some years since he and his wife split up. The home is orderly in the way I've come to expect from lone ranch hands, the order deriving from objects arranged tightly against walls as if there were but one way to set out a room, and things, like the prairie itself, a little weathered and dusty but not cluttered. The furniture seems set down in some permanence like an outcropping of pasture rock: here a grayed doily and there a plastic flower gone off its color — the presence of a woman not yet disappeared entirely, and it's these remnants that make a bachelor cowboy's house lonely. I've never heard a Chase County pasture-man so express it, but I think they are drawn to things that never seem to move far from the permanent, from the eternality of birth, death, cattle coming and going, from storm, fire, injury, heat, cold.

Slim offers the living room sofa, but I ask to go to the kitchen, where chairs are closer, coffee near, and memory of good times is. We sit down to the small, bare table, oilcloth-covered, Slim with cigarettes and ashtray, and, for most of the time that we talk he keeps fixed on the ashtray as if it held what was left of his past, the ashes of his hours spent between pommel and cantle.

Of the family names in the county from the days of early white settlement, most are gone, but Pinkston isn't, and countians know the name and the moniker Slim, but not many know his christened name: Dudley. The Pinkstons pick up sobriquets like sticker weed (Windy, Brownie, Chub, Bud, Mutt), but his brother Phill has never caught anything more than an extra consonant. Slim says of himself (only) that he is over seventy. I know that he and his son and Phill run ten thousand cattle on forty thousand acres, much of it on the east side of the county where he has ridden the pastures from Jacobs' Mound to Matfield Green since he went to work for the Norton brothers in the thirties. Although never the largest nor the grandest here, the Norton Ranch has become a touchstone of the old ways, a classic not like the Duesenberg places around Matfield but more like a Model T truck.

Will Norton was the boss, a good man but a poor-riding cowboy, and Slim says: *He had a lot of knowledge. He could talk to you about religion on down. He could weld in fire — blacksmithing — could make you anything out of metal. When he was a boy he made a gun to shoot his teacher with. Never did a course. I still have a fence stretcher he made. Him and his brother Ed could lay up rock wall too. Full-blooded Irish, and they told Irish stories all day. Always bachelors, till Ed up and married late in life.*

Slim stares at the ashtray, in some sadness I think, and answers more out of duty than desire; he's not going to lose himself in the past as others do because he's somehow beyond it, as if watching it from a distant ridge: he's here and it's there. He'd be happier if I stood up and disappeared with what's left of the morning so that he could get on to Emporia, but he sits doggedly, decently, and awaits my questions as one does the second page of an exam to be passed along.

His voice is granular, a gullet full of creek-worn flint, and deep, the sort you used to hear from some villainous gunslinger in a 1930s B western, yet his face is open, the kind you'd ask to see your child to school. In my first days in the county, I often heard about Slim, and almost always after his name came an appositive, *a real cowboy*, carrying respect and distinction from the western-store, all-hat-no-horse cowboys who only dress the part as they understand it played by country singers. But if your notion of a cowhand is a *sotto voce* Gary Cooper, tall and slender, in a buttless walk down a dusty street, then you'll likely take Dudley Pinkston for a washer-dryer repairman. Yet Slim is a cowboy in the manner here: laconic, of some gentleness, almost introverted, a character shaped by the bovine nature of the animals he spends his days with. A cowboy may love his horse but his essence comes from the slow beasts he cusses.

His speech, like many others' here, is a relic from the Appalachians. Slim says: *My dad was a cowboy — I guess you'd call him that — until he got crippled. His horse hubbed him, ran him along a bob-wahr fence and tore up his leg, and then he cut up the other leg on a corn-sled knife, then he fell off a horse and broke his hip. When I can remember, he was purta near all crippled up and couldn't ride. I learned cowboyin from the Nortons. They ran mostly Texas cattle brought up to Bazaar on the train in April. Steers wasn't these yearlins of nowdays people want because they're tender — then they was three or four years old and still not any wider than from my wrist to elbow — skeletons with tails — but they'd put on four hundred pounds in a season. Them Texans shipped us the horns and we put the body under them. We'd drive them up toward the Jacobs' Mound pasture, ten, twelve miles. The train these days don't even stop at Bazaar — don't stop in the county. The cattle get trucked right into the pastures, and most of the boys are bringin their horses in by trailer. Nowdays we just drive them from section to section and later on down to the pens to be hauled away. Ain't as much horse work here anymore. Hell, these cattle comin up to us now ain't never seen a horse before, and they get crazy. Then, we used to send them straight to the packin house, but now they go to a feedlot for finishin. We never had much of this cow-calf business.*

A cow-calf operation keeps cattle year-round in the same pastures where they are bred, born, and raised. The rule of thumb is five acres for every animal, but that works only if the cattle stay in the pasture just from April to late summer. To keep them twelve months a year requires eight acres per beast to prevent overgrazing, diminished grass, and eventual erosion. And now there's another potential danger called double-stocking, where twice the usual number of cattle graze for half the usual time, but many owners leave them longer, to the detriment of the land. Slim says: *We don't double-stock. It's too much for the grass. They ain't supposed to be that many animals out there. A lot of pastures now are in bad shape because of abuse like that.*

(Now I'm remembering a rancher once lecturing me how the herds of buffalo ate and trampled the hills, but he didn't mention that bison came only seasonally and some years not at all, so that their migrations let the vegetation restore itself in a cycle that sustained plant and herbivore. And, later, a prominent countian told me: *Leave it to us, and we'll eat the hell out of these pastures.* Because of the extent of rangeland in the county, to eat the hell out of the prairie is to eat the hell out of the future, out of what has made and sustained life here since the tallgrass first arose.)

Good cowboys like the Pinkstons know the cycle must be served before the dollar, and nothing benefits the old turning so well as what might seem its great enemy. Every March, Slim and the boys go out with their firesticks or firepipes and light the forty thousand acres they oversee. *We used to just ride along on horseback and break a wooden match so it don't get hung up on top of the grass and strike it and throw it down. These days we use them farsticks that somebody around here come up with. Light the end and drag it along behind a pickup. A course, you better hadn't ought to get that truck mard in, or else with that far behind you, you're not in very good shape.*

The firestick: six to seven feet of inch-and-a-half steel pipe, the lower dozen inches commonly bent to an obtuse angle like a hockey stick and stoppered by a threaded plug with a slit filed through, and the upper end capped. The cowboy fills the pipe with gasoline, lights the grass and ignites the pipe from it, and sets off trailing fire. Raise the pipe high, and the small flame goes out. The firesticks are homemade and more efficient than matches or weedburners.

When the Pinkstons burn, they leave neatly uncharred — if there are no vagaries of wind — cemeteries, right-of-ways, fences, outbuildings, and any adjoining land a neighbor wants left in old grass. But they don't like that new problem, the Kansas Turnpike. *If smoke blows across the interstate, these city boys'll drive right on into it. They can't see ahead, and then somebody slows way down, and there's your wreck, and the insurance companies want to sue us. That highway used to be our pasture — now it's a lawsuit out there.* Slim stares at the ashtray as if it were smoky pasture, and he says, *Back-burn all you want, get all the sprayer trucks and wet gunnysacks you want, and if that wind comes up sudden and changes, everything else don't make much difference, and you're just not in very good shape.*

It's past noon and he's smoking faster as if to speed things up, but I can't leave fire alone and I ask him whether he ever saw a steer trapped and burned, and no, he never did, and not a man or truck either, but you have to watch grass that hasn't been burned or grazed for a year or two because that's when fires get big. *High grass is dangerous and overgrazed grass won't burn worth a shit. We got other problems too, like lightnen — it'll kill three or four head a year. It'll whap them directly or they'll get up against a fence and it'll hit that, and then we lose our commission and the cattleman loses his steer. There's rustlers. They stole four head last year, and it wasn't no strangers because they knew our operation — went right in the pasture with a truck and knew when to go in.*

Slim is mulling losses, and that slows the smoking. *Three years ago I got throwed. A course I been throwed before but always off to the side. This time my horse turned end over end and me with him. Broke three ribs and stove me up so, it was a couple of days before I could get back on.*

When I push away from the table he's relieved, and we begin talking about pack rats in his shed, and then I ask whether he ever wanted to earn a living another way, and he says, *I wouldn't care about book work. I used to farm alongside cowboyin — plowin with mules. Did both durin the war,* and I ask, do you like being a cowboy, and he thinks and says, *I don't know. As much as I ever did. It's a way of makin money. Ride or farm, it's not much differ- ence to me. None of it'll get you rich. A cowboy ain't nothin but a hard hand, but they ain't many tellin you what to do. Nobody much out in them hills, you see. Hell, Windy, my brother, couple years back, died out in the pasture. They found him out there and his horse by his side waitin. That's how he went.*

At the door I say that I hear he's a pretty good fiddler, and he gives a smile, the first that morning, and says, *Hell, I used to play over to Bazaar at the platform dances. They'd put some boards down in the summer and call us in. Square dancin, round dancin, a waltz, a schottische. Out would come some Sharp's Crick moonshine, or else they was home brew — everbody made that in them dry years. They'd all pass the hat, and we'd get a dollar fifty maybe. But oh hell, we fiddled. I like music with a lot of bowin. "Irish Washer Woman" — now there's a real crooked old tune.*

About the Red Buffalo

I am driving out of the west: the highway laid over a section line that deviates north or south no more than does the equator, the road straight, straight, but sometimes rising and descending, the dusk gone, and on the car radio a championship game, basketball among the crackles, play-by-play coming and going, and the drone of wind and tires and voices, and my nodding, nodding, a numbed awareness of entering the county, the wandering across the centerline not enough to rouse me, and nodding, and peace. Then: uproar of rock flying in wheel-wells and the violence of riding the shoulder and the car jolting me into fear, and I stop, my senses tumbled. Everywhere ahead in the surrounding dark, the land not separable from the black sky, stretch orange lines of fire, red-gold on jet, angles and curves, oghams and cursives of flames, infernal combustings, and a pall rising and surrounding and seeming to make the valley a smoking pit. What city of burning light is this, and how could I have so lost my way as to come into it and not know it? This must be some dreamplace of Moloch, or have I just died in a highway ditch? Along the firelines rise ignitions and expostulations of yellow cinders, my nose fills with a sweet scent of char, and, on the dimmed horizon, the big, blooded moon rises, too smoked to light anything but itself, the fire like oozing magma, marking out the lines of this plutonic landscape. I try to compose my wits.

I am standing on a ridge and looking down into a vale burning itself clean, making itself into a bowl of primeval ash like the source of the cosmos itself, and I am alive, and it's early April, and this is Kansas. Chase County is setting itself afire as it does each spring so that the prairie may remain prairie here on this moist land between woodland and plains, where, at the edge, the last line of eastern trees waits like wolves watching just beyond the pale of the campfire. I've never seen the hills burn before, and I stand a long time, at last comprehending how a nineteenth-century scoundrel would torch a prairie just for the spectacle, how another could speak of *thick, ropey air, which is seen, tasted, handled, and felt.* Then I drive on across state 150.

The next morning: I am hiking across the blackened hills amidst the smoking dung settlers called prairie coal, walking until I catch up with the back side of an unattended headfire cleaning its way across a slope like a dutiful farmhand, destroying the invading exotic plants, removing thatch, leaving behind a warmth to help release soil nutrients. As white blood cells are to man, so fire is to prairie. This pasture has been grazed hard and the headfire is only inches high. I jump it time and again, the heat up my pant legs, my boots and denim turning black; a dust devil of ash twists past coating me, and behind, lumps of scat steam like pies fresh from the oven, and I walk out patterns in the char, footprints spelling out PRAIRYERTH (a photographer's negative of a snow scene). When I stop my play, I too am a piece of carbon.

The four horsemen of the prairie are tornado, locust, drought, and fire, and the greatest of these is fire, a rider with two faces because for everything taken it makes a return in equal measure. The aboriginal peoples received the gift and made it part of their harmony here and used it as a white man would a plow to bring forth sweet and nutritious new grasses, or as a scythe to open a route over the prairie, or as a horse to dislodge deer or drive bison for harvesting, or as a cake of salt to draw the beasts within arrow range, or as a telegraph to send a message with smoking grasses. Indians, recognizing the bond between flame and prairie, seemed to understand in a symbolic way how fire shaped the grasses and plants, how a green beauty rose and evolved from wet clay as if the master hand of fire turned a potter's wheel.

Today, agronomists believe the bond is twenty-five million years old and that before white settlement these prairies saw a couple of fires every decade, a couple hundred times each millennium. Yet, even to the first European travelers, fire was a mad beast from Hades; across the West, citizens fought it, and almost everyplace they succeeded — except in the Flint Hills, where the pioneers learned of the bond from the Indians, and ranchers continued the burning although agronomists, year after year, advised against such a scorched-earth policy; but people of the Hills continued until at last even the scientists realized the necessity of fire and said the prairie is a phoenix, so burn, burn. (They recently pointed out, however, that wildfire didn't take every area each year, that it was more common from August to March when grassland animals and plants were less vulnerable; biologists on the Konza Prairie Research Natural Area sixty miles north of here have also learned that the greatest diversity of native organisms occurs with fire every fourth year, a schedule that also lessens the deleterious effects of agricultural burning on the atmosphere.)

An old cowman of the region wrote a few years ago:

> The squaws would weave a large ball of this long-stemmed bluestem grass, and then the men would take their braided-hide lariat rope and throw it around those bales or balls of grass and set it afire. Then they would ride just as far as they could, dragging that ball of fire.

For whites, the means have varied: some pulled along a burning tire or a bundle of corncobs soaked in coal oil or a long, smoldering stacker rope; some still use a welding or propane torch, a kerosene weedburner, even an army-surplus flamethrower; but, more and more, it's the firestick.

Now, I'm walking on far in front of the flames, and I'm remembering the fellow who dropped his pistol and set fire to the prairie to find it. To prove a point, I light a match and drop it, but it only consumes itself, and five others do the same: this overgrazed place won't take the fire. Instead of grasses, ragweed, broomweed, and spiky-podded entanglings of buffalo burr grow, and the pasture is so bare I could hit fungoes for an hour and never lose the ball unless it were to land in a cluster of eastern cedar or Osage orange or honey locust, those first trees to steal the grassland, the ones that turn a prairie into a viciously thorned scrub lot that wood rats will take to but not a prairie chicken or upland plover. Those trees, vanguards of the woodland, if they grow large enough to cast their deadly shade, can break the back of the red buffalo, prairie wildfire.

In my pocket a dozen more matches: if the wind shifts and turns the fire across my course, these vestas will enable my escape: light a circle, step downwind, and follow your flames out, or stand within the island of ash (an Indian method and a better one than crawling into a disemboweled horse). Not long ago, two pasturemen without any matches got caught when their pickup mired in and they had to run for a swale and lie down in hopes the blaze, like a tornado, would pass over them, and it did, but they lost the truck and the skin off their backsides.

I wish I'd known George Washington Starkey, a countian who poked into the curiosities of this place and described several of them before they vanished. His English parents settled here in 1871, and twice wildfire burned them out. George wrote this in the thirties for the *Historical Sketches:*

> *Prairie fire was the most dreaded enemy of the early settlers. One time, two men were going through the county and accidentally set out a fire. They were overtaken by settlers and questioned and one of the men was hanged.*
>
> *Most people would plow two furrows around their [hay]stacks and improvements. They would plow one furrow about fifteen steps away and another about ten steps farther out, then they would burn the strip between. This they called a fireguard, and when the prairie fires came they would set fire outside the guard and that would burn out to meet the prairie fire.*

In September of 1878, the *Leader* reminded the mayor of his duty to burn a fireguard around Cottonwood Falls.

William Sayre of Cedar Creek left this:

> *It was in February, 1876 — I was but seven — a very windy day, and the hay was rolling off the top of our barn, and my father got the first whiff of prairie fire smoke. That smell meant something in those days when the bluestem grew as high as your head and hadn't been burned over for years. Father commenced to plow the guard so he could burn it off, [and he] and a few neighbors had finished the burning when the fire came. I was standing at the south window of our one-room loghouse when I saw it coming over the hill. The flames were leaping twenty feet into the air. I darted out of the house and crossed the creek on the ice, which was thick but rotten. The water was about a foot deep and every few steps I would break through. I got to the nearest neighbors, the Beverlins. Their woodpile was on fire, set by firebrands from our barn, which had been carried over the treetops a good fourth of a mile. Mrs. Beverlin was going to the orchard with her twin boys. She piled the three of us up and put a blanket over us. The smoke was choking [and blinding] us.*

My mother took my brother and went down the hill to the creek and stayed under the roots of a large tree. Everything we had burned but the house. We found one big fat sow breathing her last, and they butchered her that evening. Everything in the house was black with smoke, and cinders drifted just like snow over the creek bank two feet deep. My folks had lived there ten years, but it was like starting all over again.

And, in 1873, living near Gladstone was Mrs. Richard Phillips, who watched a wildfire take the family's barn and then approach their home. The men had used up all the water in the well and the house. As the fire, a grizzly ravenous from hibernation, licked the walls, she grabbed the only wet thing left, ran outside with it, and dashed it over the flames: she had just enough cream in the churn to save her home.

Atop the Mound

What I cherish I've come to slowly, usually blindly, not seeing it for some time, and that's just how I discovered Jacobs' Mound, a truncated cone sitting close to the center of the Gladstone quadrangle. This most obvious old travelers' marker shows up clearly from two of the three highways, yet I was here several days before I noticed it, this isolated frustum so distinct. I must have been looking too closely and narrowly, but once I saw its volcano-cone symmetry (at night in the fire season, its top can flame and smolder) I was drawn to it as western travelers have always been to lone protuberances — Independence Rock, Pompey's Pillar, Chimney Rock — and within a day I headed down the Bloody Creek Road until the lane played out in a grassed vale. Some two aerial miles west of the mound, I climbed a ridge and sat down and watched it as if it might disappear like a flock of rare birds. That morning four people told me four things, one of them, the last, accurate: the regular sides and flattened top of the knob prove Indians built it for a burial mound; Colorado prospectors hid gold in it; an oil dome lay beneath it; and, none of those notions was true.

I walked down the hawk-harried ridge and struck out toward the mound, seemingly near enough to reach before sunset. Its sea-level elevation is fifteen hundred feet, but it rises only about a hundred from its base and three hundred above the surrounding humped terrain. In places the October grasses, russet-colored like low flames as if revealing their union with fire, reached to my belt and stunted my strides, and there were also aromatic asters and false indigo, both now dried to scratching stiffness. From the tall heads of Indian grass and the brown stalks of gayfeather, gossamer strung out in the slow wind like pennants ten and twelve feet long and silver in the sun, and these web lines snagged my trousers and chest and head until, after a mile, I was bestrung and on my way to becoming cocooned. Gray flittings rose from the ground like winged stones and threw themselves immediately into invisibility — I think they were vesper sparrows. Twice, prairie chickens broke noisily and did their sweet, dihedral-winged glides to new cover (Audubon said their bent-down wings enable the birds to turn their heads to see behind as they fly). I stopped to watch small events but never for long because the mound was drawing me as if it were a stone vortex in a petrified sea.

There are several ways not to walk in the prairie, and one of them is with your eye on a far goal, because you then begin to believe you're not closing the distance any more than you would with a mirage. My woodland sense of scale and time didn't fit this country, and I started wondering whether I could reach the summit before dark. On the prairie, distance and the miles of air turn movement to stasis and openness to a wall, a thing as difficult to penetrate as dense forest. I was hiking in a chamber of absences where the near was the same as the far, and it seemed every time I raised a step the earth rotated under me so that my foot fell just where it had lifted from. Limits and markers make travel possible for people: circumscribe our lines of sight and we can really get somewhere. Before me lay the Kansas of popular conception from Coronado on — that place you have to get through, that purgatory of mileage.

But I kept walking, and, when I dropped into hollows and the mound disappeared, I focused on a rock or a tuft of grass to keep from convoluting my track. Hiking in woods allows a traveler to imagine comforting enclosures, one leading to the next, and the walker can possess those little encompassed spaces, but the prairie and plains permit no such possession. Whatever else prairie is — grass, sky, wind — it is most of all a paradigm of infinity, a clearing full of many things except boundaries, and its power comes from its apparent limitlessness; there is no such thing as a small prairie any more than there is a little ocean, and the consequence of both is this challenge: try to take yourself seriously out here, you bipedal plodder, you complacent cartoon.

I came up out of a hollow, Jacobs' Mound big now on the horizon, and I could feel its swell in my legs, and then I was in the steep climb up its slope, and: I was on top. From the highway I'd guessed the summit to be the size of a city block, but it was less than a baseball infield, its elliptical perimeter just a hundred strides. So, its power lay not in size but rather in shape and dominion and its thrust into the imagination.

I sat and looked. The thousands of acres that lay encircled around the knob I really didn't see, not at first. I saw air, and I said, good god, look at all this air, and I recalled a woman saying, *Seems the air here hasn't ever been used before.* From a plane you look down, and from a mountain you look down, but from Jacobs' Mound you look out, out into. You're not up in the sky and you're not on the ground: you're nicely in between, at the altitude of those who fly in their dreams and skim roofs and treetops. Jacobs' Mound is thrush-flight high.

And then I understood: I like this prairie county because of its illusion of being away, out of, and I like how its unpopulousness seems to isolate it. Seventy percent of Americans live on two percent of the land, but in front of me, no percentage of them lived. Yet, in the far southeast, I could see trucks inching out the turnpike miles, the turbulence of their passage silenced by distance. And I could see fence lines, transmission towers, and dug ponds, things the pioneers would have viewed as marks of a progressive civilization but which to me, a grousing neo-primitivist, were signs of the continuing onslaught. The view I had homesteaders would have loved, and the one they had of unbroken vegetation and its diversities I would cherish. On top of the mound, insects whirred steadily, and the wind blew in easy continuousness, a drone like that in a seashell at the ear. In the nineteenth century, the Kansas clergyman and author William Quayle (who once wrote, *In a purely metaphorical sense I am a turnip*) traded his autograph for an acre of prairie, and, yesterday, I thought him a thief, but now, seeing the paltriness of an acre, I figured he was the one swindled.

On his great western expedition of 1806, Zebulon Pike crossed the Flint Hills just south of this big knob, and he surely couldn't have resisted climbing this rise for a good look around. In later years, perpendicular to his course ran an old freighter road and stage line that cut between here and Phenis Mound across the county line and five miles east. Near its base, a century ago, farmer John Buckingham plowed up a small redwood chest, took it home, pried it open, and found some old parchments, one marked in crude characters of eccentric orthography advising that nearby a buried sword pointed to the spot on Phenis Mound where lay a cache of golden nuggets. Buckingham thought it a prank until he remembered plowing up a rusted saber the year before; but his and others' diggings yielded only what the inland sea put down a quarter billion years ago.

People connect themselves to the land as their imaginations allow. The links of Chase countians to Jacobs' Mound, at least in an earlier time, were more calligraphic than auricular, and at my feet lay proof: a piece of limestone, palm-sized and flattened like a slate and cut into it a reversed J surmounted by an upside-down V: perhaps a cattle brand. In the days of first white settlement, people rode out here in buggies and hayracks, filled their jugs at one of the springs below the mound, picnicked on the summit, and scratched their names into the broken stones. I looked for more: nothing. Then I turned over a small rock and there, in faint relief under the low sunlight, JOHNY, and on another, MAE, and then I began turning stones, their hardness against one another striking out a strange and musical ringing, and I found more intaglios weathered to near invisibility but the letters uncommonly adroit. The mound was so covered with bits of alphabet it was as if Moses had here thrown down his tablets.

And then from the dark, granular soil I turned one that froze me: WAKONDA. In several variants, Wakonda is a Plains Indian name for the Great Mysterious, the Four-Winds-Source-of-All. Then my sense returned: an ancient Indian writing in Roman characters? I looked closely and could barely make out W KENDA running to the fractured right edge. Perhaps once: W. KENDALL. I put it again face-down so that it might continue its transfer into the mound.

Across America, lone risings have been sacred places to tribal Americans, places to reach out for the infinite. Where whites saw this knob and dreamed gold, aboriginal peoples (it's my guess) found it and dreamed God, and it must have belonged to their legends and gramarye, and they surely came to this erosional ellipse as leaves to the eddy.

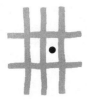

On the Town: Courthouse

December, nearing Christmas, in Cottonwood on Broadway, and I'd just come up out of the dim courthouse basement, away from the nineteenth-century census books, and I turned to the cupola to see whether the clock was working: no, the four-forty of the last year. Then I noticed the low noon sun casting the shadow of the clock tower as if it were a gnomon right down the brick street, and the surmounting flagpole was a penumbral lance pointing north to the little river as it had for 116 Decembers. On that shortest day of the year, the cupola shadow told the hour if the clock didn't, and, on that solstice, it also served as a heliotrope. From cellar to cupola (once there was an old bison skull in the attic), the courthouse bespoke time and the continuance of patterns. I had been below, lost in it all, among the faded and measured scripts that recorded deeds and misdeeds, among the whits of a communal past stacked on bending shelves, one of which held trial evidence: a bottle of formaldehyde and in it a man's bullet-pierced brain.

Years ago, a deputy clerk, Carrie Breese Chandler, slipped a one-page letter to the future under a floorboard in the courthouse hall (her husband, the county treasurer, was himself installing new flooring — without pay). She wrote of the Santa Fe Railroad at last laying track toward Matfield Green, and she said the Falls had electric lights and sewers. She (who had hidden as a child under her mother's staircase when Indians dropped by the farmhouse) recalled watching antelope on the near hills from the third-floor oval window of the courthouse, and she wrote of boys crawling through that port above Broadway to whip around the high and narrow cornices *at an alarming pace,* and she wondered whether the buffalo wallows would still remain in 1973, the courthouse centennial, a half century away. Workmen discovered her little time capsule in 1950 and added a sheet of their own and put the letters back under the oak floor.

A couple of decades ago, near the winter solstice, a circuit in the electric clock in the cupola shorted and set fire to the tower. People stood all over town and watched the flames in the sky, and a man said, *I'd almost rather it was my home,* but the volunteers extinguished the blaze in less than an hour. Instead of tearing off the charred cupola — an architectural detail superfluous now that a siren on the jail warns of tornado, fire, and every Wednesday the stroke of noon — the people rebuilt it and replaced the clock.

Under that bell tower, five generations have been probated, adjudicated, arbitrated, had their property evaluated and assessed, been registered and wedded and divorced, have come for band concerts and ice cream socials, to escape tornadoes, to ask in drought and grasshopper years for hominy, sorghum syrup, dried apples; on the front steps, they've seen their farms and houses go under the sheriff's gavel, and inside they've been locked up and set free, and a few have come to know themselves better here than in any church: scratched raggedly into the paint above the steel jail door (Dante into the Inferno): PRAY AS YOU ENTER. In the vaults are multitudes of figures and compilations, and some walls and the third-floor window recess are also ledgers inscribed and dated; high and low are books, names, lists, labels, and words even scrawled on the jail water heater: THIS IS A HOT WATER HATTER, and below, an arrow pointing to the gas flame and: THIS IS A CIGARETT'ES LITER. On the metal walls of the dark cells are tallies of days served and figurings of days remaining (the subtractions wrong). Cut into a door a man's crime: SHOT HIM IN THE ASS 4 TIMES. Other infractions etched into the steel table: HERE FOR AUTO THEFT and 60 DAYS FOR DESTRUCTION OF PROPERTY and POSSION OF DRUGS. Also: THE BEGGINNING OF KNOWLEDGE; a hand releasing a bird; a naked and headless woman, her vagina labeled; and, on the table top, a scratched-in *trompe l'oeil* of an opened book: on the left page, THE STORY OF WONDER HORSE, on the right, PART ONE BEGINS ON PAGE THREE.

Now: I am standing on Broadway at the tip of the looming winter solstice shadow, and I'm looking at how things seem to rise from the old river crossing, up the red bricks in an easy ascent that passes through the courthouse doors and up the hanging, spiral walnut staircase that makes a complete turn with every floor, up the ladder to the bell tower and on to the topping grillwork. The town seems to approach the building as a subject would his sovereign on a dais. Life here tends toward those bright, tooth-hammered walls with bush-hammered quoins, toward the stones quarried only five blocks west, where now the small, worked ledge above Spring Creek (its source once the town water supply) is concealed in the brush, and where stood the kiln to burn limestone for the mortar. The building has been cut from the hill it stands on, and perhaps no other courthouse in America has traveled so short a distance from bedrock to hall of justice.

In 1859, a few blocks away stood the first courthouse, a log cabin that was also the school, and near it the first jail, once a doctor's office not much bigger than a wagon bed. The cabin disappeared and, it seemed, so did the jail until Whitt Laughridge, the realty agent and president of the historical society, happened across a reference in some old minutes of the county commissioners which led him to a small, empty house: in the right angle of light, he could see cut stone under the stucco; he had found the first jail, maybe the oldest building in town, hidden in plain sight for a century.

Following the Civil War (the enlistment rate here among the highest in the nation), countians held court in a church, but only judgment of another kind seemed fitting there, so veterans, whose notion of civic duty had been honed by the war, conceived, designed (John Haskell, the architect of the state capitol, was once an army quartermaster), and erected something that appears almost too splendid in this unornamented town. What they did with that building, so seemingly lifted from a nineteenth-century Paris avenue, was to make a county out of four boundary lines, to focus a random identity, to embody common ideals in a symmetrical and substantial Second Empire monument of native stone covered by a red, standing-seam mansard roof that pushes a bell tower from the shallow valley to just above the encircling prairie crests. The next generation would say of those Union men, *They builded well,* and that phrase became the county motto.

On the evening of the courthouse opening, citizens (hopeful it would attract a rail line) came to tour it, to feast from laden tables in the jail and dance under the embossed-tin ceiling of the single courtroom, and for this they paid a dollar and raised a hundred dollars for a county library they shelved in the courtroom. (Carrie Chandler wrote of taking a book up to the deep, oval-window recess on the third floor and curling up next to the high view and reading *The Alhambra, Mr. Midshipman Easy, The Corsican Brothers.*) A few years after the opening, some of the celebrants returned to that chamber in 1894 on a less felicitous occasion: a *Courant* pressman got drunk and killed a high school senior, the son of a former Falls mayor, and hid himself in a ravine east of town. Night came on, weather threatened, and the people grew tense. But, before the storm hit, the pressman turned himself in, and the sheriff rang the tower bell to announce the custody and calm the town. The next night twenty-five masked citizens went to the courtroom, forced the release of the prisoner, marched him in silent and military order to the new railroad trestle over the Cottonwood, and hanged him. Carrie Chandler wrote: *Excuse was made for the lynching that so many murders had gone unpunished by law.* Since then there have been no further bridge parties, but several murderers have been tried, only to walk out the front door of the courthouse. In surrounding counties, some people still say, *If you want to kill a man and get away with it, do it in Chase County.*

Those who have been remanded out the back door of the second-floor courtroom into the rear wing that is the jail have found escape almost impossible from the two-foot-thick walls of stone (here and there the mortar half chiseled away) locked together by steel pins; the floor and ceiling of the twin cells are two-by-twelve-inch oak slabs turned narrow side up and covered with sheet iron. In the first years of the courthouse, a prisoner did escape by the classic method of working a window bar loose and lowering himself on a twisted blanket, but since then the jail has been so secure that the state closed it in 1975 for not having a good fire escape. One countian said to me, *What the hell? That's what a jail is — a place you don't escape from.*

The sheriff's family no longer lives in the three rooms below the jail, nor does his wife cook prisoners' meals, nor do his children play in an empty cell or hold slumber parties in the courtroom. The children no longer ring the cupola bell for fire, tornadoes, the Fourth of July, and New Year's Eve, but when Sheriff J. V. Gilmore's daughters lived here, they pulled the four-story rope to the five-hundred-pound bell for nearly two hours on the day the Third Reich surrendered, and that evening, to a lone jail inmate, the town toper, they carried a celebrative beer. Other children remember the prisoner who made up a crossword puzzle using the sheriff's name and details of the county, and in the twenties a young daughter held an Elmdale Moonshine Party, where she and her friends entertained themselves by pouring twenty-two gallons of confiscated white mule down the courthouse drain. Over the years, the sheriff's children (one of whom was born in the room beneath the jail) watched prisoners break rock behind the building, saw deputies kill copperheads in the hallways (five in 1878), peeped in on marriages, and in the vault read the signatures of Lincoln, Johnson, and Grant and their amanuenses, and watched clerks record items in tall ledgers, and they, little deputies, went to the attic and scribbled on the walls and rafters and made them too part of the record. At night, all of the sheriffs and wives and children lay in their beds and heard across the iron floor above the sad pacing of jailed men.

Now: it's a year since I began telling winter hours by the cupola shadow, and it's easier today because the cedars that filled the front lawn and concealed much of the courthouse have been pulled up. A hubbub over the trees had existed since the early days; this last round took fourteen months, full-page newspaper ads citing Joyce Kilmer and alluding to the devil, and a lawsuit before the issue disappeared with the trees. I'd known that citizens here do not suffer change in silence, yet how is it, I wondered, that people who hate a cedar, that thief of pastures, can fight so long to preserve twenty of them? It seemed they were beginning to think like the Osage, for whom the red cedar is the tree of life. Then I realized: those trees were a part of the courthouse, pieces of the solid and distinctive building holding deed to their lives actually and otherwise, and the cedars, like the building, were proof that things endure, if not forever, then at least long enough to keep the present recognizable. And, as if to point up the link, Howard Schwilling took home one of the cedars to turn into a grandfather clock case for the courthouse.

This respository is not an old pickled and shot brain hidden away, but a living communal memory, a means of entering the past, the core of civic identity, a stack of chambered stone that bonds the people and sometimes binds and bends them to the general will. If outsiders have mocked countians for living in a removed and windy land, no one has ever laughed at that Second Empire building made from the hills it oversees.

Thrall-Northwest

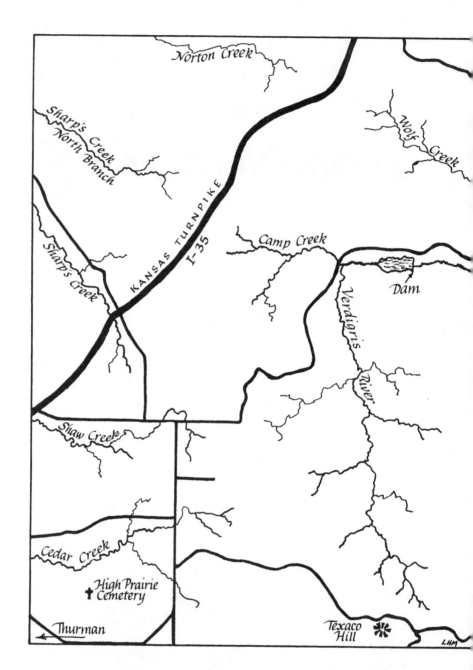

THRALL-NORTHWEST QUADRANGLE

From the Commonplace Book:
Thrall-Northwest

The once great prairies with their fruits and wildlife nourished our nation through its weak infancy. They nourished it again through its reckless and wasteful adolescence. The nation has now reached a maturity which should make it capable of recognizing that the prairie can no longer give that which it does not have and that as man destroys it he destroys himself.

> — Eugene M. Poirot,
> *Our Margin of Life* (1964)

You must not be in the prairie; but the prairie must be in you. That alone will do as qualification for biographer of the prairie. . . . He who tells the prairie mystery must wear the prairie in his heart.

> — William A. Quayle,
> *The Prairie and the Sea* (1905)

[Arrowheads] cannot be said to be lost or found. Surely their use was not so much to bear its fate to some bird or quadruped or man as it was to lie here near the surface of the earth for a perpetual reminder to the generations that come after.

> — Henry David Thoreau,
> *The Journal* (1859)

The machinery for dreaming planted in the human brain was not planted for nothing. That faculty, in alliance with the mystery of darkness, is the one great tube through which man communicates with the shadowy. And the dreaming organ, in connexion with the heart, the eye, and the ear, composes the magnificent apparatus which forces the infinite into the chambers of a human brain, and throws dark reflections from eternities below all life upon the mirrors of that mysterious camera obscura — the sleeping mind.

> — Thomas de Quincey,
> "Suspiria de Profundis" (1845)

The dream is a little hidden door in the innermost and most secret recesses of the soul, opening into that cosmic night which was psyche long before there was any ego-conciousness, and which will remain psyche no matter how far our ego-consciousness extends. For all ego-consciousness is isolated; because it separates and discriminates, it knows only particulars, and it sees only those that can be related to the ego. Its essence is limitation, even though it reach to the farthest nebulae among the stars. All consciousness separates; but in dreams we put on the likeness of that more universal, truer, more eternal man dwelling in the darkness of primordial night. There he is still the whole, and the whole is in him, indistinguishable from nature and bare of all egohood. It is from these all-uniting depths that the dream arises.

> — C. G. Jung,
> Psychological Reflections (1953)

Dreamtime is not past, present, or future, but a continuum — a stream of knowledge closely binding all aboriginal people with the land and each other.

> — Madelon Rosenfeld,
> "Dreamtime" (1988)

We can know the dark and dream it into a new image.

> — Starhawk,
> Dreaming the Dark (1982)

He felt that men were too weak to make any mark here, that the land wanted to be let alone, to preserve its own fierce strength, its peculiar, savage kind of beauty, its uninterrupted mournfulness.

> — Willa Cather,
> O Pioneers! (1913)

Cross Creek belongs to the wind and the rain, to the sun and the seasons, to the cosmic secrecy of seed, and beyond all, to time.

No man should have proprietary rights over land who does not use that land wisely and lovingly.

> — Marjorie Kinnan Rawlings,
> *Cross Creek* (1942)

What bothers us about primordial beauty is that it is no longer characteristic.

> — Robert Adams,
> "Truth and Landscape" (1981)

There is a Kansas character, and its roots are found in the midwestern rural traditions of hard work, struggle in the face of adversity, frugality, practicality, individualism, democracy, and environmental irresponsibility.

> — Leo E. Oliva,
> "Kansas: A Hard Land in the
> Heartland" (1988)

The disappearance of a major natural unit of vegetation from the face of the earth is an event worthy of causing pause and consideration by any nation. Yet so gradually has the prairie been conquered by the breaking plow, the tractor, and the overcrowded herds of man, and so intent has he been upon securing from the soil its last measure of innate fertility, that scant attention has been given to the significance of this endless grassland or the course of its destruction. Civilized man is destroying a masterpiece of nature without recording for posterity that which he has destroyed.

> — John Ernest Weaver,
> *North American Prairie* (1954)

About eighty percent of Chase County is used for native range. This native range has been used to ninety percent of its capacity since 1900.

> — James T. Neill,
> *Soil Survey of Chase County, Kansas*
> (1974)

The best conservationalists I know as a whole are the ranchers in the county.

> — Luke Austenfeld,
> Letter to the editor,
> *Chase County Leader-News* (1985)

No living man will see again the long-grass prairie, where a sea of prairie flowers lapped at the stirrups of the pioneer. We shall do well to find a forty here and there on which the prairie plants can be kept alive as species. There were a hundred such plants, many of exceptional beauty. Most of them are quite unknown to those who have inherited their domain.

Conservation is getting nowhere because it is incompatible with our Abrahamic concept of land. We abuse the land because we regard it as a commodity belonging to us. When we see land as a community to which we belong, we may begin to use it with love and respect. There is no other way for land to survive the impact of mechanized man.

> — Aldo Leopold,
> *A Sand County Almanac* (1949)

You can grow a prairie facsimile in five or ten years. But some scientists think it could take two hundred years to reconstruct the intricate prairie ecosystem. Others think five hundred. Still others, never.

> — Dennis Farney,
> "The Tallgrass Prairie: Can It Be
> Saved?" (1980)

Native tallgrass prairie is the rarest of all North America's biomes. . . . [It] is a singular system defined by climate, weather, size, and the interactions of fire and grazing bison. Because those factors are no longer functioning in a balanced whole anywhere in North America, true tallgrass prairie can be considered to be extinct as a natural, functioning ecosystem.

> — John Madson,
> "On the Osage" (1990)

Except by the measure of wildness we shall never really know the nature of a place.

> — Paul Gruchow,
> "A Backyard Robin, Ho-Hum" (1988)

City people who use the countryside can do much to help maintain its beauty and prevent its deterioration by spending their money to keep it attractive, whereas most working farmers can no longer afford the luxury of doing so.

City folk grow bored fairly quickly when left to their own devices in the country, and they demand entertainment; nature alone is not enough for them.

> — John Fraser Hart,
> *The Look of the Land* (1975)

Again and again we respond, knowing our words will have little effect, knowing that [prairie] park adversaries will continue to cling to these claims and contentions despite their stunning illogic, knowing that we are challenging a set of myths, myths which, although assailable by simplest reason, remain impervious to it because their roots extend to these people's skittish mistrust of any and all "intruders" — from coyotes to the Federal Government.

> — Tim Amsden,
> "Points of Contention" (1975)

Of a government hostile to the individual, [Kansans] cannot conceive.

> — Carl Becker,
> "Kansas" (1910)

Everyone profits from the success of industry. In our area, local industries provide jobs, improve incomes and generate business. It is the responsibility of every Chase Countian to support local industry and to urge new industries to locate here, or someday, there will be a whole lot of nothing.

> — Long-running advertisement,
> *Chase County Leader-News*
> (1985–1988)

Oh God! that one might read the book of fate,
And see the revolution of the times
Make mountains level, and the continent,
Weary of solid firmness, melt itself
Into the sea! and, other times, to see
The beachy girdle of the ocean
Too wide for Neptune's hips; how chances mock,
And changes fill the cup of alteration
With divers liquors!

> — William Shakespeare,
> *Henry IV, Part 2* (1600)

If there is magic on this planet, it is contained in water.

> — Loren Eiseley,
> *The Immense Journey* (1946)

To follow a creek is to seek a new acquaintance with life.

> — Peter Steinhart,
> "The Making of a Creek" (1989)

Digressions, incontestably, are the sunshine — they are the life, the soul of reading; take them out of this book for instance — you might as well take the book along with them.

> — Laurence Sterne,
> *Tristram Shandy* (1767)

Name, though it seem but a superficial and outward matter, yet it carrieth much impression and enchantment.

> — Francis Bacon,
> *Essays* (1625)

A name is at most a mere convenience and carries no information with it. As soon as I begin to be aware of the life of any creature, I at once forget its name.

> — Henry David Thoreau,
> *The Journal* (1860)

Did you think there was nothing but two or three pronunciations in the sound of your name?

> — Walt Whitman,
> "What Am I After All?" (1867)

It took a long time to learn how to spell Kansas.

> — John Rydjord,
> *Indian Place-Names* (1968)

The name of this tribe is variously spelled Kanzas, Kansas, Cansas, Konzas, and Conzas; and to cap all absurdity, they scarcely know themselves by any other word than Kaw. Should the Territory be erected into a slave state, it might be advisable to adopt this latter as the title, being the ominous croak of the raven.

> — Max Greene,
> *The Kanzas Region* (1856)

Since we have Hoosiers and Suckers and Pukes in the older states, it may be questioned whether we shall not have Kaws in Kansas.

> — Jacob Ferris,
> *The States and Territories of the Great West* (1856)

Kansas, as now accepted, written and spoken, is one of the most beautiful Indian words adapted to use in the English tongue. As a name for a state it is unequalled.

> — William E. Connelley,
> *A Standard History of Kansas and Kansans* (1918)

We are often asked, "Why do you call your city Kansas? — it is stealing a name which does not properly belong to you but to the Territory." Such is not the fact. When this city was laid off and named, it was called after the river at whose mouth it is situated, and the immense trade of whose valley it controls. Kansas Territory was then called Nebraska, and when it was divided by act of Congress, they stole our name. We trust the public will hereafter stand corrected. We are the original and genuine Kansas, and intend so to continue.

> — Editorial,
> *Kansas City* (Missouri) *Enterprise* (1856)

Women achieved the right to vote in stages in Kansas. They could vote in school elections after 1861 and in municipal elections after 1887, the year Susanna Madora Salter of Argonia became the first woman to be elected to the office of mayor of any town in the United States. The right of Kansas women to vote in state and national elections came eight years before the Nineteenth Amendment.

> — Leo E. Oliva,
> "Kansas: A Hard Land in the Heartland" (1988)

[Living history] is an imaginative creation, a personal possession which each one of us, Mr. Everyman, fashions out of his individual experience, adapts to his practical or emotional needs, and adorns as well as may be to suit his aesthetic tastes.

> — Carl Becker,
> "Everyman His Own Historian" (1932)

In the Quadrangle:
Thrall-Northwest

I have climbed here: the view from Texaco Hill, rising one mile from the very southeast corner of Chase County, is of aerial Kansas. North and south you can look along the eastern escarpment of steep slopes, flattened uplands, and rounded hills, the more distant ones fading to blue as if a real cordillera rather than a mere cuesta, and you can understand two early names for the Flint Hills: the Kansas Mountains and, when their origin became understood, the Permian Mountains. I won't press the point because I could walk in twenty minutes to the bottom and back up to this crest. To the north lie several spring-fed creeks, linked like rootlets, merging here to form the Verdigris River, of some fame in its lower reaches.

Before the turnpike cut into the northwest quarter of this quadrangle in 1956, only three hilly rock roads wrenched out twisted courses through the pastures and the oil fields that edge up to the county corner from the east and south and stop almost exactly at the border as if carrying contraband. A few wells now pump just inside the line, but, a half mile farther on, the oil-bearing shoestring sands, once beaches of an ancient sea, stop. From these jacks coughing out their one-cylinder *putt-putt-putt* and from several more in the extreme northwest come thirty thousand barrels of crude, which put Chase eighty-first among the ninety-two Kansas counties producing oil. The five contiguous counties all pump more, the smallest output twice as much and the largest sixty-six times greater; the relative paucity of Chase petroleum, beyond its economic effect, has left this corner pleasantly unmessed to show off its elevated scenery.

Texaco Hill, elevation 1,650 feet (four hundred above the broad eastern valley), is the highest place in the county, and from here I can look north along the front of the scarp to the place where Zebulon Pike and his soldiers entered the Flint Hills in the fall of 1806 on their way to reconnoiter the newly acquired central plains and make a permanent peace between the Kansa and Osage. He was the first person to map and write about the county and, maybe, the first white (surely the first American citizen) to enter it. Lacking the capacity of either Meriwether Lewis or William Clark to perceive and evoke, Pike, perhaps taking his view from this very prominence, limned the Chase terrain in two brief entries, one just descriptive enough to give a lasting name to the big escarpment: *Passed four branches and over high hilly prairie*, and, the next day, *Passed very ruff flint hills. My feet blistered and very sore. I stood on a hill, and in one view below me saw buffalo, elk, deer, cabrie [antelope], and panthers.* His "flint" was, more accurately, chert, but no one here regrets the error: a resident said to me yesterday when we were talking about whether panthers had actually returned to Chase as several reliable countians claim and I mentioned Pike's misnaming the rock, *Like hell. I'm not living in any Chert Hills.* Indeed, to natives, the eponymous stone, in an emphasizing tautology, is *flint rock.*

Sixteen years later another government explorer, Jacob Fowler, passed through this corner on his return from Santa Fe. Writing nearly illegible characters of his own invention, Fowler's terse entries are in a sometimes logical, sometimes daft orthography:

> *wensday 26th June 1822. We sot out Early pasing over a Rich Roleing Pirarie to a Crick With Some timber — taylor killed two deer — We maid 8 miles [north] 15 East It Rains Heavely —*

> *thorsday 27th June 1822. Set out Early Crossing five Cricks all Runing South East Some timber on all of them one twenty yds Wide the Cuntry as ushal Rich and Roleing —*

Five miles due west of me, on a high and wind-struck hill that can sling a ridge-riding harrier a hundred feet upward in a couple of seconds, is High Prairie Cemetery, the most isolated burial ground in the country. Because the nearest village, Matfield Green, lies some distance away, I had never understood those desolate markers, so many of them above the graves of young women and children and infants, the dated chunks of native rock being testaments to the high mortality of birth and childhood. I couldn't make sense of this far cemetery until I rode the quad with Joseph Hickey, a former New Yorker, now an anthropologist at Emporia State University. Joe was coming into the middle years with his hair as black as pasture ash, his eyes like faded blue denim. He said, *You walk around here, and you begin to believe you're the first to pass over any given spot, but you aren't, of course. Indians lived in this watershed for at least six thousand years, from the Archaic era through the Ceramic and on to the historic tribes — Quivirans, Wichitas, Osage, Kansa. A short view of time distorts the emptiness up here. These uplands and especially the creek bottoms have been full of occupation since before King Tut.*

Hickey had nearly finished writing a book called *Thurman in the Flint Hills*, about the human life along the hollows of the westward-tending creeks that merge with the South Fork of the Cottonwood just west of the quadrangle. If human occupation here is long, particular settlements have been brief: Indians apparently made only hunting camps, and a white community built around the continually shifting neighborhood post office lasted only seventy years. For a place of good — if limited — shelter, water, soil, timber, fruits, and game, a land of linked and pleasing valleys surrounded by rich and uncorrupted prairie, the repeated pattern of brief settlement is odd. Joe said, *Thurmanites saw land and community in practical terms, things that could be discarded if they didn't provide immediate benefit. They were wanderers who pursued the western illusion that riches and a better life were always over the next hill. Thurman, really, was only a neighborhood that followed wherever the post office went.*

External evidence of Thurman is gone now except for a school used as a garage and a derelict farmhouse once the first post office: the scattered homes, the blacksmith shop, two schools, and post offices have disappeared; the cultivated fields have vanished under grasses to become what the countians call *go-back land*. Today, ancient lithic artifacts are more abundant than homesteaders' remnants. Joe said, *We can excavate more from the Ceramic culture than from star-route Thurman. These were poor settlers in the bottoms — we're talking burlap-bag shoes. Their world was cloth, wood, and some iron. About all that remains of the first Thurman are discolorations in the soil.* I said, that's something else we have to relearn — how to make a culture that will completely oxidize, how to let earth, air, fire, and water remove us to mere stains.

We rode and wandered the place as Joe talked Thurman into existence again. I asked about the lone and pitiful little hill cemetery, and he said, *The upland belonged to outsiders — the government, railroads, speculators — all of them absentee landlords, although Thurmanites at times used it as communal grazing land. Pasture churches and cemeteries didn't take up valuable cropland in the narrow bottoms. But High Prairie was built by stock raisers during the Great Cattle Boom of the 1880s. The community was at the center of several big ranches — before the boom busted. Land ownership here has always been peculiar. An itinerant speculator, William Thurman, set the pattern in the 1870s when he bought acreage and turned around and sold it at a nice profit. To this day, a lot of these uplands have never been owned by Chase countians. But one thing has been consistent through all the years of white settlement: just about everybody has treated the land as only a commodity to make a buck off of.*

This corner of the county is a place of energy transfer. The oldest is nutrient passage from sea to rock to soil to grass to ungulates to man, and next is that of generation to generation; now oil gets drawn from the shales, natural gas courses the pipelines from western Kansas to Chicago, high-tension lines hump electric power east to west, microwave relay towers kick along information between the coasts, and there's the railroad and the interstate, these last five all striking about the same angle across the county. In a place as apparently still as the under-rock itself, transit and translation lie all over this quiet corner.

I stood atop Texaco Hill once before on an early trip into the quadrangle Thrall, a name seeming to describe my response to this high prairie, despite my knowing Thrall was only a Greenwood County ghost town of rusting remains from the oil boom of the twenties. I came off the hill that autumn afternoon, went back to the road, drove away, stopped, walked out into the grasses and stirred a coyote into a long-legged lope, went on toward the promise of another overlook, hoofing far and looking back to find the high-pole gate, my lone landmark, lost in the broadly curving upland I'd thought so level, and then all I had was a surround of horizon. I felt the misgivings of a sea swimmer gone out too far, and the grasses slapped their russet sameness against me like waves. I thought: don't walk circles, walk straight — no place in this county is farther than five miles from a road. Killdeer rose and veered and wheeled and squealed, and the grass shortened as it approached a ledge of caprock, and then the upland cleaved and just fell away to space above the east valley, and I had found the scarp again. I followed it to a vantage where the southern horizon seemed to have been pressed from both ends and crumpled into zigzags. It was the best spot I'd ever discovered to sit along this high edge of the West and look deep into the East: beyond the county, on what was once pure prairie and only that, now lay a road-checkered woodland lapping at the scarp like a dark green, usurping ocean, an inundation of eastern things moving toward the hills and carrying seeds baneful to prairie. The twentieth century was edging in, threatening, and mostly what stayed it was fire.

I thought, stop and fix this image, and as I started to sit I saw at my feet the figure eight in stone: parallel to the ridge, tangent circles looking like the sign for infinity drawn in flint. Wasn't it clear that two people had sat here and watched the spread valley when it was a grassland of hoofed and horned beasts, all the while knapping out their razored points to let that ruminant blood? The only chert nearby was this figure of gray, curved flakes the size of thumbnails. The old sea had not left these stones.

Under the southwest wind, I sat down inside the loop and merge of lines of no start or end, and I lost sense of the late afternoon, and my mind seemed to fall into the circles and away. I think I dozed, because the next thing I remember was the dusk sunk into an oppressive sky, and the gone-too-far alarm coming on again. Then I was up and trying to keep along the dark ridge and walk a straight course. A few days earlier I'd heard about a man miles from his ranch in this very area who'd fallen from his horse and lain with a broken pelvis through the night; he tried to keep from passing out so when the pickup trucks came looking they wouldn't run over him.

The prairie was a wet burden, and I kept feeling as if I were down, below, under, and the grasses dragged: a sea-bottom walker through beds of kelp. I began stumbling, and I thought, hike a figure eight and the cowboys will find you next spring. Then, as if I were not walking in my sleep but sleeping on my walk: in some lightless, soundless dreamplace, obscure forms seemed to pass by in pale luminescence, opalescent figures everywhere. My lower body sogged in the cold dew, the upper half in hot sweat. Then something rose from nowhere and snagged me and pulled me down: I'd come to a fence, a road, and, farther, the car. I was woozy that night and thrashed through the distortions of fevered and vertiginous sleep.

That's my memory of the figure eight, but now I understand it in a different dimension; another energy transfer happened, one I hadn't realized: I'd come into the prairie out of some dim urge to encounter the alien — it's easier to comprehend where someplace else is than where you are — and I had begun to encounter it as I moved among the quoins, ledgers, pickled brains, winds, creek meanders, gravestones, stone-age circles. I was coming to see that facts carry a traveler only so far: at last he must penetrate the land by a different means, for to know a place in any real and lasting way is sooner or later to dream it. That's how we come to belong to it in the deepest sense.

Of Recharging the System

The superstitious might conclude that the fellow used up his luck in surviving the war, although he'd been shot at only once, the time he got curious about a volcano crater north of Saipan and nosed his C-46 transport down *into* the cone for a good look. A Japanese soldier put a 9.5 millimeter bullet into a hydraulic line, and Larry Wagner suddenly had to horse the heavy plane up over the crater rim and turn it back toward the base, but the flying was more difficult than dangerous, and, in the end, there was no flaming crash, just a pretty good story, the kind every wartime pilot earns. After the war he went home to Kansas City, Kansas, got a job in a bank trust department, married Martha Cable, and they had a daughter and son. He was blond, lean, vigorous, and respected for his honesty and friendliness.

One afternoon in 1953 he went to the doctor, after feeling punk for a few days, and at the back of his mind lay a dark coil of foreboding, an anxiety everyone knew then, and he asked the physician, *Is it polio?* The doctor wasn't sure and gave him some pills, primitive antibiotics, and Larry Wagner drove home and told Martha to take the children to his mother's, and he went to bed. At about five that afternoon he got up to go to the bathroom, and he just fell over. His legs wouldn't work. His mother helped him up. Three hours earlier he'd walked four blocks, and now, abruptly, he'd just taken his last steps ever. He was thirty years old. At one in the morning he found himself not breathing worth a damn, and his mother called an ambulance to take him to the hospital where he went into an iron lung, and the next day he heard the diagnosis: bulbar poliomyelitis, a disease more common among children.

Six months later, when he left the iron lung, he had only a most limited use of his right hand, and his arms and legs had become mere danglings as if made of cloth like Raggedy Andy's, and he required a respirator to breathe. He would say later, *I'm one of the lucky ones — I can cough. I can keep the lungs clear.* He has since learned to use muscles not normally employed for breathing so that he can get by on his own unless he needs to say more than a couple of sentences, and then someone must place in his mouth a respirator hose to fill his lungs so he can expel his words: his sentences begin strong and fade with the air supply. Larry is well read and articulate and doesn't speak in brevities to accommodate himself. When he talks, he holds the plastic tube between his teeth, clenching it coolly and waiting for the respirator to catch up with his urge to finish the thought. This man of quiet reasonableness, who can raise only a couple of fingers, has been one of the prime movers to establish a Tallgrass Prairie National Park in Kansas.

He was sixty years old when I met him, a practicing attorney specializing in documentary law, the drafting of complex trusts and realty transactions. He said to me then: *It's one of the things I can do without humiliation, especially when I have a secretary who can just as well wash my hands as take dictation.* Unlike some wives who marry hale men and then suddenly find themselves with a quadriplegic, Martha has stood by him, and their children are grown now and at last can see the remarkable in their father, who, says Martha, *by all rights should be dead.* In Chase County, a few people have wished he were.

Some time ago: I am in the back seat of the Chevrolet Suburban, and next to me is Elaine Shea, a Kansan from New York who fell in love with the Flint Hills during a thunderstorm on her way home from a football game in the sixties. That rain may ultimately prove to be one of the important cloudbursts in Kansas history, so significant is her contribution to prairie preservation. Larry sits in the front, the respirator behind, his head gently strapped to the seat back, and his father, Ray, is bounding us over a section of pasture near the Verdigris River. Ray is eighty-five, looks sixty-five, drives as if he just got his license. Behind me is an ice chest full of fried chicken, potato salad, sliced tomatoes, and chocolate cake — our K (as in Kansas) rations. I'd like to get into them now, but Elaine says,

No way. Next to the ice chest, collapsed neatly like a card table, is an electric rocking-bed that Larry will use in the motel tonight; thirty-six times every minute it will tilt him like a teeter-totter to approximate the action of his lungs. Without it, when he fell asleep, he would suffocate, since he must breathe consciously.

Larry has just told me that he reads by balancing a book on his right knee so that his right fingers can turn the pages. Elaine says, *Sometimes he sits outside, and I put his chair across the breeze to turn the pages*. Appropriate for a Kansan, I say, and she nods, and I ask, how about a piece of fried chicken in this nice prairie breeze, and she says, *Cool it*.

Larry is showing the land he hopes will one day become the first national park in Kansas, the first federal one given to tallgrass prairie, that essence of America, that landform still unrepresented in the park system. The formal proposal has again died in Washington, killed off by Kansans, and prospects look poor as ever since the idea first appeared in the twenties and resurfaced every decade. Larry explains things, clamping the air hose jauntily between his teeth the way Franklin Roosevelt used to clench his cigarette holder, and he waits for the machine to catch up; Elaine fills the gaps with information about STP, Save the Tallgrass Prairie, a group begun in 1973. The National Park Service originally proposed eighty sites, then trimmed those to three, all in the Flint Hills, the last long-grass acreage of any size remaining in the country. Once there were four hundred thousand square miles of tall prairie (about the area of Texas, Oklahoma, and Kansas combined) over the middle of America; but, of that, plows, cows, and towns have left only three percent or less, much in fragments along right-of-ways and in neglected cemeteries, all pieces too small to convey the essence of prairie: horizon-to-horizon grasses and blossoms interrupted only by the rise and fall of the land itself. A hundred grazed acres do not constitute a prairie any more than a hundred pruned trees comprise a forest, and, in spite of what Emily Dickinson wrote about a single bee making a prairie, its essence of immensity does not lend itself to microcosm. STP worked hard to keep the proposal from dying in the bureaucracy.

Of the three final sites selected, one lies mostly in Oklahoma at the tail end of the Flint Hills, another in the northern Hills, and the third is right here under our bouncing seats, under the fried chicken I've been unable to work back into the conversation. This site, which includes all of Chase County south of the turnpike and smaller portions of three adjoining counties, has the highest priority because of its splendid escarpment, negligible population, varied soils, and three watersheds rising within the site that would lessen outside pollution. The recommended acreage of the park has varied over the years, although a tract ten by ten miles is the smallest that would allow a rich restoration of a native prairie in its diversity, from water bears to bison; that much is necessary to control visual contamination in a place where you can see twenty miles sitting down. Other tallgrass preserves around the Middle West are "pocket" prairies, an oxymoron if you ask me: grand scale is necessary to know what red hunters and white pioneers must have felt as they, like bits of flotsam, moved across the marine-like swells of grass.

A few people believe the conservation effort here is pointless, since the interstate has already hacked into the eastern slope that's also crossed by two sets of high transmission lines, six pipelines, and several microwave towers, but other parts of the Flint Hills have been hit even harder by reservoirs, a power plant, military installations. The Chase site is the best of what remains. Anyone who thinks, as some here do, that the changes technology and an increasing population make on the land have ceased in this corner has not been paying attention to the twentieth century. I read about things like aerial fertilizing of pastures, a process that would alter the balance of native species, and I ask myself, what threats are coming that I haven't even imagined yet? Today, a casual traveler through the county must look hard to find grass he can truly describe as tall.

Every major conservation group in America has backed the park proposal, but this support has been stymied by a group of cattle raisers called KGA, Kansas Grassroots Association, which urged the state legislature to pass a resolution calling for Congress to ignore the idea. Some members of the association quickly turned the issue into an emotional uproar with fright tactics, and, where logic failed, they substituted vituperation. The poisonous assertions were effective, because they rarely got into the news or formal discussions and could work unchallenged on the street: *You're gonna see your cemeteries moved. Your daughters won't be safe.* In the thirties, when Chase countians wanted a fishing lake, they applied successfully to the Works Projects Administration, but after they learned that some of the men building the lake would be blacks, the citizens dropped the idea for twenty years. Not everyone responded to the park proposal on those terms, of course; one Cottonwood man who didn't said to me, *If you want to kill off something here, all you do is throw in the word colored.* There was other ugliness: Larry Wagner received abusive and threatening phone calls, and the wife of one prominent countian, at a town hall meeting, grabbed a map from an elderly professor explaining the issues and shredded it.

The formal arguments of the KGA were these: people would be driven off their land, acreage would be dropped from the tax rolls, beef production would decline, honky-tonk development (Six Flags over the West Forty) would trash the place, a federal bureaucracy would be an incompetent steward. But the strongest ally was the old hostility toward government born out of a fear of diminished individual rights which pervades the West. After the words *communists* and *coloreds*, the most potent is *feds.*

The KGA held that ranchers had maintained the pastures for a century and more, and it saw the park proposal as a threat to a way of life central to American history. Proponents answered the KGA objections by tailoring the plan so that no family would have to move or lose its right to pass on its land, and transient grazing (less destructive and more in keeping with history than the recent year-round cow-calf operations) could continue in areas of the park; federal entitlements from off-shore oil drilling and the money the park itself generated would more than compensate for property tax losses. Proponents pointed out that the land taken out of beef production would amount to less than one third of one percent of Kansas pasturage and that any disfiguring peripheral development could be controlled through zoning, covenants, and scenic easements. They said to judge the government as an incompetent steward depends on whether you look at the Park Service or the Forest Service — the record of the former is as good as the other's is poor.

The fear of federal tyranny should never have been much of an issue, since just three Chase families lived on land they owned within the tract, and the single change for them would occur only if they decided to sell their acreage — then the Park Service would have right of first refusal. But some people who merely leased pasture might have to find other grass. A peculiar aspect of the debate was that most of the opposition leaders had no connection with the site itself, and others were not even Chase countians, yet they were able to intimidate any resident who disagreed with them through that unspoken and universal tyranny of village life: *You gotta live*

THRALL-NORTHWEST   111

with us. At the height of the debate, a Wichita reporter talked to merchants in Cottonwood Falls and claimed he found several favoring the park, but he could not get even one to speak up. Some people around Kansas came to believe that self-serving nonresidents were manipulating Chase County out of a rare and nonpolluting opportunity to broaden its economy and share more of American prosperity, while others lamented losing a chance to put the lie to the nightmare Kansas of *In Cold Blood, The Wizard of Oz*, Pike's "desert," drought, and grasshopper infestations. Here was an opportunity to show the beauty of the native land and to ease that Kansan defensiveness deriving from outsiders' ignorance of the place.

The association argued that prairie should be preserved privately, and park proponents held that individually owned plots were dangerously subject to intrusion, that private protection could succeed only temporarily. The KGA suggested a prairie parkway of linked highways and scenic overlooks, and, in fact, such a system came about until the issue seemed dead, and then the county highway department pulled down all the route markers but for the one in front of the courthouse. The association claimed that ranchers, out of self-interest, would always maintain the health of pastureland (their record so far is mediocre), and proponents said what needed preserving was not grazed fields but an entire ecosystem: of the sixty-some native grasses here, cattle raisers are interested in five; to them, the hundreds of other plants, those diverse and necessary ornaments of the prairie, fall almost entirely into the category of "weeds." A pasture is as far from a balanced native prairie as is an overgrown Cottonwood Falls back lot.

Now: at last the fried chicken is out, and Elaine says, *We agree with KGA in wanting to preserve a century-old way of life, but we also want to preserve one that's twenty million years old, but we've failed by barging in here as "experts," tramping around and mapping people's land, and not making them part of things right at the beginning. Although we had broad support, the perception of us here was as city people from Johnson County, the place known across the state as the home of spoiled brats of all ages. We lost control of the terms of the discussion early, and with them eventually went the tallgrass park. The sad thing, when the issue began to die here and the effort shifted to the Oklahoma site, Chase countians began calling us, hoping STP would buy their land.*

And Larry says, *It's a loss for America, for Kansas, and for almost everyone in Chase,* and, as his air dwindles, he says, without waiting for the machine to catch up, *I like them very much. Good people.*

How things stand now: some Kansans, who believe that both ranching and complete ecosystems must be preserved, are trying to work through education and conservation easements to show people how all lives here sooner or later depend upon natural diversity. They are trying to point out how the worst tyranny will come not from a federal park but from an impoverished people and a depleted land.

Larry Wagner spends more time now overseeing his farm southwest of Kansas City that he and his father bought in 1963, a place with a few acres of virgin ground, a buffalo wallow, and restored grasses and plants. The last time I was with him, after he told me he would soon convey, with the financial help of others, the farm to the Kansas park system, he said, *As a thick cover of natural vegetation began coming back in the late sixties, it pulled more precipitation into the aquifer, and two springs, dry for years, started flowing again. All we did was to help the system recharge itself.*

Down in the Hollow

Texaco Hill humps up at my back, looms up dry in the heat. I'm on my way down into a northerly inclined hollow, and I've just stooped to a snow-on-the-mountain, its white-margined blossoms not yet open, to test the milky sap once used (so I've heard) to brand cattle, and I've dribbled out a small circle on the back of my hand, and I'm waiting for the flesh to liquefy or whatever it will start to do before I wipe it off. I've been crouched so long, watching, that a harrier seems to have taken me for a rock, because it just slipped the ridge wind and beat to a hover close enough I can see its hot eye of golden ice. Collapsing its wings like a parasol, it drops hard into the blue-stem, thrashes, then labors up out of the hollow to catch the wind, and hooked into its nerveless, ebony talons is a small, curled, limp-tailed something, and in the grass lies a fluff of bloodied fur. The Mysterium has opened for just a moment, and I've glimpsed inside, and it's deflected me from my search for the headwaters of the Verdigris River.

I'm taking a water walk, hiking down among the intermittent streamlets (on this summer day they are just damp fingerings) that converge somewhere in here to set the river off on its ocean course: down to the Arkansas, the Mississippi, to the Gulf, which will return it on laden, leaden clouds. I've been reading about Chase waters, and I'm here to blend books and facts. Because the oldest visible things in the county lie along this river dell, I keep finding beginnings, and these rocks keep bringing me back to water, the fruit of the wind. (Had we named our planet more accurately, we might have called it Hydro.) I'm coming down an eroded escalator, dropping deeper into an extinct Permian sea, a narrow warp in time in this warped seabed, each step a thousand years further back, and I'm moving from the era of the great Permian extinctions toward the yeasty abundance of Carboniferous life lying below me, some of it liquefying into combustibles. From a clinkered slope I've just picked up a fossil, a shark's tooth, a small crescent that looks like a tiny leaping dolphin; for two hundred million years it has lain locked in the shale, and now it moves again in my sweaty, salty shirt pocket as if it were once more a piece of a saw-toothed maw gliding along in the time when these rocks could be swum. Every so often it sticks me, seems to bite my chest as if to get to my blood. When it had its last meal, the Appalachians were rising, the Rockies were at sea level, and the continents lay sutured into Pangaea. Chase County is forty-six hundred miles from Paris, but then it was about three thousand miles closer.

I'm walking down into an old marine world: in their journals, early white travelers wrote of the prairie, using a single metaphor as if it were the only one possible — *the ocean of grass* — and no wonder, since this land is *like* the sea and it is *of* the sea. The characteristic shape of the hills, the stacked trapezoids, takes its substance from the old ocean and its form from rain and ice; the prehistory of Zebulon Pike's and Stephen Long's American desert is a study of waters. I'm a hiker through antique seas that have become stone cages of a marine zoo: crinoids, bryozoans, brachiopods, gastropods, pelecypods, ostracods, trilobites, and vertebrates that left behind only their razory teeth. But most abundant of all are fusulinids, single-cell invertebrates now turned to calcite tests that are almost the signature of Cottonwood Limestone. (In the walls of the Chase courthouse and the capitol in Topeka, those billions of things appearing to be grains of wheat were once creepers of the sea. Kansas paleontologist Christopher Maples told me, *Fusulinids were incredibly abundant — the housefly of the Permian: they came along, went bonkers, then got snuffed in the Permian Extinction when seventy percent of the taxonomic variety was wiped out. Their evolution, beginning to end, was very rapid.*)

I must for a moment speak in numbers: the average annual precipitation here is thirty-two inches, and that means the square mile surrounding me gets five hundred million gallons of water dumped on it yearly, enough to fill the new water tower at Cottonwood Falls twenty-five hundred times. The entire county receives about four hundred billion gallons a year, and that would fill this square mile to a depth of nearly two thousand feet. Things vary of course: in the flood year of 1951, 768 billion gallons came down, and two years later during the big drought only 261 billion gallons. In the early days especially, the number of farmers tended to rise and fall with the precipitation — the more of one, the more of the other — and neither the apocalyptic horsemen nor mechanization nor the lure of city jobs has so pushed people out as inches of rain.

The main watercourses of Chase look like the sprung tines of a fork thrust into a squarely cut piece of beefsteak that is the county, and ninety-five percent of the surface water leaving here goes out eastward on the central tine and handle, the Cottonwood, and on to the Neosho and the Arkansas. The Verdigris River, hardly more than a brook in Chase, drains only some thirty square miles of the county as it cuts, in leaving, an upside-down L. Of its 280 miles, just a dozen lie in Chase, one of them now under a small impoundment. The upper Verdigris is very much a Hills creek, with its peculiar color of transparent gray like faded flint, that hallmark hue of these upland streams. Sometimes the water runs a shade closer to oxidized copper, and I think the word verdigris, "green-gray," describes it well, but I've read that the name comes from the Osage Indians, who today live south of here and who call it *Wa-ce-ton-xoe*, "gray-green-bark-waters," perhaps an allusion to shale banks the color of sycamore trunks. As does the etymology, local pronunciation allows interpretation: VURR-duh-gree, VURR-duh-griss, and my own preference, like rainfall, varies from day to day.

Walking again: I've come to a mossy seep, not far above several runnels resolving themselves farther down the hollow into a confluence that I take, at least on this dry day, to be the headwaters. The seep is a lateral crack, a long crevice like a slender something left between the pages of a closed book. I can't insert even a finger, but still the broken ledge drips, *tick-tick-tick*, like a water clock, and I set my tin cup under it, and now the seep goes *ting-ting-ting*, a small bell. I wait. The snow-on-the-mountain hasn't marked my hand, and I'm not branded, and I'll have no acid scar to tell stories about. *Ting-ting-ting*. This county is a leaky place, its stone sea shot through with fissures and fractures, concavities and crannies, holes and vugs, crazed layers of jointed limestone between strata of shale, all of it like a stack of sliced bread holding water until there's too much, and then draining itself in hidden slopes. This one is a mere dripping — now it goes *tuck-tuck-tuck* — but, twelve miles west of here, Jack Spring, the biggest in the county, lets go about a hundred gallons a minute, so it takes old Jack, drawing from the largest cave system in Kansas, nearly a decade to return what falls on its square mile each year. There are many other springs, and most of their cold pools sprout a toothsome and peppery watercress; in season, I've munched my way from spring to spring as if pub-hopping. West of here also rise several artesian wells, one of them once strong enough to push its water up to the second floor of a nearby farmhouse. These hydraulic details matter, since a summer-flowing creek in an upland pasture can be miles away; the ranchers' old solution was a stock tank and windmill, but the Aermotors and Dempster Annu-Oileds are gone like last year's rain, and now bulldozer-cut ponds, cheap to build and maintain, pock the county. Thoreau thought a lake to be the earth's eye; if he's right, then Chase County, born blind, now sees better than Argus.

The cup, *tock-tock-tock* as if again counting time, overflows, and I drink my Adam's ale and set the tin noggin back to catch a draft for my hot neck, and once more, *ting-ting-ting*. Years ago the citizens of Cottonwood Falls laboriously laid a four-mile-long cypress pipeline to tap water from a spring in the distant hills; I've drunk the cold sweetness from that western rock and eaten the watercress there, and I understand why they went to the trouble in that day when people attended to the tastes of water as the Irish do their stout. You can still see the cypress pipes here and there, but they are full of mud. The town drinks now from the not-so-sweet Cottonwood alluvium, a water so hard, a woman told me, that she *might as well wash with gravel.*

My cup fills, and the droplets, like a campfire, mesmerize me: the patter, the patter, the pattern, the pattern, slightly changing, the patter, the pattern. *Tick-tick-tick-tick.* I'm down in a hollow where a river begins, I'm between ledges where a source drips steady as if being long and slowly wrung, I'm between layers of rock and shale, they between gone seas; the wind carries in the rain, the water flushes along organic acids that eat the permeable stone back into liquid and send it again toward the far father sea; the solids come in and head out, just pausing; all around me are absorptions and percolations, everything soluble, the grasses sucking the mutable rock and transpiring, everything between forms of liquidity, and all things forms of liquidity: the harrier a feathered bag of nutrient waters falling onto the furred sack of sapid juices, thirsty for hot rodent blood it can turn into flight; and what was I but a guzzling, sweating bag of certain saps waiting to give up its moisture: press me dry, powdery dry, and you'd have a lump of mineralized soil, about enough to pot a geranium.

Tell me, O Swami of the Waters, in a word, what is the essence of life? Saith he, *Borrowed.*

By Way of Spelling Kansas

A couple of sentences of personal testimony (thoroughfare readers not happy on byways may proceed to the next chapter): I've carried one name for all of my life and another one for twelve years less than that, and I've come to see that while the two names attach to the same man from the epidermis out, on the inward side — the soupy side, my physician grandfather called it — the names point to men of different inclinations, dissimilar alignments, fellows of unlike silks whose souls are as chalk to cheese. One is a kind of dreamer who often darkly transmutes and even undoes the work of the more orderly man, the one who always squeezes the tube from the bottom, always wipes his shoes before entering. Actually, I believe there are more than this pair: when the Populist congressman "Sockless" Simpson of Medicine Lodge, Kansas, misspelled his hometown while running for office, he said, *I wouldn't give a tinker's durn for a man who can't spell a word more than one way.* I think I'm like that about interior selves.

Many tribal Americans believe that a person turns into his name, partakes of its nature in such a way that it is a mold the possessor comes to fill. When names lose their first meaning, as they have to most Americans of European descent, that mold becomes only a handle for others to move us around with. I think places also take on aspects of their names, at least if they touch something genuine to begin with. If you've never visited the twin towns of Chase County, I could give you a quick tour of each and then ask you to say which is which, and you would not call Cottonwood Falls

Strong City or vice versa. They have filled out their names, become them. A decade ago, before the big feedlot at Strong closed, that town filled out its name in an additional, olfactory way.

Imagine: I set before you two bouquets of prairie flowers, both pinky white. One dangles elegant blossoms like little trumpets while the other has only small, tightly clustered blooms that you must look at twice to notice. I ask you to guess which one is larkspur and which bastard toadflax. The names, appearances, and your responses converge: larkspur is the one of obvious beauty. But what if we go beyond appearances and I ask you to eat the fruit of one, to take of its essence, and I tell you that one is poisonous but the other used to be an Indian dessert? You must choose, and, while you do, read on.

Another question: in a word, freely associating, speak your response to the name Kansas. Now, what if the state carried one of the other labels linked with it: Quivira, Osage, Shawnee, Arapaho? Years back, someone proposed the territory be called Cherokee. Do these labels fit your response? On maps, Kansas has been Terra Incognita, Nuevo Mexico, Louisiana, Missouri Territory, Oregon Territory, Nebraska Territory, Indian Territory, Platte Country, and the Great American Desert, and its epithets have been Bleeding and Drouthy, and it's been the Grasshopper State and the New Garden of Eden. There's some historical accuracy in all of these but little in this one — Kansas — and the confusion from the misnomer shows even today when the people here insist on calling the Kansas River the Kaw while pronouncing the Arkansas River "Our Kansas." Ethnographers call the eponymous Indians the Kansa, and the native people now call themselves the Kaw.

For years my grandfather practiced medicine in Kansas City, Kansas, in the lower Kaw Valley — never the Kansas Valley — and he missed no chance to correct anyone who dropped a syllable and pronounced his town "Can City" (he also insisted that the double s in Missouri was a sibilant, as in Mississippi); but there is precedent for calling the city, state, river, and tribe Can. There's also precedent for calling them Canips, Ka-Anjou, Kamse, Kay, Konzo, Quans. Had history bent in a slightly different course, the professional football team on the Missouri side of the Big Muddy could have been the Chanchez City Chiefs. The possibilities increase when you include names whites have confused with the word Kansa: Accances, Arkansaw, Excanjaque, Okanis, Ukasa. To have adopted any of these dozen versions would have changed more things here than just maps and phone directories, because never can the image belonging to Karsa be the same as that of Kathagi or even Kunza.

In this territory, Coronado sought out the Guas (probably the Kaws), La Harpe visited the Canci, Bourgmont met the Ecanze, George Sibley traveled among the Konsee, and the Lewis and Clark expedition encountered the Kanzus (the most accurate spelling for our pronunciation) but they and their men spelled the word eleven other ways. That eminence of historical thought, Francis Parkman, on his map of the area identified the natives as Kanisse. None of these men spoke the language of the Kansa, a Siouan dialect, and today we are not sure any of the earliest explorers asked the people what they then called themselves, a different question from asking other tribes or whites what *they* called the Kansa.

I've come across 140 ways to spell Kansas, and, if you include the confused Ac-, Es-, Ex-, Ok-, Uk- forms at times applied to the tribe, I've found 171 variations that employ every letter of the alphabet except b, f, and v. The question comes up, if whites couldn't get a three- or six-letter name correct, what else couldn't they get right? The meaning of the word for one thing: Kansa and its forms have been translated as wind, windy, wind people, south wind people, those-who-come-like-wind-across-the-prairie, swift, swift wind, swift river, swift water, smoky water, fire people, plum people, disturbers, troublemakers, filthy, and cowards. Dispense with the freak translations like the last four, and you have a people defined by three of the four ancient elements.

Six full-blood Kansa, all men and all but one over sixty-five, are still living but none of them can speak more than a few words of the old language; they use almost exclusively the word Kaw for the tribe even though they know their parents called themselves *Kōn-say* (a spelling I've never seen except in my own notes); the n comes out almost as a w and the second syllable nearly disappears, so that you can imagine an illiterate French trapper believing he heard "Kaw." The first uncontested written reference to the tribe appears on Père Marquette's 1673 map where the word is Kansa. In nearly all of the 171 variants, one thing remains constant: a voiceless velar usually followed by a nasalized *ah*. Whatever butchering of this basic sound by whites, the Kansa seem to have accepted it, and one uppity Anglo said the people tolerated the word Kaw because they were so degraded, but I wonder how many Indians he thrashed for mispronouncing *his* name. Tact is a more plausible explanation for their tolerance.

The six surviving natives, most of whom live across the state line in Oklahoma near the last Kaw reservation, accept "People of the South Wind" or "Wind People" as the meaning of the name, even though that definition derives from a time long ago when the Kansa, with the Osage and several other now separate tribes, belonged to a bigger Siouan group living in the upper Ohio River Valley (some ethnologists believe those people were descendants of the ones who built or later used the great earthen mounds of that region); in the early sixteenth century, this larger tribe moved down the Ohio to the Mississippi and then up the Missouri, fragmenting as they migrated, until the Wind People arrived at the junction of the Kansas River with the Big Muddy.

Even before the great migration, the word Kansa referred to a gens whose totem was the wind; that the Kansa would one day give their name to a state famous for its winds is only a wonderful coincidence, although to me it goes beyond: in the Siouan family of languages, the Four Winds, the Great Mysterious, is commonly Wakan or Wakanda. Yet the everyday Kansa word for wind is quite different: *ta-dshe*, and the Osage form — the two peoples understand each other as a Kentuckian does a Cockney — is *ta-dse*. The Osage called the Kansa *Kan-the*; in my Osage dictionary (for the Kaw there are only a couple of old word lists), the term for swift is *kon-tha-gi*, plum is *kon-dse*, horse is *ka-wa*, and human being, a common translation of many tribes' names for themselves, is *ni-ka-shi-ga-ego* (*ni* means water or river).

I suppose, over the last four centuries, that this place called Kansas has come, like a murky chunk of softened glass, to fill the mold of its name, and I believe that today we see it through that now hardened form descended from unlettered explorers, careless map printers, and travelers and settlers who deemed red people worth no name but heathen. Had any white asked, we might have learned more about the name the Kansa may have once called themselves: Hutanga. We might also understand what it meant to them instead of having to rely on a twentieth-century Osage dictionary: "big fish" or "big water-dweller." Now, whatever links may have once existed between the word *hutanga* and the Kansa's most sacred object in historic times — a conch shell — are lost.

Given the erosions and eradications of history, I incline to Sockless Simpson's view: any people who can spell their homeplace only one way probably aren't worth a tinker's durn, and I append the 140 variations of the name for the Wind People as homage to their richness:

Cah	Cau	Kansais	Kathagi
Can	Caugh	Kansars	Kau
Cancas	Causa	Kansas	Kaus
Cance	Cauzes	Kansaws	Kausa
Canceas	Caw	Kanse	Kausas
Cances	Caws	Kansea	Kausau
Canceys	Chanchez	Kansees	Kausaus
Cancez	Chanzes	Kanseis	Kauzas
Canceze	Chonsa	Kansers	Kauzau
Cancezs	Consa	Kanses	Kauzaus
Canchaz	Consez	Kansez	Kaw
Canchez	Conzas	Kansias	Kaws
Canci	Ecanze	Kansies	Kawsa
Cancis	Guaes	Kansis	Kawse
Canes	Guas	Kanson	Kawsies
Canips	Ka	Kansus	Kawza
Cannecis	Kaal	Kantha	Kay
Cannes	Ka-Anjou	Kants	Kemissi
Cans	Ka-Anzou	Kanza	Kensier
Cansa	Kah	Kanzan	Kenzia
Cansan	Kahsah	Kanzans	Konaz
Cansas	Kamissi	Kanzas	Konsa
Cansé	Kamse	Kanze	Konsans
Canses	Kan	Kanzeis	Konsee
Cansez	Kançake	Kanzes	Konsees
Canssa	Kanças	Kanzez	Konses
Canza	Kance	Kanzis	Konsez
Canzan	Kances	Kanzon	Konthe
Canzas	Kancez	Kanzus	Konza
Canze	Kanees	Kaos	Konzas
Canzee	Kanisse	Karsa	Konzo
Canzes	Kanissi	Karsea	Kunza
Canzez	Kans	Kas	Quans
Canzon	Kansa	Kasas	Quaus
Caso	Kansae	Kase	Quonzai

And the flowers — your answer? If you chose to eat the bastard toadflax, have another helping. If you chose for euphony and ate larkspur, you're going to need an emetic of pokeweed root. Bastard toadflax by any other name would be sweeter, and so would our perception of it.

On the Town: The Emma Chase

Broadway, west side, a storefront window, and painted on the plate glass a cup of steaming coffee, morning, Cottonwood Falls, the Emma Chase Café, November 1984: I'm inside and finishing a fine western omelet and in a moment will take on the planks of home-made wheat-bread — just as soon as the shadow from the window coffee cup passes across my little notebook. The men's table (a bold woman sometimes sits at it, but rare is the man who sits at the women's table) has already emptied, and now the other one too. On the west wall hangs a portrait of a woman from the time of Ruther-ford B. Hayes, and she, her hair parted centrally, turns a bit to the left as if to answer someone in the street, her high collar crisp, her eyebrow ever so slightly raised, her lips pursed as if she's about to speak. (Someone calls out from the kitchen to the new waitress, *On your ticket, what's this U.P.?* and the girl says, *Up*, and from the kitchen, *You can't have scrambled eggs up.*) The portrait is of *the woman history forgot*, Emma Chase, who said, *You can't start a revolution on an empty stomach.* She was not wife, daughter, sister, or mother of Salmon P. Chase, the great enemy of slavery and Lin-coln's chief justice, whose name the county carries. Emma stands in no man's shadow but in the dark recess that the past mostly is. In this county, she's famous for having been forgotten; after all, who remembers it was on the back of one of Emma's envelopes that Lincoln outlined his Emancipation Proclamation? That's been the story in the Falls, anyway.

Most countians now understand that Emma "A-Cookie-in-Every-Jar" Chase has the reality of an idea and an ideal. When Linda Pretzer Thurston decided to open the café a couple of years ago, she cast about for a name, something local, something feminine, and she searched the volumes of the *Chase County Historical Sketches* for an embodiment of certain values but came away unsatisfied by or unaware of the facts, such as those of 1889 about Minnie Morgan of Cottonwood, one of the first women in the county elected mayor and *the* first — and probably the only one — to serve with an all-female city council. Minnie has stood in a few dark historical corridors herself: her daughter's biography of the family in the *Historical Sketches* speaks of wild plums and a neighbor who threw her family's clothes down the cistern to save them from a prairie fire, and it mentions her father's founding of the county newspaper the *Leader,* but it says not one word about Minnie's mayoralty or her advocacy of woman suffrage. There has not been a female mayor since.

So, the café had no name until one night at the family supper table Linda and her identical twin said simultaneously in response to something she's now forgotten, *The Emma Chase!* Soon, newspaper ads for the café printed Emma's chocolate chip cookie recipe, and they asked townspeople to search their attic trunks for information about her. One day Whitt Laughridge came in with a large, framed portrait of an unidentified woman he'd found in the historical society vault. Thurston said, *Yes! At last we've got Emma!* Unsatisfied with history, she had invented a persona and then had to invent ways to get people to accept the name. Her ads and fabricated history worked so well that she, who grew up five miles west in Elmdale, *she* became to the citizens *Emma down at the café,* and she doesn't mind.

There are other things she does object to, such as the racist joke a fellow told a while ago at the men's table and to which she said loudly from across the room, *Did you hear that one at church, Ray?* and sometimes to sexist comments she'll recite from the café refrigerator, covered with stick-on slogans like a large, upright bumper: THE ROOSTER CROWS BUT THE HEN DELIVERS or WOMEN'S RIGHTS — REAGAN'S WRONGS.

Linda Thurston is trim and pretty, a dark strawberry blonde given to large, swinging earrings; today she wears a pair of silvery stars almost of a size to be hoisted atop the courthouse cupola for Christmas. She sits down across from me to see what I'm scratching in my notebook. Now I'm copying what is on her coffee mug:

I HAVE A B.A., M.A., PH.D.
ALL I NEED NOW IS A GOOD J.O.B.

Her doctorate is in child psychology, she is thirty-nine, divorced, and has a son, John. She calls across the little café to the new waitress, *We can't do scrambled eggs over easy.*

We talk, and then she brings the guest book to me. In it are names from many states and also from Russia, Italy, Israel, and she says, *My friends say I'm the white Aunt Jemima of the women's movement, a radicalized, storefront feminist whose job is to get cowboys to eat quiche Lorraine even if they call it quick lorn. I'm an aproned militant known for scratch pies, soups, and breads, the one who's taught a waitress Lamaze-breathing on a café floor.*

A man, his spine crumbling with age, his eyesight almost gone, comes up and holds out a palm of change for his coffee, and Linda takes out thirty-five cents, forget the tax.

Three years ago she and her young son lived near Kansas City, Kansas, where she worked with battered women and handicapped children, some of whose fathers couldn't remember their child's name; they all were poor city people who lived anonymously. She was also president of a large chapter of the National Organization for Women, and she campaigned and typed and marched. When Ronald Reagan became president and inner-city social programs started disappearing, she found herself depressed and beginning to wonder who the enemy was, where the battlefield was, and she didn't understand why ideas so apparently democratic and humane were so despised and thwarted, and she was no longer sure what it meant to help the disadvantaged or to be a feminist. Women seemed in retreat from action to the easier, safer battles of awareness. Things were retrogressing.

On a trip home to Elmdale she learned that the old and closed Village Inn Café was for sale, and she looked it over, found a broken-down and fouled building, and, suddenly, a fight against dirt and dilapidation, enemies you could lay your rubber-gloved hands on, looked good, especially when she heard the county-seat citizens wanted a pleasant place once again to sit down with a coffee and find out whose cattle it was that went through the ice, whose horse had sent him over the fence. A group of Broadway businesspeople met in Bell's western clothing store and offered to buy the café building and lease it to her until she could pay for it — after all, she was a native — and so Linda Thurston decided to live out her fantasy of running a little homey restaurant, and she moved back to

Chase County, where, she hoped, *the Hills could heal.* Her friend Linda Woody, a state lobbyist for NOW, had also wearied of the struggle against Reaganism, and joined her, and the once dingy, moribund café became unofficially the Retreat for Burned-Out Social Activists, a place where the women could serve homilies, history, and cold pasta salad.

Linda Thurston says: *I saw it as a haven of rest from political struggles, a place I'd have time to write up my research. If we could undermine a few stereotypes along the way and wake up a few people, that was fine too. I've never seen my return as going home so much as going forward to my roots, but I don't think I'll stay long enough to grow old here — unless I already have. I believe when the time comes to go back to whatever, I'll know where that is. I've learned you can go home again, but I don't know whether you can stay home again.*

Refurbishing the café became a community task: the seventy-eight-year-old furniture dealer power-sanded the chipped floor, the clothier painted, a drywaller showed the women how to mud plasterboard. They came to love the exhaustion of such work. Then they got to the Wolf stove, which yielded its encrusted grease to no woman, man, or method from scrapers to torches. One day two fellows came in with an idea: they dismantled the range, put it in the back of a pickup, hauled it to the county highway yard, turned a steam hose on it, and reassembled it into the beauty of new sculpture, and someone happily wrote on the blackboard Thurston had set up to list possible names for the place: the Clean Stove Café. Also on the board were the Double L, the Quarthouse, and Soup and Psychological Services, this last already beginning to have some meaning.

The women did not flaunt their politics, and the town was enough impressed with their hard work to ignore their ERA NOW! bumper stickers, and strollers stopped in to watch the work or help out or just pour themselves a cup of free coffee. After six weeks of reconstruction, the women papered over the street windows to create suspense for the opening a couple of days later while they completed last details. In a county where beef stands second only to Christianity, where gravy and chicken-fried steak are the bases from which all culinary judgments proceed, the women offered eggplant parmigiana, linguine with clams, gazpacho, fettuccine Alfredo — and chicken-fried steak. Business was excellent, and the first day they sold out of pasta primavera, and the women were certain they could keep their pledge never to serve french fries or factory white bread. All their eggs came from Chase farms; on weekends, in season, they prepared calf fries fresh from county pastures (and tolerated jokes attendant to feminists grilling ballocks), and they catered meals to businessmen in lodge meetings and ranch hands at corrals.

Linda says to me: *Scratch cooking all the way. The highest compliment is a woman saying, "This is as good as I make at home." But the men bitched all the time about no french fries or white bread so we gave in and cut our own fry potatoes and baked our own white bread, but, still today, if you want a grilled cheese between a couple of slices of Rainbo, you'll just have to go someplace else. That's the only little thing we haven't compromised on.*

We've never changed our deeper values because we refuse to divorce being café owners from our feminism. We're tolerated for it and sometimes we're defined by it: I heard a man ask his friend what a crêpe was and why something like that would even be on the menu, and the waitress told him, "They're for the ERA." And that's right. We employ only women, and we try to bring to them what we've learned. In the first days of the café, a wealthy lady told me there were no battered women in the county, and she believed that, but she's been misled — the problem is just buried. Not long ago at the health fair in the school gym we sponsored a display about services for abused women and children, and we found out later that some people were afraid to stand in front of it because a neighbor might think they were abused. And one day a woman said to me, she was holding back tears, "You ought to get out of here — the longer you stay, the worse you'll feel about yourself as a woman." Maybe that's a minority view, but it's valid. The other side is that people here are still close to their pioneer ancestors, and they all can tell stories about strong and capable grandmothers. For a long time women have owned businesses in the county, so we're accepted, but then the café isn't a hardware store or a transmission shop.

The young waitress has just given a single check to a man sitting with two women, and Linda explains to her to give each person one, and she says, *Don't assume the male always pays,* and to me, *Separate checks also protect privacy — people watch and read something into who picks up the tab.* I ask whether lack of privacy isn't the worst thing about a small town, and she says, *And also the best. I love going to the post office in the morning and knowing everybody. The only time we honk a car horn is with a wave. It's touching when somebody asks about my son or my dad's health. We can't afford not to care about other people in a place this small. Our survival, in a way, depends on minimizing privacy because the lack of it draws us into each other's lives, and that's a major resource in a little town where there aren't a thousand entertainments. There's an elderly man who lost his little granddaughter to a drunk, a hit-and-run driver, a few months ago. Every time the old gentleman comes into the Emma Chase, he retells the story, and every time people listen. What's that worth to a person? Or to a community? A café like this serves to bond us.*

I'm scribbling things down, and she watches and says, *Growing up in this county I learned not to ask questions. If people want you to know something, they'll tell you.* I say that I must be a popular fellow, what with a question mark in every sentence, and she says, *You don't count. You don't live here. Besides, the word is out that you're in the county. You'll be tolerated even if they do think you're about a half bubble off plumb.* She watches me write that down, and she says, *We can't afford to ostracize each other just because we don't like this one's politics or the way that one raises her kids. You can get away with it in a city — picking and choosing — but here we're already picked. Participation by everybody discourages change, and the radical gets cut off. But if we give aberrant behavior a wide berth we don't usually reject it completely. Every merchant on Broadway can tell a story about some petty shoplifter whose pilfering has been ignored to avoid a bigger problem. For an outsider it's different: if you — yourself — would espouse something terribly unpopular like government ownership of land they'll just question your sanity, but pocket a candy bar and they'll have you arrested. If I do either one, it would be just the reverse. We have limits, of course. The first and most powerful enforcement is gossip and scorn. They're the sap and sinew of a small town.*

When she gets up to ready the kitchen for lunch, I ask whether she or the Emma Chase has ever been scorned, and she says, *You'd be more likely to hear that than I would.*

Now, late afternoon, October 1988: the painted coffee cup still steams on the window, and stalwart Emma Chase looks over the stacked chairs and onto Broadway, and the dank odor of an old and unused building slips between the locked twin doors. The café has been closed for nearly a year, and there's nothing more than a hope of somebody reopening it, although everyone is tired of coffee in Styrofoam cups and factory cookies in the Senior Citizens' Center a few doors down. Linda Woody has gone to Washington as a NOW lobbyist, and Linda Thurston is sixty miles up the road at Kansas State University, an assistant professor in rural special education. The café is for sale, and she's asking eight thousand dollars less than she paid for it, in spite of its becoming known as one of the best small-town eateries in the state, in spite of a Kansas Citian's offer to underwrite the franchising of Emma Chase cafés.

I've just returned from lunch with her in the student union, where she said, *Standing in front of that big Wolf stove I kept remembering my degree and how useless it was becoming with every fried egg. I'm forty-three, and I'm ten years behind my colleagues. I worked long hours at the café, and my feet hurt all the time, and I got arthritis in my hands, and finally I realized I didn't want to work that hard day after day and still not earn enough money to send my son to college. Every other businessperson on Broadway has at least one additional source of income — the furniture dealer runs a funeral parlor, the owners of the two dress shops have their husbands' incomes, the filling station man has another in Strong City. The Emma Chase would support one frugal person, but it wouldn't even do that without weekend city people. Tourists coming to see the Hills, bicycle clubs — they kept us alive after we earned a name around the state by being special. But there were local folks who never came in, and I'd ask them what it would take to get them inside, and they'd say, "We let the kids decide where we're going to eat out, and they choose McDonald's." How does a box of toys in the Emma Chase compete against television commercials? And there's something else: good home-cooking is common in the county. Franchise food is the novelty, especially when it's twenty miles away. What our café offered, city people wanted, but they also wanted clean floors, and the cowboys were afraid to come in and get the floor dirty.*

I asked, was it a loss, and she said, *I lost some money and something professionally because I never found time to write, but I realized my fantasy, and I was at home for the last two years of my father's life. And I got to live again according to the dictates of rainfall and the price of cattle and grain and the outbreaks of chicken pox. I was part of a community rebuilding its café, and working with those helpers let me see men again as people instead of the enemy. It meant something for my son to go to school with children of neighbors I went to school with. And — I think I can say this — because of the café, I see my femaleness differently: now I think feminism means being connected with other people, not just with other feminists.*

She was quiet for some time, and then she said, *There were losses, no question, but there was only one real failure: we never did get the farmers to eat alfalfa sprouts. They know silage when they see it. Maybe we should have tried it with gravy.*

IV
Fox Creek

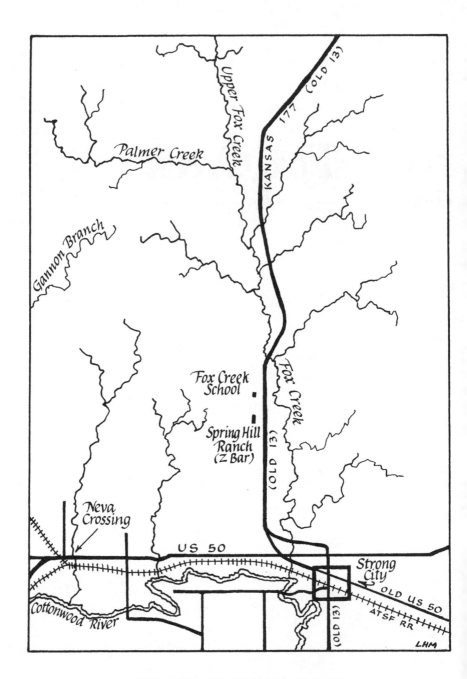

FOX CREEK QUADRANGLE

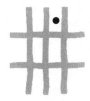

From the Commonplace Book: Fox Creek

The charge has been persistently made that John Brown and his men wantonly and fiendishly mutilated the dead bodies of the persons killed [near Osawatomie]. This charge has been made by the bitter personal enemies of Brown. It will be remembered that the men were killed with short, heavy swords at night. The victims evidently tried to ward off the blows with their hands and arms, and as they were wholly unprotected, the swords severed fingers, hands, and possibly arms. No blow was struck after death came to the misguided men. This is expressly stated by [Brown's cohort James] Townsley. In some of the works prepared for the purpose of defaming the memory of John Brown, the last statement of Townsley is published at length, but that portion of it which says the bodies were not intentionally mutilated and were not struck after death, is omitted, as is also that portion saying that the killing was a benefit to the Free-State cause.

— William E. Connelley,
John Brown (1900)

In face and form [Salmon] Chase was a model for president of the United States. Six feet in height, broad-shouldered and well built, with a finely shaped head, a handsome face, and a courtly manner, he looked a leader of men. And fine qualities were behind this imposing front. Methodical, hard-working, and efficient, he quickly rose to prominence. . . . But if the years brought a considerable measure of achievement, they also disclosed defects of mind and character. As Chase rose to prominence a certainty of opinion, a touch of pomposity, *and a tendency to sanctimonious smugness became more and more pronounced. When confronted by the necessity of making great decisions he sometimes showed a distressing tendency to straddle. He lacked a sense of humor, and he lacked charisma. Despite his desire to serve his country and mankind, he had no appeal to the hearts of men.*

— Glyndon G. Van Deusen,
Encyclopedia of American Biography
(1974)

Chase is about one-and-a-half times bigger than any other man I ever knew.

— Abraham Lincoln,
A remark (1863)

Reading [Chase's] diaries we find how he chided himself on his sinfulness; how at times he declined communion from self-distrust; how he was equally disturbed if at other times his unworthiness failed to oppress him; how he repeated psalms while bathing or dressing.

— James Garfield Randall,
Dictionary of American Biography
(1929)

And upon this act, sincerely believed to be an act of justice, warranted by the Constitution upon military necessity, I invoke the considerate judgment of mankind and the gracious favor of almighty God.

— Salmon Portland Chase,
The Emancipation Proclamation
(1862)

The Democracy is not democratic enough yet.

— Salmon Portland Chase,
Chase Papers, Library of Congress
(1868)

The underlying idea of [Chase's] public life was to bring the law up to the moral standards of the country, and to make both moral standards and law apply to black men as well as to white men.

— Albert Bushnell Hart,
Salmon Portland Chase (1899)

"Yer see, Andy, its bobservation *makes all de difference in niggers. Didn't I see which way the wind blew dis yer mornin'? Didn't I see*

what Missis wanted, though she never let on! Dat ar's bobservation,
Andy. I 'spects it's what you may call a faculty. Faculties is different
in different peoples, but cultivation of 'em goes a great way."

> — Harriet Beecher Stowe,
> *Uncle Tom's Cabin* (1851)

Charles Aldrich, the first colored man to come to Chase County . . .
was of the type of the old southern Negro slave. He was always polite
and respectful in his manner and retiring in his disposition. . . .
Charley [arrived in] Cottonwood Falls in 1866 and spent almost all
of the rest of his life at this place. He was for many years in the service
of J. W. McWilliams as stable boy, houseman, valet, and general chore
boy. It was often said of him that he was as faithful to his master as
was Mr. McWilliams' dog, which was a real tribute.

> — Obituary,
> *Chase County Leader* (1923)

Most residents spend their lives without ever being affected by a
tornado — or ever observing one.

> — F. C. Bates,
> "Tornadoes in the Central
> United States" (1962)

[The Coyote to the Young Indian Hunter:] Whenever you take a
beast's body, give something in return. How can a man expect much
without paying something! If you do not give creatures the where-
withal of changing being, how can you expect them to relish your
arrows! So, whenever you slay a game creature, offer him and his like
prayer-plumes — then they will feed you with their own flesh and
clothe you with their own skins.

> — F. H. Cushing,
> *Zuñi Breadstuff* (1920)

The [coyote or prairie] wolf is no moralist, only a committee of ways
and means to get what himself wants.

This wolf bark is like the laughter of a child maniac, repetitional,
meaningless, remorseless, a laughter without joy in or behind it. The
cry is a wandering voice of the prairie levels; disappearing and reap-
pearing among the billows of a rolling prairie, but is mirthless, insistent, uncanny.

The wolf is careless of any man; and his lope, than which nothing could be less routine or more care-free, less stilted, less an acquisition, or more an extemporaneous procedure, is the heedlessness of the prairies, the needlessness of wings, the playing with the ground as if it were a jest, with waggish head thrown over the shoulder as to insult your laggard speed. The wolf-leap is the prairie in cruel motion, not creeping like feline hypocrisy, but the vagabond swing of a wild, elastic delight in the unfenced wonder of the prairie. The wolf is a prairie child.

— William A. Quayle,
The Prairie and the Sea (1905)

The prairie wolf . . . is a sneaking, cowardly, little wretch, of a dull or dirty white color, much resembling a small, short-bodied dog set up on pretty long legs. . . . His usual provender is the carcass — no matter how putrid — of any dead buffalo, mule, or ox that he may find exposed on the prairies. He is a paltry creature.

— Horace Greeley,
An Overland Journey (1859)

The coyote is a long, slim, sick and sorry-looking skeleton, with a gray wolfskin stretched over it, a tolerably bushy tail that forever sags down with a despairing expression of forsakenness and misery, a furtive and evil eye, and a long, sharp face, with slightly lifted lip and exposed teeth. He has a general slinking expression all over. The coyote is a living, breathing allegory of Want. He is always hungry. He is always poor, out of luck, and friendless. The meanest creatures despise him, and even the fleas would desert him for a velocipede. He is so spiritless and cowardly that even while his exposed teeth are pretending a threat, the rest of his face is apologizing for it. And he is so homely! — so scrawny, and ribby, and coarse-haired, and pitiful. When he sees you he lifts his lip and lets a flash of his teeth out, and then turns a little out of the course he was pursuing, depresses his head a bit, and strikes a long, soft-footed trot through the sagebrush, glancing over his shoulder at you from time to time, till he is about out of easy pistol range, and then he stops and takes a deliberate survey of you; he will trot fifty yards and stop again — another fifty and stop again; and finally the gray of his gliding body blends with the gray of the sagebrush, and he disappears. All this is when you make no demonstration against him; but if you do, he develops a livelier interest in his journey, and instantly electrifies his heels and puts such a deal of real estate between himself and your weapon that by the time you have raised the hammer you see that you need a Minié rifle, and by the time you have got him in line you need a rifled cannon, and by the time you have "drawn a bead" on him you see well enough that nothing but an unusually long-winded streak of lightning could reach him where he is now.

But if you start a swift-footed dog after him, you will enjoy it ever so much — especially if it is a dog that has a good opinion of himself, and has been brought up to think he knows something about speed. The coyote will go swinging gently off on that deceitful trot of his, and every little while he will smile a fraudful smile over his shoulder that will fill that dog entirely full of encouragement and worldly ambition, and make him lay his head still lower to the ground, and stretch his neck further to the front, and pant more fiercely, and stick his tail out straighter behind, and move his furious legs with a yet wilder frenzy, and leave a broader and broader, and higher and higher and denser cloud of desert sand smoking behind, and marking his long wake across the level plain! And all this time the dog is only a short twenty feet behind the coyote, and to save the soul of him he cannot understand why it is that he cannot get perceptibly closer; and he begins to get aggravated, and it makes him madder and madder to see how gently the coyote glides along and never pants or sweats or ceases to smile; and he grows still more and more incensed to see how shamefully he has been taken in by an entire stranger, and what an ignoble swindle that long, calm, soft-footed trot is; and next he notices that he is getting fagged, and that the coyote actually has to slacken speed a little to keep from running away from him — and then that town dog is mad in earnest, and he begins to strain and weep and swear, and paw the sand higher than ever, and reach for the coyote with concentrated and desperate energy. This "spurt" finds him six feet behind the gliding enemy, and two miles from his friends. And then, in the instant that a wild new hope is lighting up his face, the coyote turns and smiles blandly upon him once more, and with a something about it which seems to say: "Well, I shall have to tear myself away from you, bub — business is business, and it will not do for me to be fooling along this way all day" — and forthwith there is a rushing sound, and the sudden splitting of a long crack through the atmosphere, and behold that dog is solitary and alone in the midst of a vast solitude!

— Mark Twain,
Roughing It (1871)

[The coyote] is a brute which is entitled to respect from his very persistence in knavery. Contemptible in person and countless numbers, he forages fatness from things despised of all others. [He is] the *figurehead, the feature, the representative of the broad and silent country of which he comes more nearly being master than any other.*

— James W. Steele,
  The Sons of the Border (1873)

The ugly, repulsive, sneaky coyote skulks in force, filling the night with frightful howls. Chilling. Yet hunters and trappers welcome the howls: when they stop, watch out for Indians!

— Ernst von Hesse-Wartegg,
  "Across Kansas by Train" (1877)

The stomach from one [coyote] taken on the Fort Riley hunt in 1948 contained sixteen meadow mice. . . . A low [mice] population of twenty per acre on a hundred-acre meadow or pasture will consume twenty-two tons of grass or eleven tons of cured hay each year. . . . The percentage of coyotes that have ever raided a chicken yard in Kansas has never been great and the number that have killed a sheep or a calf has been extremely limited.

— Otto W. Tiemeier,
  "Winter Foods of Kansas Coyotes"
  (1955)

As a scavenger of dead animals, the livestock industry may receive protection through reduced exposure to contagious diseases and parasites. Considering the economic benefits coyotes provide to the agricultural industries, improved management of [coyote] populations may be indicated.

— John B. Mulder,
  "Food Selection by Wild-Caught
  Captive Coyotes" (1979)

God sleeps in minerals, awakens in plants, walks in animals, and thinks in man.

— Sanskrit apothegm
  (c. fourth century B.C.)

It would imply the regeneration of mankind if they were to become elevated enough to truly worship stocks and stones.

If he who makes two blades of grass grow where one grew before is a benefactor, he who discovers two gods where there was only known the one before is a still greater benefactor. I would fain improve every opportunity to wonder and worship.

> — Henry David Thoreau,
> *The Journal* (1856)

Was there ever a time when these immense masses of calcareous matter were thrown into fermentation by some adventitious moisture; were raised and leavened into such shapes by some plastic power; and so made to swell and heave their broad backs into the sky so much above the less animated clay of the wild below?

> — Gilbert White,
> *The Natural History and Antiquities of Selborne* (1773)

The sublunary world is divided for the alchemist into three kingdoms: the mineral kingdom, the vegetable kingdom, and the animal kingdom. . . . The rhythm of the animal kingdom is that of everyday existence. The rhythm of the mineral kingdom is that of the ages, of life calculated in millennia. As soon as we contemplate the thousands of years of existence for minerals, cosmic dreams come to us.

> — Gaston Bachelard,
> *La Terre et les Rêveries de la Volonté* (1948)

It is the mysterious power possessed by stone, the manner in which it linked the cosmic order with our own inner search for order, that accounts in large part for its architectural importance.

Stones, gems, to be understood, must be dreamt about, and whereas the flexibility and adaptability of wood allows us to use it without understanding its basic nature, stone demands that we think of origins.

> — J. B. Jackson,
> "Stone and Its Substitutes" (1984)

Why not look "into" the earth?

> — Gretel Ehrlich,
> "Landscape," introduction to *Legacy of Light* (1987)

What are the natural features which make a township handsome? A river, with its waterfalls and meadows, a lake, a hill, a cliff or individual rocks, a forest, and ancient trees standing singly. Such things are beautiful; they have a high use which dollars and cents never represent. If the inhabitants of a town were wise, they would seek to preserve these things, though at a considerable expense; for such things educate far more than any hired teachers or preachers, or any at present recognized system of school education. I do not think him fit to be the founder of a state or even of a town who does not foresee the use of these things, but legislates chiefly for oxen, as it were.

If we have the largest boulder in the county, then it should not belong to an individual, nor be made into door-steps.

We cut down the few old oaks which witnessed the transfer of the township from the Indians to the white man, and commence our museums with a cartridge-box taken from a British soldier in 1775.

> — Henry David Thoreau,
> *The Journal* (1861)

Mobility and change are the key to the vernacular landscape, but of an involuntary, reluctant sort; not the expression of restlessness and search for improvement but an enduring patient adjustment to circumstances. Far too often these are the arbitrary decisions of those in power, but natural conditions play their part and so do ignorance and a blind loyalty to local ways, and so does the absence of long-range objectives: the absence of what we would call a sense of future history.

> — J. B. Jackson,
> "Concluding with Landscapes" (1984)

With every great idea comes a gaggle of mediocre minds who oppose it. It was so with the creation of virtually every national park in the United States, from Yellowstone to Yosemite, from Kobuk Valley to the Everglades.

> — Kim Heacox,
> "A Poet, a Painter, and the Lonesome
> Triangle" (1990)

We are creatures of endless and detailed curiosity. We are not sufficiently enlightened by abstractions devoid of flesh and bones, idiosyn-

crasies and curiosities. . . . We revel in the details of history, because
they are the source of our being.

> — Stephen Jay Gould,
> "George Canning's Left Buttock and
> the Origin of Species" (1989)

This fascination with the quotidian is one of the habits for which
biographers are regularly chided by critics, who, craving plot and
dramatic tension, dismiss the daily as mere besotted inclusiveness.

> — B. L. Reid,
> *Necessary Lives* (1990)

A close examination of any object is a graphic description of the level
of intelligence, manual dexterity, and artistic comprehension of the
civilization that produced it.

> — Richard Latham,
> "The Artifact as a Cultural Cipher"
> (1964)

The least the historian can do with any historical fact is to select and
affirm it. To select and affirm even the simplest complex of facts is to
give them a certain place in a certain pattern of ideas, and this alone
is sufficient to give them a special meaning.

> — Carl Becker,
> "Everyman His Own Historian" (1932)

The commonplace is the thing, but it's hard to find.

> — Andrew Wyeth,
> *The Helga Pictures* (1987)

The passion for inheritance is dead.

[Today] knowledge — saturated in historical memory — is displaced
by information, or memory without history: data.

> — Cynthia Ozick,
> "T. S. Eliot at 101" (1989)

In the Quadrangle:
Fox Creek

If you've ever put an ax to a black-walnut log, you know how the wood splits suddenly, seems to leap apart as if looking for release, and you know how the cleaving follows a gentle and slight humping away from the perfectly straight so that there's only a decurving regularity. Fox Creek divides this quadrangle into east and west rather evenly, with only the easy deviations that you find in split walnut, a tree common in these vales. State route 177, paralleling here the old Kaw Trail, follows the stream from the north county line, near where the Indian agency once stood, to where the highway crosses U.S. 50 at Strong City a mile and a half from the bottom of the quadrangle, which the Cottonwood River demarks. Other than 177, the roads lie along the river valley and leave the hills above Fox Creek a place of a few ranch trails and lone slopes of prairie chickens and coyotes: you can walk farther in a cardinal direction without encountering a road here than any other place in the county. And north of the Cottonwood, even on a stormy Tuesday night, you'd likely find more people along the quiet highway than in the few Fox Creek homes, all of them solitary ranches. On the fifty-some square miles above the river, only a couple of dozen people live, yet several of the most notable ranches lie along the creek and its tributaries, and chief among them is the Z Bar, now the center of another land-use fight. North a half mile, on a hill above the highway and in splendid isolation, as if it were some old aerial cargo that had slipped its restraints and fallen onto the blankness, is Fox Creek School, a one-room, cut-limestone building of

1882, the bell tower set so cleanly against the sky and the silhouette so archetypically native that it has become an emblem of prairie America. Its quintessential shape and location have even made travelers think it a reproduction: you've seen it in your imagination.

The first white man to build a dwelling in the county — Seth Hays, trader to Indians and outfitter to the Santa Fe Trail — sent a Kaw down from Council Grove along Diamond Creek in 1854 to find some good winter pasture for his trail oxen; the Kaw found it just below the junction of the creek with the Cottonwood near a ford long used by Indians. This first improvement (so the citizens call farm structures) was the cabin of Hays' overseer; today, what remains is but a nearly imperceptible hump in a bottom bean field just southeast of where the Superior branch of the Santa Fe line intersects highway 50, a junction called Neva Crossing. In 1937, George Washington Starkey, the farmer and antiquarian of whom I've spoken, numbered the worn logs, dismantled and hauled them to the park in the Falls, and reassembled the sixteen-by-sixteen-foot cabin. In time it fell into disrepair, and some citizens took it down and piled it by the rail line to await money for restoration; but a track fire got it first (I've heard that members of the city council, finding the thing more an eyesore than the oldest building in the county, set the blaze, but I don't believe it).

When Seth Hays, great-grandson of Daniel Boone, ran his cattle station here, Chase was part of a now nonexistent county named after Henry Alexander Wise, the dueling, cursing, slaveholding governor of Virginia who closed his term in 1859 by hanging John Brown at the very time Lincoln was campaigning in Kansas. As sectional unrest moved across the eastern part of the state, counties named by the pro-slavery "Bogus Legislature" (its statutes were later fired out of a cannon into the Missouri River) began shedding place names associated with the southern cause. Although Brown was at his fanatical bloodiest in Kansas, where he supervised the hacking to death of five pro-slavery settlers seventy-five miles east of here, he was, and to some extent still is, an honored figure in the state for his unyielding attempts to provoke emancipation. To local abolitionists like Samuel Newitt Wood, a settler and lawyer from Ohio who printed the first newspaper here in 1859 under a cottonwood tree near the falls, the Virginia governor's action constituted defamation of a grand cause; that year, through the work of Wood, the southern half of Wise County joined with a northern piece of Butler County to become Chase County.

A distant relation by marriage of Wood, Salmon Portland Chase,

Lincoln's frequent rival as well as his secretary of the treasury (and, later, chief justice), began his career in Cincinnati. He was an ardent supporter of Kansas Free Soilers, a lawyer who defended so many fugitive slaves that opponents called him *the attorney-general for runaway negroes.* He was counsel to John Van Zandt, the original of Kentuckian John Van Trompe in *Uncle Tom's Cabin*, the whilom slaveholder who frees his blacks, buys land for them in Ohio and then turns his farm into a stop on the underground railroad, sits back on his porch, and enjoys his conscience. In a confrontation made coincidentally peculiar by the county names, it was Governor Salmon Chase who responded to Henry Wise when the Virginian threatened to invade Ohio to thwart purported attempts to break John Brown out of jail after his raid on Harpers Ferry. And it was Chase, despite his belief that the Emancipation Proclamation was too weak, who wrote the last paragraph of it, the one calling for men to judge the action. He was such a vigorous and eminent opponent of slavery (later a proponent of Negro suffrage) that anti-Lincoln groups put him forward for president. As chief justice presiding over the court of impeachment of Andrew Johnson, Chase probably saved the president by insisting on proper judicial procedure. He helped preserve the Union through his intelligent work as secretary of the treasury, and he originated the national banking system, organized what is now the Bureau of Engraving and Printing to help finance the Civil War, and it was he who modified a phrase from the fourth stanza of Francis Scott Key's poem "The Star-Spangled Banner" and put it on American coins: "In God We Trust." A friend named the Chase National Bank, now the Chase Manhattan and the second largest in the country, after him. Yet the legacy of Salmon Chase has no more popular currency here today — not even in the historical society — than the ten thousand dollar bill bearing his portrait. In a county he never saw, that ignorance is sad, since it's the only one in the nation named for him.

It was along Fox Creek, a decade after the Civil War, that Sam Wood's daughter-in-law, Zilphia (a descendant of Roger Williams), one morning heard a scratching on her cabin door. She looked through a chink in the logs to see a Kaw warrior called White Eyes, a man she knew the army was offering a reward for. Food, especially meat, was so scarce she had nothing to share. Although she was alone, she was afraid *not* to open the door. White Eyes asked to "borrow" a knife, and she handed over her biggest one and stepped back. He looked at it, rubbed a finger against the dull edge, looked at her, said nothing, and left. Some weeks later, hearing a thump outside, she frantically figured what to do, but there was no place to hide. She unlatched the door but something heavy lay against it. The small woman leaned into it, the door slowly opening, until she saw blood on the threshold. Cautiously, she peeked out, and there lay a freshly killed deer, and thrust in it was her sharpened butcher knife.

A few mornings ago, not far from where Zilphia Wood lived, I found along the road a slender cottonwood sapling that a highway crew had slashed back and forced into an elbow, and I cut and trimmed it into a walking stick. For months I'd been hunting the right shape and dimension of cottonwood, that tree of life the Plains Indians made into sacred staffs. I stepped off a few paces to test the stick in the hills, and it felt so right in the hand, swung forward so truly, and so pleasingly balanced me like an outrigger that I kept walking until I ended up down along Fox Creek, where much prairie life exists narrowly in the bottoms. Things lay still and silent: had the rocky plates of the earth's surface shifted a millimeter, I'd have heard the grinding. Then a fulvous shadow moved toward the stream, and I froze and waited expectantly to see my first fox in the county, and I thought how fine it was that even yet the truth of a name could linger on. Then a bronze shape emerged, a coyote slipping from the brush to drink. There was no fox. (A few days afterward, I learned the creek carries not the name of an animal but of an early settler, Edward Fox, who stayed here only two years.) I sat down, disappointed, and whittled on the walking stick, and my thought wandered off and ended up on Flora Avenue in Kansas City, Missouri, in 1949:

My father kept his books in two cases flanking the fireplace. Among the volumes on torts and liens, covenants and contracts, was a Harvard Classics edition of Aesop's *Fables*, and another book, thick and forest green, full of pictures: *American Wild Life Illustrated*, a WPA compilation sponsored by Fiorello La Guardia and filled with arcana about, says the introduction, "those forms of life which at some stage in their development possess a notochord," a thing human beings lose before leaving the womb. My father explained notochords to me in a way that let me see the brotherness in the Brer Rabbit and Brer Fox stories. Once past the preface of *American Wild Life*, a nine-year-old can follow along, as I often did cross-legged on the floor in front of the shelves, sometimes the fireplace warming me. This book, which I still have, led me toward certain attitudes and away from others. It was almost an Aesop itself — minus the morals but not without an ethic. I read how a fox will shake pursuing hounds by running along a stone wall, or by crossing a freshly fertilized field, or by jumping onto the back of a sheep for a ride that will break the trail of its glandular-scented feet, and how a fox will test thin ice before moving out to the center to lie circled in its insulating tail while the heavy hounds break through into the cold water. And there was this paragraph:

> *The fox shows its true genius in ridding itself of fleas. Taking a stick in its mouth, the fox submerges slowly in a pool of water. As it sinks, the fleas move upward to drier regions. When only the wood remains above the surface, the fleas desert the sinking fox to take refuge on the raft. Thereupon the fox releases the stick, leaving the fleas to their fate.*

For people who like to dichotomize the world, here's mine about woods folk: houndsmen or foxmen. The image of Reynard riding smartly away on a ram's back left me long ago on the side of wildness over domestication in whatever forms.

But the reality of foxness remained for me a thing of words until one morning in 1949 when a friend of my mother came to visit wearing a fox stole, its eyes stuck shut as if in an afternoon doze, and I found myself in one of those childish muddles of repulsion and fascination as if the woman were Medusa herself. While the adults talked, I crept into the bedroom and pulled the skinned fox from the piled coats, and I was surprised by its sad weightlessness and its opened and varnished mouth. In caution, I stroked its glossy back, then curled the stole under the bed and stuffed a dust bunny between its rows of small, fierce teeth. It was this last act that got me into trouble: my mother tolerated the covert protest, but she didn't let pass an embarrassment to her housekeeping.

After the Sixteen-Sixty-Six Beast

This happened first (in Darla's Fun Center, the lone bar left in Cottonwood): a worn man in coveralls, the tatters revealing that he was neither cowboy nor farmer, seasoned his sandwich of raw hamburger on white bread with Tabasco, and he said, *All I need now is a few shakes of gunpowder.* I asked what he meant, and he said, *Black powder's what I'm talking about. The old boys used to feed it to their coyote dogs to make them fierce — put the fight into them.* I asked what a coyote dog was (the word coyote here rhymes with "my coat"), and he told me and said there weren't many left around here now, but Paul Evans over east of Strong, on past Deadman's Corner where they found that corpse years ago, he had the best ones, and he was a true oldfangled coyote man, quiet, but a good fellow. They are hunting dogs that run down the quarry, a sport descending from the old-time "wolf" drives (a prairie wolf is a coyote). The whole thing sounded so medieval, so Chaucerian:

> A huntsman there was, a most worthy wight,
> And nothing more loved he than hounds in flight.

This happened second: I am going to see Evans, it's early December, and a big red Christmas star lights the front of the small farmhouse and directs me over the black road. Paul and Leola, his wife, are not far from sitting to an early supper, and, after we talk about their six coyote dogs, they say to join them. The Evanses are in their early seventies but appear a decade younger, their faces shaped by the prairie wind into strong and pleasing lines. They have no children. Paul speaks softly and to the point, and Leola is animated, the kind of woman who can take a small, smoldering story and breathe it into bright flame. Paul listens to her in barely noticeable amusement and, from time to time, tosses her tinder. The meal is a Charolais roast beef from their herd, mashed potatoes, pickled beets and candied cucumbers, and Paul's specialty, cottage cheese dressed with corn syrup, and I have two helpings of each but for the last. I've been in the field all day, and it was cold, and, in all my time in the county, I've been asked to join a meal only a few times. We sit happily and there is time for stories.

Leola says: *It was 1949, May. Paul was home from the Pacific. We'd made it through the war, then this. We were living just across the county line, near Americus, on a little farm by the Neosho River. One Friday night I came upstairs to bed and Paul gawked at me. He said, "What the dickens are you doing?" I was wearing my good rabbit fur coat and wedding rings, and I had a handful of wooden matches. It wasn't cold at all. I said I didn't know but that something wasn't right, and he said, "What's not right?" and I didn't know. We went to bed and just after dark it began to rain, and then the wind came on and blew harder, and we went downstairs and tried to open the door but the air pressure was so strong Paul couldn't even turn the knob. That wind had us locked in. We hunkered in the corner of the living room in just our pajamas — mine were new seersucker — and me in my fur coat. The wind got louder, then the windows blew out, and we realized we were in trouble when the heat stove went around the corner and out a wall that had just come down. We clamped on to each other like ticks, and then we were six feet in the air, and Paul was hanging on to my fur coat — for ballast he says now — and we went up and out where the wall had been, and then we came down, and then we went up again, longer this time, and then came down in a heap of animals — a cow and one of our dogs with a two-by-four through it. The cow lived, but we lost the dog. We were out in the wheat field, sixty yards from the house, and Paul had a knot above his eye that made him look like the Two-headed Wonder Boy. Splintered wood and glass and metal all over, and the electric lines down and sparking, and here we were barefoot. Paul said to walk only when the lightning flashed to see what we were stepping on. We were more afraid of getting electrocuted than cut. We could see in the flashes that the second story of the house was gone except for one room, and we saw the car was an accordion and our big truck was upside down. The old hog was so terrified she got between us and wouldn't leave all the way up to the neighbors'. Their place wasn't touched. They came to the door and saw a scared hog and two things in rags covered with black mud sucked up out of the river and coated with plaster dust and blood, and one of them was growing a second head. The neighbors didn't know who we were until they heard our voices.*

Paul says, *That tornado was on a path to miss our house until it hit the Neosho and veered back on us. The Indians believed a twister will change course when it crosses a river.*

Leola: *The next morning we walked back home. The electric clock was stopped at nine-forty, and I went upstairs to the one room that was left, and, there on the chest, my glasses were just like I left them, but our bedroom was gone, and our mattress, all torn up, was in a tree where we'd have been.*

Paul: *We spit plaster for three weeks. It was just plain embedded in us.*

I'm thinking, what truer children of Kansas than those taken aloft by the South Wind?

Leola serves her coconut cream pie, a delectable thing calling for a second round, and she says, *I came out of the tornado with my rings, and then, six months later I was in the kitchen when Paul called he needed help with a calf. I took off the rings and put them in a teacup — three of them — a wedding band, an engagement ring, and another diamond ring. That evening I was making a pie and dropped a piece of leftover dough in the cup. I'd forgotten about the rings. I didn't use the dough, and the next day I dumped it into the dogs' trough. That evening I went to put the rings on, and I remembered, and I was out in that dog pen right now. The wedding band was in the trough, but the diamond rings were gone. I don't need to tell you what I did for the next week.*

No, you don't need to tell what you did, Paul says, and I say, what did you do? and Leola thinks a moment.

I went from pile to pile and I panned for gold, and no prospector ever had worse luck.

Says Paul, *I'd let a couple of the dogs out for an hour. Those rings are out in that prairie somewhere.* And I say, a wise old Indian told me, what the winds taketh not, then willeth the dogs.

This happened third: a mid-December morning, early and cold, the prairie lies coated in hoarfrost, the whitened hills like worn crystals, the grasses spiky with rime, and Paul says iced pastures will show up a coyote well. We're in his dog wagon, a cracked-windshield pickup, the bed holding the old plywood dog box with a flop-down door that Paul can release from the cab by pulling a slender cable called a jerk rope. If we encounter a coyote, Paul will yank the line, and the five hounds, whose slender skulls are now thrust through a narrow window in the door as they watch the frozen slopes, will bolt to hit the ground running, and the chase to death, canines after canine, will begin.

Paul wears a decade-old Resistol (a workingman's Stetson), rolled and stained and salty as all get-out, and sewed to its inside are two pieces of red bandanna that he can tie under his chin to keep his ears warm and his hat on in the wind. He calls the strips *ear floppers*. He has on a knocked-about denim jacket. If you've seen Glenn Ford in the western *Jubal*, you have a notion of what Paul is like: the outfit, the courteous manner, the reticence. He says of his hat, *It's lost its shape, but that's no worse than me*, and I say it has plenty of shape, just not the factory shape, and he says, *Like me*. Under his lip is a pinch of Red Man so small that I don't notice it for an hour, and he never spits. He began chewing to control his thirst when he was a teenager picking up hay on a go-devil in July.

In 1932, when he was fifteen, with seven dollars in his pocket, he jumped a freight train at Strong City and rode to Trinidad, Colorado, to look for ranch work but didn't find any, so he climbed a train back toward home. During the warm days, he'd take off his belt and strap himself to the top of a boxcar and doze; one afternoon, as he slept, a hobo lifted his last three dollars and his souvenir postcards. At night, to escape the cold, he'd climb down into an empty freight car and pull two big, conical banana-baskets together and sleep inside like a larva, warm and hidden. When he got home a week later, nobody had noticed he was gone. Unless you count his navy days, that was the only thing like a vacation he's ever taken. (During the war, he wrote Leola from the Pacific: *Get all the going out of your system before I get home — once I get back to Chase County, I'm not leaving there again.* She told me, *He's nearly kept his threat.*)

Now we're bouncing over the hills, and Paul explains: in the county there used to be coyote and jackrabbit roundups, often organized by a Sunday-school class; men would form four two-mile-long lines in a loose square and walk toward the center, driving animals before them, and, as the perimeter tightened, the shotguns would begin blasting and the clubs thrashing. Paul rode behind with dogs on a long lead and would turn them on jacks or coyotes that slipped the lines, and, after the square closed, there might be half a dozen dead coyotes and a hundred rabbits. Now the hares are gone and the coyotes much diminished, and people are too lazy (he guesses) to walk that far, and maybe it's just as well, since the whole thing was more extermination than sport.

Paul went on his first hunt with one of his father's farmhands, who drove a Model T roadster with his pair of sight dogs (they hunt visually) perched atop each front fender like chrome ornaments. The quarry was jackrabbits, and the method was to leave at dusk and drive the pastures until the headlamps picked up the reflection of eyes, and then off the hounds would go. Paul was seven and liked the chase, but there were so few coyotes in those times he didn't see his first one until he was fifteen. As they increased after the "wolf" drives declined, he began to dog-hunt them from horseback and later from a 1934 Ford with a hound box in the trunk cavity. Only once did his father go along, and, of the violent ride that comes with sighting a coyote, he said, *At first I was so damn afraid we wouldn't see one, and after we saw one I was so damn afraid we'd see another.* Following their marriage, little Leola usually joined Paul and one time even went off alone on horseback and brought back a pair of coyotes hanging from her saddle horn.

Now: we ride a ridge, then edge down, the truck tilting laterally, a bit precariously I think, cross a pond dam, climb again, then down, make a zigzag course across creeks I'd have thought impassable, rise again to hit an eroded and invisible cattle trail that slams the wheels hard, stop for me to open a gate, and on, another gate, and all the time I marvel at Paul's navigation over this grassland that to a novice carries the sameness of face as a sea. He has no compass: on a cloudy day, he takes his direction from the wind and gets lost only with an abrupt shift of the blowing or on a foggy day when there is no wind. The frost has disappeared except in the shadows so that humps of limestone cast long, white umbras, and soon those too are gone, and the tawniness returns to the grass and the coyotes will be harder to see. The odometer on the old truck shows fifty-five thousand miles. Paul believes no more than six thousand have come on roads and that he rides about five thousand miles a year in the pastures; in a half century of hauling the dogs over the hills, he's traveled a quarter of a million roadless miles inside one county. I ask how many coyotes that equals, and he says without having to figure it, *Sixteen hundred and sixty-five.*

The dogs: they are greyhounds crossbred with heavier staghounds (that name bespeaks their medieval origin, although the most famous American staghound was General Custer's pet killed with him at the Little Big Horn); the lighter animals give speed to the strength and aggressive temper of the larger dogs. A pure greyhound will often merely chase a coyote, but a thick-hided, big-chested staghound will go for a kill. Usually, the younger and faster cross-breeds catch the quarry and turn it to fight as the older ones, the throat dogs, close in to pin it and finish things off. The first time I walked into the Evanses' yard and past two big hounds, I did so with trepidation, but their disposition was that of a beagle; yet to a running quadruped of almost any sort they are deadly, and if a stray mutt happens to wander into a chase, it's likely done for, but a fleeing child they would ignore. Paul's dogs, the males weighing up to eighty pounds and capable of running nearly forty miles an hour for a couple of minutes, are faster over broken ground than greyhounds, and if Paul can get the truck within three hundred yards of the quarry, the dogs usually will close the distance to make the kill. If coyotes dispensed with their habit of continually slowing to look back and, instead, kept on the dead run, more of them would escape, since their stamina and awareness of the terrain are superior to the hounds'. As it is, the dogs miss only one of ten, and that one escapes usually by getting into bottom timber or a pond. A single dog against a lone coyote, typically weighing less than half the hound, could not likely kill it; although Paul has never lost a dog in a fight, they all soon end up with scarred faces. He carries a roll of duct tape to bind slashed flesh and lacerated feet and dew claws torn by the rocky hills, but not long ago, when a dog ripped its tongue running through a barbed-wire fence, he could do nothing but let its suffering heal it.

Paul hunts only from mid-October to mid-March when transient cattle are out of the pastures and coyote pups are grown, and he hunts not because of a fascination with coyotes or their beauty or the loveliness of their loping but because he likes to see the hounds run. He says that when he gets too old to ride the hills, he guesses he'll drive up to Abilene, the self-styled "Greyhound Capital of the World," to watch the dogs chase mechanical rabbits. In the county, there is only one other sight-dog hunter left; Paul says, *Things are harder now. Every year more locked gates, more cow-calf operations so the pastures don't empty. And if you're not as old as I am, you even need a license these days.* He's watched the coyote population go from absence to abundance to decline, and in the early eighties he saw his first case of mange. Each year it's increased. He's seen the bounty system disappear and the value of pelts rise and fall, and he knows how a trapper using scent can clean out an area. The market was high in the forties and fifties when the Russians were buying pelts to use in army coats: *Ice won't stick to coyote fur.* Even when the market was up he never trapped or dug pups out of a den, and he's never poisoned a coyote. There is no gun in the truck: if he needs to administer the coup de grâce to a coyote, he does it with a tap from a little hammer. One time the dogs tore open a female and he found three pups alive in the womb, and he wrapped them and took them home for Leola to nurse with an eyedropper, but Harry, Larry, and Mary didn't live long. Several years ago he was moved when he saw a male coyote drag its belly along the ground to distract the dogs, to give itself up while its mate ran to cover.

We ride up on a north-facing slope, a place on this day of southeasterlies where a coyote can get out of the wind, where it can smell trouble from one direction and see it in the other. The morning is nearly gone, and the coyotes will soon cease moving unless they feel the vibration from the truck, but the slope is empty and Paul says, *We should've jumped one by now,* and my relief balances my disappointed curiosity.

Now, coyote: yipping, ululating, singing, freely, freely, night-flute coyote, long leggedness through blackness, (moonless), silent, pausing, yipping, far responding, quick legs, freely, padded feet, coyote feet, pausing, silent padding, pissing, running, swinging head, pausing, back-looking, (tallgrasses frozen, frosted), cold fur erected, coyote singing, sings-long-dog, coyote, coyote, golden-eyes-coyote, canine, climbing, singing, sweetness, song dog, breathing darkness, (hiding darkness), yip-yipping, nose-to-sky-coyote, singing, sweet-throat-beast, coyote jaw, coyote teeth, looking-always-coyote, running, singing the darkness, long-song-dog call, coyote, coyote belly, waiting, watching, wanting, coyote eyes, eye this, that, this scent, scenting, sending, sensing, pausing, pissing, breathing, smelling, sniffing, snooping, nosing, silent-feet-coyote, earth-feel-under-foot-coyote, nose to wind, canid, canid, coming something, belly, belly, belly, passing, pausing, halting, creeping, softly, soft, tricking, thumping, coyote heart, pushing, pumping, pulsing, coyote blood, beating-beating, pouncing! snapping! Rodent! — belly, belly — trots-along-coyote, and: (going night, going cover, going, sky rising), ridge-line-coyote, runs-far-song-dog, thin, thin, muscle-bone, (and this, coyote, this: now, they come):

West of the Z Bar Ranch we ride onto an expanse rising westward, and Paul says only and quietly, *There,* and lets me find the distant, gray loping, and he steps on the accelerator, and we take off in axle-crashing pursuit to close the gap, and the coyote keeps moving in alert nonchalance, pausing to watch our progress, and Paul says, *I can see the shine on the skin — it's got the mange.* We gain ground in a tumult of barking as the hounds see the coyote, the lunch pails are in the air and my hands are on the ceiling of the cab to keep me from cracking my skull, and my heart is in my throat as if I were the quarry, and Paul reaches up and pulls the jerk rope as if to request a trolley stop, the barking ceases, and, in prodigious leaps, long catapults, the hounds hit the prairie, become linear blurs and in an instant they are thirty yards away, and the coyote's tail is straight out and it's streaking now to no cover we can see, and the dogs terrify a deer into leaping a fence and running toward us, and then Paul says, *Oh no,* and two stray dogs have come from nowhere but the hounds this time are not distracted, and from the still prairie, suddenly, racing in four directions, there are five hounds, two dogs, one coyote, a deer, and a pair of men in a truck.

A fence cuts us off, the chase drops into a draw, we can see nothing, and we get out and try to listen. Only the wind. We wait. Our pulses calm, and then Ferd, a young white dog, comes up, its chops bloody, and Paul says, *They got it,* and Ferd nuzzles my pant leg and smears me with coyote blood to initiate me, mark me with evidence, and then Ribbon, a white female, trots up, chops red, and both dogs draw their snouts through the grass to clean them. They are breathing too hard to drink yet, their hot vapor visible in the cold air. Then we see Jack in the distance, and we crawl under a fence, walk down the draw, and there by three lone elms lies the lead dog, the old master of the kill, Red, tongue hanging, rib cage rising and falling heavily, seeming pleased like a terrier that gets the rat, just a good old dog that wants its belly scratched, and before him, so blending with the grass that I almost step on it, lies the coyote, its limbs stretched fore and aft as if still trying to outrace the hounds, its maddened lip curled to show a tusk, its head mangled but the skull not opened, and in its side is a long, fierce rent, like a rip in an old shirt, and there are punctures in its thighs, but the worst is the mange that has left its back half hairless. This one would not have survived the winter. Paul says, *I'd guess Red got to it first, hit it in the hams and flipped it, then bit it behind the head, then the other dogs got on the back legs and stretched it out. That was it.* And I say, sixteen hundred and sixty-six.

I ask whether coyotes yelp during the fight, and he says he never heard it, and I ask if the mange keeps the dogs from eating on the animal, and, no, they won't touch it once it's dead — they won't even eat coyote meat out of their feed pans. We walk back to the truck, and it's noon, and Paul, thinking of the stuffed lunch pails Leola made up, says, *Eating out here's the next best thing to the race. Sometimes we build a fire and set a can of chili in it.* I have to ask, at last, have you ever eaten coyote, and he says, no, he never has.

Above the Crystalline Basement

Underneath eastern Kansas lies a range, the Nemaha Mountains, and just now I am walking up what would be the foothills of its steep eastern face. I'm near the western edge of Fox Creek quadrangle and following a ridge track above Gannon Branch that I hope will lead to an oil well, this one a dry hole drilled years ago. In my pack is a hefty wrench that I plan to use to uncap the pipe and open a little window, a porthole, onto the old buried mountains, ones from the time of the Ozarks and the Black Hills. When the Rockies were still prostrate, one theory holds, the Nemahas rose and then eroded as the Appalachians reared up to relieve the crustal pressure, the birth of one being the death of the other. (A geologist told me he thought the tourist bureau should erect signs where highways enter Kansas that would say: MOUNTAIN BURIAL PROJECT NOW COMPLETE.) Although I'll be looking at their crests, I'll be peeping into a deep corner of the county basement, and I realize I'll no more see the Nemahas than a man in total darkness his hand, but I want to see *at* them, three thousand feet down, and I plan to sniff the vapors rising from them and drop a small stone down, count seconds until I imagine I hear the pebble bounce onto the granite ridge, that old igneous exudate from the earth's first time. The Nemahas disappeared from view four hundred million years ago when the continents lay as one, and animate life had gone only so far as to cover itself with scales and free itself from the necessity of returning to the ocean to remake its generations; these mountains were already old when life began going from a legless world to a footed one, when lungs were something new.

It was well-drillers who found the Nemahas, and the only men to have seen them are those who pulled up the cuttings that penetrated the granite. In Chase County, of the nearly four hundred gas and oil wells drilled, only a couple of dozen reached the Precambrian rock of the Nemaha Ridge, the crest today six hundred feet below sea level and much eroded from what it once was. A Kansas geologist a half century ago said the Nemahas *must have been originally one of the great ranges of mountains of the earth.* With their nearly vertical eastern flank and their much less precipitous western exposure, I imagine them in their first days looking like the Tetons. Kansans, whose name almost means flatlanders in the minds of their countrymen, are not surprised at living atop a four-hundred-mile-long cordillera, since they have always understood that unexpected Kansas must be sought in its remoteness, a place you find only with effort. Yet I haven't told even one of them that I am out to "see" the great subterranean mountains of Kansas at the bottom of a half-mile-long, six-inch pipe. What's more, since there is no granite in the county except that in the Nemahas, I hope to identify a few bits of them around the well, and I'd like to walk out of here with a little piece of mountain in my pocket, a granite nubbin whose age is reckoned not in millions of years but in billions; in my pocket will be some of the raw material elsewhere broken down to become the bones of this place of Prairyerths.

In front of you imagine on the floor a thick book, like an encyclopedia, and atop it seven slender books; push the books to your left so they slide down to overlap like shingles on a roof: the encyclopedia is the Precambrian crystalline core, here thrust up into a mountainous fold, and the books atop it are the seven periods of the Paleozoic era that describe Chase County; all of this is to say that on top of the antediluvian granite rest the marine-made layers of sedimentary rock, mostly successions of shale and limestone, old sea floors that have since been slightly tilted. The leaves of these volumes of rock are the individual strata that compose the county, here rubble-strewn, there fertile, arable here, only grazable there. Once, probably, three additional volumes lay atop this slipped stack, but water and wind have sent them eastward.

The uppermost of the seven books represents fifty million years of sediments settling to the bottom of a sea that came and left again and again like a quarreling lover. The history here is this: a sea transgressing, regressing, transgressing, in and out, up and down, higher, lower, always advancing, withdrawing always, and always leaving something behind, the sea conceiving stone, and the rock bearing living things that turn mineral solutions — calcium carbonates — into shell and bone, and bone becoming stone again, and that too waiting to become again; and everywhere cycles, and cycles within cycles, and the sea laying down strata like shrouds over the old life, and then the corrupting winds and waters coming to resurrect it. The Nemahas rose, were partly eroded, subsided, and were buried, all of this happening in the Eastern Hemisphere; and then, slowly and passively like a casket, the range got carried into the Western world to come here — to what appears a permanent resting place — where the thirty-eighth parallel crosses the ninety-sixth meridian; so, in this way, Chase County, Kansas, migrated from the far other side just as its human inhabitants were to do. In the half century since I was born, this hill has moved at about the rate a fingernail grows, some four feet farther west — about the distance from my heel to my hip — as has everything else around it, the Cottonwood, the courthouse, the brass bedsteads.

Here, except for the river valleys, the issue of the old inland sea is Permian limestone and shale laid down a quarter of a billion years ago, long before the rising of the great saurian world of giant jaws. To walk the Flint Hills is, in a sense, to walk where the evidence of the last 250 million years — the shape of the hills themselves — shows only as does the hand of the sculptor on the finished figure: to see Michelangelo's chisel and his dusty grip, look at the swell of David's buttock, the incurve of his back. The ancient aspect of this terrain derives, in part, from the last quarter billion years' appearing to have gone off and left only a carved artifact behind, and, sometimes, I think the citizens absorb that aspect: they often seem to be people from another time, people who desire permanence over continuity, who just happen to find themselves surfaced in an era of X-rated movies, the Internal Revenue Service, Styrofoam burger boxes, and nuclear medicine.

Now: I've stopped walking and have sat down to take a pull from my canteen, to look about and consider my trouble in finding the well I figured would be near these stone ruts of the old drillers' track. The day is quiet, and the western slope above Gannon Branch seems to invite a long roll down its easy contours of grasses, a hill smoothly stretched like a circus tent caught full of a breeze and pulling against its ties. This place is not what the aboriginal world was, but you can sense something of that other period, the dominance of a landscape that seems to be at rest and in place and immutable but for the seasonal changes of its colorings. This illusion of stasis is its power over us, our newness among all the oldnesses, we such nervous tenants afraid of endings. A far, narrow black line that is a barbed-wire fence looks absurd, so humanly small, a thing as foolish as a fence strung over a piece of sea: ownership is too paltry for the long reach, horizontal and vertical, of these hills.

Chase County is as it is because the Permian seas were as they were: the condition of those waters supplied the matrix for the shape of the terraces and ridges where the cherty sheets of rubble that give the hills their name protect beds of shale from storm and fire and plow. In the valleys, man can eat directly from what the soil gives — corn, wheat, fruits — but on the hard uplands he needs the intermediary of four-stomached animals, and in that small link, these citizens see themselves (truck mudflaps say CAT-TLE COUNTRY), but the linkings go no further back, and the residents don't picture themselves as children of the Permian seas. They understand their living in the hills but not the hills living in them, and so the deeper links are broken and don't inform their conscious life. The connection would seem to be more apparent than it is, since it's so easy to mistake a distant piece of limestone for a skeletal something, or a bleached steer-bone for a chunk of limestone. (The Canopic jars holding mummified pharaonic innards are, appropriately, cut from limestone as are the pyramids themselves.)

I'm guessing, but I think a telling in this county of the story of Deucalion and Pyrrha — repopulating a postdiluvian world by throwing the bones of their mother, common fieldstones, over their shoulders to make new people — would receive blank stares, and the tale would have neither the power of myth nor the truth of geology. Yet the fact remains: limestone is a rock not unlike bone; the fact remains: the chemical nature of the old seawater produced a stony land that produces good grasses that produce good, hoofed protein digestible to man. Flint Hills beef is a 250-million-year-old gift, yet the sense of history here goes back only to 1850 or sometimes a little further to the time of lithic weapons, and then it ceases. Even the three most noted buildings — the courthouse, the

Z Bar Ranch home, and the Fox Creek School — made as they are
from that primeval, thickened Kansas sea cut and laid up into walls,
even these buildings do not carry the people's connections beyond
the nineteenth century. The sense of the past here is abbreviated,
and it lies separate like a severed limb.

The rubble on this ridge is Wreford Limestone, a fragmentary
rock derived mostly from sea plants, and so better suited for railroad
ballast than courthouse walls, and the well-diggers' track is full of
it and broken flint. No one knows certainly how flint, its hardness
greater than steel, forms within soft limestones that will dissolve
in a bowl of apple-cider vinegar. Typically here, the flint develops
in elliptical spheres, nodules to remind you of sponges, and some
geologists, in fact, believe that ancient sponges provided the "seed"
for flint (I like its formal name: cryptocrystalline quartz, and I
imagine: the Cryptocrystalline Hills). I've just picked up a piece of
blue-gray flint, the color of deep seawater under clouds, and I try to
imagine spongeness; but how could something so soft, absorbent,
open-textured, and weightless ever be transmuted into a thing so
hard, impermeable, heavy, sharp-edged, and capable — if I strike it
against another — of releasing sparks? (Surely those sponges were
the kind more like coral.) Fire from the old sea, as if the silica, a
Prometheus, had stolen it away from the igneous granite god and,
through all the long changes, held it close until I set it loose again
in a place and day so distant from its inception.

Before the children of Europe took these hills, the people who
walked here believed stones to be alive because they carried heat,
changed their forms, and moved if you watched long enough. To
them, rocks were concentrations of power and life; all over the
world, where people have not forgotten the wisdom of primitivism,
they touch sacred stones to bring fertility. But here, when a bottom
farmer limes his fields with "inert" granulated rock, in his chemis-
try there is no informing poetry, no myth. Yet, to think of rock can
be to dream origins and be reminded of the old search for the
philosopher's stone, that elixir basic to all substance.

Now: my topographic map shows I've walked too far, and I turn
back and try to look where I've overlooked before, and I rewalk, my
hopes dwindling, and then there is something not right, a thing that
doesn't blend, and I've found the wellhead. In my delight, it's a few
moments before I see the concrete cap, and for me, except in imagination, there'll be no approach to the Nemaha Ridge, the true Kansas Mountains, no looking down toward the crystalline basement

lying at the far bottom of this tube of darkness, three Empire State Buildings below, no sniffing that source granite warmed by the earthern heart and covered with the sea gift. There are some places you don't go, some journeys you can't make. But now, in my pocket, like an old coin often spent, is a chip of the Nemahas.

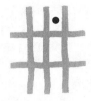

Outside the Z Bar

The American prairies and plains eat pretension and dreams of aristocracy with the slow patience of inevitability, corrupting, eroding, and quite dissolving them in some places, and in others leaving only a carcass as a kind of memorial, a monument, a memorandum. Drive the rock roads of Chase County and you can see old, cut-stone walls of abandoned houses roofed and unroofed, windows broken and gone even down to the frames; in the houses still having roofs and floors, you'll find gnawed holes and in a corner a large pile of brittle sticks like a few baskets of laundry dumped and left; these wood-rat nests are the last insult: spheres of scat spreading and deepening over the parlor, the kitchen, the bedroom, in a final defiling of the wish for nobility.

Around the county there are a dozen or so of these houses, all built between 1870 and 1890 of native stone, always cut and usually dressed. A few of them are small, no more than four rooms, and, seemingly, designed as the walls went up, as if the owner told the mason, I have this much money — do what you can but do it well, and the mason did, so that even the humblest of these somehow partakes of the timeless stone, and these small shells are the saddest ones. The other houses, larger, are mostly still occupied; of them, sitting above Fox Creek a couple of miles north of Strong City, is the finest, Spring Hill Ranch, now often called the Z Bar. Its 112 years of occupancy are about to end, and with them ends the capital expression in Chase of an American hunger for the trappings of landed noblesse.

Of all the gifts from these prairie hills, humility may be the greatest, but it apparently wasn't what Stephen F. Jones, with his so common last name, was looking for when he came into the county with his family and black servants (once slaves in his and his wife's families) and two thousand head of cattle; Jones arrived with big money (*Dollars sticking out of every pocket*, said an old countian) and grand, southern notions. He wanted from the hills, it seems, an American fiefdom. Born near Nashville, Tennessee, in 1826, at twenty-three he went to Tallapoosa County, Alabama, to work on a cotton plantation where he married Louisa Barber, who *followed his fortunes from that time forth*. They went to Texas to farm and ranch, and eighteen years later moved to the Arkansas River Valley of the Colorado plains and continued farming, ranching, becoming rich. In 1876, for reasons I haven't been able to discover, along with much else about the Joneses (why was his brand an N?), they reversed the usual pattern of settlement here by emigrating from the West with much money and many possessions — in fact, with everything for a ranch except land, and they soon also had that, seven thousand acres along Fox Creek. On the western slope above the stream and just below the crest that opens to an extravagance of horizon, Jones laid out his ranch home near the spring that untypically issues from a hilltop as if its water were highborn. He bought the big grassland at his back and the wooded valley before him so that he came to own the horizon too.

In constructing his house and a half-dozen outbuildings into a composite collection from a single material — limestone quarried on the place — he hired so many workmen that travelers on the Council Grove road would take the hubbub for Strong City and stop and try to find lodgings. Completed, the three-story house of eleven rooms seemed larger than it was, probably because of the triple-terrace garden he set in front of it. Yet the place is not pretentious: maybe it's the hugeness of prairie and sky that subdues things, gives them a human if not a humble scale. Like the house, the barn is three stories and built into the slope, a feature not seen by Jones' workmen since the hillside dugouts of the first settlers. Twin ramps, high and steep, rise to the top floor of the barn so that a four-horse team can enter and turn around inside or continue through to the other exit; attached to it was a big doubleheader windmill that could both thresh and grind. When Jones finished the immense building he learned that its length fell two feet shy of being the biggest barn in the state. His workers constructed a chicken house with a barrel-vault ceiling, a combined smokehouse and springhouse, and a cut-stone privy with a cupola and arched window to light three seats (one half-height for children). He surrounded it all with twenty-six miles of English-style stone fence that he believed would be rat-proof. His manor was complete.

Jones then founded the Strong City Bank, bought into a lumber and hardware business, had a five-acre orchard planted, helped develop English Herefords, and also raised Shorthorns, Galloways, Hambletonian trotters, Berkshire and Poland China hogs, some sheep, and put three hundred acres into cultivation. Five years after entering the county, his holdings could be matched, or nearly so, only by J. R. Blackshere on his Clover Cliff Ranch eight miles west. In a time when a farm of a quite prosperous countian could be valued at fifty thousand dollars, Stephen Jones' holdings were worth two hundred thousand.

At sixty-two, twelve years after arriving here, he sold Spring Hill, and he and Louisa moved to Kansas City, Missouri, where he built another house, this one also of Cottonwood Limestone shipped all the way from Chase County. A quarter of a century later, this man, who had lived in six states and gotten rich in four, came back to Kansas to die. I've been told that, in his last years, he used to sit alone on a small stone wall along Cottonwood Street in Strong City and watch automobiles pass by. A countian said, *It was a pitiful sight.*

Today there aren't many countians who can tell you what the carved letter J above the cornice of the house stands for, and hardly anyone recalls Jones' daughter Christiana, who stayed on in Strong City, although a few remember his granddaughter Colie, who married William Yoast Morgan, son of the first and only woman mayor in the county, the man who sold the *Emporia Gazette* to William Allen White and who later wrote the "Jayhawker in Yurrup" travel books. (Morgan had the capacity to turn a phrase: about Holland, he said, *Some of the land looks lower than the rest, but none looks higher.*)

The ranch: old highway 13 passed thirty or forty feet closer to the lowest terrace than does the newer and straightened and renumbered route 177, but both highways split the small valley, really not much more than a long and broad hollow. The roads approach Spring Hill laterally, when the ranch layout calls for a long, frontal entrance, one that would let the place rise on its levels in the eye as does its wealth in the imagination. The terraces are long and narrow and parallel to Fox Creek running beyond the east line of trees; the wall of each terrace is of cut stone, and atop the lowest is a wrought-iron fence, only knee-high to mark out the estate but not block the traveler's view, and on the highest terrace is a circular stone fountain once served by the spring but now filled with soil. The home, built by some of the men who worked on the courthouse, seems to be a descendant, with its Second Empire Parisian urbanity and its red, standing-seam mansard roof articulated by dormers. On each end of the front side are twin projecting gables, and a crenellated cornice joins the roof to the rock shell of undressed cut-stone of regular dimensions cornered by tooth-hammered quoins. The oblong and columned first-floor porch, the element that makes the place look like a home instead of a small courthouse, opens to the east vale. Grillwork once topping the gable is gone, but above the cornice remains this:

A.D.   J   1881.

The J stands inside a shield as if a crest. I have never been permitted inside the house, but I understand it has been modified, remodeled away from grace to practicality, the commonplace absorbing the fanciful and superfluous, as the twentieth century often does to the nineteenth.

On the north side of the home, in complementary but simplified lines, is a peculiar smokehouse-springhouse, the one above the other and joined to the kitchen by a thirty-foot tunnel once surmounted by a small tower to admit light, an eccentric thing Thomas Jefferson might have designed for Monticello. When I first began poking around the county, I heard stories about a slave tunnel at Spring Hill. The passage ran, allegedly, for a couple of miles from the house to the barn, penetrated the big ridge, then opened onto the western prairie to afford escaping blacks a jump on their pursuers. While it's true that eastern Kansas had an active underground railroad network, Jones built the house sixteen years after the Civil War ended; yet neither the anachronism nor the inability of anyone to find a tunnel other than the short one from the kitchen has dissuaded believers. Last year after a tree on the highest terrace blew over and exposed a rock-lined vault, apparently a cistern, the legend revived. Perhaps because of the mystery inherent in dark, forgotten, death-haunted secret passageways, county children come to cherish the place with a feeling only the courthouse or the big stone-arch bridge a few miles away at Clements can equal. But the truth is that Louisa Jones, after witnessing a tornado strike the house during construction, wanted a storm cellar, one she could reach without getting wet. The only blacks ever moving underground at Spring Hill were servants carrying butter and smoked hams to the kitchen.

When Jones left for Kansas City, he sold the ranch to a Strong City man, Barney Lantry, the third-wealthiest countian, who moved his cowhands into the house. Nineteen years later Lantry sold it, and then it sold four more times, at last being picked up by a Red Hills ranch outfit whose brand was Z — . Except for one interval, only tenants occupied the house after Jones. In the 1970s, the ranch went on the National Register of Historic Places. In 1989, after the Audubon Society bought an option on Spring Hill and its nearly eleven thousand contiguous acres, including the Fox Creek School two miles north, the society started working to get the National Park Service to take it over as a monument to commemorate early ranch life in the Flint Hills. When talk began about also restoring the connected prairie, the ghosts of the Tallgrass Park arose, the old arguments once more started flying, and voices from outside the county were again abundant; but this time many countians spoke up in favor of preservation (not just of Spring Hill but of themselves), and they refused to be intimidated by KGA members who disrupted public hearings and videotaped anyone advocating the monument. (One bold citizen called the association the KGB, and another asked, *If you KGA boys are so opposed to federal this and that, why do you accept agricultural subsidies?*) The councils of the twin towns even passed a resolution supporting the proposal, and most countians hoped the Kansas congressional delegation would soon introduce a bill to establish the monument.

The dreams of a cattle baron came to this: eight years of blooded horses, candelabra, black servants bearing silver trays, and then a century of mostly hired hands and absentee and corporate owners, the home become tenant housing and now headed toward ownership by every American. Whatever else these hills tolerate from Anglo culture, they do not long admit the phantasm of squiredom, and yet some people here, despising and fearing possession in common, wish for the return of a cattle king to rescue the ranch from fellow citizens they imagine descending on them.

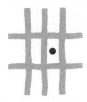

On the Town:
Gabriel's Inventory

The old Dunkard preacher and his wife came into the county in 1856, their wagon full of what they had imagined in Indiana they would need in the new land. It was a good load, and, once across the Mississippi — in Hannibal, Missouri — Gabriel Jacobs traded his horses for oxen, powerful but tractable beasts that would graze where horses would not, animals born to pull eastern chattels into the West. Traveling with Gabriel and Elizabeth were three daughters, a son, and two sons-in-law, and waiting for them along the creek that would soon bear their name was the eldest boy, who had arrived the year before. Why Gabriel at seventy-three headed west no one knows now, but one countian wrote, *They must have heard some glorious and promising story about Kansas.* The first Sabbath after the Jacobses arrived in the creek hollow, they observed the Dunker custom of mutual foot washing, and Gabriel took as his sermon text Nehemiah 2:20. "The God of Heaven, he will prosper us; therefore we his servants will arise and build."

While living out of the wagon, near a spring just above the creek, Gabriel built a two-story log house of walnut and oak (furniture woods today) with a fieldstone fireplace, and he built animal pens and broke the ground and sowed corn, cane, and buckwheat, and Elizabeth planted vegetables. The crops did indeed prosper the first two years, and then there was nothing you could call rain for a year and a half, and, in the autumn of 1860, old Gabriel fell ill, and in October he died, done in by the long drought. His sons built a walnut coffin from a tree on his farm and fastened it with wooden pins, and then, since his death was the first in the settlement, they had to set out a cemetery. He died intestate, and William Holsinger, another Dunkard preacher and the administrator of Gabriel's estate, filed an inventory of Jacobs' possessions.

I've seen the movies and paintings, and I've looked closely at those portrayals of prairie schooners making their cumbrous way into the West, and I've always wondered just what the hell really was in those things, what precisely it was that broke their hickory axletrees. Then and now, when people travel through unknown territory, their baggage is a packing up, an assembly, of their fears as much as of their expectations. Gabriel Jacobs died only forty-two months after riding behind his oxen into the nearly uninhabited land, so it would seem his estate inventory is very much a listing of the burden in that wagon and of several things he must have made soon after arrival, and it is also, with some dreaming, a tour of the Jacobs farmstead: the things hung, shelved, stacked, and set in some order in the kitchen, the bedroom, the barn.

The inventory, kept in a third-floor room of the courthouse, is a tidy, inked script on six sheets of narrow paper glued end to end like a scroll. I give it exactly, adding only a few clarifications:

> one large yoke of Oxen one red and one red with white face
> one small yoke of Oxen one black and white and one roan
> one cow & Calf cow red & white
> one cow & Calf cow roan with red calf
> one Spotted 3 year old heifer & Calf
> one red cow
> one Black & white yearling Heifer
> one Red & white yearling Heifer
> one Red heifer 1 year old
> one Stack of Hay
> one Stack of Hay and Corn fodder
> one crib full of fodder
> 4 log chains
> 1 Mall & Wedge
> 2 Sledge hammers
> 2 Hoes
> One mare
> 2 set of harness
> 1 Saddle & Bridle
> 1 Curry comb
> 1 pair of Stirups

1 Horse Brush
1 Waggon Doubletrees & neckyoke
1 pair Breast chains
1 hay Rack
1 log Sled
1 Manure fork
1 old waggon lock
1 lot of lumber
1 Harrow
2 Shovel Plows
1 Stiring Plow [stirring]
1 Breaking Plow
1 Kiln of Lime
1 Feed Trough
1 Manville [planting device]
2 Pothooks
1 Keetle
2 Corn Cutters
1 crosscut Saw
1 Tenant Saw [tenon]
1 Half Bushel
1 pair Match Plains
1 pair of small Match Plains
1 pair of Steelyards
1 Brace & Bitts
2 Hatchets
4 Chisels
1 Monkey Wrentch
1 Gague [gauge]
7 Augers
3 Gouges
4 Wash Tubs
1 Shovel
1 Keg of Vinegar
1 Tar Barrel & Tar
1 Keg of Lard
1 Pickle tub & Pickles
1 Keg of Molasses
1 Tar bucket
2 Ox Bows
1 Box old iron
3 Planes
1 Frow
1 Tenant Saw
2 hand Saws

1 Pair Compasses
1 Pair Blacksmith Tongs
1 Rope
1 Mowing Sythe & Snath [scythe handle]
1 Butter Keg
1 Sausage Tub
1 Bunch of Flax
3 whet Stones
2 Axes
1 Pair Pincers
1 Cole Chisle
1 Trough and meal
1 Box
1 Work Bench and Skrew
1 Drawing Knife & Shaving horse
1 Hammer
1 Gringing Stone [grinding]
1 Sled and water Barrel
1 Streacher Chain [stretcher chain for yoking oxen]
1 Buck Saw
4 Big Hogs and 11 Shoats
9 Acres of Wheat in the ground
1 Basket
1 square
1 Brass Keetle
4 Wooden Pails
1 Pair Candle Moles [molds]
2 Milk Strainers
1 Cooking Stove & Utensils
2 Beds and Bedding
1 Chest
4 Coverlids [coverlets]
3 Bed quilts
1 Lounge and Tick
1 Spining Wheel
1 Shot Gun
2 Sacks
1 Vinegar Barrl and Vinegar
1 Box and Sweet Potatoes
1 Barrel
2 Bushels Seed Corn
3 Bushels of Wheat
100 pounds Flour
150 pounds Meal

3 Bushels Corn
1 Clock
1 Bed & Bedding
1 Stand
1 Table
1 Cupboard
1 Chest
7 Chairs
2 Milk Pans
3 Milk Crocks
4 Milk Buckets
6 Tin Cups
1 lot of dishes and Crockery
2 Smoothing Irons
1 Wooden Churn

In addition to the animals, there are nearly two hundred items here, a complete household except for Gabriel's personal effects. But I wonder about the absence of chickens and chamber pots; and, from the spellings, repeated on the more carefully written appraisement, I wonder, did they pronounce kettle as "keetle" and coverlet as "coverlid"? Not a single object is superfluous, nothing an amenity or luxury. I've seen little else in the county that so quietly speaks of austerity and the fight to survive and the interminable toil in a small nineteenth-century prairie household where there is not one thing to ease a long winter day, fill a quiet hour, not a single book (other than the presumed Bible), not a fiddle, not so much as a jew's-harp. Of course, a bucket can suggest the drudgery of milking or a fine afternoon of berry picking, a bridle plowing or a Sunday ride. About the Jacobs place was no frippery or frillery, and of their possessions, by my reckoning, there are only a half dozen you wouldn't commonly find on a Chase County farm today if you consider descendants of the older tools and implements.

The appraisement valued these chattels at $515.65; the sixty-five cents is important because it represents a half-dozen items. The hammer was valued the lowest at a nickel and the two yokes of oxen the highest at sixty-five dollars each. Elizabeth apparently kept all of the food and kitchen items and two beds and coverlets and the spinning wheel and four washtubs and two cows and calves, but she sold the log house and went to live with her children up on the creek, where she disappeared into the anonymity of plain life.

V

Bazaar

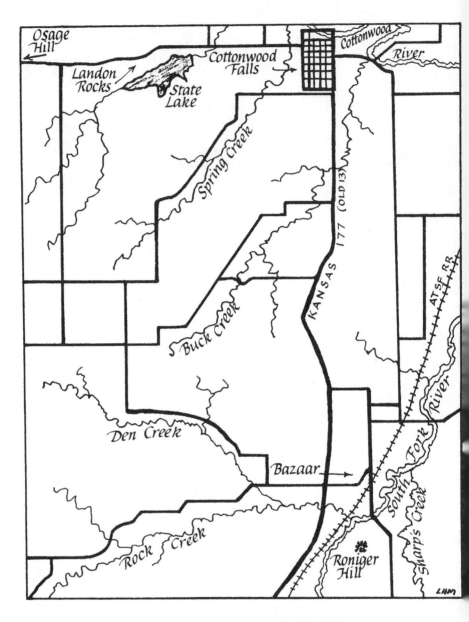

BAZAAR QUADRANGLE

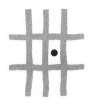

From the Commonplace Book: Bazaar

Beyond all the self-conscious lamentation over the passing of rural America, beyond the shallow romancing over a time that never was, lies a real awareness of some unique values of small-town life — certain relationships among people, between man and the land. These values are not better than those of city or suburb, they are simply different. They are values worthy of respect and preservation — values that some people would like to share today. The villages and small towns of America are not dwindling and disappearing because their values are no longer meaningful, but because they no longer work economically, no longer provide the level of services and amenities that most of us demand. No dramatic violence is being done to rural America. It is withering away because it has little function in modern life. The question of whether it can be brought back to health is at base a question of whether it can once again be brought into the mainstream of American life, of whether it can be given a meaningful function. And if it can, there still remains the question of whether the cost would be worthwhile.

— Robert B. Riley,
"New Mexico Villages in a Future
Landscape" (1969)

Perhaps the blurring of provincial lines and the need for everyone to identify with the human condition in general will have positive results for the future, but preservation and promotion of local, state, and regional traditions will continue to make life more meaningful.

> — Leo E. Oliva,
> "Kansas: A Hard Land in the
> Heartland" (1988)

Love a place like Kansas and you can be content in a garden of raked sand.

> — Earl Thompson,
> Garden of Sand (1970)

The right scale in work gives power to affection. When one works beyond the reach of one's love for the place one is working in, and for the things and creatures one is working with and among, then destruction inevitably results.

> — Wendell Berry,
> "Out of Your Car, Off Your Horse"
> (1991)

Q. There are about 1.3 billion cattle on the earth. The caloric equivalent of the food they consume would feed approximately how many human beings?
A. Nine billion people.

> — Bill Adler, Jr.,
> The Whole Earth Quiz Book (1991)

A fundamental characteristic of Kansas individualism is the tendency to conform; it is an individualism of conformity, not of revolt.

> — Carl Becker,
> "Kansas" (1910)

And of each one the core of life, namely happiness, is full of the rotten excrement of maggots.

> — Walt Whitman,
> "Thought" (1871)

When I recline on the grass I do not catch any disease,
Though probably every spear of grass rises out of what was once a catching disease.

> — Walt Whitman,
> "This Compost" (1881)

In its original state, the tallgrass prairie — also known as the true prairie — was probably the most dramatic of all American grasslands, [yet] the designation "true prairie" is ironic, because the tallgrass prairie has a tenuous hold on being prairie at all.

> — Lauren Brown,
> Grasslands (1985)

I think the prairies will die without grass finding a voice. Its democracy may be against it.

Prairie grass never seems to know anybody.

> — William A. Quayle,
> The Prairie and the Sea (1905)

Compared to trees, shrubs, or forbs, grasses seem unfathomably plain. They fail to inspire interest or stir the imagination. We look at prairie and we see a great emptiness, a void that staggers the psyche and leaves much too much room for a mind to wander.

> — Randy Winter,
> "Nature Notes" (1987)

Every American has the right as part of his cultural heritage to stand in grass as high as his head in order to feel some small measure of history coursing his veins and personally establish an aesthetic bond with the past.

> — William H. Elder,
> "Needs and Problems of Grassland
> Preservation" (1961)

Grass is the most widely distributed of all vegetable beings and is at once the type of our life and the emblem of our mortality . . . the carpet of the infant becomes the blanket of the dead.

> — John James Ingalls,
> "In Praise of Blue Grass" (1872)

Grasses are the greatest single source of wealth in the world.

> — Agnes Chase,
> First Book of Grasses (1959)

Grasses are the overseers of the soil.

In the battle which we call agriculture, grass is the first line of defence.

Of all things the most common, grasses are the least known.

> — J. C. Mohler,
> *Grasses in Kansas* (1937)

Every recorded, primitive civilization in the world was built directly on wild grasses supplemented by their cultivated kin.

> — Leo Edward Melchers,
> *Grasses in Kansas* (1937)

Grass is the only soil builder of any consequence among the natural vegetation that originally covered this continent.

Grass is that indispensable form of plant life without which civilization, as we know it, would not exist.

> — Sellers Archer and Clarence Bunch,
> *The American Grass Book* (1953)

The basis of human proliferation is not our own seed but the seed of grasses.

> — Evan Eisenberg,
> "Back to Eden" (1989)

The voice said, Cry. And he said, What shall I cry? All flesh is grass, and all the goodliness thereof is as the flower of the field: the grass withereth, the flower fadeth: because the spirit of the Lord bloweth upon it: surely the people is grass.

> — Isaiah,
> 40:6–7 (eighth century B.C.)

Climb this immense knotted cord, take one fact after another, and you will progress from the vibrio to the constellation. The immanent marvel has its own cohesion. Nothing is wasted; no effort is lost. The useless does not exist. The universe has what is necessary and only what is necessary.

> — Victor Hugo,
> *The Toilers of the Sea* (1866)

Most of the evidence, such as it is, reveals that the Plains repelled the women as they attracted the men. There was too much of the unknown, too few of the things they loved. If we could get at the truth we should doubtless find that many a family was stopped on the edge of the timber by women who refused to go farther.

If one may judge by fiction, one must conclude that the Plains exerted a peculiarly appalling effect on women.

The plain gives man new and novel sensations of elation, of vastness, of romance, of awe, and often nauseating loneliness.

— Walter Prescott Webb,
The Great Plains (1931)

For these [Kansas pioneer] women, life was far from easy. The endless hours of back-breaking toil left little time for rest and leisure. Day in and day out, they worked in the house and in the fields to produce the basic necessities of life and to build a future for their children. At first, the heavy work load seemed almost unbearable; it was physically exhausting and emotionally draining. Over the years, however, most women learned to abide the drudgery and monotony which filled their lives.

— Joanna L. Stratton,
Pioneer Women (1981)

In reading [pioneer women's] diaries we come closer to understanding how historical drama translates into human experience. Through the eyes of women we begin to see history as the stuff of daily struggle.

— Lillian Schlissel,
Women's Diaries of the Westward Journey (1982)

Loneliness, thy other name, thy one true synonym, is prairie.

— William A. Quayle,
The Prairie and the Sea (1905)

By listening to a particularly individual pattern of words, catching a tell-tale emphasis, or recognizing that something is being said which the speaker may not ever have been able to say before, there is a recognition of the infinite possibilities and experiences lying just under the surface of things.

> — Ronald Blythe,
> *Characters and Their Landscapes*
> (1982)

Living in Kansas is a contradiction.

> — Graffito noted by James Shortridge,
> University of Kansas, Watson Library
> (1970)

In the Quadrangle: Bazaar

The tracks: slicked with mist and starting to freeze, and the train coming on and passing, and I bending to feel a rail warmed and dried by the heavy freight heading toward California, and then I cross the line running along her backyard, and just behind me, where the depot once stood, there is still the Santa Fe sign: BAZAR, an old spelling, and its brevity odd in a county where village names can have more letters than people, although here the hamlet has double its characters. I walk up to her house — white frame, two stories. On the grass in the cool of the October morning under the big and broken tree, windfall pears lie decaying, sweetening the air until it seems sticky, and edging the circumference of the pears is a fairy ring come up overnight, its yearly reappearance as regular as the arrival of the herons (later she will comment on it and the annual joy it brings her, and she means, *Things like this hold me here*). West down the street are weed-grown, bleached, falling wooden buildings and houses, these once the cattle town, and now not even half a dozen of them occupied, and due south, just a gray looming in the mist, is Roniger Hill. With the sweet corruption in my nostrils I remember for a moment how I came down off that hill with a shape in my head, and: she is at the door and saying, *Pleased to see you again.* She is eighty-five, reaches a small hand of agate translucence to wipe the mist from my sleeve, and she looks a bit wan, and I am asking would another time, and she says, *No, it's Friday. I call Thursday my day, when the papers and magazines arrive. Tomor-*

row is house-cleaning and personal-grooming day. Then we are in the dim room: gray linoleum, plastic-webbed aluminum chairs, a desk stacked up, the soft exhalation of her Warm Morning bottled-gas stove and atop it a kettle sending up a vaporous arm as if beckoning.

This is Blanche Schwilling. She was outside late last night to watch the comet again, and she says, *It isn't much now, not what it was in 1910.* Maybe the stargazing has thrown her off today, she is saying, because an hour ago she had to drop down on the aluminum chaise in the middle room to try to gather herself, and then she got up to write from memory a few lines from a childhood reader: *Keep plodding — 'tis wiser than standing aside,* and so on; but she still felt, she says, *dizzy as a pet coon.* She is small and lightly boned like a finch, has an enlarged heart, has buried two husbands and one son, and now she works to keep the times from burying Bazaar, the oldest village in the county. For twenty-eight years she was postmaster — never she a postmistress, that irksome word — the last one before the government soon closed down the p.o., took away the stamps, canceled the zip code, and said by its action that Bazaar was no longer a real town; and some people agreed, since the school also had been closed, because rural people know that those two elements constitute a village even more than a grocery and filling station. But there remained the Methodist church against the west hill, and when they tried to close it Blanche rallied the citizens, a victory made easy because of the quaintness of the building that still lures city people to be married here. Yet countians understood that it wasn't a frame building keeping together Bazaar — population twelve if you count those in the near hills — it was little Blanche. A woman said to me, *When Missus Schwilling goes, so will Bazaar. She holds things together with her own two hands.* Between the alternate-Sunday visits of a circuit preacher, it's up to Blanche to conduct a devotional, and every Sabbath she rings the bell, but, she says, *Nobody hears it except those of us already there, but I guess that's who it's for.*

At the turn of the century Bazaar was the terminus of a Santa Fe spur and one of the largest cattle-shipping points in Kansas. From its pens — now also gone — grass-fat steers went down the line to end up on dinner plates in Kansas City, Chicago, New York. The village sits nearly at the juncture of Rock Creek and the South Fork of the Cottonwood in the southeast corner of the quadrangle; six miles north is the Falls, near where highway 177 leaves its course through creek and river bottoms to rise onto the hills almost at the center of Chase, bypassing Bazaar and then dropping into the vale of the South Fork and heading toward the southern county line. The river and large streams here — Rock, Buck, Spring — and the roads that follow them strike similar southwest-northeast courses; only Den Creek runs counter. Sharp's Creek also comes in contrary, but just the mouth of it nips into the quad; with no other village near, inhabitants along the farther reaches of the stream belong to Bazaar. To it, then called Frank's Creek, in 1860 came John and Nancy Sharp of Tennessee, who had freed their slaves and headed west only to be driven eastward again by the great drought and subsequent starvation that forced out thirty thousand other Kansas immigrants; but the Sharps held on near Missouri and returned to the Flint Hills with the rain. A year later John died and left Nancy with their thirteen children. She raised sheep and planted cotton and made herself a small gin, spun wool and cotton together, concocted dyes from oak and walnut bark, and sold the cloth in Lawrence and thereby kept the children alive, and some of their descent today live along the creek. People say that before she died in 1884 Nancy, who had learned to extract essences and life from the rocky land, cut a goose quill and with ink made from pokeberries put her X to her last testament.

In the kitchen Blanche is setting out a tray of chocolate chip cookies, dried apricots, pumpkin seeds, white mints, and a pot of hot water for Scripture tea. I ask what that is, she hands me a baglet, and at the end of the string is a paper octagon and this: *As cold waters to a thirsty soul, so is good news from a far country. Proverbs 25:25.* I read it aloud, and she smiles so that I know she selected it, and I ask her about the sign above the faucet: NOT FOR DRINKING ONLY FOR WASHING, and she says, *It's from the cistern.* Drinking water she hand pumps each day from her well, ten strokes this morning, but twenty in dry weather.

We are in the small middle room with its seven doors. Blanche tells me about things: one of the doors leads to the old sitting room, which in 1944 she turned into the post office, and behind that door the p.o. is as it was on its last day: the photograph of President Richard Nixon, the 1974 calendar stopped on April, the rates still posted, the watermark (four feet up on the wall) from the '51 flood that unglued the stamps, the glass-front boxes, the scales, the little bell of Sarna that customers jingled to summon her to the counter — all still in place. Behind the counter, in the linoleum, two worn ellipses that give proof of her days standing and sorting and counting that never earned even the minimum wage for what the postmaster general considered a part-time job: for her those ellipses are ten thousand days when first-class postage rose only seven pennies. (She speaks of hearing old grassmen tell about the earliest post office here, a mound east of town where lay rocks inscribed with family names: anyone returning from Emporia left neighbors' letters under a stone.) Beneath her counter is a small box of glass shards from the site, a few miles west, of the plane crash that killed Notre Dame coach Knute Rockne in 1931; and there's also a glass bottle turned to opalescence and embossed WONDER-FUL EIGHT (once containing who knows what elixir) that she dug from her little vegetable garden in the backyard near the old *cyclone cave,* which she refuses to enter, preferring to take shelter in the ninety-first Psalm: *Thou shalt not be afraid for the terror by night, nor for the arrow that flieth by day.*

Just beyond this storm cellar near the tracks lies the path to the depot she walked ten thousand mornings at six to wait for the Doodlebug, the one-car "train" carrying only mail, passengers, and cream. On the crossing at the corner of her yard, two years after Rockne crashed, Postmaster John Mitchell died lugging his laundry over the tracks when he stepped in front of an engine one January
• night; but, she wonders, how do you accidentally walk into a whistling locomotive? They found the frozen body the next morning. His wife was an ignorant woman, they say, smoked a corncob pipe, and John hid away his education: in his toolbox he kept a cardboard tube and in it were his postal commission and another paper; one afternoon when a federal inspector examined Mitchell's certification, he saw a rolled-up diploma with John's name on it and, in surprise, he asked why a Yale graduate would be in this godforsaken place, and Mitchell grabbed the papers and threw them back among the tools and said, *Forget it.* Neighbors suspect a link between that sheepskin and John's death on the tracks, but the only explanation now has to be what you invent.

Blanche: *Martha Leonard came here with her husband and two sons in 1857 from Pennsylvania, and she died the next year, the first white death recorded in the county, but they say she named the town after her shop back east where she sold fancywork and infants' clothes. Later a postmaster changed the town name to Mary, but it didn't stick.* By the way Blanche phrases that, she means, We're too eccentric for that name to fit.

She says, *Bazaar began up on the old trail a half mile west, where*

*our last schoolhouse is, up next to the cemetery. The first stone
school was up there too, one room. It was the heart and we were
the blood of Bazaar. They did everything in the building: voting,
ciphering matches, spelldowns, cotillion dances, singing lessons,
moot courts, magic-lantern shows, literary societies.* (She doesn't
say it, but I've read about the Utile Dulce Society that met there: on
one occasion, the *dulce* was an interpretation of "Hiawatha's
Wooing," and on another the *utile* was a demonstration of a sausage
grinder.) *They held church in the room, and grange meetings. The
schoolhouse record book states the building was to be open for
anything from a political meeting to a monkey show — sometimes
probably about the same thing. Funerals too: the teacher would
gather the children in the back of the room during the service, and
later they'd see the coffin carried out the door and across the
schoolyard to the cemetery.*

She is pausing now and watching the misted morning press on
the windowpanes, the day seeming to have not enough light in it to
give to the room, and she says, with vigor, *So what did we do with
that rock schoolhouse? We tore it down. We only left one step. But
they didn't get our last building when they consolidated the district. We kept it for a community center. They didn't get it.* And
I'm thinking how the highway department did get the massive
triple-arch bridge over the South Fork a mile east, among the finest
stone spans in the Middle West; largely because of one nonresi-
dent's complaints, the county bosses refused to let its beauty and
history stand alongside the new bridge.

Blanche says, *The railroad built to here in 1885 to reach the
pastures, then stopped. We were the end of things and boomed up
to seventy-five people. Then in 1923 the tracks were laid on
through, and we were soon on the main line, but it wasn't enough,
especially when trucks started hauling the cattle — that was about
it.* So, what remains is the inertia of existence, Blanche Schwilling's
will not to let go, and the few women of the village who continue
collecting rags and gathering to tear them to make rugs to sell at
their annual benefit called the Bazaar Bazaar.

I ask to see the upstairs, and she lets me lead: one room piled and
the doorway labeled DISASTER AREA and pasted to the wall is a
newspaper clipping about Zebulon Pike passing nearby and another
with a photograph of her in a tiara when she was the centennial
queen of the courthouse; a second room for her diaries she's kept
for seventy years and her hobby collections: *I've labeled them from*

A to Z: N is napkins, H is handkerchiefs. P is my favorite, my potpourri of prayers. I ask what Z is, and she says, *Zip code cancellations.* And her bedroom under the roof-sloped ceiling, the walls close: tidy, sparse, only a chair and steel bed with a white coverlet over the little concavity in the mattress where she sleeps in the fetal position, a string from the pull chain on the naked bulb in the ceiling to the bedstead, and an old mirror with the silver mostly gone as if all its reflections had worn it through.

We are again in the middle room. *When Carrie Chandler lived down here, she jumped when she had a chance to move to Cottonwood, and someone asked, "But you'll be buried in Bazaar, won't you?" and she said, "I've been buried here long enough."* It's a story I've heard several times because it so encapsulates for the citizens the challenge of living in the old hamlet. Blanche, as she has for the last couple of hours, sporadically taps her small right shoe on the floor as if counting time, and she says, *I could never be buried here long enough unless I missed the Resurrection,* and she speaks of her two years teaching school on Osage Hill where she taught as many as five students, of the greeting cards she sells although she ends up using most of them herself, of her late-hours tatting in front of Johnny Carson, of how she'll doze off in the aluminum chaise until two A.M. She rises from her chair and crosses the dim room, puts on her hearing aid as if to listen for the mist against the windows or some ethereal footfall on the porch. She takes a page from an envelope and passes it to me: a typed sheet, her obituary.

In Ecstasy

The pink polish is chipped on the sixteen-year-old girl's fingernails, and dried blood is caked around the cuticles: she grasps the scrotum gently and pulls it taut and with a scalpel cuts off the tufted base and throws it down, reaches deep into the sac to find the testicular cords, jerks them loose, and drops the testes into the clouded water of a gallon jar holding another three dozen. The whole operation is nearly bloodless. Cheryl will cut calves but she refuses to brand them — *that* she leaves to the others. In my nostrils is the smell of burnt Hereford hair, an odor that takes getting accustomed to, and white smoke from the electric branding iron swirls up for a few moments, then blows clear; on the little bull's haunch is a flying ⅃⁊ the raw skin shining brown like new harness leather. Linda leans and thrusts a hypodermic needle into the haunch.

Through all of this the four-month-old bull has lain silent, but when Arlene puts the electric iron to its skull to burn off the buttons that would grow into horns, and smoke swirls again, the animal bawls keenly. Then it's all over, and the calf table — a hinged chute that clamps and lays out the Hereford — swings back upright and opens, and the little fellow shoots across the corral and looks around in confusion, and somebody calls out in falsetto, *Welcome to steerdom!* The five women move the next animal toward the calf table, but this one is recalcitrant, and Jane says, *Come on, sugar,* and it takes a step or two and then throws its heavy little skull against Cheryl's head, and she drops to the dust, and it's a few minutes before she can continue. When she does there is no vengeance in her work. Throughout the hot June morning none of the all-woman crew has cussed or kicked the animals. If you've ever watched men castrating, branding, dehorning, and inoculating cattle, you know it just isn't done this way.

Jane Beedle Koger owns these calves and the land they graze on; she is thirty-five, dark blond, about a thumb's length taller than five feet, and she often does things the way they aren't done. Consider her corral attire: a pink pith helmet, high-top pink sneakers, an emblazoned T-shirt, WE'RE OUT TO WIN OUR SPURS. Earlier she said seriously to me, *My views aren't always in tune in here, so I keep them turned down.* While she usually hires only women to work cattle, she does employ one man to help with her two hundred acres of feeder crops, but now that the last little bull has been cut I'm the only intact male in six miles, and one of the women has just flashed the knife toward where I sit watching above the calf table and says, *Next?* and another says, *Forget it — he's a canner,* meaning an animal too old to bring a good price, the kind Koger believes goes into most franchise burgers, and somebody says, *Couldn't even get a Little Mac out of him.*

Jane Koger has awakened feminism in her employees as Linda Thurston helped awaken hers, and this morning she said, *Agricultural knowledge doesn't pass on a Y chromosome — it's learned behavior, and if a cowboy can learn to work cattle, anybody can. I mean, his idea is, "If it don't fit, get a goddamn hammer." When a woman is around animals, her nurturing instinct comes out.* Jane knows that any cowboy who didn't scorn such talk would be ridiculed, and she also knows that, in spite of her early success, men here still say an all-woman operation can't last long; her response is to quote native son William Allen White: *My advice to the Women's Clubs of America is to raise more hell and fewer dahlias.* She raises only a little of the first and none of the other, but she does raise three hundred crossbred Herefords. She can see no reason for rodeos that only perpetuate adolescent male myths about cowboys and encourage a moronic masculine desire for dominance over dumb animals: *Some of these guys are so bright they can't even see when they're running a pasture calf to death.*

When the cattle are again on the grass, we climb into her Jeep, and she hands me the jar of ballocks rolling sluggishly in the thick water as we bounce back to the ranch, where she will clean the little creamy ovoids, heavily veined with purple and looking like nothing so much as nighthawk eggs, and to her friends she will dole them out like Godiva chocolates. As for herself, she's never eaten one.

I've known Jane for a year or so, occasionally seeing her along the desolate roads near her pastures in the southeast part of the county, but it was only a couple of weeks ago that I went to her home in Bazaar after I heard her crew was going to cut and brand. That evening we stood and talked on her back porch, and she said abruptly, *Do you eat red meat?* and I thought she was setting me up as she likes to do, and I said, if it's brown, and she said, *I just got some steaks today.* We went inside and she began fixing two mail-order strips. Jane doesn't eat her own animals; about that she said, *Inconsistency is just great,* and she put the cuts on the grill and said, *I grew up eating beef twice a day. Now maybe it's once a week.* Jane Koger's six-thousand-acre Homestead Ranch, a third of which she leases for transient grazing, goes mostly to her year-round cow and calf operation where she allows eight acres to each animal, twice the transient ratio.

She grew up in Cottonwood Falls. Her father, Evan, a Yale graduate in English literature, is an heir to one of the big ranching operations in the state, a place partly comprising land bought from the New York Rockefellers by her great-uncle, the son of a Kansas immigrant from Connecticut in 1883 who became wealthy in banking and realty speculation. On that ranch in the Gypsum Hills of southwest Kansas, Jane and her sisters used to spend summers working cattle. Her mother is a native countian and a descendant of the Norton Ranch family. When Jane went off to the first of several colleges, she vowed never to return to Kansas; she studied some religion but never graduated, although she did earn her pilot's license. At a tiny Nazarene college in Idaho she realized the Flint Hills still held her even after eight years, and a novel gave her the final urging: *Evan challenged me to read* Atlas Shrugged, *so I did, and Dagny Taggart became my mentor. I thought if she could run a railroad and succeed while playing by men's rules, I could operate some outfit. She woke up in me the importance of ethics in business and the dangers of compromise. So I came home to run my railroad, which turned out to be a ranch, and I've been motivated — like Dagny — by anger at people saying, "You can't."*

Evan Koger saw several reasons for not buying Chase pastureland at more than the fifty dollars an acre he had last paid years earlier, and he refused to help Jane buy back land once in her mother's family. She said to me, *I figured it was better to buy it and lose it than never to try. Evan antagonized me to success. He'd say, "Jane, you can't do it. There are things you just can't do." But I knew that, because we're not as strong as men, we don't have to be as dumb, so instead of muscle we use a come-along to pull a calf from the uterus, or we get a front-end loader to move a chute. Gears and ratchets and hydraulics are great equalizers. The upshot of all this was that, with my sister Kay, I committed to a quarter-of-a-million-dollar debt to the Federal Land Bank. I was twenty-five then. Evan gave some seed stock. Later I bought out Kay's interest — she and her husband run a ranch up at Hymer. After my grandmother died I bought her home, this house, and remodeled it a little, and now I've reassembled a lot of family land. When I'd proved a few things — had succeeded almost in spite of Evan — then he contributed some more land. I've taken a rancher's short course at Kansas State — my family calls it a short rancher's course — and I've attended a stockmen's school in Texas, and I read. Still, people here think I've had it all handed to me. They say Evan Koger was born with a silver spoon in his mouth, but his kids have left him with a plastic fork.*

She set out the steaks and rice and broccoli, and I said that I'd heard she had one of the biggest ranches in Chase among those who run their own cattle, and she said, somewhat absently, *I suppose,* and then, *People here sit around and compare how poor they are, see who's the worst off. I mean, being successful in this county is suicide. Nobody wants you to succeed. People get together and tear you down, and that used to bother me until I realized it wasn't just me they tore down — I saw that, if they could chew me up and spit me out as a potential failure or whatever, they wouldn't even pause before going on to the next person. They'll get around to you too. I just don't understand it: they talk about economic development in Chase and at the same time they don't want anybody to achieve anything.*

I said someone had told me that in spite of all the low-income families here, there were a dozen countians worth more than a million dollars out of a population of only about three thousand, and she nodded and said, *But this is still a great county for not taking risks and not having a good time. Before my parents moved away, they belonged to the Over Forty Club, and all they did was have good times. There's nothing like that around now. A lot of these people don't know what they have because they've always lived here, and it's the only world they know so it looks typical and ordinary. That's sad.*

Later she would say, *Last year a colt was born in the early morning, and I was there with it. That afternoon I was in New York, on Broadway, buying a ticket for* The Search for Signs of Intelligent Life in the Universe, *Lily Tomlin's one-woman show. I was standing in line with trash blowing around, bag ladies limping by, everything shoulder to shoulder, and I was thinking of that wet colt in Chase County, Kansas, and I felt I knew how different this place is and what it's worth. I love New York, and one of the reasons I love it is that it shows me what I have in this county.*

To the end of helping city people explore the tallgrass country and understand where their Whoppers and tenderloins come from, for several weeks each year Jane opens the Homestead to a few women; for sixty dollars a day, a visitor can eat and sleep in the old south ranch house on Thurman Creek and loaf about the prairie, or she can join the crew and help work cattle, even down to castration. Jane said: *I like people, but I live where there aren't many, and I want to share some of this prairie — a few people at a time. But to get outsiders to see the beauty, they have to ease back and stay for a while. This place comes to you slowly — or maybe we come slowly to it. I want women to see the reality of my operation, and, if they're not afraid, they can watch a pregnancy check or watch the electro-ejaculator go up the bull's rectum, and they can help measure testicles to determine if he's fit to service my cows. People should understand at this basic level what has to happen to put a burger in their mouths. The women who come in here are great. They ask all the questions you hope nobody will ever ask, like "How do you make silage?" They don't mean, how do you cut and pack it — they want to know how caramelization works. They want to know about drugs and chemical enhancements in my beef, and I tell them I use antibiotics only by injection. They're necessary to inoculate against pinkeye and influenza, and I put antibiotics into cattle feed only during the three weeks of stress following weaning. Hormones I don't use at all, and no ear implants. I tell these women they should get after the cattle industry because too much shit goes into beef — not nearly as much, of course, as goes into hogs. If it was feasible now, I'd raise only natural beef. I'd feel better about organic meat, but ranchers' traditions and consumers' unwillingness to pay a few cents more makes it difficult. When the Europeans announced they wouldn't buy American beef because of possible dangers to humans from animals laced with hormones and drugs, I cheered. I mean, when will we wake up?*

After we finished the meal and pushed our chairs from the table, she said, *There's no public access in the Flint Hills worth talking about so my "internships" — the real name is Prairie Women Adventures — help out, and I have some control over who explores my land. I think a private response like this is better than the prairie park, even if I can only take five or six people a week.*

I said, you're an assault-rifle radical until the park comes up, and then you turn into a shoot-that-clock reactionary, and she said again, *Inconsistency is just great. You know that my grandmother was one of the leading park opponents, but I've never been opposed to maintaining grassland, although I am against overrunning the place. You've got two million acres in Yellowstone, and now they're moving out bears instead of Winnebagos — that's mismanagement I don't want to see happen here.* She was warming up, and what she took to be my view on issues may have altered her words somewhat. *I like Aldo Leopold's idea of stewardship: just because the recorder of deeds says the land is mine doesn't really make it mine, but in this county I'd rather admit I'm a feminist than an environmentalist. People tolerate me — they even expect me to be a feminist, but being an environmentalist is just not an acceptable mode of behavior, although one day ranchers and conservationists are going to be on the same side. Already we both agree that the place can't be opened to Winnebagos or tourist strips and still survive.*

For the third time the phone rang, and for the second time she said, *No, he's here,* and when she sat again, she said, *I've learned that I can't get the land to do what I want it to do. Mostly I have to follow what it wants to do, so it's my responsibility to learn how the prairie lives. If the land wants fire, I give it a match. I'm a manager, that's all, and basically what I am is a bug manager — what I'm really interested in is my cows' digestion, and that's a result of microorganisms in soil and water and stomachs. Basically, this is a bug ranch. Don't thank a rancher for your steak, thank bugs.*

I leaned toward the floor and said, thank you one and all, and she groaned and with her pink sneaker kicked my chair. She said, *Look: one day I'm going to write an essay called "Maggots and Rattlesnakes," and the idea will be that we're all in this together, even the things we may not like. Maggots are an integral part of my world where I have dead animals and disease. I need all kinds of decay — my business depends on it. My crop is really grass, and cattle are just the means to harvest and package it.*

I said that not everyone here saw things that way, and, especially, the absentee landlords did not seem to act as stewards, and Jane said, *The bad thing about absentee ownership is the system of payments where the managing cowhand receives a check from the cattle owner and then the cowhand pays the landlord. We need to reroute it so that the cattle owner pays the landlord, who will inspect the pastures to protect her investment, and then she'll pay the cowhand. The way it is now, in the short term, overgrazing gives more dollars to managers and cattle owners.*

I asked whether absentee owners didn't often treat their land like old-time bonds where all the investor did was clip a coupon and send it in, and she said, *It's hard to care about what you don't see. A couple of years ago I wanted to double absentee owners' taxes, which would have included Evan, and the county treasurer said she'd go along if I could convince my father. Well, goodbye to that idea.* Jane sat quietly for a while, I picked up the plates, and she said, *If anyone anywhere should be environmentalists, all of us here should: if we lose the land's productivity, we've lost our hope of living on here.*

Out along the near tracks the Santa Fe horned and dieseled through Bazaar, its noisy regularity a kind of Big Ben to the hamlet. She said, *Ask one last question and then go home,* and I asked what was so special about the Flint Hills. Picking and handling her words carefully as if they were newborn, taking her time, she said, *These hills are so everlasting. I get bored with the work sometimes but never the place. But you need an excuse to stay on, and ranching is one we all understand.* And a moment later: *I've come to see that if I sit still, things and people will come here. Even canners like you,* and she was quiet and then said, *Maybe that's the religion I left Kansas to find.* There was a silence, and when I thought it safe, I said, and then you tapped the heels of your ruby slippers three times, and she let fly a pink sneaker, and she said quietly, *Nevertheless.*

After I was out the door and in the cool and dewed night, a chuck-will's-widow calling from a wooded slope, I noticed for the first time her Jeep license-plate letters: IMNXTC.

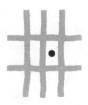

Beneath a
Thirty-Six-Square Grid

Items found, things dug up, oddments of the grasses like shards under a digger's grid:

CRIBBING ARISTOTLE. Earth, air, fire, water: the fruit of these ancient elements here is tallgrass, and from it proceeds the way of life.

THE VIEW FROM THIRTY THOUSAND FEET. If, in June, you look down from a jetliner on Chase County, ninety-five percent of what you see will be grasses — native, alien, cultivated, wild.

ONLY ALFALFA IS NOT. Of the four major crops here, three are grasses — wheat, sorghum, corn. The major pursuit, beef, absolutely depends on grass. You can see how, given the present American diet, grasses stand between us and hunger.

IN ABSENCE OF POISONS. In North America, tallgrasses probably began evolving about twenty million years ago, most likely in tandem with herbivores, against whose teeth grass has not the usual vegetative defenses of toxin or spine but instead only cellular structures containing silica — microparticles of "sand" — that strengthen the plant and also wear down the teeth of grazers, a defense that would seem as effective as a holdup victim's breathing hard on the gunman's cold pistol to corrode it. Yet, if you take a field knife of finest steel and cut a couple of armfuls of prairie grass, you'll find the blade dulled as if you'd dressed out a buffalo.

ERTHS. The soils of the American grasslands, according to one old taxonomy, belong either to the Prairyerths — lying generally east of the ninety-sixth meridian in the North and the ninety-seventh farther south — or to the more western Blackerths. Chase County lies among the Prairyerths close to where they meet the Blackerths of the mixed-grass region. Tallgrass is to Prairyerth as cypress to swamp, caribou to tundra.

SNAPSHOT. I am on an upland in a fine stand of little bluestem and some buffalo grass, a place of full light where the only shadows are poor, tiny, fleeting: a few leaves of wild indigo, a spider web, the flight of a bird.

WHY THE BREADBASKET. The Prairyerths and Blackerths are deep soils, lightly granular, relatively nonacid, unleached, with full stores of humus and minerals. Weathering (wetting, drying, freezing, thawing) and deeply penetrating roots (especially those of the grasses) that "stir" the soil provide nearly every element favorable to plant growth. This mixing of climate and earthen crust has made the middle of America the most plenteous agricultural region on the planet.

THE WESTERINGS. The signature of the long prairie, big bluestem, probably originated in the valleys of the Appalachian Mountains, although its character is better suited to the climate and landforms farther west; its migration recapitulates the grand plate movement of the crustal rock it comes from, and it's also an analog of human passages: red and white.

ETYMOLOGIES. Unlike unrelated and non-native "Kentucky" bluegrass, the name bluestem is self-evident if you look closely at the lower end of a leaf where it branches away in purplish blueness from the stalk; you will also understand an earlier and more accurate, if less elegant, name: bluejoint. Look at the seed head of spread prongs on big blue and you'll understand its other names — turkeyfoot, turkeyclaw — and watch the heads of little blue turn to white silkiness in the autumn and you'll understand its other name — prairie beard grass — and its Latin generic name: *Andropogon*, man's beard.

FORGET THE BLUE GRAMA. Of the nearly seventy species of native grass growing in Chase County, the cattleman cares about five: big and little bluestem, Indian grass, switch grass, and sideoats grama. Many ranchers consider that a sufficient diversity.

LIKE THE CHINESE ARMY. On upland ranges away from wooded vales some ninety percent of the vegetation is grass, yet three quarters of the species are nongrasses: the dominance of grass lies in its bulk, not its variety. The native forb with the largest number of species, about as numerous as the grasses combined, is the aster, yet its members are nearly invisible.

SNAPSHOT. I am up on a ridge. In spite of the rise and fall of the hills, the grass gives such openness that it distorts elevation and turns this land into mere length and breadth, into an apparently horizontal place, a myth you can truly dispel only by walking cross-country.

WERE IT NOT FOR ROOTS AND CUDS. The work of Chase is the turning of soil and cellulose into humanly digestible carbohydrate and protein. If this immense conversion of sugars were to fail, only a half-dozen quarrymen could earn a living.

VESSEL OF WRATH. Although humankind's most commonly concocted beverage, beer, comes from a grass, the native grasses of the tall prairie are too deficient in sugars to serve as a source of brewing malt. Were Kansas known for barley instead of beef and wheat, local notions would be different, and Carry Nation would not likely have chopped up her first saloon thirty-five miles from here.

HEKA HO! GENERAL CUSTER. With its growth tissues protected, tallgrass attracts grazers and fire to itself, thereby turning apparent enemies into allies that help destroy seedling trees and non-native broadleaf plants, the real rivals of long grass: the Kansa inviting in the cavalry to subdue the Pawnee.

THE ANTHILL PRINCIPLE. Some tallgrasses keep sixty percent of their weight underground and seem to treat the world of sunlight as alien and dangerous, a realm to enter as a spinster does the stock market, venturing only a portion at a time on a few blue chippers, yet ready, if they fail, to cut her losses and get out. Big bluestem invests germ so conservatively that some prairie botanists have never found in the wild a big blue seedling.

THE LESSON OF BEASTS. The survival of mammals on a grassland where cover is scarce depends upon at least one, commonly two, and sometimes three facilities: herding, burrowing, running. Native peoples dominated the plains when they developed all of them: clans, earth lodges, horses.

SNAPSHOT. It has just rained, and I'm walking a drenched crest where the little bluestem has turned nearly to amethyst, as it does on a wet October day (people accustomed to city lawns are surprised to see tall prairie respond to autumn with subtle hues of cinnamon and wine, like an oak-hickory forest, and showing more rich colors in some years than others, like maples). This hill has no intermediary horizon of trees so I am the highest thing, a solitary projection, and the roundness of the sky seems nearly accessible: the grasses allow me the illusion I can raise my arms to stir the bowl of heavens, and that notion makes my blood regret the long, ancestral years of skulking in the forest.

NO SOFT FOCUS. In the early days of settlement, when countians used the words *flint hills*, they meant upland pastures as distinct from cultivated bottoms, but the term broadened and came to include the whole of the two-hundred-mile-long, east-central rumpling across the state. Academics' later attempts to name the region the Bluestem Hills failed, and that's odd, since flint breaks farm implements, slices tires, cuts up stock, injures people, and contributes virtually nothing to the natural exchange that makes the land abundant here. It's as if we were to chuck out the several epithets of Lincoln — Honest Abe, the Great Emancipator, the Man Who Saved the Union — and happily call him Old Wart Face.

THE ORTHOPTERAN CHORUS. In October the dominant sounds in the tall prairie are the raspings and clicketings of grasshoppers, katydids, and crickets; everywhere among the long stems cling translucent-winged, jointed-bodied creatures with serrated jaws that can eat the hickory handle of an ax. Like a cook who wants her pie eaten but not gobbled and so leaves a few pits in the cherries, grass laces its moist cellulose veins with silicon it takes from Permian stone: seawater become rock borrowed by bluestem to blunt the jaws of bugs.

WHAT ZEB SAID. After Zebulon Pike explored the center of the Heartland, he wrote in his 1808 account: *From these immense prairies may arise one great advantage to the United States, viz: The restriction of our population to some certain limits, and thereby a continuation of the Union. Our citizens being so prone to rambling and extending themselves on the frontiers will, through necessity, be constrained to limit their extent on the west to the borders of the Missouri and Mississippi, while they leave the prairies incapable of cultivation to the wandering and uncivilized aborigines of the country.* In 1871, General George Custer said in *My Life on the Plains: [The] tide of emigration . . . advanced toward the setting sun, slowly but surely narrowing the preconceived limits of the Great American Desert and correspondingly enlarging the limits of civilization. At last the geographical myth was dispelled.*

LIKE AN APOTHECARY. From the first, countians have believed

that limestone imparts to the grasses their remarkable capacity to fatten elk and antelope, bison and cattle, and the earliest geological report on Chase, by Major Hawn in 1865, attributed the thick stands of bluejoint to *gypseous clays* and spoke of several theories scientists were offering for the link between "gypsum" and the robust *vegetable economy:* the mineral serves bluestem as gastric juices do a stomach, stimulates its circulation like a tonic, supplies an invigorating spritzer of water and carbonic acid, promotes soil fermentation like yeast, fixes ammonia as calcium does bone, or acts as an exciting power to the saps like powdered unicorn horn to the old lover.

ANDROPOGON AND MEN'S BEARDS. From wind comes the sea, from it shelled creatures, from them stone, from it grasses, from them the bison, from it the hunter: a Plains Indian sometimes speaks of *the grandfather winds.*

SNAPSHOT. West of Bazaar and north of Den Creek, the grasses lie over the hills like a blanket over a sleeper, retaining the dominion they once had everywhere about. They slow my walking although this surface growth is only three months old; yet, below ground, the root systems are older than the big cottonwoods in the hollow. The prairie hides its age by peeling off its face every year and showing each spring a new one, but the cottonwoods can only swell, gnarl, extend, and break. Humankind has long seen trees as reflections of itself, and we have imagined gods in them and cut deities and holy objects from them; we will eat and build with grasses but not worship them, will see them as metaphor but not divinity; it is this separation, I think, that can create such unease when we confront the prairie. Gods may rise from oceans and clouds, but I've heard of none rising from grasses, and this is peculiar because, unlike oceans or heavens, grasslands so evidently die and are reborn, and because, although less evidently, they are the place where our kind was made.

O BRAVE NEW WORLD. Big bluestem spreads over the prairie mostly by cloning itself through lateral underground stems, its rhizomes having the capacity to replicate themselves for a century or more; it also, but less frequently, reseeds itself through sexual means, so that a slope of big blue contains both clones and seedling offspring. Could a man do this, say a Shakespeare, his precise genetic duplicate could sit down today and share an ale with his great-great-etcetera-grandchild.

HUMDRUMITY. If we judge from their many journals, nineteenth-century travelers in their first miles of crossing the prairie were astonished, appalled, and confounded by the grassed endlessness west of the ninety-fifth meridian even though they were expecting it; but their awe almost never opened to perception, turning instead to recitations of numbed miles over grass, grass, grass, from here to Tedium.

CAVEAT EMPTOR. During one year of especially good rains, Cottonwood Falls realty agent Whitt Laughridge tried to show a prospective buyer some pasture, but the bluestem was so high they couldn't see the tract. He told me: *We drove into it and had to turn around and drive out. He didn't buy it, so I guess he didn't recognize it as pasture.*

THE BOOK OF NATURE. Grasses and broadleaf plants coexist closely by sharing light and soil nutrients at different levels and different times of the year; in spite of relentlessly fierce competition, species so balance themselves that a big increase of one at the expense of others hardly happens unless there is outside disturbance. In mature grassland the communities are diversely full yet in equilibrium, but I haven't heard of any prairie politican seeing or caring to apply the parable.

THE LAST DEFENSE. The third-greatest enemy of the tallgrass is not fire, disease, herbivores, high wind, heat, cold, ice, freezing, or flood — it is drought, the force that shapes the prairie, the power that grasses roll their leaves against and counter by treating the world above ground as a treacherous place to be only tolerated, as if they understood the prepotency of drought over their second great enemy, trees. Against the biggest enemy, Western man, they have a lone defense of waiting him out, surviving in neglected pockets like those World War Two Japanese soldiers who were still creeping out of jungles a quarter of a century after the surrender.

SNAPSHOT. I am atop a hill that opens onto a circle of horizon without a single tree interrupting it. Over the last fifty years it's become a view harder and harder to find here, and I have yet to meet a longtime resident who does not say that there are more trees than ever before: seventy-six-year-old Frank Gaddie of Bazaar said, *It's got so I hate a tree.* When I first began looking around the county, I found the wooded vales, several of them reminding me of Vermont, the loveliest places in Chase, but since then, while I've not lost my pleasure in wooded hollows, I've come to cherish absolute treelessness.

THE RED AND THE WHITE. Range biologists classify species of

prairie vegetation as "decreasers" or "increasers" according to the response of a plant to agricultural practices. All of the native tallgrasses are decreasers when faced with heavy grazing, trampling, frequent mowing, plowing, even fertilizing. With their decline come the increasers, the imported grasses — fescue, brome, bluegrass. Decreasers, increasers: bluebirds, English sparrows; prairie wolves, hounds; ghost dancers, Moral Majorities.

BLUE BABIES. Unlike native grass, an alien increaser frequently needs fertilizer and irrigation to survive the vagaries of the prairie. The last time I stopped for gas on the turnpike, I saw a small sign on the door: *Matfield Green Service Area has exceeded the 10.0 mg per liter limit allowed for nitrate in drinking water*, and it warned of cyanosis, a disease caused by, among other things, fertilizer runoff.

BRAZIL. A burr oak here may live 150 years and take fifty more to decompose; for those two centuries it keeps most of its nutrients locked within itself, giving up only a smidgen each autumn in its acorns and leaves; but that superficial mat of fallen vegetation — if it isn't carried away by wind or rain — inhibits circulation of water and air and allows only a shallow recycling of nutrients. Although an oak sends down a deep taproot, the tree scarcely alters the subsoil, and that's why earth in a cleared forest can quickly lose its shallow fertility: had the Heartland been largely woods instead of prairie, America might now be what the Amazon is becoming.

LEVIATHAN. A clump of big bluestem penetrates deeply into the subsoil and carries some nutrients up and deposits them and hauls others down and stores them; the old passages of decayed roots open the soil to percolation and aeration; the brief cycle of an individual plant accelerates the process, while the thick surface network of rootlets (something that can hardly be washed or blown away) sponges up moisture and foods: in these ways the tallgrass builds soil from rock debris. As a whale surfaces for air, so big blue comes up for sunlight, but it too belongs mostly to a netherworld.

GO-BACK LAND. After pioneers had all the rich bottom acres in tillage, the second generation of countians began breaking sod on less steep hillsides and planting corn, oats, wheat, barley; for a time the plants grew on the marginal cropland, and, just before the great drought of the thirties hit, about eighty thousand acres here were under cultivation. Because most of the plowed land lay in the protected bottoms and nearly all of the remainder of the county was grass-covered, Chase fared better than many other areas; nevertheless, when the dust years finally ended here, one quarter of the cultivated acreage, mostly slopes, was on its way back to grass. It was as if, said an Oklahoma biologist, *Nature had withheld rain to rid herself of the unworthy.*

SNAPSHOT. On a rare day of near windlessness, I am sitting on a ridge that opens toward two smaller hills so similar they seem reflections. Unlike a forest, a grassland lets sound carry, and I can count distant prairie voices: a harrier, a meadowlark, an upland plover. Each calls in plaintive phrases as if it admitted the prairie solitude into its notes. When the air does move, it pulls from the bending grass around me a soft outrush like a deep breath slowly vented, the wind giving voice to the grass, and it lending a face to the wind.

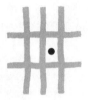

Within Her Pages

Elisha Mardin of New York came into the county in 1859, only four years after the first white settler, and made his home a few miles northeast of Bazaar and began buying livestock primarily for market in Chicago. In 1861, when he was twenty-eight and full-bearded and thinking himself well enough established, he went to Bloomington, Illinois, and, two weeks before Christmas, married Elizabeth Ann Frank. She was eighteen, small but sturdy, attractive. Sometime in 1862 Elisha brought his Quaker bride in a wagon to Chase, where they set up near Bloody Creek and lived for a decade and witnessed the clearing and tilling of the bottoms, but the upland they saw only in its aspect of the last ten thousand years.

On May Day, the bride began keeping a diary — a small thing, three by five inches — to my knowledge the earliest surviving record of daily life in the county. Elizabeth's entries cease the day before Christmas, and there is one three-and-a-half-week hiatus in October, and one November page is missing. Her 210 postings, the longest no more than five telegram-like sentences, are all in the plainest of declarations, without punctuation, and in a homemade and changeable spelling; her cursives are here tidy but elsewhere collapsing as if she were tired or writing on her lap; the entries are dispatches from a quiet prairie frontier during a time the country was fighting its internal war. She apparently kept no later diaries, although Elisha maintained one the following year, his beginning a week after Elizabeth's stops and mostly covering livestock business, with occasional mentions of *choring around,* burning pastures, sowing flax (a crop now unknown here), trading with an Indian for a pony, building a branding pen, helping home friends *pretty tight,* drilling with the militia. In May he writes this typically terse entry: *I went up to the falls & over to Bazaar after a band of garillas got back about two oclock in the after noon.* But what had he seen?

Elizabeth shows herself doing traditional tasks of a frontier wife, often helped by a hired woman, and this suggests a modest affluence. She writes with a detachment that has the strength of direct and unadorned statement, and, other than weather, she rarely evaluates anything: the woman who appears within her pages is one adjusting quickly to the prairie; if she is happy to see her walls plastered or a new cellar cemented or a cistern dug, she keeps mum. From time to time she does speak of weariness and not feeling well, but otherwise she and Elisha and her friends enter and exit as if in tableaux vivants. Her lack of intimacy — except for two expostulations of loneliness — suggests that Elizabeth recorded only what she was likely to forget rather than, say, her sorrow at the unexpected death of her helping woman's husband. Although writing just for her own ends (on her birthday she remarks merely on sewing and weather), she still confides nothing that could embarrass her in front of someone coming along later, such as a voyeur from another century.

Seen together, her little penciled accounts go against the conventional notion that pioneer life was all toil and burden, an eking out of drudging survival and little else: Elizabeth's pleasures may have been simple, but they were abundant. Where Gabriel Jacobs' inventory suggests days of hard work, Elizabeth's pages reveal horseback trips out to Jacobs' Mound, canoe rides on the Cottonwood, and overnight visits with friends.

Here is a month of entries, May to Christmas, 1862:

Sunday, May 4: *was home all day reading a book it was a very plesant day*

Wednesday, May 7: *I helped to wash   we had a large washing I got very tired lisha came home it was a plesant day*

Friday, May 9: *Molly and I ironed all day Elisha went to town* [Emporia] *I am so lonsome it is a plesant day*

Tuesday, May 13: *I was in bed all day nearly till in the evening then I worked at the babies skirt it was so warm*

Saturday, May 17: *it was very unplesant day I did not do*

much of eny thing only to help do the cooking and do the patch-ing

Wednesday, June 11: *Koke [a friend] Elisha and me went up south fork a goose berrying   it was very warm we went on horseback*

Saturday, June 21: *I went a goosebarrying in the fore noon and I went to see the soldiers drill in the after noon it was a plesant day*

Tuesday, June 24: *I cut carpet raggs there was to gentlemen here for dinner it was a plesant day they commenced the cellar*

Tuesday, July 1: *Molly and I washed in the fore noon we fixt the clock so that it would run*

Thursday, July 3: *We baked some cakes and roasted a pig to take to the fourth it was a plesant day*

Friday, July 4: *we went to the dinner we had a good dinner a good speach there was a good menny folks there*

Monday, July 7: *I was not very well   I had dreadful soare lips finished the cellar went to the garden*

Wednesday, July 16: *I made a sheat and cut out a pair of drawers for Elisha it was a plesant day*

Tuesday, July 22: *I made me a under waste I went to Fowlers and took tea and went to Prathers and stade all night*

Tuesday, August 5: *I worked at lisha shirt   Elisha went to Emporia coke killed a pig Molly and I dressed it*

Saturday, August 9: *Molly and me went after plumbs and grapes I got a letter from Sarah [her sister who would later join her]*

Saturday, August 16: *I don the ironing and picked the grapes for pies*

Monday, August 18: *I done the morning work   swept the yard we had company Mr Davis and Mason*

Wednesday, September 17: *Mandy washed Miss Jacops [Gabriel Jacobs' daughter] was here   I went with her to Mollys Frank took sick*

Sunday, September 21: *I wrote a letter to lin [another sister] in the fore noon and went to Mollys in the evening   Frank died in the night*

Monday, September 22: *I went to Mollys and done the work was there all day came home and went back   sat up all night*

Tuesday, September 23: *I went to the graveyard   went to stouts for dinner came home and was very tired and sick*

Wednesday, October 29: *I was at home   Elisha was sick tended to Elisha   worked to my quilt Manda came home*

Monday, November 17: *I lined my muffetees Elisha and linly*

went to Emporia   Hodgin went to Gipson for some eggs   got a
dozen and a half
    Thursday, November 20: *Manda washed and I worked at the
shirt in the fore noone and then I done the other work*
    Monday, December 1: *I fixt me a skirt ready to quilt   I had a
sore finger   I could not sew*
    Tuesday, December 2: *I did not do much of any thing only
tend to the work*
    Friday, December 12: *we cleaned some of the [hog] guts for
soap grease   it sprinkled rain*
    Sunday, December 14: *at home all day   we rendered out lard
in the morning   it was a glumy day*
    Friday, December 19: *I baked ten pies and fore kakes   it was
a very plesant day   we had rain in the evening*
    Saturday, December 20: *The folks went home   I went to bed
at eleven and slept till four*

Three days before Christmas, Elizabeth left on a long visit to her
parents in Illinois, and Elisha later joined her there briefly. In his
diary of the next year, he mentions Elizabeth not even two dozen
times, yet in the memoranda section of her diary she copied out
this:

> *Remember me Oh*
> *pass not thou my grave*
> *Without one thought whose*
> *Relics there recline*
> *The only pang my bosom*
> *dare not brave*
> *Must be to find*
> *forgetfulness in thine*

    Her early entries about making baby clothes and her frequent
spells of not feeling well suggest a pregnancy, but their first child
was not born until a decade later when the Mardins had moved forty
miles south, out of the county, to Eureka; none of their three daughters ever heard anything about a miscarriage, and they believed the
baby clothes were gifts, perhaps to be given along with the meat the
Mardins took to war widows in Emporia. Elisha, despite his numerous entries about being sick, lived to be eighty-three, but Elizabeth
died a few weeks short of her fiftieth birthday.
    I first read her diary, in typescript, on a flight to Los Angeles; as
we flew over Chase County, I thought how odd to hear Elizabeth
Mardin's words in a machine she would have found incredible and

how, surely, she never dreamed her hours of boiling hog fat and baking wild mulberry pies would one day move in the mind of someone riding five miles above her homestead on a morning so pleasant the sky showed the edge of darkness of deep space, that indigo of stratospheric flight. Seated next to me was a friendly and loquacious woman well into her eighth decade in whose face I imagined an older Elizabeth. When she spoke, as if to remind me of her presence, she put her hand on my wrist, and I was surprised how something of so little flesh could be so soft, so heated, but her insistent conversation at last led me to pass her the typescript for, I hoped, a long and close reading. When she finished somewhere above the Mojave Desert, she returned Elizabeth's diary and said, *How far we've come from it all.*

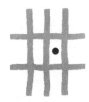

On the Town: A Night at Darla's

I am sitting at the bar, a compact L-shaped thing of ten stools, and I am by the wall, almost pressing myself against it as if trying to be invisible, but that's foolish, since I'm jotting down items. Such activity in this place is most conspicuous, but ducking into the men's toilet for notations is out of the question, so I'm trying to disguise my scribbling by occasionally copying figures from a State Board of Agriculture *Annual Report* manifestly open on the bar. It's just past six in the evening, and conversations flow past me, riffles against a creek-bank stone.

I'm in Darla's Fun Center, called the Long Horn Bar when I first visited Chase, the only taproom left in Cottonwood, and one of three in the county. A century ago the taverns here bore English pub names: the White Swan, the Blue Goose, the Dolly Varden (a woman's hat, a dress, a trout, or a coquette in *Barnaby Rudge*), and the distance between Dolly and Darla may measure how far we've come. Darla's, a few doors down from the Emma Chase, is a couple hundred feet beyond where the tip of the courthouse cupola shadow ceases on the winter solstice. Above the front doorway is a Pepsi sign holding a ragged starling nest, and inside the door and tossed down is a paper dinner plate; on it in a mixture of upper and lowercase letters: *bAcK aT FiVe*. The smudged paneling on the walls seems more to bespeak the age of the building than to cover it, and near me, just beyond arm's reach over the bar, the cash register stands open as if brisk trade didn't allow for time lost

opening and closing it. There are nine customers here — three are
ten-year-old boys playing the video game — and there's the bartender, an ursine man of late middle years whose air of apparent men-
ace is undermined by his perpetual lifting with his tongue and
thrusting forward his lower denture, which then unrolls his nether
lip; occasionally he removes his plates altogether to make a grotesquerie of his face to amuse the boys. He smiles seldom in spite
of his wisecracks, but he suffers more from annoyance than anger;
he wears an adjustable billed cap that says FECES OCCURS, and
I think of grammarians who'd like to counter with hats reading
SUBJECT-VERB AGREEMENT.

Near my stool is an empty number-ten green bean can used as a
spittoon, and at my elbow the cue-chalk jug holds a twenty dollar
bill a customer has left for a pool stick when the salesman next
comes around. In various places are gallon jars of brined things —
turkey gizzards, sausages, eggs, dill pickles, jalapeño peppers — and
there's also a large bottle of Tabasco; after five o'clock, other than
the corner grocery and the quick-stop that hasn't yet opened, these
jars hold the only food for sale in town. I've been in the cold
wind most of the day, and I'm happy enough to order a paper towel
of pickled gizzards, which I slice with my pocketknife. I have a
glass of three-point-two malt beverage, called beer in Kansas: I've
not developed a taste for something known as a *red one,* beer mixed
with a slug of tomato juice so there's *something* to taste. (Still,
I should be grateful: Kansas, forever long on temperance, once
banned even near beer, and the last commercial brewer in the
state, John Walruff of Lawrence, peddled his beer as a health
beverage called Celebrated Stomach Invigorator.) Darla sells no
wine or hard liquor. The three pool tables are idle and so is the
domino table and also the men's toilet, the door always remaining open (unless a stranger goes in), a useful practice, since the
three-point-two beer makes for soddenness before drunkenness.
After dark, the peeing behind pickup trucks on Broadway that so
annoys some of the citizens is really a problem of mathematics:
one toilet plus twenty imbibers times three-point-two equals
outside.

I am copying down a hand-lettered sign posted by the blackboard:

WANTED: SET OF COMFERTABLE KITCHEN CHAIRS
WOULD PERFER SET OF SIX
WILL SETTLE FOR FOR.

Feigning concentration, I then copy down a few figures from the *Annual Report*, and later a headline on the major front-page story in the *Leader:*

JANITOR APPLICANTS INTERVIEWED.

A fellow with two silvery teeth alternating with two missing ones that give his smile the look of a '49 Buick grille says to a middle-aged woman who taunts him (and I write it down while looking at the *Report*), *Be nice to me or I'll date your daughter,* and she says, after having gotten the words straight, *You're so dumb, if you fell in a barrel of tits you'd come up sucking your thumb,* and he, *You're so ugly we're all hoping that wind don't blow off your clothes.* In fact, the woman is fair of face and a wind is more likely to blow the hide off a heifer, her cowboy shirt and denims fitting as they do: what could be soft folds and drapings are creases like blades. She says, *At least I ain't so ugly I got to tie a bandanna over Old Paint's eyes fore I get on.*

The people listening are attentive not so much to the memorized put-downs as to the possibility of real friction, but it stops there. They all have known one another for years, and they keep their ripostes to whiskered raillery and corn, covers that nevertheless express irritations and yet do not bring to light truly poisonous things they know about each other. The mutual protections are as genuine as the subsumed hostilities, with more ragging than real ridicule, yet all of them — except me, the unknown outsider — sit on a land mine another person can detonate at any moment, even though they are more likely to come to blows, knowing the child's chestnut about sticks and stones is opposite actuality: their learning this comity is the first lesson of survival in the village. The result is laughter with little joy, and the shoes of every citizen carry old and unseen pebbles that make each countian, in his own way, limp along privately.

A fellow comes in and says, referring to the courthouse clock still stopped at four-forty, *I don't drink until after five, but I can't wait another year,* and someone grouses, *I'm gonna climb up and move that damn clock hand myself just so he'll quit saying that,* and the other in self-defense, *You can't drive a dry cow over a creek.* I'm writing these things down while cagily noting *Report* figures on swine production when the bartender steps up and thrusts his dentures as if pointing at me: *The owner says it's okay if you mark things down. I called him and told him what you was doing and he says you're likely that book guy.* Several people turn to watch, and

I can think of nothing to do other than order another draft of Stomach Invigorator. A man who wears a big trophy belt buckle that says WILD BULLCUTTIN' comes over: *I'll give you something to mark down, and this is truth. A guy here decided to raise bullfrogs for the supper table, and he was going to start with a dozen he'd catch. He got to figuring how they breed, and, before you knew it, he was titty-deep in frogs. He was going to have so many when he went to truck them out the police would stop him at the weight station. Now, this guy thinks a little different than you and me.* (A woman offers, *Like his antenna has fell down.*) The man says, *I'm telling you the truth. He's thinking, "If I haul them frogs alive and loose in the truck, all I got to do is watch when the inspector looks at the scale and then give that trailer a whack with a big stick and send all them frogs up in the air, and I can drive on."* The man watches me for a moment, then stubs a thick thumb on my notebook, *Mark it down*, and I do, and soon interest in my pencil wanes, and I'm just another outsider again, at the edge.

It's seven o'clock, and a man walks in and stands a bit forlornly at the bar; his eyes are lusterless like old buttons, and, in a phrase I heard yesterday, *he's been around the sun bettern fifty times.* His clothes are soiled and shabby. Someone is talking about a good coon hunt, and the forlorn one says to no one in particular, *All I ever caught was a limb in the face,* and walks out, leaving his beer; he soon returns with a loaf of white bread and a three-pound package of raw hamburger under his arm. He tears open the wrapper and lays a slice on the damp bar, digs his long and blackened nails into the meat, wads it and presses it down on the bread darkened by his hands, sprinkles Tabasco over it, the sandwich now red, white, and black; I've seen him do this once before, and I remind him to add the gunpowder. He smiles and lays out another slice, digs his begrimed fingers into the meat, mashes it down on the bread, pushes it to me, and excuses his hands: *Had to get into a crankcase today, but I only peed twice.* The sandwich is an act of generosity, not a challenge; I'm thinking about it, and the woman who has been taunting the men turns to him and watches in theatrical revolt and says, *Nothing worse than raw hamburger unless you're a dog,* and he says, *Being dead's worse,* and she, *Not in your case,* and he looks at me to plead his sanity, and I ask for the jalapeño jar, and the woman watches us bite into the sandwiches and says, *Arf-arf.* The fellow moves over to sit next to me, I order beers, and he says to the woman, *Did you hear about Harold dying from eating mountain oysters?* and she looks up in surprise, *What!* and he, *The bull fell over on him*, and the men break into laughter at her getting lured into such a hoary joke, and she coughs out a flat-voiced *Ha-ha-ha*.

We eat, and I think, thank god I'm hungry. Someone tells about a beach party thrown by people who wouldn't set foot in Darla's: how, on the sand "greens" of the golf course, they scattered mussel shells from the Cottonwood, strung out an old tennis net, and stuck a mounted fish in it. For much of this evening, conversation has been propelled by an undercurrent of sexuality that occasionally roils the waters: at one point the woman of the filled cowboy shirt attributes her proportions to nightly butter massages of her breasts, and, suddenly, something dangerous breaks the surface, but the bartender quells it with, *I use to make my old lady drink goat milk to make her butt better*, and someone says, *Well, we know now that don't work.*

Later: a man picking his teeth with a pocketknife stops probing to say, *They had this mule tied up in the trailer to haul down to Matfield, and Jimmy had been in the corn squeezings. It was at night. Jimmy was a tough old cowboy — cleaned his ears with bob wire. He'd return your strays and steal your wife. So he gets up on the jenny, and they're going down the road — a rock one — and he yells to the driver, "Speed it up!" and gives the mule his heels, and she set to like you never seen and throwed him plumb over the side, and he come up with the worst case of gravel-rash short of being skinned. They stop at the first farm and ask the old boy if he's got anything for all them cuts. "Maybe I got a cure for him," he says. Now, he remembers something about Jimmy — don't know what, but I'll bet it was about a woman. Farmer was real polite, and he leads them out to the barn and tells Jimmy to get down to his shorts. It hurts like hell just to pull them jeans off. The farmer says, "This looks like the right stuff for you," and pours a jug of screw-worm treatment over him. I'm telling you Jimmy was tough, but he run to the horse trough and jumped in, and that cold water hurt just as bad, but he sure got healed up.*

The bartender sends packing some boys trying to sneak in a can of beer; the place pauses to watch, and then the hubbub resumes, and a fellow is talking about an absentee landowner, and he says, *On three different years, she didn't like the pasture fees, so she refused to rent anything. For all the acres she owns, that's almost three quarters of a million dollars she just threw away.* The owner is well known in the county and widely disliked, so they defame her parsimony toward hired hands with stories: how, too pinchpenny to buy a hair dryer, she hangs her long gray locks out the window to dry in the summer sun; how to work hard and ask for a raise is to get fired. A bulgy man says, *Year or so ago she was up here to see her grass in her goddamn limousine, and they was out in the pasture, and she got out for something and lost a goddamn diamond earring, and so she and her goddamn chauffeur crawl around that pasture, hunting that goddamn earring. Never found it.* The listeners do not laugh but nod, for this is proper retribution.

It's after eleven, and the relative good humor of seven o'clock begins to disappear, and an aura of malevolence begins rising like ground fog. People are straggling out, and a man looking at the crankcase hands of the hamburger fellow says, *You look like a nigger backwards: backs of your hands is white but your palms is black,* and another man, who had been chided for missing the Catholic soup-supper, says, *They was a woman here wanted someone to help with her baby, and all she could find was a mammy, but she worried about her touching the baby until she seen the mammy's palms was white as snow, and so the mammy got to raise that child.*

The noise of departures protects this iniquitous warren of confabulators, and a man says, *That mammy's boys was both murdered in Strong City,* and someone else says directly to me, *They's been several niggers killed here that nobody stood trial for,* and an old fellow says, *No, both them two white boys was tried, and one of them was sent up — the only murder conviction in this county in my life.* The first says, *The other guy shot the colored boy in the back of the head and got off on self-defense — convinced the jury the guy use to wear his hat backwards.* I am thinking, for some reason they want me to know this.

The place goes suddenly quiet with the last door slam, and we all stand locked in the guilt of an evil topic, and nobody knows what to do until a fellow says, using his words to cover his exit, *Ed, you better be at that nut fry tomorrow,* and Ed hooks himself to those words and gets pulled out the door and calls a bantering farewell that someone else hooks on to, and, like a string of caught fish, they're all pulled out into the night. I'm standing awkwardly alone. The bartender pushes out his lower plate as if pointing toward the door, and he adjusts his FECES OCCURS hat, and then I'm outside too.

VI

Matfield Green

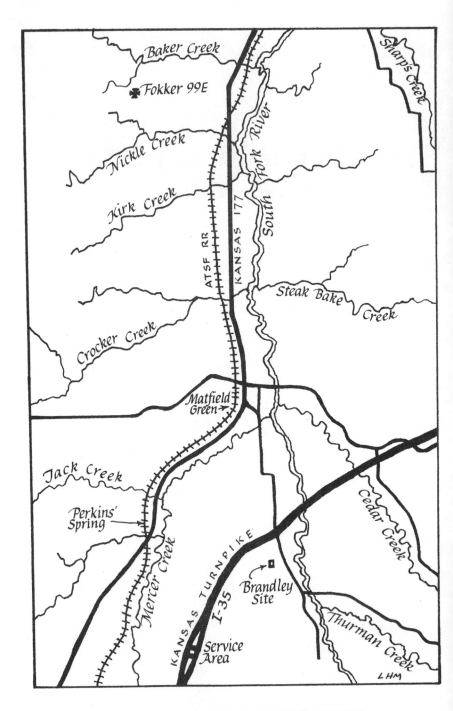

MATFIELD GREEN QUADRANGLE

From the Commonplace Book:
Matfield Green

The Power of the World always works in circles, and everything tries to be round.

> — John G. Neihardt,
> *Black Elk Speaks* (1932)

The incomprehensible takes up too much room for any to be left for the improbable.

> — Victor Hugo,
> *The Toilers of the Sea* (1866)

We do not ride upon the railroad; it rides upon us. . . . Did you ever think what those sleepers are that underlie the railroad? Each is a man, an Irishman, or a Yankee man. The rails are laid on them, and they are covered with sand, and the cars run smoothly over them.

> — Henry David Thoreau,
> *Walden* (1854)

Track crews lived along and maintained each of the six- to eight-mile sections into which the Santa Fe divided its line. The crew would spend most of its day reinforcing weak roadbeds, tapping down loose pins, replacing worn ties, and clearing the right-of-way of weeds, grass, and debris. The foreman was also responsible for daily inspection of the entire section, meaning that every day, every mile on the system was examined. The section foreman had to be a man of some experience and common sense, but the track laborer needed little skill beyond being able to hit a spike with a hammer. It was universally considered a most inferior and arduous form of labor.

As long as a man was white and not a Chicano, he could engage in any type of railroad work and aspire to advance. . . . The Santa Fe held open its doors for jobs and advancement to men who offered hard work, loyalty, talent — and a white skin.

> — James H. Ducker,
> *Men of the Steel Rails* (1983)

November 21, 1913 — The Santa Fe was teaching foremen one hundred Spanish words used in track-laying and construction work so they could give orders to Mexican laborers.

> — Jennie Small Owen,
> *The Annals of Kansas: 1886–1925*
> (1956)

Tradition says a railroad is only as good as its track, and in this the Santa Fe is supreme.

> — Merle Armitage,
> *Operations Santa Fe* (1948)

Within the prairie the conditions of life are severe. . . . After thousands of years, the species have adjusted to the environment. The plants, with few exceptions, are remarkably free from disease, regardless of weather, and are little injured by high winds or extreme heat. They may be harmed by late freezing or — infrequently — be stripped of their leaves and battered to the ground by hail, but they rarely or never are killed. Those that were unfit have disappeared.

> — John Ernest Weaver,
> *Prairie Plants and Their
> Environment* (1968)

During recent years we have heard much about the great and rapid changes now going on in the plants and animals of all the temperate regions of the globe colonized by Europeans. These changes, if taken merely as evidence of material progress, must be a matter of rejoicing to those who are satisfied, and more than satisfied, with our system of civilization, our method of outwitting Nature by the removal of all checks on the undue increase of our own species. To one who finds a charm in things as they exist in the unconquered provinces of Nature's dominions, and who, not being over-anxious to reach the end of his journey, is content to perform it on horseback or in a wagon drawn by bullocks, it is permissible to lament the altered aspect of the earth's surface, together with the disappearance of numberless noble and beautiful forms, both of the animal and vegetable kingdoms. For he cannot find it in his heart to love the forms by which they are replaced; these are cultivated and domesticated and have only become useful to man at the cost of that grace and spirit which freedom and wildness give.

> — W. H. Hudson,
> The Naturalist in La Plata (1892)

The people of the European race in coming into the New World have not really sought to make friends of the native population, or to make adequate use of the plants or the animals indigenous to this continent, but rather to exterminate everything found here and to supplant it with the plants and animals to which they were accustomed at home.

> — Melvin Gilmore,
> Uses of Plants by the Indians of
> the Missouri River Region (1919)

It comes to pass that farm neighborhoods are good in proportion to the poverty of their floras.

What a thousand acres of compass plant looked like when they tickled the bellies of the buffalo is a question never again to be answered, and perhaps not even asked.

> — Aldo Leopold,
> A Sand County Almanac (1949)

Man can grow some of the native grasses but he cannot recreate the unique variety of different prairie plants, each kind suited to a particular niche in the prairie. Once gone, replacement of animal life is equally difficult.

> — Donald Christisen,
> "A Vignette of Missouri's Native
> Prairie" (1967)

During the past six hundred million years, the natural background rate of extinction has been about one species per year. Around the world now, the rate is estimated to be one to three lost every day —

*perhaps as high as one species every hour — and the trend is acceler-
ating. Scientists predict that by the early twenty-first century, we will
witness several hundred extinctions per day.*

— G. Jon Roush,
"The Disintegrating Web" (1989)

*It is of importance to seek out these primitive races and ascertain the
plants which they have found available in their economic life, in order
that perchance the valuable properties they have utilized in the wild
life may fill some vacant niche in our own, may prove of value in time
of need or when the population of America becomes so dense as to
require the utilization of all our natural resources.*

— John W. Harshberger,
"Phytogeographic Influences in the
Arts and Industries of American
Aborigines" (1906)

*[Buffalo gourd] is one of the plants considered to possess special mys-
tic properties. People were afraid to dig it or handle it unauthorized.
The properly constituted authorities might dig it, being careful to
make the prescribed offering of tobacco to the spirit of the plant,
accompanied by the proper prayers, and using extreme care not to
wound the root in removing it from the earth. A man of my acquaintance in the Omaha tribe essayed to take up a root of this plant and in
doing so cut the side of the root. Not long afterward one of his children
fell, injuring its side so that death ensued, which was ascribed by the
tribe to the wounding of the root by the father. . . . When I have exhibited specimens of the root in seeking information, the Indians have
asked for it. While they fear to dig it themselves, after I have assumed
the risk of so doing they are willing to profit by my temerity; or it may
be that the white man is not held to account by the Higher Powers of
the Indian's world.*

— Melvin Gilmore,
*Uses of Plants by the Indians of the
Missouri River Region* (1919)

*The [Indian] women gathered [tipsin, or breadroots] by digging them
out of the sod by means of digging sticks [and] when [the women]
went out to the prairie to dig tipsin, the mothers would show the
children some of the plants and call attention to their appearance and
habits. Noting the branching form of these plants, the mother would
say to the children: "See, they point to each other. Now here is one:*

notice the directions in which its arms are pointing. If you go along in these directions and look closely you will find other plants in line with the direction of each pointing arm."

The children were interested and eager to show their own alertness and ability, and so they were happily busy in finding other tipsin plants for their mothers to dig. Of course, if the children followed any of these lines and kept close watch they would soon find another plant. The pretty fancy of the plants pointing to each other stimulated the lively interest of the children.

— Melvin Gilmore,
Prairie Smoke (1929)

Much energy can be spent harvesting prairie turnips [or breadroots]. In fact, I have sometimes just quit digging when the soil was so hard or gravelly that it required a pickax. It seems amazing that the roots are able to penetrate such hard ground.

— Kelly Kindscher,
Edible Wild Plants of the Prairie
(1987)

The rock formations of this [Kaw] region are limestone and sandstone. The Amorpha canescens was the characteristic plant, it being in many places as abundant as the grasses.

— John Torrey,
Catalogue of Plants Collected by
Lieutenant Frémont in His Expedi-
tion to the Rocky Mountains (1843)

We have deprived nature of its independence, and that is fatal to its meaning. Nature's independence is its meaning.

— Bill McKibben,
The End of Nature (1989)

There is something preternatural about unknown lands that seizes the imagination of certain visionaries. Promoters, opportunists, reformers, businessmen, and even crackpots are attracted to the unknown mag-net and often see it as their particular El Dorado, awaiting nothing more than the touch of their hands, the power of their money, and the fruits of their skills to achieve incalculable wealth.

— John Leeds Kerr,
Destination Topolobampo (1968)

Railway enterprise is a cure for the social and political problems of modern life. Poverty, revolution, brigandage, religious persecution, and social singularities disappear before this all-powerful agent. When armies and legislation are powerless, the locomotive-engine does not fail of success.

> — Albert Kimsey Owen,
> from a Topolobampo promotional
> pamphlet (c. 1880)

It is true original investors [in the Kansas City, Mexico & Orient Railway] lost about twenty million dollars, but my excuse for the only unsuccessful venture I have ever organized in forty years of business is that a revolution is an abnormal thing and cannot be reckoned with as a contingency of progress.

How grateful we should be that the Federal Reserve Bank is at hand and that financial panics can no longer be made to order.

> — Arthur Edward Stilwell,
> "I Had a Hunch" (1928)

History is a social expression of geography, and western geography is violent.

> — Bernard DeVoto,
> A Treasury of Western Folklore (1951)

While no people endure the reverses of nature with greater fortitude and good humor than the people of Kansas, misfortunes seemingly of man's making arouse in them a veritable passion of resistance. . . . Grasshoppers elicited only a witticism, but the "mortgage fiends" produced the Populist regime, a kind of religious crusade against the infidel Money Power.

> — Carl Becker,
> "Kansas" (1910)

Then it was remembered that of the dozen or more cold-blooded murders committed in this county during its history every murderer was acquitted except one, and he got off with a comparatively light sentence. These acquittals were not the result of lack of evidence, but through the "smartness" of attorneys who with the aid of plainly manufactured testimony, deluded the jurors; that while the man who stole a half cheese was sent to the penitentiary for five years, no perpetrator of a great crime was ever punished.

*Everyone knew that the evidence against [George Rose] would be
circumstantial and that if methods successfully employed in previous
trials should be adopted by the defense, he would be turned loose.*

— *Chase County Leader,*
"A Terrible Crime: Karl Kuhl Shot and
Instantly Killed by George Rose, a
Drunken Printer" (1894)

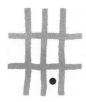

In the Quadrangle:
Matfield Green

Only two dreams — sleeping dreams — from my childhood remain, and, forty years later, they still hold the sharp focus of a view-camera photograph exposed at f/64: one was a piece of aerial fantasy, the other industrial archaeology, and each occurred only once. In the first, I went aloft in a wingless, propellerless orange crate mysteriously powered by a small, spring-wound clock without hands that could keep me airborne, just above the rooftops, as long as I kept winding it. In the other, I dreamed I uncovered beside our neighbor's picket fence a section of forgotten rail line — ties, tracks, spikes. This dream of finding history buried in my own yard, I believe now, set me out on my first walk in Chase County. But, tramping along some months ago, I was remembering only a strange and exotic thing I'd heard citizens mention, the Orient grade, an alleged rail route partly built but soon abandoned that ran through the county; evidence of it was purportedly visible around Matfield Green, even in the backyards. I say purportedly because I'd driven in the area several times to look for the grade and had found nothing, and so I put the line in with fanciful folklore about Zebulon Pike's stone fort and a house porch stained by a murdered man's blood that would never wash clean.

I pieced together these improbabilities about the Orient line: Missouri businessmen in 1900 decided to open a route to China by building a railroad from Kansas City to some forsaken Mexican town on the Gulf of California from where ships would open trade with the Far East. It seemed to me that anyone who could believe such a scheme existed could believe in a route from, say, Boise, Idaho, to Uxmal, Yucatán, to tap the African ivory trade. Yet hints about the track grade kept cropping up, and, after failing to find it on my walk, I decided to treat it as a puzzle on the grid, a crossword of blanks and clues where the game is to avoid turning to the back for the solution: I refused to ask people to show it to me, *if* they could. The search for phantasmagoria — grails, fountains, unicorns — runs deep in men, often producing things even more unexpected than the phantasm, so I made the Orient grade mine. Looking for the ludicrous allows our dreams — and sometimes dreams of others — to lead us.

I was walking about three miles north of the southern county line along route 177, which I first knew as Kansas 13, and which, to the amusement of the older residents, I still call 13 because 177 is a numeral and nothing more, but 13 is an ancient character, a glyph, an image charged with history, superstition, legerdemain, necromancy: if I say "thirteen," things rise inside you, but 177 is only three digits leading to the next county. I was walking and thinking about this, composing some of this sentence, or at least the bones of it, and then I began remembering it was this section of old 13 that had convinced me that Chase County held something I wanted to know. Something else happened on this little asphalt meander among rock walls and coffee trees, a stretch, as in most of the county, of billboard-free highway, the kind of road homeward Americans dream of: driving it in the mid-seventies, I wondered whether a traveler could cross the United States on nothing but back roads like this one. Three years later, trying to step out of the knee-deep shambles of what was passing for my life, I took off on such a trip with the hope that following new, physical maps could change the dream cartography a mind wanders in; that tour went on for thirteen thousand miles through thirty-eight states.

When I returned here in October of 1984 and was walking the Matfield road in search of Og (so I'd taken to calling the Orient grade), I realized that, while circumnational journeys are fine, I might have reached a similar destination by staying within a single American county, even one of seeming spareness like this one. The new challenge, as my quest for Og would soon reveal, was, to reword Thoreau a bit, to travel a good deal in Chase County, and the requisite to that was to go slowly, almost inch by inch, on foot. And so, I was on Kansas 13 again, looking for Og but hoping to find, as always, connections: I had gone out and come around, but I was still hunting for links — this time along a route where the way was too broken for anything but feet, a stout walking stick, and some dreaming.

The Matfield quadrangle is much like the topography just to the north, both taking their character — their genius — from the South Fork, which splits the quad north to south as nicely as a halved melon, although the traveler along route 13 misses the similarities because just south of Bazaar the road drops off the uplands into the little river valley and follows it along on the west bank to Matfield, where it branches southwest down the vale of Mercer Creek, then rises again onto the prairie and heads out for the oil fields around El Dorado. On each side of the South Fork the prairie spreads out almost entirely unmolested by roads but dissected by a dozen major creeks that flow in just a bit aslant of true east or west. The turnpike cuts the southeast corner, and the surprise in this open land is that you rarely see the toll road until you cross it (throughout Chase, the pike hardly shows up once you leave it). The pattern of streams and roads in the quadrangle reflects that of the county as a whole, but here the configuration is reversed and inverted, as New Zealand is to Italy. South of the turnpike and near old Thurman sits the Booster Station, where Cities Service in 1930 built a little settlement to tend the machinery of the natural-gas pipeline, a feudal village to serve the manor. The place is now a ghost town and the big compressor building, its pipes bending up from underground into the light like serpents cast out, lies with the uneasy quiet of the haunted, the machines more or less now minding themselves; but countians still speak of the Booster baseball team and the whang-leather arm of Chick Shaft, a pitcher Cities Service hired as an oiler so it could win itself a championship.

Route 13 also follows the Santa Fe line through most of the quadrangle, the two lying side by side like old lovers, one humping up over the other here and the other humping over there, and the citizens often fix nearby places in relation to these crossings as if they were lone navigational marks on the trail like Courthouse Rock. North of Matfield and a couple of miles south of the first overpass — near the confluence of the South Fork and Crocker Creek from the west and, from the east, Steak Bake Creek (despite the culinary appearance, the name comes from settler Ely Stakebake) — there is a house made from an old railroad passenger car. Not far away and beside the tracks is a long, cast-block building

once home to Hispanic rail workers; empty now except for stack-
ings of things, it's the only Santa Fe bunkhouse left in a county
where there used to be one every half dozen miles. The citizens still
refer to these houses without plumbing, electricity, and insulation
as *Mexican shanties*. The bunkhouse near Matfield is the last vestige of railroad moguldom hereabouts, and only a few people who
remember that life remain in the county.

Near these sorry dwellings are two large frame homes: first, the
old Crocker place with its long and angled porches, hipped and
gabled roof, and a three-story round tower that was later covered by
a portico and fluted columns; this pretense, incongruous on the
prairie, so overwhelms things nearby that it's easy to miss the
earlier and smaller Crocker home immediately north or to take it
(as I did) for a half-sized child's playhouse. Second, on down the road
is the Rogler place, Pioneer Bluffs, with its 1870 rock wall and a
parallel row of cottonwoods named after the presidents (only Lincoln is still alive). A couple of miles south of Matfield stood a third
place, the Brandley home, one of the largest frame houses in the
county until it burned to the ground in the twenties. These estates
were the south-county expression of the wish for prairie plantations
manifested at Spring Hill.

Henry Brandley (born Brandli), a young Swiss who had been a
ditch digger in Indiana, walked into Chase from Iowa in 1859 with
his friend, an Austrian, Charles Rogler, and they were joined later
by Erastus Crocker, who lost a great toe at Appomattox (Rogler
served only a hundred days, but Brandley saw action in the West
and caught a Ute arrow in his arm that left him with a permanently
crippled hand). Following the war, these men began making money
and going (or sending sons) to the statehouse, and they formed a
club of three: one countian said, *They intermarried until who-laid-
the-chunk.* But, as the twentieth century pressed in, things began
changing and the inevitable classlessness of prairie life exerted itself; today the Brandley place is a mere depression on a slope, the
Crocker home sold out of the family, and the Rogler house closed
and apparently on its way to becoming a museum. To look at the
stories of the upper South Fork, it seems that no family got very far
from the dirt floor of the log shanty it started in, and that has
happened so often across the county it's as if the prairie lets nothing
rise far from itself.

On that October day in 1984 when I was walking north on Kansas
13 toward Matfield and finding Og nowhere, I was distracted by an

old roofline showing above a somber grove, and I headed off west toward it; along an abandoned and overgrown piece of highway I found some small outbuildings piled with wood-rat nests and chewed pods from coffee trees. From under a rotting board that I disturbed crawled a fat black-widow spider missing a leg, and nearby lay a dead heron, decay turning its freakish beak and legs into something out of a Hieronymus Bosch painting; a few yards beyond stood a derelict farmhouse of gnawed rat holes, and across the old roadway rose the steep and wooded slope of the western uplands. Cut into the hill was a small stone springhouse with an arched doorway, and from it and a culvert alongside came an outrush of water. The thing opened like a dark, evil maw issuing the sound of far waters moving in turbulence as if riled. Although the day was warm and my thirst up, the water seemed such a voice of lurking malignance that even the hominess of the springhouse ledge, which once held a churn of butter or can of milk, did not lessen the aura of a thing not right. I stepped out of the cool damp hole and, still bent from the low ceiling, slowly straightened, then recoiled violently before I realized that what stood above the springhouse was not a horribly burned man but a tall and charred tree stump, its pair of stubbed limbs like arms upraised in warning. I headed back to the road to get away from the gloom of overgrowth and the infested buildings. In the county are many campsites Indians used for centuries, yet this homestead around Perkins Spring hadn't lasted sixty years, and I figured my unease came from some notion about white men's inability to endure, about their incapacity to live with the land, people who were *users of* and not *dwellers in.* That no one today could find this little acre of the wooded and watered valley a pleasant place to live in — maybe that's what cast the darkness. Or was it the other way around — a darkness driving people away? I hiked on up the sunny road and wondered what my price would be to sleep a single night in that bane of a house with its sinister gurgle of water.

I came to the big curve 13 makes below Matfield, and I was thinking how this road seems to promise much but releases it slowly, letting its past seep out so that you must collect it drip by drip, a cup of old water shot through with the exudate of lives: the collecting and drinking of such seepings is one of the most human things we do, and it is the source of our hope for continuance. Even though I had not drunk from Perkins Spring, merely confronting its dark presence had started changes.

About halfway around the road curve reflecting the bend in Mercer Creek is a stand of big sycamores; stacked among their sparse limbs, seventy feet up and clinging precariously to the higher forks and outer lateral branches, were a dozen blue-heron nests, some of them big enough to hatch a brood of human infants. This colony began in 1953, but it descends from a heronry a few miles east on the Verdigris that has been used for a century, its remote location once kept secret by cowhands. To the people of the upper South Fork, nothing shows the end of winter more than the coming of the massive wings of great blues and the courting clapper of their clumsy beaks, the heavy bills grasping and shaking sycamore branches as if to drive winter on north.

I was walking, and now and then a pickup rolled past, driver staring, rarely waving. When I stopped once to see if a certain rise might be Og, a fellow pulled up and said, *Trouble?* by which he meant, *Are you trouble?* and I said I was heading to Matfield, and to indict me he said, *Ain't many to walk this road,* and that was something I knew: walking here is eccentric; even when the citizens take an outing in the hills they go by truck, and to walk along a road is to suggest poverty or peculiarity.

Matfield sits on the western side of the South Fork, against the brow where the uplands drop to the river terraces and then rise again a half mile eastward to run brokenly to the Flint Hills escarpment. The hamlet is snugged in enough to make me believe that, with a terrific heave, I could throw a rock up and out of the valley onto the uplands; it is this compression of river and trees and simple dwellings, hidden from the prairie sweep, that gives the village its unornamented, if decrepit, charm and keeps its name from being a hoax.

Matfield Green, the words spelled out in rock letters high on the eastern slope, got its name from settler and first postmaster David Mercer of Kent, England, who remembered a place called Matfield, a collection of fine houses around a big green where he played cricket, just east of Tunbridge Wells. If by "green" you understand a mowed sward at village center, then the Kansas Matfield is greenless, but with the grasses around it for miles, a common here would be like a pond in Venice. The hamlet has burned several times, the last big fire in 1933 when, people believe, a windowpane concentrated a beam of sunlight in the second floor of a shop. Much of what has been here is gone, yet Matfield retains just enough structures to be picturesque in the prairie manner: a couple of old false-front stores, two closed brick schools, some empty and some occupied houses (the best a 1905 catalog kit house with restored fretwork), a steepled church, and a pair of old-style canopied filling stations on 13, once known as Reed Street. The west-side station is shut up, but the other is now the Hitchin' Post bar, appropriately run by an English woman who follows the country-pub and old West custom of putting the convenience out back; I don't know where the last American tavern privy will be, but the Hitchin' Post has a chance at national history.

Things coalesce accidentally sometimes, and words end up saying more than they were meant to. The story of Matfield and the tenor of its life have been shaped by two things: murder and the long promise of a railroad. Wayne Rogler, a former state senator and the last of the three great families here, says he once counted up seventeen died-with-boots-on killings around early-day Matfield. From that, you can see how, without intending to, promoters celebrating the grandest moment of the town, on the last day of July, 1923, linked those forces in a newspaper headline advertising their awaited emergence and rise to urban prosperity:

SEE MATFIELD GREEN AND DIE

Matfield Green, the last great cattle town without a railroad, after waiting half a century, has
realized her dreams and has a railroad and will
celebrate the event by a rousing
OLD TIME PICNIC

After failed attempts by several rail companies to build through Matfield, the promoters were still cautious and hoped for the Lord's mercy should the train come in *sideways instead of endways*. The promoters did not mention it, but the old town plats show that citizens had been ready for years to pick up their present streets running the due compass directions and set them down realigned with whatever angle the tracks might take.

On that Tuesday in July, from morning until dark, the people turned out to watch the Santa Fe crew lay track; they brought basket dinners and shared free watermelon, put their children in footraces, set sons to busting broncs, played against Elk for the county baseball championship; all day there were concerts and that evening a platform dance. Although citizens did not know it, Matfield was at its zenith of exuberant optimism: their hopes — *the dream* — was that material progress hauled in on trains a mile and a half long would be followed not only by money but also by civility. For a while, the railroad did indeed seem the harbinger of economic and moral progress: incomes rose, murders dropped. Then came paved highways and truck transport, and by midcentury the only thing Matfield could get from the Santa Fe was a whistle blast, and the Saffordville Syndrome began, and today Matfield Green, population thirty, has less than it had sixty years ago of everything except abandoned buildings. But it hasn't seen a man shot down in years: maybe at least part of the dream has been realized; maybe some of the freight, if not the train, did come in sideways after all.

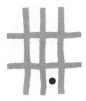

En las Casitas

In the narrow river vales of the county, the fields lie in squares and rectangles of row crops, fence lines darkly outlining them with small trees; from above, in autumn, the pattern is of strips of plaid cloth showing through long rents in the burlap of the prairie. Beside one of these tears, which is the South Fork Valley, and up on its western terrace high enough to give a view down on the vale road and the cropped grids, sits a low stone building, gray and grim like a barracks. It has eight rooms, ten doors, five chimneys, and is built like a double-footed L on its side, ⌐‾‾‾¬, and between the two longer end rooms is a roofed porch, and in front of it, a covered well. The stone blocks are, in fact, concrete cast to look like hewn rock. The place sits above old 13 just north of Matfield and a hundred feet east of the railway cut. Built without plumbing or insulation by the Santa Fe in the twenties, the building is the last of its kind in the area. I've heard it called the *Mexican bunkhouse, laborers' quarters, trackmen's houses, section hands' dormitory, company housing.* No one has lived here in some years, but once five Hispanic families did, and now the ceilings are shucking off their plaster down to their thin lath ribs, dropping pieces onto a miscellany of piled junk; window lights are missing, doors tied shut with twists of wire, and dirt lies so caked to the floor that the cold wind stirs no grit as it haunts through and gives the place an occasional voice — a slapped gutter, a shaken door, a rattled pane. Once there were ten clusters of trackmen's houses scattered somewhat regularly along the line, and from them every day, regardless of weather, men went out to tend the track, even on Sunday when a walker followed the right rail halfway to the next section quarters and returned on the left, all the way hammering down loose spikes, tightening bolts.

Fidel Ybarra never lived in these Matfield quarters, and I have found no one still in the county who did, but he spent thirty-one years in the even cruder company houses at Gladstone, ones the inhabitants called *las casitas* and the Anglos *Mexican shanties;* sometimes still, even Fidel calls them that, but he pronounces it *chanties* as if they were pieces of some old folksong from the sea. Now he lives in Cottonwood on the corner of Pearl and State streets, two blocks west of the courthouse, in a white bungalow, the first place he's ever had plumbing. It is late October, and in his small yard the long pods of the catalpa swing like pendulums in the slow wind, and the wahoo tree is about ready to split open its four-cornered berry capsules, and on the cramped front porch Fidel has stacked curious stones he has found along the Santa Fe tracks, and in the little bay window the morning sun warms the cockatiel into some whistlings and cage tapping. We sit at the dining table with its damask-patterned plastic cover.

Fidel is a compact man but not stout, his face nicely rounded, and he has a small, meticulously cut trapezoid of a mustache that resembles a silhouette of the Pyramid of the Sun at Teotihuacán, a place he has never seen although he was born a few miles south of it. His right eye is glass and seems fixed in a way that makes him appear to look through and beyond you, but it is the left that you must follow to read his meaning, his passions. He is sixty-three, and he and his wife, Teresa, an attractive woman whom he calls *the Missus,* have seven children, all living out of the county; they are clerks and businesspeople who have only the rudiments of the Spanish language. He is eleven months retired from forty-four years as a Santa Fe section hand, two decades of which he worked alongside his father, Nasario. Fidel ended as he began at eighteen, a trackman, and it's the only real job he's ever known. In 1927 when Fidel was a year old, his father brought him and his mother from Mexico City to Laredo, Texas, where they waited until Nasario saved up forty-six dollars for passports; then they caught a ride to Plymouth, Kansas, just across the Chase line. After fourteen months there, Nasario got drawn into some kind of scuffle and began going by Fidel Almanza, his father's first name and his mother's last; to get beyond the trouble, he moved the familiy to Gladstone, to the "little houses," and that's where Fidel grew up. He liked to watch the old locomotives blow off steam, but, since it was impossible for a Hispanic, he never wanted to become an engineer. In 1948, he brought his bride, born in the Mexican barrio of Emporia, to Gladstone, and eleven years later he became an American citizen.

Fidel and I are talking about those times, and his answers are ever so lightly gilded with Mexican rhythms and tones. He says, *Those houses at Gladstone were made of one-by-twelves, and the gaps between the boards were covered with thin wood strips. Tarpaper over the roof. No insulation except my mother's wallpaper. We had two rooms, about fourteen by twenty — that was the whole house. After the kids come along there was twelve of us in there. No electricity, no running water. There was six other chanties, some just one room, and all we had was one outhouse with two doors, a men's and women's, and just one seat in them: thirty people and two seats. We had a pump for water. But Santa Fe didn't charge us nothing to live there, and in the winter the company sent in a car of old track ties and pieces of depots and boxcars, and we'd unload it and chop the wood up for our stove, but the place was still cold.* Teresa calls in from the next room, *Oh yeahhh. If we went to Emporia to visit overnight, when we came home everything was frozen.*

Fidel smiles at that and says, *Then in the summer, when the reefer cars come through and throwed off the old ice on the siding, we broke it up and put it in our icebox. And one day thirty-six reefers of potatoes derailed at Gladstone.*

I ask did he like living in those little houses, and he says, *I didn't mind. A lot of farmers around us didn't have no plumbing neither,* and I say, but they had more than two rooms, and he answers, *When my kids complain, I tell them, "You should've lived when I lived back then." After the war we still just had kerosene lanterns, so I went to a company boss and told him if the houses were fit to live in they were fit to have electricity, and after a while we got it. And in 1950 I went and asked for propane stoves, and later we got them too. If I'd thought about it, I should've got Santa Fe to put an electric pump in the well.* And Teresa calls, *Look around and you won't find any fireplace in this house — I'm not going through that again — the dirt,* and Fidel says, *No more busting up wood.*

I ask just where in Gladstone the houses were, and Fidel takes the back side of a ten-million-dollar sweepstakes entry blank and draws a map, but the page is too small, so he goes to the kitchen and returns with two sheets of typing paper precisely taped end to end like a scroll. He lays a yardstick on it and draws twin parallel lines across the top that are train tracks and then freehands in curving parallels that are the diverging routes, and he begins talking as he draws in sidings, bridges, the control tower once at Elinor junction, cattle pens, the Strong City hotels (one an old Fred Harvey House), the section hands' houses there (putting roofs on each one). He labels every item and gives measurements and distances, even the mileposts around Gladstone and Matfield, and he lists the trackman's tools and defines them:

> Spike maul — to drive spikes
> Claw bar — to pull spikes
> Lining Bar — to use to raise track also to line track and other
> various uses

and so on through wrenches and hammers and jacks, and he writes how rail sizes in his years went from eighty-five pounds per three feet to 140 pounds. The houses at Gladstone he labels with arrows pointing to each one:

> Dad lived here →
> I lived in Middle one →
> We didn't have no Electricity till 1945
> Went to Miller School there Grade 1–8

As he limns in Gladstone, he X's the house where a younger brother, during some horseplay, threw a toy hatchet into his right eye. Each time he tells of an incident about a *chanty*, he touches his pen to the building and leaves a mark, and soon they are full of inky points like little residents.

He draws and loses himself in the map, and he forgets to speak, sometimes only nodding an answer, sometimes writing it as part of the drawing:

> I went to work for A.T.S.F. in 1944–1988
> Section Hand — Tamp Track

I watch his large hands, hands for a spike maul, labor their history onto the map, and I ask whether he has driven a spike in every mile of track in the county, and he pauses and calculates and says, *Way more than that,* and he pens in the laborers' quarters at Matfield, and says, *I could take you out and show you just about every place*

I drove a spike, and the idea is that it was a hard task, the kind of work you remember. He says a mile of track has 3,200 ties (we figure 300,000 in the county) and that he's done something to every one including replacing many of them.

I watch his map fill in. Artless and accurate but for its scale, it is a portrait of sixty years spent along the skinny rail corridors of the county, but it is a trackman's picture: bridges without rivers, curves without trees, villages only sidings with labels like trackside signs, and Chase without hills, a level place of inclines you can't perceive. And he draws on and turns it into a picture, chart, chronicle, handbook. The clock has struck off the hour again, and he keeps drawing. Then he seems to begin to rise out of his cartograph slowly, and he speaks more and nods less, and something between us, a caution, has disappeared, the way it will between people who travel some distance together.

Teresa passes by, looks at the map, and lays a finger on the middle house at Gladstone where she lived next to Fidel's parents, and she says, *It was okay there, but it was lonely, and there was no privacy,* and she is not self-contradictory. She says, *The tracks were so close that the engines shook the house, and cinders blew in, and sometimes pieces broke off trains and crashed by the houses: Fidel's little brother got hit by a loose wheel cover.* Then she leans close to the drawing, and she too seems to enter it, and she says as if from some distance off, *In summer, I pumped water into a tub and let it sit in the sun all day, and when the sun went down and the water was warm, then I started washing clothes.* Fidel says, *The only running water we ever had was the flood in '51,* and Teresa draws out a long *Ohhh. It came up so fast, and all the men were gone except a neighbor, a colored man. He was on vacation. He came up to help, and I passed him my baby out the window, and he held him above the water and took him to higher ground, and when we all got out, I saw how scared the man was, and I thought, "Oh God, I gave him my baby."*

Fidel says, *At first the company wouldn't let us have gardens, I don't know why — nobody asked in those days — but later it was okay, and we grew green beans, tomatoes, corn, sweet peppers, hot peppers. And if a hobo come down the tracks, my father gave him tortillas and beans.*

I ask, were you poor? *We knew we were Mexican but we didn't call ourselves poor because we had jobs.*

I say, you knew you were Mexicans? *In Cottonwood or Emporia,*

Topeka too, we couldn't get served in restaurants, but at some places you could take food out or go around to the back to the kitchen. We couldn't get no haircuts neither. Then one day when I was in high school in Cottonwood, I guess in 1941, I was walking down the street past the old bank, and the barber come out of the basement where his shop was, Jim Venard was his name, and he starts talking to me, and he says, "Who gives you your haircuts young man?" and I said, "My dad — nobody here will cut it," and he says, "You come to me. I'll cut it. Bring anybody else." *That was a breakthrough. During the war things changed, especially afterwards: guys figured if they were good enough to fight for the country, they were good enough to eat in a café instead of in the alley. But we never had it as bad as the colored people. Whites let us in earlier.* I ask him about the war. *I couldn't enlist because of my blind eye, so I worked on the track then: seven days a week, ten hours a day, sixty cents an hour.*

Several times he uses the word *breakthrough,* and his idea, unarticulated, is that whatever changes have occurred came about one person at a time — a barber giving a haircut, a café owner offering a table, a foreman asking for electricity, all of them bucking the wind on their own and not waiting for jurists to catch up with justice. Fidel says, *Things were like that, and we went along with them, but it was hard on us.* I ask how life is now besides having insulation and a toilet, and he says, *Some older white people remember the way things were, but they keep hush, but I remind them. I tell them, "It isn't like the old days when you had power over us — now it's going to be the other way around. In time, the Caucasian race will be the one dominated." I tell my kids, "We had to take it back then, but you got the Discrimination Board in Topeka."*

He speaks of twice confronting men who had, on separate occasions, grabbed his youngest son and torn his shirt. *I told them both, "If you've got any problems with my boy, I'd like to settle them now." And I said to one, a coach, "This isn't like back in the dirty thirties — this is more modern now." Coach said he was sorry, and I told him, "That don't get it anymore." I should've took him to Discrimination.* After a moment, Fidel says, *Nobody paid for the shirts.*

He is telling all of this while he keeps fixed to his map, and as he speaks, he draws in the ties of his tracks, a couple hundred little hash marks. At first I see them as tallies of wrongs, but when he keeps making them even after the topic changes, keeps laying down those little sleepers, I think: of course, the most important element in a trackman's work is the crosstie — that piece holding the railroad together, the predicate between subject and object, the linking between soil and rail. A trackman's days go to battling ties; as feet are to a walker, so ties are to a train. (Later I would recall ancient Aztec picture maps that used narrow parallels with footprints drawn between to indicate roads. In a like way, Fidel's map is primitive — of a first time.)

He does not fill in all of the space between his rails with ties but stops as if the time has come to put up the mauls for the day, as if to leave some work for tomorrow, and he looks over his document. I can't tell what he thinks its worth is, but then he gives me the answer: in the left corner, right under his good eye, he draws a small rectangle and in it carefully prints *By Fidel G.* **YBARRA**, and he adds his postbox number, street address, zip code, and ten-digit phone number (four digits put through local calls). He rolls it, presents it to me (and I'm thinking, of all the papers countians have handed me, this map of a man's territory is the finest because it is the most wrought). He accompanies me to the sidewalk, where the catalpa-pod pendulums swing slowly, and Fidel nods a so-long, and his right eye looks past me, past the courthouse at my back, on past everything in the hills.

Ex Radice

We are walking, you and I: it is the warm season, but one such as cannot exist because this day is April and May, June and July, and autumn presses against spring right through the fullness of midsummer. The prairie reaches out in bloom all at once and more: we can see plants in their entirety, can look into the soil as if it were sky, see roots in their descent, their webbed complexity, and we can penetrate the fibrous darkness below us where most prairie living goes on. We have power to do this, and we understand it is possible only in a dreamscape. It is useful to remember that the planet is a ball of dark never more than half wrapped in light, where darkness is the rule, light the exception; remember also that with our sleeping, blinking, wakingness spent in darkened places, we, like the prairie, live most of our days in nights.

We are walking then. We have walked here before. You may have sensed this, and you may have recognized some things here and about and suspected it. Once I saw a cutaway drawing of the inner ear titled HOW WE HEAR, and it struck me that the illustration confused the how of things with their apparatus. I am trying to avoid that as I tell you something about my writing and reading: when I walk this prairie county I often mutter words, phrases, and notions that eventually turn into this book, and I never think of this as talking to myself or as being a half bubble off plumb. That the words must travel far and alter form does not change things: you have often been with me, and sometimes when I am struggling to reach you it happens that I dream you. Certain kinds of writing and dreaming are intertwining things, like wild grapevine up the trunk of the plum tree: from the same dark soil, different fruits.

For the past several days I've been reading how tribal peoples took their health — body and mind — from prairie plants: how they ate them, used them to allay fever, heal wounds, stanch hemorrhage, ease pain; how, with them, they cleansed themselves, decocted fragrances and love charms; how they decorated themselves with seeds and pigments (but, given the respect they accorded the *flower nations*, how they rarely picked a blossom just for its beauty); and how they often apologized and left an offering to harvested flora. Of the several hundred herbaceous plants native to this place, rare is the one Indians did not employ in some way, yet most of their ample botanical knowledge — much of which is not mere folk wisdom but empirical learning about alkaloids, glycosides, resins, proteins, and so on — has been lost; of what remains, little has been examined to distinguish superstition from science. Yet I tell you from experience, I have eased a burned tongue with seeds from black samson, taken direction from a compass plant, and cleansed my hands with buffalo-gourd pulp.

These past few days I've been home looking at some forbs and legumes I've brought in from the prairie, and I've eaten parts of some and brewed several extracts according to old receipts: one of them I couldn't bring myself to swallow (a writer most fails when he loses nerve), but another I drank two cups of. Soon I lost my legs and had to lie down, and my mind seemed to tumble as if old tethers broke, and I dozed off into some grassland dream, and when I woke all I brought out of it was a recollection of an entanglement of long and numerous yet nearly invisible tendrils of a radiating vine; also in my head were the first six words of this chapter. I have wobbled to a chair, and I've followed those six words to this point because I believe they are the issue of darkness and that concoction, something come from minced and steeped prairie root: had I dreamed of God I could talk about *deus ex radice*, but it is you who came out of the root.

So: we are walking in an impossible season, and we are looking at totems of this land, more certain emblems of the long prairie than any other things but the tallgrasses themselves. The place is in them, and, in their ways, they carry the place. We are walking and looking, heading ourselves only in the cardinal directions, the native paths of approach to the Primal Urge.

East: *Silphium laciniatum:* listen: where these yellow rays of blossoms once grew in abundance ten feet high, some prairie tribes refused to camp, believing that the plants drew down lightning, yet during electrical storms the people burned the dried root to ward off thunderbolts (the plant is not so plentiful now, and lightning must seek fenceposts instead). Now, look within the soil and see the ten-foot taproot growing like a great carrot: from it the original prairie peoples made extractions to treat rheumatism, scrofula, constipation; and from it also came a diuretic, diaphoretic, expectorant, antispasmodic, vermifuge for their ponies, and a general tonic for listlessness for both people and horses. In several dialects its name translates as "big medicine." Indian children, in season, broke open its stems and collected the balsamic resin and chewed it like gum, and even the first white children in the county used to fan out on the hills on their way home from school and collect the candy, the plants being the only sweetshop in the neighborhood. This passing of useful botanical knowledge from red people to white is the exception not just because whites often scorned such wisdom, but because medicine men and Indian women, the keepers of much of this knowledge, had little commerce with settlers; and also, surely, lore must have been deliberately withheld from a people taking away the land, so that the thieves got the big machine but not the operating instructions.

White men also learned that this plant turns its long and rigid leaves on edge and points them toward the poles as if to gather only morning and afternoon sun; from this habit, whites used it as a cynosure on landscapes that could seem featureless to lost travelers, and they called it compass plant, pilot weed, polar plant, and also rosin weed and gum weed. It is not so easy to find here today unless you get into a hay meadow or a neglected piece of ground, because cattle take to it as did bison and red men.

South: *Cucurbita foetidissima:* I will tell you: when I began walking the county, I came upon this strange plant several times, and one day I asked a farmer what it was, that huge thing spreading green tentacles over his rock fence, and he said, *Some goddamn old vine.* Later I looked it up and learned it was buffalo gourd (but not why so named, since bison don't eat it), also called coyote melon, fetid gourd, wild pumpkin; and I found that to the Osage this goddamn old vine was *mon-kon-ni-ki-sin-ga,* "human being medicine," and I shall show you why. But first, see how it lies low, crawls, trails itself, raising only leaves and its yellow-star flowers;

see how it takes the ground as if it were flood, its copious spreading not so much growth as flow (and in the worst drought it will continue pushing its deep greenness, as if little more than encased water, over other vegetation turned the color of dust). It radiates itself over a fifty-foot diameter, and, were you to cut the long tendrils and tie them end to end, you could lower them from the observation deck of the Empire State Building to the sidewalk: there would be enough to do this eight times, all of that growth achieved in just five months, where the annual rainfall may be fifteen inches.

If you like, crush the prickly leaves and smell them and understand why the scientific name is "gourd-most-foul"; take the fruit — little yellow spheres with light stripings pole to pole as if geographers' globes — break one open, and rub the moist, stringy pulp on your hands, and the saponaceousness, smelling sweet like pumpkin, will cleanse them like soap. Save the seeds — their protein we can eat — and put extra gourds in your pocket: we can fashion them into rattles should we need to attract the ears of the Grand Mysterious.

Watch how I grasp the plant, lift it from the soil, and haul it into the light as if I were an Eskimo pulling a seal through its ice hole: nearly two hundred pounds, the weight of a large man and something of his shape too (now you understand the Osage name). I ask you, have you heard medieval lore that the mandrake root screams when pulled from the earth? I ask you, do you believe in the doctrine of signatures? Do you have pain in your feet, in your head? An Indian healer could take a piece from the part of the root that approximates the place of your discomfort and prepare you a remedy. But the mystic properties of *mon-kon-ni-ki-sin-ga* and their uses, I think, are lost utterly. Now, say this: Some goddamn old vine.

West: *Psoralea esculenta:* you see grasses are taller here, flowers more bountiful, their kinds more, and you feel a sense of the aboriginal you can wade into. This slope has not been grazed for several years, so it is a good place to look for Indian breadroot, also called, in English, more than a dozen other names, and every comparative label is inaccurate: wild turnip, prairie potato, ground apple, scurf pea. In fact, it is related to beans, although I find the taste of it fresh from the soil more like a raw peanut, but other travelers thought it similar to a carrot, Jerusalem artichoke, or white radish, and one even said it tasted like horseradish. Of the names, I like the Winnebago best, *tdo-ke-wi-hi*, "hungry," which stands in contrast to the Latin: "edible scabbiness" (*psoralea*, as in psoriasis).

Whereas buffalo gourd advertises its tuber, breadroot hides away its little bulb for most of the year by letting wind break its stem near the ground so that it goes bounding off, spilling its seed. But, for a few weeks in late spring, it raises five-fingered leaves just above the new grass, as if calling for attention like a waving hand in a crowd. The tuber, usually about the size and shape of a hen's egg, lies a few inches beneath the surface; it was these small swellings of carbohydrate that Indian women were prying from the earth with fire-hardened digging sticks and trimmed elk antlers on the morning of the battle of the Little Big Horn, and you might like to think of the high-arched arrows that brought down the cavalry's arrogance as powered by bison haunch and breadroot.

Digging a prairie turnip doesn't have the romantic thunder and blood of a buffalo hunt, but it was just as important to the plains peoples, and, although they would likely have survived without breadroot, their life would have been different: their stories and legends (the maiden who wielded her digging stick so avidly she dug through the earth and fell into the sky), their sports, health, names on the land, the look inside tepees where dried breadroots hung braided in strands like locks of the horsemen. Some prairie tribes made their way into bison country on annual hunts along courses determined by the richest slopes of breadroot as if they were oases. The people put pounded root into soups; they blended it with sliced bison stomach or beaver tail (Lewis and Clark's favorite meat); they pulverized dried flesh and added marrow and sun-dried cherries to breadroot flour; they mixed the roots in stews of yellow calf or venison or fattened pup; from them they made buffalo-berry pudding or coal-baked flatcakes; and sometimes they peeled off the leathery skin and ate them like fresh apples. Today, cattle have reduced the number of breadroot plants, and the effort of wrenching the tubers from hard soil has turned modern tribes to bagged flour and sweet potatoes and saltines; but, five years ago at Wounded Knee, South Dakota, I swapped a Lakota man a dozen prime Missouri Jonathan apples for a pair of dried breadroots the size of quail eggs.

During their expedition, Lewis and Clark often traded for "white apples," and Lewis wrote the first description of them and their preparation but concluded with this: *The white apple appears to me to be a tasteless insipid food of itself, tho' I have no doubt but it is a very healthy and moderately nutricious food. I have no doubt but our epicures would admire this root very much, it would serve them in their ragouts and gravies instead of the truffles morella.* And journals of many early western travelers mention breadroot: Pierre-Antoine Tabeau (*all the wandering nations leave regretfully the districts where the prairie turnip grows abundantly*), John Bradbury (*very palatable even in a raw state*), Henry Brackenridge (*something of the taste of the turnip, but more dry*), Thomas Nuttall, Edwin James, George Catlin, Prince Maximilian (*a wooden dish was set before each of us, containing boiled beavers' tail with prairie turnips . . . it did not taste amiss*), Charles Murray, Victor Tixier, John James Audubon, Edward Harris (*more Farina than a Ruta baga*), Father de Smet, Rudolf Kurz, Randolph Marcy, Isaac Stevens (*a soup, made of buffalo and Typsina, a species of turnip . . . was rich and greasy but quite palatable*).

We are dreamwalking so we can call forth breadroot for you to see, but I must tell you, in all my ambles about the county I've not found it often, and I've fretted over its decline, but a friend and botanist, Kelly Kindscher, has given me some hope: when he hiked across Kansas six years ago, just northwest of the county he found an Indian breadroot coming into blossom right in a forgotten rut of the Santa Fe Trail. So, the esculence shows its doggedness.

North: *Amorpha canescens:* say this word as we walk, speak it, and try to call forth the thing named: *te-hu-to-hi.* It is Ponca and means "buffalo-bellow plant"; *te-hu-to-hi* came into blue flower when the far-distant bison bulls came into rut and the cows into heat, a concomitant passing of seed by blossom and beast, and so *te-hu-to-hi* was an almanac showing the people when to head for the hunting grounds.

White settlers heard the long and slender lateral roots snap on the blade of their breaking plows, pop sharply like old bootlaces drawn too tight, and they named the plant prairie shoestring. Other homesteaders, seeing the gray hairiness of the leaves, called it lead plant and believed it drew its color from ore deposits beneath it as if its deep roots worked the alchemists' dream of transforming lead into a kind of prairie gold. Now, take the leaves home, dry them slowly, steep them, and, from their leaden color, watch appear a golden tea of pleasing taste. The native lore says that also from those leaves can come a tonic for pinworms, a wash for eczema, and it says the stems can provide a moxa for neuralgia or rheumatism (if you have courage): take a dried sprig, strip it, wet one end to affix it to the place of discomfort, light the other end, and let the stem, like a slow fuse, burn to the pain. If you wish to approach health more spiritually, crush the dried leaves to a powder, mix in a bit of bison tallow, tamp and light it in a sacred calumet, and send your prayer for health with the smoke rising skyward.

When John Charles Frémont crossed Kansas in 1842, he wrote of the prevalence of lead plant, and Lieutenant John James Abert four years later on his exploration said it was so abundant he usually didn't record its presence. When botanist John Weaver studied the tall prairie two generations ago, he found lead plant still abounding, in some places sixty plants to a square meter and growing thicker than the bluestems. But you and I, were we to leave the dreamwalk and hike the actual land, would find a county cut by cattle trails: *Amorpha* indicates healthy prairie, and its absence reveals severe disturbance to the original vegetation, and this loss is significant, since its deep leguminous roots fix nitrogen in soil. Nothing so demonstrates that this is land under domination of white men as springtime hills absent the purple flowers of lead plant (and, again, you see how rangeland and native prairie are as different as pasture to a feedlot). Were tribal people to return, it would be a lean land they would have to live on.

I must tell you this: last year a county farmer, complaining about the Kansas Fish and Game Commission restocking areas of the Flint Hills with native animals, said to me, *What the goddamn hell are they doing putting antelope back in here for? Everything we worked a hundred years to get rid of, they're bringing back.* No Anglo engine, not even the plow, has so effectively cleared the Hills of their old diverse abundance as the steer: to harvest all the prairie into franchise burgers is a respected practice, goes the thinking, and to some the setting aside of a portion where nature can answer only to itself is waste rather than the creation of a seedbed of biological diversity for a future time. Survival here means getting through next Monday, and children born on Tuesday will later be on their own. Another countian: *What kids don't know, they won't miss.*

Someday you may walk the prairie not in the soft light of a dreamscape but in actual fact; if, then, you want to see *te-hu-to-hi* or *tdo-ke-wi-hi* or *mon-kon-ni-ki-sin-ga,* or other flower nations that gave life for eight thousand years to people living in a land never even remotely close to being used up, seek them in an overgrown cemetery. But if you stay in a white man's old burial ground long enough, this darkness must come to you: his way of life is the land's death and his way of death is the land's life.

Via the Short Line to China

Being dreamed about is not the same thing as walking in someone else's dream, the latter much more rare, but one day when I was rambling along three miles east of the Falls and not far north of Gladstone, I stepped straight into a fellow's dream and felt it full upon me for several hours. It came about through the progression of these details: a list of murders, a serendipitous hike, the flight of a heron, and a man long dead who laid through the county a rail route to China on the advice of pixies. The pursuit of such progressions is a good way to travel: start with a single, near destination, follow it to the next one revealed, and continue until things lay out their own map for you, something you see in Indian file over your shoulder rather than in front of you beforehand.

That morning I went into the courthouse to try to draw up a list of every murder committed in the county, got daunted when I saw the volumes I'd have to pore through, but, before I quit, learned that James Fisher, the first settler in Chase and an eccentric bachelor, had been bludgeoned to death with an iron bolt and robbed in his cabin at the juncture of the South Fork and the Cottonwood. Here is the 1871 account in the *Leader:*

> *About 4 o'clock in the morning [James Fisher] fell asleep, when he was struck a violent blow on the head. He sprang upon the floor, and a violent struggle ensued, in which the assailant succeeded in so disabling Mr. Fisher as to suppose him dead. He*

then wrapped him in a blanket and pushed him under the bed
and endeavored to conceal the blood upon the floor by covering
it with ashes; Mr. Fisher however so far recovered as to creep to
the door and call for help, bringing his neighbors to his assis-
tance.

I came out of the courthouse into an early spring day of deeply
blue sky not yet yellowed by pasture burning, and it crossed my
mind to let the wind blow the dust of ledgers off me, so I headed
out to look for Fisher's cabin site. Hoping for a foundation corner,
a hearthstone, something, I found nothing, and I ended up idling
by the cold meeting of the waters, and I realized how little of
the Cottonwood you commonly see because of its deep, narrow,
wooded channel through the county. I clambered up the bank and
began breaking my way through the tangles along it in a kind of
river hike. Just west of the railroad bridge over the Cottonwood, I
came out onto a tall and massive and marvelously laid stone abut-
ment with a matching one on the bank opposite, the cut rocks as
big as any you can find here. It was apparent the abutments were
old yet never used and that somebody had gone to considerable
expense for no purpose. I'm as susceptible as anybody to the romance and mystery of hidden ruins, especially ones in rock. I made
my way back to the road and got asked the usual question by a
fellow in a pickup, *Trouble?* and I told him about the abutments,
and he said, *It's the old Orient line,* and moved on, and I thought,
Old Og again, the *ignis fatuus.* I walked and considered, and finally
I said, find it or bury it.

I headed down to Matfield Green where, allegedly, Og showed on
the land like a faint shadow, and I pulled over near Perkins Spring:
even in the light of noon, the old farmstead lay in a forbidding
murk, an evil looming again, and I decided not to go in to fill my
canteen. (That night when I was drinking a Guinness in Emporia
with Joe Hickey, the Thurman anthropologist, I told him Perkins
Spring was the only spot in the county where, for no apparent
reason, my flesh starts creeping, and he said, *There's a story that*
when the Perkins place was an old-style tavern on the stage line to
El Dorado and Wichita, guests got waylaid there. And one of the
Perkins boys said his mother put up Jesse and Frank James one
night. Waylaid? I asked. *Murdered,* he said, *but I haven't found any*
evidence, and I said, I have.)

I walked up old 13, surprised by how far the leafless trees let me
see into the woods along Mercer Creek, and I began anticipating a

good look at the heronry — the season was perfect for visibility and activity. At the Jack's Creek bridge, I stopped to watch a great blue step fastidiously along a shoal, but when I tried to edge closer it jumped and somehow got its six feet of flapping wings up the tree-encumbered creek. Following its flight, I saw a strange, narrow, earthen, truncated pyramid usually covered by foliage; behind me in the roadcut lay the same form, each with some perfection to its angles. Although I was noticing it for the first time, I knew what it was: Old Og, my will-o'-the-wisp, the Orient grade broken open by route 13; I'd driven and walked right through it a dozen times before. In front of me, here in the middle of Kansas, lay a trackbed leading to Cathay — from Kansas to Kansu. Sometimes it's more invigorating to have your disbelief broken than to have it confirmed. In this most unlikely of places, the Chase County prairie, I'd found an overgrown and almost forgotten route to the court of Hung Wu; to the Hall of Luminous Benevolence, redolent of tables laid with sliced eels caught by cormorants; to eunuchs serving ginseng pickled in rice wine, lotus-seed mooncakes, Fungi of Immortality; to rooms with carved walls hung with scrolls painted in inks made from gamboge and powdered pearls; to hidden closets holding jade vials of dragon-bone elixirs; all in a land of the Sixty-four Hexagrams and the Five Poisons; a land with the drunken Wu Wei fingerpainting bold pictures of cats capable of driving out rats; a place sequestered by a great stone wall filled with rubble and clay and the pounded-in bodies of dead workers.

In the intoxication of discovery, I climbed the grade of Old Og and set off down the Orient Road now thronged with the exotic purplescence of redbuds, yet knowing, somehow, I was still in Chase County. Later, when I tried to describe to a cynical friend my hike down another man's dream, he said, *Is that the secret of happy travel in Kansas — imagining somewhere else?* Two-dimensional Rand McNally travelers who see a region as having borders will likely move in only one locality at a time, but travelers who perceive a place as part of a deep landscape in slow rotation at the center of a sphere and radiating infinite lines in an indefinite number of directions will move in several regions at once. But to him I could think only to say that there are 140 ways to spell Kansas.

The man who raised twenty million dollars to build this Orient Road to tap the agricultural wealth of the American Southwest and the mineral resources of northern Mexico along a route to a new Pacific port, Arthur Edward Stilwell, was a devout Christian Scientist who took his moral tutelage from churchmen and his business counsel from imps in the dark, whom he called *the Brownies*. One night he awoke suddenly when he heard them advising him to make the terminus of a railroad he was building (today called the Kansas City Southern) not Shreveport, Louisiana, but a new town he would build on Sabine Lake in Texas: to my knowledge, Port Arthur is the only American city founded on the advice of gremlins.

A few years later, in 1900, he lost control of that railroad to "Bet-a-Million" Gates, a man of easy ethics, and Stilwell, forty years old, despaired so much from his setback that he considered shaving off his large sideburns, things of pride to which he attributed some of his early success because of the air of gravity and maturity they gave him. Casting about for reasons for his failure, he read in a newspaper this sentence by George Ade: *If a man is cross-eyed it is a great detriment; if a man is humpbacked it is an act of God; but if a man wears side whiskers it is his own fault.* Stilwell deliberated and then acted. Some years later he said of that moment, *I stood at another crossroads in my life — on one side the wisdom of George Ade and on the other my beautiful whiskers, locked in a death grip. Ade won. But I decided no profane hand should participate in the final rites over this facial appendage which had played its part in constructing the Kansas City Southern, and that I myself should officiate.* (As Port Arthur is the only city founded on the advice of pixies, so is the Southern the only railroad founded, in part at least, by sidewhiskers.)

Soon after, an acquaintance met the freshly shaved Stilwell on the street and said in surprise, *I've heard about your trouble, but I didn't know it was anything as serious as this.* In truth, it was no longer so serious because the dream voices had spoken again. At a testimonial dinner to lift Stilwell's spirits (he undoubtedly knew this to be a double entendre) at the old Midland Hotel in Kansas City, the encomia went on until one o'clock in the morning; then he took the podium among the potted palms and American flags. He was later to say of that moment, *I had been for a long time perfectly conscious of my reputation for making rather unexpected moves, and, to utilize a modern expression, I was now playing this presumed faculty off the boards.* He accepted a silver loving cup and said a few predictable words about losing the Southern, and then, abruptly, he stunned the large audience: *I have designed a railroad sixteen hundred miles long which will bring the Pacific Ocean four hundred miles nearer to Kansas City than any other present route.* His friends said: *He's lost both his railroad and sidewhiskers, and now he's talking about bringing oceans to the prairie. His troubles have unhinged him.* But the next day he raised a half million dollars to found one of the last long railroads built in America.

He planned to construct his Kansas City, Mexico & Orient Railway to the natural harbor at Topolobampo, Mexico — to be renamed Port Stilwell — on the Gulf of California. If voices spoke the notion to him at night, they were apparently lifting ideas from other people, especially the civil engineer Albert Kimsey Owen, who had built a utopian community at Topolobampo and settled it, in part, with Kansas farmers unhappy about the growing social destruction caused by big American corporations. For some years, various men had advocated a route from the middle of America to a West Coast port closer than San Diego, Los Angeles, or San Francisco — even if it was, like Topolobampo, farther from China. But these other men lacked not so much the counsel of spirits as the capacity to move men to believe in a nearly mad dream of Columbian proportions: to make Kansas City the eastern terminus of a trade route with the Indies and Orient. They also lacked Stilwell's capacity to sell speculative securities and to manipulate reporters and editors. In his youth, he learned his trade by peddling his own patent tonic, and later he made good money selling to laborers cheap housing on an installment plan like insurance (the press loved his slogan: *You can live in your endowment policy and raise chickens in its back yard*).

In face and figure and force of personality, Arthur Stilwell might have been the son of Prince Otto von Bismarck: large, Teutonic, great mustache, the power to rouse in men a lust for lucre. In fact, he was the son of a Rochester, New York, jeweler, Charles Stilwell, a business failure as unlike his son as Charles was *his* father, Hamblin, an owner of Erie Canal packet boats, an investor in the New York Central Railroad, and a vigorous and wealthy man who liked to tell his grandson stories of the building of the canal and the Central. Arthur grew up measuring his achievements not with a jeweler's calipers but with a railman's odometer. One of the last things he wrote in a career full of books, articles, poems, songs, photoplays — all dictated by his *Corps of Spirits* — was this concluding paragraph to a six-part autobiography in the *Saturday Evening Post* called "I Had a Hunch" (editors discouraged talk of Brownies): *When I was twelve years old, I told my grandfather I would go forth and build a railroad. I did not tell him I would go forth and build seven or eight. But in those days of long ago my hunches, like myself, were in their infancy.* It must be a mark of some success not to know for certain how many railroads one has founded. In fact, he built four, two of them minor lines.

Stilwell's plan for the "Orient Short Line" was to acquire right-of-way from Kansas City to Topolobampo immediately but begin building between Wichita and Presidio, Texas, on the Rio Grande so he wouldn't arouse competitors in Missouri. Although he drove the first spike on the Fourth of July, 1901, at Emporia, the track ran west just a mile to a long dirt grade through Chase and on toward El Dorado in Butler County; eastward to Kansas City the railroad existed, as it does today, only as a dotted line on maps; but between Wichita and Alpine, Texas, and in places in Mexico the track went speedily down. Stilwell made a deal with a transpacific shipping company, and the railroad began earning money, although not enough to offset construction expenses. He knew the Orient line and the land it opened for speculation (where he could make huge profits) would be of little worth until the railroad could be linked to the ocean: preeminently standing in the way were the Sierra Madres and the instability of revolutionary Mexico. If nocturnal voices proffered inventive ideas, they didn't give any guidance in management, apparently never counseling him to treat one of his contractors, Pancho Villa, with respect; of him Stilwell said, *Whenever I met him on the railroad I carefully avoided inviting him into my private car. I could never quite reconcile myself to any close contact with Villa. He was a horrible-looking fellow, always greasy and dirty.* There is a well-known photograph of the revolutionary — in a suit, shoes shined — sitting on the steps of an Orient day coach, taken about the time he blew up Stilwell's Mexican silver mine; to the day of his death, the American never understood why Villa did not simply expropriate the mine, as he did everything else.

In 1912 the Orient went into receivership and Stilwell went out as president. That year, before Congress began enacting its great antitrust legislation, he and his wife, Jennie, who had never failed him, moved to New York City, and he gave a speech in Carnegie Hall to a thousand people. He said, *The money trust has been chasing me for fifteen years because I was successful, and at last they have thrown my road into the hands of receivers. I tell you, gentlemen, this country could be ruined within two weeks if the group of men who control the currency of the country in New York wanted to do it. It is perfectly awful to think that in this country, supposed to be free, that a man trying to be on the level and do the right thing is persecuted and almost ruined by this system. Because I had the idea that a railroad was built to serve the people, I was hounded and persecuted. The New York financial interests who have been fighting me knew I was a dangerous man. For sixteen years I have been followed by detectives. Every friend I meet is given a note telling him to have nothing to do with me. If I go to a club with a friend, that friend is handed a note saying I am no good. My only object is to have the Golden Rule dusted off and put back into practice — that's all I ask.*

To a degree, Stilwell was right that Wall Street had helped block his success, and he was also correct when he said a few days later, *Building and running railroads in Mexico is a terrible thing.* (Especially if you pay more heed to Brownies than to Pancho Villa.) And there were other problems: the lucre of the Orient, at least then, was more fable than fact, and the wealthy American and British investors underwriting the project were more interested in making money than in building a railroad; as they began backing away, even the force of Stilwell's salesmanship, the primary asset of the Orient line, could no longer buy the time the project required.

Soon after his railroad went into receivership, a New York elevator fell with Stilwell in it, leaving him an invalid, a symbolic accident a nineteenth-century novelist would cherish. He withdrew from business and spent his last years writing, his books advocating what were then ideas on the fringe: trust breaking, the abolition of the Monroe Doctrine, pacifism (he urged in 1915 that a first step toward disarmament would be the sinking of all warships on Christmas Day), a Jewish state in Palestine. He at last confessed to attending voices in his dreams, and, about himself, he wrote, *"Is the Author a spiritualist?" In the common acceptance of the term he is not a spiritualist and he has read very little on the subject, [but] he is a spiritual-list. He lists for spiritual messages.* The New York press, seeing good copy in such parlance from a railroad magnate, came to him for many interviews; even to the end, Stilwell could talk himself into the news. After admitting to his sprites, he wrote a verse:

> *Do you wish to know where the Brownies stay,*
> *Who romp all night and in moonlight play,*
> *A merry happy little band?*

They live on the shores of Slumberland.
They live on the shores of Slumberland.

From their apartment in the Esplanade Building on West End Avenue, Arthur and Jennie watched the Orient struggle along under its receivers, men of small daring and without advice from night messengers, but men with some savvy; William Kemper, of the famous Kansas City banking family, personally made several million dollars by buying out jumpy stockholders cheap and later selling the railroad to the Santa Fe in October of 1928. Except for the Sierra Madre portion and one other in Mexico and a seventy-mile section just north of the Rio Grande, Stilwell's Orient Short Line was then complete from Wichita to the sea. The Santa Fe soon finished the American gap and then sold the Mexican trackage, and a third of a century later, Mexico surmounted the Sierra Madres and opened its line: Stilwell's dream route was complete except for a hundred and some miles across the Flint Hills and into Kansas City, a portion the Santa Fe had already laid its own rails over, in places nearly touching the old Orient grade.

Arthur Stilwell, whose Brownies had also given him advice on how to live to be 140, died halfway there, and he missed by twenty-five days seeing the Santa Fe take over his dream, and so did Jennie (whom the night had revealed to Arthur some half century earlier). Immediately after Stilwell died, she called upon the spirits to help her reach him. A few days later, she stepped out of a twelfth-story window of the Esplanade; her note said, *I must go to Arthur.* Some reports held that Stilwell had only a thousand dollars at his death, while others claimed he was a millionaire, but a will has never been found, nor have the cremated remains of the couple, despite a long search by officials in Port Arthur (someone finally suggested, *Has anyone checked with the boys from Slumberland?*). I know nothing about the whereabouts of Stilwell's ashes, but I know where the monument to his oriental dream is: it's a pair of massive cut-stone abutments on the Cottonwood River in Chase County, Kansas, which never carried a single locomotive.

That spring afternoon when I was making my way along Old Og's back and was still entangled in the redbuds, I heard water running below me, and I stumbled down the steep grade to its source. I stood there in surprise: in front of me was the Perkins springhouse, that dismal thing, and I saw the hill the water issued from was no hill at all — it was the Orient grade itself. Stilwell's crew had buried the original spring and built that dark and evil-looking conduit. I climbed the grade again and followed its slow ascent onto the tree-less upland toward the oil town of El Dorado, "the golden place" that would have let Arthur Stilwell finish his dream had the Spirit Corps mentioned what lay below his tracks — the biggest oil field in Kansas, one discovered only three years after he lost the Orient line.

As I hoofed along I wasn't thinking about black gold so much as water: I had refused again to fill my canteen. What could it be that disturbed the peace of that copious spring? It wasn't, really, a legend about tavern guests getting waylaid for their money; and it wasn't, really, the presence of Jesse James; and it wasn't just some spiritual-list's mumblings about silver mines and golden rules, a speculator possessed of the old European lust for the riches of the Indies, that avarice at the heart of the stealing and corrupting of the American land; and it wasn't just night-dancing hobs down in that darkness. Something else, stronger and more ancient than any of those, was in there. When I was a couple of miles down Old Og, I thought I knew: what also loomed in that dismal and aggrieved wood was my memory of a native people who found the greatest gift in the grass-lands to be clean water in perpetual flow. With that spring, Mr. Stilwell and his dreams played hob.

On the Town:
Versus Harry B. (I)

THE ROMANCE

This is what we know about a certain dark event in 1898 near Matfield Green, where there have recently been three unsolved murders: a man on horseback rides down the dirt-packed lane just south of town. His name is Frank Rinard, and he is a hired hand on the Captain Henry Brandley place. It is Sunday, July the twenty-fourth, dusk. Neighbors see him pass on his way to the Brandley farm on the western terrace of the South Fork, a favored piece of ground. Rinard (pronounced *Rine*-erd) is about twenty-one, unmarried, a local man, and he is on his horse, Bender.

The captain, a Union army veteran whose left hand crippled by a Ute arrow is a kind of always evident campaign ribbon, has retired from the Kansas senate and now develops his realty investments. In less than thirty years he has become one of the wealthiest and most influential countians. He and his second wife, Elizabeth, have eight children. (His first spouse died several months after they had married and taken up housekeeping in his log cabin.) Lizzie is a pretty woman with thick, glossy hair, her Teutonic eyes of such transparent blue they could almost be window glass. She is shrewd and determined and a member of the school board, and she is disappointed that their eldest son, the third child, Harry, has shown no interest in his education. When he was two years old, he fell into a well and would have drowned had a young woman not climbed down in after him. Now he is twenty-four and unmarried.

What is about to happen will concern him and his strikingly comely seventeen-year-old sister, Pearl, and the man riding the horse. It is common knowledge that Miss Pearl pays more than passing attention to Frank Rinard, and he to her, but as a farmhand his prospects are ordinary. Several times the two have been seen walking toward the Brandley quarry, where men are cutting stone for the foundation of the big house the captain is building to replace the log home he put up after staking a claim here. Miss Pearl was also observed in the hired hands' bunkhouse above the barn, when she and Rinard sat on his bed as he showed her pictures. One of her five sisters is married to Edward Crocker and another is seeing his younger brother, Arthur; the history and achievements of the Crockers match the Brandleys'. Power and influence have been building on the upper South Fork since the end of the war.

Young Brandley has ridden in from the ranch house at Jack Spring, four miles west, where he lives and works. He has brought in his laundry, and as he talks with his mother in the kitchen, hired hand Cecil Richards comes in with the fresh milk and interrupts the conversation — seemingly at an inopportune moment — and leaves. Some time later, hour not certain, Harry heads back to the ranch while his fifteen-year-old brother, Bob, arrives from Matfield, fixes himself something to eat, and then goes to the south porch to sit alone. Daisy Brandley, a couple of years older than Pearl, sits talking with Arthur Crocker on the unfinished foundation of the new house. She will marry him, and he will become a state legislator. The eastern sky darkens, and the crickets and bullfrogs start up. It is about nine o'clock.

Frank Rinard rides onto the place, heads to the barn and unsaddles Bender, but does not unbridle him. Then: from near the granary and hog lot comes the loud report of a large-caliber gun. The night goes still for some moments, then the gentle sounds of the vale resume. Gunshots are not especially unusual. Again the dark is staggered, this time by a woman screaming and moaning. It is Lizzie, and she is saying, *Someone's been shot! Is it Bob? Is it Bob?* Her son runs to her and says he isn't hurt. He doesn't know who fired the gun.

There is confusion. Bob and Daisy and Arthur Crocker go toward the barn. Near it lies a body. Arthur raises the head and sees it is Frank. He's been shot in the face. He lies weltering in his blood. He is unarmed, and no one sees any gun near him. In the turmoil, the men take Rinard up to the porch, where they can see bad powder burns on his face, and within minutes he dies. Lizzie sends John Knowles, a farmhand, for the doctor. An hour or so later the captain arrives, apparently from his real estate office in Matfield. Around midnight, the Brandleys hear a horse gallop through the gate, but the captain tells Knowles not to follow — by the time he gets a horse up, the rider will be gone. About daybreak Lizzie sends Knowles, a cousin of Rinard, to tell Frank's father of his son's death.

THE GUN

On Monday, the twenty-fifth of July, an inquest is held in Matfield and Harry Brandley summoned. The coroner has extracted a single forty-four-caliber slug from Rinard, and the county attorney asks Brandley to show his pistol. He rides off to get it, returning shortly. In his forty-four are six live rounds, five tarnished and one brightly new. Harry says he shot at a coyote on Thursday, but the gun seems to have been fired more recently. He says he often carries the pistol to protect range cattle. The attorney asks whether he objects to Rinard's attention to Miss Pearl, and he says no, he and Frank are on good terms, but someone challenges his assertion (in a small community, the one thing neighbors know about is bad blood). There are no other suspects. Circumstantial evidence is strong enough for the justice of the peace to call for Harry's arrest and have him taken to the jail in Cottonwood.

The community is tense: people remember the hooded men who, four years earlier, pulled the confessed murderer George Rose from the courthouse jail and hanged him under a Santa Fe trestle because they doubted justice would be done, and those men, the belief is, were not hoodlums but eminent citizens. Reporting a few days later the preliminary hearing on the Rinard murder, the *Leader* writes that emotions are unlike anything seen here before and crowds composed of an unusual number of women throng the courtroom.

Over the next nine months, the witnesses are many and the evidence voluminous but the trial of *The State v. Brandley* ends in a hung jury, one man holding for acquittal, and the attempt to impanel a second fails altogether. Believing Chase countians prejudiced against them, the Brandleys want a change of venue to Emporia, where the captain has several influential friends, but the *Leader* claims:

> If the attorneys for the defense are responsible for the statement that "Chase County is against Brandley," they utter what is not true for the purpose of excusing their own failures. The attorneys for the defense at no time seemed to appreciate the

status of their client. They attempted to belittle the prosecution from the start and when they could not ridicule witnesses for the state they resorted to abuse and badgering, and one of the defendant's attorneys appeared to be more interested in making the audience laugh than in proving the innocence of his client. Brandley's case was undoubtedly badly managed. A change in management of his case and not a change of venue is what the defense needs.

Finally, in March of 1900, the motion is granted, and on the fourteenth of May a second and decisive trial begins in Lyon County. The crowds, still marked by a large number of women, continue in Emporia, and the reasons are evident: the son of a wealthy landowner and real estate investor, a senator and war hero, accused of shooting down a poor farmhand sparking his sister: privilege versus the people, Romeo dying for Juliet in a family feud.

VII

Hymer

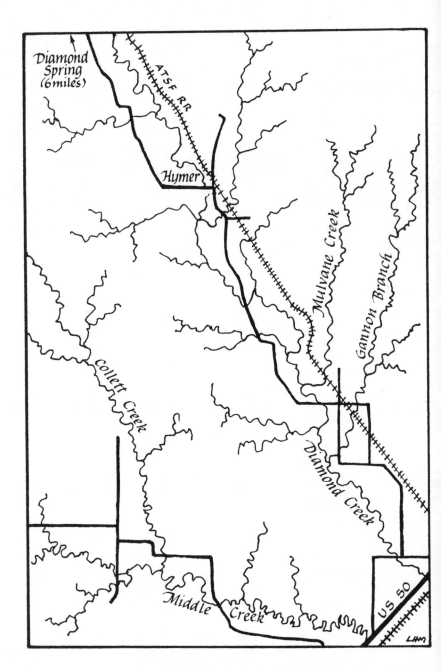

HYMER QUADRANGLE

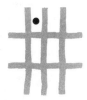

From the Commonplace Book: Hymer

Life was not only a process of rediscovering backwards.
> — D. H. Lawrence,
> *Sea and Sardinia* (1923)

Did you guess any thing lived only its moment?
> — Walt Whitman,
> "Song of Prudence" (1881)

If a stone appeals to me and elevates me, tells me how many miles I have come, how many miles remain to travel — and the more the better — reveals the future to me in some measure, it is a matter of private rejoicing. If it did the same service to all, it might well be a matter of public rejoicing.
> — Henry David Thoreau,
> *The Journal* (1856)

I found that when the moment was right, by concentrating on some external object, an arrowhead found on Scratch Flat, for example, or the running walls or foundations of the area, I was able to perceive something more than a simple mental picture of what some past event was like. I not only could see the event or the place in my mind's eye, but would also hear it, smell the woodfires; and sometimes, for just a flash, a microsecond if you care to measure things, I would actually be there, or so it seemed. This is nothing like the experience with the madeleine in Remembrance of Things Past; *what I would sense is the reality of an event that I could never have witnessed. Nor is it anything mystical; I don't claim to have experienced these things in some previous existence. It was simply a heightened awareness or perception of the way things must have been.*

I began to talk about our western bias concerning the structure of time. I said that [we] think of time as linear, flowing from past, to present, to future like a river, whereas the [Pawtucket-Micmac Indian] Nompenekit thinks of it as a lake or pool in which all events are contained.

> — John Hanson Mitchell,
> Ceremonial Time: Fifteen Thousand
> Years on One Square Mile (1984)

Human beings inherit little History but many histories. The past bequeaths a small nest egg of stable, undisputed facts and a thick portfolio of speculative issues — divergent, ever changing interpretations — because presents and futures alter pasts. . . . No one can predict the future of the past.

> — "Notes and Comment,"
> The New Yorker (1989)

We are inclined in America to think that the value of monuments is simply to remind us of origins. They are much more valuable as reminders of long-range, collective purpose, of goals and objectives and principles. As such even the least sightly of monuments gives a landscape beauty and dignity and keeps the collective memory alive.

> — J. B. Jackson,
> "Concluding with Landscapes" (1984)

[Landmarks] stand for continuity, community, identity, for links with the past and the future. In the contemporary American community these roles are what counteract our mobility and fragmentation and forgetfulness of history.

Stone was a way of establishing the passage of time in terms comprehensible to rational men.

> — J. B. Jackson,
> "Stone and Its Substitutes" (1984)

Limestone is among the chief blessings of Kansas.

> — Horace Greeley,
> *An Overland Journey* (1859)

The true-born rockman (for they are born, not made) has always been one of the finest characters in England, with a farmer's patience, a woodman's imagination, and the constructive vision and balanced mind of a mathematician. Of old, without infringing the boundaries of his legitimate craft and often unable to read or write, the rockman could do wonderful things. Even today they do not easily put pen to paper, and probably there are few people more inarticulate, few people whose mental processes are less formulated. They have always used an instinct as completely unconscious as that of an Eskimo at a seal hole. Looking at rock and its position, they will arrive at an equation demanding mathematical formulae far beyond their conscious calculation. They will say, putting a finger on the spot, "The shot will shift it here," but remain quite incapable of telling you how they arrive at that perfectly accurate judgment.

> — Dorothy Hartley,
> *Made in England* (1939)

A landscape is where we speed up or retard or divert the cosmic program and impose our own.

It is here in the United States that we see the largest and most impressive example of neo-classic spatial organization. Our national grid system, devised by the Founding Fathers, represents the last attempt to produce a Classical political landscape, one based on the notion that certain spaces — notably the square and the rectangle — were inherently beautiful and therefore suited to the creation of a just society.

Instead of being a blueprint for the ideal Classical democratic social order, the grid system became simply an easy and effective way of dividing up the land.

> — J. B. Jackson,
> "Concluding with Landscapes" (1984)

Perhaps only the stone wall of New England equalled the hedge of the Middle Western prairie as an essential man-made part of a distinctive historical regional landscape. The Kansas part of that landscape

*rivaled that of New England in durability [until] make-work activity
in the 1930s stript the area of most of its hedges.*

> — Leslie Hewes,
>   "Early Fencing on the Western Margin
>   of the Prairie" (1981)

*The Indians give an extravigant account of the exquisite odour of this
fruit [of the Osage orange] when it has obtained maturity, which takes
place the latter end of summer, or the beginning of Autumn. They
state, that at this season they can always tell by the scent of the fruit
when they arrive in the neighbourhood of the tree, and usually take
advantage of this season to obtain the wood; as it appears not [to] be a
very abundant growth, even in the country where it is to be found. An
opinion prevails among the Osages, that the fruit is poisonous, tho'
they acknowledge that they have never tasted it.*

> — Meriwether Lewis,
>   Letter to Thomas Jefferson (1804)

*Much had been expected [by Lewis and Clark] of the Osage orange,
called by them the Osage apple, for fabulous tales had been spread
about it in the East. After they saw it, however, the explorers lost all
interest in it; it did not in any way fulfill their expectations, being
useless for timber and producing no valuable fruit.*

> — E. J. Criswell,
>   *Lewis and Clark: Linguistic Pioneers*
>   (1940)

*You cannot civilize men if they have an indefinite extent of territory
over which to spread. . . . Civilization can best be effected when the
country is hedged in by narrow boundaries.*

> — George McDuffie,
>   Speech before the U.S. Senate (1843)

*I was led to see the utter impossibility of a proper social organization
of society, so long as the want of fencing material compelled the people
to form broken and scattered settlements on the margins of groves and
streams, while all within was left a solitary waste. . . . I then thought
that the greatest moral, intellectual, social, and pecuniary benefactor
would be the man who should first devise some feasible mode of*

fencing. Accordingly . . . I commenced a series of experiments with hedge plants.

— Jonathan B. Turner,
The Prairie Farmer (1847)

There is a curious logical connection between civilization and rain. All along the frontier, Indians declare that the white man brings rain with him. Thirty years ago, Missourians living on the opposite bank of the river thought the soil of Kansas good for nothing on account of its rainless climate. Since the young state was settled, it has suffered only twice from dry seasons, and of late good crops and increasing rains have dispelled all apprehensions.

— Albert D. Richardson,
Beyond the Mississippi (1867)

Kansas is the only state I have encountered that has made a census — even an estimated census — of the number of its tree inhabitants. For its 86,276 square miles, the population of trees has been set down as about 225,000,000. . . . How many are Osage orange trees nobody knows. But the number must be high.

— Edwin Way Teale,
Journey into Summer (1960)

There is something primitive about the name "barbed wire" — something suggestive of savagery and lack of refinement, something harmonious with the relentless hardness of the Plains.

— Walter Prescott Webb,
The Great Plains (1931)

Prairie and sea plant no other hedgerows than the sky.

— William A. Quayle,
The Prairie and the Sea (1905)

The true character of the spirit of an age is better revealed in its mode of regarding and expressing trivial and commonplace things than in the high manifestations of philosophy and science.

— J. Huizinga,
The Waning of the Middle Ages (1924)

You must never undertake the search for time lost in the spirit of nostalgic tourism.

— Gregor von Rezzori,
The Snows of Yesteryear (1989)

[Captain Henry Brandley] was charitable, kindly, a big man in every respect, and left an honored name in his part of Kansas.

— William Connelley,
Standard History of Kansas and Kansans (1918)

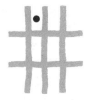

In the Quadrangle: Hymer

Twenty-four years ago in a secondhand shop, I bought a mantel clock with Roman numerals, a small Seth Thomas made of oak; its brass pendulum, knocked about for nearly a century, by chance had taken on the features, down to the grin, of the man in the moon. The clock didn't run until I cleaned the old lubricant from its gears and reoiled it, and then, once again, it began keeping good time, slowing down like a tired worker only on Sundays when I rewind it. Whether it was my cleaning or the idiosyncrasy of the clock itself I don't know, but it distinctly goes *tock*-tick, *tock*-tick, as if its hours flow in reverse. Had American Indians — whose notion of time is so much more unified and unlimited than the European conception — ever built clocks, I think theirs would run like this one, its hands moving forward while its voice speaks backwards. If, in your sleep, you sometimes dream of, say, a dead parent living again or of yourself as older or younger than you are, then you may have an inkling of the breadth and depth and oneness of Indian time.

A few years ago while I was watching the moon-faced pendulum grinning and *tock*-ticking, I began wondering who before me had watched it: what had things been like in that other house when the clock was new and the pendulum smooth and featureless? From then on, merely watching old Seth was not enough for me, so I tried to dream up a past for it, but, without my knowing a few certain details, it was as if the clock had no real past at all. What I wanted

was at least one definite fact about its former days that could under-
pin my imagination (even Sherlock Holmes needed Dr. Mortimer's
walking stick to recreate him, to imagine him). When I next passed
through the Illinois town where I had bought the clock, I stopped to
ask about its history, but the shop was out of business, the owner
gone, and I was cut off from Seth's first hundred years, cut off from
the dreamtime it carried; now it was a book with pages forever
fused, not to be read again. In the quarter century or so it has *tock*-
ticked for me, of course, it has begun to carry my own dreamtime,
those nights and days that have given a certain lunar terrain to my
face too, but that span isn't deep enough: I am grown beyond wading, and now it is fulfilling only to swim.

The American disease — and I'm quoting someone I can't recall — is forgetfulness. A person or people who cannot recollect
their past have little point beyond mere animal existence: it is
memory that makes things matter.

At about the time I began poking around in Chase County, my
father had a stroke just as he was happily telling me over the phone
of his plans for a Thanksgiving visit. Several days after that moment
of suddenly garbled speech that marked its happening, he still
wasn't sure who I was; he recognized me only as a man and not as a
son. It was the most difficult thing ever to pass between us. One
afternoon, his speech not yet unjumbled, I gave him a pencil and
asked him to write who he was: in fear, afraid of his aphasia, of
failing and what it would mean, he took it and, slowly, unsteadily,
marked out his name, his once well-formed letters, which I had
tried to emulate as a boy, now tumbling into each other, falling
down. I asked him to write my name. He faltered, then he did it,
and I asked him to put down what I was to him: he did nothing,
seemed confused, his expression the same as when the physician
had pressed alternately to his left leg the point or eraser of a pencil
and asked whether it was sharp or dull, and my father, slurringly,
could only guess. Then he began moving his right hand, the other
good now just for weighting the paper, and he marked down something. Uneasily, I picked up the pad, and I could make out, *My boy.*
I looked at him. The right half of his face was smiling. For a while
longer, anyway, we had escaped the obliteration of our shared past,
the thing that bound us.

Not long afterward I walked in the hills around what was once
the town of Hymer, Kansas, but that abrupt and painless temporary
erasing of my father's memory was most of what I encountered

here. A few days ago, I returned to walk again, now trying hard to step out of my own dreamtime, and I worked to see:

The quadrangle has the common Chase topography, vales and uplands. Diamond Creek, largely the outflow of Diamond Spring on the Santa Fe Trail seven miles north, runs the length of the quad at a north-northwest angle, and, to the south, Middle Creek (precisely midway between the Cottonwood River and Diamond Creek) comes in almost due east-west, and these creeks and their tributaries, as water does everywhere here, shape the course of things. The Superior branch of the Santa Fe Railroad, now little used, follows Diamond Creek, and the only two roads of consequence keep to the fluvial vales and their cultivated fields.

In Hymer, the only hamlet the quad has ever had, the Saffordville Syndrome is complete, and a casual traveler passes through unaware that the little 4-H building is the relocated and rebuilt depot, the last vestige of the village. In one sense, there never was a Hymer, Kansas: the town name, actually, is Hegwer, but a postal clerk misread the original handwritten application for a post office (scrawl the word and you'll see how the misreading happened), and residents never bothered to correct it, perhaps because they thought themselves lucky to get away with Hymer, considering that the fellow who had suggested his wife's maiden name of Hegwer was Kasimir John Fink: to ask for a correction could have meant ending up in Finkville.

Kasimir (here pronounced Keezmer), a yodeling German immigrant, came into the county from the California goldfields in 1858 with five silk top hats and not much else. He built a cabin along the perpetual flow of Diamond Creek and began courting Medora Hegwer, who worked in a Council Grove shop serving the Santa Fe Trail trade, but she refused to marry him because his cabin had a dirt floor. One morning Kasimir John took his ox wagon up to the Grove and bought a load of lumber and a marriage license, and that afternoon he returned to Diamond Creek, his bride perched atop her future oak floor. Some years later, after Kasimir John came back from the Civil War, he and his sons quarried stone on their place, constructed a lime kiln, cut black walnut and burr oak, built a large home, and lined the walks with lilacs and roses. The house, abandoned now, inexplicably faces into the north wind, but, even yet, in June the lilacs are thickets countians drive out to see, breathing the sweetness, sniffing old Kasimir John's world.

It was toward the Fink place I was hiking, telling myself some of

the old Hymer stories to keep from thinking about my first disheartened walk here, from remembering how fast memory can be
stricken and how easily goes with that erasure the only thing we
can take to our deathbeds, the only thing that we might be able to
slip across to the other side — if other side there be. But I couldn't
leave myself and enter the land, and I grew irritated that I was
turning the jaunt into some kind of hack-jack self-therapy, and I
cursed the dismal Hymer sky. I thought, walk in the stories of this
place: Medora Hegwer Fink's sister, Henrietta Boenitz, coming into
the county with her thirteen children, most of them trooping behind the oxen-drawn wagon; her refusal to build a fire on the ground
(Hegwer women were persnickety), and her asking husband and
sons to take down the new stove she had just bought in St. Joe and
set it up along the trail; Henrietta, in the crowded wagon, bedding
down the youngest girl in the butter churn; all of them taking
comfort in the dust of wagons two days ahead of them and two days
behind; and, after the family settled in, some Kansa Indians slipping
up to the cabin one night, their faces blackened with charcoal for
war, and chanting and dancing around a tall pole dangling a blond
scalp, only to disappear with the darkness.

But the stories didn't work very well for me, and I walked on, the
sky dimming like my mood. Then I remembered that in the little
rucksack I carry on my tramps, somewhere among the notebook
and pencils, binoculars and magnifying glass, camera and canteen,
field guides and raisins, was a thing I'd bought a few days earlier and
still had not used: a truck side-mirror, the small convex kind you
stick on. I'd recently read about an eighteenth-century traveler's
device called a Claude glass that served to condense and focus a
landscape and make it apprehensible in a way direct viewing cannot. When the English poet Thomas Gray first crossed Lake Win-
dermere, he reserved his initial view of the other side for his Claude
glass by blindfolding himself on the ferry. Maybe my mirror could
rearrange things and show me, so memory-ridden, what I was having trouble seeing.

I pulled out the thing and walked on slowly, watching in it the
hills compress and reshape themselves into something different,
and what happened was strange and invigorating: in the glass the
Chase prairie somehow took on the aspect of my first views of it,
and I began to feel again the enchantment of those early encounters.
By looking rearward, it was as if I were looking back in time, yet I
was looking at a place where left was right, a two-dimensional

landscape I could see but not enter: the prospect was both real and impossible, it was there and it wasn't, and I entered it by walking away from it. If I turned to look, it was gone, something like the reverse of the old notion that when we turn our backs the universe suddenly disappears, to reappear instantly only when we look again. If I extended the mirror far in front of me, I — or a backward image of me — joined that turned land, a dreamscape that could exist only in my palm, a place behind I could see only by looking forward: I was hiking north and traveling south. And then, stumbling along as I was, I realized that ever since I'd come down off Roniger Hill and begun walking my grids I'd been traveling much the same way, and I realized that forward or backward didn't matter so much as did the depth of the view, a long transit at once before and behind: the extent of cherishing depends upon the amplitude of the ken.

My grid walking half complete, I understood this: I'd come into the prairie, this place of long and circling horizons, because of a vague and undefined sense that I lived in shortsightedness; I saw how the land, like a good library, lets a fellow extend himself, stretch time, rupture the constrictions of egocentrism, slip the animal bondage of the perpetual present to hear Lincoln's *mystic chords of memory*. If a traveler can get past the barriers of ignorance and forgetfulness, a journey into the land is a way into some things and a way out of others.

The dark north sky kept coming on until it gathered the light as if bagging it, and I lit out for cover, the wind flattening the grasses as if treading on them and small, fierce raindrops like spines angling down hard, and I breasted a ridge above Diamond Creek north of where Hymer had once been, came to an old rock house, unroofed, unfloored, unwindowed, and I sat down against a wall in the shelter of the hypotenuse of windblown rain. The house, a compact L, was of cut and dressed limestone blocks of regular size, the quoins nicely bush-hammered, their craftsmanship now peculiar in its isolation and collapse, and I wondered whether the stonecutter had ever imagined a day when his work would come to this, a shell empty but for the rubble of the roof and plastered walls, an immense buffalo-gourd plant taking the interior as its own. Had the mason ever imagined his work inhabited only by wet sky and a vegetable with a human-like root? I could see in the stone of the west threshold gently curving striations cut by a door opening and closing, opening and closing, the kind of marks a glacier leaves as it grinds across an expanse of living rock, and cut small but deeply into one wall, this: *1889* — ninety-nine years earlier; the second generation here (the first having no time for stonemasonry beyond hearths and chimneys), the one inspired by the courthouse to carry its perdurable craftsmanship into the open prairie with rock homes the third generation would begin leaving for balloon-frame houses. These abandoned Permian stone places, despite their unpretense, partake of timelessness from the rock, the material of cathedrals and castles and capitols, and their decay seems sadder than that of a wooden derelict because the hopes and labor of their builders appear to have fallen farther. Plaster had broken away to expose the date hidden high on the wall, and *that* suggested the mason had indeed imagined someone coming along when the stones would start their return to earth; but, as though he thought his work signature enough, he had not left his name.

A pickup rolled by at a good speed down the valley road below the house. Idling out the storm, I took my pencil and notebook and figured where that truck would be if we pointed it into space and let it roll along at sixty miles an hour for ninety-nine years, permitting the driver only stops for gas and a few interplanetary cheeseburgers: halfway to the sun. At a mile a minute, that's how far I was from whoever chiseled in that date, that mileage stone. And what if I got up from this house and walked — time out only for naps and milk shakes — for ninety-nine years? I'd be a million miles away.

We measure distances short and long with time — a six-minute walk, an eight-hour drive, a star twenty light-years away — so maybe we should also measure time with distance: it changes things. A million miles on foot is farther than ninety-nine years ago, and perhaps a truer indication of the gap between me and the fellow who laid up the wall now warding off the rain-shot wind. I had no face for him, but I did seem to have his hands in the cut stones, and I sensed him in the very way I wanted to do with the first owner of my Seth Thomas clock but could not, lacking even the simplest of evidence — a fact or two salvaged from the universal amnesia that wants always to take from us what we have endured to learn, forever seeking to pry away that long root of our humanness.

I sat. I didn't need, really, to know which particular lintel of limestone the mason laid up when he was thinking of that pretty woman who had turned to look at him, or which rock dropped on his thumb and thereafter left it a prophet of damp weather, or which course he mortared the day when he kept hearing his dead father's perpetual advice on taking time to lay things true: those details weren't necessary here for dreamtime. Just the blocks themselves, his handmarks still evident on them, were sufficient, and his old stony presence on the prairie hill was enough to extend my walk by a million miles.

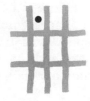

Underneath the Overburden

Within our blood move spirals of genetic inclinations bobbing like old messages in bottles cast into the sea: when I was eleven or twelve and scribbling out some kind of theme, I mentioned that I wanted to become a writer and a stonemason; the teacher asked whether I didn't mean writer *or geologist*. I didn't, and she thought the combination unlikely, but then neither she nor I knew about Robinson Jeffers. When I became the one, I didn't entirely forget the other but subsumed it by laying amateurish rock walls here and about from time to time. One day my father mentioned that his great-grandfather had transposed the Old Testament into couplets, a task that sounded so appalling to me that I got curious about the man, my only forebear ever to make a dollar by writing. I went in search of him, David Grayston, and found an English immigrant who earned his way into the West by doing stonework on the Erie Canal; I came across evidence that he descended from people who, for generations, had worked with a gray semiprecious stone found in Yorkshire — hence the name Grayston.

I followed his trail deep into the Ozark hills and eventually came across a woman nearly a century old who remembered Grayston's accent and the stone troughs and herbal remedies he made and sold from his wagon; later I found a copy of some lyrics he wrote, ones accepted by the Missouri legislature as the state song; but his biblical versification I've not yet seen. Having discovered this fellow of rocks and words, I felt I'd fished out and uncorked one of the bottles bobbing in my bloodstream, and David Grayston's message was: My pen and chisel, their marks are upon you.

I went in search of other occupations of forebears on my English and Irish sides. Not one of them followed any field that I have utterly no capacity for or at least interest in: no mathematicians, electricians, mortgage bankers. Now, I confess there is room for error here, since, if any of us goes back just twenty-five generations, say to the time of Chaucer, standing behind us are two parents and sixty-seven-million-and-some grandparents. Still, I like to think that in a cultural way ontogeny recapitulates phylogeny, and I believe that I would never have written this book without a stone-cutting, versifying great-great-grandfather. Perhaps I'd never have written at all, and surely I'd never have sought out this particular piece of prairie, because, after the thrall of the grassland itself, the thing that lured me here was stone architecture: the adroitly laid rocks of the courthouse, the Cedar Point mill, and the bridges, banks, homes, fences, cattle chutes. Once I came to understand that these things were only one expression of what undergirded the place — geologically, biologically, and historically — then my quest turned toward the bones of the land, toward the hard seed from which this prairie and its peoples grow. Whenever we enter the land, sooner or later we pick up the scent of our own histories, and when we begin to travel vertically, we end up following road maps in the marrow of our bones and in the thump of our blood.

I can't say that these notions were consciously before me as I walked around the quarry five miles up the much bent Middle Creek Road in the southwest corner of the quadrangle, but they were bobbing around somewhere inside, and they eventually led me to a question, which led me to Mac Stilley. The quarry, named Thut's (pronounced Toots), on the topo map looks remarkably like the muscular arm of a stoneworker bent at the elbow, fist clenched, biceps flexed, ready to wield an invisible hammer. The works hook around a low ridge between Collett and Middle creeks, and from the road you see not the cut hill but massive rectangles of rock stacked high and suggesting Stonehenge under construction. Because the ledge of the Cottonwood formation in Chase slopes gradually up to break through the surface, building-stone pits are commonly shallow, and they little disfigure the terrain. Typically, three to four feet of overburden, a dark and granular soil, must be removed to reach the flat beds that form naturally regular fault-lines a quarryman will use when he slabs off his big blocks. In the best exposures, like the one in the Middle Creek quarry, the ledge is so evenly thick it looks like poured concrete five feet deep. As a countian said, *That Cotton-wood rock's just waiting to become a building: about all you need to do is to set it up and run in the plumbing.* The stone, exceptionally uniform in color, largely free of holes and veins and flint nodules, seems to be composed almost entirely of fusulinids, fossils that reveal the bed was laid down in deep water rather than in the more shallow and warmer seas of other formations here. Its nature and distinctive qualities as building stone are a result of its parentage and later ancestral forces that literally came to bear on it.

Thut's quarry has been inactive for some time, and these stacks of stone, removed from the ledge years ago to await dimensional cutting, form a labyrinth with walls rising eight feet above my head and narrow lanes twisting and often turning into dead ends with only a couple leading through to the other side.

I walked those passages one afternoon, my curiosity balanced by unease as I imagined my footsteps jarring a stack loose to squash me like a bug between two fallen bricks. The blocks are of such size that big flatbed trailer trucks can carry only a couple of the smaller ones at a time. I made a sharp turn and came into a hidden chamber where, out of the wind, the December sun warmed the enclosed air and struck a golden light against the stones as if to heat them with color. A sanctum. I sat down, made notes, scouted the sky with my binoculars. Across from me I noticed a prophylactic, and I wondered what *that* would be like in here, lovers hidden in a maze cut from the ancient seminal sea.

I walked out of the meanders and followed a path to a ledge of living rock, the place where the last quarryman apparently stopped work. At my feet and running ten yards as true as a meridian was a quarter-inch fracture centered on a drill hole the size of a silver dollar. Although Chase quarrymen often remove blocks in the traditional way — sledge and wedge — this fracture resulted from explosives. The configuration was utterly simple, a line and a dot, ——————•——————, like a musical note bestrung on its staff, a lone pearl on a strand: I couldn't take my eyes from it. Nothing in the quarry so revealed the skill of the worker who had packed in a charge and, effortlessly and almost silently, broken off whole a big and splendid thirty-ton rectangle of the 250-million-year-old ocean.

I sat and looked at it and wondered whether there was any chance that the man who had made it was still alive, still in the county, still capable of speaking about the old craft of shooting stone. I went off in search. (When I told this story to a friend, a fellow who also loves stone and of whom I'll speak later, he said, *You were looking for old David Grayston.* But I don't think so, although I may have been hunting his strong and elemental craft and his sense of stone, because it was those that drew me to this simple configuration of hole and cleft.)

I drove to the Falls and began asking around, and I got sent back up the highway, until I ended up in Elmdale, which sits at the bottom of the Middle Creek Road. I went to a small frame house, old and worn and almost hidden by big ricks of carefully cut and stacked cordwood: slippery elm, hackberry, ash. A woman, looking sorrowful, answered the door, and I explained my mission, and she thought about it and then let me in.

Now: the closed room, dark but for a dim ceiling bulb, is thick with heat and the scent of humanity and burning logs in the old stove. The woman disappears, and I stand confused in the oppression of warmth and obscurity, and I can scarcely make things out in the small and heaped-up room; then a low, umbral Ozark voice from a corner, *You alookin for me?* I can just discern a slumped form in a chair, and I tell the shadow I'm hunting the Middle Creek quarryman, and the darkness says, *I done the last work, and I done the first. I shot that whole quairy.* I've found my man: McClory Stilley.

He switches on a small lamp that illuminates him only from the chest down. He wears denim coveralls, the left pant leg folded up at the knee and safety-pinned near his hip. On the small table by his worn chair is a peach can of tools, a pocket watch, a penknife, a pipe, a tin of tobacco, a pack of cigarettes, a coffee-can ashtray, and an old radio that must have once carried the voices of Fred Allen and Fibber McGee. We speak a few things, and he says pull up a chair, no use standing, things like this take some time, and I move a rung-back chair close in front of him, his knee nearly touching mine. In expectation, he raises himself a little, prepares himself, and the slowness in his voice disappears. My eyes adjust: I can see a long and wearied face, gaunt, and gray hair cropped close. He says he is sixty-five. *I used to be a better worker than I am now. I've had fourteen surgeries: I'm cut up all over. In the veterans' hospital, they had my heart completely out on the table, and they rebuilt it and put in all new leaders. I've had heart attacks for three or four men: you're alookin at man come from the grave. Circulation*

*problems: good blood but bad pipes. Sometimes of a night I reach
down to rub my left leg, and the only thing down there is the pain.
But I'm still ahangin on, still split my own farwood and run my
tractor and keep the lot mowed across the street, where they have
the Fourth of July picnic. I take care of the volunteer far trucks:
start them up once a week. I guess I been very fortunately.* Several
times over the next couple of hours he will use that phrase.

Mac holds his cigarette between his thumb and index finger and,
with his darkened little finger, knocks the ash into the coffee can.
He's telling me he was born in Arkansas, Eureka Springs, grew up
on a farm, took work in an Ozark quarry in the late thirties, learned
the trade. He says, *First machinery I run was a sledgehammer: one
man held and turned the drill — a churn drill — and two of us hit
it with sledges. That was to make the hole for the black powder,
and that's where I learned to shoot rock. I come into Kansas in the
fifties and up here in nineteen-and-sixty-two, and a few years later
they opened that quairy up on Thut's. That's as good a Cottonwood
rock as you'll find, and I shot it all, but most of the quairies here
was plug-and-feather work.*

In a series of shallow holes drilled along a line, the quarryman
puts in steel shims, the feathers, on each side of a wedge or plug,
and then taps them tighter and tighter up and down the line and
then stands back as if waiting for the first kernel to pop, and suddenly, if he's done the work right, a narrow fracture opens along the
length of the aligned holes, and the stone can be lifted out. But the
method Mac practiced is different: *After you've catted off the dirt
over the ledge and took your air hose and blowed the rock clean,
you find how the seam is arunnin, and you take your straight-edge
and square and draw your lines to the size the boss wants. Up at
Middle Crick we used a jackhammer to make the powder holes —
takes about five minutes to make a four-foot-deep hole to near that
natural seam you find in Cottonwood rock. You angle down. Then
you put your reamer on the jackhammer and drive it down and
pull it, and you've got them wings that gives the direction to your
break.* He takes a pencil and draws the reamed hole: —●—. *Then
you clean out the dust, load in the black powder and the fuse, and
tamp it tight with rock and dust. That's it.*

I ask whether he completely filled the holes with explosive to
break something so big, and he says, *If it's gravel you're awantin.
No, you put a little in the palm of your hand — say, a tablespoon-
ful, that's all — gauge it more or less dependin on the size and*

grade of the rock. Now, if you load her a little too heavy, she'll snap right in two or break some other wrong way. Since strippin down to the ledge is the most expensive part of things, you don't want to ruin too much rock.

He seems to shuffle off a few years and take on the strength and the mind of a rockman one more time. I ask, isn't it dangerous? and he says, *I never used matches. I used a Camel cigarette — nothin works better. There's no danger in it atall if a man knows how to read his seams and use his powder and takes his own cautions. A course, I was always very fortunately.*

We talk for a while about shooting rock, Mac sometimes drawing a device or technique to explain, and he is pleased to be considered competent and knowledgeable although it has been a dozen years since he last put a Camel to a bunch of fuses and watched a ledge *open up like a big old watermelon.* We talk about all the churches, schools, banks, even the Eisenhower Library at Abilene, each constructed of rock he'd shot, and I tell him I've read about Chase stone going to build the statehouse in Topeka, a reformatory, two military posts, three Kansas courthouses, four Missouri River bridges, a hundred Santa Fe Railroad bridges between Chicago and Albuquerque, a cathedral in San Francisco.

I ask how he figures limestone is created, and he says, hardly pausing, *I been told in my period of life, at one time this here was all under water, but, a course, I wouldn't have no way aknowin whether that's right or wrong,* and I ask whether he thinks it's right, and he says, *One time up there at Middle Crick, I shot a block, and when the forklift picked it up, in the rock they was a petrified fish — twenty-two, twenty-three inches long — it looked like a big old catfish. I didn't think much of it, but the men that was aworkin for me was just about carried away. They couldn't get over that fish abein in the rock. We run into a couple of others. I never did keep one, but I think Harvey Stark took one home. I know it's somethin you won't never run into very often. You ask me, and I'd say that was a normal fish when it went in there, and whatever caused the rocks to be where they're at, that's what petrified him in there. This rock — Mother Nature put it here — it come here — it was here — I don't know. But it'd be quite a history.*

He's uncomfortable that he can't pencil a diagram to explain fish in rocks for me, but he knows what I'm asking of him, and he puts down his cigarette and stokes his pipe the better to help recollection, tamps it down precisely as he must have done his powder, and then puts the Camel to the briar bowl and transfers the fire, and he says, *I'll tell you what I liked: when you take one of them rocks out, you know when you walk down on that bare ground you're the only man alive that's walked there that people knows about.*

I ask how he felt about quarry work, and he says, *I was very well interested in it. It raised my kids, montained my family. You might say I've got a lot of that limestone rock in my veins.* He's watching to see whether his answers are satisfactory, and he's edgy that they might be insufficient. *Limestone is somethin you get interested in and somethin you learn to like, and then you become part of it. You know every move to make: just how to mark it off, drill it, load it, shoot it, and then you see a real straight break, and you feel good. If they's some quairymen that says nobody can shoot more than a couple of blocks at a time, and you shoot thirty in front of their eyes, that gives you a feelin you cain't explain, and I done it.*

When I get up to put my chair back by the stove, he says, *I got more time if you need it,* and I say, when it warms up, how about a trip to Thut's quarry to show me how to shoot rock, and he says he'll do that. But in June, Mac died. A month later when I passed the quarry again, I stopped and went back to the figure ————•———— , and I thought of it as his epitaph, one scribed in the last block he shot, now cleaved and wonderfully squared, the ground beneath not yet having taken the first footfall of man. When that step would occur was only a question of time: Mac's Cottonwood rock was ready for somebody sometime, waiting only for the plumbing.

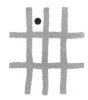

With the Grain of the Grid

Had the courthouse clock been working, I wouldn't have stopped in Whitt Laughridge's office to ask the hour, wouldn't have gotten it from a most peculiar timepiece and then ended up some miles away and walking into a green bit of fossil history. I had begun the day with my usual pedestrious approach: set a small goal and let the destination find me. Goals are looser things, less tied to schedules, more amenable to circumnavigation than destinations, which seem to call for the straightest course possible: the one serves exploration, the other arrival. My goal that day was to find the site of Shipman's gristmill somewhere at the foot of Osage Hill just east of Elmdale, but I ended up farther south, hunting an Osage orange tree, also called hedge.

Perhaps because the fruits of the hedge had just come into ripeness and were bountifully before the countians' eyes, a day earlier a man had said to me that old Jack So-and-so *wasn't worth a bushel of damn hedgeballs*, that is to say, utterly worthless. So, when I went into Whitt's office (he said, *Come on in. We're not doing anything but sitting here lying to each other.*) and got the correct time from a hedge apple, I shifted my goal around to follow this new stacking of events. On his old office counter, which has had as many stories passed over it as Darla's bar top, sat a small clock with two wires stuck into the polar ends of an Osage orange, the fruit of *Maclura pomifera;* I was suspicious and pulled a wire loose and the clock stopped, and I realized it was running on the galvanic response from the acid. Whitt said, *We finally found a use for hedgeballs*, and an elderly fellow said, *How many would it take to crank up my '58 Ford?* and another said, *A hunnerd hedgeballs wouldn't far up your old engine.*

The destination hunting me that early autumn Tuesday, I figured, was not Osage Hill but an Osage orange: sometimes traveling orders get bollixed in their passage. For the last year, whenever I happened across the trees, I always looked for a good walking stick, but *Maclura*, like my jaunts, usually takes a digressive course in sending its branches out: they twist, turn, bend, bow, warp, hook, crook, curve, deflect, and arc. Now, a certain kind of contortion in a natural walking stick can be handsome, but the sinuous limbs of Osage orange commonly impart springiness when what you want is rigidity. Nevertheless, inspired by Whitt's hedgeball clock, I took off in hunt of a length of *Maclura* about a meter long and an inch thick. Even given the fair number of hedgerows left in the county, finding a proper stick is considerably more difficult than it might seem. Thinking I was hunting only a shaped branch, off I went and soon found myself exploring the lines of the county and the direction of sleeping bodies here, and ended up walking, you could say, through the mind of Thomas Jefferson.

Like the Osage orange and my ramble, I must first curve around things, must pour a few drafts of old lore, because without them arrival means little: *Maclura* came into the county not long after the Civil War, carried by a number of the early settlers who, above all else, wanted both domesticated stock and cultivated fields untrampled by cattle, ungrazed by horses and goats, and unuprooted by hogs. A gallon of seed, claimed an immigrant's guidebook, would enclose eighty acres. For the most part, these people had neither the time nor money to lay up the abundant fieldstones here into fences (few places have loose rocks of such regular squares and rectangles begging to be laid into walls as those of Chase County), nor could those homesteaders afford much lumber, since the bottoms held only enough for some fuel and a few houses and barns; protecting even forty acres of wheat with rails was out of the question. The smooth-wire fencing of the time was variable stuff, soft in one span and brittle in another, so that heat or cold or an insistent cow could break it. These settlers, as their numerous letters to newspapers prove, believed that civilization followed not a free-range steer but rather a moldboard plow, and they believed that a good fence was not just an earmark of civilization but a precursor of it. Sooner or later, to gain the land, to make it theirs, to try to free it from Indian prerogatives, to prove up a homestead claim, to make it truly productive, they had to have fencing as they had to have plows. Before Robert Frost said it, they believed that something there was that didn't love a wall, that wanted it down, and that something was wilderness, the abode of the devil in Christian thought. They also believed that good fences make not only good neighbors but progressive communities. They understood that, while fences separate animals and crops, they link people into a utilitarian webbing. Rich land without readily available fencing was often the last to be taken up, and, as prairie farmers learned, the correlation between fences and profits was direct: you harvested only what you could protect, and a plow without a fence was a hammer without a nail, a rifle without a cartridge.

The first Americans to practice agriculture in a big and fertile but nearly treeless and rock-free place, the farmers of central Illinois, tried and rejected sod walls and ditches with embankments for fencing; then they looked to their English ancestors and considered hedges: all they needed was a plant adaptable to the vagaries of prairie weathers, one that would grow into a fence at once *pig-tight, horse-high, and bull-strong*. They tried willow, black walnut, cottonwood, honey locust, mulberry, privet, gooseberry, sweetbrier, crabapple, arborvitae, and several roses, all with indifferent success. In 1839, Professor Jonathan Turner of Jacksonville, Illinois, a preacher with both a mystic and scientific turn of mind — he once said he could not persuade himself that *the beneficent Creator had committed the obvious blunder of making the prairies without also making something to fence them with* — began working with a plant native to an area between the middle portions of the Arkansas and Red rivers. By 1847 Turner was advocating and selling this plant, until then known primarily as the finest wood in North America — maybe in the hemisphere — for making archery bows, a tree that French trappers called *bois d'arc*, one that some Ozark hill people, even today, call bodark, or more literally, bowdark or bow wood, although now the old names derived from Indian archery have mostly yielded to those linking it with Anglo fencing. There was coincidental logic here: just as the tree provided bows and clubs that helped Indians eat and defend territory, so would it as fencing help white settlers. Professor Turner proposed calling *Maclura* prairie-hedge plant, and he said, *It is our plant — God made it for us, and we will call it by the name of our "green ocean home."*

Referring to it as Osage apple, Meriwether Lewis wrote the first description of bow wood in a March 1804 letter to Thomas Jefferson that accompanied some slips from a tree in the St. Louis garden of the famous Indian trader Pierre Chouteau, who had grown them from seeds obtained five years earlier from an Osage man who had carried them three hundred miles; there is evidence that many of the Osage orange trees now growing in the Northeast descend from those in Chouteau's garden, a place visited by several early travelers, including the botanists John Bradbury and Thomas Nuttall, who both wrote about it in their journals. In a message to Congress two years after Lewis' letter, Jefferson mentioned the possible use of the plant as hedge fencing; since it was from his mind that came the township-and-range system — the great American grid, an expression of eighteenth-century rationalism if ever there was one — it seems that he understood the importance Osage orange could have in establishing agricultural and political dominion and in enforcing it on the face of America west of the Appalachians. Once Jefferson read the reports of the Lewis and Clark expedition, he knew his system would require in the plains something like *Maclura*, a living embodiment of the gridwork of the new civilization; it would be what a constitution is to a government, what a police patrol is to a neighborhood: a thing defining, delimiting, enforcing.

Thomas Nuttall, the so-called father of western American botany, gave an account of the plant in 1811 and named it after his wealthy friend William Maclure, a philanthropist and geologist who lived for some time in that nidus of early western science, New Harmony, Indiana, home then of the Geological Survey, the agency responsible for laying the national grid over the land. This chain of linkings from *Maclura* to William Maclure to Jefferson's grid is, I assume, largely chance, yet the overall interweavings of connections from Osage bows to township-and-range are a result of the nature of the tree itself.

Maclura pomifera is a monotype, the sole member of its genus in all the world, although in preglacial times it had many close relatives. Like Indian breadroot, its several comparative popular names are misleading, for it is neither an orange (sometimes called mock orange) nor an apple (sometimes called horse apple) but rather a distant relative of the breadfruit and mulberry. (During nineteenth-century attempts to introduce silk culture into eastern Kansas, farmers fed *Maclura* leaves to caterpillars, but the worms spun out inferior silk.) While the leaves resemble those of an orange tree, its fruit, so intriguing to anyone seeing it for the first time — or any ten-year-old needing a softball — is typically about the size of a grapefruit, its ripened color between that of a lemon and a lime; but the heartwood is a wonderfully grained ocher that provides another name, yellow wood. Hedgeballs seem to repel insects (countians place them in basements and under kitchen counters), yet quail, squirrels, and pack rats will gnaw through the thick flesh, heavily charged with a milky and resinous sap, to eat the nutlets. On Stephen Long's great western expedition of 1819 and 1820, the botanist Edwin James wrote of the sap, *We were tempted to apply it to our skin, where it formed a thin and flexible varnish, affording us, as we thought, some protection from the ticks.* Timothy Flint in 1828 probably explained the effectiveness of the sap as a repellent when he said of the fruit, *Tempting as it is in aspect, it is the apple of Sodom to the taste.* So, I conclude, to say a hedgeball is quite useless is to ignore keeping time, feeding wildlife, repelling roaches, warding off tick-borne fevers — not to mention procreating trees for Indian bows and Jefferson's grid. But, as for providing softballs, I concur: a hedge apple is as worthless as old Jack So-and-so.

It is, of course, the wood of *Maclura* that men have for several thousand years admired: one of the heaviest on the continent, a cubic foot of it in a natural state weighs more than half that of an equal size chunk of limestone, and it is nearly as hard, taking the edge off a lathe chisel or saw blade immediately; yet the wood is two and a half times stronger than white oak while still marvelously flexible: an Osage orange bow made from a good sapling properly seasoned and strung with bison sinew could drive a dogwood arrow up to the fletching into a buffalo, and to this day some archers believe the wood superior to yew, the stuff of the famed English longbow. On his 1811 Missouri River journey encouraged by Jefferson, John Bradbury said the price of a bow made from *Maclura* was very high: a horse and a blanket.

White men, having little use for bows, made Osage orange — when they could find straight trunks — into wagon axles, wheel spokes, pulleys, tool handles, the keel and ribs of at least one river steamboat, the world's first chuck wagon, telegraph poles, insulator pins, police billy clubs, and railway ties: in an experiment by the Pennsylvania Railroad, sleepers of oak, chestnut, and catalpa decayed in a couple of years, but *Maclura* ties in virtually new condition were in use almost a quarter of a century later. Even though the wood is so hard, so impervious to bugs, so incorruptible that some

American streets were paved with yellow blocks of Osage orange, it is still supple and responsive enough that dowsers witch for water with forked branches of it. Because of its potential heat, farmers have to learn to use it sparingly to keep its intense fire from destroying a metal stove. Indians showed settlers how to use the wood and shallow roots, brightly orange like washed carrots, to concoct tinctures, dyes still utilized early in this century to turn doughboy uniforms olive drab.

But it was another aspect of the Osage orange that, for a time, made it important to rural Americans living between the Wabash and the hundredth meridian: thorns: not stubby and hooked like a rose's or long and maleficent like the vicious spikes of the honey locust, which inflict pain that continues for hours after getting stabbed, but rather modest inch-long spines of just the right length and strength to turn away fleshy creatures without lacerating them, unless we speak of mice caught and rammed down on a hedge thorn by a loggerhead shrike (I once came across a small *Maclura* dressed out in several tiny rodent skulls as if some cannibalistic homunculi had been marking their territory). If its thorns are perfect instruments, nearly so also is its capacity to adapt to the climates and soils of the prairies, its ability to grow from either inexpensive seed or seedlings, its resistance to insects; once established, it takes to pruning by thickening its zigzag lateral branches and sending up vertical shoots that can grow forty inches in a year. A trunk that gets too big can be cut for firewood or a gatepost: countians speak of cedar, catalpa, honey locust, and coffee-tree posts for barbed-wire fencing lasting a man's working life, but one of hedge can last his *and* his children's. They also talk about old cowboys trusting in the longevity of the wood, year after year hiding a bottle of whiskey for long prairie nights in the hole of a loose Osage orange fencepost.

Chase County lies just north of the native range of *Maclura*, so the prehistoric aspect of these hills was free of them, yet today, especially on the uplands of the southwest quarter, they mark off the prairie with their long and dark rows, the trees sometimes enclosing and shading section-line roads — a splendid gift for a walker in July — and in other places making a stroke right across the land like the narrow signature of some long-gone farmer whose field boundaries they yet reveal. The trees began reaching the county in the early 1870s, putting an end to both stone fences and old disputes between farmers and ranchers that, across the prairies, took the form of hedge bounties and herd laws, the bounty paying people up to $128 a mile to plant and maintain living fences, and the herd laws requiring stock owners to contain their animals: it took time and litigation before Kansans widely decided to follow the English precedent of holding responsible, not farmers for fencing animals out, but stockmen for keeping them in. Because Chase County has never had a herd law, farmers usually protected their own crops, and some progressive cattlemen also realized that strong fences help safeguard bloodlines of good cattle from a stray bull or a tick-infested herd carrying Texas fever.

But the rows of *Maclura* still standing reveal more than the ancient battle between tillers and herdsmen: some time after American explorers began sending back reports on the prairies and plains, a notion developed that this land was treeless because it was without trees. Knowing that a mature grove can transpire much moisture, people came to believe that to plant trees was to increase rainfall by raising the humidity (the nearly constant winds that absorb and disperse transpiration didn't enter their thinking), and so one argument held that living fences of Osage orange would bring rain: of the four basic elements any seed requires — sun, soil, water, protection — half came with the territory, and *Maclura* could provide the other two while at the same time disrupting the desiccating winds. These ideas gained strength from the frequent above-average precipitation during the settlement years in eastern Kansas. The first historian of Chase County, H. L. Hunt, praising the white man's husbandry in changing the land from a *desolate waste*, wrote: *That our county has undergone a decided climatic change since its first settlement is evident from united report of early settlers, who say that when they first settled here, they could not raise potatoes without mulching the ground to keep it moist, that corn was a very uncertain crop.* These homesteaders, new to the region, saw the great drought of 1860 as typical weather rather than as a brief phase of a greater, more humid cycle.

Chase hedgerows are a little over a century old now, and not one of them is any longer actually a hedge: untrimmed for years, they are lines of forty-foot-tall trees full of gaps (some made by cutting out posts to carry their successor, barbed wire) and therefore useless as fences, although valuable as windbreaks and wildlife cover. Farmers cuss them, now so overgrown and their roots unpruned, because they shade crops and draw away moisture a couple dozen feet into a field, sapping as many as two acres of crops per mile of hedge. Cowhands gripe about cattle ceasing to graze on summer afternoons and taking to the grass-thin shade of a hedgerow: Slim Pinkston told me, *You play hell to get a hot steer out of there where he cain't eat and put on weight.*

In its first years, hedge is troublesome: it requires effort to establish a fence, and, under good conditions, it takes five years to grow enough to turn away stock; a line of twelve-inch seedlings I planted in Missouri four years ago, despite care, still wouldn't stop a diapered infant. Young plants are vulnerable to drought, fire, gophers, and cattle. Even once established, a row must be continually patched in and cut back almost annually if it is to serve as a barrier.

Although Osage hedge quickly appeared in abundance across the tall prairies, its era as an agricultural tool was even briefer than that of river steamboats, and what the locomotive did to paddlewheelers, barbed wire did to the hedge-apple fence: made it a lovely, comforting, historically rich anachronism. It is probably not coincidental that the invention of barbed wire occurred in Illinois, not far from where Professor Turner proved Osage orange to be good prairie fencing, and it even seems that Joseph Glidden, from whose 1874 barbed-fence patents modern wire descends, took his idea from the shape of a thorned branch of *Maclura* (nature generates, man elaborates: from the gourd, the canteen).

Long past the introduction of cheap and effective steel fencing, countians continued planting Osage orange because, I think, something deeper moved in them, an urge that barbed wire, the devil's hatband, can never fulfill: a living fence of hedges and trees gives a feeling of enclosure to a people still at heart woodlanders, people who, even in later generations, found the vastly open expanses overwhelming, threatening, and they knew, whatever else these uplands are, they aren't cozy; the prairie novels of Willa Cather are full of this discomforting omnipresence. But a farmstead and its lane, tidily hedged in, could give the sense of a snug and intimate English farm, and the family could look out to a distant tree line demarking their boundaries to see all they had given their lives to and see encompassed their real capital, their investment, their defense against the precarious world beyond them. Osage orange, as much as a deed, showed what was theirs, marked off for the world their accomplishment, their contribution to civilization. Property lines were invisible things, but a row of windbreaking Osage orange, standing like guardsmen, gave proof.

The enclosures also enforced things: before the fencing of the prairie, homesteaders made their own roads to town, to church, to the neighbors, and tracks lay haphazardly over the place, each family needing its own crossing over a creek, its own grade over a hill, and everyone moving in frequent trespass. A workable system of bridges and roads and an upholding of property rights demanded organization beyond the mere following of a few old, established upland trails and valley lanes; it seemed to require Jefferson's grid: as curbstones are to a suburb, so was Osage hedge to the prairies, as it came to mark out routes and channel citizens onto them, laying down a pattern that so shaped lives that people began to build their new houses in alignment with the now visible grid. They set out their furniture accordingly, dressers and bedsteads against walls running only in cardinal compass directions, so that, still today, Chase County sleeps north-south or east-west, the square rooms squared with the world, the decumbent folk like an accountant's figures neatly between ruled lines, their slumber nicely compartmentalized in Tom's grand grid.

The dreaming citizens lie comforted that outside their walls run the township-and-range lines, their defense against a fruitful and transgressing nature perpetually threatening erasure and apparent disorder. That's why, if you ask me, they retain the so discernible Osage orange hedgerows, and it's also why they cut and poison and burn and bulldoze those *Maclura* that break ranks and take higgledy-piggledy to the open pastures rightfully belonging to the aboriginal and faceless grasses and forbs. And that's also part of the reason, even if it is unperceived, why countians line up on Broadway in the Falls and stand through a June thunderstorm to get a plate of Chase bison barbecued over old hedge fenceposts.

And it may explain why a Missouri visitor one autumn Tuesday will tramp about for hours in search of an Osage orange walking stick, and, at last finding a proper shape, shred his arms getting it out, why he will trim and dethorn and smooth it and oil its hardness to a gleaming. It's why, thereafter with it in hand, he will walk the county a bit differently, holding not just a stick but also a synecdoche of the place.

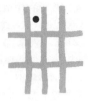

Around Half Past

The western hill drops down sharply to Diamond Creek Road, and a ledge provides a small bench. I am sitting on it, up above things it seems, watching the empty road. Not much is happening other than the saps rising, the creek running, the wind ruffling a nighthawk trying to keep clamped on to a barbed-wire fence. A car comes along, slows, stops, and a man and woman get out, look across the vale, and he points at something, and she looks in that direction and puts her arm around his waist, pulls him against her, and they laugh and drive on. I sit and watch, nearly invisible, the eyes of the blind hills: in that private moment, so unwittingly (and now widely) shared, what brief thing happened down there to give them delight? Did he point out where he first saw her on horseback, where he got the tractor stuck, where they would one day build a house? The moment seemed nothing much, more mere fact than meaning, an ordinary occurrence, the sort of thing that composes most of human life, the kind of insubstantial detail lost to historians and left to dreaming novelists.

I'm thinking how much I'd like to witness on this spot some happenstance between a man and woman five hundred years ago, thinking how time turns the mundane to significance. Or maybe it's that time clarifies the value of the commonplace: archaeologists excavate tenth-century middens and last-century privies and then display the old refuse in glass cases in marble-floored museums. Was a woman's embrace less than a pre-Columbian coprolite?

It is about two-thirty in the afternoon, the fifth of April: if I came to this little coign of vantage at half past two for the next month, the next year, how would my view of the prairie change? For days on end, zoologists sit behind blinds and observe animals, so why doesn't someone become a site watcher? I consider it, consider the discomfort, the boredom, the time — the very things that make for changed perceptions — and I know I lack the will to carry it out, and, truth to say, that bothers me.

I am hiking on in some restlessness, and then: what if I gathered hours and became a collector of half past twos? If I recorded what I saw between two and three o'clock every day I am in the county, would it add up to an album of hours? I'm walking and thinking about it, and I begin to see the assemblage of moments as one of the illustrations in a child's book: a bird's-eye view of a house in cutaway, with members of the family doing this and that: mother carving a pumpkin, father lighting his meerschaum, junior putting the propeller on a model Hellcat, sister hunting the gerbil hiding behind the chair, a lawn robin pulling at a worm.

Now: it has been twenty months since I sat and watched the Diamond Creek Road, and I have assembled a notebook, and from it I give you in random arrangement this selection, a compendium of humdrum, a cutaway view of Chase County, Kansas, in the late 1980s:

September 28: in the cool sun of late morning, a fisherman sits whistling (more breath than notes) on a small dry spot on the old milldam at the Falls. He has just caught a large bullhead, but a few minutes ago he lost a flathead catfish that he believed everted its stomach to pitch out the hook. It was not, of course, as big as the eighty-three-pounder a fellow caught years ago before the big oil spill (that winter the river didn't freeze properly for ice skating). In the man's bait bucket are seven small cricket frogs that he caught earlier on Sharp's Creek. (Over this dam, a few months later, a high school science teacher and his son will try to shoot the drop in their canoe: it will overturn and the man will strike his head and be pulled into a frothing eddy, and the fifteen-year-old boy will be unable to help, and he will watch his father drown as his mother videotapes from the bridge.)

February 3: at the Emma Chase (where an elderly woman just said to her friend, *You drink water like a bird*), the conversation over coffee at the men's table is about a courthouse clerk who has turned down a raise of $8.33 to her monthly check of $1,066.67. Last year she refused a $37.50-a-month raise. Her action and comments about the farmers' economic struggle will be reported in the *Kansas City Times: Agriculture supports Chase County, and I can't understand why [the commissioners] could give raises when the people who are paying the wages aren't making it.* She also doesn't understand why the county commission, to save money, has torn up blacktopped roads and put them back in gravel but still gives raises to road workers. When I go to the courthouse to talk to her about it, she says, *I have nothing to say. It did nothing but cause trouble.*

March 12: Dorothy Selves pulls from the glass exhibit case in the county historical society museum a ledger from the Hinckley House, a hotel long gone from Cottonwood. The book, next to Captain Henry Brandley's quill pen, always lies open to Monday, 18 May 1874; in a clear hand, the first entry is this:

Brigham Young & 27 Wives . . . . . Salt Lake City, Utah.
Below the name are other travelers from Denver, San Francisco, Niagara Falls, Saratoga Springs. Mrs. Selves makes a photocopy of the entry, believed here to be genuine. (Later I will send it to the historical department of the Mormon church in Salt Lake City, and the reply is two sentences: *We are afraid that the signature in question is an example of 19th century farcical humor penned by some wag as a joke. While Brigham Young (1801–1877) traveled many miles within the Great Basin Region, after his return from the Midwest in the fall of 1848, he never again set foot east of the Rocky Mountains.* When I report my findings to some historical society members, they are not much pleased, as if I'd stolen away a piece of history or the exhibit, but one man says, *I like the truth better: who'd make a joke in a hotel register?* They say it wasn't Brigham, but, hell, somebody came through here — *and he got away with keeping a bunch of women up in his room. That's what happened.*

July 7: I am at the counter of Whitt Laughridge's office (a man once said to me, *Stand here long enough, bud, and you'll hear every story in the county,* and Whitt said, *More likely every lie*). Someone tells a choice story about a neighbor, and Whitt is surprised to hear it so long afterward, and he says, *That's what I get for going to Florida.* A boy brings in a funeral notice, a three-by-seven-inch card announcing the death of a countian. Notices are useful in a place with only a weekly newspaper, where burials draw sizable turnouts, especially if the weather is bad and people can't get into the fields;

funerals, in fact, are such social occasions that the bigger cemeteries have privies. A fellow so bent and wrinkled that he looks as if time just wadded him up stares at the slender card and says, *Another shingle off the old roof.*

January 28: outside the Flint Hills Restaurant, a truck stop on the highway at the edge of Strong City: the mercury-vapor lamps cast a deathly green luminance into the dismal fog as if it were night; horses stamp restively in a trailer, and a pair of mutts pace the bed of a pickup; on the rusted bumper of an old Pontiac from Butler County is a sticker: OIL FIELD TRASH AND PROUD OF IT. Over-the-road rigs idle out their smudgy dieselings, their air brakes expelling, their running lights little auras of red and yellow, and trucks leave and arrive, some of the two thousand a day passing here. Inside, in the cigarette smoke, the Sunday papers from Kansas City and Wichita lie separated and spread on the counter and tables, and over them truckers dressed to be cowboys eat and laugh (the real cowboy in the corner is dressed more like a trucker), and the waitress brings them plates of food running up her forearms, and one fellow hears something surprising and says, *Well I'll be switched.* I'm eating a western omelet filled with chilies, cheddar, and diced tomatoes, topped with salsa; it takes up half the big platter, the other side occupied by a hillock of hash browns, and it requires two glasses of milk to get it down (this is what happens when you skip breakfast and lunch and walk around half a day). A teamster, his road-shaken guts sagging like old drapery, gets up to leave, and, looking for the door, walks the wrong way in the L-shaped room, then turns to the windowless east wall, then turns toward the windowless north wall, turns again, and then mumbles, *How'd I get in here at!*

March 13: while I'm gassing up at the station on the turnpike near Matfield, I talk to a young actor from New York City who's driving to Los Angeles and seeing the West for the first time. I tell him that parts of the movies *The Gypsy Moths* and *Bad Company* were filmed here. Referring to the highway department sign a few miles up the pike,

ENJOY SCENIC
FLINT HILLS
NEXT 31 MILES

he says, *I kind of like a place where the scenery has to be called to your attention,* and I say that some travelers see the sign and, when they arrive here, ask, *Where were they!* We go into the burger stand for a soft drink, and I ask him how things out here look to him, and he says, *Last week all I knew about Kansas was that it's dry and flat and takes up two pages in the road atlas.* I ask what he feels like on the prairie, and he says, *Forty-eight hours ago, I was in Times Square. Now it seems I've been dumped out of a tall glass bottle — sort of uncorked and poured out.* I ask, what do you think of life horizontal? and he says, *I guess no one here has dreams of falling.*

September 30: I often do this: take a sandwich and a bottle of Guinness into a county cemetery and, eating and sipping, walk along reading tombstones. Today I'm in the largest burial ground here, Prairie Grove, a mile west of Cottonwood on the Osage Hill Road. This Arlington Cemetery of Chase County holds a power over me, I assume because I've come to know stories about so many of the people stretched out beneath me (could I rouse a couple of dozen of them, I think we could rewrite — correctly — western history). A woman of middle years is setting a wreath of plastic somethings on a grave, and as I pass I say hello and she scowls and nods in reluctance. A few minutes afterward, leaving in her Chrysler, she drives close, opens the electric window an inch, says, *Please! This is not a tavern*, seals herself in again, and rolls on. Then I come to this marker:

MARGARET REPLOGLE SHORE
1921–1977
"THANKS FOR STOPPING BY. SEE YOU LATER."

I raise a toast. That evening I learn that Margaret's family denied her request to have jazz played at the funeral.

April 5: I have stopped in Elmdale to ask directions to a remote prairie-chicken booming ground; a couple of men look up from the papers of some business deal they are transacting on the hood of a truck. One gives directions, gets corrected by the other, then corrects the correction, and, finally, with information so correct as to be impossible to follow, I ask whether the small sedan I'm driving can get over the ruts and rocks, and one fellow says, *I was awonderin when you was agonna ask the important question*, and the other says, *He couldn't get that little thing over a cow pie*, and the first one bends down and looks at the clearance, and he rises and says, *Hell, Eddy, he ain't agonna get it over a wet fart.*

December 12: in the Senior Citizens' Center on Broadway, there is a discussion about countians' driving to Emporia to shop, and a man, not in the least meaning a double entendre, says, *The main business of this town is dying.*

October 10: (notebook entry) I'm sitting on a knobby hill with at least a six-mile-long view in every direction, the afternoon without winds as if they had been bound up, the grass stock-still, and I cannot see the slightest movement of anything anywhere: in the visible hundred-and-some square miles, *nothing is happening.* It's as if the entire scene has been cast in a Steuben crystal sculpture and eternally stopped except for the tiny scratching of my pencil across this notebook page — good god, I'm the only thing *happening* here. Ten minutes later: no — in my miniature vision, I've been watching for visible events, not unseen processes. Significant "happening" is process occurring behind a screen of mere, if overwhelming, presences. What I see as stasis is, in fact, moving, and if my pen wiggles along faster than the fractional creepings of the continental plate and rooted mats below me that are a slow and grand erasing of what I see now, its movement counts for little when compared against the imperceptibilities going on here, forces completely remaking this place second by second, inch by inch. A traveler (who cannot even remotely detect the thousand-mile-an-hour spinning of the planet he rides through space at sixty-seven thousand miles an hour, to say nothing of its solar and galactic movements and its precession) writes in his notebook *nothing is happening.* Man muses, God guffaws.

June 3: at Bonnie & Clyde's, the Strong City bar, I hear a man say, *That big old hog wouldn't get out of the truck. Wouldn't budge. Now, you know Tom's a poor-tempered sonofabitch to start with — kicks his help about as much as his hogs — so he grabbed that sow by the ears and pulled, and just as he did, Bobby, his hired hand, hit her on the hams with his cattle prod. That jolt went through them pig ears into Tom, and he started jumping around, flailing, cussing: he thought he'd been stung by a hornet. Bobby realized what happened, so he started jumping around, acting like he'd been got by a hornet too.*

April 8: Charles Ireland, the retired superintendent of Chase schools, and Whitt Laughridge and I are walking around the few crumbled remains of Kenbro, a twenties and thirties oil boomtown just across the line in Greenwood County. On the north side we come to some broken concrete and a few bricks and rusting pipes that mark the site of the home Charlie grew up in. He tugs on a piece of metal and tells how the company houses, made of wood, were tied down with long hoops of steel wrapped over them, like cord around a package, to keep the flimsy things from blowing away. When he comes to a small depression at the end of a walk, he says, *This was Hamilton. That's what we called the outhouse — I don't remember why. We'd say, "Well, I got to go to Hamilton."* He smiles but on the way home is very quiet.

May 31: the Cottonwood Falls clothier stands behind and leans on the men's suit rack, and he stares out into the brightness of empty Broadway. I've often seen him there, immobile as a mannequin, practicing the prime requirement for making money in the town: patience. I cannot imagine living here and walking past his eternal gaze, wearing a suit I did not buy from him.

November 2: one of the most frequently used references in the county is the big 1908 county plat called *Methuselah's Map,* in the window of Whitt Laughridge's realty office. It hangs in the narrow room across from his collection of prairie grasses on the south wall. This afternoon I asked him what caused the big stain on it in township twenty-one, range eight, near Bazaar, and Whitt says, *Years ago, Methuselah used to hang in the insurance agent's office here, right behind old Abe Conner's chair. He spent a lot of time tilted back in that chair, sleeping. That splotch in twenty-one— eight is Abe's hair oil.* (From then on, whenever I pass the office window and see the stained map, Mr. Conner, forty years gone, is asleep against it.)

May 8: do I only imagine that countians prefer to sit away from windows? In a bar, a café, a shop, the citizens cluster in the back, especially in an old commercial building, its length commonly three times greater than its width. Is it that they have had too much sky and openness? Does some atavism draw them to the darker, safer, more temperate rear of the cave, the café?

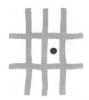

On the Town:
Versus Harry B. (II)

THE TRIAL

Ninety years later, *The State v. Brandley* has not yet died out, and I hear countians speak of it, not necessarily with accuracy but with notions: that Captain Henry Brandley gained his first wealth by waylaying guests who stopped over at his log house, a station on the old stage line before Perkins' tavern replaced it; that he made enemies in his acquiring land and handling of mortgages; that son Harry was innocent and forced to stand trial for the real killer, his mother (abetting this idea is the murder of a man six years earlier committed by his wife's lover, who, trying to throw off suspicion, wore a sunbonnet and a *Mother Hubbard dress*); that Frank Rinard's bloodstains on the Brandley porch and barn door never went away, and thereafter, the place and family were damned.

It seemed there was more here than just a murder. I remembered Jane Koger talking about how nothing so vexed countians as financial success, how one could be forgiven almost anything except making big money: was it possible that the citizens wanted to punish not a murderer but an uppity plutocrat? If the Brandleys really did object to Rinard, weren't there easier solutions than murder? I went to the courthouse and began going through the big books, and I found a few journal entries about bail, subpoenas, jury selection, changes of venue, but the one book giving details of the trial was missing. Another question arose: had the captain or his eldest daughter, Clara, who wrote much of the early history of the upper South Fork, seen to the disappearance of records? (After all, Clara was prone to polishing some pioneer deeds while ignoring nefarious ones.) Perhaps, but then again the county records are carelessly maintained (a teacher recently found lying on a hallway floor the coroner's inquest of the Knute Rockne plane crash). A clerk told me that the Brandley material would have followed the trial to Emporia and then *should* have come back.

I went to the Lyon County Courthouse, and James Hoy, a professor of English at Emporia State University, who has a special interest in the folk culture of the Flint Hills and who grew up a few miles southwest of the Brandley place, joined me. We made our way through the microfilm, then a clerk took us to a storage room behind the courthouse; it was an unheated, gritty, sorry room cheaply partitioned off from a county garage. When I saw it, I knew the quest was in trouble: the Chase records were not there and neither was any of the Lyon County material of the trial. The so-called mysteries people read and watch should be called riddles because they contain solutions; true mystery is a bottomless thing, and we were in one.

Only a single avenue remained: Jim came up with accounts of the trial in the *Emporia Gazette* (William Allen White's paper) and the *Daily Republican*. I want to tell you what happened to Harry Brandley, but I must warn you: the accounts are fragmentary (*Little testimony has been given that is of much interest*), in error (consecutive sentences have Elizabeth as Harry's mother *and* his wife), and incompetently written (vague pronoun references and tangled grammar obscuring the simplest of facts).

Jury selection began on a Monday afternoon nearly two years after the murder: those opposed to capital punishment or conviction on circumstantial evidence were excused, and the state seemed to win the first round. The trial, as it developed, repeated the proceedings in Cottonwood. Harry sat between the captain and Lizzie, within the railing. The first witness, a surveyor, presented a map of the murder scene, and four following witnesses testified to seeing Rinard riding toward the Brandley farm about sundown, and then Arthur Crocker described finding the body. The coroner came on to say that Rinard had been killed by a single bullet that entered the center of his face and ranged down into his neck: he concluded that this angle indicated that the shot came from above Rinard and that powder burns on his face suggested the gun was about eighteen inches away — or twice that if the victim was sweating.

On the second day, the state worked to show that Frank and Miss Pearl were frequently together, and the defense did not challenge. Then the prosecution brought forward one of its key witnesses, John Digman, who told of a dance in January preceding the murder: Rinard and Pearl were sitting in a window, and Digman pointed them out to Harry and said, as best he could remember, *They're having quite a conversation — you better fix that,* to which Harry said, *I'll fix it all right,* and walked away. The defense held that Harry was the floor manager who arranged the dancers and that he separated the couple, and then his counsel moved to strike all of Digman's testimony, since the incident had occurred six months before the murder and proved neither malice nor threat. Following the long argument, the judge sustained the motion.

Over the next two days were these events: the state called Charles Fisher and asked him to repeat a conversation he had with Rinard; at last it seemed the dead man would be heard, but the defense objected, motion sustained. Brandley's counsel then moved to strike all testimony bearing on relations between Rinard and Pearl, again sustained. The state had lost its evidence of motive and now it would have to prove guilt without it.

The prosecution called on W. H. Dosier to relate a conversation he had with Harry several weeks after the murder. Dosier said, *He came to me to sign an affidavit for a change of venue and said that he wanted to be tried by twelve men. I said that if his father had done what he ought to have done, Harry never would have been suspected: when two other murders occurred in the neighborhood, his father had offered a reward, but when a man was killed at his own house he had ordered the hands out to work the next day. Harry said that if his father had done what he ought to have done, the damned dog would have been left lying in the hog lot where they found him.* The defense moved to strike the testimony but was overruled, yet the state never again raised the question of the captain's unusual action.

Hired hand Cecil Richards testified that on the evening of the murder, when he carried the fresh milk into the Brandley kitchen, he heard Harry say to his mother, *I'll fix him,* but he did not know who "him" was. The state seemed to be working motive again, but it permitted the witness to change his testimony from the first trial and the defense went after him. The *Daily Republican* reporter commented on Richards: *He was badly confused and finally said he did not know what he had heard.* The incompetence of the prosecution seemed to be helping Harry as much as his counsel.

The defense called several witnesses to establish the common-
ness in Chase of carrying pistols, a number of them forty-fours.
Then it tried to prove good relations between Harry and Frank. On
the fifth day, a man testified that the captain disappeared for a while
some time after the murder, but the prosecution did not pursue that
question either; in fact, the state seemed to have no questions at all
for the captain. Witnesses spoke of hearing Harry's horse, Roxie, an
animal with a distinctive gait, leave the farm just before the murder,
but none of them actually saw him riding her. The defense called
its leading witness, Bob Handy, Harry's assistant at the Jack Creek
Ranch, where Brandley alleged he was at the time of the murder.
Handy said he arrived there about one A.M.: *I got to Harry's and
found Harry in bed, asleep. I shook him and wakened him up,
telling him Frank was shot. He asked me if they had help over there
and who all was over.* But Brandley, oddly, did not return to the
farm, only a forty-minute ride away.

At last a central figure took the stand. About the events of the
evening of the murder, Elizabeth Brandley said: *Harry came up to
the east gate and hitched his horse. I went into the northeast room.
He asked me for some handkerchiefs. He also told me he wanted
some underclothes. I got out some and mended them, and he took
them, went and changed them and came back. We talked about
who was to be hired for teacher. I also, while I was at it, mended a
shirt for Frank Rinard and Frank Calvert. I talked of Bob going to
school, of his crops and prospects. While we were talking, Cecil
Richards came in with the milk. There was no such conversation
as Richards testified to. When I began mending I could just see to
thread a needle, and afterwards finished by lamplight. The last he
said was: "I'll sell my crops this fall, pay every penny I owe and be
a man." He went out then, and I should say it was about nine
o'clock. About an hour after I heard a shot. After Harry left I
thought of the milk and was just going down in the cellar to strain
it, when I heard the shot. I came out, heard a gurgling sound and
knew someone was hurt. When I came out I missed Bob, and I
began to scream as I thought it was him that was shot, and I said,
"Is Bob shot?" When I got to the gate Bob came up and touched me
on the shoulder and said, "It is not me. Is anyone hurt?" Then he
and Arthur Crocker went to the body and said it was Frank. I told
them to take him to the house. They laid him down, and I felt his
pulse and saw he was dead. We sent for a doctor.*

Then Miss Pearl took the stand: the defense asked her whether she knew why Cecil Richards changed his testimony, and she said Richards was angered that *the Handy girls stuck up for Harry so and were so proud that he wanted to take them down.* The state apparently accepted this damage quietly, and no one asked Pearl about her relationship with Rinard or whether her family opposed his interest or where she was when the murder occurred. The spectators must have wondered why the prosecution was holding back and what they were waiting for. Pearl did not testify again.

The captain went to the box and retold the known facts, adding only that he arrived at the farm about an hour and a half after the murder. Neither side asked him to account for his whereabouts during the murder or where he went in the middle of the night or whether he opposed Rinard's attentions to his daughter.

On the final day, at last, Harry Brandley took the stand. He repeated the story already pieced together by both sides, adding nothing new, and he concluded, *I was not on Father's place when Frank was killed. I was at home in bed — and I did not shoot him.* During cross-examination, his counsel asked about his conversation with W. H. Dosier, and Harry said: *I asked Dosier to sign an affidavit for a change of venue to Lyon County. I explained to him my cause for wanting the change. He said he did not want to, as he had been summoned as a juror. I told him he had heard a lot about it and could not sit. He said he had heard some, and I told him he had already made up his mind. He then went on to say that he had heard that Mr. Brandley had not treated the body right, but had left it on the porch. I asked him where he had heard about that, and he could not say. I then told him that a lot of dirty dogs were running around trying to injure me and my family. I further said that if they had done as the law required, they would have left the body where they found it until the coroner came and took charge of it, or a doctor, but that they had carried it to the house and did all they could for it. And that is the extent of the conversation with him.*

Throughout the proceedings, the opposing lawyers had been at each other. At one point, when defense attorney F. P. Cochran was on the stand, A. L. Redden for the state asked whether he carried a gun, and Cochran answered, *Yes sir, ever since I came to this western country. I also carried one during the war,* and Redden sneered, *Oh yes, you were a nice, brave soldier,* to which Cochran said, *Yes sir, I killed as many of them as they did of me.*

The newspapers commented on the excellence of both sides in

their final pleas, Redden for the state implying that his opponents had played *an underhanded game*, and John Madden for the defense drawing applause for his eloquence. But the reports leave unexplained the captain's peculiar absence from court on that last day, although the *Republican* reporter implies that he was with influential Emporia political friends. He did return in time for the verdict.

At ten past five on Monday, a week after the trial started, the jury left the courtroom. The spectators, including William Allen White's mother, who had once taught school in Chase County, remained. On a first, informal vote only two jurors spoke for conviction, and discussion began. Less than an hour later the jury returned. The foreman passed the verdict to the clerk, who read it aloud, all the while young Brandley, sitting with his parents and sisters, held a strained composure, staring blankly, everyone turned toward him. He listened, and then he broke, dropping his head down on the table, crying like a boy, paying no attention to the applause shaking the room. Then he rose, flushed and wet, his friends congratulating him, and he shook the hand of each juryman. Lizzie came forward and invited them to join the family for supper and dancing at the Wigwam. The captain arranged to have a photograph made of the twelve men, and the *jollification* went on well past midnight. The Brandleys, it seemed, were free.

The next day the *Gazette* reporter wrote: *Today the Brandley family returned to Chase County, and another Chase County murder mystery is still unsolved.*

VIII

Elmdale

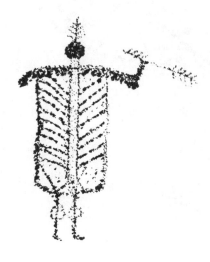

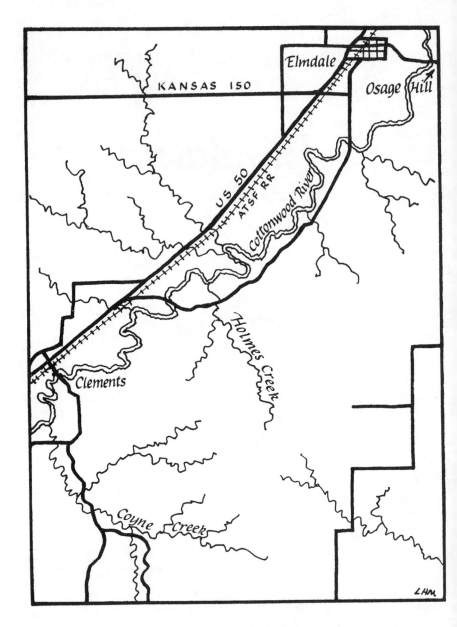

ELMDALE QUADRANGLE

From the Commonplace Book:
Elmdale

A lot that goes on out there is invisible to us. Some of it's visible to science, some of it's visible to mystics, some of it's visible to local inhabitants, but much of it is unreachable, uncontainable. I think of it as having authority because its order is, at least in some places, still innate. It's part of what we call "God." It is the face of God.

> — Barry Lopez,
> "An Interview," *Western American Literature* (1986)

Fellow citizens, we cannot escape history.

> — Abraham Lincoln,
> "Annual Message to Congress" (1862)

Without a living past, we have only an inert present and a dead future.

> — Carlos Fuentes,
> National Arts Club speech (1988)

How will we know it's us without our past?

> — John Steinbeck,
> *The Grapes of Wrath* (1939)

(Bravas to all impulses sending sane children to the next age!
But damn that which spends itself with no thought of the stain, pains,
dismay, feebleness, it is bequeathing.)

> — Walt Whitman,
> "By Blue Ontario's Shore" (1881)

Stupids find the nowhere-road
Dusty, grim, and slow.

> — Vachel Lindsay,
> "On the Road to Nowhere" (1912)

When you sit in council on the welfare of your people, you must
council with the seventh generation in mind.

> — Onondaga Chief Oren Lyons,
> Long Island University lecture (1990)

The land belongs to the future.

> — Willa Cather,
> *O Pioneers!* (1913)

Possunt quia posse videntur. [They can because they think they can.]

> — Chase County High School motto in
> 1908 [Vergil, *The Aeneid*, 19 B.C.]

Chase County High entertained an old jinx last Friday night when
Hope invaded the home field. For a number of years now, Chase had a
very difficult time winning from Hope. Friday night was no exception,
but this time it was the many penalties that made victory difficult
rather than the opposition on the field. Every time Chase would make
a long advancement, a penalty would nullify the gain.

> — Sports page,
> *Chase County Leader-News* (1955)

The Gladstone 4-H Club met Monday, May 5, 1987, at the Methodist
Church basement. Five members and two leaders answered roll call
of "your favorite flower." Mary Jones led us in the song "An Austrian
Went Yodeling With Plenty of Action." Mary M. taught us how to
play "Passing Grapefruits." Even parents participated in this exciting
game. The meeting was adjourned to refreshments of melted marsh-
mallows on fudgegrahams brought by Jerry Jones.

> — Marcy Griffin,
> *Chase County Leader-News* (1987)

County life in Kansas is not entirely monotonous.

> — Charles Moreau Harger,
> Original source unknown (1902)

A major export of Kansas has been its talented youth.

— Leo E. Oliva,
"Kansas: A Hard Land
in the Heartland" (1988)

We all know that our country is economically stagnant and losing ground in population and maintenance of basic services. Ranchers and farmers who already have a guaranteed occupation and business and professional people who already are making a living should be joining forces to insure there will be some room or some reason for anyone else to want to be left in Chase County in the decade ahead. Maintaining the status quo means our country will die. It's that simple. And those arguing for that might as well get out their shotguns and put ol' Chase County out of her misery now.

— Editorial,
Chase County Leader-News (1990)

A people living with nature, and largely dependent upon nature, will note with care every natural aspect in their environment. Accustomed to observe through the days and the seasons, in times of stress and of repose, every natural feature, they will watch for every sign of impending mood of nature, every intimation of her favor and every monition of her austerity. Living thus in daily association with the natural features of a region some of the more notable will assume a sort of personality in the popular mind, and so come to have place in philosophic thought and religious ritual.

The cottonwood [the Plains Indians] found in such diverse situations, appearing always so self-reliant, showing such prodigious fecundity, its lustrous young leaves in springtime by their sheen and by their restlessness reflecting the splendor of the sun like the dancing ripples of a lake, that to this tree they ascribed mystery. This peculiarity of the foliage of the cottonwood is quite remarkable, so that it is said the air is never so still that there is not motion of cottonwood leaves. Even in still summer afternoons and at night when all else was still, they could ever hear the rustling of cottonwood leaves by the passage of little vagrant currents of air. And the winds themselves were the paths of the Higher Powers, so they were constantly reminded of the mystic character of this tree.

The Sacred Pole of the Omaha was made from a cottonwood. This was an object which seems to have had among that people a function somewhat similar to that of the Ark of the Covenant among the ancient Hebrews.

— Melvin R. Gilmore,
*Uses of Plants by the Indians of the
Missouri River Region* (1919)

[Prayer before cutting the sundance lodgepole:] *Of all the many standing peoples, you O rustling Cottonwood, have been chosen in a sacred manner: you are about to go to the center of the people's sacred hoop, and there you will represent the people and will help us to fulfill the will of* Wakan-Tanka. *You are a kind and good-looking tree: upon you the winged peoples have raised their families: from the tip of your lofty branches down to your roots, the winged and four-legged peoples have made their homes. When you stand at the center of the sacred hoop you will be the people, and you will be as the pipe, stretching from heaven to earth. The weak will lean upon you, and for all the people you will be a support. With the tips of your branches you hold the sacred red and blue days. You will stand where the four sacred paths cross — there you will be the center of the great Power of the universe. May we two-leggeds always follow your sacred example, for we see that you are always looking upwards into the heavens. Soon, and with all the peoples of the world, you will stand at the center: for all beings and all things you will bring that which is good.* Hechetu welo!

We choose the cottonwood tree to be at the center of our lodge [because] the Great Spirit has shown to us that, if you cut an upper limb of this tree crosswise, there you will see in the grain a perfect five-pointed star, which, to us, represents the presence of the Great Spirit. Also perhaps you have noticed that even in the very lightest breeze you can hear the voice of the cottonwood tree; this we understand is its prayer to the Great Spirit, for not only men, but all things and all beings pray to Him continually in differing ways.

— Black Elk (recorded by Joseph Epes
Brown),
The Sacred Pipe (1953)

In almost any other portion of the country the cottonwood would be the least desirable of trees; but to the Indian, and, in many instances which have fallen under my observation, to our troops, the cottonwood has performed a service for which no other tree has been found its equal, and that is as forage for horses and mules during the winter season, when the snow prevents even dried grass from being obtainable.

In routing the Indians from their winter villages, we invariably discovered them located upon that point of the stream promising the greatest supply of cottonwood bark, while the stream in the vicinity of the village was completely shorn of its supply of timber, and the village itself was strewn with the white branches of the cottonwood entirely stripped of their bark. It was somewhat amusing to observe an Indian pony feeding on cottonwood bark. The limb being usually cut into pieces about four feet in length and thrown upon the ground, the pony, accustomed to this kind of "long forage," would place one forefoot on the limb in the same manner as a dog secures a bone, and gnaw the bark from it. Although not affording anything like the amount of nutriment which either hay or grain does, yet our horses invariably preferred the bark to either.

> — George Armstrong Custer,
> *My Life on the Plains* (1872)

These appearances [of cottonwood] were quite reviving after the drairy country through which we had been passing.

> — Meriwether Lewis,
> *The Journals* (1805)

We cannot visualize what the cottonwood [once] meant because we are too far from it all.

> — C. M. Older,
> "The Cottonwood" (1938)

The white man does not understand America, a red man wrote. *The roots of the tree of his life have yet to grasp it.*

> — Amy Clampitt,
> "The Prairie" (1990)

We live in succession, in division, in parts, in particles.

> — Ralph Waldo Emerson,
> "The Over-Soul" (1841)

Wherever one is, the place has its conscious genius. Man has lived there and brought forth his consciousness there and in some way brought that place to consciousness, given it its expression, and, really, finished it. The expression may be Proserpine, or Pan, or even the strange "shrouded gods" of the Etruscans or the Sikels, nonethe-

less it is an expression. The land has been humanized, through and through: and we in our own tissued consciousness bear the results of this humanization. So that for us to go to Italy and to penetrate into *Italy is like a most fascinating act of self-discovery — back, back down the old ways of time. Strange and wonderful chords awake in us, and vibrate again after many hundreds of years of complete forgetfulness.*

> — D. H. Lawrence,
> *Sea and Sardinia* (1923)

You have to have nerve to live in Kansas.

> — Pat Reid [Floyd M. Gurley],
> *White Thunder God* (1947)

The facts are available to all, but the patterns they form depend upon the point of view of the observer. Surely the patterns are as valid as the facts themselves, because they make rational and comprehensible a way of life which has too often been considered erratic and strange. They are merely a diagram of functional processes, a reconstruction of folkways. Though the pattern is made up of facts, it differs from them as an assembled machine differs from a dismantled one.

> — Walter Prescott Webb,
> *The Great Plains* (1931)

History is the big myth we live, and in our living, constantly remake.

> — Robert Penn Warren,
> *Brother to Dragons* (1979)

From gossip the book-writer sucks a goo called information to cement edifices of assertion with.

> — Hugh Kenner,
> *Historical Fictions* (1990)

In the Quadrangle: Elmdale

Some places a traveler never really enters no matter the number of times he passes through; Elmdale, on the Cottonwood River near the junction of Middle and Diamond creeks, has ever been such a place for me. I wonder whether my failure has anything to do with the rainy afternoon, some years before I began my rambles in the county, when a speeding car, just outside the village, nearly crashed headlong into me. That's the nearest I've come to getting rubbed out on a two-lane highway, a miss that perhaps set something else in motion: since then, Elmdale for me is a place of erasure, a village that seems to lose its inhabitants every time I arrive, as if they were wraiths that could come and go on whim. I always have the sense that the vaporish citizens are standing behind their old curtains to watch me from narrow openings, waiting until I move on: they are like the jungle Tasaday who for so long hid themselves from the twentieth century.

I have, of course, entered the three or four businesses yet surviving on much dwindled Main Street, where the little buildings are mostly shuttered even to Elmdalians now that the Saffordville Syndrome and floods and diesel power (steam locomotives no longer stop for water) have reduced the population from three hundred to eighty. I've been in the small and picturesque stone bank, in the post office, the corner grocery, and the trading post on the highway, but these encounters have been hardly more than a meeting of somnambulists: a bottle of cold pop gets passed over the counter and a few words spoken, but when the sleepers awake, they believe nothing really happened, as they believe dreams don't "really" happen. At other times the encounters seem removed even as they occur, having in their actual moments the quality of memory, of a thing previously accomplished; they are events I witness from behind a scrim of prior time as if a present moment here is already long gone so that I cannot effectually touch the place any more than I can, say, Kasimir John Fink's sweating hand as he planted lilacs at his Diamond Creek home. I've wondered whether the sensation — if it isn't the result of nearly having crossed to the other side here — is evidence that a man dies in certain places before he dies in others, dying in pieces *and* places. Maybe I've already, so to speak, gone west in Elmdale, Kansas. Maybe *I'm* the wraith here, a temporary ghost.

Once, before I was aware of this little Bermuda Triangle of my soul, I almost had a real exchange. Some people I'd met in Cottonwood, a retired couple (not far from permanent wraithdom) who visit their old home in the moribund village only a few weeks each year, invited me over to pick up some memoirs; late for an appointment in Bazaar, I hurried a stop in Elmdale. Their house was old and worn, the yellowed shades drawn, and the June humidity seemed to hang like stalactites and drip darkly from the high, dingy ceilings. I had the notion that everything leaned just a little — joists drooping under me in damp rot, rafters sagging, doorjambs surrealistically akimbo — and yet these two people welcomed me as if to a soirée, and they did what I'd not encountered before in the county: they offered me a drink, a good whiskey. I was new to the place and its ways then, and, not realizing what the invitation meant, I rushed on to Bazaar. We never met again, although we did exchange a couple of letters about Sam Wood (I learned that he wanted to die in Elmdale).

Now, innocence gone, I offer this traveler's advice: should you ever find yourself in Chase County and have a good whiskey proffered, accept: it is a rare gift. I told this story to my friend, of whom I'll yet speak, whose mind is as eccentrically contoured as you can find among those of us walking at liberty, and he said, *You violated a fundamental rule of the road: you refused hospitality. As you well know, Plains Indians took umbrage at ungraciousness. Your insensitivity put the kibosh on you in Elmdale — forever.*

Most probably, such talk is nonsense, yet between Elmdale and me something *is* different. If you've walked through a gallery in a

big museum and unexpectedly found yourself alone among un-
shrouded mummies, with their mirrors and combs and golden
toothpicks on display, and then gotten the willies as if ancient souls
resented your voyeurism, you have an idea of me in Elmdale. Still,
a village that I can never really catch in the throes of existence is an
unwonted gift of the road, and its lure is this strangeness, something
I've chosen not to monkey with by forcing it into actuality. Elmdalians and I will remain sleepers.

At the heart of this dreamtime is an incident I missed by nearly
ninety years, yet it's something I've never found distorted and dis-
connected like my own encounters. Clara Breese, a former schoolteacher, and her husband, owner of a general merchandise in the
village, sent their daughter, their only child, off on the Santa Fe to
the normal school at Emporia in the autumn of 1903; pretty Julia
Breese suffered from incipient tuberculosis, but she was uncommonly bright, an apt pupil, and she did well in her studies even
though she wrote her mother to *ask God to help me to perceive
readily in Arithmetic* (some of us understand divine intervention as
our only hope with numbers). Julia wrote her parents often, and the
letters evoke every now and then her collegiate life in a time of
hoop skirts and patent medicines, but mostly they are piled up with
gratitude and duty and piety, so much so that, when I read them in
the little book entitled *Julia*, which her mother had published in
1905, I nearly smothered in righteous goodness, and I wished for the
girl to complain, or pull a prank, or sass the arithmetic professor.
Perhaps Julia knew she was dying — the letters can be interpreted
that way — and felt a seventeen-year-old girl's last days were not
proper for anything beyond safe and standard nineteenth-century
Christian joy — that is, a gratitude that things are no worse in our
dark and transitory vale. She did not finish her first year. Late on
Christmas afternoon in 1903, she and her parents arrived in San
Antonio with hopes the dry southwest Texas air would cure her.
Two weeks before the vernal equinox of 1904 Julia died. Clara
Brandley said that Mrs. Breese never recovered from her daughter's
death, and the mother wrote in a notebook: *We can only fancy what
a welcome we'd give her if she came back.*

All of this is by way of background to a couple of letters Clara
Breese did not include in her memoir of Julia; I saw them only once,
yellowed pages I transcribed, and, perhaps in the doing, as if an
incantation, created the core of my Elmdale dreamtime: for me, the
village now lies in it far more so than it does in township nineteen-

south, range seven-east, immediately southeast of the Santa Fe
tracks and U.S. 50. These are parts of two letters Clara sent to Julia
in early September:

> Business has been reasonably good. I have a nice basket of
> grapes — wish you had them. I sold John Holmes six bottles of
> prickly-ash bitters for five dollars — he thinks his stomach is
> out of fix.

> I got up late and have gotten breakfast, washed the dishes,
> brushed the front porch and dining room, emptied the refridge
> pan, fixed up the bedroom, slopped the chickens, fed the cat
> three times, and now can step on the porch without a howl
> greeting me. Visited an hour or so with Maxine, washed my neck
> and combed my hair, and gave Edith her instructions for the
> forenoon's work. I did that twice since it was to nicely dust the
> dishes and shelves and counter and rearrange the dishes. I know
> that where she dusts she doesn't rearrange things. I expect her
> to improve a lot under my charge. I want to know, are the plaids
> showing much in the windows in common goods? I suppose
> stripes are past.

Although the Breese store is gone, their house still stands on
Main, and, whenever I pass through, Clara is on that porch, pausing
in joy of work accomplished and the high expectations for her
daughter's health and studies: Clara slows her tasks to write Julia,
hot dust rises from someone passing down Main, and the morning
lies closed in by the steady sawing of katydids as if they were
cutting off the last days of summer to stack them for the coming
cold. Clara wipes the wet cloth over her white throat as women
once did, and she runs the cool around and over the back of her
neck, and she is ignorant of this: her days of contentment, her times
with Julia alive and not a memory, are draining away invisibly like
a leaking sinkhole pond until there will be only the small cleft in
the bottom, hardly enough, it would seem, to let so much pass
through so quickly.

So.

Other things, of course, have happened in Elmdale, and I've heard
a few stories about them, but I've never found anyone like Clara to
infuse them. Indians widely believe that the past belongs to everyone, but only the proper storyteller can open it, and archaeologists
know that in any dig some shards remain mute, isolated, and dis-
connected, waiting for other hands to come along and discover their
pattern and reassemble them.

For example: in August of 1897, when her daughter was eleven,

Clara Breese woke in the night to two explosions and roused her husband, who alerted five other men who heard two more explosions while they were dressing and taking up their guns. The men surrounded the little bank on Main, and, in the deep darkness, fired willy-nilly toward it while the unseen burglars went out the front door with drafts, postage stamps, and seventeen hundred dollars. With the dawn, the citizens could see they had plugged good the buildings on each side of the bank, but *it* they had hit just once and the thieves not at all.

In August of 1989, soon after I had photographed the fine Cottonwood-stone bank with decorated Ionic pilasters, a robber entered it at half past ten in the morning and slipped a note to a teller, the employees just then entirely women. Neatly typed on the paper — actually an envelope torn in half — was this:

> *Very quietly*
> *VERY quickly*
> *Fill this bag with money, big bills first!*
> *No alarms or I shoot: your choice*
> *Now MOVE!! Quietly — quickly.*

The thief walked out the front door with about twice as much cash as ninety-two years earlier, but by eleven o'clock a new deputy (in hot water for wrecking a police car in a chase the night before) sped over Osage Hill and arrested him a few blocks from the bank and found the money in a hole. The accused man, who fancied himself a writer, denied the robbery, but police later found the other half of the envelope in his car: the return address on it was the Kansas State Penitentiary.

Five miles southwest of Elmdale used to be Clements (drawing upon memory or stories, citizens still apply the name to a mostly empty piece of gravel road): other than a fine, tin-sided building — closed up — and an old Quonset hut, Clements, Kansas, belongs to dreamtime, a result of the Syndrome and one too many fires alternating with floods (if you're ever looking for a place with a number of villages built in stupid locations, look no farther than Chase County: such happens when whites refuse either to heed the lay and insistence of the land or to listen to Indians). About the time of the last Elmdale holdup and fifty-eight years after burglars robbed the Clements post office of twenty-nine cents, police broke into the Quonset hut and arrested three men brewing up methamphetamine, a drug called crank that they planned to sell in Topeka.

But Clements today usually makes the news because of the splendid twin-arch, camel-back stone bridge over the Cottonwood a half mile out of what was town; it's a somewhat secluded span often considered the loveliest bridge in the state and, after the courthouse, the structure most cherished by countians; yet, despite its being on the National Register, a battle over its survival is imminent: a man told me, *The dang highway boys got that triple-archer over to Bazaar, but they're going to play whaley getting this one. If you thought they was an uproar over them courthouse cedars, watch what happens here.* Not far from the bridge, but five years before it was built in 1886, a terrific March hailstorm and high water hit Ed Holmes' low-lying log cabin, and silt covered several deep piles of hail; that Fourth of July he and neighbors unearthed the still frozen hail to make rare cold lemonades and thunderstone ice cream. For people hunting measures of American progress, this happened not far from where the crank was concocted.

Between Clements and Elmdale is Clover Cliff Ranch, another National Register site, its 1883 stone house and big barn and outbuildings once nearly the equal to Stephen Jones' Spring Hill; now the barn is gone, the land broken up and sold off, and travelers along U.S. 50 see only the handsome two-story rock house against the side of the low bluff. It was otherwise in 1912 when Vachel Lindsay, thirty-three years old, passed through the county on his long walk from his home in Illinois to New Mexico, earning his way by trading poems he carried in an oilcloth rucksack. In a time when the likes of countian Adam Ice put up skull-and-crossbones signs near Clements as warnings to hoboes, Lindsay came down the Cottonwood Valley one June afternoon as he followed the highway and Santa Fe tracks, which here for some miles exactly parallel each other like lines strung between telegraph poles. He found his back labor easier to trade for a meal than his poetic ones, especially during alfalfa harvest. I believe I understand his encounter at Clover Cliff, which he misnames; here is a picture from his book *Adventures While Preaching the Gospel of Beauty:*

> *Much of the country east of Emporia is hilly and well-wooded and hedged like Missouri. But now I am getting into the range region. Yesterday, after several miles of treeless land that had never known the plough, I said to myself: "Now I am really West." And my impression was reinforced when I reached a grand baronial establishment called "Clover Hill Ranch." It was flanked by the houses of the retainers. In the foreground and a little to the side was the great stone barn for mules and horses.*

Back on the little hill, properly introduced by ceremonious trees, was the ranch house itself. And before it was my lord on his ranching charger. The aforesaid lord created quite an atmosphere of lordliness as he refused work in the alfalfa harvest to a battered stranger who bowed too low and begged too hard, perhaps. On the porch was my lady, feeding bread and honey to the beautiful young prince of the place.

Lindsay's long walk through Kansas, nevertheless, created in him an extravagant idealism apparent in his book with its proclamations (so like Walt Whitman's, when, thirty-three years earlier, he rode over the tracks Lindsay walked), euphoric assertions about how the villages of middle America will soon abound with craftsmen, artists, philosophers, great-hearted statesmen. Nineteen years after his tour, Lindsay died from drinking Lysol.

The quadrangle: in the way that is almost a pattern here, a watercourse cuts the quad nearly centrally. The Cottonwood flows in from the southwest to turn eastward around the big foot of Osage Hill, a nearly level-topped ridge that goes beyond hillness in its massive breadth and length. It is a rampart that more than any other thing marks off the eastern part of the county from the western half, the occidental side of Chase showing fewer people and a less troublous past, an area that appears to me less under the domination of human history; the white past, especially, seems to lie not so densely here. Except for the small river valley, the topography is more even, less tumultuous, having the quiet of deep seawater rather than the noise of a steeper coast that is eastern Chase, where the continuous re-forming of the hills through erosion is more evident. And so it is that, in this county anyway, history assumes the aspect of the land it arises from and occurs upon.

As the Cottonwood passes through the quad, it so twists upon itself that it flows toward every point of the compass, a half-dozen times turning completely around as if changing its mind about yielding its waters to the Atlantic. One afternoon, below the high south-side limestone bluffs, I paddled between the deeply cut banks of the Cottonwood, and I thought my compass had gone awry, so quickly did the needle swivel. Yet the railroad and federal highway that follow the river, never more than a mile from it here, strike nearly perfect and unyielding forty-five degree angles to true north, and state road 150, a highway built in the Franklin Roosevelt years largely with shovels and wheelbarrows to give more men work for a longer time, runs precisely east and west. Passage across the quad, then, is either by angles or arcs: people waste not an inch of time, but the laggard river is a traveler that finds arrival nothing more than the consequence of its reluctant flux.

If ever there was a homebody of a river, it's the Cottonwood: even in flood it heads not so much downstream as out laterally. Most of the time it would hardly move at all if not for the overriding crustal plate that has lifted western Kansas some three thousand feet higher than Chase County; in this way, the sluggish and relentless slipping and de-forming of the great crusts are the forces that propel the Cottonwood out of the county, and what is happening a few miles under the Front Range of the Rocky Mountains helps determine the shape of, say, Osage Hill, which, in its turn, helps determine what has happened on it. So the citizens of Elmdale are the children of many parents, and tectonics is one of them: raise the Rocky roof-beam higher, raise it faster, and Elmdale, Kansas, is a different town, maybe never a town at all.

The Cottonwood, by seeming to turn itself into sloughs and oxbow ponds, masks its usual slow but strong persistence eastward: only one other river in the two-hundred-mile length of the Flint Hills in Kansas has managed to cut through them. And, almost certainly, every few years the Cottonwood rises to thrust itself violently into the laid-down hills as if aroused to ravish them. But then it falls back, detumesces, metamorphoses itself into a gentler, more feminine thing: supine, languid, fecund. As Yang it cuts a face into the hills, and as Yin it suffuses that visage with life.

Throughout the quadrangle, and in the north especially, gas wells were drilled about the turn of the century, with more coming in the forties and eighties; before the First World War, Elmdale was surely the smallest hamlet in the country to have gas lamps along its eight streets. The second of its two newspapers, a thing born and gone in 1909, was the *Gas Jet*. At that time many citizens called the town ELL-um-dale, and even still I hear older residents say it that way, but when the twentieth century closes that fossil pronunciation (which I think derives from Cornish immigrants to America) will be gone, as are Tuh-PEEK-ee and Em-POR-ee. Like the hills and the human days spent in them, countians' words lie in a watershed where the course of things is seepage, drainage, erosion, and then deposition in some unknown place farther away. Could I ask Clara Breese, I think she would say, *Indeed*.

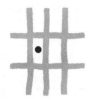

Up Dead-End Dirt Roads

One morning when I was walking a couple of miles south of Elm-dale at Camp Wood, more than a hundred acres of timbered vales and grassy uplands given for a retreat for young people in 1916 by Stephen Wood, Sam's brother, I found an uncommonly well pre-served brachiopod still resting in a piece of its once soft seabed, both now turned to stone. I took the fossil down to the creek to wash it off, and a boy and girl, about nine years old, came up to watch. I told them what it was, the boy unimpressed but the girl curious, and she asked whether people ever became fossils, and I said yes, but even the oldest ones were a hundred times younger than this shell. I tried to suggest 250 million years by telling them the hundreds of miles this shell had traveled since it had clamped itself closed for the last time, and the girl asked how far the shell had moved since she was born, and I said about the distance from your heel to your big toe. She was disappointed to have lived so many years only to find it had gone no farther than that. The boy believed nothing I was saying. Then she said, *Where will things be when I'm old?* I flipped a pebble a few feet away and said, about there, and she said, again disap-pointed, *I wish it could go farther*, and I said if your bones last as long as this shell, you'll be getting near Hawaii.

I liked her attempt to imagine tomorrow as yesterday, her own bones become stones. I had just been reading Vachel Lindsay's brave pronouncements about the coming surge of prairie youth into phi-losophy and artistry, and it came to me that I should try to take a little time-hike myself, one where the destination would be Chase County of a coming day. I went to the high school in Cottonwood, up to the second floor, and asked the librarian, Carol Glotzbach, whom I'd met before, whether she could assemble a few students, a cross-section of juniors and seniors, to talk about their future here. I went to the principal and told him that we would need to use the library after hours, and he answered some questions: enrollment was 180, grades ten through twelve; more than three quarters of the graduates would at least try college; discipline was not a problem, nor was substance abuse, if you excluded boys spitting tobacco behind the radiators. He believed inspiration the greatest battle.

After classes, eight students came to the library, where I'd brought some pop and chips as poor recompense for taking away the first good spring afternoon. Four lived in the out-county, two were Hispanic, one black, one a Finnish exchange student, none from a wealthy family. Carol Glotzbach said to me, *You wanted typical Chase kids — I'd call these typical, although the ethnic balance is different from the school. This place is almost entirely white.*

The students and I talked awhile, and I was struck by their deference to one another and by their good looks. I asked them to write down, privately, a sentence saying what kind of work they'd like to go into and another describing themselves so that a stranger might recognize them. We shot the breeze a few minutes, and then I turned on a tape recorder and let things roll along. It was a little colloquy that by its nature encouraged responsible talking but discouraged more private comments — things I probably could not repeat without giving the teenagers bogus identities, a common ploy of oral historians. The seniors were T. W. Burton, Marko Hirsimaki, Shannon Lopez, Jeremy Smith, and the juniors Kendra Dawson, Raymond Galvan, Glenna Grinstead, and Shawn Potts. They said these things, and this is how Dub Burton described himself:

(*Jobs: cowboy, electrical engineer, jet pilot. T. W. is a tall, lean, dark-complected male, never serious, easy going, carefree.*) He said, *I like working alone. I love working with cattle, but there's no future in it now. Unless the older people should start dying off, there's not going to be any future for me here in ranching, but I'd give my right arm to do that. I don't even like coming to town — I prefer to stay out there where I'm at, but I don't see any future for me here, so I'm thinking about finding something else to go into — don't know what it'd be. My parents and teachers — seems like they pressure me, wanting me to go to school, but I don't really* want to, but I know I'll about have to. If I could, I'd love to have my own place, but this is the first year my dad's told me — he's a ranch foreman down by Matfield — he said I'll have to find something different. I'll always be looking for something here though, but I think I'm going to have to go someplace else. I'm hoping not to get any farther away than Wichita. You know, when somebody from the outside buys up land here, they'll bring in new people to take care of it usually. I don't know, maybe I'll go to Wyoming. He stopped, looked up, smiled, and he said, I'm just thinking, my stepmother used to work in the restaurant on the turnpike down by Matfield — it was a Howard Johnson's then — and she said people would come through from out of state, and they'd go, "I don't know how you stand to live in this hellhole." Well, I guess it's bred in us, like ducks to water.

Shannon Lopez (fashion merchandising: Shannon is an easygoing, unpredictable type person. She is dark-skinned, dark hair, green eyes). In a year, I'll be gone from here. I lived for a while near San Francisco, and I love a city. But I'll come back for rodeo — I don't ride — it's just that we live in Strong City across from the rodeo grounds, and we sit up on the roof of our house and listen to the rodeo. That's the only thing to come back for. I don't like this town — I mean, what's this county ever done for us? People are more concerned with the roads than with us. And, you know, the only way to meet new people here is to get out of the county — if you have a car. They're so behind on the times that they won't accept new things — even some young ones can be negative too. Like, new students have to meet higher standards to be accepted in our school: everybody knows the new students, and if they don't come up to your standards, they're pushed aside, put down in a lower class, and people won't talk to you. I made more friends in a summer in California than I have here in twelve years. In a city you can be yourself — in Chase County, if people don't agree with the way you are, you get talked about, not talked to. I mean, kids gossip more than adults. I hate that about Chase. There's no privacy: if you do anything, the whole county within a day knows about it. If I come to school in clothes that I like, people say, "Oh my god! Look what she has on!" In a city they don't do that. And when that guy came in to talk to us on AIDS, after the program was over, there were suddenly two or three senior girls who supposedly had AIDS, just because they asked a lot of questions. There are other things too, like if you're Mexican, things are different.

When we moved here when I was in the first grade, we had people coming by our house, yelling stuff, cussing my mom out. My brothers were in high school, and guys would come by and try to pick fights with them. They'd yell, "Get out of this town!" It was really bad. Nobody would talk to us. It hasn't really changed.

She was working at not crying and was irritated with herself for not merely speaking in simple anger. *People — teachers — make remarks, and it hurts us. We really don't have to put up with it — if we wanted to do something, we could probably get some teachers fired. I mean, there are teachers in this school that admit they're prejudiced, but if they'd switch places with us they'd realize how it feels. You sit there and you have to laugh at the jokes.* She stopped again, the other students averted their eyes to give her some privacy, and she continued, *Kids say, "If you're not full-blooded white, you shouldn't even be over here."*

Jeremy Smith (*computer repairman, musician: Jeremy is a little short; great personality; he likes to have fun, and he likes his music*). *I live down around Wonsevu with my foster parents, but I'm from Wichita — my family is still there. I've been here four years, but I'll be going back to Wichita after I graduate.* He paused and said quickly, as if to face the issue but not dwell on it, drumming fingers as he spoke, *I hear some teachers telling racist jokes too, but I get along with white people fine — sometimes I forget I'm even black, and I live with a white family here. In Wichita, my parents used to have to go down and take my sisters out of school because of stabbings going on, but things aren't like that in Chase County. I've never been in a racial fight here. I'm not bragging, but I'm accepted because I have so many talents — I play drums, guitar, I'm in forensics. There's only one other black person in the school — a guy — there aren't any black girls. But if I date a white girl in Chase, they say, "Why don't you stay with your own kind?" So, my girlfriend lives in Wichita — but she's white. I think the prejudice is mostly with parents. When I'm with kids, it's fine: if I went out with a white girl here, I don't think the kids would mind, but the parents would about have a heart attack. Things have been all right, and people have helped me out, like when my neighbor — he's white — totally rebuilt my car engine, and he just had me pay for the parts. He did all the labor free.*

Marko Hirsimaki (*physical education coach, naval cadet, engineering: Marko, that athletic-built young man owns friendly and outgoing mind, of course, with some kind of inside trouble*). *Here I*

live near Wonsevu and Burns, but in Finland I live north of Hel-
sinki, maybe one hundred fifty miles from Russian border. I come
from the forest with lakes. When I first saw Chase County, Kansas,
I thought that I'm in the wrong place: there was some mistake.
Then I thought of it as some kind of challenge: it's my place, I have
to live now here. I had all kind of dreams about U.S.A., then I
came to Chase County and found it was some kind of nightmare. I
was disappointed. I don't know if I'll bring my parents here to see
things — I know they'll get mad. It wasn't what I was waiting for.
I said that his words reflected those of many Nordic immigrants
who settled in central Kansas in the nineteenth century and that he
was recapitulating history. He said, Yes, but you know, I'd like to
meet more strangers, but that's impossible here, but I don't want
big city — one night in New York City was enough, it was driving
me nuts. There are some nice places here: one is right by river —
grass and trees and clear water, like some kind of dream. And the
courthouse — in Finland we don't have very many old buildings
left like that. If you don't look at houses here, it looks exactly like
in those old movies: some cowboys riding to the sunset. I'd like to
do that. I thought I come to U.S.A. to see some kind of paradise,
but then I realized it's not any better than Finland. Now, I love
Finland more. We do many things even better than you do — of
course, some things we don't do. But the kids, they can't realize
that. They live in a small community, they think there is only one
way to go, that there isn't any other way. I think that's bad: you
have to know there is something different, to learn about life.
Before school started, at the first football practice, kids were very
curious about me. Someone said, "Is he some kind of Russian?" I
said, "No — don't kill me yet." It made me mad, it made me sad.
They ask, "Do you have toilet paper there?" But I learned it's easier
to teach students about Finland than the teachers — they seem
limited.

Glenna Grinstead (probably a housewife on a ranch or working
for a business: Glenna is a short, petite girl with an energetic
personality and a ready smile. Dressed in her western outfit, she
has a warm look and an ornery look in her eyes). I live near Cedar
Point. My father is a feedlot manager and my mother is a secretary
at a health care center. The future — I know it's hard to find a job
here, but I want to go into ranching. I'd like to have a little land. I
spend a lot of time at Camp Wood — it's my favorite place in the
county, especially sunrise there, it's so beautiful. I don't know

about sunsets — usually I'm so tired I don't pay any attention. There's nothing better than being outside, on a horse, riding along with grass up to your stirrups, or out shagging cattle, or helping a sick calf — it gets a feeling in my heart, like, this is just right, I'd like to do this all my life. But that's going to be hard because people are going under. To keep a living you have to have an outside job almost. It's real hard. The future — I don't want to leave. I mean, this is a good place for families, but people here are so closed-mouth, it takes forever to get to know anybody, the adults especially. It seems hard to start over. My parents had so much trouble when they came here: people think, "You haven't lived here all your life so you have no say in this matter." If I have to leave I might go to Montana or maybe a ranch in Colorado but no cities. I mean, if you compare us to kids that live in a city, the majority of us have had a lot more responsibility. I think we're a lot more prepared to go out in the world. The things we've got, most of us have gotten them ourselves — we've earned them.

Raymond Galvan (*Ray is a pretty laid-back mellow kind of guy, who is in a rock & roll band and likes to ride motorcycles as one of his many different hobbies. He is about five-nine and has black hair and brown eyes*). *I live in Strong City. My dad works for the Santa Fe. I don't think there's a future in Chase County for me. I'm a musical kind of person — I play the bass guitar. After I graduate from high school, I'll probably move to Wichita: I've got some family there, my brothers. I might get a job in a music store, making speaker boxes or something, or else get a job laying carpet. If I could go anywhere, I'd go to L.A. That's one place you can really get a band going — all the record companies are there. I wouldn't mind coming back just for the heck of it for rodeo, otherwise, I don't know.* He started a couple of sentences, broke them off, then said, *I just wish people here would keep their mouths and ideas to theirselves. It just kind of builds up.* He didn't want to say what he referred to.

Kendra Dawson (*interested in business: Kendra is a blonde, blue-eyed junior, fun and outgoing. She participates in a number of activities and sports*). *I live in Cottonwood. My dad is a rancher and farmer and my mother is a housewife. My grandparents and great-grandparents have all lived here. If I get married to a farmer or rancher I'll stick around, but if I don't I probably won't stick around. I couldn't live in a big city — I'd have to find a place similar to this, but maybe where people don't pass judgment so* bad. Like when they first had that deal for birth control down at the health center on Broadway: if anybody saw you just walking down that block, since there's not much else there, they would probably assume you were going to get birth control pills, and talk would start. And this new church on the highway, the one that broke off from the Homestead Friends church — for everybody who doesn't go there it's called just "the church." Everybody talks about it: "What they do out there isn't right." If you're seen going in, everybody starts talking about you. I don't know what the problem is other than maybe people leaving other churches, but whatever it is, it's stupid. Shawn Potts muttered, It's change — the county won't accept change, and Kendra said, It's an older community, and they just don't make transition very easily at all. She listened to Shawn, her boyfriend, confirm separation of generations, and she said, We had a good girls' volleyball team this year, we went sixteen-and-four, and we've had two second places in state competition the last couple of years, but nobody bothered to come out and watch us — nobody supported us, maybe fifteen people in the stands. Older people, except for your family, just don't have much interest in us. I asked her if she were to stay on here, what she would change, and she said, I wish we could get rid of the Podunk image most people in cities build up about places like this. Even though Emporia's only thirty minutes away, to them we're like back in the hills — no electricity, no running water.

Shawn Potts (I'd like to run my grandparents' farm and ranch. Shawn enters as a man sitting good in the saddle — as a rancher he loves the out-of-doors and cattle). I live west of Strong City. I like the springtime when the Flint Hills is burning and at night when the fire glistens off the water — that kind of depicts the country around here. And the courthouse is special, but with it being here so long people take it for granite. I like the togetherness of this county, especially in the country with the ranchers and cattlemen: when you're out and you have trouble, there's always a neighbor that'll come help you. Somebody talked about problems meeting people, but if you move up Diamond Crick it's like a welcome party: everybody brings new families things — but if it's not up Diamond Crick maybe things are different. This is a good place to raise a family because you can know more people than in a city. But the high school teams the community doesn't back unless you're real good, especially a football team. Last season we got behind twenty-one to nothing to a weak team, but in the fourth *quarter we got our heads in the game and got together and wound up winning twenty-eight to twenty-one, but the people watching us had went home. The next day half the county thought we'd lost.* Someone said that even the rodeo was having problems now with local support, and Shawn said, *The rodeo takes people back to what this county really is — it takes them back to what it's come from and what it's been. I think people ought to wake up and realize how neat this place is, and how much work people went to to build things like the courthouse and the Z Bar with all the tunnels, and Clover Cliff, and the bridges. If the ground could talk, if the ground could talk . . .* We waited for him to finish, and finally I said, what would it say? and he shook his head. *You stuck me now. I guess it would give the good, bad, and ugly. Somebody could dig up all the neat and bad things about this place, I guess, but it's something nobody's ever going to find out because they haven't kept enough records.*

When the janitor made his third sweep past the library doors, the clunk of his mop an announcing of the hour, I reached to turn off the recorder, and Shannon Lopez said, *Wait! We need a club where high school kids can go and dance. Everybody complains about drinking, drinking, high school kids drinking. Then that party got busted last weekend, where there were kids down to fourteen drinking. All the adults complain about it, but they don't do anything.* Someone interrupted, *They ride their horses down Broadway in the rodeo parade with a six-pack hooked on to the saddlehorn, and then turn around and tell us not to drink.* Shannon said, *There's nothing, not one thing, to do on weekends here — I mean, you can go to Darla's and play pool, play video games, and that's it. Adults say if there's a club for us there'd still be drinking. I think it would cut down drinking a lot.*

Suddenly everyone was talking, and Kendra said, *Nobody will go to the trouble to get one started,* and Shawn, *People never take interest to do it.* And Dub, *There's just too many older people that won't accept change,* and Ray, *Some of them complained about the new pizza place even before we got it. They didn't want something new — they thought it'd bring in more businesses, more people,* and Shannon, *They're scared to open new places because they think it'll steal business from the places we already have,* and Shawn, *But new stuff helps improve other businesses. Competition helps.*

I asked whether any of them had urged their parents to get a club started, and they all fell silent, and somebody said, *It's easier just to complain.* Glenna said, *I always think: why go to a party? All you're going to do is get in trouble or everybody is going to be talking about you.*

I asked why parties seemed to be so much trouble, and Shawn said, *Alcohol. Kids find a dead-end road, and light a fire, and stand around and talk and listen to music, and drink — beer mostly, but some whiskey and schnapps too. Then there was that raid last week.* Dub said, *During rodeo, the adults block off Broadway and listen to music and drink — the same thing they get after us for on a dead-end road.* Jeremy said that the girls liked to stand together at these things and sing along with one special song. When he mentioned it, they all began talking, describing the scene: pickups and cars pulled together, the fire opening a primitive circle in the prairie night, the music thumping, the boys calling out, the girls knotted and singing along, loud and in a peculiar key: "You Shook Me All Night Long."

Days later, when I listened again to their words, it seemed I heard a vision of a future Chase County very much like the one they knew, the difference being their absence from it. And I remembered a grammar school teacher here once telling me, *I wish we'd learn to love ourselves less and our children's future more.*

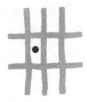

In Kit Form:
The Cottonwood Chapter

Now: you are dreaming, walking in your dream, here in the hills, alone. If you continue you will find what I have hidden for you, if you want it. The time is October, and you are far south in the quadrangle, dreamwalking up to a crossroads, and you see the big and isolated cottonwood tree; the massive bole you cannot encompass even halfway around with your arms (its grandness keeps it from ungainliness), its bark furrowed deeply as if plowed, the whole tree stubbed down by the wind, the branches thick as trunks of lesser trees, the lower ones curving nearly to the earth; the leaves, toothed spades, little mirrors throwing shimmered light, dangle so brightly yellow at sunrise and sunset that you can believe you never really saw true yellowness before, not even in ingots hot from the furnace: it's as if the leaves have used the summer to leach color from the sun, and now, as the days cool, they release their pent heat through their yellow light. Take a book and sit beneath the tree and read and see the pages turn golden as if they too receive the old and sponged-up solar extravagance. The cottonwood grows just beyond the crossroads in a damp draw, and you will find here the dream-kit I have left you, and in it the pieces I've gathered but not assembled, because they are to be yours, things for you to put your imprint on, but there are no directions. All I want is to show you some of what is in a name, to cut it open to reveal how meaning accumulates like sap rings in a tree trunk, each year deepening the name, thickening it.

The writer writes, but there is no real book until the reader enters a shared dreamtime and makes the connections. So: start in the middle and read outward, start at the end and read upward; it is yours to make: design, whittle, cut, snip, tie, glue, trim, rasp, paint, grow vexed, cuss, and pitch it across the room (we will then share one more thing): it is yours to show how the pieces can fit together, perhaps even to demonstrate how the job *should* be done:

a few years ago, an easterner moved to the Flint Hills during a drought and worried about the land he'd bought; he went to bed — his first night on the prairie — and outside his window was a cottonwood; a breeze came on to stir the heat, and he heard the sound of rain, and he rose to go to the window: the leaves moved in the dry air, their shaking and soft clattering like raindrops; later he said, *The wind in that dry tree was a promise*

the largest cottonwood in Kansas has a trunk twenty-seven feet around and reaches ten stories into the air, and its deepest roots lie another four stories below

the Plains Indian, at least before the coming of the Europeans, had a use for nearly every part of a bison, even down to its spirit (when the red man finished with a buffalo nothing was left but memory of it, and that he used also); the animal provided him what a white man might find along the main street of a town: food, lodging, tools, medicine, recreation, religion; and these gifts also came from the cottonwood: bison to tree is as river to vale; and, as if to point up the link, sometimes a cottonwood will grow up in the dampness collecting in an old buffalo wallow; Christians may understand the power of such a conjunction to an Indian if they imagine a sapling from the Tree of the True Cross arising from a footprint of their Fisherman

the eastern cottonwood, *Populus deltoides*, has other names: cotton tree, whitewood, and necklace poplar, this last from the hanging catkins that look like a strand of green pearls; and, in fact, Indian children tied catkins together and wore them around their necks, and sometimes they dangled catkins from their ears like emerald pendants

Lewis and Clark accomplished much of their grand expedition seated in the hollowed boles of cottonwoods they cut into pirogues; they carved out two trunks at the mouth of the Missouri River and six more during their first winter stay at Fort Mandan, which itself was built almost entirely, possibly even the chimneys, of cottonwood: the palisades, roofs, tables, benches, beds, shelves; they heated the small rooms with cottonwood, and over its coals they cooked sides of bison, deer, antelope, biscuits, coffee; the next season, when they needed to portage around the great cataracts of the Missouri, they made trucks with cottonwood wheels and spent eleven days hauling eight heavy dugouts, each some thirty feet long, around the five falls

a Mexican calls the cottonwood *alamo*

in June, the Cottonwood River can slow, seeming to avoid the heat of quick movement, and, as if to insulate itself, will lie nearly still and quilted over with the white fluff of cottonwood seeds, and a swimmer comes from the water covered in wet down; unlike many of the other common native trees here — oak, hickory, walnut, hackberry, redbud — the cottonwood depends for its dispersal not upon mammals and birds but upon the two oldest things in the hills: wind and water

when Illinoisan John Wright in 1842 was looking for a tree suitable to use as a living fence on the prairie, a farmer suggested cottonwood, but Wright said, *Something not quite so old-maidish would look better*, and he thought that the tree had about it *too much primness and mustn't-touch-me sort of air*

in a single year a cottonwood sapling in an ideal riparian location can grow twice the height of a man

although things have changed today, this mustn't-touch-me tree, with its nearly grainless, featureless white wood, once furnished (despite its inclination to warp and check and its only moderate strength) rafts, cabins, barns (studs, joists, rafters, floors, bins, cribs, mows, stalls, troughs, but not shingles or siding), churches, hotels, coffins, fences (in a big tree are a thousand rails, said an immigrant's guidebook; but in contact with soil, cottonwood posts seem to melt), wagon bodies, saddletrees, chicken coops, egg crates, strawberry cartons, flour-barrel staves, excelsior, plywood, newspapers, basket veneer, iceboxes, ironing boards, trunks, cigar-box linings, woodenware, matchsticks, ice cream sticks, and (so appropriate for an offshoot of the wind) kite sticks

the cottonwood has almost no defenses against things eating or cutting it other than its fecundity

some Plains Indians, like the Hidatsa, believed shadows cast by cottonwoods possessed intelligence and would counsel a troubled person; while all *the standing peoples* have voice, few are so sweetly loquacious as the gentle and generous cottonwood one summer, near the southern county line, a cottonwood outside a boy's bedroom died, and the rest of the summer he had trouble falling asleep in the new quiet

the Timber Culture Act of 1873 gave 160 acres of land to any settler who would plant ten of those acres to trees; because a cottonwood requires little care, grows quickly, and stands well against drought, blizzard, wind, and heat, Kansans commonly planted it to claim their free land: it was the mortgage tree

a countian found his air conditioner not working well; he removed the grille and discovered across the fins a strange gray blanket, and he pulled it away, a perfect rectangle the size of a cradle: it was a knitting of cottonwood fluff; that fall he cut the tree down

grasses murmur but a cottonwood seems to be the articulating of the tongueless wind: to take comfort in this garrulity is to use the sound and not let it go wasted

settlers once cut white inner pulp from the tree and made a delicacy called cottonwood ice cream; but no one remembers the recipe, and people no longer know how to eat a cottonwood

taxonomists cannot agree whether the eastern and western cottonwoods are one species or two or perhaps more; the structural variations in even a single grove may be evidence of genetic drift — a most American thing — or it may be that the cottonwood is quite genetically plastic, an ancient survival device (and an emblem for future continuance); whatever the case, the tree is not likely to become a symbol for the shaved-head, new *über-alles* boys

the fragrant leaf buds are fat little resinous things like droplets standing on end, and to break one open is to smell some primitive lowland long before the coming of mankind; from these buds Plains Indians boiled down a yellow dye to color arrow fletchings

in 1937 the cottonwood became the Kansas state tree; some citizens wanted a flowery something, like the hawthorn of Missouri or the redbud of Oklahoma, and they complained, but there is an honesty to Kansans born of a long and necessary practicality: the legislature voted for a typical, working tree

its riverine life: sometimes a storm shears off a living branch and it is carried downstream where it may snag along a sandbar and take root; a Missouri hiker recently testified: he cut a staff from a cottonwood and trimmed it to shape and walked all afternoon with it, then stuck it into a riverbank, and when he passed by weeks later his staff had rooted and leafed; Aaron cast down his rod before

Pharaoh and it turned into a serpent; a walker sunk down his stick and it became a tree

in western Kansas, were it not for the cottonwood, the old plains joke would be true: *the state tree is the utility pole*

to cure gastric upsets caused by drinking alkaline water, Indians showed whites how to make a cottonwood remedy; trailman Charles Goodnight, inventor of the chuck wagon (he made the first one out of Osage orange, not cottonwood), wrote that cowhands *would get the inside bark, boil it to a strong tea, and drink liberally. It was a hell of a drink, a wonderful astringent, and a bitter dose. But it was a sure shot*

from the sap, early-day farmers made cottonwood syrup

some prairie citizens believe that a cottonwood calls lightning down upon itself because it carries so much water; the tongue of the great fire-bear lapping up honey

after the Civil War, when Kansans were building the capitol in Topeka of Cottonwood Limestone (four nouns, one thing), the blocks lay piled about the grounds; when construction finished, landscapers found a fair-sized cottonwood growing next to where a pile of stone had been, and some people said the seed arrived stuck to a block from Chase County (for a tree that moves its generations by wind and water, a seed transported by stone from the old Permian sea was indeed a novelty); others said one of the stakes tying down an old wooden crane had rooted itself; the landscapers left the sapling, and it grew into the preeminent tree in the state: the 1928 book *Trees of Kansas* has a picture of it on the cover with the caption *Kansas' Best Loved Tree, the Statehouse Cottonwood*

the catkins furnish food for quail and prairie chickens and grouse, and meadowlarks (the state bird) take the silky fluff to line their ground nests, and Indian children pulled the moist cotton out of the capsules to chew like gum

around the turn of the century, urban people looked for a tree that would withstand coal smoke in their cities, and they found the glossy varnish of cottonwood leaves shucked off soot (rain off the goose), and the trees thrived; in fact, they grew too big for the confines of streets and yards

in his 1828 description of the western states, Timothy Flint said of the cottonwood, *when these are cut in the winter, the moment the axe penetrates the center of the tree, there gushes out a stream of water, or sap; and a single tree will discharge gallons;* if there is a rot pocket, this can indeed happen, and the trunks may also discharge a jet of methane that can be lighted like a lantern

a cottonwood reaches its mature height in the first half of its typical eighty-year life and then spends the remaining years spreading its crown as if it understands what other plains-life needs from it is not verticality but protective breadth; as it opens outward, it prunes its branches, and beings underneath receive a beneficent blend of sun and shade; yet the tree itself thrives on no protection other than a damp swale; not growing well in close proximity to other trees, it seems to want nothing between it and the sun and wind, and, by taking from these, it intercedes for other life: a shield against the blade of the wind, a rampart against the arrows of the sun

not only Lewis and Clark but also fur traders and frontiersmen paddled into the West in cottonwood pirogues and dugouts; the Kansas Indian trader Frederick Chouteau said that a pair of four-foot-circumference cottonwood logs seventy feet long could be lashed together to carry fifteen tons of cargo; later, Missouri river steamboatmen fired their boilers with cottonwood, and overland travelers relied on it, and surveyors laying out Jefferson's grid marked certain section corners by driving a cottonwood stake or planting a sapling; the conquest of the West would have happened without the tree, but it would have happened differently and probably less felicitously

curling the roundly triangular leaves into cones and pinning the edges together, Indian children made toy tepees, and the shape was so accurate that the Lakota holy man Black Elk believed that in an era long before him people had learned how to cut the pattern for a bison-skin tepee from the shape of the cottonwood leaf

travelers on the Santa Fe and Oregon trails, once past the ninety-sixth meridian, learned to watch the horizon for a grove or even a lone cottonwood: it was a beacon, a beckoning (NEXT SERVICES 30 MILES); since the trees grew mostly near streams, springs, or seeps, they were signposts of water, of grass for animals (one countian describes covered wagons as grassoline-powered), of firewood, of shade, even of news when preceding travelers left notes folded into the bark; a hollow in a bole might hold honey, and the trees gave the woodlanders comfort, joy, and a spiritual relief from the long and unnerving open miles; the perpetual shaking chuckle of the leaves, a liquid sound that could almost quench a thirst, seemed a promise of the mountain forests so far away; for two generations of plains travelers, the cottonwood was a wayside inn in the four volumes of the *Chase County Historical Sketches* there are a few poems written by the citizens, and one third of them are about cottonwoods; this emphasis may derive from the habit of the tree separating itself from wooded vales and taking to draws in the uplands where it assumes prominence by its isolation: to prairie people it becomes an obvious metaphor, a thing to be personified in a land where almost nothing else so obviously can be

although the cottonwood is to the Osage orange as soft is to hard, round to sharp, chalk to marble, medicine staff to war club, homesteaders used both trees for shelter belts and believed both would increase rainfall (neither tree, of course, can bring rain, but the cottonwood does reveal where the once and future rains sleep)

a Missourian came into the county and so loved the cottonwood that one spring he went to the river and picked from a sapling some small leaves, sweet and aromatic; he dried them, ground them in a handmill, and ate them on scrambled eggs and poached fish, and others he crumbled in his palm until they smelled sweet and mixed them with his favorite English tobacco to smoke in his pipe

young Indian women placed the tip of a cottonwood leaf between their lips and pressed the sides of it to their nostrils with thumb and forefinger, and then, expelling their breath through their noses (said the old prairie ethnobotanist Melvin Gilmore), *they vibrated the leaf in such a way that very sweet musical notes were produced, birdlike or flutelike*

at the coming of the white man, the valley where Council Grove is today was primarily a clustering of big oaks and elms; of the individual trees now commemorated there — the Treaty Oak, the Post Office Oak, the Custer Elm — none is a cottonwood; within living memory all of the famous big trees have died and been lopped down to mere painted trunks: Council Grove today is a town of honored stumps

do you know the origin of the English maypole?

six sentences from Black Elk: · *The spirit said, "Behold the circle of the sacred hoop, for the people shall be like it, and if they are like this, they shall have life-force, because there is no end to this hoop"* · *The sacred hoop means the continents of the world and the people standing as one* · *They put the sacred stick into the center of the hoop, and you could hear birds singing all kinds of songs by this flowering stick, and the people and animals all rejoiced and hollered* · *Depending on the sacred stick we should walk, and it will be with us always; from this we will raise our children, and under the flowering stick we will communicate with our relatives — beast and bird — as one people: this is the center of life of our nation · The sacred stick is the cottonwood tree · This tree never had a chance to bloom because the white man came*

Across Osage Hill

One Saturday afternoon I was in Buck's Drive-Inn up on highway 50 at Strong City to revive myself with a milk shake after walking around Osage Hill, and I was staring out the window at highway travelers when a nearby, slow conversation chinked with snarls broke into a squabble about something, and I heard the woman say, *What've you ever done with your life?* She was speaking to a man nearly my age, whom I knew to be her brother. He said, *There isn't enough time to tell you all I done in my life,* and the woman turned away and stared out the window at the highway, and he stared out too, and so did I: three people staring out at the passage, all of us fixed on what he'd just said.

That night, on my long drive home, I thought of the tiff and the man's defense, and I began wondering how long it would take to tell my half century of life. The next morning, Sunday, I went to the porch where I sometimes read the paper or write but more often just watch the woods. I set out a tape recorder and a digital timer with an alarm, and my mind wandered off, and I muttered sentences, and when I felt a kind of rhythm in it, I pressed on the recorder and timer; for sixty seconds I described my every motion and tried to do the same for my thoughts (I scratched my knee but I was watching an oriole pull the tough threads from a yucca leaf and carry them to the nest she was weaving in the big sycamore). The telling on tape of that minute took, of course, sixty seconds, but listening to it, I realized that for an audience other than myself all the important information was missing: why I was sitting there doing this, where I was and what it looked like, felt like, smelled like, how the yucca threads in a few weeks would hold four plump nestlings and the parent through a hard rain, why that minute was worth paying attention to.

I took up a pencil and paper and began trying to give a description of those sixty seconds as a novelist might, and when I hit six pages I stopped — not because I was finished but because I was so far from finishing. I read the pages aloud, doing it as if I had a listener, and that took a little more than ten minutes. I totted up and figured: even an abbreviated retelling of one hour of my life would take ten hours to relate, and one working day — could I remember it all — would, with an hour of rest each day, require a week to retell, and that meant a single year needed seven years, and my half century of waking life would consume 350 years, about the time from the *Mayflower* till now.

While I may pass my life in continuity and completeness, I comprehend it only in discontinuous fragments; of the lives of people around me my understanding is utterly fractured and piecemeal: scraps, shavings, smithereens. Family or friends tell me a story in a few details, and I say, I see. Even more than autobiography, biography and history and literature and all the arts are far-flung bits reassembled into an illusion of completeness so that we comprehend only by orts. Put a strong magnifier to, say, Dagwood Bumstead's face in the Sunday funnies, and, in a sense, you'll see that he isn't really there — mostly what's there is white page rather than little dots of red ink. Our incapacity to see what is truly before us allows us to perceive the cartoon man in something like a hallucination.

A cousin of mine, a metallurgical engineer, worked for a while on a doctorate in particle physics at Kansas University until he had a kind of breakdown; not long ago he told me, *I kept going after matter — structures — and I kept going until I saw that when you go inward far enough there's almost nothing there. Everything is space with tiny pieces strung out only in propinquity to each other. My crisis was about learning to live in the interstices by hugging up to little particles.* He left physics, although he stayed in engineering, and became a Christian Science reader.

I'm not really concerned here about human understanding as hallucination; what I have to say is about Osage Hill, but I must do that through a kind of equivalence to the pointillist spots of ink that compose Dagwood's face, my words serving as daubs that may allow you to enter a kind of dreamtime where you can pass across the Hill. The subject of this chapter, I suppose, is really its method. To American Indians who believe that the past is to a people as dreams are to a person, stories are the communal snaggings of generations, the nets that keep people from free-falling toward pointlessness, as did my cousin, and they are also the knots of matter that help people into dreamtime, where the listener, the traveler, can imagine he sees links between smithereens; from that hallucination, everything that we value arises. I'm speaking about shards and grids and crossings, about that great reticulum, our past.

That Saturday before I went to Buck's for a chocolate milk shake, I'd been walking around on Osage Hill, writing down notes, talking to myself (*about a half bubble off plumb*), quick-sketching a few details, and taking two photographs. It was April, and from the west, low and heaped clouds fat as galleons slipped in only to break open on the flinty ridges and spill their cargo, an airy blueness that rolled on east: it was a day of two skies and one weather. I carried my cottonwood stick and my usual haversack, but my real equipage was a mind full of stories I'd heard about Osage Hill, pieces of the *real* hill, a Platonist might say: with the greater framework now lost, they were more chips of narratives than whole tales, icons without an iconography, isolated pictographs that can remind a person and involve him in more than they actually were themselves; they were small configurations that had to be continually reinfused and reinvoked to keep them from becoming indecipherable. I believe Indians fear loss of meaning — that is, memory — beyond all other losses, because without it one can love nothing. After all, love proceeds from memory, and survival depends absolutely upon memory.

Osage Hill, lying between Cottonwood Falls and Elmdale, is actually a long and massive ridge extending several miles from the southern end of the county northward to stop abruptly only where the Cottonwood River comes in askew of due west and, in its last grand shift of course, takes a true easterly run to the Neosho River. The western slope of Osage Hill, coincidentally lying atop the granite Kansas Mountains, the Nemaha Ridge three thousand feet below, is much steeper than the gentle rise on the east, and the five miles of gravel road between the two towns is mostly straight although not level, and it crosses the ridge at its highest point to give one of the fine valley views in the county; it is this vista, above all else, that has made the hill special to the people: as early as 1885 couples came here to be married in the high pasture.

In the initial days of federal highways, this road was a stretch of U.S. 50 before it got moved a couple of miles to the north, down into the valley floor to ride around the base of the hill, as do the tracks of the Santa Fe and fishermen floating the Cottonwood. The first death from an auto accident in the county happened on the east end of the Osage Hill road in 1908 when William Romigh — Lizzie Brandley's brother, a man who once beat out Sam Wood for county attorney by four votes — one autumn Sunday drove his brand-new Oldsmobile runabout (which he was just learning to handle) off into Spring Creek, and the seventy-six-year-old got pinned under the upside-down car in a few inches of water and drowned. Several years later, at precisely the same place, another man ran off the straight road into the little creek and died. But passage here is much older: a rock-ledge ford, one of the two or three important Indian crossings over the river, lies at the bottom of the western slope, and near it the tribes, especially the Osage, camped on their treks into the nineteenth-century bison ranges that once began fifty miles west. To stand on the end of the hill overlooking the big angle of the river and to see both ways along its dogleg valley, to look down this fluvial breaching of the Flint Hills (the only other gap is the much larger Kaw Valley) and also to look up the vales of Middle and Diamond and Fox creeks and see the commingling of waters, is to realize the special strategic and spiritual significance Osage Hill held for tribal peoples in passage; it is fitting that, of the very few Indian place-names in the county, this preeminent location bears one.

I've already spoken of Seth Hays, the Santa Fe Trail provisioner who built the first cabin in Chase for the overseer of his wintering oxen, but I haven't said that the building was at the base of Osage Hill; so, depending on your views of white westering and genocide, the ridge is either a kind of a triumphal monument or a cenotaph. (George Starkey, the man who, years later, dismantled and reassembled that cabin in the city park at the Falls, crashed his steam-drawn thresher on a wild descent of the hill in 1905 and was severely burned when he was pinned against the boiler.) Behind Seth Hays came a generation of wagons that often stopped at a burr-oak grove below the ridge, a place that later became a picnic ground for the citizens of Elmdale, where, on the Fourth of July, farm boys having no firecrackers would push boulders down the slope, and those rocks, so goes the story, became tables for later picnickers.

At the ford, called Osage Crossing, Joshua Shipman in 1870 built a dam and gristmill, and to it Russian Mennonites from Marion County hauled their wheat and corn, and children ran and hid and stared at the men of strange words and hanging black beards that caught the wind. The water behind the milldam became a good fishing and swimming hole (kids jumped their ponies in) and ice-skating pond and also a place to drown. Shipman in 1882 built a new and bigger mill that burned in 1906, and later his dam washed out, so that today you find only a few cut stones to mark the site. Whitt Laughridge told me that near the crossing was a rock, now buried, with three footprints left by a dinosaur wading a muddy shoal: ponderous, claw-footed reptiles sloshing where aboriginals hunting bison would one day cross, where goggled drivers would test a new roadster to see whether it could climb the hill in high gear, where farmers would haul produce in Model T trucks, some of them with gravity-fed carburetors that made them take the steep western face of Osage Hill in reverse. Paul Evans, the coyote hunter, told me when he was a boy living near Elmdale he and a couple of friends every August used to lie in wait among the oaks for the farmers' old trucks loaded with watermelons to start up the hill (this before the road was straightened and the grade lessened in 1972): because of the clutching mechanism of those trucks, the driver had to keep moving and hold his foot to the low-gear pedal to make the laborious, grinding ascent, and he could only watch as Paul boarded the back end and pirated off a couple of choice melons; it was a kind of toll for using the road.

On the morning I was on Osage Hill with my lading of stories and hoofing around not far from where the telephone relay tower stands (now one of the good navigational points in the county), it seemed that most of what I knew of the hill had to do with passage and semiotics: precisely midway east and west across the county, it has been a high hub around which waters and men and their events turn, a still point drawing transit and tales to it as the quiet eye of a tornado draws atmosphere. It is a centripetal force of a hill, yet it has neither the classic symmetry nor arresting isolation of Jacobs' Mound; in fact, from the valley, it doesn't particularly stand out. It's the kind of rising that moves you only after you've surmounted it and *then* discovered it's there, and, in this sense, it's a hill only when you're on its western side: I've wondered how many travelers come to the vista above Elmdale and say, *How the hell did we get up here?* Aboriginal peoples give attention to natural places with steep edges, and, I think, that attraction is not yet entirely erased even in city dwellers who may work on some twentieth floor.

My hiking that morning on the hill as I walked in its stories was a try at entering it and partaking of its identity and life, at being infused with its old, cryptogrammic presence.

A few weeks later, Whitt Laughridge and I were talking about Osage Hill and the road over it, and he said that he thought he'd identified an old Hockaday sign on a fencepost there, and I was surprised because I'd just read something about Hockaday and his signs, so we drove out, and I picked up a rusted and riddled metal plate now devoid of any markings, and we took it back to the county museum. I was as pleased as if we'd unearthed a piece of a temple at Chichén Itzá, not so much with the object as with the unexpected link it had revealed between Osage Hill and a man whose bubble often floated far off plumb.

F. W. Hockaday, called Woody, was an auto-supply dealer in Wichita in the early days of motoring, a time before highways carried numbers, when "maps" were instructions: *left at the big oak; go one mile; right a quarter mile past red barn on south.* Woody was a small and bespectacled fellow who could take up a cause with a fervor beyond most people. When it came to roads, Woody thought like a Roman, and he decided to measure and mark the major highways in Kansas; since he was paying for it, he would make his auto-parts store mile zero — this, of course, occurring before the U.S. Zero Milestone was set up in front of the White House on the eastern end of highway 50. He toured around nailing up rectangular metal signs two feet long showing a large red H on a white background, a directional arrow, the name he'd given to the highway, and the next town. We all know that a driver, no matter how veteran, never happily accepts losing the road: if he's delighted with the wit of some signs —

A MAN
A MISS
A CAR — A CURVE
HE KISSED THE MISS
AND MISSED THE CURVE
BURMA-SHAVE

— he becomes devoted to anyone sending him, as the needle edges toward empty, off down the right route. Even though Woody's markers created thankful customers, he became obsessed with his signs and put more and more auto-store income into them, until by 1917 he'd spent at least sixteen thousand dollars on his project; two years later he contracted to mark thirty-five hundred miles of road from Washington to Los Angeles. He began numbering highways (Kansas 96 was his auto-supply phone number) and issuing maps with "his" routes marked in red, and he spoke of *the Hockaday National Roads,* and he even began asking farmers to paint the name of the nearest town on their barn roofs to help aviators. Eventually his expenditures and time away from Wichita did his business in.

Thereafter, he had to take respites in sanitariums. In 1938 in Oklahoma City he tried to jump into President Roosevelt's car, he said, *to shine FDR's shoes.* Woody was declared insane and sent off for another rest. In the forties, he became an antiwar zealot and went around visiting American Legion posts where he would tear open a pillow and sprinkle the behatted old warriors with down and call out his message: *Feathers are better than bullets any day!* The slight, myopic fellow was regularly thumped by police, and he finally died, sixty-three years old, in a sanitarium only an hour from where I live in Missouri. To Plains Indians the red road is the good road (the opposite of the blue road of the self-concerned). I wish I could have talked to Woody Hockaday about his red highways, and I'm sorry that the proposal in 1954 to name the Kansas Turnpike after him went nowhere.

As Whitt and I were wiping off the old Hockaday marker and hoping to find some ghost of a word, which we didn't, he said, *This reminds me: in the late thirties or a little later, every summer up on Osage Hill there used to mysteriously appear a sign that would say something like* GREAT IS THE WHITE THUNDER GOD *and another year maybe* THE THUNDER GOD IS COMING. *Dick Iliff, the old newspaperman, knows the story.*

The next day we talked to Iliff, and he lent me a book privately printed in 1947, titled *White Thunder God,* by Pat Reid, a name Iliff assumed to be a *nom de plume.* In the novel is a photograph of a pleasant-looking man and this caption:

> *Rev. Floyd M. Gurley*
> *"Thunder God" to the Pedro Martir Indians.*

Gurley, said Iliff, had gotten into trouble in the county in the early thirties, and, some years later, this book had mysteriously appeared in the *Leader* office.

I went to the courthouse and, in the first big index I opened, my gaze fell right to Gurley's name, both the clerk and I taken aback by the immediacy of what could have been a long hunt. She brought out the file, and I read through the papers of his arrest and conviction for arson and his commitment to prison for three years at hard labor; and there was, signed by Governor Alf Landon, Gurley's Citizenship Pardon, a document he apparently never wanted. There was also something the clerk had never before seen in a file: attached to the original complaint a photograph of Gurley that confirmed his connection to *White Thunder God*.

Unless a transcript of proceedings exists, criminal court files often don't reveal the story, so I went to the historical society and read old issues of the *Leader*; at first the case seemed to be a simple crime of revenge and confession: twenty-four-year-old Gurley, a motorman for the San Francisco streetcar company, returned in the summer of 1932 to Butler County to visit relatives and court a fourteen-year-old girl, the younger sister of a pretty woman he'd lost to another fellow a couple of years earlier. In August, allegedly for lover's vengeance, he went to the isolated farmhouse on Coon Creek, about twelve miles south of Osage Hill, where his first love lived with her husband, and burned it to the ground while they were away. When the sheriff arrived, Gurley ran into a cornfield, leaving his luggage and Model T coupe behind, and hurried back to his job in San Francisco. A month later he waived extradition and was returned to Cottonwood, arriving at three in the morning after two days on the train; without sleep, he underwent an interrogation that lasted eighteen hours. The exhausted man finally confessed. The day before he was sent off to state prison, he married his fourteen-year-old sweetheart in the courthouse; with that, reports in the *Leader* about Gurley cease, and the easy simplicities of a crime and punishment vanish: why would a girl marry a man who had just burned down her sister's house? Why would parents of a minor consent to such a marriage? The criminal file indicates that they all testified at the hearing, but would they give witness against a man about to become husband and son-in-law? Was a confession forced from him?

Looking for an answer, I started reading *White Thunder God*, a peculiar novel of humane if unorthodox values written barely well enough to be readable, its style suggesting an author who had some experience stringing together sentences but not narratives: a preacher, a reporter, an ad writer. The story was an amalgam of the more preposterous aspects of James Hilton (*Lost Horizon*) and

H. G. Wells (*When the Sleeper Awakes*), all daubed over with nudism, vegetarianism, biblical fundamentalism, anti-Darwinism, and anti–New Dealism; in other words, a book of some appeal in the darkly Reaganized days when I was walking around Osage Hill.

The story, set in the late thirties, is about an American missionary to the Indians of the northern end of the Gulf of California (a little beyond Arthur Stilwell's Topolobampo); the unnamed and undescribed protagonist is a simple man who manages to enter a secret utopian community sequestered inside an old volcano in the San Pedro Mártir Mountains of Baja California; the inhabitants are women nudists, well-formed vegetarians of Amazonian strength who look one quarter their age and who live on milk, strawberry shortcake, and vanilla ice cream, all picked from trees. The utopia is not precisely a gynecocracy, since it is ruled by the kindly and wise White Thunder God, a shadowy but extramortal man who visits on the same cycle as the appearance of the seventeen-year locust. At first the author tries to blend Mexican Indian and Christian myths but finally his fundamentalism overtakes everything except his anger: using his words like cudgels, he vituperates against clothing (*a root of evil*), drinkers (*raving, swearing drunkards*), cigarette smokers (*vile, fuming addicts*), eaters of meat (*makes them vicious and blood lustful*), banks (*the sin of usury*), police (*Gestapo*), laws (*If you are poor and have no capital you have no rights*), FDR (*Roosevelt the Damned*), Kansas (*the Land of Sunshine, Sunflowers, and Sons of* ——), and the governor (*Landon the Louse, Terrible Tyrant of Topeka*).

Alf Landon, in life, was an oil magnate who defeated John Brinkley, a pseudo-physician who became wealthy transplanting billy-goat glands into impotent men and selling rejuvenating medicines. Landon proved to be a progressive Republican with some sympathy for laborers and drought-stricken farmers, a governor who believed in conservation and who opposed a resurgent Kansas Ku Klux Klan. In 1936 Landon ran against Franklin Roosevelt and won only Maine and Vermont in the worst electoral loss in history; but in 1978 his daughter, Nancy Landon Kassebaum (who now represents Chase County), became the first woman initially elected on her own to the United States Senate.

The women utopians in Gurley's novel take their ethics from the Thunder God and their science from a speaking flame, a kind of radio that intercepts broadcasts from the planet Venus. As utopians tend to be in novels, the citizens are impassioned only for knowledge and justice; they are logical, intelligent, reasonable, unmilitaristic, aloof, and humorless; they respect only the Indians of Mexico, a few of whom they let visit their volcanic sanctum. The missionary, his sect unnamed, learns that Thunder God is suffering from tuberculosis in a concentration camp in the *land of creeping shadows*, somewhere east of Wichita. He volunteers to find the god and deliver to him a hollow crucifix filled with a curative powder. He sets out, travels far, comes down off the eastern face of the Rockies into western Kansas, then suffering from the curse of a drought laid on the state by Thunder God. The pilgrim, for so he has become, agonizes his nightmarish way along dust-clogged highway 50, and he witnesses repeated acts of brutal police enforcing insane laws. At last he arrives in the valley of the Cottonwood River cutting through *the weird and legendary land of creeping shadows*, and he passes through Strong City (*one would have to be strong to live there*) and into Cottonwood. The river is dry and the falls silent:

> *The little town itself was likewise dead and its streets all choked with shifting sands. It was a beautiful little town with lovely homes and great shade trees. They had been shade trees before the leaves blew off, that is. The town, like the old mill, spoke of a glorious past, back in the days before it turned its hand to fighting for booze and usury. Today it was just another mass of shifting sand with dry tree skeletons and houses projecting up above the dust level.*

He marks off the chapter with a pair of skull-and-crossbones as if it were a bottle of poison.

In the courthouse he learns how Thunder God was sentenced to prison with only a hearing, and a clerk tells Pilgrim why there was no trial:

> *If he defended himself or opposed the District Attorney in any way he would be sent off into slavery for the rest of his life. On the other hand, if he pleaded* nolo-contendere, *or non-contending, he would only get a year. Naturally, everyone nowadays pleads either guilty or* nolo-contendere.

During a trial, Pilgrim watches a witness sworn in:

> *That judge, in his blatant ignorance, actually believed that by having a witness swear that his witness was going to tell the truth would make it true. Evidently he believed that if a person planned to give perjured witness the person would hold up his*

hand and say: "I solemnly swear to tell lies, whole lies, and nothing but lies."

He didn't call it witness, however, but testimony. This, of course, meant that the witness was swearing by his testicles. It seems that in the early days a person called a "testator" stood by the witness with one hand upon a testicle, and had him swear to tell the truth. If he "testified" to false "testimony" an operation was performed, so he could never swear in court again. Perhaps this had its merits at that.

Before he can resume search for Thunder God, he witnesses in Cottonwood a charivari, or shivaree (*such heathenism*), a medieval wedding celebration, something like Halloween without masks that came into the county with French pioneers and survived here until World War Two (Whitt Laughridge had to push his bride down Broadway in a wheelbarrow).

Every so often Pilgrim's anger has sharpness: of innumerable Kansas laws, from fishing to marriage licenses, he says: *First they pass a law against things, and then they sell you a license to break the law for a certain length of time.* As he rides the train out of Strong City he listens to a radio:

The air seemed to be full of aimless vocalists broadcasting to the world their soughing self-reproach for being constant failures with the opposite sex. Along with these were interpolated numbers of vacuous mutterings and howls about sex-starvation. . . . All were set to nursery tunes of five or six notes.

Pilgrim at last finds Thunder God hanging by his wrists in the penitentiary at Lansing, and he delivers the curative. Years later he returns to the hollow volcano in Baja and discovers the god living there quietly but preparing for a great departure; on the evening of the ninth of October, 1946, White Thunder God paddles a canoe far into the Sea of Cortez where a spacecraft picks him up and hies him off to Venus. Pilgrim cites San Diego and Los Angeles newspaper stories about the appearance of a spaceship, and his book includes a photograph of the vehicle (looking remarkably like a B-2 Stealth bomber) crossing the face of the moon.

As a novel, *White Thunder God* is not noticeably sillier than much of the fare in an airport book rack today; but, as a defense of a possibly innocent man who served three years at hard labor seventy-five miles west of Osage Hill, it enters another dimension, a deeper one, and it becomes another knot in the net, another ligament tying muscle to bone, people to land. Like a tale not forgotten, its force ramifies:

One morning soon after my hike there, I was driving over Osage Hill to Elmdale, the stories of dinosaurs and Indians and watermelons and Woody Hockaday's red highways and Thunder God's anger turning in my memory like leaves in a gyre of wind, and as I went up the gentle eastern side, I noticed on a recently burned slope what seemed to be an old message spelled out with rocks, and I stopped. I thought I could faintly discern in the char like a palimpsest:

LANDON F—   —OU.

What the hell, I thought, after a half century White Thunder God strikes again? I crawled under the fence, went up the hill, looked closely at the message, and paced it off — eighteen feet high and more than two hundred long. Clearly, the rocks had been laid in place years earlier. I went back to the car and climbed on the roof to photograph it. Although some stones had slipped out of position, and the last five letters were nearly invisible, I could now decipher the words: LANDON 4 GOVERNOR.

I thought, this hill is an earthen bottle of messages from far travelers, a lode for paleographers, and I headed back to Cottonwood and went to information central, Whitt's office. He was sitting by his collection of grasses taken from the eastern side of Osage Hill. He said, *That state land out there hadn't seen fire in years, and then a week ago they burned the brush on it, and the rock sign popped out. The last time Landon ran for governor was '34. I think most everybody who was here then had forgotten about the thing.* He paused a moment, and, *First we find the old Hockaday sign and now this one. Who knows how many more signs are out there?* I said I didn't know how many, but I was sure they were all over the place — it was just that we couldn't read many of them any longer.

At the end of the summer, on Labor Day, some high school students rose early, went out to Osage Hill, and neatly whitewashed the letters they had begun calling *the Landon Rocks*, to make them wonderfully legible.

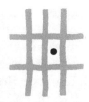

On the Town:
Versus Harry B. (III)

THE HOUSE

If you've ever driven Interstate 35 between Kansas City and Wichita, you have passed right in front of what was once the large lawn of Captain Henry Brandley's new home, and you've been within a thousand feet of the very ground where Frank Rinard was shot in the face, but you can't see much because of the cedars and pines the captain planted as if he knew the turnpike would one day open things to public view.

My temptation is to say nothing of the Brandleys' now remains other than the evergreen grove, when in fact the captain himself is here, or at least his dust lies between his first wife and Lizzie, and close to daughters Ruby and Flora Belle and son Harry in a tiny fenced plot made dim by overgrowth and the darkness cast by the big cedars. The old log home and its bloodstained porch are gone and so is the grand frame house of bay windows, porches, chimneys, and a central tower, the home the captain was starting when Rinard was murdered and which was just being finished when Harry returned a free man. Cap Brandley, the immigrant Swiss, called it Helvetia, a name countians found highfalutin and refused to recognize.

I've heard tales of the captain's seeking solitude in the isolation of his fourth-story tower, sitting up there with only his bottle and dog (he gave the hands the day off when it died), staring out over his holdings, things a man could rely on, and remembering events a man could defend himself against — Utes, Confederates, the South Fork (he and his brother watched from a tree one night as a burning lantern on an old trunk floated around and around in their flooded log house, and each time the lantern passed the open door his brother said, *There she goes,* but the next morning the lantern and cabin were still there), the sky (once he got caught in a prairie hailstorm and held a flat rock over his head like a bumbershoot while his friend Charlie Rogler tried to take cover in a haycock and was beaten senseless — and perhaps remembering his simpler days as a splitter of rails and a digger of ditches, and recalling his first winter in the county when he lived on only corn bread and salt-cured wild birds.

In the months following the trial, Cap could look from his tower westward to where laborers were building the grade for the Orient Railway, which he believed would make his real estate investments skyrocket. I've heard tales of the old campaigner drinking too much up there and coming down to concoct some sort of hangover remedy from dried rabbits he kept in the cellar. I've heard that the home-place, following the bloodshed, was cursed: the log house burning to the ground the year of the trial, the captain drinking himself unconscious and dying in the stall of the Matfield livery barn ten years afterward; Lizzie gone three years later; and three years after her, Harry (having spent the rest of his days sitting with his back to walls) found dead at forty-two in his barn, apparently from self-poisoning; and eight years after that, Helvetia, occupied by tenants, mysteriously burning to the ground in the middle of the night. But Miss Pearl, the lovely dark sun around whom events turned, escaped: she married and lived into her eighties, outlasting all of them.

Today, what remains of Helvetia is a grassy swale and a few outlines of rock walkways. But down the slope to the east stands a small structure, the lower half of native stone, the upper of oak planks painted with red lead: depending on your view, it is ironic or fitting that the last remaining Brandley building is the barn where a hired hand was murdered. It is a simple but quaint thing in the Flint Hills vernacular style, the sort of barn that on a snowy evening belongs in a Currier and Ives print, were it not for the door with the dark blotch believed to be Frank Rinard's ineradicable brain blood.

THE LEGACY

Now: I've been here several times before to try to piece the mystery together, and I've walked the place and tried to imagine its events and earlier aspect; today I've brought a copy of a description Harry's eldest sister, Clara, wrote twenty-eight years after the murder about their life on this very ground, and I've been using it to check details and create dreamtime:

> *Here in the old house the children grew to maturity. They romped and played in a backyard shaded by box elder trees and one gorgeous morello cherry tree at the well. Here roamed the chickens, the young turkeys and geese, the dogs with their puppies, the cats with their kittens, and even the white rabbits with their young.*
>
> *There was a front yard filled with cedar and cherry trees. Here purple lilacs and old-fashioned roses bloomed, and clove, pinks, and annual flowers in their season. Bird boxes on high poles to make them safe from cats were there and filled with chirping colonies of purple martins in early summer. Swift-winged swallows built their mud nests under the eaves. A latticed porch was covered with grape and scarlet trumpet vines where, in the hottest weather, hummingbirds whirred in the air, sucking nectar from the long tubular blossoms.*
>
> *These scenes live in the memories of the children raised there, and now and then some vagrant scent of new blown rose or pink recalls it all, rekindles the past, recreates the old scene anew, with over it and in it and saturating it an all-pervading sense of the presence of Mother, Mother, Mother everywhere.*

But the presence that saturates and rekindles the past here today is something else, something full of unresolved questions: from such a distance, could Mother really have heard the blood-gurgle of a dying man? Why didn't Father offer a reward? Why didn't the captain, with his power and wealth, try to help his son by finding the murderer? In a community so small and known to each other, how could a killer conceal himself? With miles of isolated country around, why would Harry shoot Rinard in the Brandley backyard? Why did the judge strike all testimony of motive? Why was Rinard's friend not allowed to testify? Where was Miss Pearl on the night of the murder? Why didn't the captain have to prove his whereabouts, and where did he go in the middle of that bloody night? Why was the cross-examination of the Brandleys so cursory and the prosecution so manifestly inept? In a time of growing Populist and Progressive sentiment, were some countians, roused by the captain's wealth or a European hauteur, more interested in revenge than in real justice?

The questions the trial raised, perpetually damning in their irresolution, may have served some residents even better than a conviction: looking at all the evidence, it's difficult to believe that Frank Rinard's murderer was not in the courtroom when the clerk read the verdict, but to conclude that the killer was the man acquitted is much harder.

I think many countians feel justice was finally served: of the three great families of the upper South Fork, the Brandleys rose the highest and fell the fastest and farthest, and, unlike the big places of the Crockers and Roglers still standing handsome nearly a century later, the Brandley estate is come to a small, weedy cemetery, a stained barn, and tales continually retold as if poisons to keep privilege from taking root. The vengeance of the people is the long persistence of rumor, where the living haunt the dead.

IX

Homestead

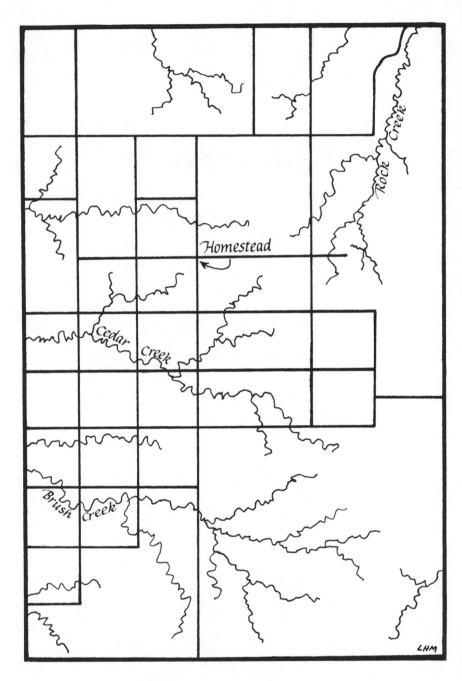

HOMESTEAD QUADRANGLE

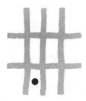

From the Commonplace Book:
Homestead

There is a saying here that freaks are raised for export only. In one sense the saying is true enough, for what strikes one particularly is that, on the whole, native Kansans are all so much alike. It is a community of great solidarity, and to the native it is "the Easterner" who appears eccentric.

> — Carl Becker,
> "Kansas" (1910)

> *But the darkness pulls in everything:*
> *shapes and fires, animals and myself,*
> *how easily it gathers them! —*
> *powers and people —*
>
> *and it is possible a great energy*
> *is moving near me.*
>
> *I have faith in nights.*
>
> > — Rainer Maria Rilke,
> > "You Darkness That I Come From"
> > (1899)

It is a queer sensation to experience a storm out on the open prairie.

> — Ernestine Franke Huning,
> *Diary* (1863)

Our maps have indeed grown less speculative, less interested in the elemental possibilities of the Earth's skin. They are drawn by computers from satellite photos, and that suggests that the Earth has lost its capacity to keep secrets. The natural features are buried under the gridwork of roads and the blur of names. Maps become a means of getting past things, of threading the ganglia and writ of modern life. We tend to look at them for what we want to avoid, rather than what, in good fortune, we might discover.

There is not much fable in a landscape we cannot enter.

— Peter Steinhart,
"Names on a Map" (1986)

Since the world beyond Kansas has been so well guidebooked, the only trip left us is inward.

— John Krich,
New York Times Book Review (1989)

The universe and all it contains does not advance along a linear or planar path. It expands and grows volumetrically outwards and must, at the furthest limit, rupture, split, collapse, and disappear. But at a point, beyond this limit, what should have vanished reverses its course and reappears, now moving centripetally inward, contracting and condensing. What has form vaporizes at the limits of development to a void, and the void condenses into a form and reappears in a never-ending cycle of contraction and expansion. I liken this pattern of development to the wheel of Dharma or a cyclone because it is identical to a cyclone or tornado, which compresses the atmosphere into a vortex, expanding and growing as it rages furiously, then eventually disintegrates and vanishes.

— Masanobu Fukuoka,
The Natural Way of Farming (1985)

Until all the desirable lands and the prairies were fenced and claimed, the early settler's philosophy and reaction to loss of natural resources was to use it up and move on.

— Donald Christisen,
"A Vignette of Missouri's Native
Prairie" (1967)

Time was when all a man had to do was just farm eleven and a half months, and hunt the other half. But not now. Now just to belong to

*the farming business and the hunting business ain't enough. You got
to belong to the business of mankind.*

> — William Faulkner,
> "Race at Morning" (1955)

*As machines replace skill, they disconnect themselves from life; they
come between us and life. They begin to enact our ignorance of
value — of essential sources, dependences, and relationships.*

*The work of [agricultural] production is immediately profitable,
whereas the work of responsibility is not. Once the machine is in the
field it creates an economic pressure that enforces haste; the machine
concentrates all the energy of the farm and hurries it toward the
marketplace. The demands of immediate use eclipse the demands of
continuity. As the skills of production decline, the skills of responsibility perish.*

> — Wendell Berry,
> *The Unsettling of America* (1977)

*The substitution of machinery for labor, and then larger machinery
for existing equipment, has been a fact of midwestern life for a century. The causes of the cycle are complex, but a nagging shortage of
farm labor is partly responsible. Young people head for the cities, so
the farmers have been forced to go with more machinery and economies of scale. The results are $30,000 tractors and 600-acre midwestern
farms, accompanied by a rural landscape that is dotted with abandoned houses, obsolete outbuildings, and rusting equipment. The pace
of change has been incredible. Those who can remember the area even
a decade ago find many things totally different and feel tinges of
nostalgia, in spite of the obvious advantages of the present situation
in production efficiency. Farming as a "way of life" is about gone in
the United States.*

> — James R. Shortridge,
> *Kaw Valley Landscapes* (1988)

*It was difficult for Kansas farmers to comprehend that there had been
only two eras of sustained agricultural prosperity since statehood: one
just before and during World War I and the other during and just after
World War II. . . . They have often been forced to choose whether
[farming] has to be a business or a way of life, especially with the
trend toward larger farms, exploitation of the soil, and pressure to
pursue quantity rather than quality.*

Many farmers like to point out that in the old days, if a farmer's son was not smart enough to get a job in town, he could always farm; while now, if he is not smart enough to farm, he can always get a job in town.

> — Leo E. Oliva,
> "Kansas: A Hard Land in the
> Heartland" (1988)

Few things in nature have a greater human appeal than a family of gallinaceous birds. The whole scene from the hatching of the first young [of the prairie grouse] to the departure of the brood is one brimming with thrilling incidents. The motherly interest of the old bird when the first youngster pokes its head through the breast feathers and gives a contented peep, as it picks at its mother's bill or her eye, is an event never to be forgotten. Then the unexpected poking of a downy head through the plumage, first at the side, then through a rear window, and perhaps two youngsters surprising each other as they appear simultaneously, all are experiences that make a long vigil in the blind well worth the effort. As more of the young hatch they become more daring and may vigorously compete for a position on the mother's back. They make repeated attempts to scale the slippery feathered dome, and finally when one does succeed he has an unmistakable look of triumph. All these things seem to have a truly human aspect, and surely the most skeptical cannot help but take an anthropomorphic attitude toward their behavior.

> — Alfred Otto Gross,
> *Life Histories of North American
> Gallinaceous Birds* (1932)

The flavor of the prairie chicken's flesh is as wild as its prairie flight. Its tang is caught from the wayward prairies, a wild flavor as strange as bison flesh, the prairie become sapid.

> — William A. Quayle,
> *The Prairie and the Sea* (1905)

I have joined several times in the deer hunts, and more frequently in [prairie] grouse shooting, which constitutes the principal amusement of this place. . . .

I was lucky enough the other day, with one of the officers of the garrison, to gain the enviable distinction of having brought in together seventy-five of these fine birds, which he killed in one afternoon; and although I am quite ashamed to confess the manner in which we killed the greater part of them, I am not so professed a sportsman as to induce me to conceal the fact. We had a fine pointer, and had legitimately followed the sportsman's style for a part of the afternoon; but seeing the prairies on fire several miles ahead of us, and the wind driving the fire gradually toward us, we found these poor birds driven before its long line, which seemed to extend from horizon to horizon, and they were flying in swarms or flocks that would at times almost fill the air. They generally flew half a mile or so, and lit down again in the grass, where they would sit until the fire was close upon them, and then they would rise again. We observed by watching their motions, that they lit in great numbers in every solitary tree; and we placed ourselves near each of these trees in turn, and shot them down as they settled in them; sometimes killing five or six at a shot, by getting a range upon them.

In this way we retreated for miles before the flames, in the midst of the flocks, and keeping company with them where they were carried along in advance of the fire, in accumulating numbers; many of which had been driven along for many miles. We murdered the poor birds in this way, until we had as many as we could well carry, and laid our course back to the fort, where we got much credit for our great shooting, and where we were mutually pledged to keep the secret.

— George Catlin,
*Letters and Notes on the Manners,
Customs, and Conditions of the North
American Indians* (1841)

When I passed through [Kansas] Territory it was being devastated by a scourge of locusts, or grasshoppers, as they are here called. In many places they covered the soil with a moving mass, and filled the air like snowflakes on a snowy day. At a roadside station, the train was not able to start till they had been swept from the track. The growing crops were cut off, the trees stripped of their leaves, and the cattle were starving for want of food. The alarming extension of this insect pest, which has ravaged Kansas, Nebraska, and the neighbouring states for the last two or three years, is plausibly explained by the destruction of winged game on the prairies. The nidus of the grasshoppers is the sage brush desert, at the foot of the Rocky Mountains. Their flight westward was checked by myriads of prairie-fowl [Tympanuchus cupido], which devoured them greedily. The opening up of rapid railway communication between the western country and the eastern seaboard has led to these birds being killed in countless numbers for sale in the New England states, and for exportation to Europe.

The barrier which previously existed to the spread of the locust was thus removed. It affords a curious illustration of the intimate relationships which now unite distant nations, to find that an addition to our supply of food in England should bring disasters to cultivators of the soil at a distance of five thousand miles.

> — Samuel Manning,
> *American Pictures* (1878)

Prairie chickens probably contributed more to homesteaders than the buffalo ever did.

> — Gerald Horak,
> *Kansas City Star* (1975)

Someone wrote that the prairie chicken's booming was of great comfort to the pioneer. I can't imagine why. Many things can be said of prairie chicken noise, but by no measure is it a comforting, civilized sound. It is a lonely, wild sound made by a lonely, wild bird. It has the quality of an ancient wind blowing across the smoke flap of a wickiup — companion noise to an Indian courting flute and the drum of unshod pony hooves on bluestem sod. In all of modern America, there is no more lost, plaintive, old-time sound than the booming of a native prairie chicken.

> — John Madson,
> *Where the Sky Began* (1982)

A grizzled country of narrow fertile lowlands and wide, depressing uplands, which smiles a few days in the spring and relapses to sullenness during the remainder of the year; a country with cattle on a thousand low-flung and menacing hills, and the green and purple of alfalfa in threads between. That's where Knute Rockne died.

> — Jay E. House,
> *Philadelphia Public Ledger* (1931)

So died the great Viking of football on a high hill overlooking a prairie, at the crossroads of the old forgotten stage road and the new highway of the air, and at his bier, keeping vigil on the hilltop stood, not the Four Horsemen of Notre Dame, but four sun-tanned horsemen of the plains forcing back from the tangled wreckage a gaping, curious crowd.

> — William Allen White,
> "How a Viking Died" (1931)

*(Talk as you like, he only suits these States whose manners favor the
audacity and sublime turbulence of the States.)*

> — Walt Whitman,
> "By Blue Ontario's Shore" (1881)

*In the free states, we give a sniveling support to slavery. The judges
give cowardly interpretations to the law, in direct opposition to the
known foundation of all law, that every immoral statute is void. And
here of Kansas, the President [Franklin Pierce] says: "Let the com-
plainants go to the courts," though he knows that when the poor
plundered farmer comes to court, he finds the ringleader who has
robbed him dismounting from his own horse and unbuckling his knife
to sit as judge.*

*The President told the Kansas Committee that the whole difficulty
grew from "the factious spirit of the Kansas people respecting institutions which they need not have concerned themselves about."*

> — Ralph Waldo Emerson,
> "On Affairs in Kansas" (1856)

*The state of controversy respecting the existence of slavery in [Kansas]
Territory is well known. Those who would prefer a home where politics are undisturbed by any strong element of agitation had better go
into the more northern territory. Nebraska will furnish room for immigrants for many years to come.*

> — Jacob Ferris,
> *The States and Territories of the Great
> West* (1856)

*The settlement of Kansas was made in the throes of a political revolu-
tion; and the character of her people and their acts must be gauged
by a state of embryo war leading up to a war which had no parallel in
the civilized world. We were but a few years removed from a condition of public sentiment when, even in the most enlightened portions
of the North, the attempt to disdain slavery at all had been met
with tar and feathers, lynching, and many other modes of torture.
Even in enlightened Boston the clamor of the mob of "men of wealth
and respectability" had hardly passed away when the very elite
of that city pursued the poor fugitive [slave] Anthony Burns and delivered him up to the slave power. . . . [Until] the passage of the
Kansas-Nebraska organic act, it was dangerous to express sympathy*

with the slave anywhere, and peril of death to do it near the border slave states.

> — John Speer,
> "Accuracy in History" (1898)

The origin or genesis of states is usually obscure and legendary, with prehistoric periods from which they gradually emerge like coral islands from the deep. Shadowy and crepuscular intervals precede the day in whose uncertain light men and events, distorted or exaggerated by tradition, become fabulous like the gods and goddesses, the wars of heroes of antiquity. But Kansas has no mythology; its history has no twilight. The foundation stones of the state were laid in the full blaze of the morning sun, with the world as interested spectators.

Philosophers and historians recognize the influence of early settlers upon the character and destinies of a community. Original impulses are long continued, like the characteristics and propensies which the mother bestows upon her unborn child. The constant vicissitudes of climate, of fortune, of history, together with the fluctuations of politics and business, have engendered in Kansas hitherto perpetual agitation, not always favorable to happiness, but which has stimulated activity, kept the popular pulse feverish, and begotten a mental condition exalted above the level monotonies of life. Everyone is on the qui vive, alert, vigilant like a sentinel at an outpost. Existence has the excitement of a game of chance, of a revolution, of a battle whose event is doubtful. The unprecedented environment has produced a temperament volatile and mercurial, marked by uncalculating ardor, enterprise, intrepidity, and insatiable hunger for innovation out of which has grown a society that has been alternately the reproach and the marvel of mankind.

> — John James Ingalls,
> "Kansas: 1541–1891" (1892)

Was slavery the rule and freedom the exception, or freedom the rule and slavery the exception?

It was evident that the great question, "Shall freedom or slavery become national?" was to be settled upon the plains of Kansas.

> — Samuel Newitt Wood,
> Kansas Historical Society Address
> (1886)

He was one of the heroic band who threw their lives between the infant state of Kansas and the demon of human slavery and success-

fully fought off the monster, notwithstanding it was supported by the whole power of the Federal Government.

> — Margaret Lyon Wood,
> *Memorial of Samuel N. Wood* (1892)

We are disposed to like Kansas; moreover, we believe in Kansas, for she will, at some future day, accomplish much greater things than party quarrels or Wakarusa Wars. . . . Give her, we say, but a sufficiency of true-hearted and able-bodied Anglo-Saxon men and women, every-day working-people, not fine ladies and gentlemen, not broken-down politicians, or pot-house-ranting filibusters, and we will venture to predict that the moral atmosphere of the Territory would clear itself from its impurities within six months' time; but above all things, let the men who are to till those yet unbroken acres and ere long make the laws of the state, which is soon to take her glorious place among the proud sisterhood of the Republic, be conservatives. *For it is a well-established fact, that as Radicalism is the disorganizer, so is Conservatism not only the pacificator but the absolute preserver of the frontier. And we feel assured that if those who claim to be the best friends of Kansas — and in saying this we reiterate our disclaimer of any sectional leanings — would but be satisfied to attend to their own affairs and let border disturbances alone, it would be infinitely better for the Territory and a real blessing to its inhabitants. Nations, like individuals, derive but little benefit from officious outside interference, however well intended it may be.*

> — George Douglas Brewerton,
> *Wars of the Western Border, or, New Homes and a Strange People* (1860)

*On the levee at Kansas City stood a sort of omnibus or wagon, used to convey passengers to and from Westport, upon either side of which was painted in flaming capitals the words "*BORDER RUFFIAN.*" Standing about in groups, or running in every direction, were numbers of the men who claim for themselves that gentle appellation. A description of one of these will give the reader some idea of their general characteristics. Imagine a man standing in a pair of long boots, covered with dust and mud and drawn over his trousers, the latter made of coarse, fancy-colored cloth, well soiled; the handle of a large bowie-knife projecting from one or both boot-tops; a leathern belt buckled around his waist, on each side of which is fastened a large revolver; a red or blue shirt, with a heart, anchor, eagle, or some other favorite device braided on the breast and back, over which is swung a rifle or carbine; a sword dangling by his side; an old slouched hat; with a* cockade or brass star on the front side, and a chicken, goose, or turkey feather sticking in the top; hair uncut and uncombed, covering his neck and shoulders; an unshaved face and unwashed hands. Imagine such a picture of humanity, who can swear any given number of oaths in any specified time, drink any quantity of bad whiskey without getting drunk, and boast of having stolen a half dozen horses and killed one or more abolitionists, and you will have a pretty fair conception of a border ruffian, as he appears in Missouri and in Kansas.

> — John H. Gihon,
> *Geary and Kansas* (1857)

Idealism must always prevail on the frontier, for the frontier, whether geographical or intellectual, offers little hope to those who see things as they are. To venture into the wilderness, one must see it, not as it is, but as it will be.

> — Carl Becker,
> "Kansas" (1910)

In the Quadrangle: Homestead

I'm not going to hide this from you: I don't much like the Homestead quadrangle, lying as it does with all the mystery of a checked tablecloth, its section lines marked so clearly by square fields and roads cut into the high and flattish topography that they show up in satellite photographs. To drive the gridded acres here, except for a single mile in the most northeastern section of the quad, is always to be aligned perfectly with true north or precisely ninety degrees off it; that there are only four compass headings on the Homestead roads is an emblem of this area of wheat and milo and some overgrazed pastures, a forlorn place filled with evidence of mankind but mostly empty of men: a dried-up water hole on the veldt where you find only tracks of its inhabitants. In this place, I end up talking to myself to disrupt both its desolation and my sadness at seeing the grid so heavily laid onto the land. The lines I look for are imagined ones linking seens with unseens, heres with theres, nows with thens. I've wondered whether I could ever set this quad before you in some fairness to it and its oddlings, things I've had a hard time finding. I haven't even been able to learn the origin of the name Homestead beyond its being three widely separated wooden buildings — school, community hall, Friends meetinghouse (the post office is gone); this is the only quadrangle that never had anything you might call a village, and today there are barely enough residents for an ice cream social.

One evening I sat in a small and dreary motel room, where I

stayed from time to time, and studied the topographic map of
Homestead, stared at this piece squared into Jeffersonian perfection.
I saw how all but one of its eighteen section lines had a road along
at least part of its length; looking at its pattern was as interesting as
staring at a wire hog-fence. For a fellow laying out his little travels
around a grand grid, I was baffled with the imaginary become real,
inked lines turned to cut-in roads, and I disliked that perfect scotch-
ing of the prairie which imprisoned the place and fenced me out; it
was a net to ensnare the land and haul dark mysteries like a load of
pilchards into the light (as a caught fish learns, the important thing
about a net is not the interstices but the web of lines). In my time
in the quad, I could never find a way to escape through the gaps into
where the real place might lie, and I seemed equally incapable of
turning the grid into a screen that might sift out artifacts.

I stared at the map and got annoyed and cussed it. I poured out a
couple of inches of straight cornmash made along the Missouri
River from limestone spring water, and I went outside to the ice
machine; it was broken, so I muttered back to the shabby room.
Then I remembered several smooth rocks I'd picked up in the quad
that morning, and I brought from the car a couple the size of grouse
eggs and rinsed them and put the cool stones into the tumbler of
bourbon. If you like whiskey and prefer it truly neat, cold rocks are
better than melting ice. I set the map up again and sipped and
listened to the clinking stones, the whiskeyed rocks, the rocked
whiskey, and I recalled an afternoon some weeks earlier when I'd
dropped a chip of Chase County limestone into a glass of cider
vinegar and watched it fizz, and, over the next couple of days, saw
the rock disappear by a third: the county dissolved.

I rattled my tumbler and watched for another transformation,
rolled the stones around, jiggled them, and sipped in full hopes I
was drinking some of the bones of the quadrangle I was fenced out
of. In the sixteenth century, Europeans ground up dried flesh and
bones of Egyptian mummies and infused them into concoctions
they drank to ward off death. You see what I'm suggesting about
some prairie elixir curing my dead-end approaches to Homestead: if
a traveler can't penetrate a place, maybe it can penetrate him;
sometimes he must let his theres come to him.

I tried not to look at the map but rather to *watch* it so that it
might assume a presence, but it lay motionless, full of ink barriers.
I walked around it, circled it, and I took out my homemade Claude
glass and turned it on the grids, now tiny curving things almost

disappearing in their smallness, and then an idea: why not erase the lines?

The only way I knew how to accomplish that was to go back into Homestead at night and noctivagate the encroached quad, let darkness conceal the intruded place, let my dimmed vision turn a graphpaper land into a blank sheet that might open to dreamtime. After all, no place on a map carries more mystery than its blanknesses, the *terrae incognitae* old cartographers inscribed with "Here Be Strange Beasts." Night travels permit you to forgo certain baggage — pretenses, preconditions, assumptions — and they can let you cut loose from some moorings, even go a little loony under the privacy of darkness: when you disorient yourself, the country changes, often for the better, and sometimes you can then encounter it directly. Purblindness might work.

So, the next evening I went out to erase the barrier, to slip through it, to circle the mystery somehow, let the spin of night hours hook me around the place to show me its nether side; maybe I could find a way to travel it as a moon does its planet. Then, perhaps, would arise oddities of the Homestead night.

Now: I am walking, and it's just that time when owls take to their perches to wait for the last drop of day when even their silhouettes disappear into edgeless night and you can't distinguish wings from the dark carrying them. Like the owls, I've dozed much of the afternoon to earn wakefulness. I'm starting out from near a small tree that I came across last October: the thing was bare and empty then as now, its stark isolation stopping me. While I sat some distance away trying to sketch it into a notebook, a robin flew in, and the tree looked as if it had sprung a new leaf, an autumncolored one; then came another robin, and some more, and quickly a dozen leafed the tree in orange feathers and got it with song: the Mysterium calling, flaunting itself and its sleight of hand. Then the birds were gone, the whole thing so astonishing that some minutes later I could doubt I had actually seen it.

I'm using the remembered power of the tree as a doorway, and I'm walking, kit on my back, a small flashlight (to write by) around my neck, a cottonwood stick in hand. On down the graveled road, off onto a grassed lane, the moon still far from rising, the grid not yet disappeared although subdued like a map stained with india ink. I'm passing a squared grove of coffee trees, sure evidence of a house once here (in this county, clusters of the three C trees — cedar, catalpa, coffee — are virtual tombstones to vanished homesteads): settlers grew coffee trees for fenceposts and sometimes ground up the large brown beans and brewed them as a substitute for coffee; Plains Indians, using syringes made from animal bladders and hollow leg bones of prairie chickens, dried and pulverized the bark and mixed it with water for an enema. I am walking: a couple of miles west of here is another kind of tombstone, a rock tablet over the spot where eight men died when an airplane fell out of a windy sky in 1931.

The road blurs in the descending night, but it's still an evident roadway, marked out on one side by a line of Osage-orange hedge grown huge, and I'm working to see the lane in its fullness, not as a flat line of two dimensions but a thing running in three — or four — dimensions, a cartographer's mark encircling the planet: the due-west course I'm on could be the first leg of a journey to Yosemite and on across the sea, to Yangyang, South Korea; over the Great Wall, into the Chinese interior, across the Caspian Sea, down the length of Turkey, past the Parthenon, into Palermo, Sicily; along the southern edge of Don Quixote's La Mancha, the Atlantic, the Azores, Baltimore. This road is not an isolated parallel but a piece of the conflux of the greater grid, a planetary circumscription to read: far in front of me right now a Korean must be walking toward his noon meal, and behind me in the dawn an Athenian coming from a tryst, and along this line someone lies sleeping in Maryland. A road become a long circumferential is less forlorn than a short dark strip a walker finds himself on. Stopping to make a note:

> Straightness in Kan illusion, short-sightedness — grid here not plane figure but chunk of webbed circles — isn't it obvious squared-up Kan isn't planogram but piece of sphere? Kansas is bent.

I cross under a fence into a harvested sorghum field that should have never been plowed into this erodible slope (countians call tillage *broke land* — the meaning ramifies). The furrows and stover are bad footing, and I fall and have to grope for my stick. And on, scaring a prairie chicken into a shattering batter of wings. With my stick leading my plowed-field gait, I look like a walking tripod. A rustling: switch light on: a little, humpy, quick-footed shadow rolling from side to side: raccoon.

Back to the road again, moving along too fast, slowing down, under another fence, stopping, pulling out a small pad from my kit

and sitting down on it in the dewed grass. (A walker displaces the
territory as a swimmer does water, but a quiet sitter is a dropped
stone and his ripples subside and water laps back in: submergence.)
Yesterday I heard that a period of meteor showers has begun, and I
lie back, arms behind head, a cushion of flesh, and I watch, but only
the slow slippage of stars. The darkness is as complete as it will get
and the silence the same, so perfect that a lier-back can listen for
the planets in their transit, but what I hear is my watch ticking
down. (Thomas Merton wrote, *Whose silence are you?*) I smell the
sweetness of fallen hedgeballs: eyes yield to ears and nose, an ani-
malizing of a man.

Heavy scratching in the dry grass: in the flashlight beam a large
beetle that neither speeds nor slows nor diverges from its own
course toward Yangyang, and behind it another bug angled to miss
the entire Far East, and then a cricket hopping onto my leg: lie still
and the place will swarm you. As a secretary of under-life, I make
notes of these things. Boston Corbett, after he shot down John
Wilkes Booth in Virginia, came out to Kansas where he would lie
on his back, rifle locked toward the sky, and shoot hawks; I'm lying
here in hopes the stars will shoot. The quiet is so immense that it is
oppressive, and it seems the whole prairie has paused to listen to
me — my breathing, heartbeats — and this is the peril of night
travel: it can remove everything around you and throw your attention back inward as if darkness were a black mirror. I am here to go
the other direction, to find not an egocentric orbit but an eccentric
one. Self-advice: escape, heed the sky as the countians do.

Then, across the blackness, a slash of keen-edged light, and it's as
if I've been lying inside a great gourd deftly sliced open by a long
and gleaming blade that quickly withdraws. Then there is another
meteor, its track shorter and less bright, and, over the next minutes,
more star-chips glancing off the black dome, hail off a tin roof, but
all this falling in universal silence. From the west an owl call, then
a high and wavering warble of a coyote, a yipping answer, then the
owl again, and it seems the white intrusions have stirred things into
turmoil, the silent dark abruptly strung with light and voice; then
it's all finished, and it's one more moment you could doubt you
actually encountered, an occurrence of no more substance than a
dream remembered.

I am walking, following the roadway by feet rather than eyes,
checking my compass: southward this section line is a path to
Corpus Christi and the ruined Zapotec pyramids of Monte Albán,

and: the Pacific (just missing the Galápagos — Melville's *Encantadas*, Darwin's finches), the South Pole, Indian Ocean, Mandalay, the Himalayas, the western desert of Mongolia, the white heart of Siberia, the North Pole, Lake Winnipeg, and Fargo, North Dakota, and home again, home again: Homestead.

Eastern sky warming in yellow light, moonrise begins, breaks the horizon, still a few days from fullness but big in the low sky (only in coming up and going down does its size fit the prairie). I can see the road for some yards ahead now, and it grows even brighter, strangely so, and behind me gravel crunches: a car approaching, slowing alongside, stopping, the sheriff's deputy saying, *Where you going, fella?* I can't resist it: I'm on the road to Mandalay. He says, *You mean Cassoday?* I'm unable to think of a believable explanation for walking an empty, isolated lane at two in the morning, and he says, *Are you from Missouri?* (how does he know that?) and, yes, and, *Is that your vehicle way back there, xzw-064?* Yes, and, *Aren't you that there book writer?* Yes, and he nods, that apparently explaining everything, and he rolls on, slows again, and calls, *Of course, this road don't go through to Cassoday,* and he's gone, and I'm thinking how a fellow widely considered a half bubble off plumb gets out of much tedious explanation.

At three o'clock the moon disappears behind a cloud bank. I haven't encountered much, and I head back to my starting point. In the car, rolling gently, the headlights glaring off the road and reflecting across the dashboard, and then (how could it be?) a silhouette scurries across the dash, and I'm coasting, stopping, reaching slowly for my flashlight, and there in the beam, on the passenger seat back, are two minutely gleaming eyes. Both of us, I and the mouse, frozen. And then it, without panic, is gone as if I'd dreamed it too. I'm opening doors, emptying the car of maps, books, cameras, tape recorder, everything into the road, then I'm inside and thumping the seats, crouched and stamping and yelling the mouse out (and thinking, if the deputy comes along now, even being a book writer won't account for this).

Rain begins to fall, and I'm packing up again, and off down the road, headlamps glaring: it's a night of small eyes giving me back my beams transmuted into green and yellow and red cabochons, and I wend a slow course among the gemmed heads, and they watch, I watch, we all watch, an eye-laden night. Next to me a scrabble of sharp feet and a small arched silhouette across the dash again, and around to the seat top beside me. Why does it keep moving toward my head? Is it going to run for the darkness between shirt collar and back of my neck? I'm trying to figure what a man does with a live rodent under his shirt, tiny claws into his flesh, the panicked scrambling of them both for an exit: two cornered creatures. I'm about to be vermined. I'm driving sixty-five, the car yawing in the loose gravel, and I force myself to slow (not so many men die from mice in their shirts as from speeding on rock roads), trying to enforce a calm, trying to reason: how could it get into the car? Think! A true *fleder-maus!*

On the road a possum makes an accustomed dangerous, unhurried, stupid crossing, then another, hunched and pulling and gnawing, its hairless rattail a stabilizer, yellow eyes glowing, and I'm speeding again, wondering how I got so far from the highway. Am I circling? I'm driving with my shoulders drawn forward to pull my collar against my neck, hunched like an old geezer, and I'm thinking, a mouse on the floor is a mouse, but a mouse at eye level is a beast, and I'm remembering how George Orwell's Winston Smith was terrified into Big Brother's conformity by torturers holding caged rats to his face. I'm reasoning, or trying to, how could (really now) a mouse get into a car? Surely there's no unknown species, some rare leaping prairie kind attracted to automobile dashboards. At least it isn't (is it?) a wood rat, which will take to a vehicle as readily as a teenager. This all must be the workings of a mind that has stayed up too late, exposed itself to too much moonlight. A thing imagined. (Do I hear gnawing?)

Then the darkness suddenly fractures, and out of the jagged rupture flies a sharp and intense light, and then it's gone like a lantern dropped overboard; then thunder, big raindrops hitting hard, and: fracture, flash, blast: and again. At the wheel a hunched madman stamps his feet to keep a varmint at bay, his radio socking out hard to terrorize things into immobility. Then the sweet asphalt of highway 13, and speeding again. Up the county, north, east, neck aching from the distorted and ridiculous posture, rain bashing down. At long last, the glow of Emporia. I'm into the all-night market and trying to find the right aisle (Health Aids? Pet Supplies? Sporting Goods? Cleaners? Where's Verminalia?) The clerk punches the cash register: one chunk of longhorn, one mousetrap. Apparently accustomed to bizarre purchases at four in the morning, she says nothing but only looks at the wet man with the lunatic eyes.

I am driving back through the rain-blown night toward my dismal room, and on the car floor beside me is a set trap. Here, mouse.

Shoulders still up under my ears. Down the highway: on the road to Mandalay where the flying mouses play, and the moon comes up like thunder.

In the dank motel, I pour out a sourmash on the Chase rocks, get into bed, and I have this question: did I manage at last to enter Homestead, to slip through an interstice, to find the quad through subtraction? I don't know, but I'm thinking that I got into someplace far enough at least to find absurdity, and that too is a destination.

And so.

The next morning, Wednesday, the trap untouched, I truly began to wonder whether I hadn't hallucinated (from the Latin, *hallucinari*, to dream). I drove to a car wash and vacuumed up sandwich crumbs and left the trap set. That evening it was still cocked. Thursday morning I got into the car and headed out to meet Lloyd Soyez, who farms in the west county, and when I reached over to the passenger side for a pencil, I saw the trap: there it was, upside down, and protruding from beneath it two small, stiff legs and a hairless tail.

Beyond the Teeth
of the Dragon

This can never be known for sure: a farm boy of French descent from up on Middle Creek may have changed postwar Europe beyond calculating. In late August of 1944, Lloyd Soyez drove his M-24 light tank (his crew named it Falstaff after he bought them a keg of beer as an apology for throwing a track) down the Champs-Elysées as the first Americans entered Paris to secure bridges and streets, and he remembers grinding past Notre-Dame. On his second or third day in the city, he took up a strategic position near the Grand Palais as part of the guard protecting a parade celebrating the eviction of the Nazis. He and four other men were seated on Falstaff to watch Charles de Gaulle come down the boulevard. From the top floor of the palace, where some German soldiers were temporarily imprisoned, came a crackling cough of machine-gun fire. Lloyd says: *They were trying to shoot down General de Gaulle, so us guys in the tank jerked back the bolts on our machine guns — thirty calibers — and opened fire on them palace windows. That put an end to it. We probably done the right thing, but we didn't have orders to fire. Word come down real fast to pull them gun barrels out and put clean ones in, and that's what I done, so when they come around and inspected they couldn't find anything because we had slick barrels — that's how we avoided a court-martial.*

Lloyd Soyez is seventy years old now, and he lives near Cedar Point on the uplands a couple of miles west of the northwest corner of the Homestead quad, but he has farmed many locations in western Chase. We are standing in front of his home, a double-wide, and strewn around it are forty-two pieces of farm machinery — tractors, planters, disks, hay rakes, five-bottom plows, balers — and there are another forty things behind the house; many of these eighty-two machines still function. Lloyd is retired but he occasionally helps the two of his sons who farm with plowing and harvesting. He is a big man, although not so big as he was a few years ago when a physician told him, *Lose weight or you'll become a cripple.* In eighteen months he lost seventy-five pounds, and now he weighs just under two hundred. He also quit smoking: *I told everybody, "Next time I catch a good winter cold, I'll quit." I finally caught one and I quit.* He has two gold-capped front teeth, and he is wearing a spotless Resistol XXX Beaver (a sixty-dollar hat, forty less than a comparable Stetson) and clean coveralls, a mix of clothing that reveals his days as both a cowhand and a farmer. He's a man of immediate friendliness who is pleased to talk, and, as is common in the county, he won't try to answer questions he doesn't know the answer to.

The wind strikes across the uplands, and we get into his pickup and drive to the Town and Country Café in Florence, just west of the county line. I ask him how German prisoners happened to have machine guns in their cells, and he says, *The windows of the top floor of the Grand Palace had bars on them, and the Nazis saw the time when they might be locked in there, so they hid the guns in the walls before we come in.*

Lloyd is neither a braggart nor a liar, and he speaks of his action with diffidence but also with pleasure. *After Omaha Beach, we had fun going into Paris because the Free French had run out most of the Germans by then. We spent a week in Paris, and then the fun was over. We headed off toward Germany at twenty-two miles an hour in the tank. Then we come to the Dragon's Teeth — concrete tank-barriers along the border, part of the old Maginot Line. We pulled up to wait for bulldozers to mound dirt roads across them, and then we drove right on over the Teeth like they were just furrows. But from that time on, things were hard. Now, you've seen pictures of people running out to wave little American flags at our troops rolling in, but in Germany, when we passed through, they waved swastikas at us — I never saw any pictures of that.*

Finally, we got behind the lines. One night near Aachen I was on a foot patrol. I spotted a German infantryman aiming his rifle at somebody behind me. He had his weapon angled way up, so I got

down and took a shot and missed, and then here come from him a
rifle grenade bouncing in against my chest and rolling away and
then exploding. He had that gun up to arc the grenade in on me —
he was aiming at me the whole time. That explosion lifted me off
the ground and shrapnel hit me in the hands and chest. The next
thing I knew, the lieutenant was saying, "Jump up and get in the
timber! You're on your own now!" I crawled several hundred yards
back to our post. I had to sneak around our sentry so he wouldn't
shoot me by mistake.

When a man has a chest wound, they taught us in first aid to
prop him up so he can breathe, and you never give him water. The
sentry and two others come to help me, and he told them to keep
me down and give me water — now there was a boy who didn't
pay attention in class. They were drowning me. I was shaking my
head, and I tried to say, "Prop me up!" but the sentry — he'd won
a Silver Star the week before and figured he knew everything
now — he said, "Don't pay any attention! The man don't know
what he's saying." The medics got there and set me up against a
tree to keep the blood out of my chest. I had a punctured lung.
Right now, in this very café, there's a piece of a German grenade
next to my heart. I've seen it on x-rays. And here's another one.
Lloyd holds up his right thumb, and in it is something black like a
peppercorn. I ask about the missing index and middle fingers on his
left hand, and he says, smiling now, *That wasn't the Germans'*
work. An old combine took them, and it would've got my arm if I
hadn't had the strength to jerk my hand out. I was stout as a bull
then.

After the grenade explosion, Lloyd was in an army field hospital
four months, then returned to his unit; from there he went un-
scathed all the way to Berlin. He sustained his most severe army
injury not in battle but in basic training when he damaged a knee
on the obstacle course. A couple of years ago he had the joint
replaced, and for a year received a hundred-percent-disability check.
To his dismay, he hasn't been able to ride a horse since. *I could've*
got a discharge after basic and come back and farmed with my
brother, but I was young and ready for the army, so I hung on and
made it through the war. I say, so did Charles de Gaulle.

Lloyd Soyez pronounces his name the army way, as if it were
Spanish, Soy-YEZZ, and ignores the French, Swah-YAY. (As he talks
about it, I imagine the young sergeant seeing Parisian girls holding
up signs: SOYEZ LE BIENVENU À LA FRANCE! and Lloyd taking

personally the common welcome.) Because it creates confusion, he doesn't like the Chase County pronunciation of his name: Sawyer. *Mother was Scotch-Irish or Dutch, but Dad was straight French. His parents homesteaded here — my people come from Paris and Alsace-Lorraine. My great-grandfather come out here to work as a freighter on the Santa Fe Trail. My dad spoke French, but none of us kids do, except for counting to ten and a few words like couteau — that's pocketknife. We tried to get Dad to teach us a little, but my folks was against it — even the schools were against it, and that's hard to believe now, but people then wanted to be American. I could have used some French when I was over there.*

He returned to Kansas in 1945 after driving his M-24 nearly two thousand miles. *That tank had twin Cadillac V-8 engines, but when I come home I was afoot. Then I bought an old cavalry horse from up at Fort Riley, and that was my civilian transportation until I got a Model A truck. I did a little cowboying for a couple of years, and I helped Dad farm. Things changed fast after the war. I was born in 1918, and I grew up riding behind a team of horses, although Dad made us walk when we'd harrow: he wanted to make it easy on the animals, but when we'd get tired we'd jump on the harrow and ride a ways. We raised wheat, corn, kafir corn, and oats — lots of oats. Dad used to say, "You can always get a crop of oats." If we had rain we could get ten bushels of wheat to an acre, but with oats we'd get thirty or forty — it was a pretty sure crop even in dry weather. We fed it to our horses, cows, hogs, and chickens. Oats was the power that broke out this country.*

He stops, measures his words: *Of course, there was some land that should've never been broke out — a lot of uplands where the topsoil is only three or four inches deep and sitting on rock to start with: it'd give you a good crop for a few years, but the wind and rain took its toll, and there wasn't floods on the uplands to leave soil behind, so they went to pot and the valleys stayed good: they've been farmed better than a hundred years. These days, we fertilize even in the bottoms — nitrogen, phosphate, and some lime. We didn't do that when I was a boy, and we didn't spray for weeds or bugs. We didn't do nothing — we just raised crops, and it was generally a poor crop. In the thirties we had our wheat blow out, and in one of them dry years the grasshoppers took our corn.*

Lloyd now owns about four hundred acres, all of it uplands, and he raises wheat, prairie hay, and some brome. This year, about a quarter of his land is in the federal Conservation Reserve Program, called CRP or, more commonly here, *set-aside* (emphasis on the first word). The purpose of CRP is to take highly erodible land out of production and put it into a protective cover like clover or native grass. County farmers make caustic remarks about being paid not to farm, but most of them participate in the plan. Lloyd says, *With government programs and an outside job in the family, you might survive as a small farmer.* Dolly May, his wife, teaches music in grammar school.

When it does come up for sale, bottomland has always been too expensive for many independent farmers like him to buy, so most of his life he has rented acreage and done custom farming as his sons do now. *A few years ago the arrangements for a bottomland field was fifty-fifty: half of the profit to the landowner. That wasn't really right, but that's the way it was. Most of the land in here rich people own — city people. I hate to say this, but some of them are kind of greedy and they want a lot of money out of their acreage. They say the land is expensive today and they have to get more, but some of them bought it when it was thirteen dollars an acre instead of eight hundred like today. But one of these days I'll be renting my land and I'll be the same way I guess, although I know one piece of bottom I farmed for ten years — I had it in wheat — and my net worth went down two thousand dollars a year. I was worth twenty thousand dollars less after farming it because I just never got good enough crops off it even with fertilizer and spraying. Of course, I had to pay for all that and half the thrashing bill and all the seed cleaning — weevils belong to the farmer, not the landowner — so fifty-fifty wasn't enough. Things are set up so that the risk is just about all with the man on the tractor. But today it's gotten harder for a landowner to find somebody to take that risk, and my boys work with better contracts, usually sixty-forty. They've got to have at least that to cover the big machinery they run.*

All the time we're talking in the café, people pass the table and speak to Lloyd, many of them knowing him from his third of a century on the county school board. When the waitress drops butter and steps in it and grumbles as she wipes it up, Lloyd says, *When I was a bachelor I used to put the* Wichita Beacon *on the kitchen floor to keep it clean; when the floor got dirty, I'd turn the pages.* The waitress wipes and mumbles, *I like it, I like it.* Lloyd says, *In those days, every winter we'd butcher one beef and five to six hogs for eight kids and the teacher we boarded. If there was ten of us at* the table, she would fix eleven pieces of steak, always just one extra. I thought I had to do more work than the others — bring butter out of the well or haul in a pail, or do something — so I figured I was a privileged character, and I'd take the smallest piece of meat on the platter and eat it right quick, and then I'd get to that extra piece. Nobody contested me for a long time, then they finally caught on.

I ask him a question I've asked dozens of people here: how was it then? When I graduated from high school in '36, a farmhand made two dollars a day, so I went out to Idaho, working the potato harvest and topping beets. Hard hours, but I made five dollars a day. I come back with seventy bucks in my pocket — well, no, I come home a quart of wine short of seventy: you couldn't buy wine in Kansas then, so in Nebraska I bought a bottle to bring Dad — he was straight French, you see. He made his own wine out of wild grapes he picked up along Middle Creek, and he aged it in our cave. He always preferred wild grapes to tame ones. It's been some time since I heard of anyone here making wine out of wild grapes, but then we fed off the land pretty good. Other things we needed, we traded for: every Saturday we took our eggs and a ten-gallon can of cream — we milked our beef cattle — and took it all to Ellumdale and sold it to the grocer and turned right around and bought groceries. We didn't have any cash to speak of. Along with the farming, Dad worked part of most every day on the roads. He was a township road boss. Back then every man had to spend one day a year working on the roads free or pay a two-dollar poll tax.

In '39 and '40, before I went overseas, I helped build highway one-fifty. It was all shovel and wheelbarrow work for thirty cents an hour. I made two-forty a day, and I'd take my road money and help the folks out: buy a sack of apples or a case of pork and beans. I wasn't married so I was only allowed to work two weeks out of four, but a family man could work every week. I had some wheat in the ground too and we got along all right.

If there's a crop I love to raise, it's wheat: you plant it in the fall and just about forget it over the winter, and with good rain you can pasture on it till early spring, then top-dress it, and in June take your crop off. At harvest time everybody is excited. It's special for us. I like to run a combine too. And I like to plant corn and cultivate, but I hate to fix fences. I'm a very poor fence mender.

I ask him how farming has changed since he walked behind the harrow, and he says, Kafir corn's disappeared — now it's milo. No

*beans then, soy. Fifty bushels of corn to the acre — now it's two
hundred. Silos are about gone — silage is put in trenches these
days. Barns are nothing but metal equipment sheds. Big round
bales in the fields — no more haymows. Gasoline instead of oats.
We didn't used to fertilize or spray. We'd cultivate the weeds out,
pulled a curler — called it a snake killer — behind our lister and
turned dirt up over little weeds, but we still had a terrible problem
with them. These days we put a herbicide on right when we plant:
I can show you big fields of corn or beans almost perfectly clean.
We never had that before. And another thing: we all don't visit
around much anymore. We just watch TV.*

I ask whether organic farming has a future here, and he says, *If I
was a young man and could make the same profit as regular farming, I'd go the organic route. I wouldn't even mind using a team
again instead of this machinery that's got so big my boys can't
hardly haul it down the road. I don't know whether you could get
them behind a team.* He thinks awhile, then, *We're hurting the soil
every year. Nobody has patience anymore to grow clover and let it
improve the ground. Farmers want all their fields making profit
immediately these days to pay for their big machinery, so you don't
come across much good land in clover.*

*After a rain now, I see big piles of foam on the Cottonwood from
field chemicals. We never used to have that. My boys got to wear
gloves and goggles to handle some of these fertilizers and sprays.
My dad's worry was plowing into a bungle-bee nest.*

I ask how he visualizes Chase farming in fifty years. *It'll be like
today, I guess. Maybe different chemicals, safer ones. I don't
know — I don't have much vision of it. I can tell you that when I
look back, a farmer's lot is better today — a smart one can become
a millionaire, or at least close to it. Maybe, of course, some of that
comes at the expense of people on down the line.*

*You can find some good changes too. We're getting away from
moldboard plows, ones that go down half a foot or more to turn the
mulch under, and we're using chisel plows that just scratch along
like a harrow and leave stalks on the surface to give protection
against wind. I think we probably should rotate our crops more
than we do, but this system of government subsidies works against
it. Now, machinery: I was twenty before we had our first tractor
and twenty-three when we got a combine, but my boys grew up in
a tractor seat. John cut his first wheat with a big, self-propelled
combine when he was six years old, and the younger boy, Frank,*

when he turned six, used to get on a tractor and follow behind me when I'd plow: he'd drive around and around the field. A neighbor one day asked me what he was doing using up all that gas, and I told him I was just like Casey Stengel getting a relief pitcher ready in the bullpen, and the neighbor said, "But the boy ain't pulling anything!" and I said, "No, but he'll know how when it's time to hitch him up to an implement."

People told me my boys would never stay on the farm because they couldn't make a living on it. Well, four of them are still here, but I think they'd have gone to the city if I hadn't put them on them tractors and later loaned them machinery to get them started. They're paying me back now for raising them to be farmers by making me help them. I know I should've learned more about all of it myself, but I was in the army. The best I could do was send our kids to college.

When Dolly was on the way to the hospital with the first child, she said, "What do you want, a boy or girl?" and I said, "Soon as you raise me three boys you can have all the girls you want." And that's how it turned out: the first three were boys, and I said, "Well, we're through," and she said, "No, I'm going to raise me a girl," and she did, two of them. And then come along the youngest boy, and I said, "We got to quit raising kids so we don't get more than we can educate." It's a good thing a couple of them helped by getting scholarships.

We leave the café and head home, and along the way he shows me the 1896 stone one-room schoolhouse he attended when the Cottonwood didn't flood and wash away the planks he crossed on. We ride and he points out enemies — cheat grass, sourdock, mule tail, sunflower, cockleburr, velvet-leaf — and we stop to see one of his sons' bean fields, Lloyd proud of its clean and straight rows. He bounces us back into a hidden corner behind a rented field: *Last year the law found somebody's mary-wanna patch in here and they cut it out. It was just a pickup load, but it was worth thirty thousand dollars. That's more than one of my boys'll make in a year off three hundred acres of beans or corn.*

When we reach his house, he drives past the jumbles of vehicles and implements that give his place the aspect of a salvage yard, and he says, *I told Dolly, "Every time I have a son, I'm going to buy me another tractor," and that's how come I got so many tractors. The kids were ashamed of the old house, so we set up this new double-wide.* At the pole barn we get out, and I follow him in to see a peculiar-looking steel-wheeled tractor, a heavy, clumsy, primitive machine, a thing Lloyd loves most after his family. I say it looks like an old tank without its armor. *It's a 1920 Avery, two years younger than me. Two cylinders, two forward gears: when you shift you have to move the whole engine backwards or forwards. She still runs.* He points to a mouse watching from atop a rear wheel, and he says quietly, *Nest somewhere in that Avery,* and I say they like wheeled things out here. He walks on. *I always seems to end up with old equipment. I guess I just take to it like them mice, but my boys won't put up with it. They've bought a lot of new or repossessed machinery, and they usually won't buy anything unless they can pay for it right then — that way, a bad year doesn't hurt them so much. They're doing all right, but all they do is work or play softball on Sunday or hunt or fish. They're coming up on thirty, and they're both bachelors. I don't know what'll come of them. Of course, I was thirty-six when I got married, and I raised a good family — well, good enough. I hate to say it, but the girls they went to school with don't know much about farming — don't care about it — and that'll make a real hard life here.*

In the Soyez living room, Lloyd pulls out a photo album full of sepia snapshots: a tank sitting in a Normandy hedgerow, the Champs-Elysées empty of traffic, young women waving alongside a road marked with tank treads, a friend dozing under a howitzer, three German prisoners standing sullenly, five bandaged Americans sitting in the Ardennes Forest, a long row of temporary wooden crosses in a snowy cemetery, a pontoon bridge over the Rhine. The artless pictures take force from events now bound safely in with white, deckle-edge borders. As I look, Lloyd says but a single sentence: *We met the Russians at the Elbe.* I turn the pages slowly, and, after a long while, I close the book, and I ask what his children think of the pictures, and he says, *They don't ever ask about it,* and then, *Come on outside.* We walk past the big combine shed that a tornado took down a year earlier (which they rebuilt more sturdily after collecting, to their surprise, insurance money). A bird calls loudly from some high grass, and Lloyd says, *Cock pheasant. I've shot a load of them with a German training rifle — a twenty-two — I brought back from the war.* We come to a small upland pond he cut in a few years ago. The water moves under the wind, and in front of us a rusting lawn chair his sons found and set up for him beside the pond, a seat he takes when he fishes for bass, perch, and two-pound bullheads. He offers it to me, and I offer it back, and we end up only leaning on it.

He says simply and without sentimentality, *I've never abused* my body much unless hard work is abuse, but I've had gallbladder surgery and diverticulitis, and I've got a piece of a German grenade next to my heart. I've got a metal knee and cataracts. I've survived one bad pasture fire and more than one tornado. If I fell off a horse today it would probably kill me, but I don't complain: a lot of buddies are over there under crosses. There's no pond and old chair for them. You asked me earlier if I liked farming: I do. I even like the gamble of it. But I know not everybody is as satisfied with it as I am, although there's things I don't do anymore: I can't even buy spray because I never took the course to get a license for herbicides and pesticides. They've made things so complicated now. You take a guy like me, I've kind of given up on most of it. I've gotten away from raising crops on my own land — I'd just as soon leave it in set-aside.

He looks at the rusted chair and taps it and says, *But I'm not ready to sit down here for good yet. When the farmers had that demonstration in Topeka at the capitol a few years ago, the family tried to talk me out of driving my tractor the eighty miles up there. They said machinery was dangerous on the highway, but I wasn't listening, and somebody said, "You know, don't you, Dad, there won't be anybody there from Cedar Point." I said, "When I drove my tank onto Omaha Beach there wasn't anybody from Cedar Point there either."*

Amidst the Drummers Desirous

Tympanuchus cupido:

1. (THE COCK):

comes the little drummer desirous, comes he to the April grounds, the booming, dancing, scratching ground, the old lek, comes he to boom *whoom-ah-whoo-om!* a mile through the stilled dawn (what ethereal sound is this across the tallgrass: beast, bird, sky, something dreamed?), comes the boomer, *whoom-ah-whoo-om!* (like far thunder or deep breath over the round lips of a great empty jug), to the hillock to tymbal the fogged morning, to the cropped rise smoothed around, trampled down, the open knoll; so have his generations done at the crossing of the equinoxes, *whoom-ah-whoo-om!* the flung call, the muted prairie anciently voiced; to dance too, to boom and jig, a fling of stepping, stamping, strutting, pivoting, legs pantalooned, the capering clawed feet rolling out their sound, the little thumping dance: one-two-three-four, one-two-three-four; comes the cock to cock the neck feathers, rotating, flashing into halos, aureoles of dark light, devils' horns, erected pinnae (his signature); to hoist the long tail, fan it, spread the festooned delta; he into displayed pomposity, puffed, puffing, inflates jugular sacs, blown tight, orange drumheads; to cock the head and beak, to blow the sacs into *whoom-ah-whoo-om!* (inflation, exhalation: the sails of a pinnace in full wind, bulging to dump it), booms again; now a second cock to join, engage, and he too blows into vociferance, moves into his antic cavort; challenger levels spine: stamping, trampling, dropping wings to drag the ground, raises orange eyebrows (grotesquerie, gaudery: fat and arched, puffed caterpillars), stomping, charges: they vault, violent volitation, feather wrecking, thudded breasts, beaten wings, juggling of birds, and down again, and challenged again, and again into the pinion-torn air: and so, they all come to dance the ground, to boom *whoom-ah-whoo-om!* come they the cocks to the parliament of fowls to transact the passage of generation: O birds, nothing more prairied than you

II. (THE HEN):
arrives to the concupiscence flaunted, the quickened avian heat, to nonchalant edges of the round boomed and danced, to pull a blade, a bud, to seem to idle in the whooming among the cocks rising; she waits to make selection, tread a territory, be treaded, taking the cock's cocking, to move in and squat low as if to get under the gambols (Audubon painted this), under the ruckus, the raucousing wing-necks, the bag-necks; she leaves the waited edge, enters the lists (called there), going down low and spread to his nuptial bows, and then their wings almost concealing the passage, and, rising cock, he: *whoom-ah-whoo-om!* she goes from the round, her circle not the boomed ground but scant dried grasses laid so poorly into a nest (its haphazardness also concealment: harrier arrives, hanging low, and she squats into a lump of dun-mottled immobility, invisibility, a hot-blooded stone); soon she lays; sits over her shelled ones, breaks the spring winds; then: she rises in front of coyote, falls, calls him to her feigned broken wing, rising, calling (coyote following), chunking herself up again and again until the damp canine nostrils lose the nidal scent; hen returns to take the sun-hammered heat, night dew; her mornings like this: head rising, surveying, she leaves the clutch, crouch-walks, head periscoping, sizing up, briskly stepping, halting, moseying, suddenly rising, locking wind under her pinions, and gone; and returning is this: gliding, circling, dropping, crouching, waiting (always this), closing the circumference as if drawing the center to her breast, orb tracking, retracing the arcs, waiting: then she breaks the circle and runs down the radius to the naked eggs, covers them like silt (she the precipitate of prairie): O thatchback, treeless thing, await your parliament pipped

III. (THE BROOD):
sod-backed bird sits twenty-two days: then *ptchweep,* and the rumped parliament speaks, she rises nervous (as a hen), bills eggs

around, stares at the holed shell calling, covers the synchrony, hides the pipping, *ptchweep!* feels under her the fracturing, dithers above; then: squirting from under her, cracked into the prairie light, grassed liberty, they swarm into the bluestem, she calls, retaining the circle, they leap onto her back, tumble of downies, she calls, and from all the calling prairie they know hers and heed it: heading out, returning, assembly, dispersing, returning to her whistle, they leashed to her voice, she holding the circle tight; and: the long-winged-shadow hover; she calls now differently, and, to these notes never heard by them before, they know to squat-freeze and blunt the harrier vision; speckled-back disappearance; then she calls for assembly, they gather, sixteen fuzzes now generated and footed and they follow from the cracked-open nest and strike a slow course away, to walk themselves into wings (one day to use only when necessary as a turtle uses its shell); she calls the bevy, holds the circle of bug eaters, commands the little parliament, calls it to order, and keeps it until full grouseness arrives; O cockettes, learn your *whooom-ah-whoo-om!*

IV. (THE DESCRIPTION):
the adult greater prairie chicken (some call it prairie hen, but then you end up with a prairie hen cock) is a couple of pounds and a foot and a half of gallinaceous bird: that is, its shape is fowl-like (large plump body and small head: a walnut atop a watermelon), its bill stout, short, slightly decurved, its hind toes or spurs elevated on the leg; the male is polygamous, the female's clutch numerous, the hatchlings downed and ready to leave the nest and peck up their own food immediately; given the ancestry of the bird, a better name is prairie grouse, but settlers tended to interpret the land in terms of edibility; grouseness means completely feathered legs, plumage of barred and mottled browns and grayed whites (a camouflage so good that it and the propensity of the bird to depend on it and take wing only at the last moment can put a hiker's heart into his throat on a quiet prairie walk); its escape flight is deceptively swift, a lovely pumping and gliding never very high off the prairie floor: a burst of wingbeats, then wings bent to gentle arcs, a sweet volplaning, and another powering of wings; quickly, the bird (its grounded plumpness sleeked for the air) is a mile gone, and this flight is so distinctive that even a novice will recognize it after seeing it once; a pair of long and dangling black neck feathers — the pinnae the male erects on the booming ground — distinguishes the species and gives

its other name, pinnated grouse; the bird eats seeds and insects, many of them noxious

V. (THE HUNTER):

Whitt says: *we were out west of Bazaar, down in Miser's old field, four of us, Jim Bell, Wilbur Mann, Jesse, and me: the Misers had their corn shocked up, the way we did then, and we all took a shock and worked it around until we could get inside it like a tepee; then, just before dawn, a prairie chicken flew in and landed right on top of the shock Wilbur was in, but he didn't see it, and we couldn't shoot at the bird or we'd hit him; I pointed up, but Willy didn't know what I meant; then I wagged my hands like they were wings, and I pointed up again, and he saw the tail; he laid his gun down and, real slow, reached up for the bird; then he grabbed for the damn chicken, tried to catch it by the legs, and off it went: we fell out of the shocks, laughing at him, and that was the end of that hunt*

VI. (THE COMMENTARY):

if there is a signature bird of the tall prairie, it is this grouse whose range before the coming of the white man was almost a map of the long grasses; early western explorers only infrequently wrote about prairie grouse, so it seems that its numbers were not large then; a Kansas biologist, Gerald Horak, who has studied the birds in Chase County, believes the grouse declined as bison were driven from the tall prairies because it depends on seasonal grazing to open the grass, and Horak thinks that settlers planting cereal crops helped the bird increase again with a new blend of grains and pastures; item: in July of 1870, two hundred prairie chickens flew right through Cottonwood, and four years later Doctor Cartter, who bought Sam Wood's house in the Falls, had a competitive grouse shoot: his team won, ninety-two to eighty-seven; item: in 1873 nearly three quarters of a million prairie chickens were shot or netted, trapped, and bludgeoned (usually at night when the birds are slow to flush), and shipped to fine restaurants in the East and Europe, five hundred birds to the massive barrel or, in a boxcar, a couple of thousand gutted and strung up on wires like laundry; the slaughter edged the bird toward extinction (a subspecies, the heath hen of New England, is gone) and several middlewestern states enacted their first-ever game laws; by 1910 the grouse population began to grow again until farmers plowed up more and more grassland during the world wars; under this remorseless cultivation the bird once again declined (an example: from 1912 to 1967 the prairie chicken population in Indiana went from a hundred thousand to extinction); in Kansas, the state with the most prairie grouse today, the bird is most numerous along the eastern front of the Flint Hills where there is a good mix of cultivated grains and permanent grass and where a number of farmers practice crop rotation, strip cropping, contour farming, and no-till plowing; Cassoday, Kansas, three miles south of the Chase line, calls itself the Prairie Chicken Capital of the World, but grouse here must compete harder against overgrazing and annual pasture burning than against hunters (who annually in the state kill fifty thousand prairie chickens); the bird thrives on moderate grazing and fire only every few years: too much of either can do it in, as can too much cultivated land; in other words, this signal bird, so easy to recognize and to anthropomorphize, is an excellent load-indicator, a sign of how much the grass country can bear, an emblem of a diverse and balanced prairie, the requirements of bird aligning with those of men: as goes the prairie chicken, so goes the prairie and its people; now, this question: the *whoom-ah-whoo-om!*, is it a drumroll for survivors triumphant or for those to be executed:

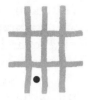

Regarding Fokker
Niner-Niner-Easy

I

Such is the power and legend of Notre Dame football and Kansas weather that commercial aviation began changing radically one turbulent morning after the two collided over Chase County, just five miles south of dead center. Things started coalescing in Kansas City, Missouri, on Tuesday, the last day of March, 1931, when one plane and eight men from the East, the West, and the Midwest gathered at the airport in a light snow. They had a single thing in common: their numbers were all soon to come up at the same moment three miles southwest of Bazaar, Kansas, a few hundred feet above route 13. It was, in truth, a day of peculiar material for a numerologist: Transcontinental and Western Air (soon to become Trans World Airlines) flight number 3; the date, 3-31-31; the plane, a Fokker Super-trimotor commissioned on 10-29-29, its registration number NC999E.

The passengers: H. J. Christen (interior design), Spencer Goldthwaite (advertising), John Happer (sporting goods), Waldo Miller (insurance), C. A. Robrecht (produce), Knute Rockne (football). People compared Rockne's current team, on a nineteen-game winning streak and unbeaten in two years, with his three other unbeaten teams, including the Four Horsemen squad of 1924; his record was 105 wins, five ties; had he lived long enough, his next loss would be only his thirteenth. A few days earlier in Florida, where he and his family were vacationing, he said he expected that thirteenth trimming to come soon. "The Rock," the forty-three-year-old Norwegian immigrant, was not a tall man, about five-eight, and never an exceptional athlete, yet he played end on the obscure Notre Dame team that beat Army, the national football power of 1913, 35 to 13. He caught a number of passes that season and predicted putting the ball in the air would change the game; he was right, and so successful were his teams at throwing that by 1931 some Notre Dame faculty and alumni were complaining about excessive emphasis on football and the deleterious effect they believed it was working on the real purpose of the university. Rockne was the quarterback for those who disagreed, as he was in finding opportunities to cash in on winning football teams. In breadline America, one reporter called him a *tremendous money maker*, a man earning more than forty thousand dollars a year through various means; on that last day of March, in fact, he was going to Los Angeles to complete promotional agreements with both the Studebaker auto company and movie producers (one film to be called *The Spirit of Notre Dame*). If much of the rest of the country was getting by on a thousand dollars a year, few people disparaged his hustle, so widely was he admired. The fundamental changes beginning that morning lay in the very admiration for an immigrant's grand success.

TWA pushed departure time for flight 3 back forty-five minutes to nine-fifteen, and that was just as well because Rockne had been hurrying all morning, trying to visit briefly with his sons, William and Knute Junior, who were coming into Union Station from Florida to resume classes at their Kansas City boarding school, but their train was twenty minutes late and Rockne had to go on; by the time the boys reached the airport, their father had just taken off. For the coach, the last day of the month began as a morning of near misses, but it would not end that way.

The weather in Kansas City changed to a slow drizzle, but Wichita, the first of five stops on the way to Los Angeles, reported improving conditions, so by ten o'clock the sky there was clear, the ceiling unlimited, temperature thirty-nine, winds a mere ten miles an hour; but the skies at Emporia, the halfway point, were more unsettled, and, for some reason, the TWA weather report omitted the barometric pressure. Flying the Super-trimotor was Robert Fry, an experienced and skilled aviator, a veteran who became a member of the Caterpillar Club by once parachuting to safety from his falling plane three years earlier in China. He was thirty-two. The co-pilot, Jess Mathias, was two years younger and had far less experience, but then his job was mostly handling tickets, baggage, and mailbags. The plane carried sixty-three pounds of mail stored loosely behind and beneath the pilots, and there was a little less than two hundred pounds of baggage, and also some sporting equipment — tennis rackets, golf clubs, balls — belonging to John Happer. The six passengers, eight short of a full cabin, weighed about eleven hundred pounds, only a moderate load.

II

The plane: fifty feet long with a seventy-nine-foot wing and weighing six and a half tons, the Fokker 10A was a large machine for the time; competitors commonly copied its design (especially Ford Aviation, although its version was entirely of metal). The fuselage, slung beneath the one-piece wing, was welded steel tubing covered with treated fabric, a material something like oilcloth; running nearly the length of the wing was a main spruce-and-fir spar, three by two feet at its center, that supported wooden cantilevers; plywood skin covered the whole wing assembly, virtually all of it secured by glue (if you've ever built a model airplane out of balsa sticks and tissue paper, you have an idea of the construction of the Fokker). Two of the tripropeller Pratt-Whitney Wasp engines hung close inboard under the wings, and the third sat forward on the fuselage nose; behind was the ten-window cockpit with excellent visibility. On each side of the passenger cabin were a dozen large, square windows, and below hung two pneumatic, nonretractable wheels. Transcontinental planes were silver and red and carried a logo (remarkably similar to the emblem of the Lafayette Escadrille of the First World War) of an Indian in a warbonnet. The plane cruised at 120 miles an hour and had a good safety record. Only six months earlier the airline had begun coast-to-coast passenger service with F-10s flying a route laid out by Charles Lindbergh; the thirty-six-hour trip from New York to Los Angeles stopped overnight in Kansas City.

Anthony Fokker, designer and builder of the F-10 series, was a blond, blue-eyed Dutchman famous for building German warplanes featuring his synchronizing mechanism allowing a pilot to fire a nose-mounted machine gun directly through the propellers with lethal accuracy. (During the war, the Germans asked him to demonstrate the new weapon himself in actual combat, and he — a friend of Manfred von Richthofen, the Red Baron — went aloft, drew a bead on a French plane, but decided to let the generals do their own killing.) I have not found figures for how many Allied planes fell from the sky as a direct result of the Flying Dutchman's genius. Two years before the beginning of commercial air transport in 1924 (the year the Four Horsemen rode over Army), Anthony Fokker moved to the United States and started building large commercial aircraft employing his favored design of single-high-wing planes made of composite materials. His success — and the competition from Ford Aviation — attracted General Motors into buying a controlling interest in his company.

III

That March morning, Fokker 99E flew the first hundred miles through broken overcast and mist, but things began to change near Emporia: the sky thickened and fog forced the plane to fly ever lower. Co-pilot Mathias called Wichita at ten-twenty-two and said, *We're flying right on the ground — there's no ceiling — we're going to head back to K.C.* TWA control in Wichita reported skies there clear but for a few clouds northeast — in the direction of 99E — with visibility unlimited and only a slight wind. At about half past Mathias radioed, *We're going to try it again. If we can't make it, we'll go back to Olpe and land.* The Olpe field was ten miles east of the Chase County line. At about this time, Paul Johnson, flying a slower mail plane that took off fifteen minutes behind the Fokker, hit the low fog and had to descend to just above the treetops; he headed off northwest where the weather seemed to be clearing, but, as he maneuvered up and down and around, he kept picking up ice that began to bow the ailerons with such weight he had to open the throttle all the way. Johnson saw the Fokker and thought it seemed to be following his climbs and drops and turns through the murk (he later spoke of *gobs of weather*); he was afraid to turn around with the other plane so close behind. Then he headed southwest. His radio and airspeed indicator iced up and he had to fly "blind," using only his tachometer and turn and climb indicators, and the engine strained under the ice. Then, abruptly, he cleared the dirty gloom and flew into sunlight, but the Fokker was not behind him.

At ten-thirty-five, Mathias radioed the tower and received another report of fair weather. G. A. O'Reilly, the Wichita operator, asked, *Do you think you'll make it?* There was no reply, and O'Reilly, getting tense, called again, *Can you get through?* Then came Mathias' voice straining: *Don't know yet, don't know yet!* A minute later O'Reilly again radioed: *Fokker Niner-Niner-Easy?* No answer.

Near highway 13, about three miles southwest of Bazaar, Edward and Arthur Baker were moving cattle on the homeplace when they heard the distant motors of a plane heading southeast. The noise passed. A few minutes later it returned and seemed now to be moving northwest, this time spluttering and backfiring, but in the low overcast the Bakers could see nothing: a brief silence, a quiet above, then a loud, thudding crash. The cattle jumped and banged into the corral. Edward climbed up on a board fence to try to see better to the west; from almost above him a long silvery and red object dropped in the slow zigzag of a falling slip of paper. The young men grabbed the nearest horses and rode all-out toward where they had seen the silver thing float down behind a treeless ridge. About a mile away they came to it, a piece of aircraft wing — broken cleanly across but otherwise hardly damaged — lying topside up. On it was NC999E. A half mile west, in a broad basin on the low ridge lay an incredible tangle of something with a tall, silvery projection like a huge tombstone. They rode fast and came up to the Fokker, heaped past recognition but for the upside-down tail assembly. Gasoline fumes hung thickly, but there was no fire and there had been no explosion.

Edward got off and tied his horse to a fence, and Arthur rode around the wreckage that lay scattered over a hundred yards. They saw four bodies lying outside the plane, the farthest sixty feet away, and they could make out two more men still in the cabin. Although there was little blood, the victims were considerably mutilated and dismembered. Without question, all six passengers were dead. Edward started to pick up some strewn mail but stopped, and his brother rode back to the house, where his father had already called the operator in Bazaar. Sometime after eleven A.M., the Cottonwood ambulance, rolling at ninety-five miles an hour down wet and unpaved route 13, made a slow, fishtailing climb over the light covering of snow on the pasture. More countians arrived and helped pick up letters, gasoline-soaked mailbags (a Chicagoan later wrote Bazaar postmaster John Mitchell to ask for a 99E letter to add to his collection of *crash mail*), and large sums of cash, jewelry, and five watches. Others had the grisly task of gathering up bodies and pieces of men in bushel baskets and gunnysacks. When a part-time deputy arrived he became ill and hung back from the mangled mess until his stomach settled.

Wally Evans of Matfield didn't want to take his Model A coupe into the muddy pastures, but when four big fellows lifted the wheels off the ground so he could put on chains, they all headed out. Later he said, *The bodies was all in pieces. They'd be a shoe with a foot in it. Bodies was strung out — just a windrow of them to the southwest. The aluminum partition between the cabin and the front end where the pilot sat was laying level with the ground — the sign was still up there telling what the pilot's name was.*

By noon, news of the crash had spread over the county, and sightseers rushed out, tearing into the muddy pasture. Then word came that one of the victims was Knute Rockne, and from then on, the crowd rolled in from a half-dozen counties: by early afternoon five planes had landed nearby, their pilots huddled and holding their leather helmets and guessing at the cause of the crash; one veteran of the World War said he'd never seen such mutilation on this side of the Atlantic. In the whine of stuck car wheels and the drone of circling planes, cowhands sat astride their horses and watched people from Wichita slog their Fords into the prairie and then get out and hurry toward the crash. They tore down the three barbed-wire fences, scrabbled in the rocky mud for keepsakes, milled about the wreckage, photographed each other standing and waving and smiling beside it as if it were the Washington Monument; they were picking up every loose thing, all the while getting in the way of men trying to gather up body parts. Stationed at the middle of the wreckage to protect it, the deputy sheriff (having recovered his stomach) was busy tearing out the Fokker's radio for a memento; John Happer's tennis rackets and golf balls were long gone. The only things people handed over were letters. One man said later, *Rockne's pocketbook was laying there just like you'd taken a corn knife on a stump and cut it right in two. There was a one dollar bill like that, just half of it, and I said, "Here's where I'm going to get me a souvenir."* Years afterward, former state senator Wayne Rogler told of a fellow walking around with a passenger's ear, and, when a friend admired it, he pulled out his knife and sliced it in half to share.

Authorities stopped a boy carrying away a carburetor and looked at it, told him he had a swell find, and let him go off with it. Then bigger things began disappearing: a man even rolled one of the huge flattened tires over the wet hills to Matfield. The eager crowd shredded the cabin fabric beyond what the crash had done and stuffed pieces into their pockets. Finally, like a great carcass scavenged by hyenas, only a skeletal plane remained: the broken frame, engines, tail assembly, the fallen wing. Harv Cox, who drove the speeding ambulance out and returned with Rockne's body, said later, *I've never seen people go so crazy in my life.* When Cox died a half century later, he still had not returned to the site; he said, *I got my fill of it that day.*

After the passengers' bodies were gathered up, searchers found the co-pilot under the forward bulkhead, but there was no sign of the captain. Somebody near Matfield claimed to have seen the plane pass overhead at about ten-thirty with a man on the wing, and a rumor arose that the pilot had abandoned his ship, but when a team of horses pulled out the seven-hundred-pound nose engine rammed three feet into the earth, under it lay Robert Fry upside down, still buckled in. Wayne Rogler said when they picked up the bodies *they were just like jelly.* Identification was difficult. Rockne's quarterback of 1929, who lived in Wichita, drove up and, looking at the rubber leg wrappings on one victim, said they had to be the ones Rockne wore for phlebitis. There was such dismemberment that, when the embalmed remains of the eight men went off on the train, the Cottonwood undertakers weren't entirely certain they had put all the parts with the right bodies.

By nightfall, the airline had finally posted guards at the wreckage, a good thing, since the next day word got out that H. J. Christen had withdrawn fifty-eight thousand dollars just before he left home and that he was also carrying half a million dollars in negotiable bonds. After searching, his wife found the money and securities, but to this day, a few countians believe someone on that muddy March morning carried off a briefcase with a fortune in it, money hidden yet in the Chase prairie. When the guards finally left the site, people went back in with shovels and dug the spot like starving men might a potato patch.

Rockne's sons, eleven and fourteen years old, came to Cottonwood with Dr. D. M. Nigro, a Kansas City friend, who confirmed identification while the boys waited in the car on Broadway. They had only been told their father was hurt in an accident. Nigro came out of the furniture store — also the undertaker's lab — sat between the boys in the back seat, put his arms around them, and explained what had really happened. The elder son, crying, vowed he would become a great quarterback.

On Wednesday, the day following the crash, there was a coroner's inquest held in the courthouse. Of the five people who heard or saw the plane go down, one of them said it fell like a meteor. The witnesses agreed on virtually every detail of the last minutes of 99E, but only one person, a garageman and sometime deputy sheriff, testified to seeing ice at the site; perhaps having a more trained eye than a cowhand, the mechanic said the pieces were U-shaped and could have come from the leading edge of the wing. The sheriff testified the co-pilot's automatic pistol had been jammed, apparently by the terrible impact, but no shells had been fired.

Airline and government officials offered little more than a recitation of the general procedures for a fatal air crash, perhaps something to be expected, especially when the county attorney said to Leonard Jurden, the federal supervising aeronautical inspector, *If I should ask any question that the Department of Commerce does not want you to answer, just don't answer.* Government policy at the time was to keep information about airline crashes secret. TWA employees (including Jack Frye, the man who would soon write the first specifications for a modern airliner) added little, their coolness perhaps abetted by the practice of requiring passengers to sign their tickets and release the company from liability. The inquest established only that the plane was flying northwest just before the wing broke off and that 99E came down in a long curve marked out by wing debris and mail sacks, and the conclusion says simply eight men *met their deaths as the result of an airplane fall; cause undetermined.* The headline the next day in the *New York Times:* UNABLE TO FATHOM ROCKNE PLANE CRASH.

On Thursday, Anthony Fokker flew to the crash scene and landed close by to examine what remained of the eighty-thousand-dollar aircraft. Under pressure because of the sensational aspect of the disaster, the federal Aeronautics Branch in Washington broke its policy of secrecy on fatal crashes and issued a hurried statement saying the missing left propeller suggested that a piece of ice from the prop hub somehow broke the blade and created stress great enough to fracture the wing. Although Fokker discounted that explanation, he searched for the missing prop by dynamiting in the cavity left by the port engine. It so happened he had personally inspected 99E the day before the accident and he rejected all implications of improper wing design or structural flaw. Of three hundred Fokker monowings built, he said not one had ever had a structural failure, and he concluded the pilot was insufficiently informed about the weather and had been forced to fly blind, a disorientation causing him to put the ship into a dangerous attitude he tried to correct with a precipitate and violent maneuver that snapped off the wing. Noting TWA rarely secured mailbags as it was required to, Fokker said weight abruptly shifting could have created problems, and he pointed out how the letters and mailbags had been strung out along the crash route. To the designer of 99E, the cause lay with the pilot, co-pilot, airline, and weather forecasters.

Thursday evening the sheriff (who had earlier let seven prisoners see the wreck and help pick up debris) recovered the missing propeller in Cottonwood from a boy who had pulled it off the salvage truck. (The few remnants went to Wichita and some weeks later sold as scrap for less than a hundred dollars.)

IV

The inadequacy of governmental attempts to find the cause was obvious, and, at once, letters began reaching the Department of Commerce and appearing in papers; the accident was so sensational the *New York Times* made it front-page news and in December called it *the year's big story.* Although 99E was hardly the first airliner to crash — the prior twelve months had seen six major accidents in the country, one taking sixteen lives and another thirteen — it was the first American disaster to kill someone as famous as Rockne. One New Yorker wrote to the *Times: If government or private inquiry shows that the airline was negligent, what penalty can the government inflict on the airline?* Newspapers, however, spent no time looking into either possible causes or the secret investigation; instead they fed the public sentimentally lionizing articles about *the death of a Viking* and pumped up peculiar details: the story about Rockne getting out of a taxi in Chicago the day before the crash and a friend saying, *Soft landings, coach!* and Rockne responding, *You mean happy landings.* And the one about why Rockne, the man who put the football in the air, no longer used the railroad: he said, *What's the use of wasting time on trains and automobiles? This is a fast day and age. I've got to get around to do things and reach places.* But the news stories, as irrelevant as they were, kept the accident before the public as much as good investigative reporting would have, and pressures on airlines and government remained strong enough that, years later, a cynical — if not cruel — Kansas Citian wrote, *The outfall of Rockne's death atoned for his hustle of collegiate football.* What happened to aircraft design and regulations after the plummet of 99E would have happened sooner or later anyway, but the changes came about earlier because of a famous coach going down near Bazaar, Kansas.

The initial result was unprecedented: the grounding of all F-10 airliners. The director of the Aeronautics Branch claimed he had been planning to ground the planes on April the first anyway (he said, *We missed the boat by one day*), but he still waited five weeks after the crash actually to do it. Less than two months later he cleared them to fly again, and a few did, but confidence in the plane was gone: TWA even pulled the engines from some of its F-10s and torched the bodies. Fokker Aircraft was finished in America, and General Motors took over and changed the name to General Aviation before leaving the business altogether a few years later, as did Ford. The demand for all-metal aircraft was national and insistent: two years after the crash the first of the DC series of airliners, some of the most reliable big planes ever made, appeared. Because the internal structure of an F-10 wing could be examined only by tearing off the sheathing, new designs for all commercial planes permitted much easier inspection. The government abandoned its policy of secret crash inquiries and records, and it received authority to investigate air accidents, hold formal hearings, subpoena witnesses, and require testimony; the unofficial removal of even the smallest fragment of a wrecked aircraft became a federal crime; and, by the next winter, commercial planes carried a de-icing substance. In fact, a couple of years after the Rock fell, the only defeated proposal to improve airline safety was a law requiring a parachute for every passenger.

V

The crash site lies a little more than a mile west of highway 177. The first time I visited it I had to be shown the way because you can't see the marker until you climb the first ridge; a sign pointing the direction is long gone, the closest fence gate is now locked, and the present owner, an out-countian, discourages visits. At the spot stands a thick marble tablet atop a limestone base, all of it about ten feet high, inscribed ROCKNE MEMORIAL and below that the names of the eight men, with the coach, alphabetically last, listed first, and the pilot's name at the bottom. The monument, fenced to protect it from scratching cattle, has been chipped at by souvenir vandals and shot here and there by gunners. The area is flattish but uneven upland, a piece of Chase County as faceless as you can find, a place visually ordinary except for its extreme austerity, and it is quiet and unmomentous, although it does have an apprehensible aura: the mystery of what actually happened on 3-31-31.

I went to the historical society in Cottonwood and looked at the relics: a large piece of the red fabric, a chunk of propeller, the pilot's Indian-head insignia pin, the cockpit nameplate, a piece of seat belt. I read the newspaper accounts; columnist "Peggy of the Flint Hills" wrote a week after the crash: *If Knute Rockne's pockets contained all the articles which local souvenir fans claim to have removed from them, it must have been that extra weight which brought down the plane.* An article four years later carried this headline: GOLD TOOTH IS FOUND ON SITE OF ROCKNE CRASH — VALUE $7. I read a 1942 story: MISSING ROCKNE PLANE TIRE TURNS UP AS SCRAP RUBBER. I talked with a half-dozen people who had been at the scene right after the accident and others who had visited it only years later; I saw in one home a wastebasket made from a piece of the Fokker rudder, and everywhere I heard as many tales as truths: *So-and-so carried off the coach's head in a basket*, and *They tied a rope around Rockne's waist to pull him from the ground with a team of horses*, and *What's-his-name years later found a human jawbone with two teeth out there.*

I noticed in the citizens a repugnance about the callous and cavalier keepsake hunting, about the distortions of celebrity and the proposals to capitalize on the horror: only days after the accident the local chamber of commerce, recognizing the most sensational thing ever to occur in the county, recommended constructing a big landing field so commercial aircraft could bring in sightseers; Emporia businessmen wanted a park on the site with picnic tables, a swimming pool, tennis courts; the *Wichita Beacon* suggested a colossal football stadium in the Bakers' isolated pasture, where each year the Fighting Irish would play *for the championship of the United States.* Slim Pinkston, whose brother-in-law was one of the four to see the plane fall, said to me, *I'm disgusted with it — it's* always "*Knute Rockne and Seven Others.*" *Them other lives was worth just as much.* And Edward "Tink" Baker, who was eighty-nine when I talked with him and recently retired from digging graves in the Matfield cemetery (his only souvenir of the crash was a pair of pliers from 99E that a trucker later stole when he learned their history), told me how his father set out the first monument, a small fieldstone. Tink said, *The Catholics put up that marker out there now. They wanted to just forget everybody but Rockne. My dad owned the land then, and he told them he wouldn't stand for that — if they wanted to include all the names, he'd let them put one up.* The much newer monument in the Matfield service area on the turnpike, however, commemorates only Rockne and his football success and doesn't even suggest that seven other men also died. But neither the monuments nor accounts of the accident say how aircraft history changed in the Baker pasture.

In all my looking, I couldn't find what actually happened to Fokker 99E while it was struggling above old route 13, what had caused the wing to break off. Then one day I came across something called "Report on the Crash of Fokker F-10A Transport Near Bazaar, Kansas." It contained excerpts from records held at Wright-Patterson Field near Dayton, Ohio. At the top of page one in parentheses this: "Formerly Classified Secret." Within, hidden among all the official words, were things I hadn't heard or read anywhere else, bits and pieces scattered about like debris from the crash itself.

Fragment one: at ten-forty on the morning of the accident, the wife of E. S. Chartier, an Emporia weather observer for the government airmail service, recorded a rapid drop in atmospheric pressure, and she looked out to see in the southwest, toward Bazaar, a dark cloud with a short pendant nearly in a funnel shape; although the sun was shining elsewhere, the cloud appeared to be an isolated weather cell called *an upper-air tornado.*

Fragment two: a week after the disaster, the supervising aeronautical inspector for the Department of Commerce, Leonard Jurden, wrote a confidential letter to the federal director of air regulation, saying he had definite confirmation from pilots (most of whom insisted on anonymity) that the F-10 series planes, *particularly the long-winged job, do set up a decided flutter in the wing when the normal cruising speed is slightly increased and bumpy air encountered.* One pilot told the inspector the flutter was so rapid wing tips would move up and down as much as eight inches and keep increasing if not corrected by pulling the nose up and throttling back; he said all TWA pilots knew about the problem but never discussed it because they were afraid of being fired or blacklisted. After examining the wing of 99E, he said that it had broken at the very center of the flexing; soon afterward the same flier brought in a nonpilot who also had observed the flutter in a Fokker wing, and, on one occasion after a severe jolt from turbulence, saw the plywood skin on the underwing actually open up. Another TWA pilot told Jurden his instructor would never allow an F-10 to exceed the cruising speed, *being afraid of the roof coming off.* Several fliers said they didn't know a Fokker pilot who wasn't afraid of the ship.

Fragment three: a co-pilot who had flown with Robert Fry many times said other aviators considered him one of the best blind fliers in the company, a man always capable of pulling through the fogs and clouds along the California coast; this man could not believe Fry became disoriented flying blind, and he was sure something unusual had happened.

Fragment four: a few months before 99E went down, an aircraft inspector complained about the difficulty of periodically examining the internal structure of F-10 wings, sealed up as they were, but Gilbert Budwig, director of air regulation, told him he saw no need for worry as long as the plywood skin stayed glued to the internal trussing.

Fragment five: a year before the crash, the U.S. Navy found the F-10 difficult to maneuver in certain situations and not entirely stable, and the service rejected it for naval use.

Fragment six: a TWA field manager at the crash site examined the throttles and found them closed and said the propellers apparently had not been turning when the plane hit: he could find no evidence the pilot had been flying at an excessive speed or had put the plane into a steep dive; to the contrary, he saw indications Robert Fry had the cool presence of mind, once he realized a crash was inevitable, to shut the engines down to lessen the chances of an explosion on impact. The spluttering and backfiring the four countians heard was likely Fry closing the throttles.

Fragment seven: Jurden wrote in another letter, *The wing broke off upwards, under compression. Examination of these [wing] parts showed that in the upper and lower laminated portions of the box spars, some places the glued joints broke loose very clean, showing no cohesion of the pieces of wood. Other places showed that the glue-joints were satisfactory. Two pieces [revealed] definite compression breaks as well as poor glueing.*

And this last fragment: federal inspectors, after stripping off the skin of one F-10 wing, discovered moisture accumulating in the interior had *caused deterioration of the glue, materially decreasing the strength of the wing, since this type construction is to a great extent dependent on glue.*

VI

Now: assembling the shards of what happened after those desperate last words, *Don't know yet, don't know yet!* Following Paul Johnson's mail plane, Captain Fry heads northwest, ninety degrees off course, in search of a way out of the murk and light rain icing the wings and beginning to shut down his instruments and radio, everything happening rapidly; the trimotor catches the tailings of the cyclonic cloud, and the laden plywood wings begin to vibrate, the stress on the spar immense; the cabin fabric shudders terribly, and port-side passengers watch the wing tip flutter ever farther and faster until it appears to be flapping, and their terror — that fear of the novice air traveler of a wing falling off — is unspeakable: and then a loud, shattering report, and half the left wing is gone, severed as squarely as if this black mayhem of a cloud concealed massive shears: the plane turns over violently: cries of the helpless men, engines going silent, the hiss of wind, the ship turning over again: upside down, the five-hundred-foot plunge begun, Niner-Niner-Easy falls into the prairie snow.

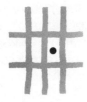

On the Town: From the Life and Opinions of Sam Wood, with Commentary (I)

THE HIGH-NOON WAGON

This is happening in north-central Ohio in 1849, and the young white man coming down the road in his four-horse wagon is about to put his cargo and himself at risk with a dangerous and rash yet logical boldness, but the young schoolteacher he is soon to meet — who will be standing in front of the small farmhouse with the decorative tomato plants (she knows them to be poisonous) — will say some forty years later when she lives in Cottonwood Falls, Kansas, *I think if I could have looked forward and seen what was in the future, I should have shrunk from it.*

It is nearly noon, and the dust rises from the slow revolution of the wagon wheels as they press into the road from the burden lying covered by canvas. Sometimes the canvas moves as the load shifts, and sometimes it speaks softly to curse the road or the entrapped heat, and after every curse comes a shushing, and the burden goes still and jostles on another mile, mute and motionless. The young driver, as if addressing his team, calls a word of encouragement, and he sits surprisingly relaxed as if he wished for an encounter, a confrontation that will draw life right to the edge. The wagon jolts, the burden grumbles, and the driver calls, *Steady!* as if the horses were doing other than plodding in sweating silence. A man can be hanged for carrying such cargo, freightage most carriers transport only in the dead of night.

Then: five horsemen, armed, ride up to block the wagon. They are hunting runaway slaves who have crossed the Ohio River and are heading north. One of the riders, the largest, says in a calm that reveals sureness and strength, *What've you got in that there wagon?* The driver turns to look at his humped cargo as if to remind himself, and then he faces directly into the squint of the big horseman and says, *I got me here a load of runaway niggers.* The riders are used to men quailing before them, and such effrontery is a surprise. One aims a pistol at the canvas and pretends to shoot it, and the men laugh and ride away, and the wagon rolls on, and the burden remains dead-still. It is not the last time the driver will speak the truth and be taken for a liar.

The wagon groans up into the yard of William Lyon, whose farmhouse is a station on the Ohio underground railroad. Lyon, a Presbyterian, has been called before a session of his church for his abolitionist work. He knows the wagon driver, Samuel Newitt Wood, twenty-four years old, a Quaker whose parents are also fervid abolitionists; Wood is not a large fellow, weighing but 130 pounds, handsome in a boyish way, his hair deeply brown and thick; he habitually fixes his gaze on people and evaluates them so intensely that he unnerves them. He looks at Lyon's petite and pretty daughter: her hair parted and drawn back, she stands beside the tomato plants with the lovely fruit she is afraid to eat. Her father uncovers the sweating burden of ten blacks and hurries them from the wagon, out of the high-noon sun and into hiding, and he comments on the risk of transporting runaways in daylight, but Wood believes in frontal challenge and the logic of the unexpected. He is a man whose conscience is not a shield but a weapon. The daughter, Margaret, a relative of Stephen Foster, hums as if her mind is far, far away and not listening to Wood tell of facing down the slavers with a misunderstood truth that saved him and the blacks. Years later in Chase County, she will tell her granddaughter, *I said to myself, there's a brave man — and a smart one. I'll catch him if I can.*

First Commentary   In May of 1854, Congress passed the Kansas-Nebraska bill, which repealed the 1820 Missouri Compromise, legislation permitting that state to draw up a pro-slavery constitution while outlawing slavery north of about the thirty-sixth latitude. The Kansas-Nebraska Act permitted settlers of those two territories to decide for themselves whether or not to allow slavery, Congress assuming Nebraska would become free soil and Kansas, heavily influenced by neighboring Missouri, would go to the pro-slavery faction, thereby keeping a national balance between North and South. Thomas Jefferson's *firebell in the night* was ringing again, and this time it would not go silent until eleven years later at Appomattox Court House, Virginia.

THE SAM CLOON

This is in Mount Gilead, Ohio, 1854: one evening Sam Wood comes home to Margaret, his wife of four years, and their two sons. He works in a law office and is about to be admitted to the bar. Although he has only a common-school education, he has discovered he can get on a porch or stump and make speeches that people will listen to, his command of anecdote more useful than rhetorical flourishes. He is a mixture of fire and frost, passion and logic, impulsiveness and vision, and he can at once mock and take mockery. He likes politics and spends much time campaigning for anti-slavery candidates, and he has little interest in leaving for the California goldfields as others here are doing; Margaret says, *Always he is reading, studying, trying to get new ideas of government.*

This evening he comes home and begins talking about the Kansas-Nebraska bill and how he sees it as a federally sanctioned means to extend slavery into the West, and then he says without warning, *As soon as that bill is passed, I'm going to Kansas*, and Margaret sits quietly, not surprised really, and she knows that she must always expect things like this from Sam Wood, and she knows that, while he likes jokes that flush into the open a person's character, he is not joking now. He asks, *What will you do?* She understands what he wants her to say, and she realizes he does not want to take her from the safety of Ohio to the tall prairie country of the border ruffians along the Missouri-Kansas line, just now the most dangerous place in the nation. Their boys are one and two years old. Margaret says, *If you're going, then I'm going too.*

On the thirtieth of May, President Pierce signs the bill, and one week later Sam and Margaret and sons have sold out and are in a wagon headed for Cincinnati: of that June morning, Margaret will say later, *The birds sang and the flowers bloomed, and the long, slender branches of the beeches seemed waving a farewell as the little family passed, going to the front, where the forces of freedom and slavery were soon to be marshaled for mortal combat.*

At Cincinnati the family boards the steamboat *Sultana* for Louisville, where they change for passage to Missouri. (Nine years later the *Sultana* will sink in the Mississippi and drown more than fifteen hundred prisoners of war just released from Andersonville and Cahaba prisons.) The going is easy. At St. Louis they get on a crowded packet, the *Sam Cloon*, and head up the dark Missouri. Passengers at first talk about the dangers — snags and sawyers and sandbars — but, once well under way, they speak of their expectations. Aboard is a contingent of Mormons heading for Kanesville, Iowa, where they will start their thousand-mile walk to the new settlement on the Great Salt Lake. Margaret watches after the boys, and Sam is all about, strolling on board almost as many miles as the boat travels up the Missouri, and especially he questions the Mormon leader, Orson Pratt, one of Joseph Smith's twelve apostles and his intellectual editor and proselytizer, sometimes called *the gauge of philosophy*, who is doing for Mormons what Wood wants to do for the Free State cause. He asks Pratt many questions about the western country.

Word comes that three passengers are ill, and, within hours, more travelers develop headaches and diarrhea, and they vomit often, bringing up something that looks like rice water, a fearful and telltale sign. Their thirsts are unquenchable, they become hollow-eyed, their skin wrinkles as if they were aging a year for every half hour, and their legs cramp, and the contractions move up to their arms and hands, and they collapse, and some slip into comas. Within hours of his first symptoms, a man dies, and then another. The passengers begin to panic, clamoring to be let off the death boat, but the river towns do not let such packets dock. Only two men are both hale and bold enough to aid the sick: Orson Pratt, who has encountered the disease on the overland trail, and Sam Wood, who has never seen cholera. He holds the head of a woman, wipes her forehead, gives her water, but she dies before him, and he moves to help another traveler. No one has the prescribed cholera medicines: pills compounded of opium, camphor, cayenne pepper, and calomel, or a rectal injection solution of sugar of lead, laudanum, and gum arabic. By the time the *Sam Cloon* reaches Independence, some of the ill have begun to recover, and Sam and Margaret and sons are well and now baptized in the dangerous waters of the border country.

Second Commentary   Across the border from Westport, Missouri, Sam Wood began reconnoitering in Kansas. Day after day he encountered pro-slavery ruffians who told stories of maimed and lynched abolitionists trying to take up residence in the territory, a place now called Bleeding Kansas even before John Brown's arrival. Sam, young and ignorant of the frontier, for a while kept his peace and listened to the rant and bully of the border ruffians, and he continued exploring. Some forty miles from Westport, well into Kansas, he climbed a huge, flattish, treeless hill and looked over the country: below, cutting a broad and backward S across the prairie lay the Oregon Trail, then called the California Road, and where it passed close to the Kaw River was a lone and unfinished log house that would soon be the first building in Lawrence; the great hill, Mount Oread, was to become the campus of Kansas University. Three miles west of the lone cabin, Wood took a claim on the California Road below the hill and set up a "house" with a roof of prairie hay and walls made from blankets and wagon-top canvas.

The family had been in the territory less than a month when Sam began writing letters to eastern newspapers to encourage settlement by opponents of slavery, people who could counter immigrants the pro-slavery men were pushing into Kansas. He continually appealed to a person's sense of justice *and* desire to make a profitable new life. He concluded one letter to Washington, D.C.: *Say to free men,* "*Come on, secure a home, and assist in this great struggle between Slavery and Freedom!*" He castigated the Methodist Shawnee Mission near Westport for the hypocrisy of trying to Christianize Indians while keeping Negro slaves; and, always, he talked the practical facts of Kansas: soils, minerals, climate, diseases, and he listed boat fares and claim fees, and he called for somebody to bring a printing press. He said:

> *Emigrants must expect to meet some hardships. We have no fine houses to receive you in; everything is inconvenient yet; settlers are generally of the right kind, with pioneer hearts. Society is good; we are all sociable, accommodating, and the person who now has the will, and meets these difficulties, and gets his choice of the land, will never regret it. Were I in Ohio today, with my knowledge of Kansas, I should lose no time in coming here, pitching my tent, building a cabin, and preparing for living. Understand me, I urge no one to come; for, as in all new countries, many chicken-hearted ones will get home-sick and leave. But if you have made up your minds and are coming, now is the time.*

Wood's letters and his increasing unwillingness to keep silent in front of ruffians made him notorious only weeks after arriving, and the pro-slavery secret societies, called Blue Lodges, began talking about him as trouble, and to this dark and dangerous fame he became addicted.

ELI THAYER AND LEMONADE

Sam Wood is returning from Westport, that ruffian cockpit, where he goes once a week to get supplies and mail and to read the eastern newspapers. This morning he heard men speak in anger about Eli Thayer of Massachusetts and his New England Emigrant Aid Company that is beginning to promote anti-slavery settlement of Kansas. East of the Wakarusa River, really a creek, Sam loses his light on the way home and pulls up to make camp. He builds a fire, eats a small meal, and, to amuse himself, he peels a square in the trunk of an old elm, and he carves:

ELI THAYER CLAIMS 20 MI SQ
THIS THE CENTER
FOR EMIGRANT AID SOCIETY

When he returns to Westport days later, he hears rumors that Thayer is in the territory and staking out land. With Daniel Anthony, his abolitionist friend, Wood stops in a grocery for a cup of water. A half-dozen armed men lounge about the store, one of them near a handbill offering a thousand dollars for the capture of Thayer, dead or alive. Wood reads aloud the poster and asks the men, *Do you endorse this?* and they say they do, and he asks, *Would you arrest Thayer if you could find him?* You goddamn bet, they say. *Well*, says Sam, *you can make a thousand dollars very easily*, and he places his hands on his eight-inch revolvers, and he says, *I am Eli Thayer — take me if you can.* The ruffians straighten but no one steps forward, and Wood and a dumbfounded Anthony leave.

As stories of Sam's provocations spread, especially after he throws to the floor a large ruffian blocking his exit from the Westport post office, some of his fellow abolitionists find the Quaker's behavior uncharacteristic and threatening to a peaceful settlement. On a later summer trip to Westport, Wood loses his friend Roff, and goes in search and finds him in a saloon. Sam steps to the bar and orders lemonade for the sixteen men there, and they come up to drink, and he says, *My apologies for treating you only to lemonade, but I never drink anything stronger. Still, I claim the right to propose a toast,* and the men assent. Roff is getting edgy knowing Wood is up to something, and Sam raises his glass and says, *Here's to Kansas and a Free State!* Roff looks at the surprised men, and then they all cheer.

Soon after, Wood writes to the *National Era* in Washington:

> *I was much mistaken in the character of the Missourians. A few* fanatics, *who were resolved to extend slavery at all hazards, seem for the time being to give tone to the whole people; but a better acquaintance convinces me that a great majority of the people condemn the violent resolutions of Westport and other places. But the die is cast. Westport will be another Alton. Blood is in her heart. . . .*
>
> *"Do you apprehend any serious difficulty with the slavehold-ers?" is frequently asked. I answer,* no; *although they have boasted and threatened much, yet they are not fools, and well know the shedding of* Northern *blood to sustain slavery here, would raise a storm that would end only with slavery itself. Northern men need not fear; all they have to do, is to be true to themselves, and not, coward-like, knuckle to the demands of these slaveholders, and padlock their lips, and "wait till the proper time to meet the question." Now is the proper time — now is the time that slaveholders are moving heaven and earth to establish slavery here; and now is the time, like men, we should meet them, and not, like cowards, cry, "Hush, be quiet; don't agitate the question* now; *wait till we are stronger."*

Third Commentary   Sam Wood left his claim on the California Road, and that autumn in Lawrence he built a home of split tim-ber — the first frame house in town — albeit only fourteen by six-teen feet (but having a wooden floor), a single room with a loft and a narrow stair that bowed under a climber. As all their homes would be the rest of their life together, the Woods' place was the ganglion of radical activity, and in this little house (on what is today Massa-chusetts Street, the main thoroughfare of Lawrence) as many as twenty people might be bedded down, and Sam's invitations were for a night, a week, a month, or what suited the traveler. The place became a station on the Kansas underground railroad: one evening a woman, escaping from a slaver down on the Marais des Cygnes River, came in, her back torn as if it were old muslin, her exhaustion her only analgesic; Margaret Wood treated the welts and lacera-tions, and she wept at the woman's agony, and she said, *Oh God, what would I do if this were my sister!*

Sam practiced a little law (defense counsel in the first murder trial in the territory), became justice of the peace, speculated in real estate as did the other town founders, and he joined John Speer in operating the *Kansas Tribune,* the first of seven newspapers he would own or edit, all of them, like their competition, primarily defenders of political and economic views; Wood attacked opponents with a rough sarcasm and sometimes facts, and from them he received the same with added flam and outright bangers. Accused of this and that, he usually ignored lies, overlooked his adversaries picturing him a treasonous, grafting coward: but even today Kansans have not yet sifted the truth of his contributions from the twaddle of lesser men who publicly reviled him.

Throughout his life, Sam Wood was relentless and bold in his beliefs, first opposing slavery, later advocating universal suffrage, and always fighting political graft; for a third of a century he was probably the most contentious man in eastern Kansas (Margaret once said were he locked in a room alone, he'd have a dispute with himself), yet, forever a believer in judicial process, he was never a hater, never a John Brown. A few years before his death Wood challenged the local nineteenth-century opinion of the man:

> *I now give it my deliberate judgment that John Brown never did any good in Kansas; that we would have been better off if he had never come to the state. His object was war, not peace. It was his constant aim to produce a collision between the Free State men and the government, which would have wiped us out in Kansas as effectually as he and his band were wiped out in [West] Virginia. There cannot be any question to a man who knew Brown as I did, that he was crazy or rather had that religious delusion that he was another Gideon, or rather, a chosen instrument in the hands of God to accomplish a great work. He died as the fool dieth, and for one I was willing to let his soul go marching on. But to have him thrust down this generation as ever being of any benefit to Kansas is an insult to the men who made Kansas free.*

MOONLIGHT RIFLES
AND GUNPOWDER GIRDLES

Ten miles south of Lawrence, Monday afternoon, November, 1855: some ninety men mill around the cabin of Franklin Coleman, a pro-slavery emigrant who has shot in the back his neighbor Charles Dow, a Free State man; the body has lain in the dirt most of the day, and Coleman has been taken into friendly custody by a zealous pro-slavery postmaster, Samuel "Bogus" Jones, recently appointed sheriff by authority the Free Soilers do not recognize. (A contemporary, John Gihon, described Bogus: *His complexion is cadaverous and his features irregular and unprepossessing. His eye is small, and when in repose, dull and unmeaning.*)

The crowd moils, yells threats, calls for retribution, and someone throws a torch against the cabin. Sam Wood and others smother the flames, and Wood climbs onto Coleman's fence and shouts to the men: *Arson and murder are the avocations of our enemies! You all know that any house here is too scarce to be burned! Don't disgrace this meeting! Don't burn the house! Do you agree?* There are still calls for a torching, but other voices shout down arson, and the crowd begins to disperse though unsatisfied. It is clear the Kansas troubles are a bed of dry tinder.

Wood then heads toward Lawrence but his pony gives out, so he stops at Jim Abbott's to rest it. While they are at supper, a rider comes in and says Bogus Jones and a ruffian posse are moving toward the Wakarusa to arrest Jacob Branson, who has retrieved Dow's body and threatened Coleman's pro-slavery friends. Wood and Abbott must walk a half mile to get fresh horses, and then they take off to warn Branson, but it's too late: the posse has him, and Wood thinks the old man will be executed. In search, he and Abbott ride into the dark prairie but cannot pick up any traces, and they return to Abbott's, where the messenger has gathered thirteen men. They open a box of eight Sharps rifles and load them; three of the Free Soilers have no guns. About two in the morning, someone hears the sound of horses far down the road, and the men hurry into the night to block the lane, and the unarmed ones take from Abbott's woodpile heavy sticks that they hope will pass for rifles in the moonlight. The posse rides up but sees the trap too late and cannot shy around the lines. With much cursing, Bogus calls out, *What's up!* and Wood answers, *That's what we'd like to know!* and asks whether Branson is there, and Bogus says he has the prisoner, and Wood calls to the old man, *If you want to be among your friends, come over here!* The posse threatens to shoot Branson, and a Free Stater shouts, *Shoot and be damned!* and Wood says, *Gentlemen, fire one gun at Mister Branson, and not a man of you will be left alive.* The old fellow rides cautiously over and dismounts, and

Wood takes the bridle of the mule and gives it a whack and says, *Go back to your friends.*

The sheriff shouts, *My name is Jones, and I have a warrant to arrest old man Branson!* and Wood calls, *We know of no Sheriff Jones in Kansas — we only know of a postmaster in Missouri named Jones.* Bogus says he has a warrant, and Wood answers, *If you must arrest him, go at it. I'm Branson's attorney. Let me see the warrant.* Jones says he does not need to show it. Six more Free State men ride up and shift the balance, and the Kansans move away with Branson, leaving Bogus (John Gihon will say later) *mad with anger and loudly vaporing in the road.* Jones goes off to report to the governor that open rebellion has begun.

The next day in Lawrence, Wood's action alarms some citizens and they are reluctant to endorse it, hoping to avoid giving any pretext for a long-threatened attack on the town. Wood volunteers to get arrested in order to try in the Supreme Court the right of Missouri to make laws for Kansas Territory. The citizens meet and reject Sam's idea; Jacob Branson offers to leave the area, but they say no to that also. Wood points out that the rescue was bloodless, but a Boston immigrant says, *I guess the tea's been dumped into the harbor again.* The townsmen talk and finally draft a wordy and Latinate resolution protesting the lack of properly constituted law in the territory and pledging themselves to resistance.

Over the next five days, more than two thousand armed pro-slavers come into Kansas, a large number of them surround Lawrence, and the residents begin digging trenches and drilling in ranks. On a December afternoon, Lois Brown, wife of the editor of the *Herald of Freedom,* visits Margaret Wood in the little slab-sided house. Jim Lane, leader of the defenders, comes in most disturbed about the small ammunition supply, and Mrs. Brown says her father has hidden a keg of powder on his place twelve miles south on the Santa Fe Road. But Lane knows, even at night, men cannot get through the blockade. Lois and Margaret volunteer to go.

The next morning the women put knitting and a large medical book in their baskets, and they climb into a little one-horse cracky wagon and set off accompanied by soldiers to the edge of town, and the ladies head south past the ruffian camps. Two miles along, pickets halt them and ask questions, and Lois inquires how to find a Mr. Burge, a pro-slaver living near her father, and the riders give directions and let them proceed. The women move slowly, stopping only to pick up an empty whiskey bottle they plan to fill with milk.

Mrs. Brown's mother feeds them a meal and gives them two pillow slips, one of which they load with gunpowder and then tie under Lois' long and full dress, giving her the roundness of pregnancy. They go on to the Abbott place, scene of the Branson rescue, and wait for a man to unearth a trunk: from it they fill the other pillowcase with more powder and some ammunition. Caps, cartridges, bullet molds, and gun wipes they stuff into pockets, sleeves, and waistbands; bars of lead they slip upright into their heavy stockings. The small women waddle to the wagon, but, gravid with explosives, they are unable to hoist themselves onto the seat and must be lifted up.

They ride back across the Wakarusa and work to resist their impulse to move fast. A few miles out, two scouts stop them, one man taking a position behind them, his rifle at the ready, the other alongside to look into the wagon bed: he finds only knitting, a medical book, and a bottle of milk, and to these young wives obviously in the family way, he says, *Excuse me ladies, but we thought you were men, and we have orders to let no man pass this road into Lawrence.* The scouts consult, the women moving along slowly, pretending boredom, and then the riders wave and abruptly gallop away; once out of sight, Margaret and Lois can no longer restrain their tension, and they roll fast into Lawrence, and the people come out into Massachusetts Street to cheer them. The ladies must be lifted out of the wagon, and an unknowing fellow will say later, *When I saw those women, I just allowed that bustles had come into fashion again for they were swelled out awful.* They go inside to shed garments and armaments, and they learn a man has just been killed crossing through the lines.

That night a strong north wind comes up and blows down tents of the ruffians, some of them taking shelter with people they came to fight. The next morning many of them begin packing up, and soon the governor, seeing the resolve and arms of the Free Staters, formally recognizes their militia, and the ruffians withdraw. This so-called Wakarusa War (which some Kansans will later consider the first engagement of the Civil War), with no battle and but a single man shot down, has been precipitated by Sam Wood's bloodless rescue partly accomplished by moonlight rifles of sticks and helped to conclusion by Margaret's gunpowder girdle. Having achieved a tottery truce that will soon collapse, the citizens ask Wood to leave for a while, and he walks to Topeka and then goes east to recruit settlers. Sarah Robinson, wife of the future first state governor, writes in her diary:

Mrs. Wood, whose husband has ever been most active in the free-state cause, and for whom the enemy feel no little bitterness, has offered her little "shake" cabin, next the hotel, for the general use. Daily and nightly the ladies meet there, in the one room, with its loose open floor, through which the wind creeps, to make cartridges, their nimble fingers keeping time with each heartbeat for freedom, so enthusiastic are they in aiding the defence.

Elk

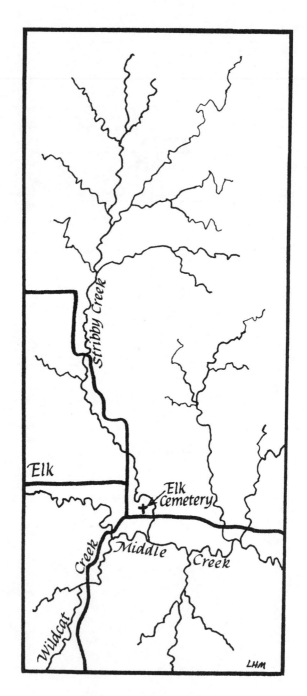

ELK QUADRANGLE

From the Commonplace Book:
Elk

Unfortunately for good history, the general public has overlooked the ephemeral, the sensational, and the pathological features of the short-lived cowboy boom days.

> — James C. Malin,
> "An Introduction to the History of the
> Bluestem-Pasture Region of Kansas"
> (1942)

Sentimental illlusions are not a good basis for national creeds, and certainly the creed of the West has been among the most sentimental of all.

> — Richard Bernstein,
> "Unsettling the Old West" (1990)

The Romans read places like faces, as outward revelations of living inner spirit. Each place (like each person) had its individual Genius — which might manifest itself, on occasion, as a snake.

> — Charles W. Moore et al.,
> The Poetics of Gardens (1988)

Land speculation here [in Kansas] is about the only business in which a man can embark with no other capital than an easy conscience.

> — Horace Greeley,
> An Overland Journey (1859)

We must allow for the possibility that we can only understand something truly by knowing its future, its fruits, its consequence.

> — Frederick Turner,
> "A Field Guide to the Synthetic
> Landscape" (1988)

Only the growth of a global appreciation for our common human past will wipe out assumptions that a site belongs to the person who temporarily owns the land above it.

> — Ellen Herscher,
> "A Future in Ruin" (1989)

We're only now learning that there's yet another, concealed danger in indiscriminately altering the environment: by inadvertently severing connectedness and thus dulling some of our own awareness, we can begin systematically ignoring our surroundings without quite realizing that our alertness has faltered; we can damage our natural systems; we can put our own safety and health in peril.

> — Tony Hiss,
> "Encountering the Countryside"
> (1989)

Now that some veils are being lifted on national-security obscurity, indications are that military facilities are major sources of toxic pollution. Military activity, it appears, has been undermining security of a physical kind, in the name of protecting the metaphysical kind contemplated by geopolitical threat assessors.

> — Wade Greene,
> "An Idea Whose Time Is Fading"
> (1990)

History is lived in the main by the unknown and forgotten.

> — Arthur M. Schlesinger, Jr.,
> Introduction to *Pioneer Women* (1981)

The dead take their names with them out of the world.

> — N. Scott Momaday,
> *The Way to Rainy Mountain* (1969)

The angels in marble make it impossible to imagine back to life the bones that are buried at their feet. Inflexibly benign, they point to heaven. . . . The historian should stay away, lest he be convinced against his will of the futility of any attempt to bring back to memory the forgotten men whose mortality on earth is here proclaimed in letters of stone.

> — Helen Hooven Santmyer,
> *Ohio Town* (1963)

Life extended into death, and vice versa. Death was not the natural end of life but one phase of an infinite cycle. Life, death, and resurrection were stages of a cosmic process which repeated itself continuously.

> — Octavio Paz,
> *The Labyrinth of Solitude* (1959)

The language of birds is very ancient, and, like other ancient modes of speech, very elliptical: little is said, but much is meant and understood.

> — Gilbert White,
> *The Natural History and Antiquities
> of Selborne* (1778)

Brave Buffalo said: "I have noticed in my life that all men have a liking for some special animal, tree, plant, or spot of earth. If men would pay more attention to these preferences and seek what is best to do in order to make themselves worthy of that toward which they are so attracted, they might have dreams which would purify their lives. Let a man decide upon his favorite animal and make a study of it, learning its innocent ways. Let him learn to understand its sounds and motions. The animals want to communicate with man, but Wakan-tanka does not intend they shall do so directly — man must do the greater part in securing an understanding."

> — Frances Densmore,
> *Teton Sioux Music* (1918)

The most important requisite in describing an animal is to be sure and give its character and spirit, for in that you have, without error, the sum and effect of all its parts, known and unknown. You must tell what it is to man. Surely the most important part of an animal is its anima, its vital spirit, on which is based its character and all the peculiarities by which it most concerns us. Yet most scientific books which treat of animals leave this out altogether, and what they describe are as it were phenomena of dead matter.

> — Henry David Thoreau,
> *The Journal* (1860)

[Harrier] flight has the notionateness of prairie winds, and the sudden detour as a change of mind, a leap straight on, and then a notionate, abrupt change in direction as if he had just bought wings and were trying what sort of wings they were.

> — William A. Quayle,
> *The Prairie and the Sea* (1905)

E. H. Forbush (1927) says: "As [the harrier] bounds up and down in the air, it seems to move more like a rubber ball than a bird."

> — Arthur Cleveland Bent,
> *Life Histories of North American
> Birds of Prey*, Part I (1937)

A few years ago the freight wagons and oxen passing through Council Grove were counted by the thousands, the value of merchandise by millions. But the shriek of the iron horse has silenced the lowing of the panting ox and the old Trail looks desolate. The track of the commerce of the plains has changed and with the change is destined to come other changes better and more blessed.

> — Editorial,
> *Junction City Union* (1867)

The most famous spring in Kansas ought to be a state shrine.

> — Kate L. Gregg,
> *The Road to Santa Fe* (1952)

We believe it to our interest to discourage the settlement of free negroes in Kansas. The two races never have, and never can associate together on terms of equality. But at the same time, if we have got to have them here, we would have them educated; we are opposed to ignorance in every shape.

> — Samuel Newitt Wood,
> *Kansas Press* (1859)

I advocate "negro suffrage" not because they are black, not because they are of the male sex, but because they are human beings and entitled to all the rights of other human beings. If women are not human beings, then they are not entitled to the rights of human beings; but if you once raise them above the brute creation and admit them to be human beings, that ends the argument.

> — Samuel Newitt Wood,
> *Emporia News* (1867)

I did what I believed right at the time, with the light that I then had, and I have no apology to make to the present or to posterity for the part I took. I concede some honesty of purpose to others. If any erred, let us throw the mantle of charity over their acts, for not until we reach that better country to which we are one by one surely emigrating and in which [we] will be emigrants and not pioneers, will the motives of all, and the whole work of the pioneers of Kansas, be justly estimated.

> — Samuel Newitt Wood,
> Kansas Historical Society address
> (1886)

Much of the best legislation of the state was originated by [Sam Wood], especially such as protects the poor and the rights of women and children.

> — Editorial,
> *Lawrence Jeffersonian* (1891)

They call Kansas the "Sunflower State," not because it is overrun with the noxious weed, but because, as the sunflower turns on its stem to catch the first beams of the morning sun, and with its broad disk and yellow rays follows the great orb of the day, so Kansas turns to catch the first rays of every advancing thought or civilized agency, and with her broad prairies and golden fields welcomes and follows the light.

> — Editorial,
> *Burlington (Kansas) Nonpareil* (1887)

For a generation Kansas has been the testing-ground for every experiment in morals, politics, and social life. Doubt of all existing institutions has been respectable. Nothing has been venerable or revered merely because it exists or has endured. Prohibition, female suffrage, fiat money, free silver, every incoherent and fantastic dream of social improvement and reform, every economic delusion that has bewildered the foggy brains of fanatics, every political fallacy nurtured by misfortune, poverty, and failure, rejected elsewhere, has here found tolerance and advocacy. The enthusiasm of youth, the conservatism of age, have alike yielded to the contagion, making the history of the State a melodramatic series of cataclysms in which tragedy and comedy have contended for mastery, and the convulsions of Nature have been emulated by the catastrophes of society. There has been neither peace, tranquility, nor repose.

Kansas was the prologue to a tragedy whose epilogue has not yet been pronounced; the prelude to a fugue of battles whose reverberations have not yet died away.

— John James Ingalls,
"Kansas: 1541–1891" (1892)

The belief that Kansas was founded for a cause distinguishes it, in the eyes of its inhabitants, as preeminently the home of freedom. It lifts the history of the state out of the commonplace of ordinary westward migration and gives to the temper of the people a certain elevated and martial quality. The people of Iowa or Nebraska are well enough, but their history has never brought them in touch with cosmic processes. The Pilgrims themselves are felt to have been actuated by less noble and altruistic motives. . . . This may smack of prejudice, but it is no heresy in Kansas. The trained and disinterested physiocratic historian will tell us that such statements are unsupported by the documents. The documents show, he will say, that the Kansas emigrants, like other emigrants, came for cheap land and in the hope of bettering their condition; the real motive was economic, as all historic motives are; the Kansas emigrant may have thought he was going to Kansas to resist oppression, but in reality he went to take up a farm.

The frontier develops strong individuals, but it develops individuals of a particular type, all being after much the same pattern. The individualism of the frontier is one of achievement, not of eccentricity.

— Carl Becker,
"Kansas" (1910)

Seldom has a community with so much vibrant idealism in its soul, so much creative potential in its mind, become so thickly encrusted with petty bourgeois mediocrity.

— Kenneth S. Davis,
Kansas: A Bicentennial History (1976)

In the Quadrangle: Elk

That many pioneers came into the American West with a pair of horses' asses directly before them is not a consideration of either historian or ordinary citizen but, so a fellow from Topeka told me one evening in the Strong City café, for a person taking one of the Flint Hills covered-wagon trips occasionally sold to tourists, farting and manuring horse rumps sweating a few feet away will be a significant part of the view from the wagon seat. I struck up a conversation when I saw him underline with purple ink and a pocket ruler a sentence in *Kansas History*, the journal of the state historical society. He was a civil engineer, squarish and short, a friendly man of pronounced opinions: after he put a good squirt from the plastic lemon into his iced tea and took a sip, he said, *I'll be damned if I couldn't eat three lemons and pee out a better juice than this.* He loved double acrostics and western history, and I think he'd read everything written on the Union Pacific Railroad. I was familiar with his arguments, but I liked his passion for them, especially his vexations about textbooks and professors.

He said, *For six generations we've given our kids a picture of the American West that's no better than the dime novels of the 1880s — nationalistic, imperialistic, romantic, and distorted till hell won't have it. Indians are either ruthless, conniving savages or noble stiffs. Pioneer men are two-fisted and upright, their women prairie madonnas. The railroads are quaint pufferbellies with lovely little whistles, tooty-toot. And what is probably the most recognizable scene of western history — two armed men facing off on a dusty street — if that ever happened, there isn't one single reliable record of it. The past we believe in is fabrication. We're informed idiots about it. The truth is, white settlers were motivated to come out here not for noble ends but self-serving, economic ones. At their worst, pioneers were genocidal and environmental exploiters encouraged by a grasping and moronic and inhumane government. And the inheritance continues.*

He had got himself exercised, and I'm afraid I abetted it when I asked whether I might jot down a few of his words. He waved his hand in what seemed to be assent and said, *The white conquest was inevitable, but that doesn't mean we have to perpetrate lies on our children. They'll understand themselves, and the threats they live under, if they can see their ancestors honestly. We harm their futures by throwing bull chips in their eyes.*

When his steak dinner arrived he kept talking, seeing the ready audience I was, although he choked once and had to pause. Projectiles of food now and then rocketed from his mouth onto me as he continued more to lecture than to swallow. He didn't blame movies, television, or popular novels for the distortions so much as a couple of generations of American historians who let the public get by with myths. *Look, these historians — they were almost all white males — they were more interested in theories than in how the butt of a horse changes the way you see things or why a certain carbine would jam and change the outcome of a battle. They were nothing more than medieval theologians deductively proving their ideas. What they gave us belongs in a Buffalo Bill Wild West show.*

He stopped to ask what I was writing down, and I complimented him on his insight and he continued, but not before snorting a particle of pickled beet onto my sleeve. *When I took that covered-wagon tour a couple of years ago, one passenger was a history prof back east, a nice guy in Hush Puppies, lots of information, but he couldn't tell a sycamore from a cottonwood, hadn't the least idea of what kind of tree to cut a wagon axle out of. He wasn't exactly sure what an ox is. He didn't know how to make hominy, hadn't ever skinned a squirrel or milked a cow — and he got paid fifty thousand a year to tell college kids about the West. A woman, an outspoken gal, asked him what the wagon-train pioneers used for toilet paper and sanitary napkins. Now I'd call that basic knowledge. He didn't know. If you'd put him in a homesteader's cabin* alone, he'd die in a month. But he told us every theory of the American frontier ever concocted.

After the waitress took away his plate, I asked him how his steak was, and he said, *I had meatloaf,* and went off again, pausing only once to pick something from a tooth (I thought, if he orders the coconut cream pie I'm moving to the next stool). He said he was glad to see a younger generation of historians working to break down nationalistic and racist and sexist myths of the West by looking at ordinary details of life and then trying to interpret them inductively. Then, *But I still haven't read anything about the realities of riding in a covered wagon for days, where you've got a pair of crapping butt ends in your face the whole way.*

He spoke about writing an account of his trip, how it changed his perception of our history and the kind of people he descended from; the title was, so he claimed, "Fair History and Farting Horses: Fundaments and Fundamentals of Our Western Passage." When I wrote that down he said, *Just so you'll know, I've copyrighted it.* I asked to read his essay when he finished it, but I've never heard from him. He continued over coffee, now taking on Kansas railroad barons, but his commentary was less heated and interesting, although it later helped me see something in the Elk quadrangle I otherwise might have overlooked.

At forty square miles — the smallest of the twelve quads — Elk has a single westward-running road that follows Middle Creek before splitting off north and south to follow two polar-trending small tributaries, Stribby and Wildcat creeks. The entire northern half, but for a single section, is without roads, and this isolated corner is a lovely reach of hollows and narrow vales dissecting the knobby land. It is a place mostly of pasturage, a good quad for getting the feel of tall prairie even if it is a bit chewed over. Because of its isolation and negligible population, much of its history has never been passed along and recorded in the Falls, the county hearth for storytelling. If you had a handful of half-dollars, you would today have enough to give one to every resident of the Elk quad. But, for about fifty years there was a village here, or at least the seeds of one, directly atop the county line so that on one side of the main street Henry Collett's general merchandise and post office sat in Chase but his blacksmith shop across the road was in Marion. Such bifurcation rarely benefits a community, and this split, dividing affairs as it did, was not good for Elk. There were never more than a dozen buildings, and nearly all of them, one by one, went down in flames (the last two, as if to close an era neatly, burned on New Year's Eve of 1930); all that you'll see today is a strip of big Osage-orange hedge along a dirt lane. When Whitt Laughridge first pointed out the site to me and said, *That's Elk,* I asked, looking right at it, Where? and I walked through the brush and still couldn't find it; later he showed me a couple of photographs of the village.

Two miles east stand the only aboveground remnants: Balch school, a fine one-room stone building (now a hay barn, the standard use here for old schoolhouses), and little Elk Cemetery, one of the prettiest in the county.

Born in London, Henry Collett, whose ancestors followed William the Conqueror into England, came into the county exactly 799 years later and walked around to find a good piece of untaken land; nine years afterward he opened a store next to his house and received a postal commission, which established the necessity for people to come into his shop. He named the settlement not for any long-gone animal but to be brief: the government required rural postmasters to cancel letters by writing the name of the post office across them; not for him the endless scrawling out some fifteen-letter town name. Collett was an astute businessman, and he made a profit from Elk, and the enterprises he set up gave a hub — a heart — to the American and German immigrants homesteading along upper Middle Creek: Collett's Gen. Mdse. and P. O. became the nexus of their lives, the single spot they all visited, the one center everyone shared. To this forum of economic and social exchange women carried barnyard and garden surplus (eggs, butter, turnips), and men brought field surplus (wheat, oats, corn). In cash-poor Elk, almost everything ran on barter. The store gave a focus of allegiance to settlers from seventeen states and seven nations and helped form them into a community where cooperation could mediate differences in language and culture.

(Digression, this from an old countian: just after World War One, when the area began declining, there was a closed-up church Elktonians used only for yuletide programs and Memorial Day services. At Christmas, a skinny Santa Claus would laugh into the small room and give six-year-old boys twenty-cent penknives and twelve-year-olds West Bend pocket watches that the boys were almost afraid to accept because of the cost: a dollar and a half, nearly two days' wages. The big cedar Christmas tree would always be left standing until practices for the Memorial Day service, when the farm children would slip behind it to pick off and eat the dusty, strung ornaments — popcorn, animal crackers — but leave the shriveled cranberries. Even after parents scolded them and threw the tree over the back fence, the children would sneak out, scare sparrows off the cedar, and again eat the decorations.)

On the north bank of Middle Creek, Collett built an icehouse, and anyone who helped cut out blocks in winter could draw a free ration in summer. His blacksmith shop would shoe an animal or fix an implement in the same day a farmer brought it in, this speed often the difference between getting a crop planted or harvested in time. Elk was the invention and expression of Henry Collett, and as his success went so did the community's progress, but, even had he lived a second life, his shrewdness could not have kept the village from dying, situated as it was in a pinfold of federal land policies, legislation that created a kind of serfdom that to this day still binds many countians. What the Cottonwood in flood did to valley towns, federal land policy did to this upland village.

Whites who entered Chase in its first half-dozen years of settlement were largely free to take whatever acreage they chose, deferring only to someone's earlier claim, but the people who arrived after the Homestead Act of 1862 were limited to a quarter-section — 160 acres — of free land they could gain patent to by building a permanent residence of specified minimal size and living in it for five continuous years (Horace Greeley wrote of one land speculator who tried to qualify by putting up a purple-martin birdhouse and reporting its dimensions as eighteen-by-twenty but leaving the agent to presume the feet.)

Most county bottomland had been claimed by 1870 through preemption or homesteading, and, to this day, valley farms are rarely more than quarter-sections. Settlers of the 1870s not only had to take their farming to the more precarious uplands but also to contend with land grants given the Santa Fe and the Missouri, Kansas, & Texas (the Katy) railroads as a kind of federal subsidy for building lines into the West. (A benefit of this program — for the county — is that it got a railroad without being long encumbered by rail bonds.) The two companies received title to thirty-eight percent of Chase, more than any other county in the Flint Hills, most of it uplands: the railroads received the odd-numbered sections, each a mile square, thereby leaving homesteaders the even-numbered pieces; around Elk the settlement pattern became a checkerboard of unconnected plots, railroads taking the black squares, homesteaders the red. Even for the rare settler who had money enough, land was hard to buy because railroad realty agents preferred selling here to big land speculators or ranching syndicates that would buy thousands of acres at a time. The people of Elk were largely locked into forty- and eighty-acre plots adequate only for subsistence farming. Young men, other than eldest sons, found it nearly impossible either to stay on the homeplace or buy neighboring land, and the consequent social disruption was serious: suddenly, the constricted rural Germany or New England that so many immigrants had come here to escape was again upon them and their generations.

At first the population around Collett's general merchandise grew and prospered — four one-room schools, a creamery, an annual neighborhood fair — and then things began to decline, partly because of irresponsible management of the shallow upland soils. There was something else: the Santa Fe and Katy finally sold two big parcels, up till then freely used as pasturage by farmers: one went to the Eastern Land and Loan Company, speculators who profiteered off railroad grants during the recession of the 1890s, commonly through lending farmers money and then foreclosing or through buying up mortgages on the cheap at sheriff's auctions. The other large parcel went to a British ranching syndicate, the Western Land and Cattle Company, headed by three men (one was the travel writer Sir William Tyrone Power, son of the Irish actor, and another Thomas Hughes, author of *Tom Brown's School Days*). The English sent their sons into the county as part of the young men's practical education. A newspaperman and former countian, Jay House, in the thirties wrote (with some exaggeration, I suspect): *Younger sons of British aristocracy were as thick around Cottonwood Falls as bass in South Fork. The county actually boasted of two or three British titles [and the] invasion had a distinct influence on the speech, intonation, and nomenclature of the county.*

People near Elk found themselves increasingly boxed in by absentee landlords whose main interest was to turn big profits, something that encouraged their buying up farmsteads. People north of Elk ended up being completely encircled by the syndicates and having to get permission to cross into the village. The British acreage, eventually comprising about twenty percent of Chase, evolved into the Diamond Ranch, named after the major creek watering it, the outflow of the renowned spring a few miles north on the old Santa Fe Trail. The ranch grew to thirty-five thousand acres before the famous 101 Ranch of Oklahoma bought it in 1900. Later, out-county Kansans purchased it and broke it into three pieces, and, to this day, nearly all of the land in the Elk quadrangle belongs to people living in cities. The largest landowner here — and in Chase — is a Texas widow whose holdings derive through her husband directly from one of the speculators of the Eastern Land and Loan Company; she owns twenty-eight square miles, nearly four percent of the county, but her ties to Chase are merely those of her local lawyer in Cottonwood. (Enclosing a letter of introduction from her Falls banker, I wrote her to ask for an interview but she returned my request with one typed sentence telling me she would not be available and did not wish to discuss her family or properties.)

Realty agent Whitt Laughridge believes nearly three quarters of the county now belongs to nonresidents, a percentage still increasing, and he says much of Chase has not for even a single day been owned by a resident. Although some of these absentees care for nothing more than the rental income, while others oversee the land with better husbandry than some natives, virtually all of the absentees take their profits out of Chase to invest elsewhere. Owners who hire local hands and buy materials in the county do, of course, make a small contribution, but the range-cattle business is neither labor- nor material-intensive: a few cowhands and salt blocks can never support Chase.

These alien landlords have little interest in the survival of county towns, condition of its roads, quality of its schools, or the acumen and honesty of its officials. Absentee dominance in this agricultural place makes it almost certain that many citizens will never be anything more than manual laborers who will live and die as hired hands, with chances for economic improvement hardly better than those of southern sharecroppers of another time. For this reason, it seems to me, making big money here is the one sin countians are slow to forgive. The nature of this landownership ulcerates the lives of many hard-working people with an insidious jealousy often turning into a meanness of spirit, an infection that gnaws at hospitality, friendship, and their sense of community; and, unquestionably, nineteenth-century federal land policies still drive out their children, especially ones with energy and imagination.

To the homesteaders who came here looking for relief from the economic and social restrictions of Europe or eastern America, such a crimping of expectations and possibilities would be depressing and bitterly ironic in this grandly open land. Surely they would curse the great Jeffersonian grid — so cage-like when seen from above or on a county plat — that has helped bring about the effectual vassalage of several hundred of their descendants in a result quite the opposite from what Jefferson had in mind when he wrote (for example): *Those who labor in the earth are the chosen people of God, if ever he had a chosen people. . . . Dependence begets subservience and venality, suffocates the germ of virtue.*

When I was in my last months of walking around Chase County, the federal government threatened to work another permutation on landownership around Elk, a turning of the wheel to bring it full circle. On the fifth of April, 1990, countians were stunned to read this headline in the *Leader-News:*

ARMY EYES CHASE FOR FT. RILEY EXPANSION.

The fort, forty miles north, is the old cavalry post where George Custer was second in command in 1867, and from it in 1890 rode the Seventh Cavalry on their way to kill two hundred Indians, half of them women and children, at Wounded Knee, South Dakota. A monument on the post describes the slaughter as *an unfortunate incident.*

Today, Fort Riley is primarily an artillery and tank training ground. The current proposal calls for the army, either here or at one of three other sites, to take by eminent domain more than eighty-two thousand acres for *maneuvers by tracked vehicles.* Thirty-six square miles of northwestern Chase may go under the tread of tanks.

Countians and other Flint Hills people, but not many absentee landlords, organized and wrote letters and editorials (a headline: HOME, HOME ON THE FIRING RANGE), their opposition virtually unanimous — if you exclude the right-wing Kansas Grassroots Association which sees a greater threat in placing a national historic monument at the Spring Hill Ranch. To many residents, the idea of turning food-producing land into a target range was insane; but, with the destruction of the Berlin Wall, many came to believe that the real future enemy of mankind was not a hammer-and-sickle soldier but a horseman called famine. The political changes in Eastern Europe in 1990 buoyed them as they saw the death of the Cold War serving to protect their prairie from tracked vehicles. But then George Bush and his industrial colleagues led America into Arabian sands, in part, some people thought, to establish a new need for tanks and weapons.

What land profiteers and railroads and foreign syndicates could not quite accomplish in Elk during the first century and a half of white settlement — the removal of people — the army now proposes to do with panzer divisions. If these Rommels of the tall prairie succeed, citizens believe, you can just about kiss goodbye the good life in Chase County. In only six generations, the history of Elk will have gone from horse fundaments to howitzer muzzles.

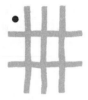

Among the Hic Jacets

Elk Cemetery, in the burr oak valley of upper Middle Creek, lies half encircled by Stribby Creek just above its juncture with the bigger stream a quarter mile to the south near where Wildcat Creek comes in. From time to time this burial ground at such a confluence of waters goes under, its location, considering all the upland surrounding it, revealing something about the settlers' unease in the grassland. The south side of the cemetery faces the road, set off from it by a low wrought-iron fence of some age, and just inside the gate is a stone carved with RUTHERFORD B. HAYES, a fifteen-year-old who died the same year as the president. A few yards northward stands an eight-foot-high shaft of gray marble commemorating the soldiers and sailors of the Civil War, a monument that went up nearly a half century after the fight ended; for some reason, people around here refer to it as *the Unknown Soldier's Grave.* Elsewhere stand or lean or lie fallen a couple of hundred other markers cut with cherubim, urns, fingers pointing aloft, and *hic jacet* biographies: a name, a pair of dates, sometimes a detail or sentiment (VATER UND MUTTER, BELOVED WIFE, RUHE IN FRIEDEN, GONE BUT NOT FORGOTTEN).

At the back of the ground, in a kind of potter's field near the soldier and sailor column, lies a flat piece of limestone, a rounded little delta that repeats the shape and orientation of the whole cemetery. The inscription, if one was ever present, is unreadable; perhaps the eroded indentations are nothing more than cuneiforms of wind and rain as if the land itself were trying to speak for whoever lies, easterly-westerly, below. I've stopped twice on late afternoons in hopes the low-angled light would pick out letters or numerals, but it hasn't worked. The nearest grave belongs to Joseph McClure, who died on the Fourth of July, 1883, at twenty-one, and the first burial here, 1871, is also close: Jabez Dart (the Christian name, reflecting his last one, means "he will cause pain").

I've said that I sometimes use cemeteries for lunch stops, where I can eat and walk and imagine the dead again above the turf by taking clues from the stones: a homemade Depression-era marker, its name etched in wet concrete by a finger; a cowhand's wooden cross hung with a horseshoe; a trainman's stone carved with a locomotive; the old miller's with a streamside mill; a grave covered with synthetic turf tacked down with golf tees, a weathered ball centered, teed up, and ready; a stone with an incised Chrysler New Yorker carrying a license plate with the wife's name: CLETA. These icons can let the dead out of the anonymous ground and set them loose in some stranger's dreamtime, but on the little limestone delta at the back of the cemetery I've found nothing like that, unless the utter poverty of the rock itself is somehow a door. After my first visit, I took to calling it the Grave of the Unknown Citizen.

At four o'clock one morning, weeks after I'd last been in Elk Cemetery, I woke from a dream, a brief thing, small and fragmentary but sharply delineated like an unearthed piece of broken platter painted with a scene: the surrounding landscape gone but the bit of image on the shard remaining bright and clear. I bring up this dream because its strange violence rupturing my sleep eventually led me on to the end of my time in the county. The topic of the dream, as I first understood it, is something I pay no attention to except perhaps to jape literal interpretations of it: the Resurrection (it's a word I even have trouble spelling, always trying to make it reserection, "things stood up"). I do, of course, believe in biological kinds of resurrecting (flesh to worm to bird to so on, and the more subtle one of genetic inclinations whereby ancestors seem to stalk our blood). If there's any other kind of journey in the beyond, it's going to expose me as a poorly packed traveler, planning as I am to go without so much as even a thought for a change of shorts. Now that I think about it, I also believe in another type of resurrection, where the living can carry along not just the legacies of the dead but also an awareness of them as people so that they, in a way, live again: Jefferson — the man — alive in township-and-range, Beethoven in a cadenza, Himmler haunting Auschwitz.

Could I have chosen the dream that night, I'd have taken a conversation with Sam Wood, or a prowl around the Brandley place the evening Frank Rinard went down, or maybe spent an hour on the masons' scaffold as they set the last course of courthouse stone. Instead I ended up in Elk Cemetery and listening to preaching (you may want to call it a nightmare): a man stood over the flat rock marking the Unknown Citizen and scraped dirt off it with the toe of his old-style countryman's boot. He was weeping yet still able to deliver a eulogy of twenty-seven words: *Lord, these are just ordinary Kansas boys, common as corn and lard. It don't seem right to make them and then go off and leave them behind.* That was it, that's when I woke and wrote it down.

Why a eulogy for someone long dead? Why *boys?* Why not boy or girl or people? With Judgment Day still ostensibly pending, how had they been left behind?

Some little time later, it came to me that maybe the dream wasn't hooked to Christian eschatology but to American history (after all, the word Lord comes from *hlaford*, literally, "bread-guardian," initially a term expressing agricultural and social arrangements). Maybe the dream was really about nourishment, death as the staff of life, perhaps an emblem about forgetfulness of source and cycle, some notion about an old cemetery becoming nothing more than a place to cast off the useless, a spiritual landfill of plastic flowers where the stones should be carved GONE BUT ALSO FORGOTTEN.

In Mexico there is a celebration called El Día de los Muertos, the Day of the Dead, deriving from prehistoric Indian rites: during it a family will picnic atop an ancestral grave, children playing with papier-mâché skeletons and cradling small gifts called *muertos* and eating chocolate femurs and tibias, fathers lounging, mothers singing softly, grandparents reminiscing, everyone sharing the repast and the past, living and dead together, the distinctions blurred, the people trying to touch time fore and aft, enter its breadth to live connectedly. To walk in an Indian-Mexican cemetery, at any time, is to see how those people fear a forgotten life, to see their belief that remembrance of the dead gives meaning to the living.

American cemeteries once lay commonly at the heart of a town, to serve as parks for contemplation (hence the abundant variations of *Think on me as you pass by*) about responsibilities necessary for continuation — about resurrection, if you like. But, by the time citizens laid out Elk Cemetery, ideas were changing, machine-age separations beginning to press in, so that the burial ground lies removed from the village, as if residents were thinking, *If I am here, death belongs out there.* They do not seem to have considered that the untwisting of death from life is an unraveling of the whole skein. It's as if they wanted to live without the awareness they would die. They seemed to ignore how the future, from day to day, is mostly remembrance.

When I was next in the county, I went back up to Elk Cemetery for another try at deciphering the eroded stone. I made a rubbing of it, and at last I thought I could make out E — S — RO — . That night I sat with the *Chase County Historical Sketches,* four volumes of nearly two thousand pages of testimony about life here, written by the countians themselves (literate expression declines from the first collection, of 1940, to the last in 1984, another manifestation of forgetfulness). I turned pages in search of — whom? Erastus Roe? Effie S. Roberts? I wasn't coming up with anything plausible, and I kept getting sidetracked in the details of the early countians' lives. Then it struck me that maybe I was, after all, finding somebody under that worn rock. I took out paper and copied down details that seemed to compose themselves into a man, a woman:

he: came into the county from New York Pennsylvania Illinois in 1859 1860 1865 rode with John Brown and took a minié ball at Pea Ridge and got captured at Chickamauga and sent to Libby Prison (so crowded there the men had to sleep on their sides on the floor and when the hardness became too much they would all turn at the same time on a signal from a leader) had to survive Libby by getting food from prisoners too near death to eat (in 1892 took the train from Chase to Chicago to see the Columbian Exposition and oh god stunned to turn a corner and find himself again in front of the nightmare the three-story brick prison reconstructed there and with his wife walked through it crowded as before and not able to believe what was happening);

heard that Lincoln once said *If I went west I think I would go to Kansas* and came into the county with a soldier's warrant for 160 acres;

she: came into the county in 1858 1861 1866 from Ohio Indiana Missouri (her youngest brother sixteen put creek stones in his boots to make himself tall enough to enlist but got no farther than Fort Leavenworth and died of pneumonia and a friend took Billy's hat and wore it at Second Manassas) came with her father by ox team with a brace of cooped chickens in the wagon and the going slow because of the milch cow tied behind and the four beeves herded along and nothing so bad as fording creeks infernal muddy banks

and had to lay tallgrass under the wheels and followed the Santa Fe
Trail to the Grove and down the old Kaw Trail;

whenever he saw an approaching prairie fire always thought how
it looked like a line of battle and got burned when one jumped the
neighbors' guard and took his pole barn and before that no rain for
eighteen months and the Cottonwood went dry and sloughgrass
covered the riverbed and won't-mention-who let a fire get loose and
it came right up the river like a flood and of course the earthquake
two years after the war and he was laying up a roof beam in the new
barn and the rumbling commencing to shake the timber and he
running to the cabin for her and she holding on to the wall and what
a racket the furniture was in;

she said about the cabin logs *the gaps was big enough you could
nearly throw a cat through them* and the door only a hung rug and
she said *the wind would come through and blow out the grease
lamp* nothing but a saucer of animal fat with a flannel rag twisted
on a nail;

sometimes the Kaw passed by and stopped to look through the
gaps and once to make friends she held a mirror up to a gap and
scared tarnation out of a painted brave and then there was laughter
like you wouldn't believe and they took turns gaping into it and
admired and chortled and thereafter when passing always stopping
to use the mirror;

(down on Cedar Creek the Kaws came out to see that new French
woman and the husband saying she was gone but the pesky redskins
waiting around and he bolted the door and hid her between two
feather mattresses for three days and took his meals on the bed so
he could slip food to her and she getting up only after dark to answer
nature's calls);

walking home one noon with her youngest and caught in a thunderstorm and ducked into an encampment and Kaw women mocked
her drenching and laughed at her baby and later he had to remind
her how she'd said she'd rather take her chances with Indians than
border ruffians (not she that woman complaining about moving on
west because there'd already been enough pioneering in Ioway) later
she saying *I never complained — I was the one wanting to come
west* and proud she never took her children out to hide in some
creek-bank hole and she wasn't the woman who heard coyotes
howling and then skulked all night in a cold thicket to escape
"Indian attack";

(didn't the children gracious sakes alive love the terror of Kaw
visits);

learning after a few years they'd settled on a railroad grant and had to abandon their place and build again just another burden to bear but not so bad as her brother's — filed on land some miles southwest but decided it was worthless and gave it up and three years later a town founded on his old claim (called Wichita);

homesick much of the time until he met her (once walked back to Illinois to see the folks) and when the food ran out their first spring together went on foot to Fort Leavenworth 150 miles and back with a bag of flour on his shoulder and hoping it wouldn't rain and had to split rails for a month to earn eight bushels of wheat;

walked in the house one evening and Land of Goshen if there wasn't a big old ratsnake unwinding out of the canary cage and no canary (she told him for the last time to get a door up);

(the woman near the Falls who was making lye soap in a kettle in front of her house and three Kaws riding up and motioning they wanted some soup and she shaking her head and saying *Soap — not soup* and they growing vexed she wouldn't share and one grabbing the stir spoon and taking a big slurp and his eyes reddening and tears welling up but without a word he passing the spoon to the next and he tasting and giving the spoon to the third and he likewise then handing her the spoon and they riding off and that was the only time anybody could remember a Kaw crying without wailing);

got good at taking perch and bass and bullheads out of creek holes and couldn't afford a gun for the oldest boy and taught him to make bird traps and figure-eight deadfalls;

those first years ate side-meat squirrel buffalo salted-prairie-chicken-breasts quail turkey biscuits cornbread vinegar-and-sheep-sorrel pie wild plums and grapes gooseberries never any coffee and instead brewed parched corn and the only condiment vinegar-sauce and the only sweetening sorghum molasses and she said *Never saw sugar after I came out to Kansas;*

every dry year the grasshoppers came and the worst in '74 ate up his crops and turned around and spit them on him and he walked in and said *Ain't never swore in front of you before but I'm going to now* and he sure did and where her beets and turnips and parsnips grew were just holes in the ground;

one July the Kaws showing up led by Loshinga and she gave out watermelons (might as well they'd steal them anyway — oh did they love it) the littlest boy staring at the braves and one of them pulling out his long knife and brandishing it and cutting off a slice of melon and giving it to Johnny and he eating and another urged on him and he ate it and another and ate it too and braves watching

and another and had to sit (let the boy learn a lesson) stomach round
and hard like a melon itself and Loshinga reaching down and tapping it and the men laughing and wiping clean their knives and each
rising and tapping the little blown belly before traveling on;

the oldest boy accidentally shooting an arrow into the face of his
Kaw friend and the mother appearing at the cabin to seek reparation
(gave her a calf);

six years after statehood he went with the governor to ask aid
from the War Department to drive out *them dang injuns* and she
said *All they ever done was scare us;*

crops busted and took work carrying mortar at the new county
capitol and setting a bright penny in wet concrete under a stone;

little girl came down with typhoid and shook so bad it broke your
heart and she wrapped her in blankets and set her outside in the
spring sun and still the little thing shook (later he said *Death come
into our house four times*) and the afternoon the child went she
chattered out *Am I dying Papa?*

sometimes the whole night she'd hear the Kaws up on the hill
where their dead lay buried wailing and moaning and that was the
worst sound on the prairie and one spring she realized she hadn't
heard them that year and she never did again;

played the melodeon and filled the place with "Blue Juniata"
"Paddle Your Own Canoe" "Money Musk" and lordy could she
make that thing sing;

took his gun and went out west of Dodge City and came back
with buffalo hides and meat enough for the winter and she joked
You ain't no better than an Indian now and that December she put
hot rocks in the sleigh and wrapped them all in buffalo robes and
they went to town;

on one hunt the boy had to stay in camp and sit there (and
grumble) and crack open buffalo shin bones to fill a two-gallon
bucket with marrow and was it good on pancakes;

always believed any man who worked wearing gloves couldn't
ever be a success (of course excepting the miller who had to keep
the feel in his right hand so he could judge the texture of millings)
wanted religion in small doses real small and got older and found he
could make a speech if they asked him and he did and he often
spoke in those later years how he saw resources being wasted by
grasping men and a friend saying *Ain't there more than enough?*

walking up the hollow that day (done it fifty times before) but
that morning the big plum thicket swirling with hummingbirds

hundreds and hundreds and she told about them all the way into the next century;

(if it wasn't one thing it was another) the youngest not two years old sitting out watching his brothers play and from the high grass came a wild hog and got him by the dress and dragged him off toward the brake and she running and screaming and throwing everything she could find until the boar dropped him;

humane assistance parcels from the East in the early years and he opened theirs to find three moth-eaten suits and three stovepipe hats and three ladies' ballroom dresses with matching slippers and he set a hat on his head and said *Dost thou waltz, milady?*

the neighbors south gave up but he told her *We'll live to see the day this land is worth forty dollars an acre;*

carried with her into the county a piece of rose root called queen of the prairie and set it out and lived to see it cover the entire front of the cabin with pink blossoms;

if it wasn't raining on Sunday and the circuit preacher got through they moved the furniture outside to make room for the neighbors and washed the children for the sermon (and nearly any day the wind was down they could hear the old bachelor who lived a mile off calling to the Lord to get him through another month praying so loud he must have figured God was deaf and one day she didn't hear that anymore either);

raised four children lost three (typhoid diphtheria consumption) but when she arrived in the county she was sure it would be snakes that got them all and she said *I learned what the Lord's real serpents is;*

grew older and sometimes he thought about selling out and moving into Strong and conducting the horse trolley and sitting down to earn a living;

thinking maybe they should move out there to Pasadena the daughter said to come on out;

reminisced about the first days how out riding he found the human teeth on the big rock and figured someone had been eaten by wolves and came to find out missus oh-you-remember lost her dentures a couple years earlier in the tornado that killed the husband just before she moved to Oklahoma and he mailed them to her and missus wrote back and said thanks they still fit just fine;

reminisced about how she put that small jar of butter down in the spring and forgot about it and two years later he cleaned the spring and found the butter and they ate it that night;

in his last years the Confederate prison sickness finally turning him into an invalid and he spent his time carving chessmen and small canteens from black walnut laid in with designs of Cottonwood River clamshell and one afternoon said to her *Everyone was young in Kansas in them days* and she said *If my eyes was good I'd think I was young* (she was eighty-four);

he died from a kick of a mule, after inhaling gas when he was digging the schoolhouse well, when high water took him and the miller in the boat over the dam at Cottonwood, at the crossing under a locomotive, struck by lightning, fell off his horse into Diamond Creek and she buried him in that homemade shirt he brought from Scotland sixty-three years earlier and she tended the grave for a decade;

outlived them all and not a day went by but what she wondered who'll attend me?

Out of the Totem Hawk Lexicon

One morning north of Elk, I was walking over an undulance of hills, the wind in my face so that I had to keep blinking, and I grew tired of it and took a rest in the lee of a ridge, a relative vacuum of quiet and warmth where I could open my eyes and my canvas coat and lie back and watch the blowing: clouds in slippage, bluestem in bondage. I dozed off, woke, sat up, and considered whether to eat or hike on.

Suddenly, over the slope, as if tethered to a cord of air drawing quickly upward, came a northern harrier, motionless but for its rising. So still was the bird — wings, tail, head — it might have been a museum specimen. Then, as if atop the wind, it slid down the ridge, tilted a few times, veered, tacked up the hill, its wings hardly shifting. I thought, if I could be that hawk for one hour I'd never again be just a man. It went into a hover near a rock ledge, twisted its tail and ruddered into position for the drop, then fell out of the wind onto what looked like a vole and began tearing open flesh. I made notes on what had just happened and concluded: hwk stlking best dun seatd. After some minutes, the harrier raised its wings but moved them only that once, and, as if again leashing itself to its invisible line, floated up into the wind (a river diver rising to the surface, catching the current) and was gone. Somewhere now the mammal heart flew in the harrier, vole turning into wings and talons, and those giving the rodent its creeping and sequestered and dark life: shapers of each other like a human making a sculpture and it making him a sculptor.

This is a chapter about hawkness and harriers, but I must tell you straight: it's a cowlick — no matter how much I comb through it, wet it down, try to smooth it into coherence, it pops up, always insisting on standing awry. When I write, I usually try to follow the directions in the images and let details point the way so that my pencil (I always begin drafting with a lead pencil as if I were drawing) is a vehicle across the map of paper, a smudged course down parallel lines, little roads, and the best part of such a journey, the reward for the isolation necessary to it, is the unexpected encounters: travel writing is a tour twice taken, and which one is more real depends on how you value dreamtime. For me, writing is not a search for explanations but a ramble in quest of what informs a place, a hunt for equivalents. (I always envy the painter never having to ask, "Understand?" Were the choice ever offered, I'd want to be a Turner rather than a Twain.)

Now: I am in the room where I write (my pencil absently scribbled "writhe"); wadded and thrown against the wall are nine sheets of paper that were various first paragraphs of this chapter. I haven't been falling asleep until early in the dark mornings these last few hot July nights, and I've become a convict of two alternating emotions, irritation and depression, because I can't find a way into the topic. I've tried all my old devices to trick words out where they can reveal a course: read some Dickens or Shakespeare or Melville's *Encantadas*, draw a picture of the subject, play my aboriginal cedar flute, lie on the floor and stretch, go outside and shoot baskets, take a shower, a walk, a nap (these days I lie dreaming I'm solving the riddle of hawkness, only to wake and find myself exactly where I began); above all, try to avoid anger. Still, I've ended up with crumpled paragraphs and the old terror creeping in that my quarry has grown too clever to be caught, that it knows what I'm after: itself revealed.

During all of this, I've resisted writing down what I am about to say (some things are easier to admit to than others) because it will probably be laughable; but, maybe, it's a way in:

Six years ago, when I was first beginning to prowl around Chase County, my wife and I visited friends in Canandaigua, New York. Of him I will tell you more later. His wife, partly of Tennessee Cherokee blood, works in vocational rehabilitation; she's a bright woman whose bubble always seeks its own plumb. Someone had recently given her a Ouija board, which, she said, had taken to calling her Z in its responses. My wife and Z played with the board one summer evening, asking questions, laughing at the answers, until Ouija said my wife would die in a car crash in 2005.

They looked around and told me to ask it something, so I did, although their hands, not mine, followed the black pointer. I avoided destination questions and asked about the new book I wanted to write: was it a good idea? Ouija answered, *YO*, which I took as yes. What would be the first words? *GOIN WEST, BRO.* What was the subject? *LAND*. Ouija gave a couple more answers, both plausible and even surprising in their insight. (I must add that I'd not then talked specifically about my project with anyone.) I asked, will there be strong help in making the book? The pointer lay still, then moved slowly, *W-A-* (moving erratically) *M-* (as if hunting a lost alphabet) *R-E*. We waited for it to finish but it lay still. I asked what WAMRE was, and the pointer sat, sat, then again slid slowly to the letters: *W-I-N-D* and stopped, then started once more and, herky-jerk, spelled *R-I-D-E-R*. I admit my flesh was crawling. I asked what a wind rider was, and Ouija quickly spelled out *H-A-W-K*.

I went outside on the porch to sit in the cool dark and collect myself. I'd recently begun keeping a Chase journal of observations and ideas — a most secret thing — that I hoped would lead me into the prairie book; in it I'd written this: the harrier rides the wind as a fish the current — it treats air like a liquid. I alone had seen the notebook, and neither woman had ever heard me speak of hawks (except in bird-watcher talk), and I'd not spoken about my new notion of hawk medicine — not in a pharmaceutical meaning but in an Indian sense, of power that can infuse a mind or a beast or a bundle of collected sticks and feathers. I was hoping my journal pages would become a medicine bundle.

You may wish to account for all of this with some easy, rational explanation; I've tried a few myself, but always I return to a belief that the source of my work is not so much reason as something darker and less comprehended, something arising from dreamtime. For the long journey into the prairie that I was just beginning, that obscure medicine had somehow already taken on the form of hawk-ness. I'm not quite saying that this figure-hawk is supernatural but rather only suggesting a less conscious mind using an emblem to reach toward a vague awareness and push it to the surface where shallow reason can look it over. (Does this sound like self-deception, hallucination? Very well, let the strict rationalist label it that and pigeonhole the hawk.)

A couple of weeks ago, I was having even more trouble writing another chapter. Then the July heat broke and I opened the windows, a cool northwesterly blew through, ruffling my paper, and I was sitting before the unmarked, lined page, and two hours disappeared in staring and listening to the singing birds; invigorated by the coolness, now I couldn't blame my trouble on the weather. Among the several different bird voices, I became aware that one came from a red-tailed hawk. I couldn't see it but for some time heard its high rasping. It was circling close. During the next hour the blank page began to fill, words being called up, lured out, duped into revealing themselves: I, starving, hovered and dropped onto them as if they were plump voles. The next day I had the sketch drafted. I offer this as an illustration of hawk medicine, even if it's nothing more than a longing conducive to useful delusion.

This week I've been hoping for another approach of hawk-radiance, but nothing comes, and I sit blunted. Have I become hooked on a talon-like voice, become its psychic prey?

Then very goddamn well, I say at last, maybe I can write around the goddamn problem: I advise myself to try again and this time speak only in names, in pictures — that's the primitive method. (Have you ever taken a photograph of an aboriginal person and seen him become angry? People not yet completely seduced by European rationalism often believe something strong but beyond the comprehension of reason attaches itself to images and names.)

I am going only to name and limn hawkness as I have encountered it in the tall prairie, where its form and habits suit themselves so perfectly to the windy and open hills as to make it a familiar of the place. This is a little lexicon, arranged not alphabetically but according to the way I've come to see hawk-figure, which in this particular case is the northern harrier, *Circus cyaneus*. The first dozen entries are recognized names, the other twelve from my dreamtime hawking. (A suggestion: when you finish reading, go outside and find a living thing you do not know the name of and look at it closely and give it one of your own making; then it will become yours to carry into dreamtime because memory depends finally upon what we create for ourselves, and, until we become nomenclators of a place, we can never really enter it.)

So:

CIRCUS CYANEUS: freely translated, "circling blueness," a Latin misnomer, for neither the males nor females are blue and their distinctive flight pattern is actually one of angles (see Zigzagger);

but, understood even more freely, the name suggests an aerial circus of feathery acrobats (see Somersault hawk).

NÓRTHERN HARRIER: if the country is open, this slender bird may be found nearly anywhere in North America, although it usually isn't any longer, and the Audubon Society has placed it on its Blue List (an early warning of endangered species); even so, in the Flint Hills it isn't at all rare.

MARSH HAWK: an old moniker given by easterners because of the former abundance of the bird over grassy wetlands; pesticides and the draining of marshes have almost made the name another misnomer; today, "prairie hawk" would be better but that already belongs to another species.

BOG TROTTER: a description of some poetic resonance, albeit of little accuracy, for such an accomplished aerialist; if you want a trotter, look to the ostrich.

HEN HARRIER: a name used by English settlers; outweighed as she is by a barnyard chicken, an American female *cyaneus* hunts not so much leghorns as prairie chickens; incidentally, while both of these tallgrass wild birds nest on the ground, *cupido* takes to the air only when it must and *cyaneus* comes to earth only when it has to: the grouse a reluctant, sometime bird, the harrier hardly needing legs or feet.

FROG HAWK: if a harrier lives near a marsh it eats many amphibians; if it's on the prairie it doesn't; analog: Bostonians residing in Kansas are not commonly called bean eaters.

MOUSE HAWK: in rearing its five to eight nestlings, a harrier pair may catch a thousand mice and voles; but many kinds of hawks prey on mice; analog: to call the French "bread people" would mislead you about Italians or Spaniards; some farmers even call the bird "mouser" as if it were an old barnyard cat.

RABBIT HAWK: since a full-grown rabbit weighs more than a harrier, "bunny hawk" might be more accurate, but then, again, most raptors catch cottontails and hares.

SNAKE HAWK: nearly any bird of prey could be called this; conversely, several species of reptiles that hunt eggs and chicks of the ground-nesting *cyaneus* could be named "harrier snake."

MOLE HAWK: it will eat a mole if it can find one above the ground; analog: the woodpecker as "peanut-butter bird."

BLUE HAWK: for the assumed color of the adult male's back; a birder who sees a northern harrier as blue has no need of colorized black-and-white movies.

WHITE-RUMPED HAWK: if you accept that birds indeed have rumps, an accurate name but of little elegance (would an Englishman want to be a "bleach-butted Briton"?); the white band, by the way, which the harrier almost flashes in its low and tilting flight, is diagnostic of the species.

Now, suggestions for renaming *cyaneus:*

SOMERSAULT HAWK: the nuptial flight of the male is a series of nosedives, often from several hundred feet down to within ten feet of the ground; one observer diagrammed it as a UUU seventy times; at the apex of each steeply bent crescent, the harrier will nearly stall before closing its wings, and then, in silence, turn head over tail, plummeting, head over tail again, still falling, only to swing upward at the last moment and barely clear the ground; sometimes also called "tumble hawk."

SKYDANCER: a mated pair may fly together, arcing marvelously, one of them rolling over to fly upside down and glide along, talons to talons; also called "ecstasy hawk."

OWL HAWK: with a facial disk of feathers that amplify sound, the nearly neckless harrier can find prey by listening almost as well as an owl; in this way, harriers seem a linking species between hawks and owls.

MORMON HAWK: the male, unlike other North American hawks, is often polygamous; there is evidence that more than two thirds of harrier hatchlings are females, which may account for the polygyny; circumspect travelers in Utah may wish to call it the "Solomon hawk."

RIDGE RIDER: even though *cyaneus* is not a particularly big hawk, the female (larger than its mate) may have a four-foot wingspan that will keep it motionlessly aloft in the gentlest of drafts where she can fix her wings to let wind do the work; speaking of the effortless high flight a harrier occasionally engages in after eating, Audubon said, *I have thought that it preferred this method of favoring digestion.*

CLOUD NESTER: the high ratio of wing surface to body weight of a harrier gives it a flight that observers time and again describe as "buoyant"; although Audubon found its flight elegant, he wrote that it *cannot be said to be either swift or strong; but it is well sustained;* even if the bird usually prefers flying low to high, it spends half of each day airborne, turning winds into perches as if it could grip the currents, something most useful in a prairie where reconnaissance posts are few; buteos and eagles soar, harriers float; these aerial corks may also be called "wind bobbers."

HANGMAN'S HAWK: viewed from below in certain lights, the contrast between the dark gray head and its lighter breast feathers gives the male the appearance of wearing a black hood.

BOMBARDIER HAWK: in their nuptial display, a pair will fly together, the female some distance below, and her mate will drop a caught rodent that she, flipping upside down, will catch neatly in her talons; when she begins building a nest on the ground or in a bush (the only North American hawk to do so) the male delivers sticks by flying over and dropping them; once she takes up brooding, he will drop food to her either on the nest or in an aerial exchange: these tactics help conceal the location of the vulnerable nest.

ZIGZAGGER: the harrier takes its prey by flying only a few feet above the grass, quartering an area back and forth, reconnoitering side to side, cutting diagonals as if loving the geometry of angles, holding its wings in a sharply upward dihedral (the reverse of the prairie grouse); upon seeing or hearing movement below, it halts suddenly as if it had hit an indiscernible wall, hovers, the long wings fanning and harrying (hence its common name) a ground beast into terrorized running and full exposure.

VIVE-LA-DIFFÉRENCE HAWK: the northern harrier is the only North American raptor exhibiting pronounced sexual dimorphism and dichromatism: the differences in size and color are so obvious that a booming prairie grouse will continue its performance or even attack a male harrier that approaches, but when a female hawk appears the grouse will freeze or flush wildly; she, one and a half times heavier than her mate, has a plumage dark and streaky like a March meadow, while he is the color of an overcast sky; although throughout most of the year both sexes spend about the same number of hours in the air, their different colorings match the element most important to survival of their kind.

INK DIPPER: moving to and fro repeatedly across the drafts, a male's long, pointed wings tipped in black look like pens inscribing words on a foolscap of air as if he were amanuensis to the wind; the ancients, trying to read the future in the flight of birds, would surely have held this scrivener of a hawk sacred; sometimes also called "wind writer."

SPIRITUS HAWK: to wind, the primal life force of the prairie, *Circus cyaneus* is the embodiment, the hot-blooded beast: token, totem, transmogrification.

At the Diamond of the Plain

When I graduated from the University of Missouri in 1961 with a bachelor's degree in literature, I had encountered in my studies nothing so absorbing as the mythic Yoknapatawpha County novels and tales of William Faulkner. In the week between my last exam and commencement, I lit out for his territory; I drove an old Ford and took along a friend whom I'd talked into going: he'd heard of Faulkner. From Columbia, Missouri, to Oxford, Mississippi, I rattled on about the Yoknapatawpha books, and Jack told stories about woods and waters (a muddy pond and a snapping turtle chomping off his great toe — that night I noticed he was fully appendaged). As we followed a route of courthouse towns (Hernando, Senatobia, Sardis) into the red-earth piney woods of northwestern Mississippi, I thought I felt a strange presence coming from the land as if Yoknapatawpha were throwing out halos from dreamtime.

We reached Oxford at dusk, drove around the courthouse square, past the gray granite Confederate statue (the half-wit Benjy always circles it three times in *The Sound and the Fury*), along the alley Joe Christmas flees down, and to a café called The Mansion, not so much because it was the only eatery open but because it bore the title of Faulkner's most recent novel. Maybe we'd find him there. Jack could talk immediately and intimately with almost anyone, and he often used his slight stammer to advantage, especially with women. He was at once friends with the waitress and announcing our plans to tour the area, using as guides Faulkner's books and the map of Yoknapatawpha County the writer drew. I asked whether he ever came into the café. Looking at Jack, she said, *I've served him any number of times.* Before we finished the meal, she had hurried home and returned with a paperbound copy, given her as a tip, of three Faulkner tales. The master had signed it. She said to Jack, *What am I going to do with a book?* and she gave it to him. He took his sweet time with it before permitting me to trace my finger over the small, vertical signature, and already I was thinking how easy it would be for a stammering college boy simply to disappear in the big Mississippi woods.

The next morning, early, someone rattled the door of our room. My shorts and face rumpled by sleep, I squinted into the sunrise: there stood a slight man immaculately dressed in a khaki sport coat, plaid tie, and in hand a huckleberry walking stick of wonderful gnarls. He said, *I hear you're wanting to see the county.* He was Malcolm Franklin, Faulkner's stepson. Faulkner himself was away in Virginia. Malcolm, in his early thirties, offered to show us around, and I immediately began a pummel of questions until Jack nudged me and whispered, *Whoa, boy!* but Malcolm answered everything, shied away from nothing. Off we went, he driving and elucidating the miles of broken barns and tenant cabins and dusty pines with details from the books: the hollow tree Mink Snopes stuffs a body into, the creek where Candace muddies her drawers, the foundation of a barn Ab Snopes might have torched. Malcolm introduced us to family (I looked closely at them for signs of the master — the small hands, the narrow eyes), and he took us to Rowanoak, Faulkner's antebellum home (but not inside because he didn't want to betray his stepfather's privacy), showed us Faulkner's favored horse, an ill-tempered mare that kicked at us (the following June the beast threw the writer, an accident contributing to his death).

We went into the woods to visit Walter Miller, called Uncle Buddy, a man who used to take Faulkner along on night hunts (on his first one, Walter said, young Bill got sick from liquor but thereafter stayed sober and listened to the campfire talk of hunters — some of them virtually illiterate — sources of what would become splendid moments in his books). Uncle Buddy led us down to a small spring, the head of Tobee-Tubbee Creek, and dipped up water to add to our dusty glasses of whiskey that cooled the June afternoon; it was a kindly water that made the best bourbon-and-branch I've ever put down. We rolled on till midnight when, at last, Malcolm let us go. Until those hours with him, I had never really known what it is to travel *into* a country, to go bodily into a topographic dreamtime.

Seldom since have I been so well prepared to see a place, or been so profoundly guided once I arrived. There are, of course, drawbacks to such preparations (disappointment from preconceptions the worst), and I must tell you that isn't the way I usually went about Chase County, where I liked to use the Columbian method: *¡Madre mía!* Look what the hell I just found! But Diamond Spring, six miles beyond the Chase line in Morris County (almost due north of Elk cemetery), I treated differently because the first time I looked for it I ended up only with nightfall. I began reading about the site to get better directions, and I became absorbed and kept reading so that, when I finally did arrive there, I'd already traveled down a couple of centuries of the spring.

For the second trip I put together a notebook of photocopies of early travelers' impressions of *The Diamond of the Plain*, the most famous oasis on the Santa Fe Trail. I suspect there are twice the three dozen wayfarers' accounts of the spring I've found so far.

At one time in my life, when I planned on becoming a nature photographer, I considered specializing in time-lapse work, an interest that grew out of fascination with before-and-after, then-and-now pictures of townscapes and landscapes. When I saw the number of historical comments on Diamond Spring, a small fountain in a small vale, I realized how its record seemed out of proportion to its physical size, and I began assembling the notebook as a kind of verbal time-lapse rendering of the spring. After I at last reached the actual site, the collected-up timebook saved me from what otherwise would have been the grandest disappointment in my million miles of American travel. Heavy grazing in the Flint Hills has today increased water runoff and decreased percolation into the aquifers so that few springs flow as they once did.

As a spring (I like the French word, *source*), the Diamond of the Plain is hardly the largest in the Flint Hills and certainly not on the Great Plains, but if you measure it as a source of written words it stands well with any in the nation, and, as a contributor to the great American historic themes of westering, red-white conflict, slavery, and the destruction of wilderness, it is truly national.

The earliest head of the Santa Fe Trail was Franklin, Missouri, now washed away. Diamond Spring lies about a third of the eight-hundred-mile way between there and the terminus in north-central New Mexico at La Villa Real de Santa Fe, the Royal City of the Holy Faith (the oldest capital in the States). The trailhead moved steadily west until it reached Council Grove, Kansas; the local chamber of commerce calls the town "the Birthplace of the Santa Fe Trail," which it manifestly is not. As that settlement grew more crowded in later years with people, wagons, oxen, and mules, travelers and traders often would assemble their caravans at Diamond Spring, so that it became both chronologically and topographically the last jumping-off point, a place at the pale of white rule, the spot where the short rolls of prairie hills yield to the much longer and broader and bowl-like swells of the Great Plains. Beyond the Diamond lay uncertain supplies of water, grass, and safety: from the spring westward, the trail passed through the fierce land of Comanches, Apaches, and Kiowa. In many ways, Diamond Spring was to the Santa Fe traveler what Plymouth, England, was to the Pilgrim — the last home port.

Now: I've planned my arrival at the site to a late afternoon in April, a common time for westward-bound travelers to arrive, since the spring was the first stop out of Council Grove, sixteen miles to the northeast. I'm walking down the private lane that serves the Diamond Creek Ranch, where I've asked from a cowhand permission to enter. The road passes just north of a worn two-story frame house, on past an old barn, and drops down a slope into a shallow hollow to ford a wooded creek, and then heads into broadly open country with a view similar to that of an April a century ago.

I've walked beyond the spring and turn around to find it where I hoped it wouldn't be — at the mutilated edge of a stony square packed hard by hooves. A concrete stock tank sits there, only a little larger and deeper than a coffin, and water wells up at its center and drains into a brook crammed with more watercress than I've ever seen before. (Because it isn't a native plant, the cress may have been planted here years ago by an early traveler.) A few yards north of the trough lies the spring itself, a concrete cap covering a submersible pump to deliver water to the decrepit house on the small ridge above. In 1876, Major Richard Whiting, the first ranch owner here, installed a hydraulic ram to supply the tenant house; now an electric machine does the job. Ranchers call such works *improvements*.

In the center of the tank, where water fairly boils up to flush it clear, I rinse my face and fill my canteen, all the time thinking about the thousands of travelers who have taken these waters since even before Stonehenge went up: from utterly unknown red people to notorious whites like Kit Carson. For nearly two centuries, the greatest peril to westering Americans was water: whether through dysentery, typhoid fever, or cholera — the black death — bad water did in more people than any other cause, and that is the reason Diamond Spring appears so often in trail history; along this route, no water between the Missouri and the mountains surpassed it in perpetually cold and clean clarity. One traveler west of here described his search to quench thirst: *We found a muddy puddle from which we succeeded in getting a half bucket full, and, although black and thick, it was life for us and we guarded it with jealous eyes.*

I pick a salad of watercress and take it and my canteen and timebook into the little copse just across the outflow brook and sit in a cool spot, my back to a slender elm. The brutalized earth around the spring is less evident here. I open the book.

Whites may have "discovered" the spring as early as 1804 either through Indian advice or by following animal trails that once led to it like spokes to a hub. Although Francisco de Coronado's long circuit into the southern plains brought him within seventy-five miles of here (where a sixteenth-century Spanish sword and chain mail have been unearthed), I believe stories that he drank from the spring to be no more than possible. Its recorded history begins four years after Missourian William Becknell in 1821 laid out an amazingly direct wagon road across the upper Southwest to tap the commerce of Mexico (Santa Fe did not come under American control until 1846). Major George Sibley in 1825 wrote a comment when his trail-survey contingent camped at the spring on the eleventh of August, a day after he met with Osage chieftains at what is now Council Grove (a name he gave) under a large oak (the alleged stump still stands) and paid the tribe eight hundred dollars in goods and chits in exchange for safe passage in perpetuity (a few days later and some miles west, the Kansa accepted the same terms).

I'm sipping the cold spring water and munching the cress as if I were a muskrat, the timebook open to the first picture; I want you to look over my shoulder and visit a place through its years (wear good boots — it's a long journey). Here's what Sibley said when he sat within yards of where I am and made his pencil notations in a twelve-by-fourteen-inch diary:

*We halted on a Small Creek where the water is Scarce & bad.
The Grazing pretty good and fuel plenty. Mr. [Ben] Jones discovered a very fine Spring about 300 yards So. E. from our camp
down the Creek. It is uncommonly large and beautiful, and the
Water very pure & cold. I have Seldom seen so fine a Spring
anywhere. After so hot a day, this fine Water was a luxury to us
all. The distance from Council Grove to Jones' Spring as measured upon our Route is 16 Miles & 32 Chains.*

Two years later, Sibley began a second survey to correct details of
the first. When he reached the spring he wasn't well enough to
continue, so the party turned around the next day and worked back
toward the Missouri River, but the men were beset with problems,
the last one a bolt of lightning that struck Sibley's tent, filling it
with smoke and splinters and leaving him temporarily deafened and
numbed. In 1839 he wrote a letter giving a longer account than does
the diary of his first afternoon here:

*The spring gushes out from the head of a hollow in the prai-
rie, and runs boldly among the stones into Otter creek, a short
distance. It is very large, perfectly accessible, and furnishes
the greatest abundance of most excellent, clear, cold water —
enough to supply an army.*

*There is a fountain, inferior to this, in the Arabian Desert,
known as "The Diamond of the Desert." This magnificent spring
may, with at least equal propriety, be called "The Diamond of
the Plain." We found it a most excellent camping place. A fine
elm tree grows near to and overhangs the spring.*

*On the 10th and 11th of June, 1827, I encamped here with my
party. During our stay I made requisition of "Big John" [Walker]
and his carving implements once more to inscribe on the stoop-
ing elm, "Diamond of the Plain," which was promptly done.
The tree has since been cut away, I believe. The fountain is now
generally known as "Diamond Spring."*

Captain Philip St. George Cooke, a few years later, said it was a
*Pearl of the Prairie — were pearls but as transparent as its cold and
crystal waters!* Sibley's words put the lie to one local notion that
the spring takes its name from a diamond stickpin found at its edge.
Otter Creek, by the way, is now Diamond Creek.

James Josiah Webb, a twenty-six-year-old who had just joined a
freighting train of *23 wagons, 40 mules, 80 yoke of oxen, and 40
men,* came into the West for the first time in late August of 1844,
and he said:

[Council Grove] being the last place where we could procure hard wood for repairs of wagons, one day was spent in cutting and slinging timbers under the wagons and preparing for an early start the next morning. As soon as possible after daylight we "catched up" and drove out, every person in camp in good health and spirits, and we greenhorns hoping we should see the Indians.

Passed Diamond spring, where we partook of mint juleps and passed a vote of thanks to the public benefactors who some years before had transported and set out some mint roots at the spring which by this time had increased to a bountiful supply for all trains passing.

Two years later, in June of 1846, Susan Shelby Magoffin, not yet nineteen and just married to a well-to-do freighter, came through. That she was the first white woman to travel the entire trail, as she claimed, may be true — no one has yet disproved her — but that she was the first woman to write an account of her journey is certain. Her husband, Samuel, twenty-six years her senior, pampered his bride on the trail with a maid, two servants, a private carriage, a big carpeted tent, and a feather-mattress bed (people commonly slept on the ground in the open or under a wagon). Susan said, *It is the life of a wandering princess, mine.* She was one of the few travelers who did not comment on the water; perhaps, camped up on the slope as she was and with servants to fetch, she never saw the fountain. Her diary entry of leaving the place the next morning and arriving at Lost Spring, thirteen miles west, is more evocative of her travel:

Ouch, what a day this is! We started in the rain, came in the rain, and stoped in the rain. Last night was a very cold night, and about day-light it commenced raining. We started at 9 o'clock having had difficulty yoking the oxen. After travelling only a mile or two the wagons stuck at the crossing of a small creek and we were detained some time, but finally got off, and arrived here by 4 o'clock. . . .

I closed a letter to Papa. It was a hurried affair, for I had only a few minutes to do it in [to give to an eastward-bound traveler], and then the wind and rain were blowing in my face, blotting my paper, and shaking me so I scarcely knew what I wrote.

This is certainly one of the "varieties of life" as well as of traveling. To be shut up in a carriage all day with a buffalo robe rolled around you, and with the rain pouring down at ten knots an hour. And at the close of this to be quietly without any trouble to one's self, into the middle of a bed in a nice dry tent, with writing materials around you and full privillege to write anything and every thing that may chance to enter one's head whether foolishness, as this is, or wisdom. We have rainy days any place and they are not more disagreeable on the plains than in N. Y. I have books, writing implements, sewing, kniting, somebody to talk with, a house that does not leak and I am satisfied, although this is a juicy day en el campo!

A few days after Susan Magoffin passed through, contingents of soldiers began reaching the spring on their way to join Colonel Alexander Doniphan and General Stephen Watts Kearny to fight the Mexicans, a war that would bring New Mexico, Arizona, and California into the Union. Of several soldiers' accounts, that of Colonel John Hughes is the most self-conscious:

> *Advancing about sixteen miles further, over high, rolling prairies, we encamped near the Diamond springs. The heat was oppressive. The most enchanting spots ever depicted by the pen of the eastern romancer possess no more charms for the youthful imagination than do the groves and the fine, gushing, transparent Diamond springs, for the thirsty, wayworn traveler on the plains. These crystal fountains derive their name from the limpidness of their waters.*

Frank Edwards, a member of the Missouri legislature, organized a cavalry regiment to join Doniphan. Going to war is not — even then — a usual way of regaining health, especially for politicians; Edwards wrote some time later of his night near the spring:

> *Oh, the breath of the prairies! When the breeze, which always rises at sundown, fans your cheek after a hot day's ride, you sink quietly to sleep, feeling that that soft delicious air is bringing health and strength to your weary body. How much I felt this can only be known to myself. One of my reasons for going on this expedition was to obtain the restoration of my health, which had been, for some time, very much impaired; and when I bade adieu to St. Louis, I hardly expected to get across the prairies alive. But I had not been a week upon them before I felt that my whole being was changed, and ere I reached the settlements, I was one of the most robust of the whole company.*

A man of whom I've spoken, Lieutenant John James Abert of the Topographical Engineers, a twenty-five-year-old West Point graduate, kept both a field journal and a sketchbook during his tour with the Army of the West. On the front and back covers of his field book he printed large: PRIVATE. Inside, his careful sentences and sensible observations, put down under the terms of hard travel, contain quotations from Pythagoras, Vergil, Horace (many trail journals suggest that soldiers were of a different cut then). He was a capable quick-sketch watercolorist, but he did not paint Diamond Spring. He wrote:

> Shortly before reaching Council Grove we passed a grave of a white man who was killed some time ago by an Osage Indian. A circular pile of rough stones marks this unpretending grave; from the crevices the ivy has shot forth. Over the whole a bent stick is leaning mournfully. When I viewed this simple grave my mind turned to the proud monuments which we see built up by the wealthy in our great cities and which are daily leveled with the ground to give place to some improvement. Here on the wild prairie the Indian and the rude hunters pass by this spot and not for the world would they remove one stone. Who now shall we call the rude man? the wild man?
>
> Continuing our march we travelled over a distance of about 20 miles, when we reached Diamond Spring. This spring is several feet across and the water makes one's hands feel extremely cold. The temperature of the spring is 54° while that of the air, the thermometer in the shade, is 87°. I procured at this place a beautiful white thistle which is of delicious fragrance. We saw a great many nighthawks and plovers. They let us approach very nigh them. We also noticed some grouse and several herds of deer.

When Regimental Adjutant Abraham Johnston came through on the eighth of July, he spoke of the abundant flow of water but added, *The horses of those who had gone in advance of us had tramped it up very much.* George Gibson, a soldier traveling with Johnston, wrote:

> Hereafter it will be necessary to be cautious how we leave the company, as we might fall in with some of the wild and savage Indians of the plains. [Diamond Spring] is an important point, as after this no timber can be found on the route to repair anything broken.

Of his night at the spring and the evening following he wrote:

> After we got up this morning, we found a small rattlesnake in our blankets. It had slept between the first lieutenant and myself and near the captain's face. It was soon dispatched for its

intrusion, and we thought but little more about it. . . . Last night all we wanted to complete our happiness was one of Joe's best juleps, a long straw, and well feet. In the morning the men were tolerably well. But it commenced raining soon after we left camp and continued throughout the day, and we were wet to the skin and did not reach camp until after night, in a severe thunderstorm. The company was very much crippled up by the long march in such bad weather, and all had to lie down and sleep in their wet clothes without a mouthful to eat, as it was not possible to start a fire with green cottonwood in such weather or to cook with rain pouring down in torrents. My feet were so swollen I had to cut my boots off, and the night was very stormy, but we were soon sound asleep. There would have been no temperance men in camp tonight if they had had spirits.

The next year, 1847, enlisted man Philip Gooch Ferguson, a twenty-three-year-old printer, gave his explanation of the name of the spring:

When we were ready to start, the captain made us another war-speech, again warning us to be on the alert, as we were now in the enemy's country. Mitchell and myself were sent ahead today as spies. We rode considerably in advance and stopped at the Diamond spring until the company came up and camped. This is a most delicious fountain, rising clear and perfectly transparent, the water being icy cold. The name of this spring, I presume, was taken from the diamond shape of the surface of the ground, at the corner of which rises the spring.

H. M. T. Powell, a crotchety English-born shopkeeper, arrived at the site on his way to the California goldfields in 1849. Fearing a shortage of grass on the more common Oregon-California Trail to the north, his group chose the much longer southern route through Santa Fe. The small, moralizing Victorian (a Missourian said his initials stood for *His Majesty's Twerp*) squabbled with his fellow gold seekers and, in the long tradition of the English traveler, groused about much that he encountered. Four days before he reached Diamond Spring, Powell came down with diarrhea from bad water and asked a fellow traveler, a physician, to help him, and Dr. Burchard gave him a concoction made from white oak bark; Powell was recovering when he reached the spring, but he still noted that Burchard was *a coarse bully, an evil tempered man.* Powell carried along a trunk of books he hoped to use in starting a school but he found no one interested. The English immigrant kept one of the best of the Santa Fe Trail journals, full of unexpected details and self-revelations, and he was also a highly capable drafts-man: among his pencil drawings of California towns is the earliest extant picture of Los Angeles. But, seeing Diamond Spring after a rainy spell in May, he wrote only:

> Scoggins much better and the girl in the Missouri Company better; self quite sick last night, but better this morning. Still very cold bleak weather. Got to "Diamond Spring" about 3 o'clock. . . . Why it would be called "Diamond Spring," I cannot tell. There is very little that sparkles about it. It boils up about the size of my arm with some force, bringing with it a consid-erable quantity of heavy black sand. I dipped up a pail full, where it wells up, and there was at least a quart of sand settled at the bottom, and the water itself is turbid. We moved on from Diamond Spring and passed along a Prairie of entirely different character from any we have yet seen; flat, with a gradual ascent along the line of the road, so that for the first time we could see a long distance ahead.

About 1850, Max Greene, a journalist gathering information he would turn into an immigrant's guide called *The Kansas Region* (with a fifty-six-word subtitle), visited the spring and left a report unparalleled in Latinate diction:

> The next place on the route, of any interest, is Diamond Spring — worthy of its translucent baptism. That spot has been squatted upon some time ago. On every knoll around it, I have an air-castle and horse-stable as tangible as Pacific Railway stock. My land patent is in sympathetic ink; but as the soil here is of poorer quality than it is a few miles eastward, and the Kaw claim is not extinguished, it may be presumed that my title to a few acres is valid — until some sensible emigrant sees them. I have no objection to good neighbors, educated in Sunday school and addicted to the chase; provided they leave me the spring, and all the stately elms that cluster along its clear-flow-ing rivulet.
>
> Aside from natural beauties, Diamond Spring has special charms for me since I came near losing the lid of my head there. Which sans circumlocution, thus: As usual in serene weather, I was out "solitary and alone." The day was sultry; and I thirsty. Momently in the hope of arriving at the spring, I was grudging along patiently; when, thinking only of information to be ob-tained, I was pleased to espy a squad of Indians hastening over the prairie by a lateral path which intersected our trail. They

*were a couple of Mishquawkie hunters and a squaw, mounted
on ponies, hung around with quaint drapery of dried buffalo
meat; and from the panoply of knives, tomahawks, bows and
full quivers, it was apparent they were returning from a successful foray upon the "prairie cattle." In single file they loped
up to my side, and came to halt with an emphatic "hi!" I returned their salute with gruff suavity; and in response to the
demand for tobacco, proferred them money (in small sums) to
conduct me to water. My proposal and the purse were accepted;
when the squaw, who was a facetious creature, lifting up one of
the bunches of buffalo tags with which her palfrey was capari-
soned, produced a gourd, and extracting the corn-cob from its
neck, signified that I should drink therefrom. Desperately dry
and ripe for rash experiment, I put the vessel to my lips, and —
took it away again; but not till I had decanted a mouthful of
warm oily liquid — which was recanted. Expostulating with my
red interlocutor, it was insisted that he should inform me where
water came from under ground and was above suspicion. To the
reasonableness of this he assented, and his explanations not
being intelligible, at length offered to conduct me to a spring
near the path by which they had come. Thinking they ought to
know if a spring really was there, and judging from "the lay of
the land" that there was, I accompanied them — to an old buffalo wallow, which, in the showery season, had been a mud
puddle. Here they jerked short their ponies, and holding up both
hands expressed profound surprise at the miracle of the fountain
which had suddenly vanished. This was too palpable a gull, and
in a cross-jaw of vernacular and Choctaw, I intimated as much;
the reply to which was a demand from my copper gentleman of
brass for silver as the price for the next spring they were to show
me. I shut down upon them with prompt denial, and refusal to
negotiate; but it was too late for that — almost. During the colloquy they had closed in, with their horses so spurred together
as to form a triangle with me in the middle. One of the trio
leaned forward and tapped a pocket with the handle of his tom-
ahawk to make the coins jingle, while from another pocket I
had the sensation of something gliding out, and turning abruptly, detected the squaw who, having slid from her pony, was
in the act of purloining my handkerchief. In an instant she
sprang back into her seat, and three tomahawks were bran-
dished over my devoted scalp-lock. It was an emergency, or bore
startling resemblance to one; and I did the best could be done
under the circumstances — laughed (sardonically). It took. The
weapons were dropped, and my late-found acquaintances join-*

ing in an audible smile, affected to treat the affair as a capital joke — which I considered it to be — at my expense. Availing myself of the respite of good humor, I set out with them in search for the other spring — back upon the same path. Arrived in the Santa Fe trail, I squared myself, and thrust one hand into a capacious side-pocket which, for all they knew, contained a Colt's revolver — but it didn't. Keeping my hand clutched there, as though about to draw out something dangerous, I tried to look bullets. Whereupon my Indian, growing diabolically impertinent, ordered me to step into the lead of their file and "go on." To have done so would have been turning my back on the enemy, and have afforded them opportunity, unobserved, to effect a perforation seriously detrimental to the healthy circulation of the blood. Not acquiescing in the programme, they waxed wroth; the veins on their temples writhed like red lizards. I remained defiant — it was all my ammunition. By a combination of gibberish and manipulations with my left hand, I proceeded to inform them that I was E pluribus unum; that there were a hundred ferocious creatures like myself coming over the next hill-top but one, and that they might be expected immediately — if not sooner. These suggestions operated. The savage game-cocks of the wilderness were ungaffed. Filing out into a side-path, they descended into a hollow. I eyed them until a grassy curve hid [them] from further scrutiny. When withdrawing my right hand, "it exchanged congratulations with the left"; and turning on my heel, I walked off fast. In ten minutes I was drinking the Diamond water more thankfully than Cleopatra ever swilled her pearls.

Soon after Greene visited, a twenty-four-year-old man — who had inspired himself to join the First Dragoons, an Indian-fighting cavalry regiment, by reading *Ivanhoe, Mr. Midshipman Easy,* the *Leatherstocking Tales,* and John Frémont's reports of his western explorations — camped nearby. Sergeant Percival Lowe reached the spring with his unit as it was moving toward Fort Leavenworth. Some years later he wrote:

Nothing of special interest occurred until we reached Diamond Springs, now in Morris county. The weather had been frosty at night and days sunny — a continuous Indian summer all the way — grass dry as powder. We had barely a quart of corn per day for each horse, and they were poor. All day we had seen little bands of Indians a mile or two off the road traveling the same direction that we were and apparently watching us. This was the Kaw country and probably no other Indians were there, and we could hardly understand why they kept aloof and watched our progress. Of course the Kaws knew our troop by the horses, and we knew they had no love for it, but were slow to believe they would attempt to do us any harm. We camped on high ground a little east of Diamond Springs, on the south side of the road. We had been very careful of fire all the way in, and here we were especially careful on account of the dense growth of grass and consequent danger of burning the camp. We had finished dinner, about two hours before sunset when, as if by one act, fire broke out in a circle all around us not more than a mile from camp. A stiff gale was blowing from the south, and when we noticed it the fire in the tall grass was roaring furiously and the flames leaping twenty feet high. Quickly we commenced firing outside of our camp, whipping out the fire next to it, thereby burning a circle around it. Every man used a gunnysack or saddle blanket and worked with desperate energy. The utter destruction of our camp was imminent, and we faced the fire like men who had everything at stake. Success was ours, but the battle left its scars on nearly all. I have never seen fifteen minutes of such desperate work followed by such exhaustion — scarcely a man could speak. Blinded by smoke, heat, and ashes, intuitively we found our way to [Diamond] creek, bathed our burned hands and faces, many of us terribly blistered. My hands and face were blistered in several places; my mustache and whiskers, the first I had ever raised, were utterly ruined; even my eyebrows were badly scorched. I could not wash on account of the blisters, and dipped my face and head deep down into the lovely spring water and held my hands under to relieve the pain. My experience was that of most of the troop. We had quite a quantity of antelope tallow, which was warmed and gently applied to our sores. Undoubtedly the Kaws had set the fire to burn us out, and while they did not quite succeed, if they had seen us they should have been fairly well satisfied. I think that Major Chilton and Lieutenant Hastings were better satisfied with the troop than they had ever been before. Men who could stand together in such a fight and win could stand against desperate odds anywhere. I was instructed to notify the troop at retreat roll call that we would start at daylight. The guards were doubled, and we rested as best we could.

Some time before 1855, a freighting and mail company built on the low ridge above the spring a stage station consisting of three two-story buildings (hostelry, store, wagon shop) and a big rock-fence corral; George Morehouse, an early-day Kansan who lived nearby, said the buildings were *the most pretentious of their kind* between Council Grove and Santa Fe. The structures, even the

corral, are gone now, and no one has done archaeological work to
discover their precise locations and sizes.

In the fall of 1856 when the station was new, an eleven-year-old
girl, Marian Sloan, came through with her mother in a caravan
heading east. It was the second of ten trips up or down the trail she
would make. In the thirties, Marian (by then Mrs. Russell) finished
dictating her memoirs not long before being run over by an automobile; the old trail traveler was ninety-one:

> The wagons were all ox-drawn and oxen do not walk as fast
> as mules or horses; however, they did walk more evenly and we
> were able to sew or even read as they ambled slowly east-
> ward.... We read and reread Pilgrim's Progress and a travel
> book written by some missionary....
>
> [Brother] Will walked all day by the wagon. Mother busied
> herself sewing ball after ball of rags to be woven when reaching
> home into a fine rag carpet. I think that the walking and carpet
> rag sewing helped them to kill the time as the slow oxen bore
> us onward. I had nothing to do but help with the carpet rag
> sewing, a task that I loathed.... I can see the hot August sun
> shining on the polished horns of the red and white oxen....
>
> There came at last an evening when our tired oxen stumbled
> to a halt at little Diamond Springs. Water bubbled from the
> earth as clear and sparkling as a diamond. It came in such quan-
> tity that a little stream had its source there. A great stone house
> stood near by, its windows boarded up, its massive door barred
> and bolted.
>
> Our wagon master went into a huddle with the drivers and it
> was decided that on account of the Border Ruffians and the
> danger from Indians that we should go into camp at Diamond
> Springs and stay there until such time as a larger caravan might
> join us or the Government be induced to send a detachment of
> soldiers to protect us. Some of the drivers argued against the
> delay. Many of them were anxious to get to Fort Leavenworth.
> However, we were guided by the decision of the wagon master.
>
> Mother tried to say that she could not see where we could be
> in much more danger on the road than in camp; but being a
> woman no one listened to her. The man said that if we were to
> be attacked by Ruffians or Indians we would have the old stone
> house in which to seek shelter. One argument led to another
> and finally it was decided to break the great lock and to enter.
>
> We used that grand, old parlor as a community hall while we
> camped there. It had a fireplace at one end and a pathetic old
> spindle-legged piano at the other. Several ladies in our party

played well and one old man had a fiddle. In the evening while flames leaped on the hearth, lilting tunes would go echoing through the empty rooms. The old man would take his fiddle out of its red-lined cradle. He would nestle it under his chin for a moment and then suddenly the Irish Washer Woman would begin ducking in and out among the smoke-blackened rafters. The old man teased the Washer Woman. The old rafters shook with the music. The fiddle would wail like a banshee, the old piano kept on a thrumming. The piano throbbed with love and longing. The fiddle filled the hearts of the children with strange mystery. Flames leapt on the hearth. Shadows danced on the stairs. Some folks danced, their shoes a clump, clumping. This is my only memory of a strange fire-lit evening when the Santa Fe trail wound like a serpent through the New World's dream vineyards.

All of us were called upon to furnish entertainment. Two drivers agreed to furnish sheet music. They appeared at the piano-end of the long room with a bed sheet in their hands. They lay down on the floor, covered themselves with the sheet and "snored." There were charades, jokes, dialogues, recitations, and songs. . . .

After two weeks at Diamond Springs our food supply began running low, but still the men refused to press onward. Perhaps there is such a thing as mass panic for one evening when the advisability of breaking camp was discussed around the fire-place and a vote was taken; most of the men voted to stay where we were. That was the evening mother arose to her small height and announced firmly that she was much more afraid of Old Man Famine than a host of Border Ruffians. She said she was very anxious to get back to Kansas City and would walk if she could go no other way. The men laughed indulgently at her fearless words, but I knew my mother meant what she said, and, when another and another day passed and still no mention had been made of breaking camp, I was not surprised when she awoke me early one morning and told me to dress quickly, as she and I were going to walk to Council Grove.

Marian and her mother reached Council Grove the next evening and found a big feathery bed in the home of a grocer. The following morning they accepted a ride with a westbound wagon train and met their caravan coming toward them: they rejoined their group and Mrs. Sloan told the wagon master that she had broken the trail as far as Council Grove and had encountered no ruffians to hurt him.

After the discovery of gold in Colorado in 1859, gold seekers began passing through. Their notations tend toward the cursory, typically commenting on the amount of water pouring forth, things, perhaps, to be expected from men in quest of bullion. The Civil War came on, and, in 1863, a dark turbulence moved down the trail, Dirty Dick Yeager, a Confederate guerrilla from Missouri. He and his bushwhackers, intent on burning Council Grove, thundered into town one evening, the residents cowering in half paralysis. Suffering from a severe toothache, Yeager sought out the dentist and promised to cause no trouble if Dr. Bradford would pull the bad molar and provide an analgesic: he extracted and Yeager took his raiders outside town. Several citizens visited the bushwhacker camp and persuaded him, mellowed perhaps by laudanum, to move on. The next night the guerrillas rode up to the stage station at Diamond Spring and attacked it, shooting, setting fire to the buildings; hit in the arm, the storekeeper, Augustus Howell, ran up Diamond hollow and tried to use his necktie as a tourniquet, but his strength gave out before he could bind himself up and he bled to death. His wife, Adeline, was shot trying to defend her husband and their two little girls, but she recovered and later moved with her daughters to Chase and remarried; now she lies next to Augustus in a cemetery near Hymer. That August, Dick Yeager joined William Quantrill in burning Lawrence.

The year following, George Vanderwalker tried in three states to enlist in the Union army but he was neither old nor tall enough, so, as a panacea (he said) for his disappointment, he joined a freight company in Council Grove to learn how to be a bullwhacker, a whip-cracking oxen handler. Some years later he wrote:

Thus it happened that on an early June day in 1864 there were dumped from a westbound coach at Diamond Springs as odd a collection of the human family as ever escaped the museums. The appearance of the bunch would have tempted the ancient mariner to cut loose from the bank and scuttle his ark had they come aboard during his high water experience. Generally speaking, they were long on everything but money, clothes, and religion.

Soon after our arrival in camp we tenderfeet were being instructed in the art of how to handle a wagon with a live end to it, and the proper manner of carrying an ox yoke and bow in yoking the cattle in preparation for hitching them to the wagons, being instructed by the wagon master and his assistant. A whip

was given each driver of the outfit, the last being about sixteen
feet in length with a "popper" (whip cracker) added and fas-
tened to a whip stock eighteen inches in length by a buckskin
thong. This instrument of torture required an almost constant
everyday manipulation by me during my first two hundred
miles of the trip before I became proficient enough in handling
it to prevent its going about my neck and hanging me.

After the Civil War, the railroads again began pushing west and
travelers used the Santa Fe Road less and less. The last trail account
of Diamond Spring I've found is a sad piece that mentions the water
not at all; Samuel Kingman, a law partner of John James Ingalls, the
future Kansas senator and author, wrote in October of 1865:

We have today the advantage of an old road to travel on. Six
miles farther on we passed Diamond Springs. The remains of 3
buildings of stone 2 stories high tell their own story of violence.
A good monument for the builder. A small room used as dram-
shop is all [that's] left fit for use save a large stone corral sur-
rounding 5 or 6 acres with a small supply of hay.

Now: the sun is a few minutes from setting, coming down just
above a short stretch of still-evident trail ruts a mile west. By the
early 1870s when the Santa Fe Railroad came through the region,
travelers had abandoned the trail (the ghost town of Diamond
Springs five miles south of here belongs only to train-depot days).
Sunflowers took to the compacted and furrowed soil, and turn-of-
the-century residents said they could get on a hill and yet see the
wagon road bending out, a long golden swath.

Dusk is already in the hollow. I'm opening a small pewter pocket
flask and pouring an inch of Missouri whiskey into my cup and
topping it with Diamond water and (unable to find any of Mr.
Webb's mint) garnishing it with cress and sipping. From the creek
timber, five deer file out: in the falling light the place takes on an
earlier aspect.

A couple of days ago, I visited Lost Spring, the next usual camping
spot west on the trail. (The second owner of the stage station once
near there won it in a card game and turned it into a gamblers' den
where at least eleven men were killed and, reputedly, two bodies
thrown into the station well.) The spring lies only seventy yards
beyond a paved road in a shallow and wooded draw, yet it took me
some time in the overgrowth to find the source, a difficulty that
accounts for one of several explanations for the name; it also ex-

pands gold seeker Charles Post's comment in 1859 (he misunderstood what people called the spot):

> *We stopped for dinner about one mile from what is known as the last spring and drank slew water and cold coffee. This spring lays about one-half mile off of the main road. We were not a little vexed when Lemm found the spring so near after dinner and we vented our wrath by drinking immense quantities of the last water.*

Lost Spring is small and reclusive, seeming more to leak than flow, and lacks the isolation of Diamond Spring; yet, overgrown and seemingly forgotten and allowing a visitor the pleasurable mystery of hunting something he knows to be in plain view, today its topographical aura is superior to the trampled and troughed pearl of the prairie. But Diamond Spring bears such an accumulation of voices and recorded events that it carries a traveler farther. To look beyond its barbed wire and plastic conduit and the electric pump rammed down its cold throat is to find a splendid American source, a spring as full of incident as its outflow is of watercress. But without its years of encrustings built up slowly like so much travertine, the spring appears a barren place indeed because a traveler now must rely entirely on these depositions to open it to the imagination and reveal its deep time, and it is these layerings that make so shameful Kansans never caring to protect or honor the spring beyond a small 1907 DAR marker. Surely this place belongs not to an absentee-owner businessman but to a whole country. To turn the Diamond of the Plain into a stock tank is the damndest thing I've yet seen here.

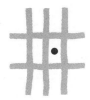

On the Town: From the Life and Opinions of Sam Wood, with Commentary (II)

Fourth Commentary In May of 1856, the truce at Lawrence collapsed, and the pro-slavers, led by the raving Bogus Jones, attacked the town and burned the Woods' house and, next to it, the new, three-story Free-State Hotel on Massachusetts Street, and much of Lawrence. John Gihon, the Kansas governor's secretary, said: *Jones himself was in ecstasies. He sat upon his horse, contemplating the horror he was making, and rubbing his hands with wild delight, exclaimed: "This is the happiest day of my life. I determined to make the fanatics bow before me in the dust and kiss the territorial laws: and I have done it, by God, I have done it."* He had, of course, done nothing of the sort, but one company of his raiders did march out of town each with a book from the *Herald of Freedom* office speared on his bayonet. This pillaging would be repeated, with far more citizens killed, when the Confederate guerrilla William Quantrill struck seven years later; given its beginnings, it is fitting that the first mayor of Lawrence was Colonel James Blood.

In the chaos I lose Sam, and I feel like the paleontologist who discovers a few fossil footprints and has only them to reconstruct the man who left them. The Woods' first daughter was born in Lawrence, and, in the autumn of 1858, Sam went alone to the falls of the Cottonwood River, where there were only two cabins, and took up a claim. He built a small log house, apparently with the help of two slaves he hired from an acquaintance, and in May of

1859 he brought Margaret and the three children to this new verge
of the frontier. While the many accounts of the border troubles give
good documentation of the Woods' days in Lawrence, their seventeen years in Chase are now only scattered — if abundant — fragments rather than whole stories, and no biographer has yet tried to
assemble the shards into the entire bowl of his time in the Cottonwood Valley; I can show you only some of the pieces and footprints
to let you imagine something more complete than is actually present. (If you will follow me in this fragmentary middle of the Sam
Wood triptych, I will get you to the story of the bizarre yet apposite
way he died.)

I cannot tell you why Margaret, in her long biography of her
husband, skips over their years in the valley where they lived longer
than any other place and where they lie buried, and this is odd: if
anyone could be said to be the father of Chase County, it is Sam
Wood, who named it and Cottonwood Falls, who helped organize
and lay out both of them, who so set his hand on the very shape and
early character and tenor of the place. I cannot even tell you in
certainty why he moved to the Cottonwood River other than to
guess that he was looking for a greater opportunity to speculate
with his own town-lot company.

Sam went into new country because he liked the essence of
pioneering — being first — as he liked founding things: he was in
on the creation of half a dozen new towns, seven railroads, five
newspapers, a couple of mining companies, and one telegraph line,
most of which had about the longevity of, say, a row of carrots.
Whenever he left the two or three high causes that molded his life,
he became an all too common American character, a fellow seemingly in pursuit of influence and money, and some of his later
eccentricities and battles look like the mere posturings of a realty
opportunist. What he was able to achieve in helping others he could
never do quite so well just for himself, and I like to imagine that the
effort he put into land promotion schemes and some small and self-
serving litigations was without his fullest passion because the consequences weren't national, the arena not large enough.

One of the first whites to perceive the agricultural potential of
the Flint Hills, Sam Wood helped to cut Chase out of Wise (later
Morris) and Butler counties and, soon after, to enlarge it twice, once
by taking a strip from Lyon County and another from Marion: the
mile-long jog in the western side of Chase is Sam Wood's work (he
got residents there to vote to leave Marion because it had a herd

law). Taking pieces from four of the five bordering counties, Sam assembled Chase like a Dagwood sandwich: a slice of this, a cut of that.

I've already spoken of his naming it after his Ohio friend Salmon Portland Chase, an abolitionist and opponent of the Kansas-Nebraska Act and a man Wood advocated for the presidency; in 1870, when Chase was chief justice of the Supreme Court, he wrote Wood: *I am glad to read such favorable accounts of the county with which you have done me the honor to associate my name,* but beyond that sentence he apparently had no interest in it. I've also spoken of the Indian notion of names coming to shape their possessor, and so, in that way too, Sam Wood's influence yet lies over the county, although, in many instances now, I find it more ironic than apt. But then, the movement from liberalism to conservatism, from a more open society to a narrower one, is the history of all Kansas.

If Sam's reason for coming to the valley was to make more money, then I believe he wanted some of that income to underwrite his causes: within ten days of bringing his family to the Chase claim, he set up a printing press under a cottonwood tree not far from the river and gave the valley its first newspaper, the *Kansas Press,* a polemical Free State organ of four pages that also promoted the new town and county (he later also brought out the second paper, the *Banner*). In his small house nearby, local Republicans met in 1859 to draw up a resolution calling for the federal government to buy a portion of the Sonoran Desert from Mexico to provide a homeland for black people; this man, who had risked his life transporting fugitive slaves on the underground railroad, had decided (as Lincoln would later) the solution to racial problems was colonization.

Sam also farmed, sold town lots, and practiced law: his defense of four settlers accused of murdering William Hugh (the first of eight men to die violently along Bloody Creek) may have brought vengeance on him when, a month later, fifty tons of his prairie hay were burned, and, soon after that, his house was robbed and torched. Whatever the cause, this is clear: Sam Wood drew fire, figuratively and literally, everywhere he went (appropriately, his Chase home had the first lightning rod in the county). A year later, during an interlude when he lived in Council Grove, his house there was set afire (he must hold the state record for houses deliberately burned from under him).

Sam, so he said, moved twenty miles north to the Grove because the battle over whose plat constituted Cottonwood Falls — his south one or Isaac Alexander's to the north — was hindering the growth of the village, but I suspect he really believed the Santa Fe Railroad would build through Council Grove rather than down the Cottonwood Valley. The town company also plied him with new opportunities to speculate in real estate and it bought many subscriptions to his *Press*, but profits were disappointing there also, and Sam ended up accepting payments in cast-off clothing, coyote pelts, and buffalo chips. He began calling for the opening to white settlers of the Kaw reservation lying just outside the village, and he published sarcastically racist editorials about Indians, yet he hoped to be appointed as the government agent to the tribe. After three years in Morris County, he saw the railroad would not follow the Santa Fe Trail but rather the Cottonwood River, and he moved back to the Falls.

He served in both the territorial and state legislatures before joining the army in 1861 and forming a cavalry company (he wanted a battalion) with himself as captain. He fought at the battle of Wilson's Creek, in Missouri, and in other, smaller engagements across the northern Ozarks, and his eleven-year-old boy joined him in the field (David was one of the youngest combatants in the war; there is a photograph of him seated on Sam's knee, father and son crossing pistols). With unproven charges of malfeasance dogging him — as they did everywhere — Sam's fourteen-month military career was as unconventional and mercurial as all his other endeavors: the army investigated one incident where he took into custody slaves owned by an English trader and, to their bewildered joy, set them free. After trying to resign his commission four times, he finally succeeded and left the army as a lieutenant colonel; he was later appointed brigadier general of the Kansas militia, but after 1862 he preferred to be Colonel Sam Wood.

He continued off and on in the Kansas house and senate, but he could never make the jump to Congress, despite his proficiency as an anecdotal speaker and his comprehension of the law and parliamentary procedure, which allowed him so to control the legislature that people called it *Sam Wood's Circus*. Opponents fought him with legal action (he once said that he had no reason to fear Kansas laws since he had helped make most of them) and twice with weapons: in the capitol, a representative, angered over Wood's advocacy of female suffrage, attacked him with a bowie knife but Sam threw him down as if he were a Westport ruffian. The Little Quaker, as opponents sneeringly called Wood, several times took his fists to adversaries.

Colonel Sam built a new house — of fireproof rock — a mile due east of the courthouse (his virtual second home); a small and unpretentious place, enlarged by a later owner, it sits on a barely perceptible rise at the edge of the river, a location so shrewdly chosen that the Cottonwood has never been inside it: of the dozen places in Kansas that Sam lived, this is the only one remaining. Although on the National Register, this oldest stone dwelling in Chase is in private hands and its survival is tenuous. Behind the house he put in a ferry, a thirty-six-by-fourteen-foot boat, the first in the county: the tolls were a dollar for a loaded wagon, half that for an empty one, fifteen cents for a pedestrian, two cents for a hog.

He opened a general store and also served several terms as county attorney: during one election, he published for six weeks a newspaper, *The Scalping Knife,* to advocate his candidacy, and in it he promised to lower the tax levy, which he did — several times. Wood never ceased arguing for economy in government, and in his later years he began suggesting methods for eliminating the national debt. He went into court to fight the four-and-one-half-mil tax to pay off the sixteen-hundred-dollar difference between the initial cost of the courthouse and some small additions to it, lost the bitter case, but finally won the argument over whose plat legally held the name of Cottonwood Falls. Today, the only obvious manifestation that once there were, technically, two towns, appears in the misaligned streets behind the courthouse: to walk along Union now and see the jogs in eight of the nine north-south avenues, as if Sam had yanked his plat twenty feet west, is to find some of his fossilized footprints.

As a vice president of the Santa Fe Railroad, he tried to bring the line right through Cottonwood and have the depot built on his property, but his opposition to a railroad bond issue that would have burdened taxpayers doomed the Falls from being on the main tracks, and the Santa Fe ended up a mile and a half north; Sam thereby became indirectly responsible for the founding of Strong City, at first called Cottonwood Station, and also the two-mile-long horsecar line that would later connect the depot with the county seat, perhaps the smallest American towns ever to have their own trolley.

He litigated with friends as easily as foes: once, during his term as road-district overseer, his eldest son brought him into court over the placement of a lane; the father fought hard but, said a countian, *he showed more pride in the plaintiff's argument than in the defense.* Sam was not only the most powerful man in Chase but also the most progressive (first corn planter, first registered cattle brand), and he was usually the most liberal, especially when the cause was women's rights, a volatile issue that got him the name of Sally Wood for his advocacy.

He always believed in the power of newspapers to further his causes, but when he left Council Grove he sold his paper, so in 1866 he brought to the Falls an old printing press, the first to come into Kansas Territory, the very one Jotham Meeker hauled up the Missouri River in 1833 to the Baptist Mission near what is today Kansas City, Kansas, to print laws and religious tracts in Indian languages. Before his death, Meeker took the press to Ottawa, Kansas (when he died Indian children sprinkled lead type like wildflowers on his grave); the old machine then went to Lawrence, where the ruffians eventually broke it up and pitched it into the Kaw, but Free State men retrieved and repaired it and put it back into service, and it later survived Quantrill's raid. Sam moved it on west to print his new paper, the *Chase County Banner* (the subsequent peregrinations of Meeker's press are as many and legendary as those of Odysseus).

The *Banner* pumped Sam's projects and promoted women's rights, a cause that drew him into as many ructions as had abolition, even though these quarrels were — the knife attack excepted — of words, many of them libelous charges from editors opposing female franchise. His response was to found the Impartial Suffrage Association and make eastern Kansas a pivot in the women's movement, and he brought to the state (and to the Falls in 1867, the year an earthquake shook the county) Susan Anthony, Olympia Brown, Lucy Stone, and Elizabeth Cady Stanton. He even persuaded Miss Stone to agree to buy his house if woman suffrage won in the county election, but it failed by seven votes and Negro suffrage by three. The election should have shown Sam that his privately professed strategy of achieving the vote initially for women and then pursuing it for blacks was backwards: in 1870 Kansas became the first state to ratify the Fifteenth Amendment (Negro suffrage) but it didn't grant women enfranchisement until 1912, eight years before the Nineteenth Amendment. Although Sam introduced a bill in the Kansas senate in 1867 to extend the franchise to females and blacks, C. H. Langston, grandfather of the poet Langston Hughes, rebuked Wood for complicating, thereby dooming, male Negro suffrage.

The center for his political activity was the small rock home with the Cottonwood River in the backyard, a house that gave roof to

Anthony, Stone, and Stanton, and, later, to another reformist woman, a young Council Grove teacher whom Sam successfully defended in court when she was charged with integrating her classroom, a case foreshadowing the national one that was to occur eighty-nine years later, the momentous *Brown v. Board of Education of Topeka.* The teacher, Mary Ann Hatten, left the Grove for Cottonwood to teach for a term, and she boarded with the Woods, where she found the meals tardy and poorly prepared and the beds, used not only by suffragists but also by men just off the cattle trails, infested. Margaret later said that young Miss Hatten was *very fussy.* The teacher moved on to Emporia, married, and gave birth to William Allen White, but her complaint may have had merit: when the Woods lived in Council Grove, a rival Kansas editor wrote that Sam had *two very nice Suffolk pigs, which, judging from his looks, he eats with, drinks with, and sleeps with,* and, years later when Sam died, an obituary writer said, *They talked about his dirty shirt and his clothes, which were shapeless. But he cared nothing for them, because he cared nothing about clothes. With all the thinking he had to do, he had no time to think of clothes.*

For a couple of years Sam ran cattle on the Chisholm Trail, then tried ranching in Texas, then began a Santa Fe Trail freighting business. In 1865 he went west to check on one of his wagon trains: near Raton Pass on a fiercely cold night, an ox kicked him and broke his leg, but he managed to get himself to the house of the legendary fur trader and trail freighter Uncle Dick Wooton, who pulled hard on the ankle while Sam, somehow keeping from passing out, drew back on his knee to set the tibia, but the fracture didn't knit properly and thereafter he had to wear a built-up shoe.

His businesses gave him enough income that five years after Charles Robinson, famous from the Border War, became the first governor of Kansas he asked Sam for a loan to build a new house, one finer than Woods' own modest place. Of the many derogatory things said against Sam, I've not found any accusing him of wealth or ostentation. In fact, he donated land and money to build a Catholic church in the Falls, even though he was neither a member nor particularly religious. In his lifetime Sam read the Bible through a couple of dozen times, but Margaret said that he believed sharing bread with the hungry was *a more holy ordinance* than taking communion. He often gave food to struggling countians, contributed hours and dollars toward establishing the library in Cottonwood, borrowed money on his own signature to lend to farmers stricken by droughts and grasshoppers, did some legal work as charity, and several times asked Salmon Chase to assist the county (I've found no record that he did).

One morning in Wichita, Sam's great-grandson, Richard, a retired industrial engineer, showed me the colonel's Civil War uniform buttons and his senate barbershop shaving mug. Richard said: *In Cottonwood Sam defended a poor war widow who was about to lose her home in a foreclosure. Her mortgage was on a table in the courtroom. As Sam passed back and forth presenting her case, he quietly tore off a small piece of the mortgage and put it in his mouth. Having no chewing gum, he was known for chewing paper: a soldier at the battle of Wilson's Creek said that Sam went into the fighting with a paper wad between his teeth. Finally, when time came for a decision in the widow's case, the judge declared a mistrial and wrote, "Cause dismissed, Sam Wood having eaten the mortgage." You can find that recorded somewhere in the courthouse.* But I haven't been able to dig it up, although the story sounds like Sam's unorthodoxy: in Lawrence he once saw an intoxicated man who owed him money stagger past his law office, and Wood ran out, tossed the drunk down, and pulled out of his pocket the money due.

The colonel sold his home and twelve-hundred-acre farm east of the Falls in 1873 to a Washington federal judge, David Cartter (who was taking testimony on the shooting of Abraham Lincoln when the president died in the next room). The judge's son, William Cartter, moved his family to Cottonwood from Cleveland (a teacher in the Falls once told William's son, *That is not how you spell Carter*) and quietly brought some wealth into the county, and he raised cattle and racehorses. For a time Sam and Margaret rented a home in Cottonwood before moving to a farm near Elmdale; there, Mary Elizabeth, the youngest child, called El Dearie, became ill on her fourteenth birthday and six days later died of typhoid. What ruffians and repeating rifles and bowie knives and lawsuits could not do — bring Sam Wood down — the death of Dearie nearly did.

He and Margaret moved on to Emporia when he bought a newspaper, the *Kansas Greenbacker*, to espouse cheap paper currency that could raise agricultural prices and ease the debts of farmers. The paper, he thought, might also advance his new political aspirations, but by the early 1880s a more settled eastern Kansas was finding the colonel's irrepressible vigor less useful, and he could not win election to the legislature, so the Woods moved to Topeka, where he could edit the *State Journal* and remain close to the power shaping Kansas.

That did not last long either, and, in 1886, he and Margaret went out to newly organized Stevens County in the southwest corner of the state, an area he had seen while traveling the Santa Fe Trail. He founded the town of Woodsdale, a self-honoring and, given the treelessness there, conveniently deceptive name. He began another newspaper, the *Woodsdale Democrat* (Sam, moving toward populism, left the Republican party as it came to represent money and privilege), and he entangled himself in a deadly fight for the county seat. Of the thirty-some such "wars" fought in Kansas, the one in bloody Stevens was the most violent, in no small way because Sam Wood lived there. To read about the American West is, so often, to discover how far fact stands from our myths of it, but the colonel in western Kansas fuses archetypes of character, scenery, and action into a story that dime novels were just then beginning to concoct and lay across all of the West.

He was abducted and taken on what his enemies called a *buffalo hunt* into No Man's Land — the Oklahoma panhandle where no government appeared to have jurisdiction — only to be rescued, as he had once rescued the old Free Stater Jacob Branson, and saved from execution. It must have seemed to the sixty-one-year-old crippled veteran that the days of border warfare, the kind of society he was most effective in, had come again and that he'd finally found the right place. With his old intrepidity and legal inventiveness, he began fighting a corrupt faction in Hugoton (named after the French novelist who so admired John Brown) that wanted the county seat, the proposed railroad, and the death of Woodsdale. But the Hugoton ring knew that even a graying and limping Sam Wood was still a formidable opponent, and the faction hired a gunman.

XI

Cedar Point

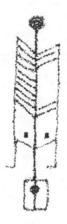

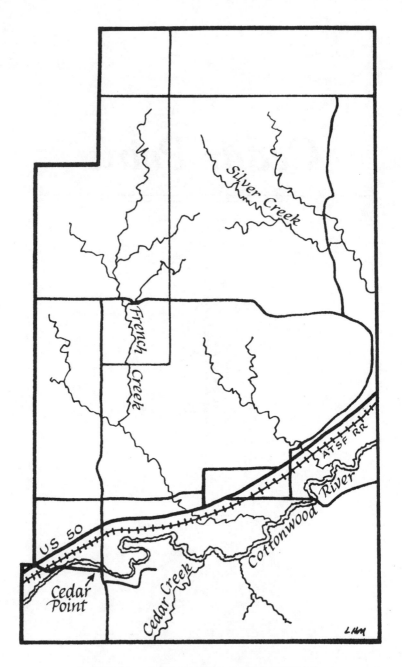

CEDAR POINT QUADRANGLE

From the Commonplace Book: Cedar Point

The spectator's judgment is sure to miss the root of the matter and to possess no truth.

> — William James,
> "On a Certain Sense of Blindness in
> Human Beings" (1899)

The Anthropic Principle . . . states that one of the constraints on the initial state of the cosmos was that it should be the kind of cosmos that could bring about through evolution observers of it that could confirm its existence and compel it to actualize itself by being observed.

> — Frederick Turner,
> "A Field Guide to the Synthetic
> Landscape" (1988)

There always comes a moment, just before the moment of composition, when a subject seems stripped of all attraction, all charm, all atmosphere, even bare of significance. At last, losing all interest in it, you curse that sort of secret pact whereby you have committed yourself, and which makes it impossible for you to back out honorably.

> — André Gide,
> Journal of "The Counterfeiters" (1926)

We must allow for the possibility that we can only understand something truly by knowing its future, its fruits, its consequences.

— Frederick Turner,
"A Field Guide to the Synthetic
Landscape" (1988)

The small country mill used to be one of the most common and important pivots of the American social and economic scene. . . . The road leading to the mill was always well traveled, as the miller was one of the most important members of the community. . . . Conversation and sociability were part of the mill's stock-in-trade, and a strengthened sense of community a byproduct of its existence.

— Douglass L. Brownstone,
A Field Guide to America's History,
(1984)

"Depend upon it, sir, when a man knows he is to be hanged in a fortnight, it concentrates his mind wonderfully."

— Samuel Johnson,
in Boswell's *Life of Samuel Johnson*
(1777)

Whoever could make two ears of corn or two blades of grass to grow upon a spot of ground where only one grew before, would deserve better of mankind, and do more essential service to his country than the whole race of politicians put together.

— Jonathan Swift,
Gulliver's Travels (1726)

The earth belongs in usufruct to the living.

— Thomas Jefferson,
Letter to James Madison (1789)

There are large tracts of land in America whose bounty is wasted because the plants which can be grown on them are not acceptable to our people. This is not because these plants are not in themselves useful and desirable, but because their valuable qualities are unknown.

The people of any country must finally subsist on those articles of food which their own soil is best fitted to produce. New articles of diet must come into use, and all the resources of our own country must be adequately developed.

> — Melvin Gilmore,
> *Uses of Plants by the Indians of the*
> *Missouri River Region* (1919)

We shall continue to have a worsening ecological crisis until we reject the Christian axiom that nature has no reason for existence save to serve man.

> — Lynn White, Jr.,
> "The Historical Roots of Our
> Ecological Crisis" (1967)

Christianity reserved spirit to men alone, and without spirits, plants and animals become mere matter, eligible for dissection into scientific law and economic advantage.

> —Peter Steinhart,
> "Ecological Saints" (1984)

If agriculture is founded upon life, upon the use of energy to serve life, and if its primary purpose must therefore be to preserve the integrity of the life cycle, then agricultural technology must be bound under the rule of life. It must conform to natural processes and limits rather than to mechanical or economic models.

Our agriculture, potentially capable of a large measure of independence, is absolutely dependent on petroleum, on the oil companies, and on the vagaries of politics.

It is likely that we will have either to live within our limits . . . or not live at all. And certainly the knowledge of these limits and of how to live within them is the most comely and graceful knowledge that we have, the most healing and the most whole.

The energy crisis is not a crisis of technology but of morality.

> — Wendell Berry,
> *The Unsettling of America* (1977)

To raise protein in a vegetable form and then feed it to an animal results not in more but less protein for us, for the animal is an inefficient converter. A rough figure for the conversion of vegetable protein to animal protein by all livestock is 8:1. For cattle, the ratio is closer to 21:1. The twenty pounds of vegetable protein that do not become meat become mainly manure, which is not used to fertilize fields, but is washed down the river.

— Lauren Brown,
Grasses: An Identification Guide
(1979)

Indirectly, the meat-eating quarter of humanity consumes nearly forty percent of the world's grain — grain that fattens the livestock they eat. Meat production is behind a substantial share of the environmental strains induced by the present global agricultural system, from soil erosion to overpumping of underground water.

— Alan Durning,
"The Grim Payback of Greed" (1991)

Fertilizers, pesticides, and farm machinery all appear convenient and useful in raising productivity. However, when viewed from a broader perspective, these kill the soil and crops, and destroy the natural productivity of the earth. "But after all," we are often told, "along with its advantages, science also has its disadvantages." Indeed, the two are inseparable; we cannot have one without the other. Science can produce no good without evil. It is effective only at the price of the destruction of nature. That is why, after man has maimed and disfigured nature, science appears to give such striking results — when all it is doing is repairing the most extreme damage.

Man is but an arrogant fool who vainly believes that he knows all of nature and can achieve anything he sets his mind to. Seeing neither the logic nor order inherent in nature, he has selfishly appropriated it to his own ends and destroyed it. The world today is in such a sad state because man has not felt compelled to reflect upon the dangers of his high-handed ways.

— Masanobu Fukuoka,
The Natural Way of Farming (1985)

So much energy is consumed by farms and in the processing of foods that by the time the average American inserts the average calorie into the average mouth, some 9.8 calories of fossil fuels have been spent, meaning that we each eat the energy equivalent of more than thirteen barrels of oil every year.

— Jon R. Luoma,
"Prophet of the Prairie" (1989)

We have worked from the outside in, to alter our environment. Now we are starting to work from the inside out, and that changes every-

*thing. Everything except the driving force, the endless desire to master
our planet.*

> — Bill McKibben,
> *The End of Nature* (1989)

*People talk about human intelligence as the greatest adaptation in the
history of the planet. It is an amazing and marvelous thing, but in
evolutionary terms, it is as likely to do us in as to help us along.*

> — Stephen Jay Gould,
> *Time* magazine interview (1990)

*Since European settlement of North America, we've gone from native
flora to mostly an exotic one, and now we are working our way back
to native, environmentally adapted plants, with, perhaps, a few genetic manipulations thrown in. Sadly, it took us two hundred years to
make this circle, and, two hundred years from now, we'll probably
still be battling the exotics that acclimated and became weeds while
we were making the circuit.*

> — Steven Clubine,
> *Native Warm-Season Grass
> Newsletter* (1990)

*All mankind is entering a new age, and world trends are beginning to
obey new laws and logic.*

> — Mikhail Gorbachev,
> A speech in California (1990)

*What is love?
One name for it is knowledge.*

> — Robert Penn Warren,
> *Audubon: A Vision* (1969)

*The very playful character of [the eastern wood rat], its cleanly habits,
its mild, prominent, and bright eyes, together with its fine form and
easy susceptibility of domestication, would render it a far more interesting pet than many others that the caprice of man has from time to
time induced him to select.*

> — John James Audubon,
> *The Viviparous Quadrupeds of North
> America* (1851)

The ideal geographer should be able to do two things: he should be able to read his newspaper with understanding, and he should be able to take his country walk — or maybe his town walk — with interest.

> — H. C. Darby,
> Lecture at the University of Liverpool
> (1946)

Kansas has had more newspapers established than any other state.

> — Leo E. Oliva,
> "Kansas: A Hard Land in the
> Heartland" (1988)

The frontier everywhere, and nowhere more so than in Kansas, was a crucible which, if it often extracted the best from men, frequently revealed their baser metals as well. Or, in other words, the American West was not only a land of new beginnings, it was also one of bad endings.

> — Albert Castel,
> *William Clarke Quantrill* (1962)

The aboriginal inhabitants of our state were called [Escansaques], "those who harass," "those who stir up," "disturbers," and it seems that latter-day Kansans — those brothers — are keeping up the record by continually working at the same old game. Possibly they have absorbed from the atmosphere or from the soil some of the elements which give them the same characteristics. . . . Kansas will be Kansas no more when she lapses into a stupid pace and ceases to stir public sentiment along lines of activity.

> — George P. Morehouse,
> "History of the Kansa or Kaw Indians"
> (1906)

[Consider] the redoubtable Sam Wood, who as soon as he plays out in one county moves into another, which he never fails to have under his control within a period of ninety days.

> — Editorial,
> *Topeka Weekly Leader* (1865)

Those who cannot answer my arguments are at liberty to use their old arguments of abuse and vilification.

In the number of rich men we now exceed the Old World. These men in many, in fact in most instances, have been made rich by class legislation by which the rich have been made richer and the poor poorer. Public officials and public trusts are today bought and sold with as little hesitancy as we used to buy hogs and sheep.

> — Samuel Newitt Wood,
> "Wood's Manifesto: An Address"
> (1891)

As a saint [Sam Wood] was bright, but as a sinner, miserable, dirty, and unreliable. . . . Upon the whole, his life was a queer admixture of joke and uncommon earnestness, of the lowest comedy and of the highest tragedy.

> — Obituary,
> *Wichita Eagle* (1891)

It has been said that [Sam Wood] had more ardent friends and more violently inclined enemies than any other man who ever trod the soil of Kansas.

> — Cecil Howes,
> *Kansas City Times* (1946)

The typical Kansas politician has long ceased to be a brave, colorful fellow who coins vivid phrases, makes symbolic gestures around which social movements can cohere and so exercises personal leadership.

In most of the key areas of Kansas I've known, the economic man has become dominant almost to the point of excluding values and interests that differ from his. There is a tacit assumption among our ruling elite that the proper major aim of all education, scientific research, and cultural activity is the increase of private profits.

[There is] the present growing national passion for the second-rate in our political life, the present insistence that everybody must think like the more reactionary of our businessmen on pain of being damned as a traitorous fellow.

> — Kenneth S. Davis,
> "What's the Matter with Kansas?"
> (1954)

God made big men and little men, but Mr. Colt made eveners.

> — Anonymous,
> Western apothegm (c. 1880)

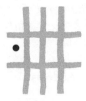

In the Quadrangle: Cedar Point

Talking with a man in Missouri one day, I mentioned I was headed out to Cedar Point, Kansas, and he, a Kansan, said, *There aren't any points in Kansas.* If you understand the word to mean sharply peaked hills, I can think of a few there, although none in Chase County. For Cedar Point, Juniper Mound would be a more accurate name.

Pennsylvanian O. H. Drinkwater came to Kansas and rode against the border ruffians and believed in John Brown and became the third settler in Chase. In 1857, while he was cutting eastern red cedars — technically, junipers — to build a cabin along a stream in the far west of the county, he suggested to a friend they call the creek Cedar. After sheltering whites during a couple of Indian scares, that first cabin, small and insubstantial as it was, became sportingly known as Fort Drinkwater. Later, when O.H. was postmaster, he canceled letters by writing "Cedar Point" across them, and, when he founded a town nearby, he transferred the name to it. I presume the "point" to be the small hill that provides a kind of protective back wall to the village, with its front gate opening onto the Cotton-wood River just north.

O. (for Orlo) H. went off as a captain with the Union army in 1863, but, a few months later, suffered sunstroke while working on a real garrison, Fort Gibson, in Indian Territory, and had to return to his place near the juncture of Cedar Creek with the Cottonwood.

Even though he never quite recovered his health, O.H. in 1867 built a log dam across the deeply banked river here and set up a sawmill. Eight years later, joined by another Pennsylvanian, Peter Paul Schriver, he replaced both with rock structures and began grinding flour to ship over all the area. Of ten nineteenth-century mills once in the county, only Drinkwater and Schriver's remains, not because it was the best but because the Pennsylvanians built it of stone. Today, one of the two finest in the state, it's big and handsome in the plain prairie manner; it's also, if not soon repaired, ready to collapse. It sits full of old milling machinery, pieces of the water turbine sunk in cellar mud.

When I first came to Chase, Drinkwater's mill so fascinated me I at once began asking questions about its history and seeking permission to go through it; a week later when I was again home I received a letter offering the stone mill to me for eight thousand dollars. The next few days I walked around the house and planned how I'd restore it while honoring its listing on the National Register, perhaps make it into a restaurant resplendent with prairie history. When reality finally took hold of me, I declined with real regret, in part because I feared for the mill. Last year, it sold to a young physician in Wichita who plans to repair and stabilize the building, dam, and machinery solely because he loves the beauty and history of the mill; he told me: *I want to leave the grain dust and cobwebs.*

Now, at this moment, I'm parked in front of the mill on the corner of Main and First: Cedar Point has six streets running east and west and four running from the river south; the railroad and U.S. 50 bend around it on the north and west, but enough out of sight so that travelers never see the village unless they turn off the highway. It's half past eight in the morning, starting to rain, and I'm sitting in the back of a small van I've traveled in for fifteen years, a clipboard on my knee. I've pulled the curtains halfway to conceal me as I watch through the rear windows. I'm on assignment.

A couple of days ago a man in Cottonwood said to me, *Nothing happens anymore in Cedar Pointless.* For years I've made a practice of seeing "nothing" because I believe the American idea of "something" usually ends up harming our perceptions and use of the land. The late New York City photographer Ruth Orkin took pictures over the years of a most ordinary intersection below her upper-story apartment across from Central Park and eventually made them into a book. My assignment here is to compress watching and time by observing intensively for twelve hours — arbitrarily no more or fewer — and enter village life only as an unseen observer. We say, "If walls could speak, the tales they'd tell": so, visualize me here as a wall, mute and impassive like those in O.H.'s old gristmill; or, if you prefer, I'm a hunter waiting in his tree-stand to nail his quarry — like him, I must sit downwind. I'm armed with a full load of patience, a small bag of French-roast espresso coffee, and a box of Fig Newtons.

The American novelist John Gardner, I think it was, said there are, really, only two plots: a stranger rides into town, and a stranger rides out of town. Because I've parked my truck around here before and thereby given it a kind of invisibility, maybe I'm inventing a third, the ultimate story: a stranger at one and the same time does both. My friend, writer Jack LaZebnik, claims there is but one plot: death approaches.

My clipboard is ready, my pencil finger itching, and I've warmed up with a couple of tallies:

> PU: 卅ㅣ
>
> AU: ‖

Six pickups have passed, two autos. I'm trying to decide whether brick walls getting wet and elms and cottonwoods moving in the wind count as action. (No, that's scenery.) Jot it down anyway; always get full information. Today, for a change, I have the time and comfort to write my notes neatly and fuss words down ever so tidily. Just so.

Nine o'clock: I'm firing up my backpacker's stove to make the espresso — not a little prissy cup but one of size — to keep me alert in the sweet thrum of rain on the steel roof and the silent mesmerism of trickling windows. My snug parlor fills with the splendid scent of brewing coffee, I hear the Santa Fe roll through the cool gray morning, and I sit warm and dry (and if I don't watch it, coziness is going to overwhelm me). Ah, life. Why haven't I done this before, be a passive reporter who sits back and lets stories come to him? What's with all this county walking? (Prop up the feet.) Here he is, a practitioner of Zen journalism, raking minutes and details into perfection as if in a sand garden.

Ten o'clock and I've just added another stroke to the PU tally; everything is in perfect array inside my unapparent post, and already I have a sense that even now, over the junipered hill, the cedared point, a stranger is about ready to ride into town, and some story will begin. Yes, we have only to wait.

Ten-thirty: The rain, probably, slows activity. When the day clears something will break, nothing spectacular, of course — after all, this is Cedar Point — but some commonplace, small yet marvelous, will open, something otherwise to pass into oblivion unremarked but for Doctor Invisible's magic bullet of a pencil that will capture it for permanent display like a trophy head: every detail is extraordinary when seen in its own deep colors. Sharpen your weapon and have it ready.

Rain: in July of 1951, the great flood stranded the Santa Fe El Capitan four days just outside Cedar Point. A woman fell ill with a gallstone attack, so Billy Brant, a young rancher south of here, puttered up in his small Cessna and landed it on a section of dry highway near the train, where a boat brought the woman to him. He flew her to an ambulance and then returned with milk and diapers for the stranded babies. A month later New York called Billy east to honor him, and three months after that he and his brother went down in the Cessna, both of them killed.

And in another July, this one in 1890, Santa Fe engineer Charley Cogswell stopped his train near Cedar Point, strode off into a pasture with an empty bottle, milked a cow, and returned to feed a squalling infant aboard.

Ten-fifty: another pickup, actually one that passed earlier. I'm starting a new category, WD: wet dogs.

Not far from these scenes and not long after World War One, there appeared in Chase the first rock sign — words spelled out in stone across slopes facing roads — this the only commercial one; the message: TALK HOME — BELL TELEPHONE. It is gone now, but the five county villages with their names spelled out in flinty limestone still retain theirs (although, overgrown as it is, the one above Clements I've been able to discern only from the air). I know an amateur anthropologist who holds that you can demark the "real" West by drawing a wiggly line connecting the most eastern towns having their initials in stone on barren hillsides; if he's right, then you must jog the line far right to include Chase, since it's the most eastern county to follow the custom (with the half-century-old LANDON 4 GOV sign a bonus).

Eleven-ten? That can't be right — it has to be later. (Tap the watch, listen to it: running?) Yes. Damn. The enemy of cross-country hiking is paying too much attention to your feet; the enemy of time hiking is looking at your watch. Advising self: pass the minutes as you would miles — enter the scenery, observe the mountain and see it move. (Why not turn on the radio just to check the time? What harm in that?) No, be here now.

So, the scenery: a stasis of wet brick and stone, leaves and branches. Once Cedar Point was a hopping village of shingled steeples and white gables reaching through the treetops, a main street of false-front shops shoulder to shoulder, where the limestone mill sent out the lull of its cascade, a fall of water you could watch from the old bowstring-arch iron bridge or perhaps from a window of the drummers' hotel. Now the population is thirty-nine, the brick school closed (last year) and also the major business, a power-mower manufacturer (this year). Today only the post office and bank and a sometime garage and the Methodist church remain alive, yet, in its prosaic way, the village retains a certain eroding quaintness emanating mostly from the gristmill and its ponded river and the persistence of its citizens in keeping their town from ghostdom. When the Cedar Point High class of '36 held its fifty-year reunion a few seasons ago, the entire group, but for the one who died young, showed up — all ten of them — each still living in the area.

Cedar Point is not yet dead, and, should some enterprise find a new use for the mill or the school or the empty storefronts, it might revive to last as long as Wichita or Los Angeles. There was a time when the government planned to build a dam across Cedar Creek south of the village to form a large lake, and for some years residents told visitors their place was the *best town by a dam site.* The impoundment has not gone through — may never go through — perhaps thereby dooming the village but preserving a long and lovely valley, a place prehistoric peoples favored, as the abundant archaeological sites attest.

Eleven-something: firing up another cup of espresso to electrocute my yawning and keep from slipping into a spell of noddins and bobbins. Sleepy is the polite, if banal, adjective for Cedar Point, but somnolent it isn't, for it truly lies in the lap of Morpheus; it's the home of forty winks times ten, the capital of Nod where you can really get down to the business of knitting up those raveled sleaves of care.

Only noon. (Has the damp gotten into this watch?) Settle back, take time in its measure, sharpen your pencil while you have the chance. Right now, over the hill, the stranger may be approaching. Not all things, of course, come to him who waits, but one or two do. (Except, perhaps, in Cedar Point?) No, believe in the stranger. (Godot's on the way.)

One autumn afternoon following a hard rain, I stood across from the mill on the other side of the river and watched the water roll over the dam. The turbulent current pushed bright yellow cotton-wood leaves toward the bank where they twisted around and down into small eddies. The little cones were like lubricious mouths slurping away, and at the bottom of one swirl seemed to be a big pair of rubbery lips opening and closing slowly, opening and closing, swallowing the Cottonwood flotsam. The lips then rose to the surface and with them a pair of bulgy eyes and an obscene orange throat — the lips working, throat gulping — and I realized a big feeding carp hung in the eddy, giving the river suction.

One-fifteen. (Another espresso to get those tissues really electri-fied?) Thanks, I will. (Fig Newton?) Don't mind if I do — and your-self? I'll bet we're making history on this spot: never before has anyone sat in a truck here and sipped French-roast espresso, eaten Fig Newtons, tallied wet dogs, and talked to himself.

(This watch grinds out the hours as exceeding slow as the mill of God does life.) Come to! Rake moments into a pattern. What would the Zen master say? (What is the sound of one mind snapping?)

Two. (How about a little walk just to stretch your legs?) And perhaps just an accidental stroll into a conversation, an incident, or maybe just the accidental quickening of time with activity? Oh, no you don't. I am a wall and one day I'll tell the story now on its way from somewhere. (How about another Newton?) After you. (An experiment like this is enough to drive one into writing fiction.) Thought: if some other observer is here, then I'm his stranger. (There's a thin tale.) That's it: think thick. Look across the street, peer into the thickness, sketch it on your clipboard, start with that cast-iron storefront:

Old Mr. Grimwood passed time there by pulling up a captain's chair under the eave each warm day to sit with a twenty-two rifle: when a sparrow (he called them *spatsies*) would squirt on him, he'd open fire.

A harum-scarum visitor once passed time here by reading store signs, and when she got to the one above the mill, the one carved DRINKWATER AND SCHRIVER, she asked her husband, *What does that mean, "Drink water and shiver"?*

Sound of the Santa Fe. The rain drumming yet. Experiment half finished. (Coffee? Drink another and quiver?)

Between the days of stone-ground flour and the arrival of rural electrification, Cedar Pointers converted the flour mill to produce direct-current electricity. Mr. Brunner passed the hours from dusk until ten P.M. by propping back in a chair and dozing, then he'd get up and go to the control board and unplug the town. One night he even threw the school board into the dark when a meeting ran long, and he refused to flip the switch on again, said it was high time to be in bed.

(Is there truth to the rumor that the earthquake, tornado, and numerous fires and floods which have hit Main Street were times of glee here, furnishing something to do?) Not at all. In fact, down at the old Pinkston place, the Anti-Horsethief Association used to stage an annual reenactment of Custer's Last Stand. (Did they see it as allegory?)

To be honest, now that I think about it, one of the things to do here, over the years, has been to witness death theatrically and actually. (For Pointers, then, sometimes there is but the one plot.) The undertakers bore names out of Dickens: the Grimwood Brothers. Captain Drinkwater's son, D.F., passed some time here by printing the *Cottonwood Valley News*, the second issue of which reported the death of his father after he was struck by a bicycle; and not long afterward, O.H.'s partner, Peter Paul, got run down by an even larger vehicle, a Santa Fe locomotive, at the edge of town where Main crosses the tracks. A year after my first survey of the county, at that very spot, four children in the same family died when a train hit their car.

Three o'clock. (How about a little nap, just to sharpen the senses?) Stand up, rouse yourself! Occupy the mind! William James once said, *Where is it, this present? It has melted in our grasp, fled ere we could touch it.* (Yes, but he never watched the corner of Main and First in Cedar Point, Kansas, on a rainy Saturday.) Were the present a hot-blooded woman, this truck would be in shambles, so long has she had me in her unyielding grasp.

Four o'clock. (Or maybe it's Orwell's thirteen o'clock.) Take away the stories, the past, and what do you have? (A dulled babbler.)

In the days of Fort Drinkwater, French settlers — including one count who had lost his fortune in republican uprisings — began arriving in Cedar Creek Valley until there were more than sixty families and annual Bastille Day celebrations (the count feigned jollity) and tornado caves stocked with wild-grape *vin ordinaire*, and at least one cabin full of books and paintings. A few descendants remain yet today, although wine cellars and July Fourteenth fêtes and *la langue maternelle* are so long gone that countians now speak of *the Lost French Colony.*

A Gallic story: Claude Francis Bichet, a carver of wooden shoes from Dijon, with wife Sophia and young son Alphonse, came into the county in 1858 after Francis spent their last two hundred dollars in St. Joe on an old wagon and a span of poor oxen. On the Bichets' first night in Kansas, one of the animals wandered off; the next morning, the family could neither find it nor make themselves understood to ask after it. Francis tried to adjust the double yoke on the remaining ox but the thing hung down and choked the animal. All he could think of was to get his shoulders under the opposite end of the yoke and carry it alongside the beast; and so, bent like bovines, *le monsieur et la madame* took turns plodding next to the ox the 180 miles to Cedar Creek Valley. (How the slow present — like a yoke of another kind — must have hung on Francis and Sophia.) A few years later, perhaps inspired by his parents, Alphonse hitched a ride to Council Grove and returned forty miles on foot, carrying on his back two factory-made windows for the Bichet cabin.

(Speaking of the French, Paul Valéry said a writer's work is never completed but merely abandoned. Couldn't journalistic experiments easily fall into a subcategory?) The difficulty with the present is that you can't shut it off like the past or future — it's a broken faucet that endlessly drenches you, only to drain away somewhere else, never leaving a deep pool like yesteryear. (Your romanticism is sloshing, my friend.)

The rain, by the way, has stopped, and a man is actually walking up Main — tally one *Homo sapiens.* All right! He pauses, looks toward the truck. Yes? (What if he comes over? Do we participate?) This experiment is one of utter passiveness. (The Dick Nixon school of reporting: stonewall it.) Here he comes, yes, yes . . . and there he goes. Didn't even slow down. (You've succeeded: you've managed to disappear in Cedar Point. Point? You've brought yourself down to a point like a receding figure.) The stranger rides into town . . . (And?) He vanishes.

Six o'clock. The hours grind and turn my thin harvest not to grist but to dust.

At last, twilight. The experiment not finished but abandoned, my perception annulled by stasis and able to find small movements but no action, scenery but no scenes, no dramatic question beyond the personal one: will I last this present out?

Eight o'clock. (Start the engine.) If Drinkwater's old mill walls could speak, I now have an idea of what they would say: *It's been a damn long century and a quarter.* And, with their hard-earned tales, they might make another observation: failing to see the distance between the memorable events that comprise one's perception of the past distorts the hell out of it.

Were the stranger to ride into town at this final minute, I know what he'd say, how he'd put the plot into motion:

Pointer : *What brings you into town, stranger?*
Stranger: *I've got a message from Captain O. H. Drinkwater: when you go west to join him, bring plenty of stories.*

To Consult the Genius
of the Place in All

In Cedar Point I heard a couple of men talking about a plot of ground near the village first planted in 1865, and one said, *I remember when that bean field was in alfalfa,* and the older one said, *Hell, I remember when it was in oats.* Today, I know of only a single, small oat field in the county. Like oats, alfalfa and soybeans are not native plants, but, while they don't quite represent a historical succession, their comings and goings do reflect changes in what we eat and the way we produce it. The Cedar Point oat farmer surely never dreamed of a crop like soybeans growing one day in his field, and that made me wonder what future crop I couldn't imagine might be there someday.

I knew a man owning land in Matfield Green but living near Salina, fifty miles northwest of Chase, who could have an answer. I'd met Wes Jackson one morning when I walked into the Wagon Wheel Café in Strong City: there he sat with Wendell Berry, the Kentucky writer and farmer; I'd read some of their splendid books, which, like *Walden,* are about sustainable agriculture with nature as the model. The three of us had come to Chase for a conference on grassland preservation. Wes Jackson, with Berry and Bruce Colman, had just then brought out *Meeting the Expectations of the Land,* but he was recognized more for a slender and influential book, *New Roots for Agriculture,* about tilled fields and human survival. We had no time then to talk beyond greetings.

After I heard the Cedar Point farmers, I went off to Wes' farm a few miles south of Salina. He cut his home, like a dugout, into the earth on a bank high above the Smoky Hill River and near The Land Institute, a teaching and experimental farm he and his wife, Dana, founded in 1976. He has a doctorate in genetics, and now, seeing the danger in homogenized agriculture given over wholly to annual one-crop fields with depleted genetic stocks, he and others at "The Land" are out to build a domestic prairie. They combine plant breeding with ecological studies of never-plowed prairie in hopes of developing *herbaceous, perennial, seed-producing mixtures as substitutes for annual monocultures* on erodible sloping ground. Jackson wants to reduce significantly our reliance on cultivation, fertilization, pesticides, herbicides, and fossil fuels. In one experiment, his colleague Peter Kulakow has crossed and backcrossed two nonindigenous species, milo and Johnson grass (a noxious weed to Kansas farmers), in an attempt to produce a plant with the strong rhizomes of a perennial and the abundant seedhead of an annual.

Wes wants to mimic the prairie to feed people without also endangering them and eroding and poisoning the earth. One of the crops that might grow someday in that Cedar Point field, if it becomes domestic prairie, could be a descendant of that "milograss." Before I left The Land, I pulled a few seeds from the new plant: they were crunchy and sweet, nearly as palatable as some breakfast cereals.

Great-grandfather Jackson rode with John Brown, and Wes, born in 1936, is a first cousin once removed to Dwight Eisenhower (who grew up half an hour away in Abilene). Wes recently brought out another book, *Altars of Unhewn Stone,* and, the week I visited, *Life* magazine had just selected him as one of eighteen Americans who are likely to be recognized in a century as "wavemakers."

Not so much a man of answers but of ideas, he's a geneticist trying to turn concepts into solutions, but he's wary of technological fixes, especially those using genetic engineering: he once said, *The philosophy that got us into trouble is not the philosophy that is going to get us out of trouble.* He comes from a family of farmers who took religion seriously, and Wes still speaks of plows and sinful pride in the same sentence: he is a practitioner of both a new agricultural and social order. A fellow of some size — people comment on his Lincolnesque hands — he seems even bigger. Someone once described his features *as rough as Cottonwood Limestone,* a suitable phrase because there is something architectural, if not monumental, about him. Since our first meeting in the Wagon

Wheel, he'd grown a beard and now he looked more like Lincoln's cousin than Ike's — especially when he delivered one of his Lincoln-like aphorisms: *We're not called to success but to obedience to our visions.*

Twice in his life physicians have told him he had cancer: once leukemia, the other time non-Hodgkin's lymphoma. The doctors were wrong. The first proved to be mononucleosis. During the second scare Jackson, with the help of the pathologist, was able (from his long experience of preparing slides) to see how faulty laboratory techniques led to an incorrect diagnosis. What he had was only a fatty tumor. To use his word, his discovering a future in doom is a *paradigm* of his work today. He said that tumor pushed him close to a personal doomsday and served to concentrate his attention. In that, there is also a paradigm.

Wes is a fine talker, a discourser really, who sends an idea aloft like a pennant, then cuts out another of complementary fabric and hoists it, then a third, until finally he has half a dozen streamers airborne, a panoply of parti-color banners that he then brings together into a union. He will say, *Now, put that on hold for a moment,* and off he goes again. He was crunching into a hard pear when I saw him, and he said, *I'd offer you one, but they aren't ripe.* Another paradigm.

It was a warm September morning: we sat near the oak-lined bank of the Smoky Hill River (which he uses as an Alice-in-Wonderland barometer that forecasts far ahead by looking backward: clear water means clear weather yesterday, but water clouded by runaway topsoil reveals not only a storm the day before but also a depletion to come). We talked — *he* talked — and the whole time dozens upon dozens of blackbirds in the branches above us were doing their autumnal yak-yak, and twice I had to ask him to repeat a sentence, the birds so poured it down on us. In the two hours we sat there, the population of the earth grew by twenty-two thousand, more than seven Chase counties.

Wes began by talking about thermodynamics. He said, *Let me ramble,* and sat quietly, organized thoughts, and then, *There are farmers running around here in Saline County who believe the oil companies have a pill the size of an aspirin that can be dropped into a few gallons of water to produce as much energy as a tank of gasoline. There's so much ignorance about energy. Hold on to that for a moment. If you take the U.S. Geological Survey data seriously, the world has left about a thirty-three-year supply of oil at* the current rate of use. If we use only proven American reserves, we have just a few months more than a four-year supply plus what the USGS estimates to be twenty years of unproven reserves. As we get closer to running dry, we may begin stretching petroleum out, but nevertheless the end of cheap fossil fuel is near. Look at the incredible infrastructure built on portable liquid fuels and you'll realize that there's a lot of dislocation coming.

Bear in mind that even though electricity is an energy form in which a hundred percent of it is available for work, given our current infrastructure and irrational settlement patterns it's simply not ready to become a substitute for portable liquid fuels. We have two alternatives. If we choose nuclear, we have to remember Chernobyl and the twenty-seven towns and villages that people should never go home to. Can we ever have safe nuclear power? I understand there's a principle in engineering which holds that, essentially, all major achievements come from failures rather than successes. If you want to cross a bridge, don't go over one that's a prototype — use one that's a derivative of lots of failed bridges. So the question becomes: how many Chernobyl accidents will we have to have in order to achieve safe nuclear power? Can we afford even one per century?

If we say no to nukes, then we've got to go with solar. Photovoltaics can produce electricity, but remember the infrastructure and our social arrangements built on portable liquid fuel. Now the news gets really bad. Several years ago, farmers came to us here at The Land and said they wanted to tell OPEC to go to hell. They wanted to turn their grain into alcohol just to run tractors and combines. At that time America had four hundred million cultivated acres, seventy million in corn, our major carbohydrate producer. All we wanted was to meet the one percent of our energy used to move machinery around fields.

It turned out that it would take not seventy million acres of corn to meet on-farm traction needs but one hundred seventeen million acres, and that would leave nothing for livestock, nothing for people. What we found, even assuming the ideal, is that we would need more than a quarter of the total agricultural acres of the richest farm country in the world just to produce and move food out the farm gate.

Can we put alcohol into our tanks to run cars and trucks at anything close to the current level? You'd better forget it. The era of cheap, portable fuel is over and we're going to live in a very *different world from now on. All right, put that on the back burner.*

Sun-powered systems have a kind of optimum ratio between the photosynthesizer and the concentrator. Imagine a field of corn as a photosynthesizer and a farmstead as a concentrator, where people, machinery, and buildings are the agents of concentration. Concentrators can work efficiently only over an area so large before expansion produces diminishing returns. When we moved from farming with draft animals to tractors (fossil fuels) the number of farms declined. The ratio became distorted beyond what we can support.

I have two stories to illustrate: George Borgstrom, the Swedish nutritionist, once spoke of the origin of cheese making in Europe: he said in a sun-powered culture, if you're using the legs of horses or people, you don't haul all that water to town when you sell your cheese. You transport only solids that count nutritionally. Had humans evolved with the level of fossil-fuel energy we have now, European cheese making might never have happened.

There's another story: Wendell Berry's farm has a steep hill going up to Port Royal, Kentucky. An old neighbor told him the tiredest his daddy ever got was the time he carried fifty rabbits and a possum up that hill. Wendell asked him, "Why didn't you use a horse?" and the neighbor said, "We only had two horses, and we tried to spare them every way we could." In other words, across the landscape, a sun-powered culture will have more carefully thought out arrangements than we have now.

By and large, agriculture is an extractive enterprise. Often, when farmers improve their land, a closer look reveals they have engaged in a kind of theft: they go somewhere else to bring fertility into their fields; whether it's a neighbor's manure or nutrients from the city, they close the loop some way. So the question becomes: what is acceptable theft?

I asked whether the motive force for change would have to be the specter of running out of oil, and he said, That and the problems with nukes, even though you can see that we're going to try to substitute nukes for oil.

By practicing any form of agriculture, the chances are humans will invert what nature is doing well. I want to learn how to invert nature less. If we are to get serious about an ecological agriculture, where nature is the standard and native prairie serves as our analogy, then we have to think about the basic unit of our study: the community — a diversity of species living together. We destroyed most of the original relationship we had with nature as we ex-

panded our gardens and plots into fields. I think that was our downfall. We began inverting over larger areas what nature does well until we turned agriculture into a fundamentally extractive enterprise. Now we have something called agro-ecology trying to correct that error, which is our current brand of agriculture. That's why it's fitting to introduce agro-ecology into economics. A native prairie or a deciduous forest is a sacred economic system. I believe it's worthwhile to compare natural systems — natural communities — with human ones. Nature engages in barter, and so do we, but we symbol makers have gone beyond and invented a metrical device called money to represent our transfer of energy and nutrients.

Capitalism arose and expanded to its highest level on a young and abundant North American continent. But capitalism is a pump, an extractive system that bases its strength on eventual exhaustion. We consume and throw away. A natural system depends on recycled materials, while an industrial one employs extraction. The late John Fischer, editor of Harper's, *wrote an autobiography called* From the High Plains. *In there, he said one way to understand the plains is as a place of mining economies: Indians dug flint, then came white hide-hunters, then buffalo-bone miners, then the cattlemen grass miners, then the agricultural soil miners, then wildcatters after gas and oil, and now water miners drilling into the Ogalala Aquifer. We European descendants have gone from one mining or extractive economy to another. Put that on hold.*

George Wald, the Harvard biologist and Nobel laureate, once said — let me get his words straight — "We living things are a late outgrowth of the metabolism of our galaxy. The carbon that enters into our composition was cooked in the remote past in a dying star. . . . The waters of ancient seas set the pattern of ions in our blood. The ancient atmospheres molded our metabolism." Keep that in mind. If we look at the Paleolithic era, that 750,000 years of human evolution, and especially the last 150,000 with the big brain, we see that humans have had agriculture for only about ten thousand years — no more than eight percent of our more recent evolutionary history. This implies that our Paleolithic predispositions — our nerve endings, endocrine system, what we are biologically — the old inclinations must still be in us. In a certain sense, we're a species out of context, and that's probably one reason we don't manage agriculture very well. I think it was Nigel Calder

who said, "If we were meant to be farmers we'd have longer arms."
We certainly weren't designed biologically to have this much fossil
energy at our fingertips. We just can't use it wisely.

So, doesn't it make sense to try to find ways to use those Paleolithic predispositions to our benefit? To look at how tribes survived? Community is civilization's upscaling of the tribe, and it
works primarily because it draws upon those Paleolithic longings
that sustained the tribe. They are somehow embedded in patterns
of human behavior. I think we once again have to take advantage
of those old inclinations.

For Paleolithic people, the tribe was a more fundamental unit
than the nuclear family. Now, I'm not saying the family doesn't
have an important role, but let's think about the possibilities of a
coherent new community by looking at the Amish. We have a
number of them near us here. They've managed to stay economically solvent during this most recent agricultural crisis. Community doesn't simply derive from aggregations of people: the Amish
create theirs through an organizing principle — the control of the
sin of pride. They believe if you curb pride, then you get leverage
on all the other sins, and they know that an individual acting alone
cannot control pride — a person needs help from the community.

A century ago, the Amish didn't appear much different from
other farm cultures around them, but with the coming of industrial
agriculture, we non-Amish thoughtlessly became dependent upon
fossil fuels and went about buying whatever was new, while they
continued to assess technology against a moral standard. For us, a
thing once possessed can't be done without. The Amish seem to
have embraced a Paleolithic reality. I'm talking about patterns as
old as our species that we've obscured by laying a technological
veneer over them. But if we will reestablish the conditions which
make community possible, most of our old predilections will come
back as gifts arriving from we won't know where.

Let me take some pots off all those back burners. We have to
confront the end of the fossil-fuel epoch; disastrous soil erosion;
chemical contamination of our food, air, and water; the development of an ozone hole as big as the United States; global warming.
Keep naming them. We have to find, as the Amish have, a way to
assess our technology against a standard that controls the sin of
pride, the desire to possess more power and goods than are justly
ours.

Hold that for a moment. We need to ask two questions: what

*will nature require of us? and what was here before we came?
Wendell Berry suggests a third: what will nature help us do? About
sixty years ago, a student in Iowa examined a tall prairie growing
next to a wheat field. He learned that native grassland seemed
designed to absorb water and allocate it according to need,
whereas the wheat field tended to throw it off. The prairie had less
erosion, lower soil temperatures generally, and so on. One of the
natural integrities of grassland is its efficient capture and release of
water. In his "Epistle to Burlington," Alexander Pope advised gar-
deners: "In all, let Nature never be forgot" and "Consult the Genius of the Place in all."*

I've looked at Chase County as the ideal place to develop a
prototype of a new agricultural community, one not based on
petro-traction and petro-fertility. The county has about eighty-five
percent grassland and fifteen percent tilled land, a good ratio for
our new purposes. A railroad runs through, providing highly efficient transportation. Because Chase County hasn't had a swelling
of population or any real industrial development, it offers an opportunity to make the transition. I imagine keeping the grassland
intact, planting bottomland to a greater diversity of species, and
farming it in somewhat different ways to try to be much less
extractive and to reduce the distance human concentrators must
travel to harvest the photosynthesizers.

I've been telling college audiences that the most exciting field for
the next century will be accounting. It always gets a laugh, but it
points out that nature lives off interest and most of humanity off
principal. Imagine that we put up a mental rope around Chase
County and say this is where our tribe, our community, will live
(and not just reside). Maybe we can even wear caps with our own
tribal logo instead of ones with the corporate overlord's. First of all,
we'll want to pay attention to ways we allow ourselves to participate in the extractive economy — and we will have to participate,
especially in the early stages. We'll need to ship both plant and
animal material out of our valleys, but then we'll have to watch
the recharge rate carefully to see that we restock nutrients taken
away. Sustainability means that we balance the nutrient budget.

This new Chase will need more people on the land, maybe about
triple the present population, about the number there in 1900.
While the industrial farmer relies on a sufficiency of capital, we,
like the Amish, will require a sufficiency of people. Labor — not
fossil by-products and machinery — will be our biggest expense.

We'll assume that people come to this new economic order because they've perceived the need for it and found it's to their economic advantage to join others.

In the first phase of transition we'll begin to free our agriculture — and our entire culture — from the petrochemical industry. Agribusiness, relying on a heavy fossil-fuel subsidy, sells packages of information because agribusiness works by homogenizing landscapes. We'll have to stop doing that and follow Pope's words — or those of the alternative agricultural biologist John Todd, of the New Alchemy Institute: "Elegant solutions will be predicated upon the uniqueness of place." Present agribusiness is incredibly simple and simplifying but its high energy destroys biological and cultural information and patterns. Historically, agribusiness has used our farms and landscapes, in Maury Telleen's words, as "a quarry to be mined."

I told Wes I'd read the other day that a farmer said, *Children who haven't walked yet have a right to the productivity of the land,* but corporate America doesn't often agree. I reminded him of his advice to young farmers preparing to deal with agribusiness: *Study Faust.* Then I asked him for details of the new Chase.

At first, we can probably continue to grow most of the crops that are there now, but we'll have to change the way we grow them. I see nothing wrong with introducing draft animals back into Chase County, where people are accustomed to using horses to work stock. A horse or mule runs on sunlight, and four legs running on carbohydrates is more efficient ultimately than a tractor using alcohol. We'll have to use creatures that utilize solar energy rather than buying finite sources of sunlight from a fossil source: solar power stored briefly in muscle rather than in a five-hundred-million-year-old oil cavern. Our traction animals could feed on the surrounding grasslands so that hillside sunlight sponsors agriculture in the valleys. Maybe there'll be a little less room in the pastures for beef if we're feeding traction animals, but we're eating too much meat anyway.

Horses and mules? I asked. Are we going back to the nineteenth century? He smiled at that.

We may have an alcohol-powered baler that's pulled through the field by horses, and stationary engines to provide highly efficient belt power for jobs like threshing, but that doesn't mean going backwards. We may also have microprocessors attached to drills for different applications of fertilizers. Some horse-drawn Amish buggies have digital clocks in them. We'll employ a lot of sublety and sophisticated technology, but, clearly, we'll also need a new sense of who we are, one that allows us to reintroduce some old technologies and not feel terrible about ourselves. This new sense will ask us to do more physical work, to use more of our own renewable biological energy: instead of jogging — there's a response to a Paleolithic disposition — we'll use that energy to produce something.

Once we come to see that we can no longer dose ourselves in the service of the industrial paradigm, then the question is: how far can we go with it? Today Americans use one-point-eight times as much energy to sponsor nitrogen fertility as we use for traction. This happens because we use natural gas as the source of nitrogen fertilizers. We'll see that it's to our advantage to use manure, both green and cow, rather than anhydrous ammonia. We can use legumes to replace nitrogen and carbon. Potassium and phosphorus and the other minerals, we'll need to replace mostly by returning human and animal wastes. To fail at any of these steps is to go back to mining the land.

And pesticides and herbicides? I asked.

If we introduce synthetic chemicals to get at some bug or pathogen or weed, we'll have to see it as a potential assault on life and ourselves. Redwoods, ospreys, Holsteins, or humans — we're all made of the same twenty amino acids and the same four nucleic-acid bases. We all had one origin. The major consideration here is not to put any chemical into the environment that our tissues have no evolutionary experience with. We must regard any new synthetic chemical as guilty until proven innocent.

We may want to get into real flood control, where we say, "We've got a twenty-year period coming up and the probability of flooding is one in this many times, so let's open the gates and let that fertility into our Chase fields rather than allow nutrients to head for New Orleans." In Europe, up until the 1940s, many hill farmers would haul the bottom furrow up to the top of the slope each year. They understood it's better to carry earth back up the hill than the bodies of malnourished children to the grave.

Let me try another run at this. The price of concentrating our sources of energy, as well as the idea that we can't afford the risks of nukes, and even the notion of getting the water out of the cheese before taking protein and fat to town — all of these imply a resettling of America. The end of the fossil-fuel epoch will mean the need for many more people in small communities across the land. Cedar Point or Matfield Green, with their closed businesses and school buildings, are victims of an "unsettling of America," to use Wendell's phrase, victims of an industrial economy which created an industrial mind that destroyed their community and their local culture. Remember, high energy destroys information of the cultural and biological varieties. Conversely, I believe that a lower energy budget can lead to a kind of reculturization of folk. I'm working on a book now called An Education to Take Home, and that's what we've been talking about — going home.

We've probably always had a little something in us causing us to wish for a neighbor's land rather than a neighbor, and a society built around a fossil-fuel-powered industrial paradigm made that possible, and thereby validated greed in ways seldom available before. Now the time has come to call that avarice for what it is, sin, and then maybe we can find ways to reward another Paleolithic instinct, the urge to help a neighbor. That too is in us. Sooner or later, we come to this question of how to resettle the land. I'll defend private ownership, but it's simple-minded to say that the best ownership is always private. There's some land that should be collective for the good of the community.

I said that Chase County homesteaders who came to claim a quarter-section at first treated the uplands as pastures held in common, but Americans today have difficulty in looking at history or evolution for ideas to solve problems.

We hold a churchyard cemetery or a city park in common and we make no fuss over those. Trouble comes when we feel our voices are being left out of managing the grounds — that's why we don't like big government. In all this, scale is crucial. Our Paleolithic urge to help a neighbor works as long as the scale isn't too big or the neighbors too distant. One of the things that makes an Amish community viable is that there are no owners of large tracts. There's a story about an Amish man who bought eighty acres and a friend asked him, "Can you make it on eighty?" and the man said, "I don't know — I know I can make it on forty." That's an Amish paradigm.

I spoke of a mental rope around Chase County as a way of concentrating on what comes in and what goes out, a reminder to ask, how far can we go in exporting nutrients for dollars? How far can we go in exchanging protein for VCRs? Right now Americans are trading topsoil for Toyotas, and the deficit shows in both the *budget and the land. Our ecological accountant will watch these things. He may tell us that to cut our deficit we'll have to rebuild some of the little electrical plants on the Cottonwood River.*

Like the ones that used to be in the old Cedar Point or Cottonwood grist mills up until a few years ago, I said.

When you have that mental rope in place, it forces you to think about closing all the loops, the cycles. Last spring I was in Strong City with a waste-management expert from Santa Barbara. He looked at those Dumpsters in Strong, and he said, "Do you know where the money they make goes? Chicago." He said the twin towns could buy a truck, hire two or three people, and keep that "waste money" right there. To him the Dumpsters were mines. Now that's a form of mining we should be doing. If we overcome our ecological illiteracy and see that answers are more cultural than technological, we can start thinking about how to take advantage of the mysteries of community and tribe and our Paleolithic longings.

I mentioned that a thing once possessed can't be done without: in our evolution, when we found a better way to throw a pot or a better oven to fire it in, our chances for survival increased. But there can come a time, especially when resources are abundant, when an adaptive trait goes too far and becomes maladaptive.

I asked, a woodpecker beak needs to be only so big? A longer one will eventually extinguish the bird?

Well, the human mind is incredibly wily when it comes to economics. People catch on fast when things get down to dollars. One of those old schoolhouses in Chase County might just be a place to gather people and develop a new world view about the second coming of the homesteader. It might be the ideal spot to explore an agriculture that can run not so much on human cleverness but on the wisdom of nature. The benefits would accrue to the land and the farmer and much less to industrial overlords.

Concerning the Glitter Weaver

One morning several years ago when I was living in a small rental house in a Missouri field, I got out of bed to answer the phone. I picked up the receiver, sat down on the couch, and a mouse leaped from beneath the cushion onto my bare foot and vanished into the kitchen. I felt its claws on my skin. I called into the phone, Hold it! while I lifted the cushion: in the new sofa was a gnawed pit, and laid out neatly like nested spoons were five pink mouslings, un-haired, eyes unopened, each uttering faint squeaks, their tiny barbed mouths opening and closing to find a hot teat. Good god, I said to my friend. In irritation, revulsion, fascination, I described what I'd found. With full seriousness, he said, *The mother won't come back now that you've upset her — you'll have to raise them.* Raise them! I shouted, and then, Will this new couch make them a goddamn good enough nest?

For the previous three months, figuring we all could get along in some form of commensalism, I'd shared the house with mice and tolerated feculence and pungent dried urine in a shoe, accepted waking in the night to see a rodent inches away scratching around the lighted face of the clock. *Calm down*, my friend said. *They're only frigging mice.* It was, of course, future frigging that gave me concern. I put the squirming nestlings onto a dustpan and carried them outside to die in the sun, but then decided a coup de grâce was more "humane" (that word we use when we're about to do something worse than bestial). I took a brick and, with one fell stroke, jellied them.

From that day on, rodents and I have had our territorial disputes, both in houses and, twice, in my little on-the-road truck; since that morning, I've been a setter of traps. I tell you all this so you'll understand my surprise when, on one of my early trips into Chase County, I found myself becoming curious about wood rats, small beasts as engaging as any here.

Still, I can't imagine that you would want to join in what I'm doing now: trying to disassemble a wood-rat nest built along and into a low rock ledge not far from Cedar Point. After all, who cares for rats? They are things we care against, like blackflies and ticks, only bigger. Last night I called my mother on her eightieth birthday and, in the course of our conversation, mentioned my plans for today. She, who often despairs of the materials that go into my writing, said, *Oh, William!* (Her maternal disappointments always turn me into William.) *Can't you find something uplifting to write about?*

In all my time in the county, I've seen many wood-rat nests but never, even once, the animal, so for me it's a kind of living fossil, something like the fusulinid tests I see in the Cottonwood Limestone of the courthouse walls, and I believe in its existence as I do in extinct sea critters: because of what they have built. For similar reasons I also believe in history. I'm trying, as I pull at this stick nest, not to break the pieces because I hope to tell you the precise number the rat has used, and I'd like to discover how the animal has interlaced them to make disassembly so difficult. I've wanted to do this since my first guided tour through the county several years ago when Larry Wagner, the Tallgrass Prairie Park advocate, gave me a wonderfully informed two days here. As his father bounced us down a lane in southern Chase, we passed an isolated Osage-orange tree: twelve feet up in it and woven among the branches was a huge conglomeration of sticks, enough material to fill a couple of fifty-gallon oil drums. If pigs could fly, they would build nests such as that one. Larry said it was a wood-rat lodge, but it looked more as if a crazed beaver had decided to go arboreal. I'd seen wood-rat nests before, but they had always been inside abandoned houses and outbuildings, at the bases of trees, along rock ledges and inside caves, and once even in the back seat of a derelict Buick. He could have told me, as believably, that a robin would just as soon build its nest at the bottom of a pond as in a tree.

Not long afterward I returned to that aerial nest and tried and failed to climb the thorned limbs. (The wood rat, weighing about a pound, is a native of this region but Osage orange is not, yet the rodent now takes to hedge like an eagle to a snag, and it may help spread certain trees into the prairie.) I found a long stick and poked at the lodge in hopes a resident would scurry out and reveal itself, but nothing stirred. Later I said to myself, you spend fifteen years killing rodents and then expect them to show themselves to you? You might as well wrap yourself in neon, the blood lust they must smell on you. Perhaps, but I'm not an eater of their flesh, as are some native peoples of the Southwest (the meat, so I hear, is better than quail).

Now: I'm laying the sticks of this rock-ledge nest in stacks of ten, but with all the breakage my count will be imprecise. It has taken an hour of untangling just to get four piles.

Countians call these animals pack rats or sometimes field rats but never trade rats, a name more common farther west. The number of citizens having a story about them is comparable to those people with tornado tales, although their favorite rodents are the rather rare black squirrels, found around here only in the twin towns. Pat Sauble, whose farm of classic stone buildings is nearby, told me of his father one night years ago hearing slow and heavy footfalls on the stair leading up to his bedroom in the old farmhouse; he lay and listened, then, with trepidation, rose quietly, got his gun, and crept to the head of the steps: he saw a wood rat struggling backwards down the risers and tugging a gunnysack with several potatoes in it: *thump, thump, thump.*

More commonly, wood rats keep their distance from people, and most of the big nests in Chase are in the relatively isolated southwest corner of the county. For this reason, as much as any other, the animals are not usually a nuisance unless you leave a vehicle unattended in a pasture for a year as one countian did: when he went to move his old pickup, he lifted the hood and saw nothing but sticks massed exactly into its shape as if they had been poured into a mold. And Frank Gaddie of Bazaar left a truck out for some time and then drove it into Cottonwood to have it worked on; when the mechanic put it on the rack and lifted it to look at the undercarriage, he found himself nose to snout with a big-eyed wood rat and whunked his head in recoiling.

These timid and reclusive animals, which keep a certain distance even from their own kind, are mostly nocturnal, occasionally crepuscular, rarely diurnal, and many countians who think they have seen one in broad daylight have, in fact, seen a Norway rat — the so-called house rat (*Rattus norvegicus*) — a destructive non-native species that has spread over all of America.

From a distance, the indigenous eastern wood rat does look something like the European rat, but it belongs to a different family and its habits and behavior are signally distinct. What Walt Disney did to the house mouse to turn it into Mickey, evolution has done to the pack rat to distinguish it from distant Old World relations: its ears are bigger and rounder and fuzzy, its tail shorter (but long enough to curl around its feet when it sleeps) and furred and not hairless and scaly; its face is a little blunter, its eyes larger and more innocent, its pelt softer and thicker and prettier; its belly and feet are white so that when it stands it looks as if it were wearing a tux and spats. But its milder disposition renders it no match for a house rat, and some of its aggressive behavior consists of nothing more than grinding teeth, vibrating lips, or rhythmically stamping feet (Thumper in *Bambi*). Unlike *norvegicus* it will not cram together or eat swill or live in filth: a wood rat in the wild usually has a separate chamber in its lodge, and special locations outside, for a latrine. (I know some Native Americans who have their own private understanding about why imported European species are so vile yet so successful.) These characteristics coupled with its preference for solitary life make it a winning little pet. John James Audubon wrote of a female and her three young he kept: *They became very gentle, especially one of them which was in a separate cage. It was our custom at dark to release it from confinement, upon which it would run around the room in circles, mount the table we were in the habit of writing at, and always make efforts to open a particular drawer in which we kept some of its choicest food.*

The pack rat earns its name from its habit of picking up objects, especially its kleptomania for bright and gleaming ones, and building them into its lodge: a bit of broken glass or china, a button, coin, bottle opener, small screwdriver. It is this avidity for glistering or metallic things that often makes it unnecessary for a farmer wanting the rats out of an old barn to bait his traps. A few years ago, a man living near the county line went to his shed to start the tractor but the ignition key wasn't hanging on its nail, and he couldn't find it anywhere about, so he had to write the manufacturer to get another; when he was cleaning an outbuilding the following summer, he found the old key and also some missing tools in a pack-rat den. He said later, *I believe if the little devil's legs had been long enough to reach the pedals, he'd have taken the tractor too.*

Dawn and Donald Kaufman, zoologists doing research in the northern end of the Flint Hills, wrote a monograph entitled "Size Preference for Novel Objects by the Eastern Woodrat Under Field Conditions": on several nights they set out tinfoil balls of four different sizes at various distances from lodges and learned that the animals preferred to make off with small and medium spheres when close to the nest but, farther away, took the biggest ones; the Kaufmans concluded that the *cost of transport increases with distance and object size and . . . large items are of greater net value than small items at the greater distance;* that is, if you have to walk a mile to the grocery you'll probably return not with one peach but a bagful. I assume that's why Sauble's wood rat quite sensibly carried off the whole gunnysack of potatoes.

The other common name, trade rat, derives from the rodent putting down some ordinary object it's hauling to the lodge in exchange for one more unusual it happens across: campers have awakened in the morning to find a pocketknife or compass traded for a pinecone or deer turd.

Yet wood rats are fussy about what they allow in their dens. One researcher noticed a laboratory specimen carry a certain stick out of its nest box; he put it back, and the rat dragged it out again, and the observer returned it, and right back out it came; after a dozen times, the scientist gave up.

The scientific name, *Neotoma floridana,* so I've read, literally means "new-cut + of Florida": a new species with cutting teeth first identified in Florida. But other accounts relate that members of the Lewis and Clark expedition were the first to write about the wood rat in 1804, when they were along the Missouri River in northeastern Kansas, and that Meriwether Lewis gave the earliest description during the winter the men spent near the Pacific coast in 1806. (It is almost certain that William Clark preserved several specimens of *floridana* and sent them downriver to Thomas Jefferson; of the 122 animal species and subspecies then unknown to science the expedition discovered, the eastern wood rat was the first.) Some years after Lewis wrote his description, the rodent received its scientific name. Now, I'm not so much as even an amateur Latinist, but I'll still suggest another translation, one that may be correct only as a double entendre or, at the least, a pun among classically educated men of the early nineteenth century who knew their Vergil: "interweave-cut/pack + glittering," that is, freely, "cut-and-pack weaver of glittering things."

To support this translation, I offer evidence from my slow-going dismantling: sticks nipped or gnawed to workable lengths (longer ones, up to three feet, show natural breaks) and so packed in as to interlink; in the conglomeration, along with a few small rocks and cow chips, are two pull tabs, a piece of beer bottle, half a tire-mashed chrome ballpoint pen, a plastic lens cap, and a spent (bright yellow) shotgun cartridge.

A lodge built in the open woods or in a tree is typically a dome-shaped structure remarkably efficient in shedding rain and keeping out predators, an abode cozy enough to attract mice, shrews, lizards, toads, turtles, cottontails — all of which a wood rat will tolerate even though it will not share quarters with its own kind. Adult pack rats regard solitary life highly enough that they exchange scarred faces and torn ears for the pleasures of hermitry. Among their ways of fighting, incidentally, is a kind of sparring in which they stand and pummel each other like tiny pugilists and, tiring, rest their paws on the other's "shoulders."

I have eight stacks of sticks now, and this tedious labor is wearing thin, and, worse, I'm beginning to suspect that the nest of soft fibers and grasses, which I should be able to see by now, actually lies out of sight underneath the ledge; with it are other chambers for storing food. A Kansas biologist, E. Raymond Hall, once opened a den to find four dozen hickory nuts, two gallons of hazelnuts, a gallon of wild grapes, a quart of dried mushrooms, and twenty sprays of bittersweet, with some of the food placed so the sybaritic little resident could reach it while reclining. But such a cache can mislead you: the vegetarian wood rat (unlike *norvegicus*, it doesn't prey on bird eggs) is a light eater, consuming daily only about five percent of its weight.

I didn't really think I'd scare up a woody, and that means, of course, I hoped I would. I've also been wishing to find a truly peculiar object stashed away (such as I've heard about them picking up): a pocket watch, perfume bottle, false teeth — something to make you say, "You found *that* in a pack-rat nest?" (In the American desert, scientists are studying thirty-thousand-year-old pack-rat middens sheltered in dry caves and crevices to reconstruct ice-age climates and vegetation that may reveal ecological effects of global changes; some biochemists even hope to extract DNA from the fossil materials.)

Not long ago I received a letter from a stranger who gave me jessie for several failures in my writing, one of them that I never include sex in my work (he wrote as if it were a subject that had never before crossed my mind), a flaw, said he, that causes me to distort topics. My first response was, let *him* — after a thorough reading of statutes on invasion of privacy and libel — walk into Cottonwood or Strong and start probing bedrooms and teenagers' back seats.

I digress here to say — but not to draw any generalizations — that in my time in Chase County I've not heard sex discussed (animal breeding excepted), and only once have I heard something approximating a dirty joke, a story alleged to be true: a female zoologist with a keen sympathy for wild animals came to the county to help a rancher having a coyote problem; she told him it was probably but a single male taking the calves and suggested not eradication but live trapping and castration; the fellow, with only slightly less than the cattleman's traditional deference in language before women, said, *Hell, lady, he's killing my calves — not fornicating them.*

But my topic (you see how the mind wanders when engaged in the humdrum — like pulling at sticks — of inquiry): I hereby answer and forever refute my correspondent's charge that I never write about sex: the retractable penis of a wood rat contains a small bone for an erection, and its testicles are so protected — except during breeding periods when they enlarge — that zoologists speak of its having a temporary scrotum. (Such anatomical design seems to me surpassingly practical even for man, eliminating, as it would, athletic supporters and the agony after a foot slips off a bicycle pedal.)

The female wood rat also has eminently sensible — if not desirable for womankind — physiological structures: four elongated teats a newborn can clamp on to with a distinctive diamond-shaped dental gap formed by closing its incisors; if five arrive in a litter, sometimes the odd baby out will fasten to and suckle the mother's clitoris. For the first three weeks after bearing young, a female suddenly fleeing the nest will drag along to safety her four — or five — clamped-on young; their toothy grip is so secure and perpetual during the pups' first twenty days before the gap disappears that, when she wants to go off alone, she must bite them in the jaw or put a foot on them to twist them loose. It may be this prospect of having offspring clinging to her nipples that makes the smaller female such a danger to her mate: following cheek-to-cheek nuzzling and several rapid-fire mountings, he will frequently beat a quick exit to escape her killing him. (One day when I was talking about wood rats and mentioned this detail to a city woman, she said, *I'd kill some sonofabitch too that wanted to run off and leave me with a couple of kids hanging by their teeth from my tits.*)

One of the reasons I'm not a zoologist, beyond soreness from hours of bent backs, is now manifest: as I begin to see I'm not going to uncover what I'd hoped for and my guilt about pillaging the small den increases, I don't want to continue. I have a dozen stacks of sticks. Trying to replace the ones I've removed serves only to break everything so I stop, but there are still enough to keep out ancient enemies: the coyote, fox, skunk, owl, hawk, all of them except snakes — but then, they get in even the best of dens.

Unlike the wood rat, a female house rat has six teats and her litter may be as large as fourteen, her gestation about a week shorter, and her estrus not seasonal but continual: in every way, she will outpropagate a pack rat. Some zoologists believe that *floridana* secures its future generations not by aggressiveness and overbreeding but by intelligently and harmoniously adapting its habitat, continuously attending its young, not fouling its nest, and perhaps even by living commensally. I'm just now remembering Wes Jackson's paradigms: for humankind, there is surely one, beyond the gathering of glittering objects, in the wood rat.

I start down the slope, turn to look at the mess I've made of the den — all for the sake of my curiosity — and I go back up to the ledge, and, about ten feet from the opening, reach into my pocket and lay down, just out of sight, the shiniest dime I have.

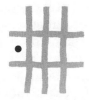

According to the Leader

Often, when the prairie weather turned sour on me, I'd go to the back room of the county historical society in the old bank building on Broadway in the Falls and sit before the microfilm machines and scroll out past issues of the twenty-eight newspapers Chase has seen over the past century and a third, some of them only ephemeral things like Sam Wood's six-week *Scalping Knife*. Usually I read the *Leader*, the sole survivor, founded in 1871 by William A. Morgan, husband of Minnie Morgan, the first and last female mayor of Cottonwood. The paper later bought out a Strong City competitor to become the *Leader-News*. Strong has also had the *Valley Echo*, the *Advance*, and the *Derrick*, and, in the villages, have appeared the Cedar Point *Pointer*, the Elmdale *Gas Jet*, the Matfield *Mirror*; in Cottonwood, the *Banner*, *Index*, *Reformer*, and *Reveille*.

While the morning rain or sleet came down against the north window of the old bank, I would disappear into those grayed pages and roam around another county. Then I'd look up, blinking, to find a noon sun and myself ready for a beer and pickled egg at Darla's, after, perhaps, just reading in an 1880s issue about tavern food at the Dolly Varden. The jolt of these dislocations, especially when I read the maladroit and solecistic expression of a current *Leader-News* as I ate my lunch, was like waking from a good dream with its brief sorrow of the little trip now ended.

Considering the time Americans pay to their daily or weekly gazette, historians' often reluctant use of our broadsheet journalism is odd but understandable, given the discomfort of sitting before a microfilm reader and all the while being aware of the immense lode waiting to be examined (a similar despair can overtake you if you have a go at the deep and even more challenging records in a county courthouse). Yet, if you really want to see how life was in America in an earlier time, to encounter it told firsthand, look to the morgue of your daily *Mirror*; if you would hear stories from your great-great-grandparents, then listen to your *Echo*. The imprint of our days, after all, is very much made by type recast. Those old six-point-Caslon chroniclers knew the tales that incline us, and, in the dim and witching light of a microfilm machine, like storytellers at a campfire, they whisper yet.

The Chase newspapers so captured me — particularly issues of the last two decades of the nineteenth century, the era that established the character of the place, the years when the county was at its summit of energy, optimism, population, and affluence — that I considered at one point how to build this book around parallel hikes over the county and down the pages of the *Leader*, through its six thousand issues, its hundred thousand pages that report on nearly all of the forty-eight thousand days white people have lived in Chase (for the three million or more days of the red people here, I'll have to turn to other kinds of records).

The early papers contain mostly national news (today it's entirely local) and packaged-in-the-East diversions; what county news does appear often tends toward now pointless single sentences: *Glad to learn that the sick are getting better*, or *Clements is taking a rest*. But every so often a county item or story glimmers briefly like a match struck in a dark room. From the *Leader*, here are a couple of dozen gleanings, gleamings:

A DASTARDLY OUTRAGE

This community was shocked last Monday morning by the report that C. C. Watson had attempted to commit a rape on a little girl, about 13 years old, the afternoon before. The scene of the outrage was the kitchen of Bauerle's restaurant, where the girl works, and during the absence of Bauerle and wife.

Watson's reputation is unsavory, but no one believed him so depraved as his fiendish attempt last Sunday afternoon stamps him.

The details of the outrage are simply horrible and

unfit for publication, and, but for the timely arrival of a boy, about 15 years old, who was attracted to the room by the noise made by the girl in her efforts to protect herself, the lecherous brute would have accomplished his purpose.

Watson has a wife and three children, is about 30 years of age, and his beastly habits have placed him prominently before the public on more than one occasion. A couple of years ago he was convicted in the district court of an attempt to commit an abortion upon a young woman who lived in his family and with whom he had maintained a criminal intimacy.

Watson's maneuvering all day Sunday is claimed by some to indicate that the outrage was premeditated. He met the girl's father early in the morning and the two eat, smoked and drank together until the middle of the afternoon, when he left the father and went to the house where the girl worked and attempted the outrage.

Expressions of indignation are loud and deep on every hand and it would require but a slight effort to induce Judge Lynch to administer summary justice, a mode of procedure it is hoped will not be resorted to, as Watson has been arrested on complaint of his intended victim, and the law, even if inadequate to deal with such characters, should be allowed to take its course.

January 15, 1885

"DAMPS"

Wm. Stone, Wm. Handcock and others were digging a well in Toledo, Chase County, and when at a depth of about 30 feet, suspended work for a few days. On resuming it Friday morning last, Wm. Stone went down into the well and was almost overcome by the "damps." He told the men at the top to haul him up. He had hardly uttered the words before he fell over partly unconscious. Mr Handcock went down into the well and tied the rope around Mr. Stone and when they commenced to haul him up he complained that it hurt him. Mr. H. then untied the rope and fastened it around himself and told the men at the top to haul him up, which they did, Mr. Stone remaining in a semi-conscious state at the bottom. After hauling Mr. Handcock out, the question was, who would venture down to fasten the rope around Mr. Stone? All hesitated to take the risk, when Wm. Stone, Jr., a lad of about eleven years stepped to the front and demanded to be let down, and down he went. Quickly fastening the rope around his father the two were drawn up and, after considerable effort, Mr. Stone, Sr. was resusicated, but at last accounts was suffering with a severe pain in his head, as was also Mr. Handcock and the heroic little boy who rescued his father from the very threshold of death.

June 11, 1885

A PLEASANT AFFAIR

In response to invitations to a rainbow party, about thirty friends gathered at the home of Mr. and Mrs. H. Collett, at Elk, on Friday evening, February 28. After the friends had assembled they were led to the dining room where an elegant supper was spread, the table being beautifully decorated with hyacinths and evergreens. When their daughter, Miss Lizzie, presented each with a cord representing some color of the rainbow and, pointing to the table, intimated that the price for partaking of the supper would be to find who was at the other end of the cord. They all most eagerly fell to work, thinking how small the price set upon such a repast. After following the cords a short time they found they led to the parlor where their eyes fell on a lovely rainbow tastefully arranged in one corner by the skillful hands of Grace and Lizzie. After much admiration and favorable comments someone remarked that when the rainbow appears the rain is over and it would be well to go on with their work.

Turning again to their task they were confronted by a mass of cords in the form of a spider web reaching from ceiling to floor, up stairs and down, no one knew where.

It was most amusing to see Bert Campbell tangled in the web and the girls tightening upon him as a spider would a fly, while Bob Reed was crawling around on the floor, looking like he had been badly knocked out in his last week's pillow fight. But all found their coveted prize and a jollier crowd never sat down to a feast, and when leaving the table each carried away a Japanese napkin with the signatures of all present as a souvenir of the occasion.

March 5, 1886

A SAD AFFAIR

About 2 o'clock, last Saturday afternoon, Ed. Jones, aged about 17 years, arrived in town with the information that his father, Isaac Jones, had hung himself in his granary, on Bloody creek.

A number of citizens, together with the county attorney, proceeded at once to the place and found the body hanging as described. From the county attorney we learned that the deceased had evidently stood on a chair, which lay overturned near by, while adjusting the rope to a rafter, after which he jumped from the chair, but the rope being too long his feet touched the ground, in which position he was choked to death. The deceased was about the average heighth, weighed over 200 pounds, and was 69 years of age.

The deceased had evidently made every preparation and contemplated the insane act for a day or more. He came to town on Thursday and called on all the merchants with whom he did business and settled all accounts. About 10 o'clock Friday morning he sent his son, Ed, and the only other person on the farm with him, up the creek to tell Si. Wilson that he might have the corn, for which Wilson had probably partly bargained. He also gave the boy $5 and told him to keep it until he asked for it. Upon returning from Wilson's, the boy, being unable to find his father at the house, went to the granary and found him hanging by the neck — dead, and immediately came to town, arriving about 2 o'clock, with the terrible news.

The deceased has undoubtedly been insane, or partly so, for a long time. He has at times labored under the hallucination that his life was in jeopardy from one and another and when thus affected would arm himself, and it is only a few weeks since he made an onslaught on two of his sons, C. W. and Scott, with murderous intent, first with a shotgun, which the boys took away from him, and immediately after with a revolver, firing twice at his son Charlie, who, to prevent the old gentleman from overtaking and shooting him, was compelled to shoot the horse which he (his father) was riding.

For this the old gentleman came to town to prosecute the boys, and not finding the county attorney, who was engaged at Strong City, he met S. N. Wood, who encouraged him in his insane hallucination and had him swear to three indictments, viz: assault with intent to kill, rioting, and [failure] to keep the peace. The county attorney suppressed two of these, and warrants were issued on the first.

The whole affair has been most painful to all concerned and their friends. The deceased, previous to his death, became more rational and expressed his regret, we are told, that the affair occurred or took the turn it did, and, no doubt, the thought of his being the victim of unprincipled advisers so preyed upon his mind that he was led to committing suicide.

March 18, 1886

A MAD (?) DOG KILLED

On Thursday night last, about 11 o'clock, while J. M. Engles and Harry Clifford were discussing the home-rule question on Broadway, their attention was attracted by a terrible racket in Holmes' clothing store. An inspection of the premises and inquiry developed the fact that a supposed mad dog was under the bed. Holmes had fled for safety to the top of a pile of goods while Charley was balancing himself on the head of the bed. Charley finally got to and opened the front door through which Clifford entered and began whistling to the dog. Clifford didn't want to see the dog half as bad as he thought he did, for when the dog came out from under the bed Clifford struck out for the front door with all the speed possible, the dog following close behind, and did not stop until he gained the top of a pile of lumber across the street, where he and the dog went into "committee of the whole" to discuss the difference between them. Engles, who was looking in at the door when the dog came from under the bed, climbed up Hotchkiss' sign post so as to give Clifford and the dog plenty of room. While Clifford and the dog were watching each other, Charley procured a loaded gun and gained the lumber pile by a circuitous route and gave the weapon to Clifford, who shot the dog, and the meeting adjourned. The dog belonged to Holmes, who is now selling clothing at cheaper prices than ever, in fact, "dog gone" cheap.

June 17, 1886

ELK NOTES

Another $50,000 rain, and still raining.

Corn is doing splendid, and indefatigable chintz bugs are of few days duration if this weather continues.

June 17, 1886

HOMESTEAD NOTES

Oh! if it would only rain — everything is so dry, and chintz bugs are not scarce in this part of the country.

We don't want any one to break their necks, but we wish they would do something to scare up some news.

A. H. Brown and John Westbay thought they saw a wolf on Coon creek one night last week. But it proved to be Harvy Mowrey.

July 15, 1886

ELK NOTES

Dry and dusty.

Unless it rains this week corn will begin to suffer.

The reaping part of harvest is about over, and now the stacks of grain begin to loom up here and there.

Rather dull after the 4th of July.

Julius Frey butchered a 3-year-old beeve last week and sold it all out before he got around. Would it not be healthier for farmers to eat more beef and mutton and less pork?

July 15, 1886

TOWN AND COUNTRY NEWS

An organ grinder struck town last Thursday whose instrument, although well arranged, was badly adjusted. The instrument played four tunes, viz: "Tickle Me with a Barley Straw," "St. Patrick's Day," "La Marseilles" and "Dixie."

July 15, 1886

ROBERT BURNS

The annual celebration of the birth of Scotland's Bard, was celebrated in Pratt's Music hall, last Tuesday night. The programme was changed somewhat from previous years and we think improved.

The attendance was not fully up to the usual "gathering of the clans," but that no doubt was the result of the threatening aspect of the weather all day, which prevented the people living in the country from attending. This had its advantages, however, as the hall was not so crowded although nearly every seat was filled, and made it very pleasant for those who did attend.

The gastronomical portion of the evening's entertainment surpassed anything of the kind ever before attempted in this city. The dining rooms of the three hotels were neatly and appropriately decorated and the arrangements were so complete that all the guests were accommodated at one sitting. The tables were beautifully arranged and before the assault was made upon them presented an elegant appearance.

[Union Hotel Bill of Fare]

STEWED
Oysters. Venison. Chicken.

FRIED
Oysters.

BAKED
Fresh Fish.

BOILED
Cold ham. Cold beef tongue. Muskallonge.

ROAST
Wild Goose. Pork. Venison.

ENTREES
Cheese. Tongue Sausage.

RELISHES
Worcester sauce. Mushroom sauce.
Celery sauce. Tomato catsup.
Lobster salad. Potato salad. Chicken salad.
Cold slaw. Celery. Lettuce.
Sweet and sour pickles.

FRUIT
Oranges. Apricots. Grapes. Apples. Dates.

NUTS
Almonds. Pecans. Filberts.

CAKE
White Mountain. Gold. Silver. Marble.
Chocolate. Cocoanut. Sponge. Lemon.
Gentlemen's favorite. Rochester jelly.
Vanilla. Fruit. Watermelon.
Ornamented fruit.

PIES
Lemon. Mince. Chocolate. Apple.

CONFECTIONARY
Gum drops. Chocolate drops. Cream candy.
Kisses. Caramels.

FRENCH ROLLS
Tea. Coffee. Milk.

January 27, 1887

CEDAR POINTERS

The new minister arrived last evening, his wife and four responsibilities will follow soon.

Little urchins are catching large catfish already; farmers are busy, the mill is running steadily, and everything booming. Even C. C. Smith has bought a cow.

March 17, 1887

TOWN AND COUNTRY NEWS

Simmons & Thorpe are putting down a stone walk from the gate to the front door of the court house.

A. B. Kinnekin had one of his hands mashed yesterday while working with a pile-driver near Elmdale.

Don't fail to go and hear Col. Copeland's lecture at Music hall on Saturday evening. The subject will be "Handsome People."

March 17, 1887

STREET CAR HELD UP

Last Monday evening, while a number of people were on the street, and an unusually large crowd were in and about the postoffice, a young man stepped aboard street car No. 2 when opposite the Corner drug store, and deliberately proceeded to abstract the day's receipts from the money boxes. The self-complacency of the young man completely paralyzed the driver and the few passengers who, spellbound at his audacity, watched him with open-eyed wonder, and before they recovered from their astonishment he pocketed the money, about ten dollars, and skipped out. The officers of the street car company inform us that that was not the first time that game has been played on them, and they propose hereafter to arm the driver.

April 11, 1895

THE SOAP MAN

About two weeks ago a smooth-tongued brass-eyed man traversed this city and Strong, carrying with him a cheap grade of toilet soap. This he offered to the "lady of the house," for one dollar a box. "A dollar and a half," said the oily tongued operator, "is the regular price, but to introduce this soap, we offer to those who buy a box, and pay the dollar today, their choice from a well selected list of valuable presents, the article selected to be forwarded to the purchaser within two weeks. This list of presents contains banquet lamps, valuable clocks and a choice collection of the most valuable articles. This, Madam, is a china plate like the china of the valuable tea set, which we can offer from this list for those who buy and pay one dollar for a box of this finest class toilet soap. We are only doing this today and it is your only opportunity." The china plate was a handsome piece of ware, and a set of dishes like it would have been cheap for ten dollars. And we are sorry to say that the feminine common sense dropped out of sight, and deluded by the wiley faker, they passed out their dollar but as might have been expected, the lovely dishes, cushioned chairs, etc. have never gladdened their vision, and fifteen cents worth of soap and a misplaced confidence is all that is left them. Will people never learn that when they hope to get something for nothing, and some traveling outfit tells them they are going to give it to them, they are sure to be left?

July 4, 1895

VANDALISM

Last Thursday night, "Hallowe'en" was made memorable by acts of unprecedented vandalism by a party of boys, or men, in this town and vicinity. The "funny fellows" confined their efforts to overturning sidewalks, changing gates and moving everything moveable. While that was more idiotic than funny, yet no considerable objection was made by the parties inconvenienced. But the malicious vandals who pulled up the telephone poles on the road running to Dr. Cartter's house, east of town, and broke the insulators, were guilty of acts that should bring down upon them the severest penalty of the law. They also burned a large sign belonging to the Smith Bros. and two of the telephone poles.

November 7, 1895

A COLORED FAMILY JAR

The residents in the vicinity of the old school house lot were startled between 6 and 7 o'clock last Tuesday evening by the hysterical screams of a woman in distress. Hurrying to the scene they found a colored man named Milton beating his wife.

Lew Heck happened to be in the neighborhood at the time and going to the small frame building south of the old school house site, he discovered the man holding the woman on the ground in the yard, pounding her with his fist, with the "hero of Franklin" standing by armed with a shotgun and Jabe Johnson rapidly approaching with a hatchet in his hand. Heck interfered and without much difficulty separated the struggling mass, which was hard to distinguish from the settling darkness.

The woman, as soon as she freed herself from the affectionate embrace of her spouse, ran into the house and re-appeared at the door armed with a revolver about 18 inches long with which she blazed away at her "hubby," who began making tracks at once to a place of safety, before Heck could secure her. The bullets, unfortunately, missed the mark and went singing high in the air over Mert Robbins' residence. That ended the conjugal misunderstanding and hostilities ceased as soon as Heck disarmed the irate female. Before anything was done toward the arrest of Milton, both he and his wife kissed and made up, and left together during the night, presumably for Junction City, from whence they came.

This place had been a rendezvous for questionable characters and bore a hard reputation. Although complaints were made to the mayor against the parties, for some reason they were left undisturbed until they "fired" themselves. Mrs. Milton had the reputation of being "a bad woman with a gun." In fact the place has been so notorious that a proposition to raid it independent of the city authorities was discussed by some of our people last week.

On Monday Mrs. Milton secured the washing for several families, and when she went away she left the clothes soaking in tubs. Yesterday several women put in their time sorting over the "wash," selecting their belongings.

January 23, 1896

A TRUE STORY

A few Sundays ago one of our ministers started for a nearby country church where he was to fill an appointment that morning, but not being certain which road to take in order to reach his parish he inquired of a passerby who mistakenly directed him down the wrong road.

The morning was warm and pleasant and although the road seemed a little longer than the good man had expected yet he cheerfully pursued his way and at last arrived at a little white church just as the pious people were closing their Sabbath School lesson. After entering the church and greeting a number of brethren the minister then took his place in the pulpit and delivered a strong and inspiring sermon to his surprised and unexpecting congregation, but who, nevertheless, listened to his good teachings with the greatest attention and reverence while a few miles away at another small, white church sat another little congregation waiting and wondering why their good minister tarried so long by the way.

At last the services were over, the clergyman descended from the pulpit, shook hands with the benevolent and grateful congregation and started upon his homeward journey, never suspecting that he had preached at the wrong church.

April 24, 1906

ARE YOU LUCKY?

In order to make a little excitement, stimulate trade and advertise Studebaker buggies, I have decided to give one of the latest style automobile twin-seat Studebaker buggies, absolutely free, to some lucky person. Here is the plan. I have two hundred and twenty-six tough raw-hide whips, the best value you ever bought in the whip line for seventy-five cents, and with each whip I will give one chance on the above buggy.

This is not a lottery scheme. You get full value for your money whether you get the buggy or not; the buggy is simply given as a prize. Come in and see the buggy and let me explain the plan to you more fully. I dare say it is the most liberal prize offer ever made to the people of Chase County, and I believe everyone who can make any use of a whip will be quick to take advantage of it. Buy your whip at once, and we will soon see who the lucky person will be.

MOORE'S [HARDWARE]

July 30, 1909

CHEWED BY HOGS

Wm. Austin, the seven-year-old son of the editor of this paper, had an experience Saturday which will probably remain in his memory as long as he lives and causes any ordinary being to shudder when it is told.

With his mother, brother and sister, he was visiting at the home of his aunt, Mrs. W. T. Glanville on the James Austin farm about two miles east of this city. About six o'clock Saturday evening the three children had been seining minnows in a small stream in the Glanville corrals a short distance from the house. William left the others and started for the house. When in the edge of a small patch of timber about a hundred feet from the corral gate, the hogs, which had been up near the gate on account of it being nearly feeding time, came running around him and in an instant had knocked him down. He yelled and kicked and fought them off as best he could. Mrs. Austin was only a few feet outside the corral and, hearing his yells, rushed to him as did also the other children. At first it seemed impossible to drive the hogs away, and Mrs. Austin stumbled and fell in trying to fight them away. This distracted their attention for an instant when his sister grabbed him and got him on his feet and they soon got him out of the corral.

In the minute or two that they had him down, they had torn the clothes from the middle part of his body and from his shoulders to his hips he had a collection of bruises and gashes, some nearly through to the vital parts of the body, which makes a person shudder to think what had been the result in a few minutes had not help been right at hand.

He had a turpentine bath and the doctor fixed him over some and, aside from being stiff and sore, he is getting along all right.

August 24, 1909

S.O.S. — MULE IN DISTRESS

South Fork neighborhood is not lacking in thrills and escapades these days. One of the latest is the story of a two-year-old mule belonging to Arch McCandless. His name wasn't "Maude," but the incident carries some of the "kick" that the famous comic puts out.

The mule, in search of water, attempted to go across an old well which was covered with boards. He got the surprise of his young life when he found himself floundering in the bottom of the 40-foot well which had about 12 feet of water in it. By swimming he managed to keep his head above the water and by braying or whatever it is that a mule does to attract attention, he soon had a crowd around the top of the well. Mr. McCandless went down into the well and fastened a rope to the mule and hitched a team onto the rope but was unable to pull him out. Vern and Paul Brant answered the SOS call and left for the scene of action in their Master Six Buick

roadster. The rope was fastened to the car and slowly
the mule was drawn to the top where eager and willing hands were ready to help him, when, snap! went
the rope, and the mule went back to the bottom of
the well. Paul Brant almost went with him but was
jerked back by members of the rescue party. The
spectators dreaded to think of the fate of the mule
this time. But in a twinkling, the mule's head came
up out of the water, seemingly back from where
he started. Arch was lowered into the well a second
time and a new rope again tied to the unfortunate
animal.

This time the mule came to terra firma and was
released. He gave a few quick deep breaths, got up,
shook himself, and ran away. He was soon rounded
up, blanketed, and put in a warm stall. Except for
two small cuts he is as good as new.

February 2, 1927

ELMDALE AREA NEWS

The community was saddened Saturday afternoon
by the death of Ed Zickefoose, who suffered a fatal
heart attack while hunting prairie chickens along 150.
It was a glorious fall afternoon; the air was clean
and crisp, the autumn foliage was glowing with every
shade of gold in the spectrum, highlighted by spots
of dark green and brown. And the hunting was good
— two shells, two birds! Ed was where he loved to
be, doing what he loved to do.

November 8, 1984

PRISCILLA CLUB MEETS

Bernice Gwyn entertained ten members of the Pris-
cilla Club at the home of her daughter, Nancy Huth,
on Wednesday.

Upon arrival, each member deposited her packet
of garden seeds in the president's basket. Bertha
Dawson, the president, gave out seed catalogs, and

each member cut out a picture of her favorite flower.

The meeting was called to order with Bertha reading the April prayer from "Guideposts."

Minutes of the last meeting were read and approved. Roll call was answered by going around the room, and each member showed the picture of her favorite flower and told why it was her favorite.

Bertha mixed up the garden seed packets, and she passed the basket for each one to take one back (if we got our own, we were to take another one). There were lots of flower seeds and some vegetable seeds for us to go home and plant. Bertha closed the meeting by reading a message of "Fifteen Ways to be Miserable."

April 24, 1986

ANNIVERSARY CLUB

The Anniversary Club celebrated their 20th wedding anniversaries this last weekend by leaving town.

Gordon and Joyce Watts, Tom and Mary Jones, and Paul and Linda Bledsoe enjoyed their taste of city life as they were hosted by Steve and Carla Gibb in their lovely home in Lenexa.

During the Saturday afternoon sightseeing tour of a nearby shopping mall, Linda and Joyce made major purchases, while Mary entertained herself on the escalators. Gordon entertained the neighbors in the early evening and then the four couples went to Tiffany's Attic for a delicious dinner. "We laughed until we cried," was the response to the production of "Life Begins at 40." Everyone in the group had moments when they could relate to the characters portrayed.

Sunday morning was spent visiting and taking a walking tour of the neighborhood. The hosting skills of Steve and Carla were stretched to the limit but they came through with flying colors and in a weak moment invited everyone back.

February 5, 1987

BAZAAR AREA NEWS

Several Bazaar men attended an insecticide dinner meeting for farmers held Tuesday evening at St. Anthony Hall in Strong City.

Jim Schwilling visited Mrs. Charles Schwilling last Wednesday and replaced a storm window blown off during the Valentine Day wind storm.

February 25, 1988

On the Town: From the Life and Opinions of Sam Wood, with Commentary (III)

THE PATCH ON THE FLOOR

This is happening in southwestern Kansas in 1891, June 21, Sunday: the dust rises from the slow revolution of the buggy wheels, and Sam and Margaret ride in silence, and she says finally, *Why don't you talk to me?* and he forces a few sentences, falls quiet again, and she asks, *Do you think there'll be trouble in Hugoton?*

She is thinking of the long friction, of the time men burned Sam Wood in effigy, of their crossing pistols in saloons and pledging to kill him; she is remembering the Hay Meadow Massacre of his supporters and the subsequent trial that Sam brought to a brilliant conclusion (lecturing the jury for eight hours) only to see the Supreme Court overturn the decision and set the murderers free; and she is remembering his friends in Topeka four days ago telling him not to go to Hugoton (and later she will learn of one man saying, *That's the last we'll ever see of Sam Wood*); she is thinking of her sister and brother-in-law, Sarah and Ephraim Pinkston, entreating Sam last night to stay in Cedar Point rather than let his respect for law get him killed; she remembers his repeated assurance that he doesn't think there will be trouble but, if there is, he must go anyway because of his bond; and she is remembering his words of a few days ago as they rode the train to Topeka when he said they should settle things and leave Stevens County and return to Chase and start a newspaper in Elmdale (his words then were slow and uncharacteristic: *We're growing old. We need each other. We have to settle down where we can live quietly and be together more).* Margaret thinks of these things and of how little money they have, but she too rides on in silence until she must press him about Hugoton and the trumped-up charge of election bribery. He repeats that he will go into town unarmed, go in without the small pistol he customarily carries but has never used, and he speaks of necessity, and then he says, *Don't talk about it.* They roll along in the pleasant day (later she will say that the ride seemed through an enchanted land — a garden of Hesperides).

When they reach Woodsdale, the place Sam calls *the Emerald City on the Plains,* an area he foresees not as a desert but as wheat country, Margaret is already looking to their return to the Cottonwood Valley. The next day neighbors come to visit, and they tell Sam not to go into the courtroom of Judge Theodosius Botkin, who keeps a brace of pistols next to his gavel, uses armed bodyguards, and has survived impeachment on grounds of drunkenness, partisanship, and fraud. The people know that if Botkin can get Sam in jail, a murder is easy to cover over. Sam repeats that he sees no real danger, yet, when a woman asks whether Margaret will go, he says, *Yes. If they kill me, I want her there to close my eyes.*

Tuesday morning they depart, Sam riding the ten miles in the buggy between Margaret and their housekeeper, Mrs. Carpenter (surely no one will try to shoot between two women), and they arrive in Hugoton (some residents of Woodsdale call it *Hogtown*) by eleven o'clock. People stare as they pass, and a small boy says, *There goes old man Wood. Don't he know they're gonna kill him today?* and an older girl says, *You talk too much.* Sam stops at the town windmill to get a cup of cool water and then heads on to the Methodist church being used as a courthouse. Judge Botkin, who holds Sam responsible for his impeachment, hears that Wood has arrived and inexplicably adjourns court until afternoon. Sam enters, looks over the docket. The judge leaves, stepping past James Brennan lounging in the doorway, and Botkin says, *Hello, Jimmy,* and he walks on toward the buggy and heartily greets Margaret, who has never met him, and heads up the street of little false-front stores. Margaret recognizes Brennan as a deputy from another county and a witness for the Hay Meadow murderers; he wears a black suit, white shirt, and he is in his thirties, dark-complexioned, mustachioed, almost handsome.

Sam comes through the door, passing close to the slouched man whose right hand is concealed to his side, and goes down the wooden stairs and toward his buggy. Brennan waits, then whirls around, draws a pistol, fires once, and hits Wood in the back near the left shoulder. Sam cries out and throws up his arms as if to cover his head and turns from the women and runs as best can a wounded sixty-six-year-old with a built-up shoe and a frame thickened by the years. In the smoke and smell of burned gunpowder, in the calls and screams, Margaret jumps from the buggy and runs, and Brennan is running and firing again, and Sam slows, and the small woman runs to get between them, and the men have half circled the church-courthouse. She once freed her husband from Bogus Jones by jerking the sheriff's gun from its holster, and she knows it's up to her now, and the men are around the other side of the church and she hears another shot and she rounds the corner to see Sam against the white wall and Brennan putting the pistol to Sam's face and firing again. The bullet enters just below his right eye. Then she is there in the acrid smoke between the men, and Sam, gasping blood, falls forward and her thin arms cannot contain him, and his weight bears them both to the ground.

Brennan runs to the street, his second revolver drawn, and a noisy crowd gathers, and in it is Botkin, and Margaret raises one reddened arm to point at the judge whom she knows hired the assassin, and she cries out, *He's the one!* But people ignore him and look to Brennan, who shouts, *No goddamn man can take me with a gun in his hand and live!* and the crowd laughs, and Brennan yells over the noise that he will surrender only to his own sheriff, and Botkin scurries about to arrange for the arrest.

Men carry Sam into the church and lay him on the wooden floor. He has been shot below the heart, in the thigh, and in the face. It is nearly noon. After a lifetime of escapes, Sam, on this morning, will not get away. Margaret closes his eyes but does not get up. She is kneeling in his blood.

Even before the body can be prepared to take to Woodsdale that afternoon, Brennan is again on the street, smirking and talking loud with some men who pay him five hundred dollars for his work. That night in Hugoton, citizens revel, knowing that Sam's murder is the death of Woodsdale, the Emerald City. Over the next several weeks, the dark stain on the church floor cannot be removed, and as long as it remains there are no services here. Finally, a workman cuts out the blotch and replaces it with a patch. Someone calls it *Sam Wood's marker.*

Fifth Commentary   Two days later, the funeral cortege, under moonlight, moved twenty miles north toward Ulysses, riding all night long to stop a Santa Fe train to carry Margaret and the casket to Cottonwood Falls. Long obituaries appeared across the country, even in New York and Boston. The next afternoon at the funeral, Sam was there to officiate: Colonel Mackey read a letter from him written five years earlier when Wood thought he would not survive an illness. Sam asked for a quiet funeral without mourning dress or ceremony (none of which he got); among his sentences of a wandering eschatology he said he wished there were a furnace available where his body *could be reduced to ashes and dissolve itself into its original elements, and not have to be buried, filling the air with noxious gases, endangering the lives of the living.* He wrote of his belief that the dead live on as conscious and distinct entities, and he said, *I am with you. I witness your every act.* Not missing his last chance to take the stump, he added, *I have tried to believe the dogmas of the churches, but the more I have tried and the harder I have investigated, the stronger I am convinced they are not true, but rather a cunningly devised scheme of the priesthood to live on the people.* In the conclusion to his long letter, he said, *Let ministers and churches quit worrying themselves about the afterlife and go to work and solve the problems of this life. If possible, prepare the people to live here.* Sam Wood, albeit by proxy, had taken his final podium and given his last exhortation against public grafters. The choir sang "Shall We Gather at the River?" and then encomium after eulogy after panegyric followed. Finally the procession started for Prairie Grove Cemetery. (A year ago, Sam's grandson told me: *When the casket reached the grave two miles away, the rear of the long procession was still leaving the church.*)

Margaret lived on in Chase for nearly thirty years, but all I know of her days after Sam is a small photograph of her sitting in a yard swing with a grandson, her face wistful. Theodosius Botkin and James Brennan never stood trial for the murder, and the judge ended up as a peddler of the Keeley Cure, a fraudulent medical treatment considerably less efficacious than the Botkin Remedy.

Now: the neat and regular road grid of Prairie Grove Cemetery has a single dislocation, a lone jog from perfect straightness; at this disruption is the Sam Wood plot and that jog is another footprint revealing the gait of the man. On his marker in fading letters: *With the peace of God around you, sleep old pioneer.* Under a big cedar nearby, I occasionally eat lunch and think about Sam's notion of *the other side* as a place separated from us only by a thin curtain through which those beyond hear everything, and I remember his Whitmanesque words: *I am with you. I witness your every act.* Just down the road a half mile is the lake that could not be built in the thirties because some of the laborers would be black, and a few yards away is a nearly markerless section where Chase paupers lie. In the same row as Sam and Margaret and their daughter Dearie (Sam's inscription on her stone: *There is no death. What seems so is transition*) lies the boy murdered by George Rose (the only man countians ever lynched), and just west lies Stephen Jones, whose single legacy to Chase is a big ranch, Spring Hill. It is fitting that Sam and Margaret lie in a dark and bloody row between the wealthy and poor.

I'm sitting under the cedar now, sipping something stronger than Sam's lemonade, and I'm thinking how he seemed to walk faster out of the nineteenth century than his friends and opponents, to walk more directly toward a bigger — if not encompassing — view of humankind that we still cannot quite accept a century later. I'm thinking how life goes these days in Kansas, that staunch outpost of the Republican party Wood helped found (he would deplore its current views). Today, Kansas, born from radical conflict, is a state first to back a war and last to join a revolution, a place once wobbling almost to toppling but now become a land of equipoise, a seeming still point at the center of a revolving nation, a state where movements end rather than begin.

Sam Wood came into Kansas with fire, and from his flames he enkindled light and engendered heat, and when he went out, so did much of that light and heat. He came into the county, marked it indelibly, left it, and returned only to lie in its flinty upland above the Cottonwood. It's a measure of things today in Kansas that so vital, significant, conspicuous, and peculiar a man has had no published biography other than Margaret's remarkably literate hagiographic book brought out a few months following his death. Even after a century, despite his being one who *builded well* a web of meaning to hold the people, he is still suspect in the county: the historical society has not so much as a photograph of him or Margaret on display. Although his life, more than almost anyone else's, is the story of the state in its first half century — slavery, war, Indian dispossession, white settlement, crusading (and self-serving) journalism, railroads, equal rights, populism — Sam Wood is still too much for Kansas.

XII

Wonsevu

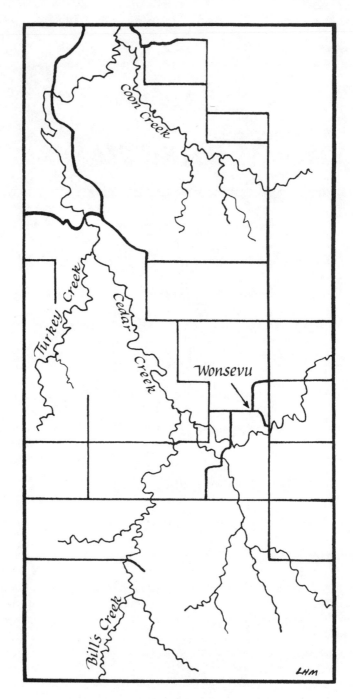

WONSEVU QUADRANGLE

From the Commonplace Book: Wonsevu

Does landscape enter the blood with the milk?

> — Ronald Blythe,
> *Characters and Their Landscapes*
> (1982)

Made by the same Great Spirit and living in the same land with our brothers, the red men, we consider ourselves as the same family; we wish to live with them as one people, and to cherish their interests as our own.

> — Thomas Jefferson,
> "To the Miamis, Powtewatamies, and
> Weeauks" (1802)

[The Indians] will vanish like a vapour from the face of the earth; their very history will be lost in forgetfulness; and "the places that now know them will know them no more forever." Or if, perchance, some dubious memorial of them should survive, it may be in the romantic dreams of the poet to people in imagination his glades and groves, like the fauns and satyrs and sylvan deities of antiquity. But should he venture upon the dark story of their wrongs and wretchedness, should he tell how they were invaded, corrupted, despoiled, driven from their native abodes and the sepulchres of their fathers, hunted like wild beasts about the earth, and sent down with violence and butchery to the grave, posterity will either turn with horror and incredulity from

the tale or blush with indignation at the inhumanity of their fore-fathers.

— Washington Irving,
"Traits of Indian Character" (1819)

What the influence of [Indian] contact and intercourse with the European has been, we all know. Where he found them poor, he left them poorer; where one scene of violence and vengeance has been seen, there many have been enacted; where he had found one evil passion, he planted many; where one fell disease had thinned their ranks, he brought those of his blood and land to reap a more abundant harvest. His very gifts were poison: selfish and inconsiderate in his kindness, he was ever bitter in his revenge and anger: he excited the passions of the savage for his own purposes, and when it raged against him, he commenced the work of extermination. He then read that the day of the aboriginal inhabitant of the soil had come and that the white man was destined to take the place of the red, and perhaps he divined well and truly; but he had no right to presume upon it or that he was to be the active instrument in forwarding that mysterious dispensation of God.

The settlement of the various portions of America, with but few exceptions, is equally in the north and the south a foul blot upon Christendom.

— Charles Joseph Latrobe,
The Rambler in North America (1836)

When the last red man shall have perished, and the memory of my tribe shall have become a myth among the white man, these shores will swarm with the invisible dead of my tribe, and when your children's children think themselves alone in the field, the store, the shop, or in the silence of the pathless woods, they will not be alone. . . . At night when the streets of your cities and villages are silent and you think them deserted, they will throng with the returning hosts that once filled them and still love the beautiful land. The white man will never be alone.

— Chief Seattle,
"Address to Governor Isaac Stevens"
(1855)

The [Indian-Caucasian] half-breeds, wherever they exist in America, almost universally exhibit a union of the vices of the two races whence they are derived, whilst their corresponding virtues are lost.

As I have looked at the white men with whom the aboriginal tribes have to deal, I have often wondered how any very happy influence upon the Indian character could be anticipated from their companionship and example.

It would be very unfair, however, to charge the United States government with wholesale injustice, or even with neglect, in relation to the native tribes. Equally unfair would it be to bring its agents under a universal censure, as forgetful of the claims of humanity, and grasping only at self-advantage.

— T. H. Gladstone,
The Englishman in Kansas (1857)

An Indian is a more watchful and a more wary animal than a deer. He must be hunted with skill.

— Colonel James Carleton,
U.S. Senate report, "Condition of the
Indian Tribes" (1867)

It seems as though the D---l had changed his residence, gone to Kansas, for certainly no such atrocities [as the dispossession] could be committed without his leadership.

— John Farwell,
Letter to Board of Indian
Commissioners (1871)

The [Kaw] tribe is now nearly extinct. All authorities will tell you that it is as impossible to civilize them as to tame a wolf. These men will not work: when you shake hands with them their long fingers feel just like the paw of an animal with a softness like hair.

— Cornelia Adair,
My Diary (1874)

Staple food sold to Indians — such as sugar, coffee, tea, and flour — are the worst that can be got, of course.

— Ernst von Hesse-Wartegg,
"Across Kansas by Train" (1877)

[c. 1878] let me give you my opinon off the indians as some off the amairkans call them. My opion is that iff the amaricans was drove

*from one coast too the other that we would be worse than the indians
have bin.*

*stop & think. when america was Discovered, the indians was hear.
How did they come hear? i belive that our maker put them hear. you
se that there was sevelr difernt tribes & there was some diference in
the tribes, the same as an ingles man & an irsh man. my openion that
theour maker gave them this country, but we was enlighten enough &
had the pour too keep Driving them back. and i know by experience
that the indians woudent bin hallf so bad iff it hadent off bin for the
white men that wood get with them and they could plot for them. that
would give these white men a chance to plunder. i know this too bee
the fact in severl cases. gest look at the indians. they was ignorent too
our ways, but yet they undr stode one another, & some one must off
gave them this [knowledge], for they all had a way of worshiping the
master. i belive that god gave them that enteligant, for God says i will
right my law up on your harts & in your minds, i will place them so
all sall no Me, from the least to the greatest. and i blave that is where
the red man got his knolej from. they all have a way off worshiping
the lord. but you wil say that they are saveges, for they fight amoung
them selves; and this is true, but dont all of the americans do the
same. and not only that, they have gred arsnells manurfactoring guns
And amunition all the while. now iff you can see the difference i
should like too kno.*

> — Matthew Flint Clarkson, Jr.,
> "The Matthew Clarkson Manuscripts"
> (transcribed 1927)

*The common saying that the island of Manhattan was "purchased
from the Indian inhabitants for the value of twenty-four dollars in
traders' goods" is not true. It is not true for the reason that the Indians
did not and could not think of the possibility of conveying property in
land. What the Indians of Manhattan did conceive was the idea of
admitting the Dutch settlers to live in the land with themselves as
neighbors, to share its benefits. But they had no idea of selling the
land for any price. No Indians of Manhattan or elsewhere entertained
at any time any such idea. Indians always said in opposition to such
proposals, "We cannot sell the land, for it belongs not to us in this
generation only, but to all our people for all time. . . ." [The Indians]
thought of the goods given by the Dutch as being merely presents
given as a pledge and token of good will and neighborly relations. The
idea of alienation of the land was never in their minds.*

> — Melvin R. Gilmore,
> *Prairie Smoke* (1929)

[Black Elk said:] The Wasichus [Caucasians] came, and they have made little islands for us and other little islands for the four-leggeds, and always these islands are becoming smaller, for around them surges the gnawing flood of Wasichus; and it is dirty with lies and greed.

Drinks Water . . . dreamed what was to be, and this was long before the coming of the Wasichus . . . and he said: "You shall live in square gray houses in a barren land, and beside those square gray houses you shall starve."

Sometimes dreams are wiser than waking.

We got more lies than cattle, and we could not eat lies.

Only crazy or very foolish men would sell their Mother Earth. Sometimes I think it might have been better if we had stayed together and made them kill us all.

I looked back on the past and recalled my people's old ways, but they were not living that way any more. They were traveling the black road, everybody for himself and with little rules of his own.

— John G. Neihardt,
Black Elk Speaks (1932)

The Kaws are among the wildest of the American aborigines, but are an intelligent and interesting people.

— Lewis Henry Morgan,
Ancient Society: Researches in the Lines of Human Progress from Savagery Through Barbarism to Civilization (1878)

The Kansa believe that when there is a death, the ghost returns to the spirit village nearest the present habitat of the living. That is to say, all Indians do not go to one spirit village or "happy hunting ground," but to different ones, as there is a series of spirit villages for the Kansa, beginning with the one at Council Grove, where the tribe dwelt before they removed to their present reservation in the Indian Territory, and extending along both sides of the Kansas River to its mouth, thence up the Missouri River . . . (near the state line), thence down the river to the mouth of the Osage River, and so on, down to the mouths of the Missouri and Ohio rivers.

— James Owen Dorsey,
A Study of Siouan Cults (1889)

We, the sons and daughters of the pioneers, are proud of the work of our fathers and mothers. They came to Kansas to help free it and reclaim what was known, when they came west, as a desert.

— Vice President Charles Curtis,
Unpublished autobiography (c. 1930)

Kansas, which was originally conceived as the red man's home, was rapidly becoming his grave.

— William Frank Zornow,
Kansas: A History of the Jayhawk State (1957)

Few Americans are devotees exclusively of the aboriginal; many are fond of the merely old.

— David Lowenthal,
"Not Every Prospect Pleases" (1962)

There has to be [an] interval of neglect, there has to be discontinuity; it is religiously and artistically essential. That is what I mean when I refer to the necessity for ruins: ruins provide the incentive for restoration and for a return to origins. There has to be (in our new concept of history) an interim of death or rejection before there can be a born-again landscape. Many of us know the joy and excitement not so much of creating the new as redeeming what has been neglected, and this excitement is particularly strong when the original condition is seen as holy or beautiful. The old farmhouse has to decay before we can restore it and lead an alternative life style in the country; the landscape has to be plundered and stripped before we can restore the natural ecosystem; the neighborhood has to be a slum before we can rediscover it and gentrify it. That is how we reproduce the cosmic scheme and correct history.

— J. B. Jackson,
"The Necessity for Ruins" (1980)

The sense of the historical past, the awareness of history and of histories, has always led a relatively precarious existence here. The nineteenth- and twentieth-century genteel snobberies about our American culture desert and historical vacuum had this much point: that the monuments, the detritus, the archives, the material leavings of the past — all the visibilia that dot and clot the European landscape — were simply not to be found here and were therefore not part of a world that Americans internalized. . . . Americans were and are quite

capable of devouring historical romances and seeing limitless num-
bers of historical movies while at the same time believing with Henry
Ford that history is the bunk.

> — Steven Marcus,
> *Representations: Essays on Literature*
> *and Society* (1990)

[Arrowheads] were chiefly made to be lost. They are sown, like a grain
that is slow to germinate, broadcast over the earth. Like the dragon's
teeth which bore a crop of soldiers, these bear crops of philosophers
and poets, and the same seed is just as good to plant again. It is stone
fruit. Each one yields me a thought. I come nearer to the maker of it
than if I found his bones. His bones would not prove any wit that
wielded them, such as this work of his bones does. It is humanity
inscribed on the face of the earth, patent to my eyes as soon as the
snow goes off, not hidden away in some crypt or grave under a pyra-
mid. No disgusting mummy, but a clean stone, the best symbol or
letter that could have been transmitted to me.

> *The Red Man, his mark* ⊏▷

> — Henry David Thoreau,
> *The Journal* (1859)

No buried nations sleep in the untainted [Kansas] soil, vexing the
present with their phantoms, retarding progress with the burden of
their outworn creeds, depressing enthusiasm by the silent reproof of
their mighty achievements. Heirs of the greatest results of time, we
are emancipated from all allegiance to the past.

> — John James Ingalls,
> "In Praise of Blue Grass" (1875)

I realized the chauvinism of the act of digging up [the Indian] graves
as if our time, our reality, and our culture, is the real thing and what
we live now is all there ever was and all there ever will be.

> — John Hanson Mitchell,
> *Ceremonial Time: Fifteen Thousand*
> *Years on One Square Mile* (1984)

The patterns made by the historian are never complete. There is al-
ways something lacking, a residue, fragments suggestive of other pat-

terns which might be formed if one only knew how to put them together or where to find the missing parts. The quest for the whole truth ends in the "innumerable puzzles, problems, mysteries, one is eternally stumbling against."

— Walter Prescott Webb,
The Great Plains (1931)

It must be added of words that they are the most inevitably inaccurate of all mediums of record and communication, and that they come at many things which they alone can do by such a Rube Goldberg articulation of frauds, compromises, artful dodges, and tenth removes as would fatten any other art into apoplexy if the art were not first shamed out of existence.

— James Agee,
Let Us Now Praise Famous Men (1939)

No doubt, Sir, — there is a whole chapter wanting here — and a chasm of ten pages made in the book by it — but the book-binder is neither a fool, or a knave, or a puppy — nor is the book a jot more imperfect (at least upon that score) — but, on the contrary, the book is more perfect and complete by wanting the chapter, than having it.

— Laurence Sterne,
The Life and Opinions of Tristram Shandy, Gentleman (1761)

In the Quadrangle: Wonsevu

On the prairie, upright sturdy things, like fenceposts, acquire an importance they rarely have in wooded country. Out here they become reminders that you are, despite having seen no other person for a couple of hours, not entirely alone: a fencepost implies a landowner, someone somewhere nearby to look after it and whatever it protects. Barbed wire across miles of open country is not so desolate to a traveler as an empty road because a fence bespeaks the continuing presence of ownership; it says, "See me or not, I'm here. This is mine." But an empty road says, in the words Spanish explorers carved in rocks of the American Southwest, "*Paso por aqui,*" "I'm passing here." No place is emptier than the one where someone has been and will not return to. A county road lies in nearly perpetual silence, but a four-strand barbed-wire fence can whisper in the wind like the strings of an aeolian harp, as if the Wind People themselves are asking after their land, "How goes it?" although a fence was a foreign, even abhorrent thing to them.

In this land where openness can sometimes begin to seem like blankness, I found myself paying attention to fenceposts, especially old wooden ones of cedar and Osage orange so bent and crooked and knobbed that I could dream them into shapes the way ancient peoples saw bears and warriors and zodiacs in the night sky. Like stars, prairie posts came to guide me. In Chase, especially in the southwestern quadrangles where the hills appear to deflate from rounded fullness, where cardinal-direction gravel roads and the pastures can look one like the next, I began naming fenceposts that served me as guides: Old Scratch's Walkingstick, Boomer's Bent Dick (looked like one), Buns Brown (nicely steatopygic), Sam Wood (all shot up), Geronimo (last two letters of Chief Paints sign rusted away), Gipper Bonzo (top rotted off), Hester Prynne (orangish lichen-covered forked post supporting another to form an A). I even started keeping a list of objects countians hung from or set atop posts, and I came to see the custom as a response to isolation. Besides the usual auto tires painted NO HUNTING and the lost hubcaps, I found a pair of red long johns stretched over a post as if to warm it, and pulled over another a woolen sock like a nightcap, and a bleached aitch-bone of a steer turned upside down to make a monster head, and an oval rock that looked as if an archaeopteryx had laid a big petrous egg atop a post.

On days of grim weather, when I found nothing of interest and began feeling desolate — especially after coming across a fence-hung sign like KEEP OUT OR U WILL B SHOT and even one with a logic that should have amused me, NO TRESPASSING WITHOUT WRITTEN PERMISSION — then those friendly and anthropomor-phic fenceposts lifted me, in spite of my belief that this prairie is more beautiful without barbed wire hacking it up and declaiming ownership of something that cannot really be owned.

The best fence object I came across was different from the others. One hot Indian summer afternoon, I was going down a county road north of Wonsevu (or what the Syndrome has left of the village) and finding little of interest. The topography here is much like the Cedar Point quadrangle. My canteen was empty, road dust stuck in my sweat and itched, and I was ensnared in a mean solitude. I saw something hanging from the top strand of a barbed-wire fence: it looked like a long-handled dipper, the kind to splash down into an oaken bucket of sweet well water. I walked to it. Swinging slowly in the dry wind was indeed an aluminum dipper, dented but not shot up by gunners like most things on fences. But why a dipper? Then I saw why: between it and the edge of the gravel road was a small conduit, and from it bubbled a cold outwash of clear water onto a little bed of watercress. An artesian well just above Coon Creek. I took the ladle, filled it, and drank from the neighborly thing. I've since used it often and learned the well was an accidental strike of an oil driller years ago.

When I was down in the Wonsevu quad in my last weeks of roaming the county, for three days I poked around to find a worthy topic. (The village name is a corruption of the Cheyenne word for deer, *vaoseva*, which literally means "bob-tail high.") All that remains now are three well-kept frame buildings: the 1885 school, a meeting hall, and a church. Finally, one afternoon, my anthropologist friend, Joe Hickey, and the geographer Charles Webb took me into a remote piece of the quad west of the village to a great stone circle on a hilltop. We looked the peculiar thing over, all of us hoping it was an ancient medicine wheel, but, we concluded, it was a geologic feature and not a grand artifact of aboriginal skywatchers.

I knew that when Zebulon Pike passed through just north of here in 1806 his Osage guides told him this was all Kansa hunting ground, and I knew that a branch of the old Kaw Trail passed by not far to the east, so I returned to the stone circle in hopes I'd missed something, but I found nothing. Then it came to me what I was overlooking was the Kansa nation itself, people who had made their slow way down the old trace after being dispossessed of their reserve to the north: the place to begin was not here but at the head of the Kaw Trail, across the line in Morris County. Archaeologists, to avoid what they call "redundancy of sampling," rarely dig every grid of a big site. So, the next day, I didn't go back to Wonsevu but went instead to Joe Hickey's classroom and called him from Introduction to Anthropology and asked if he'd like to go up to the Kaw Agency. He looked out at the day and said, *I'm finished at noon.*

Joe, who grew up in Northport, Long Island, has lived with and studied the Fulani tribe in Africa and made several films about Great Plains Indians. Soft-spoken, with a keen memory and a Celtic wit (that is, he finds a sad humor in historic inevitabilities), he is deliberate, diligent, and dedicated. After ten years of research on the Thurman Creek settlements in Chase, he began looking into the Kansa, especially their twenty-six years on the reservation in southern Morris and northern Chase counties, an area the government moved them to when an 1846 treaty forced them to cede two million acres along the Kaw River where it cuts through the northern Flint Hills. In 1873 the government compelled them to move again, this time into the new Indian Territory — Kansas was the old I.T. — now Oklahoma.

In the upper Neosho Valley in 1847, the Kansa set up three villages southeast of the Santa Fe Trail where it forded the little river, a crossing that became Council Grove. One village lay near the mouth of Big John Creek (Big John Walker was the member of

George Sibley's trail survey crew who carved the first sign naming Diamond Spring); the second village lay about six miles farther southeast, just below the present settlement of Dunlap, and the third a couple of miles farther south, along Kahola Creek near the Chase line. Toward the center of the Kansa Reserve, the government in 1861 built a two-story stone agency-headquarters, and also, along the Neosho and tributary creeks, 150-some rock cabins as permanent houses for the Indians, as well as a mill, mission, school, and council house. Only the ruins of the agency building and a few cabins remain in this valley where the people who gave their name to the state watched a ten-thousand-year-old way of life disappear, and with it their hopes for continuance.

The agency sits in the mile-wide vale of the Neosho (the book *Indian Place-Names* gives five pages to explaining the word, which, among other possibilities, may mean "clean water" or "dirty water"; the small river has also been called the Blanche, the White, the Grand, and Six Bulls); the building is just below the juncture of Little John and Big John creeks and almost directly in front of where the larger stream flows into the Neosho. The well-watered but narrow valley cuts through the rocky, tallgrass hills, and today it grows milo, wheat, soybeans. Immediately north of the agency, on a rounded and grassed ridge, stands a forty-foot obelisk of limestone visible for miles; morning and evening, it casts a long and slender shadow as if a giant sundial. In the broad base of the monument, a small crypt holds the remains of an unknown Indian whose grave the river tore open, and with him is a copper box of "historical matter" to be opened in 2025, the bicentennial of Sibley's treaty for right of passage through Kansa and Osage hunting grounds. Although the obelisk has no words inscribed anywhere on it, people call it *the Monument to the Unknown Indian.* When the Neosho exposed the grave in the 1920s, antiquarians found bones of a man and horse (the Kansa customarily strangled a warrior's favorite horse and buried it with him to ride to the far village where time doesn't exist; less honored dead received only their moccasins; today a can of chili or a chocolate bar may go into a casket); they also found numerous artifacts suggesting the man had been both a chief and a soldier in the Union army.

Frank Haucke, an unsuccessful candidate for governor and the son of the German immigrant who managed early to get title to this piece of the Kaw Reserve, convinced Boy Scouts and American Legionnaires to walk the nearby hills and gather good stones, and he paid masons to lay them up. The old Kaw at his reburial received a full military funeral: casket on a caisson, riderless horse with empty boots backward in the stirrups, and volleys from a battery of the Seventh Cavalry, the unit famous as Indian killers. A biplane sputtered over and dropped flowers on the four thousand people (whites had last gathered on the hill in 1868 to watch and cheer a halfhearted battle between the Kansa and Cheyenne — the final Indian engagement this far east); Roy Taylor, grandson of Ahlega-waho, the fine orator and last Kaw head chief in Kansas, gave a short allocution in the old tongue, a language that would never be heard here again.

A couple of years ago I went up to look over the agency and photograph it and three nearby rock cabins along the bank of the Little John Creek (it really should be the Little Big John). Charles Curtis, eighth-blood-Kansa vice president to Herbert Hoover, spent time here as a boy, a link that did not stop him from helping to dispossess the Kaw of their reservation in Oklahoma: even when this people saw one of their own reach the second-highest office in America, it worked against the survival of this luckless tribe. The agency, of cut and dressed limestone, once had twin chimneys, both now collapsed as are the west and east sides so that the sky pours in to light the one remaining fireplace now hanging to the wall with no floor beneath, its stones still rosy as if warm from burning logs; in places, plaster sticks to the end walls, both partly held upright by hackberry trees. What should be a splendid and informative historic site is merely a rather elegant ruin useful only for dreamtime. The possibilities for restoration now are remote in this place where the sense of history runs to genealogy, heirloom quilts, and embossed bottles.

Sixty feet south and also facing west stands a small one-story wooden house, sixteen by twenty-four, losing its siding to expose the adze marks on its frame timbers. Hackberrys support it too. In shape and color and condition, it looks like Dorothy's house after it crashes down in Munchkinland in the 1939 version of *The Wizard of Oz*. I have heard various purposes — council house, dispensary, home — ascribed to the little place, none of which I can verify. One afternoon I went into it. Trash lay over the floor — wine bottles, antifreeze jugs, a pair of women's red shoes (no ruby slippers these), and much rodent scat. At one time the place had been cut up into animal stalls, but the original floor plan was still evident, and, on the north wall near a small chimney, I could even yet read words on bits of newspapers pasted up for insulation, most of them stuck on sideways or upside down (would a literate person fix them like that?) so I had to wrench around to read them. I found one date, 1869, and on another scrap I could make out:

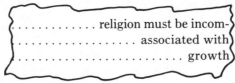

. . . . religion must be incom-
. . . . associated with
. . . . growth

and on another:

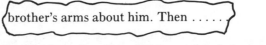

brother's arms about him. Then . . . . .

I was lost in these accidental archives when a loud thump came like a huge footfall behind me; I wheeled around. No one there. I went back to reading, and another thump. Nothing. *Paso por aqui.*

On the Indian summer day when Joe and I were headed up along back roads to the agency, I told him about the noise, and he said, smiling, *So speaks the Unknown Indian? Sometime I'll tell you about a dream I had this spring when I was reading the Kaw Reserve archives.*

We stopped at the agency and probed around, measured it before the rest fell in, and speculated on the general layout of the lost buildings. Across the road was a heap of cut stone, the remains of something neither of us could identify. Joe said, *When I first came up here just a few years ago, the walls of the agency were still standing. It was looking pretty good, and then, suddenly, half of it was down. There's been no archaeological work done here that I know of, although the state historical society once suggested stabilizing it, and I know the Haucke family wanted it preserved.*

We tried to find the site of the second Kaw mission (the first still stands in Council Grove as a state museum) but concluded it disappeared when the Missouri Pacific Railroad rerouted its track bed. Then we went a quarter mile north to the wooded bank of Little John Creek and scared up a covey of quail that startled six deer into running that alarmed a bird into a cry unlike anything I'd ever heard in Kansas. There's something weird here, I said. Surrounding one of the rock cabins were hackberry, dogwood, redbud, coffee trees, and a big clump of old pokeweed stalks bleached like skeletons. The little sixteen-by-twenty-four, one-room limestone house with dressed quoins and a manteled fireplace once had two windows and a single door, but now the roof was gone and a wall had collapsed just since I'd last seen it. The masons had laid the stone with some eye toward simple aesthetics, unlike the Kaw cabin the local Rotary Club took down to move into Council Grove a few years ago and inaccurately rebuilt. I asked Joe what had happened to all the rock houses once in the valley: *They're in fences, foundations, porches.* I muttered that if Americans recycled trash instead of historic buildings, we'd be on to something in this country.

The cabin sat only thirty feet from the creek, an odd thing, since the most repeated advice the Kansa offered settlers in Chase was not to build houses in bottoms. I asked whether this placement in the flood zone was a deliberate effort by the government to make the homes almost uninhabitable, and he said, *I doubt we could ever prove that, especially since whites built their own houses in floodplains, but the thinking behind such a scheme would coincide with what squatters wanted. The Kansa didn't take to the houses anyway — claimed they weren't healthy. They preferred their traditional bark lodges and buffalo-skin tepees, although they did apparently use some of the cabins as stables. A tepee is definitely easier to move out when the water's rising than a rock house.*

A tree had fallen and mashed in two walls of the next cabin. Joe said, *A couple of years ago, one of my students tried to get the Kaw tribe in Oklahoma interested in preserving these last few houses and the agency, but nothing came of it — I don't know why. Maybe some of them see the place as a reminder of the final days of their decline.*

I suggested that, with only six full-bloods left, it could be difficult to stir up interest in a tribe now composed of many people who are seven-eighths white or half-Cherokee or three-quarters Choctaw or what have you. Given the American penchant for honoring places of bloodshed, if the Kansa had fought their last eviction with guns and turned this place into a Wounded Knee, it might have been preserved.

Joe said, *Maybe, but only if whites had been killed too. Without that old magic word massacre, too many Americans of European descent think Indian history irrelevant — there's no emotional tie. The popular notion of what to do with an Indian site is to loot it. People want Indian commodities, not their way of seeing the world. Turquoise rings, not significant concepts.*

Back on the road, we drove toward Council Grove and past the "Madonna of the Trail" statue, her artificial-stone breasts grand enough to nurture a generation of pioneer squatters, and on to the franchise ice cream stand only yards from where the old Santa Fe Road crossed the Neosho. I ordered us a couple of milk shakes, passed Joe his, and said, fruit of the dispossession. We took them to the south edge of town, to the little park commemorating one of the honored stumps in the Grove, this one the Custer Elm, a sixteen-foot-circumference bole suffering from dry rot under its little roof; on the sign:

> GENERAL CUSTER AND HIS FAMOUS
> SEVENTH CAVALRY CAMPED UNDER THIS
> TREE IN 1867 SHORTLY BEFORE HIS
> TRAGIC MASSACRE BY SITTING BULL

Even if we ignore the pejorative "tragic" and "massacre," the "shortly before" was actually almost a decade, but then Council Grove has always been handy at making history suit its ends: a mile west of here, on another rounded ridge with a stone monument, is the alleged site (the evidence is less than scanty) of the murder and burial of Father Juan de Padilla, the Franciscan who accompanied Coronado on his trip into central Kansas in search of the gold of Quivira and returned the year following to try to convert Indian souls.

I said something about the insanity of missionaries and government agents expecting a tribal people, who had followed a successful stone age way of life for thousands of years, just to drop it along with their deepest beliefs and, in a few months, embrace industrial-age agriculture, as if Native Americans would take one look at whites and say, *Thank you for coming to save us from our long degradation, you lovely people.* The records show, to the contrary, that many Kansa considered it ruinously degrading to imitate squatters, merchants, or bigoted clergymen.

Joe, who had brought along a briefcase of documents to show me, sat down at a picnic table and said, *Given what squatters and missionaries and politicians really wanted, I'm not sure insanity is as accurate a word as insidious. The standard argument has always been that the Kansa were among the most resistant and stupid of Indians and that they refused to give up traditional ways and accord themselves with Thomas Jefferson's idea for them as "Christian-farmers." But that argument is mostly a myth perpetrated by whites who made sure the Indians failed. Traders wanted*

them out hunting to supply the fur market, squatters and speculators wanted their land, missionaries wanted their souls, and bureaucrats wanted the power and money attached to sales of Indian
land, so it became expedient to blame the Kaw themselves for lack
of progress in learning how to farm. The myth also conveniently
absolved whites from guilt and complicity in genocide. The Kaws'
failure to leave old nomadic ways was almost foreordained by
whites.

These last few months I've been reading in the federal archives
about the Kaw Reserve here — lots of letters to Washington from
agents and missionaries — and they make clear what happened
even though the history is complex, with many different people
pulling different ways. But at the heart of it was the government
forcing several land-cession treaties onto the Kansa over the years
when they were still on their ancestral grounds up along the Kaw
River. First, Congress made them cede twenty million acres —
that's the size of South Carolina — in return for two million acres
and annuities from the sale of their lands. Then, in a later treaty,
the government took that reservation away and handed them
roughly a quarter of a million acres here along the Neosho, and
then reduced that to the Diminished Reserve before finally forcing
them into Oklahoma, where the Kansa had to buy land from the
Osage. For the nineteen million acres they lost, they received a
pittance, money that wasn't a handout but the interest from sums
received from sales of their land. But it was even worse than that
because much of that pittance didn't make it back to them. All of
this done to a people who never went to war against the United
States and never broke a treaty with a government that never
entirely kept one with them.

When the Kansa arrived here after the 1846 cession, their earlier
resistance to giving up the old nomadic ways began to diminish,
especially when, a couple of decades later, whites began overrunning their western hunting grounds and slaughtering the bison that
sustained their culture. The Kaw were open to farming because the
women had cultivated plots long before even the Spaniards met
them, but it was to the benefit of whites to make sure that Indian
attempts at a new agriculture couldn't succeed: in 1860, Indians
with bows and arrows and rifles weren't going to survive, but ones
with plows and oxen might, and then they could hold on to their
land.

The first nine years on the reservation here, the Kansa had no *agent living nearby to guide them in such a huge cultural transition or give them a voice to Washington. Almost as soon as they arrived, squatters began creeping onto their land even though Kansas wasn't legally opened to white settlement until 1854. In 1855, the first resident agent wrote his bureau in Washington and requested a survey of the reservation to settle disputes over squatter claims, but all he received was a rough sketch that was useless because there were no boundary markers on the reserve. By then, more than fifty squatters had taken up Kansa land, nearly all of it in the fertile valley. Council Grove was founded within the reservation although merchants denied that fact and fought for years to prove their claim. Since virtually no whites would benefit from helping the Kansa, the government talked but did nothing significant to stop squatters from taking land. Keep in mind that there were a couple of dozen other tribes in Kansas also being dispossessed.*

All the while this went on, the Kaw were supposed to be receiving their treaty annuity of eight thousand dollars: for their sixteen hundred people, that's five dollars each. They also received two thousand dollars annually for agriculture and education: a dollar and a quarter per person. A sum like that will guarantee failure in farming and schooling.

Throughout all this Joe was pulling out documents to show me. I said that local pioneer accounts are full of complaints about Indians begging and stealing, but the usual reasons are that the Kaws were degraded savages and constitutionally indolent. I'd not found any pioneer reminiscences that speak of the livestock and crops — and land — squatters stole from the Kansa. One account even mentions the settler who kept his tobacco in an Indian skull, yet, in Chase County, there is not a single report of a Kaw harming a white.

On the Neosho, the main weapons were treaties, starvation, and whiskey. The placement of the reserve astride the Santa Fe Trail with all the desperate frontier riffraff it attracted was either misguided or criminal. The first attempt to help the Kansa here came from the Methodist mission and school where Council Grove is today, but the missionary, Thomas Huffaker, it seems, was always interested in finding where his personal financial benefit could coincide with the Kaws'. The later Diminished Reserve is mostly his work. The Indians complained that the children they sent to his mission ended up hoeing crops that he sold at a profit to other whites, and, increasingly, they resisted this forced child labor so that within three years the mission closed, but Huffaker remained to speculate in Kansa land. Even had the schools been conducted properly, a few years is hardly enough time to move a people from the Stone Age into rock houses. The second mission, down by the agency, had similar problems and didn't last any longer. Assuming that whites were sincere about these efforts, they learned nothing from their failures.

During all of this, the Kansa continued to hunt buffalo in the West because they could dependably earn ten to twelve thousand dollars a year and sometimes twice that. But the chiefs also continued asking the government to fulfill its treaty obligations and supply the plows, hoes, livestock, seed, fencing, and teachers promised them. What they received were short rations of this and that but lots of talk about a new treaty that would — this time — really fulfill promises. That's when the agency and stone cabins and mill were built. All the Kansa had to do in return was give up 176,000 fertile acres of their 256,000. The proceeds of that land sale were to pay off and remove squatters: in other words, to receive what was already theirs, the Kaw had to agree to give up two thirds of it.

After they signed the new treaty, the government failed to evict more than a few squatters and again didn't supply enough agricultural assistance even though everything was to be paid for from the Kaws' own money — which bureaucrats controlled. Worst of all, this treaty abolished tenure-in-common and stipulated forty-acre family plots. One missionary, who inspected the rocky uplands where most of the tracts were, said they were "nearly destitute of timber and water and but poorly adapted to agriculture." By forcing them to cede their lands for a pittance and then keeping much of that money from them, whites were able to assure the failure of any Kaw transitions. Some of our most revered leaders did nothing, even Lincoln, who granted the town patent to Council Grove.

I said that wherever Indians have had land distributed to them individually, sooner or later it ends up in white hands.

The buildings the government put up at that time with Kaw money were inferior, and the profits from construction went to white builders, primarily a scheming New Yorker named Robert Stevens, an associate of Sam Wood, who, by the way, was a leader in the movement to land-job the Kansa. Many border-warfare heroes became more venal when the issue was Indian dispossession. The mill never received a burr to grind corn and wheat, so it was *useless and soon began falling apart and then ended up going to a businessman who bought it for a fraction of its cost.*

Other things conspired against the Kaw. Without fencing, they couldn't protect what crops they did put in from squatters' livestock. Then there was flooding and drought: between 1855 and 1868 — the years when the epithet "Drouthy Kansas" was born — there were six droughts. In other years, floods washed away crops. And, during one winter in the 1850s, smallpox killed four hundred Kansa.

Every year, they fell deeper into debt to Council Grove merchants, who, at times, would help the Indians, since they were necessary to get hold of annuities. Many times, when a Kaw finally managed to receive a plow or ox — assuming he'd been taught to use it — he'd have to sell it right off to avoid starvation. Given the hopelessness they were driven into, alcoholism was rampant. The laws against selling liquor to Indians were so widely ignored it's hard not to see the flouting as part of a conspiracy to destroy what remained of Kansa culture.

The interest on their debt was about equal to their annuity — the merchants kept the two balanced in order not to lose anything themselves — so that most Kaw money ended up in Council Grove. It was something like the postbellum sharecropper in the South. As conditions got worse and the demands for the last of the Kaws' land increased, the governmental solution was to "persuade" them to move to Indian Territory, once again, of course, using the sale of their land to pay for it.

I was getting depressed by this history, and it got worse when three people wearing Plus Sizes fresh from some Blue Light Special drove up to pose for a snapshot in front of the Custer Elm, nearly obscuring its broad girth. I said to Joe that the general's troops seemed almost benign compared to squatters, speculators, merchants, missionaries, congressmen, and a town founded on criminal conduct.

He said, *American leadership here was nothing more than a grasping for individual gain — sometimes even among the Kaw themselves.*

I told him about the sign I'd seen near Wonsevu: NO TRESPASSING WITHOUT WRITTEN PERMISSION. It could be the title for the story he'd been telling. I said that it almost made me wish the Kansa had countered with the other sign I saw: KEEP OUT OR U WILL B SHOT.

Joe said, *The story of Indian America after Columbus is one of trespass. Did I mention that one of the early Grove merchants was Christopher Columbia and that the secretary of the interior who came out here personally to order the Kansa off their land was Columbus Delano? More apt names there never were.*

Before we left, Joe asked whether I wanted a snapshot of myself standing by the Custer Elm, and I said that although I liked the symbolism of a rotting stump as a memorial to the Seventh Cavalry, the only way I'd pose next to it would probably get me arrested for committing a public nuisance. *Not one of George's fans?* he asked, and I said I thought we remembered Custer for the wrong thing: had whites shown some of the perceptiveness of red people that his books do, the Kansa might have had a chance.

In the dusk we drove past the silhouette of the Unknown Indian monument and the dark ruins of the agency and the ghostly little wooden house. I said that had the people around here preserved these buildings, it might have called attention to their ancestors' land-jobbing. Joe doubted that many of the heirs had any idea how they came to gain title to the land. Probably so, I said — that's how you turn a faceless Indian into a loyal fighter for the Union and give him a cavalryman's funeral. That's also how, from an innocence born of ignorance, Council Grove businesspeople can concoct a "powwow" and call it Wah-shun-gah Days to hustle falsified history to tourists. (On the other hand, since Wahshunga, the so-called Last Chief of the Kansa, had no hereditary claim to the title and was a disheartened alcoholic whom whites used to sign land-transfer agreements, perhaps a street carnival with a mud-volleyball tournament and an ugly-truck contest and a couple of Indian dances performed mostly by mixed-bloods indeed was fitting.) Destroy a culture with economic weapons and then turn around and peddle bits of it to the descendants of those who reviled the Kansa but didn't mind naming the state after them.

Joe said, *I mentioned my dream of last spring when I was reading those reels of microfilm. I buried myself every afternoon from one to five in the agency records — four hours of greed, starvation, presumptions of cultural supremacy. Before I tell this, I've got to say that I'm an anthropologist — I'm not a believer in mysticism or the paranormal.*

I said I like stories that open with disclaimers.

One night, about two in the morning, Mary heard weird noises coming from me, sounds she'd never known me to make before in the night. I was dreaming I was sleeping and that I suddenly woke up and saw three human silhouettes against the sheer curtain of the big window in our bedroom. I was in stark terror, but I tried to shout for them to go away. They just stood there. I dreamed I got out of bed to see what they wanted — I knew who they were — and I pulled the curtain. Looking in at me were three Kaws in dirty, ragged blankets. Nothing but bags of bones. Then I woke up — I mean I actually woke up.

We bumped along in the dark, and I waited for him to finish. Finally he said, *I'm not sure what to make of it, but I think a dream can set you on another path.*

Toward a Kaw Hornbook

Hi-e-ye-ye! Summon them, those who knew the people in time gone, and call them to speak the story, to give testimony.

Perrin du Lac, French traveler (1802):

The Kanses are tall, handsome, vigorous, and brave. They are active and good hunters, and trade is carried on with them by the whites without danger.

George Sibley, government surveyor (1811):

The Konsee town is seated immediately on the north bank of the Konsee River, about one hundred miles by its course above its junction with the Missouri, in a beautiful prairie of moderate extent, which is nearly encircled by the river. . . . [The settlement] is overhung by a chain of high prairie hills which give a very pleasing effect to the whole scene. The town contains 128 houses or lodges generally about sixty feet long and twenty-five wide, constructed of stout poles or saplings, arranged in the form of an arbour, and covered with skins, bark, and mats; they are commodious and quite comfortable. . . . The town is built without much regard to order; there are no regular streets or avenues; the lodges are erected pretty compactly together in crooked rows, allowing barely space sufficient to pass between them. The avenues between the rows are kept in tolerable decent order, and the village is on the whole rather neat and cleanly than otherwise.

Thomas Say, Major Long's expedition scientist (1819):

The ground area of each [Konza] lodge is circular, and is excavated to the depth of from one to three feet, and the general form of the exterior may be denominated hemispheric.

The lodge, in which we reside, is larger than any other in the town, and being that of the grand chief, it serves as a council house for the nation. The roof is supported by two series of pillars, or rough vertical posts, forked at the top for the reception of the transverse connecting pieces of each series. . . . Across [rafter poles] are laid long and slender sticks or twigs, attached parallel to each other by means of bark cord; these are covered by mats made of long grass, or reeds, or with the bark of trees; the whole is then covered completely over with earth, which, near the ground, is banked up to the eaves. A hole is permitted to remain in the middle of the roof to give exit to the smoke. Around the walls of the interior, a continuous series of mats are suspended; these are of neat workmanship, composed of soft reed, united by bark cord in straight or undulated lines, between which, lines of black paint sometimes occur. The bedsteads are elevated to the height of a common seat from the ground, and are about six feet wide; they extend in an uninterrupted line around three-fourths of the circumference of the apartment, and are formed in the simplest manner of numerous sticks, or slender pieces of wood resting at their ends on cross pieces, which are supported by short, notched or forked posts driven into the ground; bison skins supply them with a comfortable bedding. Several medicine or mystic bags are carefully attached to the mats of the wall; these are cylindrical and neatly bound up; several reeds are usually placed upon them, and a human scalp serves for their fringe and tassels. Of their contents we know nothing.

The fireplace is a simple shallow cavity, in the centre of the apartment, with an upright and a projecting arm for the support of the culinary apparatus. The latter is very simple in kind, and limited in quantity, consisting of a brass kettle, an iron pot, and wooden bowls and spoons; each person, male as well as female, carries a large knife in the girdle of the breech cloth behind, which is used at their meals, and sometimes for self-defence. During our stay with these Indians, they ate four or five times each day, invariably supplying us with the best pieces, or choice parts, before they attempted to taste the food themselves.

They commonly placed before us a sort of soup, composed of maize of the present season, of that description which, having undergone a certain preparation, is appropriately named sweet corn, boiled in water, and enriched with a few slices of bison meat, grease, and some beans, and to suit it to our palates, it was generally seasoned with rock salt, which is procured near the Arkansa river.

This mixture constituted an agreeable food; it was served up to us in large wooden bowls, which were placed on bison robes or mats, onthe ground; as many of us as could conveniently eat from one bowl sat round it, each in as easy a position as he could contrive, and in common we partook of its contents by means of large spoons made of bison horn. We were sometimes supplied with uncooked dried meat of the bison, also a very agreeable food, and to our taste and reminiscence, far preferable to the flesh of the domestic ox. Another very acceptable dish was called leyed [lyed] corn; this is maize of the preceding season shelled from the cob, and first boiled for a short time in a ley of wood ashes until the hard skin, which invests the grains, is separated from them; the whole is then poured into a basket, which is repeatedly dipped into clean water until the ley and skins are removed; the remainder is then boiled in water until so soft as to be edible. They also make much use of maize roasted on the cob, of boiled pumpkins, of muskmelons, and watermelons, but the latter are generally pulled from the vine before they are completely ripe.

After the death of the husband the widow scarifies herself, rubs her person with clay, and becomes negligent of her dress until the expiration of a year, when the eldest brother of the deceased takes her to wife without any ceremony, considers her children as his own, and takes her and them to his house; if the deceased left no brother, she marries whom she pleases. They have, in some instances, four or five wives, but these are mostly sisters; if they marry into two families, the wives do not harmonize well together, and give the husband much inquietude; there is, however, no restriction in this respect, except in the prudence of the husband. The grandfather and grandmother are very fond of their grandchildren, but these have very little respect for them. The female children respect and obey their parents; but the males are very disobedient, and the more obstinate they are and the less readily they comply with the commands of their parents, the more the latter seem to be pleased, saying, "He will be a brave man, a great warrior: he will not be controlled."

They bear sickness and pain with great fortitude, seldom uttering complaint; bystanders sympathize with them, and try every means to relieve them. Insanity is unknown; the blind are taken care of by their friends and the nation generally, and are well dressed and fed. Drunkenness is rare, and is much ridiculed; a drunken man is said to be bereft of his reason, and is much avoided. As to the origin of the nation, their belief is, that the Master of life formed a man, and placed him on the earth; he was solitary and cried to the Master of life for a companion, who sent him down a woman; from the union of these two proceeded a son and daughter, who were married, and built themselves a lodge distinct from that of their parents; all the nations *proceeded from them, excepting the whites, whose origin they pretend not to know.*

Thinking the deceased has far to travel, they bury with his body, mockasins, some articles of food, etc. to support him on the journey. Many persons, they believe, have become reanimated, who had been during their apparent death, in strange villages; but as the inhabitants used them ill they returned. They say they have never seen the Master of life, and therefore cannot pretend to personify him; but they have often heard him speak in the thunder; they wear often a shell which is in honor, or in representation of him, but they do not pretend that it resembles him, or has anything in common with his form, organization, or dimensions.

They are large and symmetrically well formed, with the usual high cheek bones, the nose more or less aquiline, colour reddish coppery, the hair black and straight. Their women are small and homely, with broad faces. We saw but a single squaw in the village who had any pretensions to beauty; she was recently married to an enterprizing warrior, who invited us to a feast, apparently in order to exhibit his prize to us.

The females, like those of other aborigines, cultivate the maize, beans, pumpkins, and watermelons, gather and prepare the two former, when ripe, and pack them away in skins, or in mats, for keeping; prepare the flesh of the bison by drying for preservation; attend to all the cooking; bring wood and water; and in other respects manage the domestic concerns, and appear to have over them absolute sway. These duties, as far as we could observe, they not only willingly performed as a mere matter of duty, but they exhibited in their deportment a degree of pride and ambition to acquit themselves well; in this respect resembling a good housewife amongst the civilized fair. Many of them are tattooed.

Both sexes, of all ages, bathe frequently, and enter the water indiscriminately. The infant is washed in cold water soon after its birth, and the ablution is frequently repeated; the mother also bathes with the same fluid soon after delivery. The infant is tied down to a board, after the manner of many of the Indian tribes.

The chastity of the young females is guarded by the mother with the most scrupulous watchfulness, and a violation of it is a rare occurrence, as it renders the individual unfit for the wife of a chief, a brave warrior, or good hunter. To wed her daughter to one of these, each mother is solicitous; as these qualifications offer the same attractions to the Indian mother as family and fortune exhibit to the civilized parent. In the nation, however, are several courtezans; and during our evening walks we were sure to meet with respectable Indians who thought pimping no disgrace. Sodomy is a crime not uncommonly committed; many of the subjects of it are publicly known, and do not appear to be despised, or to excite disgust; one of them was pointed out to us; he had submitted himself to it, in consequence of a vow he had made to his mystic medicine, which obliged him to change his dress for that of a squaw, to do their work, and to permit his hair to grow.

The men carefully pluck from their chins, axilla of the arms, eyebrows, and pubis, every hair of beard that presents itself: this is done with a spiral wire, which, when used, is placed with the side upon the part, and the ends are pressed towards each other so as to close the spires upon the hairs, which can then be readily drawn out.

Edwin James, Major Long's expedition secretary (1819):

The Konza warriors, like those of some others of the Missouri tribes, on their departure on a war excursion, sometimes make vows, binding themselves never to return until they have peformed some feat which they mention, such as killing an enemy, striking an enemy's dead body, or stealing a horse. An instance lately occurred, of a warrior who had been long absent under a vow of this sort, and finding it impossible to meet an enemy, and being in a starving condition, he returned to his own village by night, with the determination of accomplishing his vow, by killing and scalping the first person he should meet. This person happened to be the warrior's own mother, but the darkness of the night prevented the discovery until he had accomplished his bloody purpose.

Paul Wilhelm, Duke of Württemberg, German traveler (1823):

Among the whites Wa-kan-ze-re [American Chief] is markedly esteemed because he was one of the first of his tribe to induce the Kansa, formerly hostile aborigines and cruel towards the settlers and fur traders, to adopt a friendly attitude and enter into trade with the Europeans. Since the beginning of this century this influence of that chief and some other respected Indians has been very noticeable. A man of more than forty, with a large, somewhat corpulent figure and a serious, commanding expression on his face, he conveys the poise and the calmness of bearing which show so advantageously in the character of the American aborigines.

Like most of the chiefs who have visited the eastern states to negotiate with the officials at the seat of the Congress, he shows in his behavior that he fully recognizes the advantages of European customs. Nevertheless, he is aware that the laws of the Europeans are unsuited to the nations close to the state of nature and that sudden acceptance of such laws would bring harm to them.

Since the weather became stormy, I had to embark in my unstable canoe sooner than I had desired, so as to achieve the opposite bank. The skill of my boatman luckily overcame the high waves on the [Kansas] river, which toyed with our hollowed-out log canoe. Since it is mandatory to maintain the equilibrium in such a canoe, persons whom one does not trust in this capacity are made to lie down flat in the bottom of the canoe, as in a coffin, and are not allowed to stir. Even so, Indian canoes upset frequently. Since the Indians can all swim like fish, this does not bother them much, and usually they are able to save their few belongings. Only rarely does an Indian or a Missouri hunter let a companion drown, but they always take the precaution to let a companion swallow enough water to make him incapable of hindering the rescuer by untimely movements.

[At the council] I had some brandy and tobacco distributed and gave the chief some presents. Whereupon he took the peace pipe and handed it to me as token of deepest friendship, at the same time delivering an address with much decorum. Naturally I could not understand its content, since the interpreter was not there. This unfortunate circumstance soon brought the meeting to a close. All the Indians arose and one after the other gave me his hand. I must say in honor of the Indians that I did not see one of them drunk, although the opportunity was not lacking, for the half-bloods and Creoles set them a bad example. All had indulged immoderately with whisky.

John C. McCoy, government surveyor (1830):

[There] was a stone building built by the government for White Plume, head chief of the Kanzans, in 1827 or 1828. . . . We passed by it in 1830 and found the gallant old chieftain sitting in state, rigged out in a profusion of feathers, paint, wampum, brass armlets, etc. at the door of a lodge he had erected a hundred yards or so to the northwest of his stone mansion, and in honor of our expected arrival the stars and stripes were gracefully floating in the breeze on a tall pole over him. He was large, fine-looking, and inclined to corpulency, and received my father with the grace and dignity of a real live potentate and graciously signified his willingness to accept any amount of bacon and other presents we might be disposed to tender him. In answer to an inquiry as to the reasons that induced him to abandon his princely mansion, his laconic explanation was simply, "Too much fleas." A hasty examination I made of the house justified the wisdom of his removal. It was not only alive with fleas, but the floors, doors, and windows had disappeared, and even the casings had been pretty well used up for kindling-wood.

George Catlin, painter (1831):

The present chief of this tribe [Konzas] is known by the name of White Plume; a very urbane and hospitable man, of good portly size, speaking some English, and making himself good company for all white persons who travel through his country and have the good luck to shake his liberal and hospitable hand.

It has been to me a source of much regret that I did not get the portrait of this celebrated chief, but I have painted several others distinguished in this tribe, which are fair specimens of these people. Sho-me-cos-se (The Wolf), a chief of some distinction, with a bold and manly outline of head, exhibiting, like most of his tribe, an European outline of features, signally worthy the notice of the enquiring world.

The hair is cut as close to the head as possible, except a tuft the size of the palm of the hand, on the crown of the head, which is left of two inches in length; and in the center of which is fastened a beautiful crest made of the hair of the deer's tail (dyed red) and horsehair, and oftentimes surmounted with the war-eagle's quill. In the center of the patch of hair, which was left of a couple of inches in length, is preserved a small lock, which is never cut, but cultivated to the greatest length possible and uniformly kept in braid and passed through a piece of curiously carved bone, which lies in the center of the crest, and spreads it out to its uniform shape, which they study with great care to preserve. Through this little braid and outside the bone passes a small wooden or bone key which holds the crest to the head. This little braid is called in these tribes the scalp-lock and is scrupulously preserved in this way and offered to their enemy, if they can get it, as a trophy, which it seems in all tribes they are anxious to yield to their conquerors in case they are killed in battle and which it would be considered cowardly and disgraceful for a warrior to shave off, leaving nothing for his enemy to grasp for when he falls into his hands in the events of battle.

Amongst those tribes who thus shave and ornament their heads, the crest is uniformly blood-red, and the upper part of the head, and generally a considerable part of the face, as red as they can possibly make it with vermilion. I found these people cutting off the hair with small scissors, which they purchase of the fur traders, and they told me that previous to getting scissors, they cut it away with their knives, and, before they got knives, they were in the habit of burning it off with red-hot stones, which was a very slow and painful operation.

John Treat Irving, traveler (1833):

The [Konza] band before us were all finely formed men; for with the exception of the Osage Indians of the Arkansaw, they are considered the most noble of the tribes which yet roam within the neighborhood of the settlements. As yet from their communion with the whites they have derived benefit alone. Too far from them to imbibe their vices, they have yet been able to hold sufficient intercourse to promote their own interest. They have thrown aside their buffalo skin robes and adopted the blanket. They have become skillful in the use of the rifle, and, except in hunting the buffalo, make no use of bows and arrows.

The two bands seated themselves upon the long wooden benches on opposite sides of the room. There was a strong contrast between them. The Konzas had a proud, noble air, and their white blankets as they hung in loose and graceful folds around them, had the effect of classic drapery.

The Pawnees had no pride of dress. They were wrapped in shaggy robes, and sat in silence — wild and uncouth in their appearance, with scowling brows and close-pressed mouths.

John Kirk Townsend, touring physician and naturalist (1834):

In the evening the principal Kanzas chief paid us a visit in our tent. He is a young man about twenty-five years of age, straight as a poplar, and with a noble countenance and bearing, but he appeared to me to be marvellously deficient in most of the requisites which go to make the character of a real Indian chief, at least of such Indian chiefs as we read of in our popular books. I begin to suspect, in truth, that these lofty and dignified attributes are more apt to exist in the fertile brain of the novelist than in reality. Be this as it may, our chief is a very lively, laughing, and rather playful personage; perhaps he may put on his dignity, like a glove, when it suits his convenience.

Frederick Chouteau, Kaw trader (c. 1835):

Wa-ho-ba-ke was a noted brave. [Once,] when the Kaws were out on hunt, Wa-ho-ba-ke was surprised when alone bathing in a creek, and shot through the body by two Pawnees, two bullets passing through his body the same instant, large thirty-two to-the-pound bullets. He fell and floated downstream. The two Pawnees sprang in and clubbed him. A blow on his head reanimated him so that he sprang to his feet in the shallow water, startling his two enemies, and causing them to flee. He then mounted his horse, which the Pawnees had left in their panic, and rode to the camp; reaching it, he fell to the ground exhausted. Having been brought back to the Fool Chief's village, he lay a long time nearly dead in his lodge. Finally he was about to die, as he supposed, and it came into his mind that before he died he must have one more ride on his best hunting horse. He called for his horse to be brought to his lodge. The Indians placed him in his saddle. He was so weak and emaciated that he could not sit upon the pony by his own strength. The Indians tied him on, strapping his legs under the horse's belly. He then started off, the pony running carelessly over the prairie. The agitation and shaking up, in this race, caused the bursting and discharge of an abscess, which had been formed in connection with his wounds. Returning to his wigwam, he immediately began to recover, and finally restored to health. This circumstance, together with his many acts of bravery, gave him great prominence in his tribe. [He died at Council Grove, of the smallpox, about 1850.]

The oldest girl is always first married. Her husband marries the younger girls successively as they become old enough, he being entitled to the privilege of marrying all the daughters for the family, a privilege which is almost universally taken advantage of. If, however, a young man declines to marry all the daughters, a second son-in-law may be taken into the family. I have seen some men have six or seven wives — sisters. They never have wives that are not sisters. If there be but one daughter, her husband has but one wife.

Victor Tixier, French traveler (1839):

The Kansa girls, much prettier than the Osage ones, looked at us without showing any shyness; their glances were even encouraging. . . . The beauty of the Kansa girls made Baptiste [the half-blood Osage guide] worry a great deal; he had a daughter who was, in his opinion, one of the prettiest women who had ever lived on the prairie. He gave her rich ornaments and made her ride his most beautiful horse, harnessed with all the luxury the savages are so fond of. He even had his daughter's name proclaimed several times. When one wants to bring a brave or girl to the attention of the public, he gives horses, arms, or red blankets to young warriors, who run about the village crying out the name of the one who has been so generous. . . . Baptiste, vain half-breed that he was, had given ten horses to have the name of his daughter, the Prairie Rose, cried out. Baptiste made it clear to us on several occasions that he did not want her to marry a savage; it is true that he refused her hand to an Osage who offered fifty horses for her. This worthy father doubtless hoped that he might make us decide to imitate the example of young Europeans who, while traveling in this country, forgot their countries and their families to become savages and to live with the young beauties whom they loved. He let us understand that our asking would be favorably received. However, the beauty of Mlle. Baptiste was thrown into the

shade by that of the Kansa girls, so the father was very critical about
the latter and always mentioned, by comparison, the wealth, the large
lodge, and the intelligence of his daughter. The poor man was going
through useless trouble, for none of us was tempted to marry in the
manner of the savages, although it is a bond which one can break
easily. Besides, the morals of the girls were not very strict. The Kansa
girls came to bathe near us; they splashed us; threw sand at us.

Nicolas Point, traveler and Jesuit missionary (1840):

It would be difficult to give an account of all the singular things we
saw during the half hour we passed in the midst of these strange
figures. A Flemish painter would have found a treasure there [in the
Kansa lodge]. What struck me most were the strong character written
on the faces of some of those about me, the artlessness, the attitudes,
the facility of gesture, the vivacity of expression, the singularity of
their dress and, most of all, the great variety of occupations. Only the
women were working and, in order not to be distracted from their
tasks, those who had children still unable to walk had placed them,
strapped to a kind of board, large enough to prevent injury to their
limbs, either in a corner or at their feet.

Some of the men were preparing to eat, which was their principal
occupation when they were not fighting or hunting. Others were smoking, sleeping, talking, laughing, or were occupied with plucking the
hair from their faces, including eyelashes and eyebrows. Still others
were attending to their hair, an occupation they seemed to find most
pleasing.

Soon I became aware that I, myself, was becoming the object of
attention, almost the occasion for hilarity on the part of the Indian
children. For some days I had given no attention to the matter of
shaving. In their estimation, the acme of [male] beauty was the complete absence of hair from the chin, the eyelashes, the eyebrows, and
the head. This was only a minor part of their grooming, but the trouble
they took to achieve the ultimate perfection in this detail of appearance is only a small indication of their vanity.

If you wish a picture of the supremely self-satisfied Kansa in all his
glory, you must imagine an Indian with vermilion circles about his
eyes; blue, black, or red streaks on his face, pendants of crockery,
glass, or mother-of-pearl hanging from his ears; about his neck a fancy
necklace, making a large semi-circle on his breast, with a large medal
of silver or copper in the middle of it. On his arms and wrists he would
have many bracelets of brass, iron, or tin. About his middle would be
a girdle, a belt of garish colors from which hung a tobacco pouch
decorated with beads, and cutlass scabbard striped in various colors.

And on top of all this would be a blue, white, green or red blanket, draped in folds about the body according to the caprice or need of the wearer. This, then, would be the finery one would see on the most envied of the Kansa tribe.

The Kansa were quite tall and very well shaped. Their physiognomy ... was quite virile. Their abrupt, guttural language was remarkable for its long and sharp accentuation of inflection. But this did not prevent their singing from being most monotonous. To their strength, shrewdness, and courage, they added good common sense, something lacking in most Indians. ... Among their chiefs were some men of true distinction. The best-known of them ... was White Feather [White Plume].

Pierre-Jean De Smet, traveler and Jesuit missionary (1840):

It is not to be inferred ... that the Kansas, like all the Indian tribes, never speak on the subject [of religion] without becoming solemnity. The more they are observed the more evident does it become that the religious sentiment is deeply implanted in their souls, and is, of all others, that which is most frequently expressed by their words and actions. Thus, for instance, they never take the calumet without first rendering some homage to the Great Spirit. In the midst of their most infuriate passions they address him certain prayers, and even in assassinating a defenceless child or woman, they invoke the Master of life. To be enabled to take many a scalp from their enemies, or to rob them of many horses, becomes the object of their most fervid prayers, to which they sometimes add fasts, macerations, and sacrifices. What did they not do last spring to render the heavens propitious? And for what? To obtain the power, in the absence of their warriors, to massacre all the women and children of the Pawnees! And in effect they carried off the scalps of ninety victims, and made prisoners of all whom they did not think proper to kill. In their eyes, revenge, far from being a horrible vice, is the first of virtues, the distinctive mark of great souls, and a complete vindication of the most atrocious cruelty. It would be time lost to attempt to persuade them that there can be neither merit nor glory in the murder of a disarmed and helpless foe. There is but one exception to this barbarous code: it is when an enemy voluntarily seeks a refuge in one of their villages. As long as he remains in it, his asylum is inviolable — his life is more safe than it would be in his own wigwam. But woe to him if he attempt to fly — scarcely has he taken a single step, before he restores to his hosts all the imaginary rights which the spirit of vengeance had given them to his life!

However cruel they may be to their foes, the Kansas are no strangers to the tenderest sentiments of piety, friendship, and compassion. They

are often inconsolable for the death of their relations, and leave noth-
ing undone to give proof of their sorrow. Then only do [the men] suffer
their hair to grow — long hair being a sign of long mourning. The
principal chief apologized for the length of his hair, informing us of
what we could have divined from the sadness of his countenance, that
he had lost his son.

Rufus Sage, journalist-traveler (1841):

A bevy of our [Caw] chief's villagers, rigged in their rude fashion,
came flocking up, apparently to gratify their curiosity in gazing at us,
but really in expectation of some trifling presents, or in quest of a
favorable opportunity for indulging their innate propensities for theft.
However, they found little encouragement, as the vigilance of our
guards more than equalled the cunning of our visitors. During their
stay we were frequently solicited for donations of tobacco and am-
munition in payment for passing through their country. This was
individually demanded with all the assurance of government revenue
officers, or the keepers of regular toll-bridges.

The Caws are generally a lazy and slovenly people, raising but little
corn and scarcely any vegetables. For a living they depend mostly
upon the chase. Their regular hunts are in the summer, fall, and
winter, at which time they all leave for the buffalo range, and return
laden with a full supply of choice provisions. The robes and skins thus
obtained furnish their clothing and articles for traffic. As yet, civiliza-
tion has made but small advances among them. Some, however, are
tolerably well educated, and a Protestant mission established with
them is beginning its slow but successful operations for their good,
while two or three families of half-breeds nearby occupy neat houses
and have splendid farms and improvements, thus affording a whole-
some contrast to the poverty and misery of their rude neighbors.

Richard W. Cummins, Kaw agent (1845):

The Kansas are very poor and ignorant. I consider them the most
hospitable Indians that I have any knowledge of. They never turn off
hungry white or red, if they have anything to give them, and they will
continue to give as long as they have anything to give.

James Josiah Webb, Santa Fe Trail trader (1847):

Two little boys from the Kaw village came into camp, and after
gratifying their curiosity and eating of the best we were able to offer
them, they commenced playing around camp and through the timber.

Their principal game and diversion appeared to be practicing with the bow and arrow, which were light and adapted to their strength and uses. The arrows were without the iron points used by the men. They showed great skill with the bow, as they would scarcely ever miss any target we could set up for them. And when they were left to themselves, they would select a mark in almost any locality within range of their bow, whether on the ground, on the body, or in the top of a tree. In case one lodged an arrow among the limbs of a tree, they would with extra arrows keep shooting at it until it was detached from its lodgment and fall to the ground. I saw them shoot a small woodpecker in a tall cottonwood tree after but a few shots, and when they had killed him, used him as a target by sticking the bill in the bark of a tree and practicing on him until he was used up.

Edwin Bryant, journalist-traveler (1846):

A Kansas Indian village was visible from our camp on the plain to the south, at a distance of two or three miles. As soon as the sun was sufficiently low in the afternoon, accompanied by Jacob, I visited this village. . . . While on the way we counted, for a certainty, on our arrival, to be received and entertained by the female elite of the Kansas aristocracy, clad in their smoke-colored skin costumes, and with their copper complexions rouged until they vied, in their fiery splendors, with the sun seen through a vapor of smoke. We carried some vermilion and beads along with us for presents to ornament the most unadorned, in accordance with the taste of the savages. But, alas! After all our toil through the rank and tangled grass, when we approached the village not a soul came out to welcome us. No Kansas belle or stern chief made her or his appearance at the doors of the wigwams. We entered the village and found it entirely deserted and desolate and most of the wigwams in a ruinous state.

We passed through and examined four or five of them. The barkwalls on the inside were ornamented with numerous charcoal sketches representing horses, horses with men mounted upon them and engaged in combat with the bow and arrow, horses attached to wagons, and, in one instance, horses drawing a coach. Another group represented a plow drawn by oxen. There were various other figures of beasts and reptiles and some which I conjectured to be the Evil Spirit of the Indian mythology. But they were all done in a style so rude as to show no great progress in the fine arts. None of the cabins which we entered contained a solitary article of any kind. I returned to our camp, disappointed in my expectations of meeting the Indians at their village and saddened by the scene of desolation I had witnessed.

Allen T. Ward, builder and missionary (1850):

I accomplished the work I had to do, build a large substantial stone house with eight rooms and two halls or passages, besides two log houses, and dug a well. This improvement is on the Neosho at Council Grove on a tract of land lately ceded to the Kansas Indians [who] are a wild, uncivilized tribe generally peaceable with the whites but at present waging a bloody war with the Pawnees; they treated us well and, indeed, seemed glad to have white people live among them, thinking they will help to protect them from the Pawnees. The Kaws need a missionary among them or else a good threshing from Uncle Sam. They have become of late very mischievous. We had to keep a herdsman with our cattle and horses all the time at the Grove till the Indians started on a buffalo hunt; whether the government with the assistance of missionaries will be able to do much in civilizing this wild nation of people is a problem yet to be solved.

The Reverend C. B. Boynton, member of a reformist religious commission (1855):

The "Mission" is merely a school, the Kaws not consenting to have the Gospel preached among them. They send a few of their children irregularly to a school in which little or nothing is, or can be done. The name of "mission" does not very well describe the thing; and this, we think, is not the only "mission" in Kansas to which the same remark would apply. It would do no harm, if this whole subject of Indian "missions" were somewhat more closely investigated by the churches. Some unexpected disclosures might be made, perhaps, by such a scrutiny, and the matter would be stripped of much of the heroic and the romantic with which it has been so largely invested. Many dreams of Christian Indian nations just budding into life on the frontier would, probably, be put to flight by a journey even through Kansas.

I had never before seen a community of real, absolute heathen, for such these Kaws are. . . . They are among the lowest and poorest of the Indian tribes — guilty of all the vices that Paul ascribes to heathenism in the first chapter of Romans — and if any new wickedness has been invented since Paul wrote, they doubtless have learned even that. In observing these miserable creatures, I was moved, sometimes to laughter and sometimes with pity, for their ignorance of all good and consequent wretchedness. In them, sin had wrought out, without much restraint, its legitimate consequences, and they afforded the most fearful evidence of its nature and its power. No such illustration of the character of man, as he is when left to himself, had fallen under my eye before, and it enabled me to estimate, as I had not previously done, what Christianity has already accomplished for the world, even where most of its influences are merely collateral. The difference between an encampment of these heathen Kaws and a Christian community, no mathematics could calculate.

The scene was enough to stagger one's belief in the unity of the race[s], and I must confess that my brotherly feelings required a little nursing, a little application of Christian philosophy as a stimulant; and I cannot declare with truth that I felt any of the movings and yearnings of that mysterious affection which, it is said, will attract kindred to each other although personally strangers. I must acknowledge that my heart did not gravitate very strongly toward my brothers and sisters of the Kaw branch of the family.

There were children of perhaps six years old walking about the public street and mingling with others and exhibiting no more anxiety about clothing than the pigs they played with. From this lowest starting point of total nakedness, the styles of dress rose upward in a series, whose culminating point was a partial covering of the body.

One thing was highly amusing and perhaps ought to be instructive. Whether naked or clothed, whether their pantaloons had two legs or only one, whether they had paint or mud on their faces, they demeaned themselves with a gravity which nothing could disturb, and their carriage was, in general, erect, dignified, and proud; sometimes even scornful. The only instances where I observed any relaxation of haughtiness were where one endeavored to persuade us to break open a closet in the house where we were staying, in order to get him some tobacco; and another undertook to sell me a coat and pantaloons, which he had probably stolen elsewhere — this last smiled, exhibited, and persuaded like an old clothes-man.

The predominant feeling was pity for these poor creatures, ignorant, degraded, and almost friendless; apparently forsaken of God, and certainly despised and abused by man. They will soon be compelled by government to treat for their lands and retire before the white man.

James R. McClure, census taker (1855):

These Indians had evidently, after [seeing the law books in my cabin and] talking over the subject, concluded I was an educated doctor and possessed the power to minister to and relieve them of any disease. I knew all this from their conduct and the signs they made whenever they came to the cabin. I also realized the danger I ran in attempting to play medicine-man, but concluded to take the risk when old Reg-e-kosh-ee told me one of his wives (he had two), Ka-lu-

wen-de, was very sick and that they had no medicine-man with them, and he had therefore called on me to cure her. With many misgivings, I requested him to bring his squaw to my house and I would diagnose her case and see what I could do for her. She was brought in with a number of other squaws. I carefully felt her pulse, examined her tongue, looked wise, took down several law books, turned [them] over, and pretended to master the cause of her trouble. During all this time the Indians watched intently every move I made and appeared to be satisfied with my professional skill and ability to cure. I then, after going alone in another place, prepared several doses consisting of flour, sugar, salt, pepper, and other ingredients, wrapped them in small papers, breathed upon them, repeated in a slow and solemn voice several Latin phrases, and then directed the chief to administer one of the powders in the morning, another at noon, and one at sundown. I did this by putting the powder in my mouth, going through the motion of swallowing it, and pointing to the east where the sun rose, where it would be at noon, and then to the west where it set. The chief understood the directions as clearly as if I had directed him in his own language.

I awaited the result of my prescription with a good deal of anxiety and apprehension, but fortunately the old squaw got well, and the whole credit of her cure was attributed to me, and my reputation as a medicine-man was fully established. I was called upon by several other Indians to doctor them, but I feared to extend my practice and experiment too often, for fear I would lose my reputation and incur their anger and resentment by having a dead Indian on my hands.

John Montgomery, first resident Kaw agent at Council Grove (April, 1855):

I think that it is absolutely necessary that . . . a survey of [the Kaws'] land be made immediately. As the settlers move in, difficulties increase. . . . The Indians, like many of the settlers, have no correct idea of reservation boundaries and are evidently claiming land that does not belong to them and have threatened to burn several cabins. I hope to receive instructions soon.

John Montgomery (August, 1855):

[The Kansa] have an annuity of ten thousand dollars which after being paid to them, is mostly laid out for provisions and whiskey, for the latter a considerable amount of this annuity is spent, and of which there is a full supply in the Territory; and they drink it where and whenever they can get it.

They are situated on one of the great thoroughfares of the West (the Santa Fe Road), where they can carry to its full extent the practice in which they are engaged for several years past, id est, the practice of "stealing." They avail themselves of every opportunity to steal not only from other people, but from each other. . . . I believe they have lost all confidence in each other; they subsist by hunting, stealing, begging. . . . The smallpox broke out amongst them and has continued fatally with the great number of them.

They plant their corn without the plow, but leave the corn exposed and uncultivated to make itself, in consequence of the drouth killing all their corn this season, they will have to have a severe winter. During the dry weather they came to the conclusion that this was not the country designated for them by the Great Spirit and that the great Spirit had become dissatisfied with them.

I am constrained to say that the Kansas are a poor, degraded, superstitious, thievish, indigent tribe of Indians; their tendency is downward, and, in my opinion, they must soon become extinct, and the sooner they arrive at this period the better it will be for the rest of mankind.

William Phillips, newspaper correspondent (1856):

It required no spirit of divination to foresee that, in opening the territory to a white population, the semi-barbarous occupancy of the finest lands by the Indians would inevitably terminate in some manner.

Some few of the more intelligent and industrious Indians may be absorbed in the population of Kansas, but the great mass can neither use nor be used by civilization.

General James W. Denver, territorial governor (1858):

There is about to be a general foray made on [the] Indians' lands. . . . If you don't send a good man to the Kaws soon, every quarter section of land in that reservation will be occupied.

Thomas Stanley, Quaker missionary (1858):

Some of [the Kaws] did plant [corn] but as it is not fenced (and if they had wished to fence it I think the settlers would have objected), it is in danger of being destroyed by the settlers' stock.

Lewis Henry Morgan, anthropologist (1859):

To my remonstrance against [the Kaws'] drinking and [my] attempt to show them that if they drank moderately they would enjoy it more, the chief asked me through the interpreter why the white men made it if it was bad for them to drink it. . . . I then told him he was not obliged to drink it because the white man made it. He replied that he should drink it as long as he lived. It was fearful to see the power of their appetites. A wine-glass full to each one in five minutes for two hours was about the allowance. I tasted a part of a glass and felt it immediately. They always took down the glass at a single swallow and poured it brimming full. It opened their hearts and tongues and I got with readiness and ease what at another time it would be hard to draw out of a Kaw Indian. They are a wild and untamed race.

Samuel N. Wood, editor (1861):

We have resided close by these delectable children of the prairies for, lo, these sixteen years, and during that time the government has furnished them, at two different periods, with oxen and all kinds of agricultural implements for tilling the soil . . . all of which have been sold for provisions and whiskey, and still the Indians are more fierce and fond of rapine and murder and the chase than ever.

Hiram Farnsworth, Kaw agent (1861):

The full-blood Indians have not a foot of land under cultivation on their reserve. They formerly raised corn and vegetables in consider- able quantities; but, the whites having settled near them, their slight fences proved no bar to stock; their crops were destroyed, and the Indians in despair abandoned all attempts to provide for their wants by cultivating the soil.

About fifteen acres have been cultivated outside the reserve — the land of benevolent persons interested in the improvement of the race. Their diligence in cultivating this gives promise of what they will do when they have fields of their own securely fenced. . . . Most of the Indians profess a strong desire to adopt the habits of the whites, but I am not over sanguine of great immediate results; they can be elevated by patient persevering labor only.

A farmer, a religious teacher, and teacher for the youth, should immediately be provided. There is no instruction of any kind in the nation.

The Kansas Indians are truly loyal to the government.

Hiram Farnsworth (March, 1862):

Whatever is done for the Indians will admit no delay. Unless they are put to farming this spring, they will be more miserably poor than ever.

Hiram Farnsworth (September, 1862):

The Kansas Indians have been provided with comfortable and substantial stone houses, which they now occupy. They have cultivated, for the first time in many years, considerable fields of corn, potatoes, and other vegetables. The new fields were broken so late that they have been of no use to them the present season. Their crops were not put in until after the middle of May, in consequence of farming implements not having been purchased until late, and then in such limited number that they were compelled to wait one for another. Had they had a sufficient number of oxen and ploughs, they would have cultivated much more land. Considering the proverbial reputation of these Indians for idleness, they have done much better than those best acquainted with them anticipated.

The school buildings are not ready for occupancy. . . . During the fall and winter there was less intemperance than formerly, but for the last four or five months it has greatly increased. Whiskey is not furnished by traders, but, for the most part, from private houses. A few have been indicted for selling to the Indians, and some have stopped. The Indians are generally unwilling to testify against whiskey-sellers.

Hiram Farnsworth (January, 1863):

This seems to be a turning point in [Kaw] history, and there is a desire on the part of many in the tribe to improve their condition.

Hiram Farnsworth (March, 1863):

Unless you can furnish the money to purchase the corn and potatoes, [the Kaw] fields will be little avail to them.

Istaleshe, Kaw chief, letter to the Indian commissioner (1863):

My Father! I am very poor and I want you to help me. . . . I have a big debt to pay and want some money left after paying it. . . . Agent Montgomery stole two thousand dollars of our money. I want it. You owe us 300 cattle, 400 hogs, 400 chickens, 300 hoes, and 300 axes.

Our great father told us we were the richest of all Indians; now we are poor.

We have had 150 horses stolen by your white children, which by the Treaty of 1825 you ought to pay us for.

My Great Father, white men tell us that you are going to drive us off to another place. We don't want to go. . . . Your white children have killed seven of my children, but I have listened to you and done them no harm.

Thomas H. Stanley, Quaker missionary (1866):

Civilization is a very gradual work, and we should not become discouraged if the great work moves slowly on.

Hiram Farnsworth (1866):

Farming among them this year has been successful, and some few take considerable interest in their work. I think there is an increasing disposition with some men to do their part of the work.

The school, which has been under the care of the Society of Friends, will be closed on the 15th. This effort to educate the Kaws has been a failure.

Whenever the school is resumed, it should be done on such a liberal scale that the scholars may be better clothed, better fed, and better cared for in every aspect than the children at home. Then the contrast will show the superiority of civilized over savage life. Simultaneous efforts should be made to Christianize the adults, otherwise the scholars, very soon after leaving school, will return to heathenism with greater capabilities of evil. The old men of the tribe see this tendency, and remark that the young men who have been to school are the worst in the tribe.

(Leavenworth) *Daily Conservative* (August, 1867):

With our routes of travel closed, with our borders beleaguered by thousands of these merciless devils whose natures are compounded by every essential diabolism of hell . . . we present to the civilized world a picture of weakness and vacillation, deliberately sacrificing men and women, one of whose lives is worth more than the existence of all the Indians in America.

Kaw chiefs to the Indian commissioner (1867):

The whites came and took possession of our places and stole our plows, harnesses, and corn, and hay that we had kept here when we left for the buffalo country last fall, and [they] have broken out our windows and have carried off the doors to our houses; the houses are now full of whites. . . . What shall we do but appeal to a generous father?

(Topeka) *Daily Kansas State Record* (June, 1868):

We have not seen the dusky forms of the noble red man of the Kaw persuasion about our streets in the last two or three days. Doubtless those sweet-scented ones that were encamped near here have gone back to their reservation. When we consider how efficient they were in "gobbling up" the putrescent animal and vegetable matter about the city, we almost regret their departure.

(Topeka) *Daily Kansas State Record* (August, 1868):

We hope that Easterners will learn that Kansas citizens are not thieves, constantly striving for an Indian war for the purpose of speculation, but that the frontier settlers are constantly in the presence of great danger so long as the Indians are permitted to remain in or come into the state.

Mahlon Stubbs, Kaw agent (1870):

[The Kaw chiefs' reply to the proposed new treaty moving them to Indian Territory] was in substance . . . "we want to see some of these promises fulfilled before we make any more treaties."

Permit me to say that this tribe, in my opinion, has been badly dealt with in former years, that they have but little confidence in white men of any class.

A. E. Farnham, military official (1870):

Fifty men with wagons came on the Kansas Diminished Reserve yesterday and are selecting claims. They say five hundred more will come today. Agent Stubbs ordered them off. They refused.

Chief Ahlegawaho (1871):

I believe my people will soon be impoverished. This I do not want to see. This is the darkest period in our history. The whites have made attempts to buy my lands, but I have never yet asserted that I wished to sell my lands.

Mahlon Stubbs (1872):

The Kaw Indians are in very destitute condition [and] are now living on corn and what dead animals they can pick up, which is certainly very unwholesome and will cause sickness and death.

They cannot become self-sufficient without means to purchase agricultural implements and stock for them to start with. They seem willing to work and a number are anxious to adopt civilized habits to some extent, but the prospect for the last eight years of having their lands sold and [with them] soon to be removed has had a discouraging effect.

Chief Ahlegawaho (1872):

Great Father, you treat my people like a flock of turkeys. You come into our dwelling places and scare us out. We fly over and alight on another stream, but no sooner do we get well settled than again you come along and drive us farther and farther.

Columbus Delano, secretary of the interior, addressing Kaw chiefs (1872):

It is the policy of the President to give to the red men a country to themselves, where you can meet and mingle together free from the interruption of the whites, and it is my duty to say to you that you must sell your lands here and select a new reservation in the Indian Territory.

Beside Coming Morning

In Oklahoma, Kay County, fifteen miles south of the Kansas line and twelve northeast of Ponca City, on a hilltop, in the distance the dammed and inundated valley of the Arkansas River turned to a reservoir called Kaw Lake: I am sitting in a maintenance shed with a grandson of an old Kansa chief in a broad shaft of sunlight sloping through the open door; it warms us in the cool wind. He is seventy-six, wears a slender mustache trimmed in the mode of the thirties: it and his wire-frame spectacles and billed cap make him appear less Kansa than he is, but his large, distinctive earlobes reveal the ancestry. From time to time he removes the hat to stroke his palm over his thinning hair; his hands are big, darkened as if oxidized, except for weathered-in networks of white like dried-up saline creeks; the fingernails are thick and broken. For twenty-eight years he was an oil field pipeline worker, although he once attended business college. In a paper sack is his lunch: a can of Vienna sausage, two slices of white bread, an apple, an orange; during the time we talk, he does not eat because he forgets about food and the passing hours. His words are soft with a slight rasp at the edges as if they were old frayed cotton, and his pronunciation is that of southwest hill country. He's six feet tall, big-boned without being burly, has had a little heart trouble, lives several miles away in Newkirk, no phone, drives a Lincoln Continental. His name is Jesse Mehojah, Jr.

A few yards north of the shed stands the old Kaw council house and south of it the dance ground, a big circle of buffalo grass with a high view of the former reservation east across the river. Yesterday I came to the dance ground with Johnnie Ray McCauley, once a pipeline welder, now a recovering alcoholic and the new substance-abuse counselor for the Kaw tribe. Polite and kindly, he too has had heart problems; at fifty-six, he's the youngest of the half-dozen full-blood Kansa remaining and the only one who still sings and dances, although he does not know any of the old Kaw songs: when the Wind People dance here, they bring in distant relations, the Poncas, to sing and drum. Johnnie has learned two Ponca songs, the Calling Song that opens a dance and invokes the Great Unknown to join the circle, and the Finishing Song that closes a dance and asks for blessing. He wants to keep alive the traditions that remain, in part because he now sees them as a shield to help fend off the alcoholism: in singing and dancing he finds strength and self-esteem. Yesterday, Johnnie said to me, *I'd like to sing them for you,* and he did, and I listened and watched the strong, uplifted face I'd seen before in the Kansa portraits by George Catlin. The songs were a gift, a moment, at last, to enter the heart of the Ones-of-the-Wind.

Johnnie McCauley is a nephew of Jesse Mehojah, the most recognized of the full-bloods. I've read about Jesse and know something of his history, but he doesn't realize it even when I help with a detail of biography or history that allows him to pull up a string of others as if I'd put a minnow on his hook so that he could haul in something bigger. Today, people pronounce his name Meh-*hoo*-jee, but he says the correct way is *Mikk*-ho-jay: you must catch the first syllable in your throat. The name means Gray Blanket, but he doesn't remember its significance. Among the old Kaws, his father was simply Mikkhojay, but, to accommodate white understanding, he added the first name of Jesse — two syllables. The father was born in the Neosho Valley near Council Grove, Kansas, on the Diminished Reserve; in 1873, when he was just four, he came with his family and five hundred other Kaws on the forced migration of 150 miles to Indian Territory, a foot journey of seventeen days. Jesse can't remember his father ever talking about the walk or the time in Kansas, but he has been up to the old reservation once, in 1925 when he was twelve, to see the Monument to the Unknown Indian dedicated. Those memories are now dim.

In the Smithsonian Institution archives, there is a cracked, glass-plate photograph of a traditional Kaw bark house, a remarkable structure the people learned to build generations ago, even before the departure from the Ohio River Valley: the house is large and circular, its five-foot-high walls surmounted by a somewhat flat-tened conical roof. In the picture, on each side of the single doorway stand a man and a woman, Nopahwiah and Pahkahshutsa, Jesse's grandparents, and in this house built near the Arkansas River soon after the exodus from Kansas, his mother was born. Nopahwiah, a descendant of White Plume, was chief of the Kahola Band, the group that lived along the northern edge of Chase County, Kansas; this branch of the tribe held out longest against the cultural erosion that worked apace once the Kaw reached Indian Territory and settled on the east bank of the Arkansas River where it enters Oklahoma. Jesse considers Nopahwiah the last blood, or hereditary, chief of the tribe.

Mehojah is the next youngest of seven children; when he was born in 1913, his parents lived in a two-story frame house on reser-vation land his father farmed. Actually, the reserve by then no longer existed, the allotment of 1902 having taken the land from the tribe and parceled it out to individual Kaws, the best acreage going mostly to the growing number of mixed-bloods. His parents attended regular church services, worked their land, and looked to the future of their children: they had become Thomas Jefferson's Christian-farmers.

One day when Jesse and his younger brother and parents were in their buggy on the way to the nearby white settlement of Kaw City, his father suffered a paralytic stroke. He lived on for some years, but the family had to move into Washungah, the reservation village laid out in 1902 as part of the allotment. Washungah was a mile up-stream and across the river on the east side from the white town. When the Army Corps of Engineers flooded the bottomland in the early 1970s, Kaw City moved up onto the bluff, and its population is now about three hundred. As for Washungah, only the council house and some graves made it out. When Kaws today talk of cultural erosion, it has an additional, literal meaning.

Jesse is speaking: *We always ate well when I was a boy. Dad and Mama knew how to preserve food, can it up. Dad would butcher an animal, and the womenfolks went out and sliced the beef into long slivers and put it over a fire and cooked it, then they hung it up on lines to cure. We call it jerky now. It was real good eating. Mama would make up hominy and boil it with the jerky, maybe add some potatoes or beans. We were efficient in preserving food. We hunted for the table — rabbits, squirrels, coons. In the summer, the river would get low and we could walk along with a pitchfork and gig channel catfish, and up on Beaver Creek we'd catch mud-*

cats and flatheads and perch. We used to take water from the creeks and springs, in big stoneware pitchers, and pass them around the table, and each of us would honor Wakonda by drinking from the sacred water. It was pure then.

As he talks he turns his thumbs slowly. Through the open door, the wind carries a peculiar wavering voice as if from some creature dying, and when I ask what bird makes that strange, pitiful song, he says, *Isn't a bird — it's wind hung up in the fence wire.*

He says, *Mama and Dad spoke English but not very good. She never did teach us two younger boys to speak Indian, although my older brothers and sisters spoke it. Mama wasn't ashamed — she was just looking at what was ahead of us, thinking of our welfare. She wanted us to learn office work and how to speak correct English, but Mama and Dad spoke Indian at home, prayed in Indian, but I and my little brother talked to them in English. I understood Indian — and I still do. When I hear Osages talking, I know what they're saying, but I can't join in. I remember hello:* HOO-way. He sits quietly, thinking. *I can't seem to remember other words now. A person lets things get away from him. Sometimes I wish I'd gone ahead and learned it. My older brothers used to speak it in the oil fields when we were all pipeliners.*

Again he reckons, then: *As far as I know, only old Elmer Clark can still speak Kaw. He's a half-breed, grew up around the Osage over east here. They speak slower than the Kaw. But the last full-bloods, none of us can speak it.*

He turns his thumbs, listens to the wind in the fence. *Now, Kansas — that's not the proper pronunciation — it's* KOHN-zay. *My parents always called themselves Kohnzay. I don't know where this Kaw come in, but that's what we are today, officially, the Kaw Tribe of Oklahoma.*

Were it not for Jesse Mehojah, there would probably not be today a Kaw tribe of any kind. When the federal government, encouraged by Vice President Charles Curtis and other Kaw mixed-bloods, forced the 1902 allotment onto the people, the tribe ceased to exist as a legal entity and most of the Kansa records went off to the Oklahoma Historical Society as if old papers from some family come to the end of its line. Eighth-blood Curtis, once a real estate developer (and like Jesse a descendant of White Plume), never lived in Indian Territory, although he saw to it that he and his sixteenth-blood children got nice parcels of tribal land at the expense of poor full-bloods.

After 1902, our land went like wildfire — to whites — and we ended up with nothing. The Osages, next to us, sold off a lot of their land but they kept the mineral rights, and that's how they became such a wealthy tribe. But we let it all get away. If I'd been chieftain then, I would've never approved of allotment because you're depriving your people. If you're a chief, then you don't think singularly. That's just born in my system.

When Jesse graduated from Kaw City High School in the thirties and went off to the oil fields, his town of Washungah, its streets named after mixed-bloods, still had a mission school, agency building, council house, and a round house where he danced in traditional costume. In the late sixties when he began losing feeling in his fingers, Jesse discovered he suffered from pernicious anemia (an irony for a red man who was about to become embroiled in issues of blood quantums), and he retired from pipeline labor and returned to home ground to find tribal buildings falling apart or gone and his people broken into factions, generally along blood-quantum lines; the ruinous tension between full- and mixed-bloods left the full Kaws dispirited and struggling to hold to old ways and communal values, while the people of lesser blood pursued aggressive and successful individualism. The problems of the Neosho Valley had not simply reappeared — they had at last overwhelmed the tribe. The great American melting pot was bubbling hard, and mixed-bloods so controlled things that full-bloods were no longer represented in what little remained of tribal organization. The rape of the Kaw realm, after almost two centuries of Caucasians, was nearly complete.

That's when ancestral ghosts began stirring things and awakening the living. With water backing up behind the dam a few miles downriver, the Corps of Engineers started moving graves in the old cemetery at Washungah to high ground twelve miles away, but the removal and careless methods of doing it angered the seventeen remaining full-bloods.

Two other things also roused them: the last intact historic Kaw structure was about to go under, and, even though their bylaws specified that council members had to be at least one-quarter Kaw, the tribe was under the control of a sixteenth-blood who was doing little for the people while pursuing a claim against the federal government for damages resulting from the 1825 treaty, money that could be collected not by the tribe but only by individuals. Jesse and a few others organized the Kaw Protective Association to watch over the interests of *the Indians*, those who fit one federal definition of that time of a Native American — a blood quantum of twenty-five percent or more. The awakened tribe persuaded the Corps to turn over a few acres of surplus land on the western side of the river and move there, block by block, the stone council house and rebuild it. With that evident symbol and the support of the full-bloods, the new group in 1973, exactly one century after the last removal, brought suit in federal court against *the breed people*, or mixed-bloods, for the right to direct the tribe. In a summary judgment, the court decided in favor of the plaintiffs; led by the full-bloods, a new tribal council appeared with Jesse as chairman. Even though they once again had legally qualified and energetic native leaders who put tribal welfare first, the assets of the Kaw consisted only of the cemetery and small council house: their original 100,137 acres of Indian Territory were gone.

They set up an office and sent representatives to Washington, where they discovered seventeen thousand dollars of Kaw money, a sum intended for tribal operations. With this as a base, they went after grants to build low-income housing at Newkirk, a few miles west of the old reservation. Establishing health care facilities and providing employment for Kaws were steps more difficult until the opening of a bingo hall at Newkirk. Now, among their several enterprises and eleven hundred new acres (none of it on the original reserve), the hall is their largest source of income. Except for the spiritual aspects, what the bison once was to the Kansa, bingo is today.

We didn't know anything about tribal government or laws or investments, but we said we're going to learn — learn good — and we dedicated ourselves. People told us, "I didn't know there was any Kaws left."

Today, in the contemporary tribal office at Kaw City, the enroll-ment ledger shows 1,550 members, coincidentally a population close to the historical number of Kansa before the ravages of the Council Grove years. It appears that Jesse, the next to last full-blood ever to lead the tribe (his younger brother served as chairman a few years afterward), has helped his people restore themselves, a success foretold in his Kaw first name, Hohm-beh-scah, Coming Morning, an image that seems to extend Gray Blanket. He and the new council made significant accomplishments — landmark achieve-ments in some ways for Native Americans — so much so that it seems fair to raise the question implicit in the growing tribal roll: what is a Kaw? Jean-Paul Sartre said that a Jew is one so considered by others; at least to the Bureau of Indian Affairs today, that is also a Kaw. The survival of the Wind People at last looks secure.

But what survives? Six full-bloods (all males and only one under seventy), five three-quarter bloods, seventy-three half-bloods, about two hundred quarter-bloods, and a few others with odd quantums above twenty-five percent: that is to say, four fifths of the tribe are less than one-quarter Kaw. Some members who come into the office to conduct business are blue-eyed blonds, others have quantums as low as 1/128. According to a full-Kaw: *Stick a needle in their finger and that drop of blood you'll squeeze out is all the Kaw they got.*

To appear on the roll, a person need only prove descent from a 1902 allottee: a single Kansa ancestor qualifies you, provided you are not also on some other tribal roll. A half-Kaw and half-Osage, say, must decide where to put his allegiance. For years, the roll was so loosely maintained people went to it and simply added their names. Now, without the benefits Jesse and other councilmen and chairpersons (the current one is a woman, only the second) helped establish, just how many of these members would bother to maintain their enrollment no one knows, although recently it has been more difficult to get a good turnout for the annual meeting. Worse, how many of these *no-bloods* (as quarter-and-aboves sometimes call them) could tell you who White Plume was or what happened up at Council Grove or could distinguish a Kaw dog dance from a Crow water dance? How many could give you even so much as a *hoo-way*?

Although a person still must be at least one-quarter Kaw to serve on the council, a time is coming when that proscription will have to change. Jesse says, *In fifty years there won't be much Kaw Indian left — there won't be much blood at all. The decision's made, and we all helped make it: I married a white woman. My children are half-breeds — but if you don't want to get on the wrong side of them, don't call them white.*

A man walks into the maintenance shed and listens. Jesse says he is his second cousin, Joe Mehojah. *Joe's a half-breed. He was tribal chairman after me, my right-hand man, but he works in maintenance now. He's my boss.*

Joe Mehojah is sixty-two, burly, squarely built, his baldness giving him the look of a Kansa warrior or a Marine grunt, both of which he has been: twenty-two years in the corps and, later, several weeks at Wounded Knee when the last federal attack occurred there. Along with Jesse, he also happened to be on Kaw business in the Bureau of Indian Affairs building in Washington when Indians took it over in 1972; both of them stayed for the seven days of the occupation until the bureau agreed to talk with the people whose welfare it supposedly oversees. A graduate of Haskell Institute, then the Indian high school in Lawrence, Kansas, Joe spent most of his early years with Native Americans of several tribes. He says, *When I was younger, my mother and I would go into a café and people would stare. They were wondering what that Indian was doing with a good-looking white woman. She used to tell me, "You're half-white, but you should take up for the Indian people." My grandmother used to tell me, "Marry an Indian, marry an Indian." And I did — a full-blood Oneida from Wisconsin. And I told my kids, "Marry an Indian," and they did. Their children married Indians, so that my grandchildren are seven-eighths Native American, but only an eighth Kaw. In fifty years, quarter-blood Kaws will be like full-bloods today. It'll be a tribe of no-bloods.*

Joe laughs before he says this: *Me, I know I'm a half-breed, but for years I blamed my father because a pretty white woman looked at him and he fell in love and married her, and then I was brought into the world. She's my mother — whatever else she is, that's what I want her to be — but I'm an Indian and I show it.*

Looking at the first two chairmen of the reorganized tribe, men who four hours ago were picking up debris, I ask why they are working out of a maintenance shed rather than in the tribal office: a silence, shuffled sentences, silence, a few words spoken for my ears only, silence. Some topics a stranger doesn't engage in without harming others. Jesse says, *If I had one wish granted for my tribe, it would be for unity, harmony, prosperity. In harmony you can prosper. Today the almighty dollar gets in the way. For some people, it's a good investment to build a chemical-waste dump on our new land, but people who've lived here and remember this land, the changes bother them because they see it turning ugly. We get so far apart, and that hurts me.*

(Later, a senior Kaw explains this much: *Tribal politics can be bad. Too much treachery. It used to be we spoke out directly, but not now. And younger ones don't go to the older members for advice. I even heard one kid say, "I wish you'd tell those elderly people to stay out of our Kaw business." He was talking about the blood Indians who rebuilt this tribe.*)

I ask, while we're on politics, why not get into religion too? Both men are Latter-day Saints. Before he goes back to cleaning, Joe recites the notion about Native Americans descending from the Lamanites, an ancient tribe of Israel that (according to *The Book of Mormon*) migrated to the Western Hemisphere. The widely accepted idea of Asian peoples crossing over the Bering land bridge he believes to be fiction. Jesse seems less sure, but he says, *About the Lamanites — that all's been brought down to me. I've been told that these lost tribes have been recorded. If it's documented, that's the way it is. But, even though we're Lamanites, I still feel we're Native Americans. I believe that every inch of ground you step on is Indian country.*

I ask Jesse whether he would do anything differently if he could go back to the year he graduated from high school, and he says, *Like what?* and I ask whether he might marry a Kaw woman.

He doesn't like the question: *You're asking me to forsake some fifty years of love.* He falls silent. Then, *To be rational, in these times you can see it would have been better for the tribe for me to have married into my own people — but who? Where was the woman for me? I was related to them all.*

Silence again but for the wind. Jesse says, *If I could go back with the voice of a chieftain, I'd advise my people to be more clannish rather than intermarrying. We all branched out and depleted our numbers — that's the sad part of the whole thing.*

The Missouria tribe is down to a pair of ninety-year-old fullbloods, I say, and then I ask, is it sad watching and waiting for the last Kaw? Jesse shakes his head. *What else? What else? We were a proud tribe. To be the last — I don't even want to think about it. If I'm the one, I'll be a lonely Indian. When your people are gone, what have you got? A void.*

Coming Morning turns his thumbs, the sun shaft gone, the air colder, the voice of the wind hung up in the barbed wire.

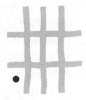

Below the Turf

One October morning I walked along Turkey Creek a few miles northwest of Wonsevu, south of where the stream joins Cedar Creek, close to the Marion County line. I turned up nothing more than the beauty of the woodbound vales and the slightly tilted grasslands rising away to the west where the Flint Hills disappear into the leveled topography of central Kansas; I took several photographs, put my field glasses on a dickcissel singing out of season, watched a meadowlark raise its wings into a little gust and, letting the wind do the flying, glide up and over a fence. Envious, I said to the bird, I hope the hell you appreciated the fun you just had.

It wasn't really so much of a windy day as a day of a hundred winds: puffs, huffs, wafts, drafts, soughs, and murmurs. The sun wasn't quite warm enough to make them entirely welcome. On the lee slope above Turkey Creek, where the winds eased in a sheltered vale I thought ideal for a campsite, I took a rest in an upland gully, a sharply banked wash eroded through an old and long overgrazed pasture. The land tilted enough to the east so I could sit somewhat concealed against the west bank of the ravine and look over the opposite side onto a run of pocket gopher mounds. I pulled out the binoculars and watched. Ranchers don't care for gophers and their burrows that can break the leg of a horse, so cowhands shoot and poison the rodents even though their tilling, aerating, and fertilizing the soil are most beneficial to the grasses and forbs and legumes cattle depend on.

Some minutes later, a gopher showed its head, then disappeared. I was upwind. I played the glasses over the high, faded moon: not quite full. I checked it against my new lunar-phase watch, a thing too nice, really, for the field: the little golden disk of moon in a blue-enameled field of pentagonal stars was nearly full too.

My friend Jim Hoy, who grew up a few miles south from where I was and of whom I've spoken, says the Flint Hills don't take your breath away — they give you a chance to catch it. I sat in that hinterland until mine was caught up, and still I sat, eyelids drooping, sunning dozily like a reptile in autumn. I reminded myself of what I'd written in my notebook the night before as directions for the next day:

> Make a little journey of conjunctions, concurrences; spend time crossing — or at least brushing past — others' latitudes and longitudes; since you can't occupy the same space at the same time they do, try occupying the same time at the same time.

I began to nod. (Once, when I fell asleep near Matfield in a little observation post like this one, a nickering horse woke me, and a young ranch hand asked what I was doing. Embarrassed to be so surprised, I said I was working and explained my interest in the county; he told me this and that; then, when he turned his horse to leave, I heard him mutter, *Wish I could get damn work like that.*)

I roused myself, played the binoculars over the quiet gopher mounds, followed the glide of a red-tailed hawk, the labored flight of a crow, and then turned the glasses onto the opposite side of the gully: exposed rootlets of grass and dried soil and, about four feet below the turf, something that didn't belong. I got up, dropped to my knees, and put on my spectacles to look closely.

A small arrowhead. An archaeologist would more accurately call it a projectile point, specifically a "side-notched bifacially flaked lithic of chert" angled downward into the soil as if driven by a falling spear. I looked it some time before I took my pocketknife and carefully removed it. No other artifacts anywhere visible, no disturbed earth to indicate a campsite. The color of a thunderhead, the point wasn't especially well made, but rather misshapen and unbalanced with its tip missing; it was probably knapped out of flint found near here — a cobble from a creek or maybe a nodule dug out of one of the ancient quarries still visible in Chase; it was an utterly commonplace point, the kind you could lay down on the bar at Darla's and stir nothing more than a disparaging remark. But it possessed one thing I'd never before encountered: given its distinctive shape and being deeply buried in uncultivated soil as it was, I was sure the last hands to touch it were at least three thousand years gone. The next hard rain would have washed it loose and removed the certainty of its long and perfect isolation. Out of the thirty centuries it had lain there, I had a thirty-minute chance at conjunction during my rest, and in that brief concurrence, the old spearman and I ended up brushing past each other.

I sat down again, the point in my palm. Here was an authentic memorial to an unknown Indian. Thoreau said in his *Journal* that whenever he found "arrowheads" he knew *the subtle spirits that made them are not far off, into whatever form transmuted.* The hunter who let that spear or dart fly surely didn't imagine it coming down nearly into the twenty-first century to be found by a man whose only piece of stone was an iota of quartz in a lunar-phase watch. Yet the hunter, who would have used quartzite for projectile points, must also have been an observer of the waxing and waning of the moon: across three thousand years, he and I were linked by three stones — chert, quartz, and moon.

Had he come to this open terrace to take gophers? (Their bones do turn up in ancient middens.) Was he looking for something larger? An elk? An enemy? (This three-centimeter-long point was quite capable of killing a bison.) Did he hit his quarry? Is that how the point broke, or was he using it broken? Maybe he lost the dart or snapped it, or maybe he just threw away the point. (I say "he" with some assurance: aboriginal hunting was universally a masculine pursuit; were the artifact a scraper or knife, the last hands to touch it could have been feminine.)

In Kansas, archaeologists recognize four general periods before the coming of Europeans and history: the Paleo-Indian, from perhaps 10,000 B.C. to about 6000; the Archaic, until about A.D. 1; the Early Ceramic, for the next thousand years; and the Middle Ceramic, to about the arrival of the Caucasian, which, in this location, was Coronado himself, who, in 1541, may have walked as close as fifty miles due west of this gully.

What little we know of these prehistoric peoples in the southern Flint Hills comes almost universally from two sources: relic hunters tramping over cultivated fields — a means of recovery that yields little information because of the disturbed context of the artifacts; or from underfunded archaeologists hurriedly exploring sites threatened by the construction of water impoundments. In the

1970s, professionals examined more than fifty locations along the Turkey and Cedar Creek drainages when the Cedar Point Reservoir project was yet alive, and, in the southeastern corner of the county, they made several digs near the headwaters of the Verdigris River before a small lake covered them. Within thirty-five miles of the county borders, archaeologists investigating hundreds of sites endangered or destroyed by half a dozen big reservoirs have recovered abundant material, although much of it is repetitive or difficult to interpret and doesn't yet add substantially to a profile of the various peoples.

But the findings do undermine a notion common among countians that the single term "Indian" accurately describes all those who lived here before 1541 as well as their descendants: yet the ancestors of the spear thrower were as different from him as the people who built the first ring at Stonehenge from King Alfred's subjects. Those who came after the hunter, some of them perhaps his distant heirs, were people who eventually made different tools, ate different foods, and prayed to different gods in a different language. The human flux through here has been of peoples markedly distinct from one another: to consider them all as merely Indians is about as informative as lumping together Henry VIII and King Tut because they were white men.

What could I surmise about the Archaic hunter who left that point above Turkey Creek? He lived in a time following widespread extinctions, when the great beasts — mammoths, mastodons, camels, huge species of bison — disappeared because of massive climatic changes and, perhaps, the relentless hunting of his more numerous ancestors (the overkill theory). Using spears and probably atlatls (the bow and arrow has been in America only about a thousand years), he pursued the lesser bison we know, and also elk and deer, as well as much small game: raccoons, skunks, rabbits, squirrels, gophers, wood rats, moles, turkeys, geese, ducks, box turtles, mussels; he took catfish, gar, bullheads, suckers, drum, chub. His people gathered grapes, gooseberries, blackberries, smartweed, Solomon's seal, and (surely) dozens of other plants which the women ground and cooked into food and remedies.

Perhaps because of the leaner times, his familial band was smaller than those of his ancestors. His dwellings were insubstantial but suitable for his life of following the seasons of the animals and vegetation. He was, generally, a less adept and artistic knapper of flint than people before him, but artisans of his time did make small clay figures, possibly deities he believed had a hand in the reduced world he lived in, beings who had taken away the great beasts he knew only from legends and songs he heard at night before the fire burned to coals and he could sleep and dream of hunting not gophers and coons but animals nearly as tall as elms, abundant as bluestem.

His broken chert point, a piece of the Permian sea, let me touch origins. It seems as if the Archaic hunter used such marine chips to make weapons, while the successor Caucasian took chunks of sea stone for apparently benign things like the commodious Spring Hill Ranch home or the Second Empire courthouse; but the point maker's path — his stone age way of life and its parallels around the globe — led to limestone courthouses and libraries: the Caucasian overwhelmed stone age people above all with writs — legal, scientific, ecclesiastical — although the weapons were the assumptions and attitudes the documents express.

That projectile point was an Archaic hunter's most lethal instrument, a thing intended for killing, but it reminded me how our most deadly instruments are really habits of mind which yield up not life but merely luxury.

That I sat in a gully eroded by overgrazing with the flint in my hand was a concurrence seeming to lead me to inevitability: I've never thought myself a determinist (too un-American), but, looking at the spear point as an expression of will and intelligence which once helped a hunter feed his little band, I wondered whether it was also something that helped him choose his destiny. The path from that flint and others like it led to 1541 and to me and my lunar-phase watch. So then, this question: could his people have chosen other ways which would have prevented their eventual obliteration? Was there any course where edged flints did not lead to Coronado?

If the ultimate use of will and intelligence is survival, then the pocket gopher across the gully had a better claim to and hope for continuance than either I or the hunter, who, were he to return here today, would immediately recognize the rodent; but what would he make of me, my wristwatch, the overgrazed pasture?

I took out my notebook and traced around the point and sketched its contours, and then, thinking how much longer than limestone walls the flint would endure, I went to a deep cleft in the dry soil and dropped the flint back into the earth.

Until Black Hole XTK Yields Its Light

Even before I came down off Roniger Hill that early morning many months ago with an image of a topographical grid in my head, the materials of this book had been moving about and arranging themselves like iron filings: I, a magnet, moved and they shifted but kept various patterns. After a few months I began to see what would fill these seventy-six chapters, although usually not how I would do it. There was only one exception, a renegade chapter that kept jibing about, slipping from quadrangle to quadrangle and, at times, even leaving the county altogether; but I wrote steadily along, slowly removing the places where it could veer off until, finally, I pinned it in this distant corner of the county, this far reach of the book.

Whenever I found a topic to give to it, to fill it with, the chapter would appear to hold that subject steady for a day but then, the next morning, the material would vanish as I realized it wasn't really what I was after. It seemed as if some trade rat of the soul would creep in at night and quietly carry off the shining subject and not leave in exchange even so much as a pinecone or deer turd.

Editors and fellow writers said forget it, go with seventy-five chapters — after all, who would miss one? The answer, of course, is that I would, and, now that I've raised the issue, you would too. Whenever I'm writing and fail or foil my instincts, I end up in regret. I began calling the chapter The Black Hole: a thing with a mystic gravitational field so intense its light can't escape to reach me. I can't see the damn thing, but I know it's there.

What I'm setting down now, then, is not the subject of this chapter, unless you want to consider topiclessness as a topic. I could, of course, pick up any number of subjects to fill out the grid, things in the county I haven't addressed: chiggers, bankers, school athletics (the Bulldogs came within a game of winning, for the first time, the boys' 3-A state championship in both football and basketball this season), the county attorney, a mammoth bone recently washed out of a creek bank, alcoholism (as in most rural places, a considerable problem), the big salamander that crawled from a courthouse wall and startled hell out of me, the Presbyterian woman preacher, dugouts, hopper-dozers (Model A's with a big catcher and trough of oil below, once used to "bulldoze" grasshoppers off crops), a night ride with a deputy sheriff, the farmer who refuses electricity. I've talked with more than ten percent of the countians, although no more than ten percent of even those three hundred appear in this book, yet all three thousand residents know at least one good tale or detail. Sometimes whom to include was easy: Whitt Laughridge introduced me to an elderly man in the Wagon Wheel one noon and told him I was writing about Chase, and the first thing the old fellow said was, *Don't go putting me in no damn book.* And the reverse, *He hasn't talked to me yet,* or the pretty woman who leaves notes on my windshield, inviting me to drop by.

These people and things are absent not simply because a book can't include everything (it's three times the length I set out to write) but rather because my explorations quite early began forming into a gestalt that seems to control what I am capable of writing about. My common sense may advise including, say, the rodeo at Strong City — after all, many people believe it to be the essence of Chase County (I find it show biz and hokum, but then those are important topics too); it's even revealing that Strong City may now pretend to be a cowboy town when in fact it began as a railroad stop (there used to be a big roundhouse and, still today, the brick depot is one of the distinctive buildings in the county). No, this gestalt permits only what *it* wants. *It* determines. You see, then, I'm not entirely in charge of this work, an occurrence writers commonly discover when they're on the right track.

So, this chapter doesn't exist: I've been thinking about doing what Laurence Sterne did in *Tristram Shandy* and printing an entirely black page. I like the idea because then the topic would be here, and all I — or you — would have to do sometime is remove the portion of ink that isn't the topic to let the chapter stand revealed, the way a stone sculptor chips away only what isn't his sculpture.

I keep having various ideas about what this black hole might mean: maybe it's an emblem of all the Chase material I haven't found or that hasn't found me. Or maybe it's a darkness waiting for a future light, material to come later, the kind of thing that will make me say, why didn't I hear that one five years ago? (If this is so, and if I and the book are still alive some years down the road, maybe I can fill the hole not as a follow-up but as a hope fulfilled.) Or maybe this chapter will one day be the spot to answer questions surely to arise: What did this book do to Chase County? What did Chase County do to the book? (Recently people here have talked to me about having an autographing party to raise money for 4-H and the historical society, perhaps in the courthouse, the one building where virtually every countian who's ever lived has been, and I like the idea, what with all the ghosts there: Sam Wood, Harry Brandley, White Thunder God, Indians, Knute Rockne's inquestors, the lynched prisoner, a future vice president, governors, and common thieves. I've said I'll do it, but citizens are wondering whether to hold off until they read the book.) At other times, I've considered the chapter a place to insert a kind of internal and preplanned afterword I might complete, say, a decade from now, when the new millennium begins, a tenth-anniversary celebration where I'll tell you the outcome of the loomings here and the fates of some of the countians you've met. On other days, I see it as nothing more than a small exit, a dark at the top — or bottom — of the stairs, or, perhaps, the kind of opening a Native American weaver leaves in a blanket for the spirit in the design to find release and travel on beyond.

When I'm writing and come across something I don't know the answer to, I pencil in XTK: Unknown To Come (XTC makes ignorance sound like ecstasy). This chapter is a big XTK. But, so that I don't cheat you of the outcome, or at least of its raw material, I include as best I can now a Tristramian answer on the next page. Have a go at it yourself. Perhaps, I having failed, you are to be its author:

XIII

Circlings

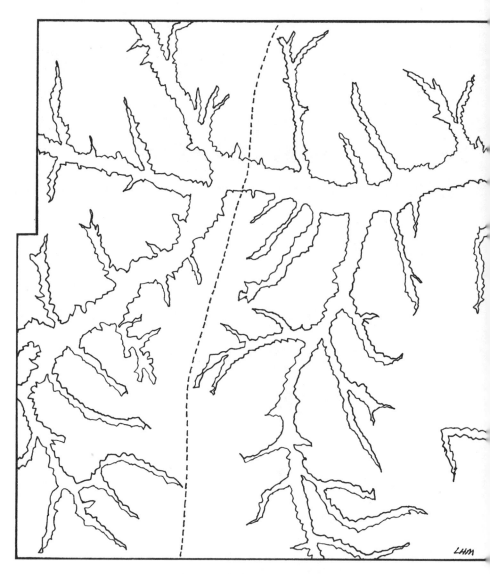

**MAJOR WATERSHEDS OF CHASE COUNTY AND
APPROXIMATE ROUTE OF KAW TRAIL**

From the Commonplace Book: Circlings

I like Kansas — that is, natural Kansas — better than I had expected to.

> — Horace Greeley,
> *An Overland Journey* (1859)

There is a look about men who come from sojourning in that country, as if the sheer nakedness of the land had somehow driven the soul back upon its elemental impulses.

> — Mary Austin,
> *The Flock* (1906)

Our last instruction to our new explorer and frontiersman is to hold ever in sight his final goal — to reveal within our innate country a land in which to live, a symphonious environment of melody and mystery.

> — Benton MacKaye,
> *The New Exploration: A Philosophy
> of Regional Planning* (1928)

The greater number of landscapes I explored, the more it seemed that they had traits in common and that the essence of each was not its uniqueness but its similarity to others. It occurred to me that there might be such a thing as a prototypal landscape, or, more precisely,

landscape as a primordial idea, of which all these visible landscapes
were merely so many imperfect manifestations.

— J. B. Jackson,
"Concluding with Landscapes" (1984)

Such concepts as karma and circular time are taken for granted by
almost all American Indian traditions; time as space and death as
becoming are implicit in the earth-view of the Hopi, who avoid all
linear constructions, knowing as well as any Buddhist that Everything
is Right Here Now. As in the great religions of the east, the American
Indian makes small distinction between religious activity and the
acts of everyday: the religious ceremony is life itself.

— Peter Matthiessen,
The Snow Leopard (1978)

The truly wise person kneels at the feet of all creatures and is not
afraid to endure the mockery of others.

— Mechtild of Magdeburg,
The Flowing Light of the Godhead
(1265)

Our faith imposes on us a right and duty to throw ourselves into things
of the earth.

— Pierre Teilhard de Chardin,
The Divine Milieu (1957)

What we are all more or less lacking at this moment is a new defini-
tion of holiness.

— Pierre Teilhard de Chardin,
Human Energy (1969)

In the same way that civilized men had cleared the earth, pruned back
the forests, planted villages, towns, and cities, so had Christianity
stripped its world of magic and mystery, and of the possibility of
spiritual renewal through itself. In cutting down the sacred trees in
the mystic groves, in building sanctuaries on the rubble of chthonic
shrines, and in branding all vestiges of ancient mythic practices vain,
imperious superstition, the Church has effectively removed divinity
from its world. But its victory here was Pyrrhic, for it had rendered its
people alienated sojourners in a spiritually barren world where the

only outlet for the urge to life was the restless drive onward — what Norman O. Brown has called the desire to become. Eventually this drive would leave the religion itself behind.

> — Frederick Turner,
> *Beyond Geography* (1980)

We deeply require an earthy spirituality.

> — Matthew Fox,
> *Original Blessing* (1983)

So I ask myself if I can still remember
How a myth began this morning and how the people
Seemed hardly to know that something was starting over.

> — Thomas Hornsby Ferril,
> *Westering* (1934)

We must come to understand our past, our history, in terms of the soil and water and forests and grasses that have made it what it is. We must see the years to come in the frame that makes space and time one.

Our philosophies must be rewritten to remove them from the domain of words and "ideas," and to plant their roots firmly in the earth.

> — William Vogt,
> *Road to Survival* (1948)

The ancients, one would say, with their gorgons, sphinxes, satyrs, mantichora, etc., could imagine more than existed, while the moderns cannot imagine so much as exists.

> — Henry David Thoreau,
> *The Journal* (1860)

Vague migratory longings spring up which find fulfilment in reflection and study. Instincts, sensations, inclinations bequeathed to him by heredity awake, take shape, and assert themselves with imperious authority. He recalls memories of people and things he has never known personally, and there comes a time when he bursts out of the prison of his century and roams about at liberty in another period.

> — Joris-Karl Huysmans,
> *Against Nature* (1884)

The imaginative experience and the historical express equally the traditions of man's reality. Finally, then, the journey recalled is among other things the revelation of one way in which these traditions are conceived, developed, and interfused in the human mind.

> — N. Scott Momaday,
> *The Way to Rainy Mountain* (1969)

Above all else, the world displays a lovely order, an order comforting in its intricacy. And the most appealing part of this harmony, perhaps, is its permanence — the sense that we are part of something with roots stretching back nearly forever and branches reaching forward just as far. Purely human life provides only a partial fulfillment of this desire for a kind of immortality.

> — Bill McKibben,
> *The End of Nature* (1989)

This is the immense threat — that when we lose one set of connections we end up severed from all connectedness.

> — Tony Hiss,
> "Encountering the Countryside"
> (1989)

Live in fragments no longer. Only connect.

> — E. M. Forster,
> *Howard's End* (1911)

The soil is the great connector of our lives, the source and destination of all.

> — Wendell Berry,
> *The Unsettling of America* (1977)

Forgetfulness of having been would be a break in the chain. We mean absolute forgetfulness; for the possibility of momentary forgetfulness, in which the persistence of the personality loses nothing, is proved by sleep. Our life on earth is probably a kind of sleep. The immortality of the soul is nothing other than the universal cohesion of creation ruling the individual as it rules the universe.

What this cohesion is, what this immanence, is impossible to imagine. It is at once the amalgam out of which solidarity is born, and the self which creates directions. It is all explained in the word, Radiation.

The interweaving of creatures with their emanations is creation. We are simultaneously points of arrival and points of departure.

> — Victor Hugo,
> *The Toilers of the Sea* (1866)

One achieves a slow, indelible intimacy with place, learning to match its moods with one's own. At such times it is as if a destination had awaited us with nearly human expectation and with an exquisite blend of receptivity and detachment.

> — Shirley Hazzard,
> "Points of Departure" (1983)

The prairie path leads to the sky path; the paths are one: the continents are two; and you must make your journey from the prairies to the sky.

> — William A. Quayle,
> *The Prairie and the Sea* (1905)

[Black Elk said:] Black Road and Bear Sings then sang a song, and all the others sang along with them, like this:

> *Father, paint the earth on me.*
> *Father, paint the earth on me.*
> *Father, paint the earth on me.*
> *A nation I will make over.*
> *A two-legged nation I will make holy.*
> *Father, paint the earth on me.*

> — John G. Neihardt,
> *Black Elk Speaks* (1932)

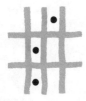

Over the Kaw Track

One thing remained to do, something I'd long intended: try to follow the southern Kaw Trail through Chase, the track once running from the Neosho agency down over the county line, just west of old 13, continuing on to cross the Cottonwood at the ancient ford near the mouth of Diamond Creek, then heading out slightly southwest toward the Arkansas River. Although other tribes probably used the route long before the Wind People, it's the path they followed into their Indian Territory exile.

And so, one Tuesday in mid-October, I gathered things up, including my friend, whom I've mentioned but not yet named. I call Clive Alexander Livingston Ralph "Scott" Chisholm by a moniker he likes, I think, because it seems to combine a vaguely Christian honorific with a historic northeastern Native American name: the Venerable Tashmoo. By birth he is Canadian, with some Ojibway blood, but he went to school in Iowa to study divinity and ended up as a college teacher of writing and an adept poet, who too often lets himself be distracted from what he does so well, render things into words. There's something Indian in him beyond persuasion, a periodic but stubborn silence that's part of his best and worst, a condition he unleashes and tethers with much effect.

I wanted him along on the three- or four-day ramble not just for our old friendship, but even more because, a few years earlier, he had retraced — alone and on foot — the route the Mormons followed in their mid-nineteenth-century exodus from Omaha to Salt

Lake City, or, as things were then, from Winter Quarters, on the Missouri River, to the Valley of the Great Salt Lake. Although some of the thousand-mile Mormon route lies just north of the Oregon Trail in Nebraska, the course is virtually the same. His walk took him ninety-one days, only a week less than Brigham Young's 1847 passage. For some time the Venerable had been writing a book about his journey, and he liked nothing more than conversation about foot travel, the West, finding one's way into the land.

We set our packs on top of my car and stood beside them on Broadway in Cottonwood: the first person to get curious would likely be the one to haul us to the county line. Gil Haug, with the Soil Conservation Service, drove up, asked the inevitable question, and ten minutes later was driving us north. At the dividing section-line fence, the Venerable and I struck out until we reached a point I judged to be either on or quite near the old track. Early-day coun-tians described the trail as two or three paths a couple of feet apart running remarkably straight, usually along ridges, from ford to ford, but today the hills are so cut up by cattle and vehicle trails it's impossible to specify any particular path as the Indians'. Even so, the track we intended to follow was not a narrow, trodden depres-sion, but a direction — one of the compass, of history, of the spirit. We were hunting the idea of the trail.

I've never begun a trip with the Venerable but that he didn't start by repacking his gear, and this one, after a dozen steps, kept the pattern. He is, though not tall, bigger than I am, and he always totes larger burdens. The bag he was about to carry across thirty-some miles of the Flint Hills I considered more of a chifforobe than a pack, a thing that can change one's destination from a place to a hernia. The clodhoppers he wore crossing Nebraska and Wyoming were the largest and heaviest pieces I've ever seen outside of the Frankenstein monster's boots: I called them his Karloffs. For our little journey he wore lightweight hikers even though his rupture sack bulged with matériel including a miniature spatula, a whisk, a bottle of Bryant's Kansas City barbecue sauce, three press cards, and a selection of gadgets from mail-order catalogs: attached to various implements he must have had six magnifying glasses, five cork-screws, and three fish scalers. He did not carry binoculars, camera, microcassette recorder, or a real notebook — I had those — but he did have the lone compass.

I grumbled while he repacked, and a big ledge of overcast I didn't like the look of let go a few drops before breaking apart as if it were old, crumbling limestone. Canada geese called and cut their usual piece of the alphabet across the sky, and he looked up, and I said the beyond calls us, marks the route, letters it, Vorward! Off we went into the grasses, the katydids sweetly rasping, a sound I'd come to love here second only to the dismal weep of an upland plover in spring. When we dropped down across the first woody hollow and sent up two dozen prairie chickens, the Venerable froze to watch their long glides, and he said, *A bird couldn't fly like that in the woods. Their flight is a revelation of their terrain: smooth and undulous.*

— Undulous? I said.

Undulating is too harsh.

The hollows kept drawing him into them — a woodland man must ease into the prairie — while I kept to the ridges where the Kansa moved. I suggested that we were having a go at participatory history, and he asked what that meant, and I said it was an effort at joining in, at trying to recapture a sense of what's gone before us, to act on history. He said, *I'm participating in valleys.*

When he came up again onto the ridge, he huffed out, *I just saw an eagle nest down there the size of Kankakee,* and he described a tree-borne wood-rat lodge. If the Olympic Committee ever introduces a competition in conclusion-leaping, the Venerable has gold-medal potential. I rambled on about the pack rat and told him its scientific name was *Rattus packalottus,* and that the subspecies that builds only in the back seats of field-abandoned sedans is *Rattus buickiensis.*

He said, *Homo bulliensis,* was gone again down into the next hollow, and I admired the labor of his descents and ascents. The Venerable has something of the build of a bison: a large and powerful humping back tapering to a small rump, short legs that give him surprising speed, dark eyes not quite sized to the head, and a little pointy chin-beard. That day, when he bent at the waist to look at something, the configuration was nearly precise, and, for those early miles, I mostly saw him not at all or some distance off as a bison-like silhouette.

He came up behind me once, deliberately, to make me jump. I told him of the old countian who said the Kaw could sneak up on game because they walked easy and didn't have kneecaps that wiggled like a Caucasian's. *These hills ought to tighten up anybody's knees.*

A mile farther he pointed to the southwest, toward Big Mound. *How far off is it?*

— Tomorrow. For tonight, I hope we can find a spring.

Set a pace, not a goal. If a spring's there, it's there.

Together we went down a ridge and back up, both of us pulling hard, our kneecaps wiggling, and I singing,

> Oh, there are no hills in Kansas
> Not even one at all,
> So if you take a tumble,
> You don't have far to fall.

When the terrain eased again, he said, *Walking in a forest, you don't see enough country, and walking on the flatter parts of the Great Plains, you see too much. But these prairie hills give you just enough land to put under all that sky. I wouldn't call this place vast — it's just balanced. And if you get tired of openness, you can take to the hollows and close up the sky, but you don't forget it. One of the best titles of books about the American West is* Sky Determines. *And, god, does it.*

Then he was gone again, off down a hill. When he came back up he had to adjust the chifforobe. *Before they had horses, how did the Kaws carry their loads?*

— Even after horses, women and dogs did much of the hauling. In 1819 Thomas Say described ten-year-old girls carrying burdens nearly equal to their weight. Of course, they tried to avoid participating in the mysteries of the hollows.

I like the way the terrain forces a kind of continuance — you can try to leave the old trails, but the land pushes you back onto them. Sane people repeat, the mad go astray. But, somewhere, the first person to find the best trail had to be a madman. God, after a couple of hours I'm already headed back into an American Stone Age.

— With a whisk and three press cards.

On we went. He asked, *What's that steady sound, that long nicketing?*

— Katydids.

Did they just start up?

— About four hours ago.

I'd forgotten how walking unbuttons you. You can't walk unconsciously for long — things thrust themselves right into your ears, up your nose. When you're on foot, life vibrates. By the time we get to the bottom of this county, I'll be hearing the hell of the place.

We went on, listening, and I watched his response to the tall prairie as much as anything. Occasionally, he'd ask the name of a grass or plant, and, for the ones I didn't know, I gave him my own names: piss weed (smell it), itch grass (rub it on your wrist), *nutmegolium* (taste it).

Once he said, *This place isn't virginal, but it doesn't seem to have been had too many times.* As he spoke, I stopped dead in my tracks, he asked what it was, and I pointed to the grass ahead. *It changes color.* He stepped closer. *It's a big circle, a disk.*

— It took me months to stumble across my first buffalo wallow, and now you've done it in your fifth hour.

The grass was a circumference slightly faded from its surrounding like a new moon. We sat down inside it, the Venerable fascinated. I called it another palimpsest and said there hadn't been any wild bison in the county since about the 1830s.

When you realize what it is, then you know for certain the buffalo were right here on their backs, rolling. Then, *God, am I sitting deep.* He lay back, rolled like a bison, paused as they do, looked upward. *I don't see anything except sky. I feel the earth, but I don't see it.*

— Coronado, when he was close by hunting Quivira, reportedly said something like that.

We think of ground being at the bottom, but this ground is in the middle, or, nothing less than at the bottom of the top. I could be floating.

We pulled out some raisins and peanut butter and flour tortillas, and ate lying down.

How do you know when the prairie is in you?

— When you see a tree as an eyesore.

He whistled low, pointed up at something: turning a high circle that seemed to reflect the wallow was a massing of red-tails. He said, *A boil of hawks — the journey begins under good medicine.*

When we were pulling on our packs again, he looked for the birds but their circle had drifted too far south to see; he said, *We live on this continent without knowing what it is or where we are.* Off he went, and I knew his course only from the prairie chickens his trespass stirred up.

I found him again, now perched on a ledge. *I feel as if I've been walking down the backbone of America.*

I said I felt as if America had been walking down my backbone. Somewhere on the far western side of the Spring Hill Ranch, we went down a grassy draw, came to a spring reduced to a small pool by the dry autumn, the watercress unpalatable. An owl rose from a lone willow and turned its neckless flight south, and I looked at the Venerable and said, Well, Brigham? He said, *This is the place.*

The draw, although holding only a few scattered trees and a fringe of scrub, was sunken enough to get us out of the wind and conceal our campfires: flames on the prairie draw people as a cottonwood does lightning. We set the tent up near the willow, and as we worked, it dropped little golden spears on us. The Venerable assembled supper, inventing, as he cooked, a dirty ditty about muskmelons and boys' procreative urges. I built a fire, then cut two staffs out of a thicket of rough-leaf dogwood. The small trees, shrubs really, tend to grow straight and of a consistent diameter, so that in its first years it provides light but strong shafts the Kansa and Osage used for arrows. In April, its blossoms yield an exotic fragrance as if someone lighted a joss stick of cheap Chinese incense. I talked about the tree as I shaped the handles of the staffs, and, around mine, cut in a ring to mark the first day. The Venerable looked at it: *Circles, circles.*

He once worked on a Great Lakes ore boat, and he said how the terrain today reminded him of water, then he sang poet Charles Olson's line: *"The fulcrum of America is the Plains — half sea, half land."*

A confusion of breaking clouds and setting sun turned the horizon to a brief, purplish circle of its own, then it was gone, and we sat down before the little fire, its slow flames seeming not to dispense the light but to gather it from the darkness as a dry cloth does dampness.

He said, *I found it hard to walk straight today. I think I kept looping as if I were walking on a big sphere that forces you into a circle. I didn't feel Jefferson's grid at all, not even when we crossed a fence. Straightness is a Caucasian's illusion. Einstein may have said that space is curved, but Indians already knew it. Your lovely grid is a great bending.*

— An obsolete word kept turning in my mind today: habitance. I think my travels here have been into habitance.

I had gathered some ticklegrass before sunset, and I stood up, misdirected his attention toward the moon, and said, O Great Mysterious, evidence yourself! and dropped the dry grass onto the fire, and, in a moment, it snapped and scintillated, and he said, *I love it.*

To coax him into real conversation, I rattled on about campfires not allowing you to do much but talk, listen, dream; I went on about how people must have first found their way into other dimensions by means of firelight. Didn't campfires create stories? He pulled out a thick, stubby Mexican blunt in a maduro wrapper, put a brand to it, rolled it in his wet pucker, and I asked whether he thought a cigar named Fellatio would sell. He said to light my fussy pipe and let the smoke do the talking, so I did, and we sat there in full-bellied contentment.

After a while he said, *When I was crossing central Nebraska on my Mormon Trail walk, I started to feel shrunk. I don't mean the weight I was losing — that's only a metaphor. I felt insignificant, but never nonexistent: my point is that I felt* more *existent. When some of my ignorance about the land began to decrease, when I started learning names and recognizing things — this was a pasque flower, that was a Franklin's ground squirrel, or whatever — my loneliness from feeling separate disappeared. Desolation was the hardest part of the walk.*

— That and lifting your Karloffs.

Those goddamn boots are a picture of what I'm talking about: massive things to protect me from the earth. But god, the companionship that was there.

From where we sat, we could see Polaris directly ahead and the Great Bear circling it as if bound to a stake.

Quit the hell scribbling in that notebook and say something. If you build a fire, feed it. Ask me why a person should walk cross-country.

— Tell me.

It frees you from wanting to own it. It liberates you. I have a theory: once Native Americans got the wheel and gave up walking, they started thinking about owning the land, just like whites. If Tecumseh had owned a Chevy, he'd never have said selling a country was like trying to sell air or the clouds.

The Venerable fired his cigar again, stoking himself now: *When I'm on my deathbed, a shriveled little walnut of a man, I think I'll be remembering my walk across the plains, not because it's the only grand thing I've ever accomplished but because it was the longest time I ever really linked up.*

He pushed some wood into the fire, and in the minutes of good light, I worked again on my notebook. He asked, *Can you put all your walking here into a nutshell?*

— Reduction is deception. Have you ever seen Hiroshige's series of Japanese woodblock prints called *One Hundred Views of Edo?* I think I've been trying to accomplish what he did.

But I want to know why you came out here.

— The question is, what drew me out here, and the answer to that is the book. Ninety-nine-point-nine to the ninth decimal of what has ever happened here isn't in the book. Its two hundred thousand words are my nutshell.

The old convenience of hiding behind the truth.

— All right, then: sacred — by that I mean venerable, Venerable — sacred understanding comes not from bearing witness but from being a witness.

I think you need both. In our own ways, we all do. The being requires the bearing.

In the dewed morning I went down to the small pool to wash, then built a fire, using the only dry tinder I could find, an old sparrow nest, and the Venerable ladled out eggs with barbecue sauce and grilled dried tomatoes. We said little. When we rolled up the tent, he composed another verse to his dirty ditty, this one about laughter as saltpeter (*Laugh ladies, laugh, then them naughty boys can't do you no harm*), and off we went.

Struggling, I barely made it to the top of the first hill and had to stop. While I adjusted my pack to get rid of whatever was gouging me in the hip, I found two chunks of limestone the size of encyclopedias. I said nothing, because in his cook kit I'd coiled up a three-foot-long shed skin of a rat snake.

We had trouble finding ridges running our way, and we felt yesterday in our legs although I thought my kneecaps wobbled less. Up the steep pitches, I sang, "Oh, there are no hills in Kansas." We would reach the top, take aim on a distant ledge or a sapling or merely a change in the color of the grass, and strike on again. Once he checked the compass, and I asked were we wandering. *This isn't a walk — it's a stagger.*

We stopped for a snack, and I told him how the old Kaws loved apples: one white traded a double handful for a pair of beaded moccasins that had taken weeks to make.

I think I saw an antelope. Is that possible here? It was. *Have you eaten antelope?*

— Never have, but Horace Greeley said its flesh was tender and delicate, the choicest eating he found in Kansas. It was the only animal here, so he claimed, that could boast of either grace or beauty.

The words of a narrow, eastern pinch-ass.

We came down along Gannon Creek and past an old cowhand's place and onto a road where we saw him working in a corral. He didn't return my wave, and in a few minutes he roared up in his truck to demand what we were doing, and I could mollify him only a little, so we just walked on. The Venerable asked if that was typical, and I said hospitality could be a different thing here than in the rest of Kansas.

Maybe this isn't Kansas. Maybe this place is only in Kansas.

We followed the north branch of the Santa Fe tracks down to highway 50 so we could cross the Cottonwood on a bridge. Abruptly he said, *I've got to have a cheeseburger.* And a milk shake, I said, and described at length what they would taste like. Then I realized he was serious.

— We're supposed to be recapitulating a piece of the Kansa experience. We're walking under the assumption that you don't really discover America until you gain some sense of its first people. A cheeseburger is only going to dispel everything we've earned.

He sat down on a guardrail, his expression fixed. I started off, stopped when I didn't hear following footfalls, and turned around: he stood along the highway, thumb up, displaying something in the other hand. I walked back. He was showing to passing cars a wallet-size press card.

— Have you lost your wits?

He said nothing. I sat down on the guardrail, relieved that we would soon have to hike on. I talked at him: even if drivers could read the card at seventy miles an hour, his dusty beard and half-demented expression of junk-food hunger would keep them moving. After a while we went on up the road, the Venerable in a silence only the dead must know, and we crossed the river, came to a farmhouse with a pump in the yard, where he filled his canteen. Mary Cahoone opened her door, and he asked her to take us to Strong City. I put my face in my hands. She got her car keys, and my heart sank. Off we went to Buck's, and the Venerable whispered *Milk shake,* and I yielded to my fate. When we walked in, the teenager behind the counter looked at me, my face surely twisted between annoyance and café hunger, and she said, *You the one dragging the cross down the road?*

— No, just him.

What cross? the Venerable said.

Some nut from Arizona said Jesus told him to drag a cross to New York City.

The cook called from the grill, *But he had a little wheel on the bottom of it — I saw it.*

The Venerable shook his head. *No, you're not putting a little wheel under me.*

We ate our cheeseburgers stacked up with extras, drank our milk shakes in silence except for my griping about one of us reading a newspaper when the goal was to slip the present. He ignored me as he did when I said if he ever went on a vision quest he'd have to do it in a booth at a Dairy Queen. Finally I said loudly, all right, now get us the hell back out there.

He persuaded a filling-station attendant on his way home to drop us off at the state lake, not far from where we'd left our trail. Seeing the picnic tables, the Venerable argued for setting up camp right there. I began ranting about cheeseburgers, cross draggers, and sleeping on top of pulltabs and candy wrappers. I jerked on my pack and headed out, but, going under the park fence, I tangled up my gear in the barbs, and the Venerable had to free me. I got up cussing, threw my bag over the fence, insulted his devotion to real walking. He said nothing but crossed the fence, and we were again into the grasses.

After a mile, I slowed down and turned to call back my apology. He said nothing. I asked if I could get off the hook.

You're off, you're off.

To recover our equilibrium, I forced some commentary, how the Kansa hated fences across their trail, how they would open them up, how whites refused to recognize generations of prior free passage although their own laws depended upon precedents.

Heavy clouds came in and quickly absorbed the light, and we set up the tent in a place not really of our choice. Wood was scarce, and we had to make do with a couple of discarded fenceposts, but, when I pushed the end of the first one into the fire, I enjoyed the symbolism. I also threw on a couple of dried cow pies, but they didn't burn worth a damn, and we talked about eastern women arriving in Kansas in the 1870s and scouring the grassland for bison chips — sometimes politely called *bois de vache* — and picking them up at first with two sticks until the women toughened and used their hands. Once I'd read an archaeologist's report on the BTUs in bison scat.

On two occasions the Venerable and I have gone to England to walk and to drink traditional ales. As we sat at the fire, he asked how a pint of Abbot's Ale would taste now. Figuring I was safe from any countian driving us to Bury Saint Edmunds, I said, oh, to be in England now that Abbot's there.

I've been thinking about English landscape today: that tidy garden of a toy realm where there's almost no real wilderness left and absolutely no memory of it. Where the woods are denatured plantings. The English, the Europeans, are too far from it. That's the difference between them and us. Americans derive from recent wilderness, although I've never liked that word — I feel wild in cities. He examined the burn on his cigar, often a prelude to a pronouncement: *Wildness makes for civility.* After a pause, *Would you call these people civil?*

— By your definition, in proportion to the wildness left here.

That night it rained hard, but a wind the next morning dried things, which was fortunate, since we had a mile of ungrazed grass to walk through that fetched up to our waists. The Venerable asked what the state bird of Kansas was, and I said the meadowlark, the same as five other western states. *That's disappointing. I'd have thought it would be something bigger, wilder — a hawk, or at the least a prairie chicken.*

— Fifty states have totem birds and not one is a raptor.

We're a Caucasian nation of titmice.

We moved steadily in the easy weather, the hill climbs seeming now little more than part of the trail. On our travels, it takes a couple of days for the Venerable to unhitch from work and custom before he really enters the journey. Besides his companionship, I'd wanted him along for the possibility of his preacherly outbursts. I thought he might be ready, so I tried to prime him with a lecture of my own: how we needed a new generation of ghost dancers who could infuse in all of us an Indian interpretation of the great chain of being. He listened but mostly walked until, northwest of Bazaar, we came onto a section-line road edged with Osage orange. When I saw him turn a fallen hedge apple into a soccer ball and boot it to me, I was ready to prime him again. I started up about how the link here between the health of the land and human welfare was so immediate — the people so directly dependent on the prairie — that I was continually surprised to see the exploitation they tolerated or engaged in; what kept things going for them wasn't really true husbandry or stewardship but their small population.

We pulled up under a big hedgerow to eat and repair our heels, and the Venerable at last launched one, and this is the gist: *You use* the word loomings, but the looming I see here is the power in the prairie itself. I feel it every step. It's inexorable. For every human violation, here and everywhere, we know that somewhere the land is subtracting from our account, and when it falls low enough, the land will foreclose on us. It holds our mortgage. It owns us. We're stupid serfs trying to overthrow the manor.

The other day you got going about "the little brown church in the vale as the imposthume," and as usual you didn't get to the heart of the matter. The canker isn't our medieval religion — it's our failure to grow out of it or reinterpret it in the light of changed times. The real imposthume is dualistic thinking: splitting and separating things rather than seeing the web. We turn creation into good or evil, body or soul, man and nature. Change those conjunctions to prepositions and see how the medieval disappears — good beside evil, man in nature, body with soul.

But you did hit on one thing when you said that we'd stay in a fix as long as we continued to believe that alleged archangels are more important than armadillos, but what you didn't seem to see is the deadliest of the seven deadly sins. Nothing more medieval than those. It's our pride that separates us from God, says the Christian, and the ecologist can also say it's pride — and greed, sin number two or three — that separates us from creation and allows us to believe that only we could possibly be the children of God. That belief alone makes us a deadly species. Exploitation is the fruit of pride and greed, and its consequence is extinction.

— May I interject something here?

No. Our extinction will be a tragedy, not in the newspaper or cosmic sense but in the literary one: pride and blindness bringing down the protagonist. If we could put on productions of the world's fifty greatest plays to an audience of eighteenth-century Native Americans, the one they would truly comprehend would be Oedipus Rex. But let me ask you, how would it play this weekend in Strong City?

— My interjection is that Emerson thought that the view a people held toward nature determined their institutions, but now the opposite seems to be at work.

And it'll continue until preachers start speaking up about a new ecological Christianity to replace our old egological one. Of all the loomings you talk about, that may be the biggest. Indians didn't worship armadillos, but they did honor their existence because *they respected what produces life. Even these stones are on their way to becoming bone.*

The wind was rising. The Venerable said, *Let's walk, Willy.* We went down the lane, left it for the grasses, came again to a short stretch of road and a farmhouse and a pump where we filled our canteens, talked with the owner, who was considerably amused by grown men hiking down-county, then we struck out again, and the canteens never felt heavier. Water, wind, hills set against us, sat on us, and we came into a vale that left no exit but a steep ascent. We stopped, dreaded it, made it bigger. I wanted to get it behind us, so I went up, using my left arm to push off my knee, my right arm leaning hard into the staff, and I was too weary to sing about no hills in Kansas. At the top, a slight depression deflected the wind, and I lay down to wait. Up came the Venerable looking as if climbing bone by bone. His tiredness worried me, but when I could make out his expression, he was smiling, and after he sat down he said, *I loved that effort up flat Kansas.* He pulled off a shoe and sock to bandage a toe. *What did you say about the Flint Hills giving you a chance to catch your breath?*

— A man who travels by horse said it. I go along with Zeb Pike: "My feet blistered and very sore."

The Venerable put a damp foot close to my face, but I was too tired to do other than stare at it.

— You've got a narrow, bending line, fed by others, running from your toes to your heel that's almost a map of the Kaw Trail. It looks like something you walked into your sole. The next time we get lost, we'll just consult your ripe foot.

Do our skins separate us or link us?

We took off again for a mile or so until, against the far eastern horizon, with binoculars we could see the old Indian monument on Roniger Hill, and in a hollow we made camp against a steep southern slope dropping down to a dry wash. I went for wood but all I could find was a crumbling pack-rat nest and a broken Osage-orange fencepost. The air was growing cold. I laid out a small stone bench against the ridge, put our bed-pads on it, and lighted the fire. The Venerable thought the site looked like our first camp, and it did, but I said the tree this time wasn't a willow but a little cottonwood.

I think we've been circling.

I was carving in the third ring on my staff. I said, what else?

Our meal was dehydrated rations he'd found on sale in an army surplus store.

— The word for this slumgullion is vile.

General Sherman didn't think so.

A coyote called a far song, and I said I was leaving my supper for him, and I pulled out a half pint of Missouri sourmash. The Venerable looked at it almost in anger. *You've had that all along?*

— We weren't ready for it. We hadn't come far enough.

What do you mean we, Tonto?

I poured two good measures, added some well-water and a few raisins for sweetening, and set our cups over the fire. Hot toddies against the night, I said.

He pulled out a Mexican blunt, I stoked my pipe, we watched tobacco smoke rise in the cold up to, it seemed, the Big Bear so low now on the horizon. The fire defended us from the heavy dewfall. *Would you say we found the old track?*

— No. Blindly crossed it, yes. Often, I think. We've been entangled in its lines the whole way.

We sat listening to the night, its voices growing fewer as the air cooled.

— Tomorrow the hills level out.

Tomorrow the tour's over, Chief.

— For me, a six-year tour here is over.

Would you say you've found revelation?

— I'd say I've found a place willing to reveal itself. I think that's worth more, even if it is easier to come by. Swami say, "River gift, not answer."

Swami also say, "Lift cup, drink Missouri sourmash, honor river."

And, with the flame-blackened cups, we did, and we watched the fire, then lifted them to the wood rat that long ago hauled in our heat, and, when its sticks were gone, I pushed in one end of the old hedge post, and we lifted cups again, and the Venerable said, *To the Wind People,* and the damp post hissed like a serpent, spit sparks, resisted its going.

Then came something I'd never seen before: a bird flew into the small cottonwood, and from its silhouette against the moon I could see it was a jay. We stared at it in disbelief, and finally the Venerable whispered, *Since when do birds fly into campfire circles?*

— Isn't just a bird.

The Venerable slowly stood, pulled me up, raised his arms, I did too, palms outward, and he said, *Old ones.*

A circled presence, like a miasma, pressed in, and how long it remained I don't know, but a meteor, the slowest falling one I ever saw, dropped right across the Great Bear like a thrown spear, and then the circle seemed to loosen, and things regained their accustomed positions, dispositions. The jaybird was gone. I pushed the last of the hedge post into the coals. Tashmoo emptied his toddy: *In all my life I never encountered anything like that. What brought them in?*

— Memory.

Ours or theirs?

Yes, I said.

In Thanks

As well as those named in the chapters, I thank these people:

Jack LaZebnik (writer and maker of writers), Larry Cooper (may the future one day sprinkle his grave with Bembo, "the noblest roman of them all"); Robert Overholtzer, Marya Labarthe, Guest Perry, Erica Landry, Peter Davison, Lois Wallace; and: Bertha Baker, Glenn Baumgardner, Cathy Beaham, Hank Beetz, Patt Behler, Mary Helen and Tom Bell, Helen-Ann Brown, Pat Broyles, Rex Buchanan, Marguerite Buffon, Orville Burtis, Jr., Jean Shaft Butler, Howard Cahoone, Sharon Cahoone, Jim Cauthorn, Wayne and Ruth Childs, Alice Clareson, Frances Clark, Joseph T. Collins, Mike Cox, Barbara Davis, Beulah Day, Tom Dennison, L. D. Dobbs, Richard Douthit, Gretel Ehrlich, Helen Norton Evans, Wayne Fields, Robert L. Foster, Lee Fowler, Joyce Garr, Don Giddings, Gayle Graham, Zula Bennington Greene, Martha Hagedorn-Krass, Mary Lu and Eldon Hainey, Karl Harder, Ken Harder, Dale Hartley, Shirley Hazzard, Mary Hickey, Mike Holder, Susan Holm, Marilyn Holt, Cathy Hoy, Marteil Hoy, Andrea Hunter, Tom Isern, Alvin M. Josephy, Jr., the Kansas State Historical Society (for permission to reprint material from its archives), June Kelly, Kelly Kindscher, Judy and Roy Knapp, Joyce Knighten, Clair Kucera, Robert Lindholm, Barbara Livingston, Christopher Maples, Wilma and Dale Martin, Scott May, James R. McCauley, Howard McClellan, Sister Jeanne McKenna, Bruce McMillen, Kathy and Ken Mildward, Jesse Miser, John Moore, Sue

Ann Moore, June Morgan, Bob Mushrush, Nancy and Stu Nowlin, Jack Odle, Ramon Powers, Charles Rayl, E. C. Roberts, Gerald Roberts, Donita Rogers, Elizabeth Roniger Rogler, Carl and Ruth Romeiser, Johnny Rufener, Bonnie Short, James Shortridge, Hugh Sidey, Joanna Stratton, Edith Talkington, Sandra Taylor, Gloria Throne, Wallace Thurston, Francis Towle, Jon Weiss, Candia Welch, Jean White, Ruth Wilson, Tom Witty, Jr.; and R. Carlos Nakai and Coyote Oldman, whose Native American flutes transported me far and long.

The author is grateful for permission to quote from the following sources:

"Tracks of the Wind" by Peter Steinhart. Reprinted from *Audubon*, the magazine of the National Audubon Society.

Discovering the Vernacular Landscape by J. B. Jackson. Copyright © 1984 by Yale University Press.

The Necessity of Ruins and Other Topics by J. B. Jackson. Copyright © 1980 by J. B. Jackson. Reprinted by permission of the University of Massachusetts Press.

"Kansas: A Hard Land in the Heartland" by Leo E. Oliva, from *Heartland*, edited by James H. Madison. Copyright © 1988 by Indiana University Press.

"An Interview with Barry Lopez," reprinted from *Western American Literature*, Spring 1986. Copyright © 1986 by Western Literature Association.

Black Elk Speaks by John G. Neihardt. Copyright 1932, 1959, 1972 by John G. Neihardt. Copyright © 1961 by the John G. Neihardt Trust. Reprinted by permission of University of Nebraska Press.

The Sacred Pipe: Black Elk's Account of the Seven Rites of the Oglala Sioux, recorded and edited by Joseph Epes Brown. Copyright 1953 by the University of Oklahoma Press.

"What's the Matter with Kansas?" by Kenneth Davis, June 27, 1954. Copyright 1954 by the New York Times Company. Reprinted by permission.

"About Books: Rereading and Other Excesses" by Anatole Broyard, March 3, 1985. Copyright © 1985 by the New York Times Company. Reprinted by permission.

"You Darkness That I Come From," from *Selected Poems of Rainer Maria Rilke*. Translation copyright © 1981 by Robert Bly.

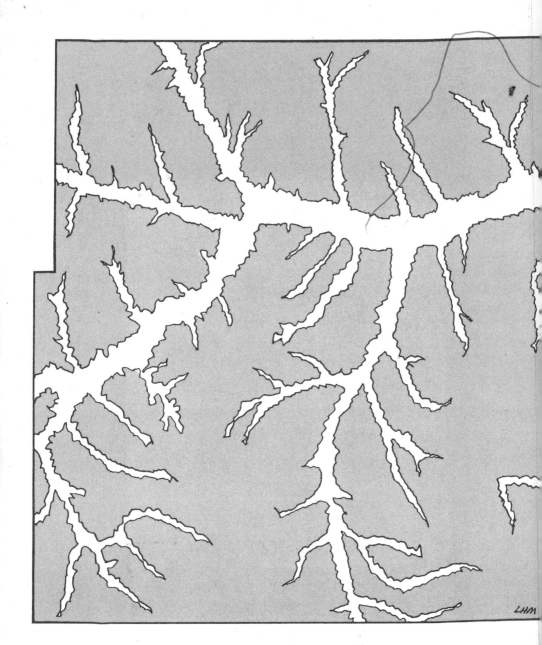

MAJOR WATERSHEDS OF CHASE COUNTY